# Problem Solving Using C:

## *Structured Programming Techniques*

**SECOND EDITION**

**Yuksel Uck**
*Miami Univer.*

**WCB McGraw-Hill**

Boston     Burr Ridge, IL     Dubuque, IA     Madison, WI     New York     San Francisco     St. Louis
Bangkok     Bogotá     Caracas     Lisbon     London     Madrid
Mexico City     Milan     New Delhi     Seoul     Singapore     Sidney     Taipei     Toronto

# WCB/McGraw-Hill

*A Division of The* **McGraw·Hill** *Companies*

PROBLEM SOLVING USING C: STRUCTURED PROGRAMMING TECHNIQUES

Copyright © 1999 by The McGraw-Hill Companies, Inc. Previous edition © 1995. Printed in the United States of America. Except as permitted under the United States Copyright Act of 1976, no part of this publication may be reproduced or distributed in any form or by any means, or stored in a database or retrieval system, without the prior written permission of the publisher.

WCB/McGraw Hill recognizes that certain terms in the book are trademarks, and we have made every effort to print these throughout the text with the capitalization and punctuation used by the holders of the trademark. WCB/McGraw makes no warranties, either expressed or implied, regarding the computer programs developed and presented in this book.

This book is printed on acid-free paper.

1 2 3 4 5 6 7 8 9 0 DOC/DOC 9 3 2 1 0 9 8

ISBN 0-256-26377-9

Vice president and Editorial director: *Kevin T. Kane*
Publisher: *Tom Casson*
Senior sponsoring editor: *Elizabeth A. Jones*
Developmental editor: *Bradley Kosirog*
Marketing manager: *John T. Wannemacher*
Project manager: *Margaret Rathke*
Senior production supervisor: *Madelyn S. Underwood*
Freelance design coordinator: *Gino Cieslik*
Cover design: *Gregg Roewski, Z Graphics, Ltd.*
Interior design: *Joel Davies, Z Graphics, Ltd.*
Supplement coordinator: *Becky Szura*
Compositor: *York Graphic Services, Inc.*
Typeface: *10/12 Times Roman*
Printer: *R. R. Donnelley & Sons Company*

**Library of Congress Cataloging-in-Publication Data**

Uckan, Yuksel.
    Problem solving using C / Yuksel Uckan. -- 2nd ed.
      p.    cm.
    ISBN 0-256-26377-9
    Includes index.
    1. C (Computer program language). I. Title
    QA76.73.C15U25   1999
    005.13' dc—21                  98-21028

www.mhhe.com

*"For Emel,*
*who has always*
*been*
*my wings,*
*and who made me*
*believe the impossible."*

# Preface

This book is intended for introductory-level college and university courses that are modeled after the CS1 course of the Association for Computing Machinery (ACM) Curriculum Recommendations. This book's primary objective is to teach problem solving using computers. For this purpose the book uses the American National Standards Institute (ANSI) standard C programming language.

This book is suitable for use by students with little or no programming background. The complete book can be easily covered in a one-semester or one-quarter introductory course on problem solving. The text can also be used for self-study by students or professional programmers.

## WHY THE C LANGUAGE

Obviously, problem solving can be taught using almost any programming language. Why did we choose C as our vehicle to teach problem solving and computer programming? There are several reasons for this choice.

1.    Since its debut in the early 1970s, C has gained immense popularity and has evolved into one of the leading programming languages in the computer software industry. Today, C compilers are available on all platforms, ranging from microcomputers to mainframes. A significant number of software system implementation projects have been–and are being–done using C. We believe that this trend will continue in the foreseeable future and that today's computer science students should be well-versed in the use of C.

2.    Another popular programming language is C++, which has been designed as an extension of the C programming language. Consequently, students who are fluent in C can easily acquire the ability to program in C++, thus enhancing their employment opportunities.

3.    C is a programming language that can be used to teach structured procedural programming techniques. It is an excellent language to introduce fundamental principles and techniques of software engineering, including structured program design, programming style, documentation, modular design, code reusability, program verification and testing, and data structuring.

## ORGANIZATION OF THE BOOK

This book is organized into 15 chapters.

- **Chapter 1** deals with the fundamental terminology and concepts of computers, their uses, hardware, software, and programming languages. It describes the C programming environment and discusses the basic steps involved in using computers to develop and run C programs. Students are exposed to their first C program in this chapter.

- **Chapter 2** focuses on problem-solving techniques. It teaches the software development method and its steps, design and representation of algorithms using top-down stepwise refinement and pseudocode, and the three fundamental program structures and their pseudocode representations.

The main objective of Chapters 3 through 6 is to teach a minimum but adequate amount of concepts and techniques that students can use for problem solving using C.

- **Chapter 3** discusses the elements of the C programming language; the structure of C programs; three fundamental data types (int, double, and char); and expression statements for interactive input using the standard function scanf, expression statements for interactive output using printf, and simple forms of the arithmetic assignment expression statement. Strings as a derived data type are also introduced in Chapter 3.

- **Chapter 4** discusses the if statement for simple selections and the while statement for simple repetitions. It also introduces the discipline of structured programming.

- **Chapter 5** deals with more complex arithmetic calculations, additional numerical fundamental data types, arithmetic errors and inaccuracies, and arithmetic and assignment conversions.

- **Chapter 6** undertakes the exploration of modular programming and function design. This chapter begins with functions that do not receive or return data, continues with functions that return values under their names, and finally teaches functions with parameters and parameter passing by value. By the time students complete Chapter 6, they know about C statement types for input, output, arithmetic, selection, and repetition, which are sufficient to solve many interesting problems. Students also develop the ability to design and implement modular programs.

Chapters 7 through 10 build on the background acquired by students up to this point and continue with additional C features and programming techniques.

- In **Chapter 7** students learn about formatted input and output.

- **Chapter 8** deals with file-oriented input and output, batch mode of processing, and data files; it discusses text files and the C language features for processing text files.

- **Chapter 9** revisits selections and repetitions, and discusses multiway selection structures using complex predicates, and examines the switch statement. It also introduces the pretest for and the posttest do-while statements.

- Next, in **Chapter 10**, students return to modular programming and study pointer variables, parameter passing by pointers, programmer-defined libraries, and modular programming using programmer-defined libraries.

Chapters 11 through 14 concentrate on data design and derived and programmer-defined data types.

- **Chapter 11** focuses on lists, arrays, dynamic variables and dynamic arrays, fundamental array operations, including sorting and searching, and higher dimensional arrays.

- **Chapter 12** discusses structures and enumerated types as two programmer-defined data types and introduces arrays of structures and structures of arrays.
- **Chapter 13** is devoted to character data, strings, and string processing.
- **Chapter 14** revisits data files and then turns to binary files and sequential and direct access file processing.
- **Chapter 15** covers recursion. It introduces recursion as a problem-solving technique, contrasts recursion to iteration, and discusses recursive functions.

The book has three appendices.
- **Appendix A** lists the C reserved words.
- **Appendix B** includes the tables of C operators and escape sequences.
- **Appendix C** contains brief descriptions of selected standard C header files and library functions.

## DISTINGUISHING FEATURES OF THE BOOK

***The book requires no prerequisite knowledge.***   Chapter 1 provides students with the necessary background on computer systems, programming, and programming languages. All other necessary background knowledge is provided gradually in the book as students learn about problem solving.

***It provides early exposure to problem-solving techniques and pseudocoding.***   Chapter 2 is independent of the implementation language. It focuses on problem solving; introduces the software development method; and emphasizes requirements specification, analysis, and algorithm design. It teaches the top-down stepwise refinement as a problem-solving technique and the use of pseudocoding for design and representation of algorithms.

***It uses the software development method for program design and implementation.*** After the software development method is introduced in Chapter 2, it is applied to problem solving throughout the rest of the book. In most of the example programs, requirements specifications for the problems are given in detail, the problems are analyzed, solutions are designed for them using the top-down stepwise refinement process, the solutions are implemented as C programs, the programs are tested, and reasonably complete documentation is provided for them. Hence students are continually exposed to the software development method.

***It provides gradual and smooth exposure to the C language.***   C is a rather complex and rich programming language, and if taught without care and in haste, may lead to a great deal of confusion on the part of the beginner. Keeping this potential problem in mind, the book adopts a pedagogically proven approach: Early in the book, in Chapters 3, 4, and 5, a C foundation is built by introducing a minimal language subset of five statements that can be used in solving a variety of challenging problems. These statements are simple input, output, and arithmetic assignment statements, the `if` statement for selection, and the `while` statement for repetition. No new statements are taught until Chapter 9, thus giving students time to reinforce the basic foundation. Beginning with Chapter 9, more advanced programming techniques and language features are added to this foundation.

***It stresses program readability, documentation, and program style conventions.*** C is generally considered to be a difficult language to teach in a first course on problem solving. Therefore, the book consistently encourages students to take a disciplined approach to program development, produce readable programs, and supply sufficient documentation with their programs. For this purpose, programming style issues and conventions are discussed in detail. Also, students are provided with example programs that use these style conventions and include sufficient in-program documentation.

***It provides a large selection of problem-solving and program implementation examples.*** Throughout the book extensive examples for concepts, C language features, program design techniques, and data design techniques are provided. All programming examples have been machine tested. These examples facilitate learning both the subject matter and problem-solving, program design, and data design techniques.

***It provides numerous complete example programs.*** With the exception of the second chapter, each chapter contains one or more complete C example programs based on the concepts and techniques studied in that chapter. There programs have been machine tested on several platforms. These programs are not esoteric; they are relevant case studies often similar to problems encountered in professional programming environments. Each example program is developed using the software development method, pseudocoding, and top-down stepwise refinement. All example programs are explained in sufficient detail. The text contains 22 complete C example programs, together with listings of accompanying input files, output files, or printouts of program test runs. By studying these programs, students see how the concepts and techniques introduced in the chapter are applied for solving problems. They also gain access to good C program examples that they can use in their program design efforts.

***It stresses the importance of program debugging.*** The ability to debug programs is another problem-solving skill that is as important as the ability to design programs. The book discusses programming errors, program debugging techniques, and strategies for defensive programming. At the end of most of the chapters in the book, debugging exercises are included to help improve students' debugging skills.

***It emphasizes program verification and testing.*** The book discusses simple program verification and testing methods and stresses their importance. Most of the example programs include sample test runs that comprehensively test the developed programs.

***It provides a smooth introduction to modular program design and functions.*** Teaching modular programming and function design to beginners is a challenging task. The book proceeds in careful steps to accomplish its goal. It begins the discussion of modular programming in Chapter 6 with simple functions that do not participate in data transfers and explains the transfer of the program control between functions. Next, it introduces functions that return a single value under their names. Then, it discusses value parameters and parameter passing by value.

The students use these techniques until Chapter 10, and are given time and opportunity to assimilate them. Subsequently, in Chapter 10, the book discusses pointer variables, and parameter passing by pointers.

***It provides the right amount of material for a first-year introductory course on problem solving.*** I believe that the entire C language should not be taught in a single beginning-level course. Accordingly, this book does not attempt to cover the complete C spectrum, but stresses only the features essential to problem solving in a first course in computing. More advanced topics, such as linked lists, stacks, queues, trees, functions with variable number of parameters, signal handling, bit string processing, and so on, are intentionally kept outside the scope of the book, assuming that they will be taught in subsequent higher-level courses.

Therefore, this book is not a comprehensive C reference book. It is a textbook for students who want to learn problem-solving using computers, structured procedural programming, and the standard C language.

***It discusses pointers in the right context.*** The concept of pointer variables is important in C programming. It is also one of the most difficult subjects to teach beginning students. I believe that pointers should be taught gradually in a CS1 course and should be taught in the right context. Rather than devoting a single chapter to pointers and discussing it in one shot, this book teaches pointers in three installments. It introduces the concept of pointer variables in Chapter 10 and shows how they can be used to pass data through parameters between functions. Chapter 11 revisits pointers in connection with pointer/offset notation for arrays and pointer arithmetic, and discusses pointers in conjunction with dynamic variables and dynamic arrays. Finally, Chapter 13 uses pointers for strings. By that time students have developed a good understanding of pointers and are ready for linked lists and pointer-based implementations of abstract data types, subjects that are commonly handled in CS2-type courses.

## ADDITIONAL PEDAGOGICAL FEATURES

***The book provides chapter objectives.*** Each chapter begins with a list of chapter objectives that provide students with a plan of concepts and techniques that are studied in the chapter and a list of problem-solving skills that students are expected to acquire when they complete the chapter.

***It provides numerous review questions.*** Each chapter contains several blocks of multiple-choice and true/false review questions, for which answers are provided immediately after each block. Review questions give students the opportunity to test their understanding of the material covered up to that point in the chapter.

***It properly emphasizes important terminology and language syntax.***    Definitions of important concepts and the C syntax definitions are separated from the text by printing them against a color background. Thus students can easily focus on them while studying or reviewing the material.

***It provides chapter summaries.***    Each chapter contains a chapter summary that consists of two sections: **This Chapter at a Glance** and **Coming Attractions**. The first section summarizes the important elements of the chapter, and the second section establishes a connection between the present chapter and the chapters that follow, thus maintaining continuity, a sense of purpose, and direction.

***It provides an extensive study guide.***    Each chapter concludes with a study guide that consists of two sections: **Test Your Comprehension** and **Improve Your Problem-Solving Ability**. Each **Test Your Comprehension** section includes multiple-choice questions with answers, which provide students the opportunity to test their understanding of the material discussed in each chapter.

The second component of the study guide, **Improve Your Problem-Solving Ability**, contains debugging exercises, programming exercises, and programming projects. It enables students to improve their problem-solving abilities in terms of program debugging, code interpretation, program design, and data design.

## SUPPLEMENTARY MATERIAL

This textbook is supplemented by a **Program Files Diskette**, which contains all the C programs presented in the book. The program files are in ASCII format.

An Instructor's Manual is available to the adopters of this textbook. It consists of teaching notes and suggestions, lecture plans, additional exam questions, and solutions to selected debugging and programming exercises.

## ACKNOWLEDGMENTS

Many people contributed to the development of this book. They include my students and colleagues at Miami University, Oxford, Ohio, who used the first edition of the book, informed me of errors they found in it, and gave me invaluable feedback on its content. I am grateful to them.

My friend and colleague, Professor Fazli Can, of Miami University, volunteered to review the manuscript; read it patiently and with great care from cover to cover; suggested many corrections, additions, and deletions; and contributed significantly to the quality of the text. I acknowledge his help, expertise, and collegiality with gratitude.

I would like to express my special appreciation to the helpful editors at WCB/McGraw-Hill, who have been instrumental in producing the second edition. They are Betsy Jones, Bradley Kosirog, and Maggie Rathke. It has been a great pleasure to work with them.

I am also grateful to many excellent reviewers provided by Business and Educational Technologies, publisher of the first edition, and WCB/McGraw-Hill, publisher of the second edition, who read the manuscript meticulously and came up with many useful suggestions. They are: Chris J. Dovolis, University of Minnesota; William H. Crouch, Old Dominion University; Chris Riesbeck, Northwestern University; Hector J. Hernandez, New Mexico State University; Naguib Attia, John N. Smith University; Mathew J. Palakal, Indiana University Purdue University Indianapolis; Sally Betz, Northern Illinois University; Marguerite Hafen, Pennsylvania State University; and Todd W. Breedlove, Oregon Institute of Technology.

This book owes its existence to Emel Uckan, my wife, my best friend, and my inspiration. She read the manuscript over and over again, corrected it, shaped it, and gave character to it. She shared this project with me from its beginning to its end, brought joy and excitement to it, and turned it into a wonderful experience for me. I am most grateful to her.

Yuksel Uckan

---

## ABOUT THE AUTHOR

Yuksel Uckan is a professor of computer science in the Department of Systems Analysis at Miami University, Oxford, Ohio. He has taught computer science for 27 years in three universities. His research and teaching interests include database systems, object-oriented programming, and data and file structures. He is the author of more than 40 technical publications and five textbooks. He would welcome comments and criticism about this textbook. His e-mail address is uckany@titan.sas.muohio.edu.

# Brief Contents

# Contents

# Appendices   726

## chapter

# 1

# Introduction to C Programming

---

**CHAPTER OBJECTIVES**

In this chapter you will learn about:

- **Computer fundamentals**
  Computer organization and hardware
  Computer software

- **Programming languages**
  Machine languages
  Assembly languages
  High-level languages
  The evolution of the C and C++ programming languages

- **The C programming environment**

- **How to use the computer to prepare, compile, link, and execute C programs**

By the time you have completed this chapter, you will have written your first C program.

---

## 1.1    INTRODUCTION

This book is about problem solving with the use of computers and the C programming language. It is your introduction to computer science—a field of study that deals fundamentally with problem solving using computers. However, you don't have to be a computer science major to be interested in this book. Today computers are used in almost all fields and professions. No matter what your major is, you have to develop the ability to solve problems, and it is very likely that you will need to use computers for that. Therefore, this book is for you; we hope you will enjoy it and find it useful.

By studying this book, you will learn how to identify problems that can be solved with computers, how to specify such problems, analyze them, and design a method of solution for them. Then you will learn how to use C to implement the method in a computer environment to get the results you want. You will develop the ability to solve problems. This problem-solving ability requires the following:

1. A knowledge of computer fundamentals
2. An understanding of problem-solving strategies and techniques
3. Proficiency in using a programming language

The programming language you will study is C. C is a general-purpose language that is powerful, rich, versatile, and exciting. The purpose of this chapter is to give you a quick background in computer fundamentals and to introduce you to C programming. The chapter briefly touches on the computer basics that are necessary for an understanding of the C environment. Then you will have your first experience with a C program. You will learn the steps that you have to go through to run C programs using a C integrated development environment. After completing Chapter 2, which deals with problem-solving techniques, you will be ready to hone your problem-solving skills.

## 1.2    COMPUTER FUNDAMENTALS

In almost every facet of our daily life, we live in close contact with computers. Whether we realize it or not, we use them as a matter of routine. They come in many sizes and shapes and do many useful things for us. If you own a digital watch, you have a computer that tells you what time it is. Your car probably has several computers that perform many different functions, such as injecting fuel into its engine, indicating that your door is ajar, and telling you how many more miles you can drive on the remaining fuel. If your telephone has a redial button, a computer in it remembers the last number you dialed. Your school has many microcomputers, workstations, and perhaps even mainframes. You probably own a personal computer at home. The examples of computers and computer applications around us are nearly endless. So what is a computer?

A **computer** is a device that can input and store a set of instructions designed to perform a specific task, input and store data, process the stored data according to the instructions, and produce output to be relayed to its user.

Some computers are designed to process a permanent set of instructions and, therefore, perform one specific task; others are more flexible and can execute various instructions. Accordingly, computers are classified as special-purpose and general-purpose computers. A **special-purpose computer** is a computer that is designed for a particular function, executing the same stored set of instructions whenever requested. For example, the computer that provides the redial feature on your telephone has only one function and one permanent set of instructions to perform its function. You cannot change its instructions. It is a special-purpose computer.

Special-purpose computers are undoubtedly very useful. However, each is designed to perform only a few specific tasks. If we want to use a computer for problem solving, since we expect to encounter many different problems to solve in our professions, we would naturally want it to be more versatile. Computers that can be used for solving many different types of problems are **general-purpose computers**. For example, personal computers are general-purpose computers. They are capable of storing and running different sets of instructions, accepting input data for each set of instruction in different forms, and producing output that satisfies various user requirements; hence general-purpose computers are more flexible than special-purpose computers.

In this book our main purpose is to develop the ability to solve different problems using computers. Hence we are interested in general-purpose computers rather than special-purpose ones. From now on, whenever we talk about computers, we are referring to general-purpose computers.

All computers can store instructions in their memory, can input and store data, can process data, and can produce output. A set of instructions that performs a specific task is called a **program**. Computer programs are written by computer programmers using special languages called programming languages. A programmer analyzes a problem and designs a program that produces the desired solution to the problem. The program must be written in a programming language so that the computer can understand the instructions that make up the program. Therefore, a problem solver, in our case a computer scientist or a computer programmer, must have a good understanding of computers, problem-solving methodologies, and computer programming languages.

## Computer Organization and Hardware

Computers are available in many sizes and different levels of capabilities. They are classified as microcomputers (laptop computers, desktop computers, and workstations), minicomputers, mainframe computers, and supercomputers. All computer types consist of many components that function together as a system to do an assigned task.

A computer system is made up of hardware and software. The tangible or physical computer equipment is known as **hardware**. Hardware for a typical computer system includes the following components: main memory, central processing unit, input devices, output devices, and secondary memory devices.

A computer's **main memory** is an electronic device that stores information necessary for a program to run. The information that can be stored in the main memory can be the machine code representations for program instructions, numeric or nonnumeric data values, pictures, sound, and so on. Each unit of information is stored in a memory cell. The information stored in a cell is the **content of the cell**. To store information in a cell and access and retrieve its content when it is time to use it, each cell must have an address. Therefore, **a memory cell** is an individually addressable memory unit that can store information. Memory cells are made up of smaller memory units called **bytes**, and bytes consist of smaller units called bits. A **bit** represents a single binary digit, 0 or 1. In most computers a byte has eight bits. Each character is represented in a byte as a particular string of binary digits called a **bit string**. The main memory of most computers consists of thousands, millions, and even billions of bytes. They are measured in kilobytes (KB), megabytes (MB), and gigabytes (GB), respectively. One KB is 1024 bytes; one MB is the product of two KBs, or 1,048,576 bytes; and one GB is the product of one KB and one MB, or 1,073,741,824 bytes.

The **central processing unit (CPU)**, also called the processor, is the hardware component that does most of the work in executing a program. The processor consists of two functional units: a control unit and an arithmetic-logic unit. The **control unit** of the processor supervises all activities of the computer system. The **arithmetic-logic unit (ALU)** is the electronic circuitry capable of performing basic arithmetic operations and comparison operations. It can carry out millions of operations per second.

We use input devices to communicate programs, data, and special instructions to the computer. **An input device** accepts information and transforms it to digital codes that the computer can process. Many input device types are available. They include keyboards, mice, touch screens and touch pads, light pens, notepads, scanners, and sensors. A secondary memory device, such as a disk drive or a tape drive, can also be used as an input device. In this case coded information recorded on disk or tape is transferred into the computer's memory during input.

An **output device** communicates to the user the solutions of problems produced by using computers. The most common output devices are printers and plotters. You can use a printer to get a hard copy of almost anything stored in the computer's memory, including the output of your programs and the listing of instructions in them. The terminal monitor, on the other hand, can provide you with a soft copy of program output or program listing.

In addition to the main memory, computers have secondary memory devices. After we design a program, we type it into a file that is stored in secondary memory. This way, the program becomes permanent, and we don't lose what we type. Also, a computer's main memory, no matter how large, has limited capacity. Sometimes a program may require huge amounts of input data. Occasionally a program's output is excessive, and we may want to save it electronically. Under these circumstances the computer's main memory may prove insufficient. In addition, because the main memory is volatile, we cannot save anything in it permanently. The solution to limited memory capacity and volatile main memory is provided by secondary memory devices. A **secondary memory device** uses a permanent, nonvolatile medium on which information can be stored and from which information can be retrieved. The most common secondary memory devices are magnetic disk drives, magnetic tape drives, and compact disk (CD) drives.

Information on disks or tapes is stored in logical units called files. A **file** is an organized collection of information. There are many types of files, including program files, data files, output files, and text files. In this book we will be particularly concerned with program, data, and output files. A **program file** contains instructions that make up a program. You can create program files and store them on disk in machine-readable form.

When you are ready to run your program, you can load the program file into the main memory and ask the computer to execute it. Although secondary memory can be used to store a program, you cannot run the program unless you copy it to the main memory.

A **data file** consists of input data of a particular structure. You can type the input data for a program directly into a data file and store it on disk. Then you can develop your program so that it gets its input from this data file. An **output file** stores the output of a program. If you want to keep a permanent magnetic copy of your output, you can design your program to send its output to an output file. Later you can obtain a hard copy of your output by printing the content of your output file.

## Computer Software

In addition to hardware, a computer system requires software to make the best use of its capabilities and to solve our problems. The term **software** is a synonym for program. There are many varieties of software. In general, we can classify software as applications software and systems software. **Applications software** refers to programs that solve some specific problems. In contrast, **systems software** refers to programs that make the computer usable and accessible to the developers and programmers of applications software. In this book we will certainly emphasize the design and development of programs for problem solving, in other words, applications software. However, we need systems software to make the process of developing applications software possible.

**Systems Software**    In general, systems software consists of programs that are quite complex and difficult to develop. Some of these programs are provided by the manufacturers of computer systems to complement computer hardware. Others can be purchased from software vendors. Some of the more important systems software, at least from the point of view in this book, are operating systems, text editors, preprocessors, language translators, linkers, and loaders.

An **operating system** is the most important software for a computer. It is the software that manages the overall operation of the computer system. Actually, an operating system consists of many component programs. These programs do the following tasks:

1. Validate that a user is authorized to use computer resources in large computer systems operating in timesharing mode.
2. Make other systems software (text editors, language translators, linkers, loaders, and so on) available to users.
3. Allocate memory and processor time to programs.
4. Manage the available secondary memory.
5. Manage disk and tape files, including creating, writing, reading, sorting files, and arranging them in directories.
6. Control various input and output devices and coordinate input and output operations.

Each computer has its own operating system. Some of the popular operating systems are the disk operating system (DOS) for IBM and IBM-compatible microcomputers; graphical user interfaces such as Windows 95 and Windows NT; the Macintosh operating system for Apple computers; the UNIX operating system, which is available for many different computer systems; and Operating System 2 (OS/2) for IBM personal computers.

A **text editor** is special software that can be used to create a text, edit it, and save it as a file using the computer's keyboard and monitor. A text editor is quite similar to a word processor—computer software that you may have used for typing term papers. The text that you create using a text editor can be anything—a letter, a report, a data file, or a program file. Most operating systems contain text editors. Also, almost all C systems (the software you will use to develop C programs) support text editors. You will need to use an appropriate text editor to create C program files and data files.

A **preprocessor** is a component of the C system triggered by a C program that contains special instructions to it. The preprocessor checks the C program file for special instructions and either includes other files in the program file or replaces some special symbols with an appropriate program text. The special instructions to the preprocessor are called **preprocessor directives**. After the preprocessor is finished with the program file, the language translation phase begins. You do not have to learn anything special to call on the preprocessor; the C system will do this job automatically if your program contains preprocessor directives. We will describe the preprocessor directives that are useful in C programming later in the book.

A **language translator** is software that converts a computer program written using a high-level programming language, or an assembly language, to an equivalent program that is in machine language. The programs that we write using the C programming language cannot be executed directly by the computer. C is a high-level language that is designed for programmers, and it is easy to learn and use. A well-written C program is quite close to a text written in English. However, a computer cannot understand C statements. It is designed to interpret instructions that are expressed in machine language. Each computer has its own specific machine language. Machine languages are highly cryptic and are quite difficult and impractical for us to learn. There is a compromise, however: we write our programs in a high-level language such as C, use a translator that converts C instructions to machine-language instructions, and then ask the computer to execute these instructions to solve the problem that the program represents.

A program that is written in a high-level language is called a **source program**. A program that consists of machine language instructions is called an **object program**. A **language translator** translates a source program after it is processed by the preprocessor, if necessary, into an equivalent object program. There are two types of language translators: interpreters and compilers. An **interpreter** translates one high-level program instruction at a time into machine code and immediately executes that code, proceeding in this manner until all the instructions in the source program are translated and executed. A **compiler**, on the other hand, first translates the entire source program into an object program and then saves the object program in a file. C is a compiling language in that it requires a compiler. **Compilation** is the process of translating a source program into an object program.

Usually, an object program produced by the compiler is not immediately executable. This fact is especially true for C programs because they typically contain references to other programs that exist in standard libraries. A **standard library** contains object codes of some standard programs (called **standard library functions**), which are provided by the vendor of the C system. Also, as a programmer, you can create programs for some useful tasks and add them to your own C library. If your C program is making use of some of the library functions, the computer cannot execute your object file, since the object program is missing the library functions' object codes. The **linker**, which is a component of the compiler, automatically combines the object codes of the needed standard functions with your object program and creates an executable machine language program, called the **load module**. The load module is saved in disk storage.

After the linker completes its task, we have an executable load module. To execute the load module, we ask the operating system to load it into the main memory. In some computer systems the loader carries out this task. The **loader** is a program that loads the executable load module into the main memory for execution. After the operating system or the loader transfers the load module to the main memory, the central processing unit begins its execution.

**Applications Software**   Applications software includes programs that are developed using systems software in order to solve problems. There are two types of applications software: application programs that you can purchase for solving special classes of problems and application programs that you can write to solve your own problems. Commercially available application programs are developed by professional programmer teams, are fully tested, and can be used directly with little or no additional programming. They include word processing and desktop publishing software; spreadsheets; database programs; graphics programs; communications software; and special-purpose programs suitable for accounting, scientific and engineering applications, education, entertainment, and so on.

In this book we are interested in the application programs that you will develop using C as the programming language. Of course, if your problem can be solved using available software, you would not develop a program for it. Ordinarily, you would not attempt to write word processing or spreadsheet software. However, there are countless problems that available software cannot handle. Therefore, society needs computer scientists and programmers, which is the reason that you are studying computer programming and problem solving.

## 1.3   PROGRAMMING LANGUAGES

We communicate with computers by using computer programs. Computer programs are written in programming languages, which are unlike natural languages such as English.

> A **programming language** is an artificial and formal language that has a limited vocabulary consisting of a set of keywords for making up instructions and a set of precise grammar rules.

Programming languages can be classified as general-purpose and special-purpose programming languages. A **special-purpose programming language** is designed for a particular class of applications. For example, Structured Query Language (SQL) is a special database-retrieval language. Programs written in SQL are intended to access and retrieve information from a database. On the other hand, a **general-purpose programming language** can be used to obtain solutions for many different types of problems.

Hundreds of general-purpose programming languages are in use today. We can classify general-purpose programming languages as machine languages, assembly languages, and high-level languages.

## Machine Languages

A machine language is the natural language of a computer. A program that is written in a machine language does not need to be translated; it is ready for immediate execution because it consists of instructions that are readily understood by the computer. However, machine languages have some shortcomings:

1.  Their instructions are extremely cryptic and are difficult to learn, even for professional programmers. Typically, a machine language instruction is a binary string of zeros and ones. The following three instructions, in the order written, form a small program for a hypothetical computer in its own machine language:

    ```
    0101 1000 0001 0000 1100 0000 0001 0000
    0101 1011 0001 0000 1100 0000 0001 0100
    0101 0000 0001 0000 1100 0000 0001 1000
    ```

2.  Each machine language instruction corresponds to a basic capability of the computer, such as addition, multiplication, or storing a value in a memory cell. Therefore, when programmed in a machine language, even relatively simple problems require a large number of machine language instructions, and we usually end up with lengthy programs.

3.  Each computer type has its own machine language. In other words, machine languages are machine-dependent. As a result, even if we develop proficiency in one machine language, we are back to square one if our computer system changes. We have to learn a new language with each new computer type.

4.  Because there is no one standard machine language, programs written for one type of computer cannot be run on another type. In other words, programs written in machine languages are not "portable."

## Assembly Languages

To make computers easier to program, assembly languages were invented. **Assembly language** instructions consist of English-like abbreviations that are less cryptic than machine language instructions. For example, the preceding machine language program might look like

```
L   1, GROSSPAY
S   1, TAX
ST  1, NETPAY
```

in an assembly language. This program is somewhat easier to understand. It instructs the computer to load into register 1, one of the special high-speed memory locations the computer has, the value stored in the memory cell whose symbolic address is GROSSPAY; to subtract from it the value of the memory cell TAX; and to store the result in the memory cell NETPAY.

A program written in an assembly language cannot be directly processed by a computer. We must use language translators, called **assemblers**, to convert assembly language programs to machine code so that they can be executed. Although, from the point of view of programmers, assembly language programming is an improvement over machine language programming, assembly languages still have some shortcomings:

1.  In general, each assembly language instruction corresponds to one machine language instruction. Therefore, programs written in assembly languages are lengthy.

2.  Each computer type has its own assembly language. With each new computer type, we may have to learn a new language.

3.  Because of variations in assembly languages, programs written using them are not portable.

## High-Level Languages

High-level languages were developed to eliminate the shortcomings of machine and assembly languages. In a high-level language, instructions are quite English-like, and a single instruction can be written to correspond to many operations at the machine level. For example, the assembly language program of three instructions given earlier can be written in C, which is a high-level language, as follows:

```
netpay = grosspay - tax;
```

Clearly, high-level programming languages are easier to learn than machine or assembly languages. However, programs written using high-level languages have to be converted to machine languages before they can be executed. For this job we use compilers, a systems software that translates a source program into an object program.

Most of the popular high-level programming languages have been standardized. Therefore, programs designed using them are quite portable. Many high-level languages have been developed during the last 40 years; not all of them have survived. Those still in use today include FORTRAN, COBOL, BASIC, Pascal, Ada, C, C++, and Java.

## The Evolution of the C and C++ Programming Languages

The C programming language was developed by Dennis Ritchie at Bell Laboratories in the early 1970s as a system implementation language. During the last two decades, it has evolved into a general-purpose language and has become available for a wide variety of computers. C combines the convenience of high-level programming languages with the power of assembly languages. In 1989, the American National Standards Institute (ANSI) approved a standard version of the C language. Currently, standard C compilers are available for many computer types and platforms. C is becoming increasingly popular in a variety of computer applications. The language has many powerful features, and it is possible to develop portable programs in it.

In the early 1980s Bjarne Stroustrup at Bell Laboratories created the C++ programming language as an extension of the C language. C++ is essentially a superset of C; C++ contains all features of C and enhances it by the addition of some new features, which if used properly, can eliminate certain weaknesses of C. Also, C++ makes object-oriented programming possible. Because C++ combines the features of C with some features that make it suitable in object-oriented programming, C++ is considered to be a hybrid language. Both conventional and object-oriented programming can be carried out using C++.

Many people believe that C is a difficult programming language and that C programs are cryptic, difficult to understand, and difficult to debug and test. These are myths. Any programming language can be misused to produce bad code. C has this reputation because some professional programmers prefer unusual, stilted, and convoluted usage. You will soon see that C is not only a very powerful general-purpose language but also a language that is quite easy to master. When C is coupled with good program design techniques, it can be used to generate programs that are well structured, easy to read, and easy to maintain.

## 1.4   THE C PROGRAMMING ENVIRONMENT

In many platforms (that is, hardware and operating system combinations), the systems software necessary to develop C application programs are bundled together into an integrated system, called an integrated development environment (IDE). A typical C IDE consists of a text editor, a C compiler, a preprocessor, libraries, and other program development and debugging tools.

The C programming environment has two components: the **language** and the **libraries**. The language includes features that enable us to carry out certain basic operations on a set of available data types. For example, by using the C language alone, we can create memory locations for problem variables, store data in them, perform arithmetic on numeric data, compare data values, and repeat a certain number of operations in a controlled fashion.

However, there are many operations that we cannot do easily, or at all, by using only the C language. For example, the C language does not have a feature that directly computes the square root of a numeric value. Admittedly, we can develop a program for this purpose; however, computing the square root is a frequently done operation, and it would be better to have a feature in the environment. The good news is that we can use a standard function, `sqrt`, to compute square roots. This function is part of the C standard libraries.

In general, a **library** is a collection of routines that can carry out operations that are not part of the language. A library supports and extends the C language and makes life easier for the programmer. It enables us to avoid "reinventing the wheel" by providing us with routines, which we would have to develop otherwise. There are two kinds of libraries:

1.  Standard libraries, which consist of a basic set of routines common to all C compilers.
2.  Programmer-defined libraries, which contain routines developed by C programmers.

Programmer-defined libraries are important, and you will study them after you develop sufficient programming skills. At this point we are interested in the standard libraries.

The C standard libraries are actually a collection of several independent libraries with distinct names and purposes. Examples of C standard libraries are the `stdio` library, used for interactive input and output operations; the `math` library, which contains some standard mathematical functions such as the square root, logarithm, and trigonometric functions; and the `string` library, which is needed for character string processing. You will learn about many standard libraries in this book.

Each such library consists of a header file and some object programs corresponding to the routines (functions) declared in the header file. A header file contains declarations of some values and functions; it is a text file, which means that you can read it and print it. You will find all the standard header files in the *include* directory of your C system. Most header files have the extension `.h`, as in `stdio.h`. If you open the *include* directory of your C system, you will see them listed; open any of the standard header files using a text editor (such as the Notepad in Windows), and you will be able to read its content. Header files contain, among other things, declarations, written in C, of some values and functions included in the library.

To use a standard library, say, the `stdio` library, a statement such as

```
#include <stdio.h>
```

must appear early in the program. This is not a C statement. Because it begins with the symbol #, it is understood to be a preprocessor directive, an instruction to the preprocessor. This particular directive instructs the preprocessor to include in the source code the content of the standard header file `stdio.h` so that in the rest of our program we can do interactive input and output. The preprocessor combines the content of the header file `stdio.h` with our program and passes the control to the compiler. Provided there are no errors in our program, the compiler produces an object program. After compilation, the linker links the object programs corresponding to the standard functions in the `stdio` library to our object program and generates an executable load module. Now that we have the load module, we can request a program execution.

## 1.5   HOW TO USE THE COMPUTER TO RUN C PROGRAMS

This section deals with the steps that you must follow to enter, compile, link, and execute a C program. Although, in principle, many of the steps are common, some depend on the computer, the operating system, and the C IDE that you will use. Because there are many different computer systems, operating systems, and C IDEs, we cannot possibly cover the operational details for all of them. Here we provide only the general steps; if you need assistance on the specifics of your systems, use your C IDE documentation.

### Accessing the Computer

If you are using a personal computer in stand-alone mode, all you have to do is to turn on the computer. Another term for turning on the computer is **booting** the computer. For security reasons some personal computers require the user to enter a **power-on password**. In this case you must type your assigned password and press the Enter key. Shortly afterward, you will see either a prompt (such as C>) or a graphical user interface (such as Windows) displayed on the screen. If you have a prompt, the operating system is ready to accept commands. If you have a graphical user interface, you must learn to use it.

If you are using a central computer or a server on a network, you must log on to your account. To use the computer system, you must have an account, identified by an account number and a password. Before you are allowed to access your account, you must convince the computer that you are the legitimate owner of that account by typing your account number (or user name) and password correctly. To protect your password, while you are typing it, the computer will not display it on the screen. After you prove that you are an authorized user, you will face the operating system.

## Using the Editor to Prepare Program and Data Files

Now that you have the operating system at your disposal, you may call on a text editor so that you can enter your program. The text editor may be a part of the operating system or a component of the C IDE. In the latter case, you will have to invoke the C IDE and then choose the option that will enable you to create a new program file.

At this step you will need to assign an appropriate file name and file extension to your program file so that the operating system and the C system can identify and process it. File naming conventions depend on the operating system that you are using. However, in most cases a file name is an eight-character name consisting of letters, decimal digits, and some special characters, usually beginning with a letter. Normally, the file extension for C program files is C. For example, you can use the file name and extension combination `PROGRAM1.C` for a C program file. `PROGRAM1` is the file name assigned to the file, and the extension C identifies it as a C program file.

Then, using the editor, you must enter your program statements line by line. After you are finished, you must save your program in a source program file.

Data files are similarly prepared using a text editor. They must also have a name, and the naming conventions are similar to those for program files. The file extension that you can use for data files can be anything except those that are reserved for special files, such as C. You have to know the reserved file extensions for your system and avoid using them for data files. On most systems `TXT` and `DAT` are good choices as data file extensions. After you finish typing your data files, you save them in disk storage.

## Compiling, Linking, and Executing C Programs

Now you are ready to compile, link, and execute your program. In some C systems these operations are carried out separately. In this case you must begin by calling on the compiler, which will automatically trigger the preprocessor and attempt compilation. If your source file is compiled successfully, you must next call on the linker. The linker, if successful, will create the executable load module. Now you are ready to execute your program.

Certain C systems may permit you to compile, link, and execute your programs by using one command (such as RUN.) This single command will trigger a sequence of operations that includes preprocessing, compilation, linking, and execution. The executable load module, which is created after linking, will be saved in your directory. This method enables you to execute your program again without recompiling it.

### Correcting Compilation and Execution Errors

If your program has **syntax errors**, the compiler cannot proceed with compilation. In this case it displays appropriate error messages on the screen to help you pinpoint the errors. Even if your program compiles successfully, it may contain some errors that prevent the linker from doing its task. In this case the linker will display some error diagnostics. These are called **linker errors**.

A program that has been compiled and linked successfully may still contain some errors that become obvious during execution. **Execution errors** are usually more difficult to find and correct.

The process of finding and correcting errors in computer programs is called **debugging**. To correct errors of all types, you will need to use the text editor to access your source program files. Sometimes, you may have errors in data files. They can also be corrected using the text editor. After you complete the corrections, you must save your edited files. Now you are ready to try to compile and execute your program again.

> ### Steps for Creating, Compiling, and Executing a C Program
>
> 1. Access the computer.
> 2. Use a text editor to type your source program statements.
> 3. Assign a name to your source program file and save it in disk storage.
> 4. Use the text editor to create your data files.
> 5. Assign appropriate names to the data files and save them in disk storage.
> 6. Call the C compiler and compile, link, and execute your source program file.
> 7. If you have no errors and you are satisfied with the results, you may want to get hard copies of the source program file and the program output. Then exit from the C system and log off.
> 8. If errors occur in your program, debug the program and identify the errors' sources. Then use the text editor again and make the necessary corrections in your source program and/or data files. Save your files and attempt compilation again, as in step 6.

---

## 1.6   EXAMPLE PROGRAM 1: A C Program that Balances Your Checkbook for Debit Type Transactions

It is time to see what a C program looks like. Figure 1.1 is a simple C program that you can use to balance your checkbook.

```
1   /**************************************************************
2   Program Filename: prog01_1.c
3   Author          : YOUR NAME HERE
4   Purpose         : Balances checkbooks for debit type transactions.
5   Input from      : Terminal keyboard
6   Output to       : Screen
7   **************************************************************/
8   #include <stdio.h>

9   int main(void) {
10     /* Variable declarations: */

11     double current_balance, check_amount, new_balance;

12     /* Function body: */

13     printf("Enter current balance: $");
14     scanf("%lf", &current_balance);
15     printf("Enter check amount   : $");
16     scanf("%lf", &check_amount);

17     new_balance = current_balance - check_amount;

18     printf("Your new balance     : $%f", new_balance);
19     return 0;
20  } /* end function main */
```

**Figure 1.1**    A C program that balances a checkbook

Don't worry if you don't understand this program. It will be explained shortly. Then, in Chapter 3, we will discuss all of its elements. For the time being, please do the following:

1.  Access your computer account and start the C IDE. Get into the text editor.

2.  Type the program of Figure 1.1 exactly as you see it, but don't type the line numbers to the left of the lines. Line numbers are not part of the program. They are shown in Figure 1.1 to facilitate the explanation.

3.  While typing line 2, replace the expression YOUR NAME HERE with your own name; don't worry, I won't sue you for stealing my program.

4.  Save the source program that you have just finished typing on your disk, which may be in drive A or B if you are using a microcomputer. You will have to assign a name to the program. Use prog01_1.c; note that prog01_1 is the name of the source file, and the name of the source file can be any appropriate name. But the extension of the source file must be c.

5.  Compile, link, and execute the program. If you have no typing mistakes in the source code, the following will take place during execution:

a. On the first line of the execution window, the computer will print

```
Enter current balance: $
```

and the cursor will be to the right of the dollar sign.

b. Type a current balance amount, say, `1205.47`, and press the Enter key. As soon as you do that, a new line will be printed on the screen. Here is what you have:

```
Enter current balance: $1205.47
Enter check amount   : $
```

with the cursor positioned to the right of the dollar sign at the end of the second line.

c. Type a check amount, say, `34.58`, and press the Enter key. A third line will be printed, and the execution will terminate. The final printout on the screen is shown in Figure 1.2.

```
Enter current balance: $1205.47
Enter check amount   : $34.58
Your new balance     : $1170.890000
```

**Figure 1.2**   A sample run of the program of Figure 1.1

You have successfully typed, compiled, linked, and executed your first C program. If you had problems, don't be discouraged. Just try again.

The following explains some elements of this program. We will study these elements in detail beginning with Chapter 3.

1. Strings that begin with a `/*` and terminate with `*/`, such as those in lines 1 through 7, 10, and 12, and the string `/* end function main */` to the right of the symbol `}` on line 20 are called comments. A **comment** is anything that you type, most anywhere that you like in your source code, that begins with `/*` and terminates with `*/`. The main reason for comments is documentation; they explain some important aspects of the program to its readers. If you get a hard-copy printout of a source program file, you will see that comments are also printed. However, during compilation, all comments in the source program are ignored by the compiler and are not translated into machine language.

2. Line 8 contains a preprocessor directive, `#include <stdio.h>`. This particular preprocessor directive allows us to use the `stdio` library, needed for interactive input and output. All C programs must have one or more preprocessor directives.

3. Lines 9 through 20 is the C program. In this case it consists of comments (on lines 10, 12, and 20), declarations (on line 11), and statements (on lines 13 through 19). In this example the C program begins with `int main(void) {` on line 9 and terminates with `}` on line 20.

4. Line 11 is a declaration for three variables, `current_balance`, `check_amount`, and `new_balance`. These are names that we have assigned to three program variables; the computer stores values for these variables in memory

locations identified by these names. In C every program variable must be declared. The first word, `double`, on line 11 informs the compiler that these variables are floating-point variables on which arithmetic can be performed. The compiler reserves memory locations for these variables at compile time. Then, at run time, the operating system creates memory locations for each and makes sure that values are appropriately stored in them. Note that lines containing declarations end with semicolons.

5. Lines 13 through 16 are C statements, which also end with semicolons. Line 13 is an output statement. It prints

```
Enter current balance: $
```

on the screen. This prompt tells the user of the program what to do.

6. Line 14 is an input statement. At run time, when the computer encounters the machine language instructions corresponding to this statement, it halts the execution and waits for the user to type a value and press the Enter key. As soon as the user acts, the computer assigns the typed value to the variable `current_balance`. Now `current_balance` has a value in the main memory.

7. Lines 15 and 16 are similar to the preceding two lines. They prompt the user to enter a value for the variable `check_amount` and read and store a value for it.

8. Line 17 does arithmetic to calculate a value for the variable `new_balance` by subtracting the value of `check_amount` from that of `current_balance`.

9. Line 18 prints on the screen the string

```
Your new balance    : $
```

and the value of the variable `new_balance`, which happens to be `1170.890000` in Figure 1.2.

10. Finally, the statement on line 19 returns the control to the operating system with a status code value of 0.

## 1.7     EXAMPLE PROGRAM 2: A C Program that Balances Your Checkbook for Credit Type Transactions

Now that you have some experience in C programming, why don't you try creating a program of your own, your first C masterpiece. The problem that you should solve is similar to the problem in the previous section; however, your program should balance your checkbook for deposits. When executed, your program should produce a sample run that is similar to that given in Figure 1.3.

```
Enter current balance: $1170.89
Enter deposit amount : $200.00
Your new balance     : $1370.890000
```

**Figure 1.3**   A sample run of the C program that is your first masterpiece

Here are some hints:

1. Your program will be very similar to the program of Figure 1.1. Of course, you should make appropriate changes in the comments.

2. One of the program variables will be different. Instead of `check_amount`, you should use a variable called `deposit_amount`. Therefore, line 11 will have to be modified.

3. You need to supply a value for `deposit_amount`. Thus lines 15 and 16 will be somewhat different.

4. The arithmetic statement on line 17 will have to be rewritten to update your checking account for deposits.

Welcome to C!

## 1.8 SUMMARY

### This Chapter at a Glance

- You learned about the basic computer concepts and terminology that are necessary for the rest of this book.

- You learned about programming languages and that C is a high-level language that can be used for structured programming.

- You studied the C programming environment and standard libraries.

- We discussed the steps involved in using the computer to run programs. You learned how to access the computer; how to use the text editor to prepare program and data files; and how to compile, link, and execute C programs.

- You encountered your first C program. By typing, compiling, and executing it, you acquired the basic skills for using your C IDE.

### Coming Attractions

- This chapter covered one of the two basic background elements that are prerequisites for considering C programming as a problem-solving tool. The second element is the fundamentals of problem solving, which we focus on in Chapter 2.

- In Chapter 2 we discuss problem solving in general, using computers in problem solving from a logical point of view, and the software development method.

- You will study the steps involved in the software development method: requirements specification, analysis, design, implementation, testing and verification, and documentation.

- You will learn about algorithms, which are sequences of steps that produce solutions to problems. You will study pseudocoding, a technique used to design and represent algorithms, and the three fundamental control structures in algorithms: the sequence, selection, and repetition control structures.

- We will discuss the top-down stepwise refinement of algorithms using pseudocode as a fundamental problem-solving strategy.

- After you are through with Chapter 2, you will be able to solve problems logically using the software development method and to describe their solutions with pseudocode. At that point you will be ready for a formal study of C programming, which begins in Chapter 3.

## STUDY GUIDE

### Test Your Comprehension

1. Which of the following is *not* a component of computer hardware?
   **a.** Main memory
   **b.** Operating system
   **c.** Input devices
   **d.** Central processing unit
   **e.** Secondary memory devices

2. Choose the correct statement.
   **a.** A file is an organized collection of information.
   **b.** A program file contains instructions that make up a program.
   **c.** A data file consists of input data of a particular structure.
   **d.** An output file stores the output of a program.
   **e.** All of the above are correct.
   **f.** None of the above is correct.

3. Which of the following is *not* a function of an operating system?
   **a.** Validating user authorization
   **b.** Allocating memory and processor time to programs
   **c.** Compiling source programs
   **d.** Managing disk and tape files
   **e.** Controlling input and output devices

4. Which of the following statements about the preprocessor is *incorrect*?
   **a.** It is a component of the C IDE.
   **b.** It is triggered by a C program that contains preprocessor directive.
   **c.** Preprocessing follows the compilation of the source program file.
   **d.** The preprocessor either includes other files in the program file or replaces some special symbols with appropriate program text.

5. Choose the correct statement
   **a.** A program that is written in a high-level language is called an object program.
   **b.** A program that consists of machine language instructions is called a source program.
   **c.** An interpreter translates all instructions in the source program file into an object program, saves the object program in a file, and then executes the object program file.
   **d.** A compiler translates one high-level program instruction at a time into machine code and immediately executes that code.
   **e.** Compilation is the process of translating a source program into an object program.

**6.** The systems software that is necessary for the execution of the load module is a
  **a.** Compiler
  **b.** Preprocessor
  **c.** Linker
  **d.** Loader or the operating system
  **e.** Text editor

**7.** A typical C IDE contains
  **a.** A text processor.
  **b.** A compiler.
  **c.** A linker.
  **d.** Libraries.
  **e.** All of the above.
  **f.** None of the above.

**8.** In a C program,
  **a.** Entries that begin with /* and terminate with */ are comments.
  **b.** All statements and declarations end with semicolons.
  **c.** We must have one or more preprocessor directives to use standard libraries.
  **d.** The `stdio` library is necessary for interactive input and output.
  **e.** All of the above.
  **f.** None of the above.

**Answers:**   1. b; 2. e; 3. c; 4. c; 5. e; 6. d; 7. e; 8. e.

# 2

# Problem Solving Techniques

---

**CHAPTER OBJECTIVES**

In this chapter you will learn about:

- **What problem solving is**
- **The software development method of problem solving using computers**
- **Steps in the software development method**
- **Design and representation of algorithms**
- **Pseudocoding as an algorithm design and representation technique**
- **Basic algorithm control structures**
  The sequence structure
  The selection structure
  The repetition structure
- **Pseudocoding conventions**
- **Top-down stepwise refinement of algorithms**
- **Programming errors and debugging**
- **Program verification and testing**
- **Program documentation**

By the time you have completed this chapter, you will have acquired the ability to:

- **Apply the software development method to solve problems**
- **Use the top-down stepwise refinement strategy in problem solving**

---

## 2.1    INTRODUCTION

The *American Heritage Dictionary of the English Language* defines a *problem* as a question or situation that presents uncertainty, perplexity, or difficulty. Real life is full of easy and difficult problems; so is every professional field of endeavor. To succeed in life, as well as in our professions, we should develop the ability to solve problems. In this chapter we will try to clarify the meaning of the term *problem solving*, identify the steps involved, define a methodology for problem solving, and see how we can make use of the computer as a tool in the process.

## 2.2    PROBLEM SOLVING

We can define problem solving as follows:

> **Problem solving** is the process of transforming the description of a problem into the solution of that problem by using our knowledge of the problem domain and by relying on our ability to select and use appropriate problem-solving strategies, techniques, and tools.

Let us consider an everyday example of problem solving. Early this spring your father asks you to come up with a fairly accurate cost estimate for mulching the garden. You think about the problem and soon realize that the problem description is ambiguous. You begin asking your father questions about the type of mulch to be used, how thick it should be, where it should be used, and so on. This process enables you to arrive at a better problem specification, called **requirements specification**:

> For the entire garden, shredded cypress mulch will be used. With the exception of the front lawn, all garden plots will be mulched to a thickness of 3 inches. Because you already have a good cover of pine needles under the pine trees in the back yard, 2 inches of mulch will be sufficient there. Determine the cost of the needed mulch and the labor to apply it.

Clearly the solution of this problem is expected to yield the total cost of mulching the garden, which is the output of the problem. Also, you realize that you need additional information to solve this problem. This information is the input to the problem. Because some algebraic formulas will be involved in your calculations, you use appropriate identifiers to represent the input. They are as follows:

1. *Regular_area.* The size of the area, in square feet, to be mulched to a thickness of 3 inches.
2. *Area_under_pines.* The size of the area under the pine trees, in square feet, to be mulched to a thickness of 2 inches.

3.  *Cost_per_bag.* The cost of a 3-cubic-feet bag of shredded cypress mulch.

4.  *Number_of_bags_per_hour.* The number of bags of mulch that Mr. Smith (the handy-man who will be doing the work) can spread in an hour.

5.  *Labor_rate.* The hourly rate Mr. Smith charges for mulching.

You go out to the yard and do some measurements to determine *Regular_area* and *Area_under_pines.* Then you call the local greenhouses and find out the *Cost_per_bag* of mulch. Finally, you call Mr. Smith and learn about *Number_of_bags_per_hour* and *Labor_rate.* Now, you can develop a method of solution for the problem:

1.  To compute the volume of mulch needed in cubic feet, use the formula:

$$Volume\_needed = Regular\_area \times \frac{3}{12} + Area\_under\_pines \times \frac{2}{12}$$

2.  To compute the number of 3 cubic feet bags of mulch needed for the job, use the formula:

$$Bags\_of\_mulch = Volume\_needed \ / \ 3$$

3.  To determine the cost of mulch, apply the formula:

$$Cost\_of\_mulch = Bags\_of\_mulch \times Cost\_per\_bag$$

4.  To determine the labor cost, use the formula:

$$Labor\_cost = Labor\_rate \times Bags\_of\_mulch \ / \ Number\_of\_bags\_per\_hour$$

5.  Therefore, total cost will be

$$Total\_cost = Cost\_of\_mulch + Labor\_cost$$

The method of solution here consists of five steps of calculations and an order in which these steps should be carried out. You should note that the order of the execution of the steps is as important as the steps themselves; you cannot do step 3, for example, before you do step 2. Now, all you have to do is to implement the method of solution by using a calculator as a tool to find the solution and report it to your father. However, re-alizing that mistakes are possible, you check your calculations and test and verify your solution before you knock on the door of your father's study.

To summarize, in order to solve this relatively simple problem, you used a method consisting of the following steps:

1.  **Requirements specification** You eliminated ambiguities in the problem statement.

2.  **Analysis** You identified problem inputs, identified problem outputs, and collected in-formation about the inputs.

3.  **Design** You developed a series of steps with a logical order which, when applied, would produce the output of the problem.

4.  **Implementation** You used your calculator to actually solve the problem.

5.  **Testing and verification** You checked your calculations to verify the correctness of your method of solution.

The method that you use to solve this problem is typical of the method used in solving problems in many fields. In engineering and science this problem-solving approach is the gist of the **engineering and scientific method**. In business-oriented problems it is known as the **systems approach**. You used your calculator as a tool; for a more complex problem, you could have used your computer. This problem-solving approach is equally valid for problems that require the use of computers. We will adopt this problem-solving approach with minor modifications in developing programs to solve problems, and we will call it the **software development method**. Another name that is commonly used for the software development method is **software life cycle**.

## 2.3   USING COMPUTERS IN PROBLEM SOLVING: THE SOFTWARE DEVELOPMENT METHOD

Computers can be programmed to do many complicated tasks at very high speeds. Also, they can store large quantities of information. Therefore, we can use computers as a tool in problem solving if one or more of the following conditions for a problem hold true:

1.  It has extensive input.
2.  It has extensive output.
3.  Its method of solution is too complicated to implement manually.
4.  If done manually, it takes an excessively long time to solve.
5.  We expect to use the same method of solution often in the future to solve the same problem with different inputs.

The general problem-solving method outlined in the previous section also applies to problem solving with computers. The implementation step is somewhat different, however; rather than applying the method of solution to the input data ourselves, we instruct the computer to do it. Now, the computer can execute the steps in the method of solution and solve the problem. However, we need to write a program that consists of instructions corresponding to the steps of the solution such that the computer can interpret and execute them. In developing the program, debugging it, expanding it in the future if necessary, and using it, we will have to remember certain details of the implementation. Consequently, the program has to be properly documented. Thus we add another step to the software development method: program documentation.

The software development method now consists of the following steps:

1.  Requirements specification
2.  Analysis
3.  Design
4.  Implementation
5.  Testing and verification
6.  Documentation

To facilitate the design phase in which we must develop a method of solution for the problem, we make use of problem-solving strategies. There are many problem-solving strategies that we apply, consciously or not, while solving problems. For example, if we are aware of a solution for a problem similar to the one at hand, we use it in developing our solution. We can combine two or more appropriate existing solutions for other problems to come up with a method of solution for ours. We can split the problem into several simpler subproblems, solve each individually, and then combine these solutions into one that corresponds to the solution of the original problem. This latter strategy is called **divide and conquer**. We will resort to the divide-and-conquer strategy frequently in designing methods of solution for programming problems.

Let us now explore in more detail the steps in the software development method. In the following discussions, we will consider a case study. Suppose our phone rings today, and we have an offer from QuikTax, a local federal income tax preparation service, to "Develop a computer program to compute income tax from tax rate schedules for the tax year 1998." The price is right, and we accept the job. However, we realize that the problem as stated is not clear. We start asking questions.

## 2.4    REQUIREMENTS SPECIFICATION

One of the most important steps in problem solving is requirements specification; that is, understanding exactly what the problem is, what is needed to solve it, what the solution should provide, and if there are constraints and special conditions. How precisely we can define a problem depends on our degree of familiarity with the problem domain. If we are not familiar with the problem domain, then we should either quickly acquire an education in it or contact people who are knowledgeable about it.

After interviewing the manager of QuikTax, we come up with the following requirements specification for our problem:

A taxpayer can determine his or her federal income tax by using the tax tables if the taxable income is less than or equal to $50,000. However, if taxable income exceeds this amount, the taxpayer must use the tax rate schedules. Tax rate schedules depend on filing status, which can be single, married filing jointly, married filing separately, and head of household. The following table summarizes the tax rates for the year 1998.

| Filing Status | Taxable Income | | Tax |
| --- | --- | --- | --- |
| | **Over** | **But Not Over** | |
| Single | 49,300 | — | 11,158.50 + 31% of amount over 49,300 |
| Married filing jointly | 34,000 | 82,150 | 5,100.00 + 28% of amount over 34,000 |
| | 82,150 | — | 18,582.00 + 31% of amount over 82,150 |
| Married filing separately | 41,075 | — | 9,291.00 + 31% of amount over 41,075 |
| Head of household | 27,300 | 70,450 | 4,095.00 + 28% of amount over 27,300 |
| | 70,450 | — | 16,177.00 + 31% of amount over 70,450 |

We would like to develop a program to do the following:

1.  Prompt the user to interactively enter a taxable income amount and read it. Taxable income should not be less that $50,000. If it is, the user should be prompted to reenter a correct value.

2.  Display a filing status menu that looks like the following:

```
* * * * * * * * * * * * * * * * * * * * * * * * * * * * * * * * * * *
*  FILING STATUS MENU:                             *
*  Single                          ---- 1 *
*  Married filing jointly          ---- 2 *
*  Married filing separately ---- 3 *
*  Head of household              ---- 4 *
* * * * * * * * * * * * * * * * * * * * * * * * * * * * * * * * * * *
```

3.  Prompt the user to enter a filing status code and read it. If the value entered is less than 1 or greater than 4, the user should be prompted again to type a correct value.

4.  Compute tax using the formula that corresponds to the filing status and the taxable income.

5.  Output the results including taxable income, filing status, and the computed tax as follows:

```
RESULTS OF COMPUTATIONS:
    Taxable income: 70300.00
    Filing Status : Married filing jointly
    Tax           : 15264.00
```

## 2.5  ANALYSIS

In the analysis phase we should identify the following:

1.  Inputs to the problem, their form, and the input media to be used

2.  Outputs expected from the solution, their form, and the output media to be used

3.  Any special constraints or conditions

4.  Formulas or equations to be used

Provided we have acquired a clear understanding of the problem and have a precise requirements specification at hand, the analysis phase is usually easy. For this sample problem, we have the following:

**Input** Consists of taxable income and filing status. All inputs will be interactive, and we will use the keyboard for them.

**Output** Two types of output are expected from this program: the filing status menu, as shown in the requirements specification, and the final output, which consists of taxable income, filing status, and the computed income tax.

**Constraints** The program should not accept a taxable income value less than $50,000.00. Also, the filing status code should be 1, 2, 3, or 4. If the user enters any other value, the program should prompt the user to enter a value that is in the correct range.

**Formulas** The tax rate schedule formulas are those given in the requirements specification.

---

## REVIEW QUESTIONS

1. Problem solving is the process of transforming the description of a problem into a series of steps that solve the problem. (T or F)

2. Which of the following is *not* a condition that requires that a computer be used as a problem-solving tool?
   a. The problem has extensive input.
   b. It is a mathematical problem.
   c. Its method of solution is too complicated to implement through manual means.
   d. Arriving at its solution takes an excessively long time if done by manual means.
   e. Its method of solution is expected to be used for solving the same problem with different inputs.

3. Which of the following is a part of the requirements specification step?
   a. A precise definition of the problem
   b. A specification of what is needed to solve it
   c. An understanding of what its solution should provide
   d. Determining the applicable constraints and special conditions
   e. All of the above
   f. None of the above

4. In the analysis phase we determine problem inputs, expected outputs, special constraints and conditions, and formulas and equations. (T or F)

**Answer:** 1. F; 2. b; 3. e; 4. T.

---

## 2.6   DESIGN AND REPRESENTATION OF ALGORITHMS

The next step is to design a method of solution for the problem. Earlier in this chapter we saw that a method of solution is a series of steps to be performed in a specific logical order. Another name for a method of solution is an algorithm.

> **An algorithm** is a sequence of a finite number of steps arranged in a specific logical order, which, when executed, produce the solution for a problem.

Stated somewhat differently, an algorithm is a procedure that takes a set of values as input and transforms them into a set of values as output. Obviously, not any arbitrarily constructed series of steps can be regarded as an algorithm. An algorithm must satisfy some requirements:

1. **Unambiguousness** It must not be ambiguous. In most cases we develop an algorithm so that it can be translated into a program to be executed by computers. Computers cannot cope with ambiguities. Therefore, every step in an algorithm must be clear as to what it is supposed to do and how many times it is expected to be executed.

2. **Generality** It must have generality. A procedure that prints the message "One inch is 2.54 centimeters" is not an algorithm; however, one that converts a supplied number of inches to centimeters is an algorithm.

3. **Correctness** It must be correct and must solve the problem for which it is designed.

4. **Finiteness** It must execute its steps and terminate in finite time. An algorithm that never terminates is unacceptable.

In general, algorithms have input and produce some output. It is conceivable that an algorithm may have no input. An example could be one that generates a fixed report form. However, such algorithms are rather trivial and quite rare. In practice we expect algorithms to be efficient. An algorithm that is designed for a specific computer is not worth much if it takes days to solve a relatively simple problem or it requires more computer resources, such as memory, than the computer has available.

Unless a problem is simple, developing an algorithm for it is not an easy task. In fact, it is often the most difficult step in the software development process. Also, after developing an algorithm, verifying that it is correct and efficient may be even more of a challenge. Fortunately, the ability to develop correct and efficient algorithms can be improved. One of the main purposes of this book is to help you acquire algorithm design skills through a discussion of available principles and an exposure to many examples.

Even if we can design an algorithm for a problem, it is not enough to just visualize it in our minds. As with any design problem, an algorithm design should be put on paper. In other words, we should be able to represent and document our algorithms using an appropriate language. Unfortunately, English, despite its richness and flexibility, is not a good algorithm representation language. The reason is that descriptions in English, as in any other natural language, can be rather ambiguous. As an example, consider the following attempt at describing an algorithm in English:

> Print the names of all students who are majoring in computer science and whose grade point average is below 3.00 or whose current status is *GRADUATE*.

We can interpret this description in two different ways:

1. Print the names of students who are either computer science majors with a grade point average below 3.00 or graduate students (of any major and any grade point average).

2.  Print the names of students who are computer science majors and, at the same time, either have a grade point average below 3.00 or are graduate students.

Hence the preceding verbal description is ambiguous, whereas an algorithm must be unambiguous.

Several techniques have been developed expressly for the representation of algorithms. We will discuss two of them in this chapter: pseudocoding and flowcharting.

## Pseudocoding

> A **pseudocode language** is a semiformal, English-like language with a limited vocabulary that can be used to design and describe algorithms.

The main purpose of a pseudocode language is to define the procedural logic of an algorithm in a simple, easy-to-understand manner for its readers, who may or may not be proficient in computer programming languages. As you will see, a pseudocode for an algorithm is ultimately implemented as a computer program. It can be contended that because an algorithm's pseudocode is equivalent to its implementation as a computer program, the computer program itself can be used for defining its logic. This contention is true to some extent; however, unless a user is knowledgeable in computer programming languages and the program code is well written, the logic of an algorithm is usually difficult to understand from a program. A program may be excessively cryptic because of its nature, the programming language being used, or the programmer's personal style. Also, a program necessarily contains the syntactical constraints and idiosyncrasies of the programming language. On the other hand, because a pseudocode language is free of these restrictions and forces the algorithm designer to describe the algorithm clearly, a pseudocode language is a more appropriate algorithm description language than any programming language.

A pseudocode language can be used for:

1.  Designing algorithms
2.  Communicating algorithms to users
3.  Implementing algorithms as programs
4.  Debugging logic errors in program
5.  Documenting programs for future maintenance and expansion purposes

To succeed in accomplishing its objectives, a pseudocode language must meet these requirements:

1.  Have a limited vocabulary
2.  Be easy to learn
3.  Produce simple, English-like narrative notation
4.  Be capable of describing all algorithms, regardless of their complexity

In 1966 two researchers, C. Bohm and G. Jacopini, demonstrated that any algorithm can be described using only three control structures: sequence, selection, and repetition.

Therefore, a pseudocode language must have constructs that correspond to these control structures in its vocabulary. There are no universally accepted standards for a pseudocode language. In this book we will use a simple, readable, and complete version for describing our algorithms.

Let us begin our discussion of the three basic control structures. In the meantime, we will develop our pseudocoding conventions.

### The Sequence Control Structure

> The **sequence control structure** is a series of steps or statements that are executed in the order in which they are written in an algorithm.

Figure 2.1 shows a sequence structure. The four statements in this pseudocode algorithm are executed one after another in the order in which they are written. Sequence structures are essentially built into computers. Unless we use other control structures, the computer executes all statements in a program one after another.

> *read taxable income*
> *read filing status*
> *compute income tax*
> *print income tax*

**Figure 2.1**      A sequence control structure

Sometimes it is useful to mark the beginning and end of a block of statements in an algorithm. We will use the keywords *begin* and *end*, as in the following example. You should note that the statements in the block are indented to improve readability.

> *begin*
>     *read taxable income*
>     *read filing status*
>     *compute income tax*
>     *print income tax*
> *end*

### The Selection Control Structure

> The **selection control structure** defines two courses of action, depending on the outcome of a condition. A **condition** is an expression that, when evaluated, computes to either true or false.

The selection structure requires the use of the keywords *if, else,* and *end_if.* The format follows.

> *if condition*
>     *then-part*
> *else*
>     *else-part*
> *end_if*

The meaning of the selection structure is as follows: If the value computed for *condition* is true, the statements that make up the *then-part* are executed. Then the statement that follows the selection structure in the pseudocode will be considered. If *condition* evaluates to false, the *then-part* will be bypassed and the statements in the block called the *else-part* will be executed. The *then-part* and the *else-part* can each be a single statement or a series of statements. In the latter case the statements must be enclosed in blocks using the keywords *begin* and *end.* To indicate the end of a selection structure, we will use the keyword *end_if.* Figure 2.2 shows an *if/else* selection structure.

> *if income is less than or equal to 82,150*
>     *begin*
>         *compute tax = 5100.00 + 0.28 × (income − 34000.00)*
>         *print "Tax rate is 28%."*
>     *end*
> *else*
>     *begin*
>         *compute tax = 18582.00 + 0.31 × (income − 82150.00)*
>         *print "Tax rate is 31%."*
>     *end*
> *end_if*
>
> *print tax*

**Figure 2.2**     An *if/else* selection structure

In this example the condition is *income is less than or equal to 82,150.* Depending on the value of *income,* this condition may be true or false. If it is true, then the statements

> *compute tax = 5100.00 + 0.28 × (income − 34000.00)*
> *print "Tax rate is 28%."*

which make up the *then-part* of the *if* statement are executed. Then the *else-part* of the *if* statement is skipped, and the statement *print tax* is considered. If, however, the condition *income is less than or equal to 82,150* is false, the *then-part* of the *if* statement is skipped and the *else-part,* which consists of the statements,

*compute tax = 18582.00 + 0.31 × (income − 82150.00)*
*print "Tax rate is 31%."*

is executed. Again, the next statement that is taken up is the statement *print tax.*

As you can see in the preceding example, the statements that make up the *then-part* and the *else-part* of *if* statements are indented. The use of indentation helps to visually differentiate the *then-part* and *else-part* statements from those that follow the *if* statement.

In certain decision-making situations, the *else-part* may be missing. In this case the format of the selection structure becomes

*if condition*
    *then-part*
*end_if*

This structure means that if the condition is true, the statements that make up the *then-part* are executed; otherwise, the statement that follows the selection statement will be considered. Here is an example:

*if status is equal to 1*
    *print "Single"*
*end_if*

In this example if the value of the variable *status* is 1, the condition *status is equal to 1* will be true. In this case the only statement in the *then-part* of *if,* that is, *print "Single",* is executed. It will print *Single* on the output device. The program execution will continue with the statement that follows the *if* statement. On the other hand, if the variable *status* has a value other than 1, the selection condition will be false. A false condition will cause the *then-part* to be skipped, and because there is no *else-part,* the statement that follows the *if* will be considered next.

The *if/else* selection structure is useful for two-way decision making. In case we have more than two courses of action in an algorithm, we can use nested selection structures.

A **nested selection structure** is a basic selection structure that contains other *if/else* structures in its *then-part* or *else-part.*

Consider the pseudocode in Figure 2.3. This pseudocode defines five separate courses of actions by nesting *if/else* structures to four levels. The second *if/else* structure is in the *else-part* of the first, the third is in the *else-part* of the second, and so on. If the value of *status* is equal to 1, this algorithm will print *Single*; if *status* is equal to 2, it will print *Married filing jointly*; and so on.

```
if status is equal to 1
    print "Single"
else if status is equal to 2
    print "Married filing jointly"
else if status is equal to 3
    print "Married filing separately"
else if status is equal to 4
    print "Head of household"
else
    print "Error in status code"
end_if
```

**Figure 2.3**     A nested *if/else* structure

Nested selection structures are useful for multiway decision making. However, they can get to be confusing for most programmers if nesting is excessively deep. You should exercise restraint in using nested selection structures in your algorithm designs. In general, it is possible to express a multiway selection structure in terms of a series of two-way selection structures. For example, the preceding pseudocode can be equivalently expressed using six unnested two-way selection structures:

```
if status is equal to 1
    print "Single"
end_if

if status is equal to 2
    print "Married filing jointly"
end_if

if status is equal to 3
    print "Married filing separately"
end_if

if status is equal to 4
    print "Head of household"
end_if
```

▶

*if status is less than 1*
    *print "Error in status code"*
*end_if*

*if status is greater than 4*
    *print "Error in status code"*
*end_if*

■

### The Repetition Control Structure

> The **repetition control structure** specifies a block of one or more statements that are repeatedly executed until a condition is satisfied.

A repetition (or iteration) control structure enables us to define **loops,** which are repeated executions of blocks of statements. Several forms of repetition control structures can be used in algorithm design. To keep things simple, we will describe only one of them here: the *while* repetition structure. It will be sufficient for our purposes until Chapter 9, when we will introduce two additional forms.

   The format of the *while* repetition structure is

*while condition*
    *loop-body*
*end_while*

   Here *loop-body* is a single statement or a block of statements that is executed as long as the condition written after the keyword *while* is true. The keyword *end_while* indicates the end of the repetition structure. The repeated execution of *loop-body* terminates when the condition becomes false. Obviously, something in the loop body must change a component of the condition so that it eventually becomes false and the algorithm control drops out of *loop-body*. Otherwise, we will have a **perpetual loop** (or infinite loop), and the algorithm will never terminate. It is the responsibility of the algorithm designer to make sure that the algorithm is not caught in a perpetual loop. The pseudocode of Figure 2.4 shows an example of the *while* repetition structure.

---

*print "Enter taxable income; should be greater than or equal to $50,000.00"*
*read income*

*while income is less  than 50000.00*
   *begin*
      *print "Enter taxable income; should be greater than or equal to $50,000.00"*
      *read income*
   *end*
*end_while*

---

**Figure 2.4**     A *while* repetition structure

In this example the first statement is a *print* statement, which is a **prompt** for the user, and it asks the user to enter a value for the variable *income*. The second statement reads that value and stores it in *income*. The condition in the following *while* statement computes to true if the value of *income* is less than $50,000.00. In this case *loop-body* is entered, and the *print* and *read* statements are executed. If the value supplied for *income* is greater than or equal to $50,000.00, the condition in the *while* statement will compute to false and the algorithm control will drop down to the statement that follows the *while* statement. Otherwise, the loop body will be executed once again.

To highlight the loop body visually and improve algorithm readability, the statements that make up the loop body of a *while* structure are indented.

## Pseudocoding Conventions

While discussing the three basic control structures, we have started a seed vocabulary for our pseudocode language. So far it consists of the keywords *if, else, while, begin, end, end_if,* and *end_while.* To express other types of operations that are needed for complete algorithm specifications, we must add to our vocabulary. We will be flexible, and rather than restricting ourselves to a set of keywords, we will use some verbs that essentially correspond to the basic capabilities of computers. We will adopt the keywords *read* and *print* for input and output. Depending on the nature of the statements, we will begin them with verbs such as *set, initialize, compute, add*, and *subtract*. There are two important considerations to keep in mind: the keywords must describe the intended operations, and they must be operations that a computer can perform. For example, verbs such as *visualize, sympathize*, and *dislike* won't do in an algorithm description!

Now we are ready to summarize our pseudocoding conventions.

## Conventions for Pseudocoding

1. Each pseudocode statement includes keywords that describe operations and some appropriate, English-like descriptions of operands.

2. Each pseudocode statement should be written on a separate line. If a statement requires more than one line, the continuation lines should be indented.

3. The statements that make up a sequence control structure should begin with unambiguous words such as *compute, set,* and *initialize.* Statements in a sequence structure can be grouped into a block by enclosing them between the keywords *begin* and *end.* Such statements should be indented with respect to the keywords *begin* and *end.*

4. For the selection control structure, use an *if/else* statement. In an *if/else* statement, the *then-part* and, if used, the *else-part* should be indented. Terminate each *if* statement with the keyword *end_if.*

5. For the repetition control structure, use the *while* statement and indent the *loop-body.* Terminate each *while* statement with the keyword *end_while.*

6. All words in a pseudocode statement must be unambiguous and as easy as possible for nonprogrammers to understand.

### Top-Down Stepwise Refinement of Algorithms Using Pseudocode

Now that we have a pseudocode language as a tool for designing algorithms, let us apply it to the problem of developing a program to compute income tax from tax rate schedules. As you remember, we have completed the specifications requirement and analysis phases for this problem, the first two steps of the software development method. In the algorithm design we will use pseudocode. We will also apply a program design technique called top-down stepwise refinement.

Having identified the inputs, outputs, and formulas necessary for tax computations in the analysis phase, we can begin with the initial pseudocode algorithm in Figure 2.5.

> *1  read and verify income*
> *2  read and verify filing status*
> *3  compute tax*
> *4  print income, filing status, and tax*

**Figure 2.5**    Algorithm for computing federal income tax from tax rate schedules (initial pseudocode)

In Figure 2.5 we have essentially split the problem into four subproblems, each simpler than the original problem. In other words, we used a divide-and-conquer strategy. Now we can graphically show the relationship between the original problem and its four subproblems using a diagram called a **structure chart**, as in Figure 2.6. This chart indicates that the original problem is solved if the four subproblems at the lower level of hierarchy are solved from left to right. To arrive at this chart, we started from the top, which is the original problem, and proceeded down to the subproblems, which are its refinements; hence the term **top-down stepwise refinement**. What we have in Figure 2.5 is not sufficiently detailed for a programmer to begin coding. Therefore, we will continue in this manner until we have a pseudocode that can be directly translated into a C program.

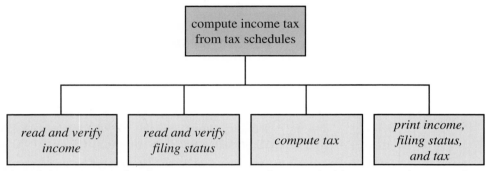

**Figure 2.6**    Structure chart for computing income tax from tax schedules (corresponding to initial pseudocode for Figure 2.5)

We will first consider the pseudocode statement in line 1: *read and verify income*. The refinement of this statement was done in Figure 2.4. After the refinement of statement 1 in Figure 2.5, we have an algorithm that is ready for implementation. It is unambiguous and detailed, and every statement corresponds to a basic capability of the computer.

Next, we consider statement 2 in the initial pseudocode of Figure 2.5: *read and verify filing status*. The logic of this statement is similar to that of the previous step. We will, however, use a different technique in its refinement. Its first refinement follows.

> *while entered filingStatus value is incorrect*
>     *ask the user to enter a correct filing status value*
> *end_while*

Here we have a *while* statement in which we expect the user to enter a *filingStatus* value. The algorithm will then check to see whether the entered *filingStatus* value is correct. If it is, the purpose is accomplished and the algorithm should exit from the loop; otherwise, it should continue asking for another *filingStatus* value. One way of implementing this logic requires the use of a **flag variable** that represents whether or not the value entered for *filingStatus* is correct, that is, whether it is greater than 0 and less than 5. Let that variable be *correctStatusInput*. In the following refinement we begin by initializing this variable to the string value *"no"*, which reflects our assumption that the supplied value of *filingStatus* is incorrect.

```
set correctStatusInput to "no"
print filing status menu

while correctStatusInput is equal to "no"
    begin
        print "Enter filing status; should be between 1 and 4:"
        read filingStatus

        if filingStatus is greater than 0
            if filingStatus is less than 5
                set correctStatusInput to "yes"
            end_if
        end_if
    end
end_while
```

The *while* statement checks whether the value of *correctStatusInput* is *"no"*. Initially, it is; therefore, the *while* condition will be true, and we will enter the loop body. The *print* statement prompts the user to enter a value for *filingStatus*, and the *read* statement assigns the typed value to the variable. The *if* statement checks whether the value of *filingStatus* is in the correct range of 1 through 4. If so, the variable *correctStatusInput* is set to *"yes"* and the loop terminates. Otherwise, the value of *correctStatusInput* remains *"no"*, and the loop body is repeated.

However, one statement in this pseudocode is not yet clear: *print filing status menu*. How do we exactly print the filing status menu? We can do so with the following series of print statements:

```
print "FILING STATUS MENU:"
print "Single                       ---- 1"
print "Married filing jointly       ---- 2"
print "Married filing separately ---- 3"
print "Head of household           ---- 4"
```

These statements will print on the screen the following:

```
FILING STATUS MENU:"
Single                       ---- 1
Married filing jointly       ---- 2
Married filing separately    ---- 3
Head of household            ---- 4
```

All we have to do is substitute the *print filing status menu* statement with these statements. We finally get the algorithm shown in Figure 2.7.

---

*set correctStatusInput to "no"*

*print "FILING STATUS MENU:"*
*print "Single                        ---- 1"*
*print "Married filing jointly      ---- 2"*
*print "Married filing separately ---- 3"*
*print "Head of household          ---- 4"*

*while correctStatusInput is equal to "no"*
   *begin*
      *print "Enter filing status; should be between 1 and 4:"*
      *read filingStatus*

      *if filingStatus is greater than 0*
         *if filingStatus is less than 5*
            *set correctStatusInput to "yes"*
         *end_if*
      *end_if*
   *end*
*end_while*

---

**Figure 2.7**    Final refinement of *read and verify filing status*

Now we consider the statement on line 3 of the pseudocode of Figure 2.5: *compute tax*. We know that there are different tax formulas for different values of *filingStatus* and *income* ranges. For each value of *filingStatus*, we write one *if* statement. The algorithm that corresponds to the pseudocode statement *compute tax* in its final form is given in Figure 2.8.

---

*if filingStatus is 1*
   *compute tax = 11158.50 + 0.31 × (income − 49300.00)*
*else if filingStatus is 2*
   *if income is less than or equal to 82,150*
      *compute tax = 5100.00 + 0.28 × (income − 34000.00)*
   *else*
      *compute tax = 18582.00 + 0.31 × (income − 82150.00)*
   *end_if*
*else if filingStatus is 3*
   *compute tax = 9291.00 + 0.31 × (income − 41075.00)*

---

**Figure 2.8**    Final refinement of *compute tax (continued)*     ▶

*else if status is 4*
  *if income is less than or equal to 70450.00*
    *compute tax = 4095.00 + 0.28 × (income − 27300.00)*
  *else*
    *compute tax = 16177.00 + 0.31 × (income − 70450.00)*
  *end_if*
*end_if*

**Figure 2.8**                                                                ■

Next we will refine the statement on line 4 of Figure 2.5: *print income, filing status, and tax*. In its first refinement we split it into three *print* statements:

*print income*
*print verbal description of filing status*
*print tax*

The first and third statements are clear and need no further refinement. The second statement, however, requires more work. We do not want the algorithm to print 1, 2, 3, or 4 for the values of *filing status*; we would like to have *Single* printed if *filingStatus* is 1, *Married filing jointly* if it is 2, and so on. These can be accomplished by a nested *if* statement as shown in Figure 2.9, which is the second and final refinement of the statement on line 4 of Figure 2.5.

*print income*

*if filingStatus is equal to 1*
  *print "Single"*
*else if filingStatus is equal to 2*
  *print "Married filing jointly"*
*else if filingStatus is equal to 3*
  *print "Married filing separately"*
*else if filingStatus is equal to 4*
  *print "Head of household"*
*end_if*

*print tax*

**Figure 2.9**     Final refinement of *print income, filing status, and tax*

We are done! Now we put all final refinements together and end up with a detailed pseudocode algorithm ready for implementation. It is shown in Figure 2.10.

*print "Enter taxable income; should be greater than or equal to $50,000.00"*
*read income*

*while income is less  than 50000.00*
    *begin*
       *print "Enter taxable income; should be greater than or equal to $50,000.00"*
       *read income*
    *end*
*end_while*

*set correctStatusInput to "no"*

*print "FILING STATUS MENU:"*
*print "Single                      ---- 1"*
*print "Married filing jointly      ---- 2"*
*print "Married filing separately ---- 3"*
*print "Head of household          ---- 4"*

*while correctStatusInput is equal to "no"*
    *begin*
       *print "Enter filing status; should be between 1 and 4:"*
       *read filingStatus*

       *if filingStatus is greater than 0*
          *if filingStatus is less than 5*
            *set correctStatusInput to "yes"*
          *end_if*
       *end_if*
    *end*
*end_while*

*if filingStatus is 1*
    *compute tax = 11158.50 + 0.31 × (income − 49300.00)*
*else if filingStatus is 2*
    *if income is less than or equal to 82,150*
       *compute tax = 5100.00 + 0.28 × (income − 34000.00)*
    *else*
       *compute tax = 18582.00 + 0.31 × (income − 82150.00)*
    *end_if*
*else if filingStatus is 3*
    *compute tax = 9291.00 + 0.31 × (income − 41075.00)*

**Figure 2.10**    Algorithm for computing federal income tax from tax rate schedules (final pseudocode)
(*continued*)    ▶

---

*else if status is 4*
    *if income is less than or equal to 70450.00*
      *compute tax = 4095.00 + 0.28 × (income − 27300.00)*
    *else*
      *compute tax = 16177.00 + 0.31 × (income − 70450.00)*
    *end_if*
*end_if*

*print income*

*if filingStatus is equal to 1*
    *print "Single"*
*else if filingStatus is equal to 2*
    *print "Married filing jointly"*
*else if filingStatus is equal to 3*
    *print "Married filing separately"*
*else if filingStatus is equal to 4*
    *print "Head of household"*
*end_if*

*print tax*

---

**Figure 2.10**

Let us summarize the algorithm design technique that we have used in this case study.

1. Use the divide-and-conquer strategy to split the original problem into a series of sub-problems.

2. Consider each subproblem separately and further split them into subproblems, progressively refining the previous versions in a top-to-bottom manner until no further refinement is possible. Stop the process when you have a pseudocode that can be directly translated into a C program.

3. Combine all final refinements of subproblems according to the logic of the original problem.

This algorithm design technique is essential to good program design. We will use it consistently in this book.

## Flowcharting

Flowcharting is another technique used in designing and representing algorithms. It is an alternative to pseudocoding; whereas a pseudocode description is verbal, a flowchart is graphical in nature.

> A **flowchart** is a graph consisting of geometrical shapes that are connected by flow lines.

The geometrical shapes in a flowchart represent the types of statements in an algorithm. The details of statements are written inside the shapes. The flow lines show the order in which the statements of an algorithm are executed. Two geometrical shapes used in flowcharting are the rectangle, which represents processes such as computations, assignments, and initializations, and the diamond-shaped box, which stands for the keyword *if* in pseudocode, with the *if* condition written inside the box.

The sequence, selection, and repetition control structures essential for algorithm design can be represented in flowcharts, as shown in Figures 2.11, 2.12, and 2.13, respectively. As you can see in Figure 2.13, there is no distinct symbol for the *while* repetition structure. It requires the use of a diamond for condition testing and one or more process boxes for the loop body.

Although, like pseudocoding, flowcharting is useful for algorithm design and representation, it has certain disadvantages that pseudocoding doesn't have. For large algorithms, flowcharts tend to become excessively large. As a result, they are quite difficult to read and the algorithm is hard to understand. Also, drawing detailed flowcharts for large algorithms is tedious and time-consuming. Therefore, we do not recommend using flowcharts as an algorithm design and documentation tool. In this book we will use flowcharts only for explaining the meaning of some C language statements.

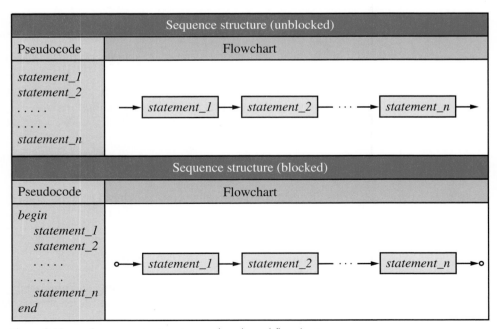

**Figure 2.11**    Sequence structure in pseudocode and flowchart

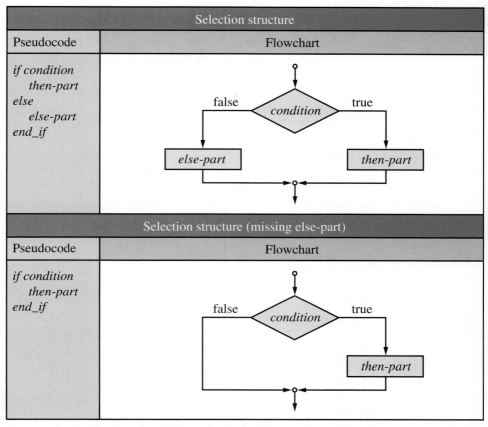

**Figure 2.12**    Selection structure in pseudocode and flowchart

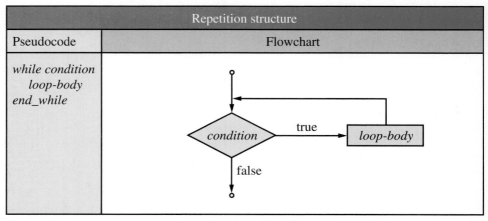

**Figure 2.13**    Repetition structure in pseudocode and flowchart

## REVIEW QUESTIONS

1.  An algorithm is a sequence of a finite number of steps arranged in a specific logical order that, when executed, produce the solution for a problem. (T or F)

2.  Which of the following is a requirement that an algorithm must satisfy?
    a. It must be unambiguous.
    b. It must be correct.
    c. It must be general.
    d. It must be finite.
    e. All of the above.
    f. None of the above.

3.  A pseudocode cannot be used in documenting programs for future maintenance and expansion purposes. (T or F)

4.  Which of the following is *not* a property of a pseudocode language?
    a. It must have a limited vocabulary.
    b. It must be finite.
    c. It must be easy to learn.
    d. It must produce simple, English-like narrative notation.
    e. It must be capable of describing all kinds of algorithms.

5.  Choose the correct statement.
    a. The selection structure requires the use of the keywords *while* and *else*.
    b. The *then-part* of a selection structure is executed if the condition associated with it is false.
    c. After the *then-part* of a selection structure is executed, the *else-part* is considered.
    d. All of the above are correct.
    e. None of the above is correct.

6.  In a *while* repetition structure, some statement in the loop-body must change a component of the associated condition so that it eventually becomes false. (T or F)

7.  In top-down stepwise refinement:
    a. We split each problem into some simpler subproblems.
    b. We begin from the top, which is the original problem, and proceed down to the subproblems, which are its refinements.
    c. We continue until we have a pseudocode that can be directly translated into a program.
    d. All of the above are correct.
    e. None of the above is correct.

**Answers:**  1. T; 2. e; 3. F; 4. b; 5. e; 6. T; 7. d.

## 2.7   IMPLEMENTATION

The next step in the software development method is the implementation of the algorithm in a programming language. During implementation we translate each step of the algorithm into a statement in that particular language and end up with a computer program. Therefore, we can define a computer program as follows:

> A **computer program** is a sequence of a finite number of statements expressed in a programming language in a specific logical order that, when executed, produce the solution for a problem.

To translate the pseudocode algorithm of Figure 2.10, for example, into a C program that can be compiled and executed on a computer, we must know at least a small subset of the C language. We begin the study of C in the next chapter. In Chapter 4 we will write a program for the algorithm of Figure 2.10. Please be patient until then. Designing algorithms is as important and exciting as writing programs in a programming language. In fact, you will eventually see that the real challenge in this business is designing algorithms. Once you develop the ability to design algorithms, writing programs for them is quite easy.

## Programming Errors

Another challenge that awaits you as a problem solver is program debugging. In Chapter 1 we defined *debugging* as the process of finding and correcting errors in computer programs. No matter how careful you are as a programmer, most programs you write will contain errors. Either they won't compile or they won't execute properly. This situation is something that happens very frequently to every programmer. You should take program debugging as a challenge, develop your debugging skills, and enjoy the process. Program debugging is another form of problem solving.

There are three types of programming errors:

1. Design errors
2. Syntax errors
3. Run-time errors

**Design errors** occur during the analysis, design, and implementation phases. We may choose an incorrect method of solution for the problem to be solved, we may make mistakes in translating an algorithm into a program, or we may design erroneous data for the program. Design errors are usually difficult to detect. Debugging them requires careful review of problem analysis, algorithm design, translation, and test data.

**Syntax errors** are violations of syntax rules, which define how the elements of a programming language must be written. They occur during the implementation phase and are detected by the compiler during the compilation process. In fact, another name for syntax errors is **compilation errors**. If your program contains violations of syntax rules, the compiler issues diagnostic messages. Depending on how serious the violation is, the diagnostic message may be a warning message or an error message.

A **warning diagnostic message** indicates a minor error that may lead to a problem during program execution. These errors do not cause the termination of the compilation process and may or may not be important. However, some warning diagnostics, if unheeded, may result in execution errors. Therefore, it is good practice to take warning diagnostics seriously and eliminate their causes in the program.

If the syntax violation is serious, the compiler stops the compilation process and produces **error diagnostic messages**, telling you about the nature of the errors and where they are in the program. Because of the explicit help we get from compilers, debugging syntax errors is relatively easy.

**Run-time errors** are detected by the computer while your program is being executed. They are caused by program instructions that require the computer to do something illegal, such as attempting to store inappropriate data or divide a number by zero. When a run-time error is encountered, the computer produces an error diagnostic message and terminates the program execution. You can use diagnostic messages to debug run-time errors.

## 2.8     TESTING AND VERIFICATION

After you translate a designed algorithm into a C program and compile it, you are ready to run it. In this phase your main objective is to convince yourself — and eventually your clients — that the program will do what it is expected to do. In other words, you will want to verify that your program is correct.

> **Program verification** is the process of ensuring that a program meets user requirements.

One of the techniques that can be used for program verification is program testing.

> **Program testing** is the process of executing a program to demonstrate its correctness.

When you begin testing your program, you may come across some run-time errors. Naturally, you debug them and run your program again. However, even output that seems correct is not a guarantee that your program is completely correct. A program must be tested using a sufficiently large sample of carefully designed test data sets such that every logical path in the program is traversed at least once. If your program contains conditional executions of blocks of code, a single test data set may not cause all program statements to be executed. You must continue to test your program until you are sure that all statements in it are functioning correctly.

Consider the algorithm of Figure 2.10 for the income tax computation problem. After you convert it to a C program and compile the program, you must test it with a critical collection of test data sets. Nine data sets are required to test every logical path in the algorithm: one for an income value that is less than $50,000, two for illegal filing status values (say 0 and 5), and six for testing the six tax computation formulas inherent in the tax schedules. Figure 2.14 shows nine sets of test data that can fully test a program based on the pseudocode algorithm of Figure 2.10.

| Test Data Set | | |
|---|---|---|
| **Income** | **Filing Status** | **Explanation** |
| 49,000.00 | – | Income must be greater than or equal to 50,000.00 |
| 50,000.00 | 0 | Filing status must be greater than zero |
| 50,000.00 | 5 | Filing status must be less than 5 |
| 50,000.00 | 1 | Testing the tax formula for filing status 1 |
| 82,150.00 | 2 | Testing the first tax formula for filing status 2 |
| 82,151.00 | 2 | Testing the second tax formula for filing status 2 |
| 50,000.00 | 3 | Testing the tax formula for filing status 3 |
| 70,450.00 | 4 | Testing the first tax formula for filing status 4 |
| 70,451.00 | 4 | Testing the second tax formula for filing status 4 |

**Figure 2.14**    Test data for testing the algorithm of Figure 2.10

Naturally, the number of sets of test data for program testing depends on the nature of the algorithm for the program. We will emphasize program testing and design of test data in the book.

## 2.9    PROGRAM DOCUMENTATION

Now that you have a working, tested program you are tempted to call it quits and look for new challenges. Please don't! For several reasons, you are not done yet:

1.  You are likely to return to this program sometime in the future to use it again, or you may want to use part of it in developing the solution for a similar problem.

2.  If you have developed this program for a client's use, he or she will need some information so that in your absence the program can be used.

3.  If you are working for a company and have developed this program for the company's software library, some other programmer may be assigned to maintain it or to make additions to it.

4.  You may eventually discover some errors in the program, and you may be required to correct them.

The significance of proper program documentation in the software life cycle cannot be overemphasized. Program documentation consists of these elements:

1.  A concise requirements specification

2.  Descriptions of problem inputs, expected outputs, constraints, and applicable formula

3.  A pseudocode or flowchart for its algorithm

4.  A source program listing

5.  A hard copy of a sample test run of the program

6.  A user's guide explaining to nonprogrammer users how the program should be used (optional)

As you will see beginning in the next chapter, our C programs will have sufficient in-program documentation in the form of comments that clarify several aspects of the program and its logic. In future chapters you will encounter other elements of design (for example, structure charts) that are also part of program documentation and add them to the preceding list.

## REVIEW QUESTIONS

1.  The implementation of an algorithm in a programming language is a computer program. (T or F)

2.  Choose the correct statement.
    **a.** Designing erroneous data for a program is a design error.
    **b.** Syntax errors are violations of rules that define how the elements of a programming language must be written.
    **c.** Attempting to store inappropriate data in program variables is a run-time error.
    **d.** All of the above are correct.
    **e.** None of the above is correct.

3.  The process of ensuring that a program meets user requirements is called *testing*, and the process of executing a program to demonstrate its correctness is called *verification*. (T or F)

4.  Which of the following is an element of program documentation?
    **a.** A concise requirements specification
    **b.** Program comment
    **c.** A pseudocode or flowchart for its algorithm
    **d.** Descriptions of inputs, outputs, constraints, and applicable formulas
    **e.** All of the above
    **f.** None of the above

**Answers:** 1. T; 2. d; 3. F; 4. e.

## 2.10    SUMMARY

### This Chapter at a Glance

*   The second chapter introduced the concept of problem solving — the process of transforming the description of a problem to its solution. To solve complex problems, we use computers as a tool and develop computer programs that give us solutions.

- A commonly used method for problem solving using computers is the software development method, which consists of six steps: requirements specification, analysis, design, implementation, testing and verification, and documentation.
- The requirements specification provides us with a precise definition of the problem. In the analysis phase we identify problem inputs, outputs, special constraints, and formulas and equations to be used. The design phase is concerned with developing an algorithm for the solution of the problem.
- An algorithm is a sequence of a finite number of steps arranged in a specific logical order that, when executed, produce the solution for a problem. An algorithm design should be put on paper. For this purpose, and to facilitate its development, we resort to pseudocoding. A pseudocode language is a semiformal, English-like language with a limited vocabulary that can be used to design and describe algorithms.
- Any algorithm can be described in terms of three basic control structures. They are the sequence, selection, and repetition structures.
- The top-down stepwise refinement of algorithms is a fundamental problem-solving strategy. In designing an algorithm, we begin with an initial pseudocode and refine it in a step-by-step manner until we have an algorithm that can be readily implemented.
- The implementation of an algorithm is a computer program. When executed, it should produce the solution to the problem.
- The next step in the software development method is testing and verification. Program verification is the process of ensuring that a program meets user requirements. Program testing, on the other hand, is the process of executing a program to demonstrate its correctness.
- The final phase is documentation. Program documentation facilitates the use of the program, future program maintenance efforts, and program debugging.
- The information in this chapter added to your problem-solving skills. Now you can come up with detailed specification requirements for problems, analyze problems, design algorithms for problems using the top-down stepwise refinement approach, and describe algorithms in pseudocode.

## Coming Attractions

- This chapter brought us to the design phase in the software development method. To implement a design, we must be fluent in a programming language. The next chapter begins the formal study of the C language and programming techniques, starting with the basic language elements. Then we gradually develop a small language subset so that we can begin solving problems completely as soon as possible.
- Chapter 3 focuses on C statement types that can be used in implementing the sequence control structures in algorithms. To this end, we cover simple input and output statements and statements that can be used in arithmetic calculations.
- Chapter 4 examines two C statements that can be used in implementing the selection and repetition control structures. You will then be in a position to implement many interesting and challenging algorithms.

## STUDY GUIDE

### Test Your Comprehension

1. Which of the following is *not* a step in the software development method?
   a. Requirements specification
   b. Analysis
   c. Design
   d. Selecting the right computer system
   e. Implementation

2. Which of the following elements of a problem solution is identified during the analysis phase in the software development method?
   a. Algorithm
   b. Pseudocode
   c. Problem inputs
   d. The programming language
   e. All of the above

3. A pseudocode can be used in
   a. Designing algorithms
   b. Communicating algorithms to programmers
   c. Implementing algorithms as programs
   d. Debugging logic errors in programs
   e. All of the above
   f. None of the above

4. Which of the following statements concerning the *while* statement is correct?
   a. It is used to define loops.
   b. The loop body is executed if the associated condition is false.
   c. When the condition becomes true, the control drops out of the loop.
   d. All of the above.
   e. None of the above.

5. Which of the following is *not* a correct pseudocoding convention?
   a. Each statement consists of keywords that describe operations and descriptions of operands.
   b. Each pseudocode statement should be written on a separate line.
   c. For the selection control structure, the keywords *while*, *begin*, and *end* should be used.
   d. All words in a pseudocode must be unambiguous.

6. Which of the following statements concerning programming errors is *incorrect*?
   a. Syntax errors are detected by the compiler during the compilation phase.
   b. Run-time errors are detected by the linker.
   c. When a run-time error is encountered, a diagnostic message is produced and the program execution is terminated.
   d. Mistakes in translating an algorithm into a program are design errors.

**Answers:** 1. d; 2. c; 3. e; 4. a; 5. c; 6. b.

## Improve Your Problem-Solving Ability

Consider each of the following as requirements specification for a problem. Complete the analysis and design steps of the software development method until you have a pseudocode that is ready for implementation. Use the top-down stepwise refinement in designing your algorithms. In each case indicate clearly the problem inputs, outputs, constraints, and formulas. Make sure that your pseudocode is clear. Also, in each case design a complete set of test data and explain why it is complete.

**7.** Design a program that keeps on reading positive numbers until the user enters a zero value and then determines and outputs the largest number.

**8.** Design a program that reads five numbers and computes and outputs their arithmetic average. Then generalize your algorithm so that it can handle an arbitrary number of numbers.

**9.** Design a program that accepts a positive integer $n$ as input and computes and outputs the product of all integers from 1 to $n$, including $n$. This product is called the *factorial* of $n$. Now modify your algorithm so that it computes any number of factorials, for as long as the user wants, and terminates if the user does not want to continue.

**10.** Design a program that computes and outputs the $i$th largest number in a group of $n$ numbers (for example, second largest number in a group of 10 numbers.) The user should enter values for $n$, $i$, and $n$ numbers as input.

**11.** Design a program that reads an integer number and computes and returns the number with its digits reversed. For example, if the input is 5643, the program should return 3465.

**12.** Design a program that reads the number of letter grades A, B, C, D and F for a student; computes and prints the student's grade point average; and determines and prints the student's academic standing, which can be high honors, honors, satisfactory, and probation according to the following table:

| Grade Point Average | Academic Standing |
|---|---|
| 3.51 – 4.00 | High honors |
| 3.00 –3.50 | Honors |
| 2.00 – 2.99 | Satisfactory |
| less than 2.00 | Probation |

In computing grade point average, assume that the weight of letter grade A is 4, B is 3, C is 2, D is 1, and F is 0. Here is a sample program run:

```
Enter number of As: 3
Enter number of Bs: 2
Enter number of Cs: 2
Enter number of Ds: 0
Enter number of Fs: 0

Your grade point average is 3.14.
Your academic standing is Honors.
```

**13.** A salesperson gets 6 percent commission on sales less than $1000, 8 percent on sales in the range $1000 through $2000, and 10 percent on sales in excess of $2000. Design a program that reads an arbitrary number of sales made by a salesperson on a given business day and then computes and prints the total number of sales, total amount of sales, and total commission earned by the salesperson. The input is assumed to come from the keyboard, and the input of sale amounts should terminate if the user of the program types 0.

**14.** Design a program that reads a positive integer and then computes and outputs all the positive factors of that integer. For example, the positive factors of 33 are 1, 3, 11, and 33, which are integers that divide 33 evenly.

**15.** Design a program that reads $n$ integer values and then determines and outputs whether the sequence entered is sorted in ascending order, descending order, or is unordered. Here is a sample dialog produced by running the program:

```
How many integers do you have? 4
Enter the 1st integer: 10
Enter the 2nd integer: 8
Enter the 3rd integer: 6
Enter the 4th integer: 4

Your sequence is sorted in descending order.
```

Make sure that your output conforms to the requirements suggested by this sample dialog. Specifically, in the first prompt for the first integer, you must have 1st, in the second 2nd, and in the third 3rd. After the third, you can use an integer followed by the suffix th, as in 4th.

**16.** A geometric series is a sequence of numbers such that each number is a constant multiple of the previous number. For example, the sequence (3, 12, 48, 192, 768) is a geometric series of five elements, beginning with 3, and with a constant multiple of 4. Design a program that computes and prints a geometric series of $n$ numbers, which begins with the first value of *first* and has a constant multiple of *multiple*. The values for $n$, *first*, and *multiple* must be supplied through input. Your program should ensure that values for $n$, *first*, and *multiple* are positive integers and should force the user to enter proper values before providing the solution.

chapter

# 3

# Fundamentals of the C Programming Language

---

## CHAPTER OBJECTIVES

In this chapter you will learn about:

- **The C language character set and tokens**
  Reserved words
  Identifiers
  Constants
  String constants
  Punctuators
  Operators

- **The structure of C programs**
  Program comments
  Preprocessor directives
  Data types and type declarations
  Named constants
  Statements
  Functions

- **How to prepare C source code**

By the time you have completed this chapter, you will have acquired the ability to:

- **Solve problems by using simple forms of C**
  Arithmetic assignment expression statement
  Interactive output statement
  Interactive input statement

- **Debug simple programs using compiler error diagnostics**

---

## 3.1    INTRODUCTION

This chapter serves as a formal introduction to the C programming language. Here we develop our second program and use it to explore the fundamental elements of the C language. This discussion of the language elements is limited to those found in simple C programs. Also, we cover the rules and conventions for typing source program files.

As shown in Chapter 2, implementation of algorithms requires at least five statement types: input, output, arithmetic calculations, selection, and repetition. One of our objectives in this and the next two chapters is to study the C counterparts of this minimal set of statements so that we can begin using the computer for problem solving as soon as possible.

This chapter discusses simple forms of three C statement types: those that we can use for interactive input, interactive output, and arithmetic calculations. These three statement types provide the tools to begin developing our problem-solving skills. By the end of this chapter, you will have a substantial amount of background in C, some competency in writing simple programs, and maybe even some affection for the language and programming.

## 3.2    EXAMPLE PROGRAM 1: A C Program that Computes City Tax

Suppose that we are asked to solve the following simple problem:

**Problem**    Develop a C program that computes the city income tax for the city of Oxford, Ohio, given a taxpayer's gross annual income.

We will use the software development method of Chapter 2 to solve this problem. First, we need a precise requirements specification.

**Requirements Specification**    Develop a program that does the following:

1.  Prints on the monitor screen a brief description of the program's purpose.
2.  Prompts the user to enter a value for gross annual income using the terminal keyboard.
3.  Reads a value for gross income.
4.  Computes the city income tax for the city of Oxford, Ohio. The city income tax is 1.75 percent of the gross annual income.
5.  Prints the computed city income tax.

### Analysis

    **Input.**  Gross annual income in dollars.

    **Output.**  The computed city income tax in dollars.

    **Formulas.**  The city income tax is computed using the formula.

        *income_tax = 0.0175 × gross_income*

***Design***    The pseudocode algorithm for this problem is as simple as that shown in Figure 3.1.

---

*print "A PROGRAM THAT COMPUTES CITY INCOME TAX"*
*print "Enter gross income: "*
*read gross_income*
*compute city_tax = 0.0175 × gross_income*
*print city_tax*

---

**Figure 3.1**    Algorithm for computing city income tax

***Implementation***    The algorithm of Figure 3.1 is so simple, it does not need any further refinement. It is essentially a single sequence structure consisting of four steps. We can write a C program that includes four instructions corresponding to these steps. The program is given in Figure 3.2.

```
1    /*******************************************************************
2    Program Filename: prog03_1.c
3    Author          : Uckan
4    Purpose         : Computes city tax as 1.75 percent of gross
5                      income.
6    Input from      : Terminal keyboard
7    Output to       : Screen
8    *******************************************************************/
9    #include <stdio.h>
10   const double CITY_TAX_RATE = 0.0175;

11   int main(void) {
12      /* Variable declarations: */

13      double gross_income;
14      double city_tax;

15      /* Function body: */

16      printf("A PROGRAM THAT COMPUTES CITY INCOME TAX\n");
17      printf("Enter gross income: ");
18      scanf("%lf", &gross_income);
19      city_tax = CITY_TAX_RATE * gross_income;
20      printf("City tax is %f dollars.", city_tax);
21      return 0;
22   } /* end function main */
```

**Figure 3.2**    A C implementation of the pseudocode of Figure 3.1

There are a lot of details in this program. For the time being, let us concentrate on lines 16 through 20. Line 16 is how we express the pseudocode instruction *print "A PROGRAM THAT COMPUTES CITY INCOME TAX"* in C. The word `printf` (read "print eff") corresponds to the instruction *print* in pseudocode. The character combination `\n` in

```
"A PROGRAM THAT COMPUTES CITY INCOME TAX\n"
```

is an escape sequence. It instructs the computer to start printing on a new line. The escape sequence `\n` will not be printed. As a result of this output statement, the line

```
A PROGRAM THAT COMPUTES CITY INCOME TAX
```

will be printed, and because of the escape sequence `\n`, the cursor will drop to the beginning of the next line on the monitor screen.

Similarly, line 17 is the C counterpart of the pseudocode instruction *print "Enter gross income:"*. It will print the prompt message

```
Enter gross income:
```

on the line where the cursor currently is.

Line 18 corresponds to the pseudocode instruction *read gross_income*. The word `scanf` (read "scan eff") identifies this instruction as an input instruction. When we compile our program, the computer will reserve a memory cell for the variable `gross_income`, and at run time it will actually allocate that memory cell for it. The memory cell for `gross_income` has not been assigned any value. Therefore, it will not contain anything meaningful. At the time our program is being executed, this input statement will cause the execution to halt. The cursor will be blinking immediately next to the previously printed message, that is,

```
Enter gross income: _
```

If we now type a numeric value and press the Enter key, that value will be assigned to `gross_income` and the program execution will continue with the next line.

Line 19 is the C way of saying *compute city_tax = 0.0175 × gross_income*. Let us assume that `CITY_TAX_RATE` is the name of a memory cell that stores the value 0.0175. The symbol `*` in this line is the multiplication operator in C. Therefore, as a result of this statement, the value of 0.0175 stored in `CITY_TAX_RATE` will be multiplied by the value stored in the memory cell `gross_income`. The symbol `=` is the assignment operator, *not* the equality operator in algebra — we will soon see that the equality operator in C is represented as `==`. The assignment operator will cause the result of the multiplication to be stored in the memory cell called `city_tax`.

Finally, line 20 is essentially the same as the pseudocode instruction *print city_tax* except it is a bit more detailed. It will cause the computer to display the string `City tax is` on the monitor screen, followed by the value that has been computed and stored in the variable `city_tax` and the string `dollars.`, all on the same line. So we may get something like

```
City tax is 326.497500 dollars.
```

printed on the screen.

Line 21 does not correspond to anything in our pseudocode. It is a C necessity and returns the integer constant value of 0 to the operating system when program execution is terminated. We examine this language element, called the `return` statement, later in the chapter.

Figure 3.3 shows a sample session obtained by executing the program of Figure 3.2.

```
A PROGRAM THAT COMPUTES CITY INCOME TAX
Enter gross income: 18657
City tax is 326.497500 dollars.
```

**Figure 3.3**    A sample interactive session for the program of Figure 3.2

The five lines that we have just explained are examples of C statements. Notice that they all terminate with a semicolon; this convention is a syntactical requirement for statements. In addition to statements, there are quite a few elements in Figure 3.2. We will begin discussing them in the next section.

## 3.3    LANGUAGE CHARACTER SET AND TOKENS

The basic building blocks in C programs are characters. The **C character set** contains 92 characters. They are the numeric digits (0–9), the 26 letters of the English alphabet, both lower- and uppercase (a–z and A–Z), space (blank), and all other printable special characters that you see on the standard English language keyboard, with the exception of three: `, $, and @.

The characters in the language character set can be combined properly according to some syntactical rules to form tokens.

A **token** is a language element that can be used in forming higher-level language constructs.

Just as we use words, which are a special kind of token, to form sentences in English, we use several types of tokens to build higher-level language constructs, such as expressions and statements, in C. C has six kinds of tokens:

1. Reserved words (keywords)
2. Identifiers
3. Constants
4. String literals
5. Punctuators
6. Operators

## Reserved Words

**Reserved words** are keywords that identify language entities, such as statements, data types, and language element attributes. They have special meanings to the compiler. They must appear in the correct location in a program, be typed correctly, and be used in the right context. The C language is case sensitive; it differentiates between lowercase and uppercase letters. For example, the words main and MAIN are different words in C. Therefore, C reserved words must be typed fully in lowercase. Some examples of reserved words from the program of Figure 3.2 are `const`, `double`, `int`, and `return`. A complete listing of all C reserved words appears in Appendix A.

## Identifiers

When writing a program, we must come up with additional words to represent and reference certain program entities. These are called **identifiers** (also known as **programmer-defined words**). Identifiers are needed for program variables, functions, and other program constructs. In the program of Figure 3.2, the words `gross_income` and `city_tax` are examples of identifiers. Identifier names in a program must be unique within the same scope and the same name space. We discuss the concepts of scope and name space later in the book. For the time being, you should make up distinct identifiers for all your program entities.

---

### Rules for Constructing Identifiers

1. Identifiers can consist of the capital letters `A` to `Z`, the lowercase letters `a` to `z`, the digits `0` to `9`, and the underscore character `_`.
2. The first character must be a letter or an underscore.
3. There is virtually no length limitation. However, in many implementations of the C language, the compilers recognize only the first 32 characters as significant.
4. There can be no embedded blanks.
5. Reserved words cannot be used as identifiers.
6. Identifiers are case sensitive. Therefore, `Tax` and `tax`, both valid examples of identifiers, are distinct.

---

Following are examples of legal identifiers:

```
student_age, Item10, counter, number_of_characters
```

On the other hand, the following identifiers are illegal:

```
student age           Illegal because of embedded blank.
continue              Illegal because  continue  is a reserved word.
17thRow               Illegal because the first character is a digit.
Principal+Interest    Illegal because of the special character  +.
```

In choosing names for identifiers, you should conform to some style guidelines:

1.  Avoid excessively short and cryptic names such as  x  or  wt. Instead, to add to the readability of your program, use reasonably descriptive names, such as `student_major` and `down_payment`.

2.  Use underscores or capital letters to separate words in identifiers that consist of two or more words. For example, `student_major` or `studentMajor` are much easier to read than  `studentmajor`.

## Constants

Constants are entities that appear in the program code as fixed values. In Figure 3.2, `0.0175`  in the line

```
const double CITY_TAX_RATE = 0.0175;
```

is an example of a constant.

C has four types of constants: integer, floating-point, character, and enumeration. In this chapter we cover only integer, floating-point, and character constants.

**Integer Constants**   Integer constants are positive or negative whole numbers with no fractional part. Although C integer constants can be decimal (base 10), octal (base 8), or hexadecimal (base 16), we will focus only on decimal integer constants. An integer constant consists of an optional plus (+) or minus (−) sign and decimal digits.

---

### Rules for Decimal Integer Constants

1.  Decimal integer constants must begin with a nonzero decimal digit, the only exception being  0, and can contain decimal digital values of  0  through  9. An integer that begins with  0  is considered an octal constant.

2.  If the sign is missing in an integer constant, the computer assumes a positive value.

3.  Commas are not allowed in integer constants. Therefore,  `1,500,000`  is illegal; it must be written as  `1500000`.

---

Some examples of legal decimal integer constants are  −15,  0,  +250, and  7550. On the other hand, the constant  `0179`  is illegal as a decimal constant because its first digit is  0; the constant  `1F8`  is illegal because its second digit is the letter  F; and the constant  `1,756`  is illegal because it contains a comma.

**Floating-Point Constants**   Floating-point constants are positive or negative decimal numbers with an integer part, a decimal point, and a fractional part. They can be represented either in conventional or scientific notation. For example, the constant  `20.35`  is written in conventional notation. In scientific notation the equivalent is $0.2035 \times 10^2$. The scientific notation in C for this constant is  `0.2035E+2`  or  `0.2035e+2`. Here the letter  E  or  e  stands for "exponent".

A floating-point constant has many forms in scientific notation. For example, the constant `20.35` can be represented as $0.2035 \times 10^2$, $2.035 \times 10^1$, $20.35 \times 10^0$, $203.5 \times 10^{-1}$, $2035.0 \times 10^{-2}$, and so on. In C these correspond to `0.2035e2`, `2.035e1`, `20.35e0`, `203.5e-1`, `2035.0e-2`, and so on.

In C a floating-point constant consists of six parts:

1. A sign (optional)
2. A decimal integer (optional)
3. A decimal point
4. A decimal fraction (optional)
5. The letter e or E followed by a signed or unsigned integer exponent (optional)
6. Type suffix f, F, l, or L (optional)

If the sign is omitted for a floating-point constant, the computer assumes a positive value. For example, `125.5` is the same as `+125.5`. If the decimal integer is omitted, a value of 0 is assumed for it. The decimal fraction may be omitted: the constants `-15.` and `-15.0` are identical. You can omit either the decimal integer or the decimal fraction, but not both. For example, `20.` instead of `20.0` and `.2` instead of `0.2` are both legal. However, for the floating-point 0, you can type

```
0.0    .0    or 0.
```

but the form (`.`) with no decimal integer and decimal fraction is illegal.

In scientific notation for floating-point numbers, the decimal point may be omitted. For example, the floating-point number `-8.0` can be represented as `-8e0` in scientific notation.

Commas are not allowed anywhere in a floating-point constant. For example, the floating-point constant `1,500.57` is illegal. You must instead write `1500.57`.

C supports three types of floating-point constants: `float`, `double`, and `long double`. Unless otherwise indicated, floating-point constants are of type `double`. The type suffix `f` or `F` indicates that the constant is of type `float`, and `l` or `L` indicates that it is of type `long double`. For example, the constant `0.125` is a floating-point constant of type `double`. If we want this value to be treated as a constant of type `float`, we must write it as `0.125F`. Writing it as `0.125L` causes the compiler to treat it as type `long double`. The types `double` and `long double` are useful in scientific, engineering, and financial applications, where either very small or very large numbers are needed.

Here are some examples of floating-point constants that are illegal in C: `12` is illegal because it is missing a decimal point; the constant `12,000.00` is illegal because it contains a comma; the constant `0.1E+L2` is not legal because the `L` designator cannot be in the integer exponent — it should have been `0.1E+2L`.

**Character Constants and Escape Sequences**    A **character constant** is a character enclosed in single quotation marks. Some examples of character constants are `'1'`, `'n'`, and `'A'`. If we print these constants, we will get `1`, `n`, and `A`, respectively, on the standard output device. For example, the output statement

```
printf("%c", 'T');
```

will print the letter T on the screen.

Most characters can be represented as character constants by enclosing them in single quotation marks. There are some exceptions, however. For example, how do we write the single quotation mark as a character constant? As the single quotation marks serve to delimit a character constant, the representation   ' ' '   is ambiguous and hence illegal. To resolve this problem, we precede the single quotation mark by a backslash,   \. Thus the output statement

```
printf("%c", '\'');
```

prints a single quotation mark on the screen. The backslash is also called the **escape character**. The escape character, along with any character that follows it, is called an **escape sequence**. We have already encountered two escape sequences: the escape sequence   \', which represents a single quotation mark as a character constant, and the escape sequence \n, which causes a new line during printing. For example, the output statement

```
printf("%c", 'n');
```

will print the letter  n  on the screen, whereas the statement

```
printf("%c", '\n');
```

will move the cursor to the beginning of a new line.

There are many useful escape sequences in C. We cover some of them later in the book. A complete list of escape sequences appears in Appendix B.

## String Literals

A **string literal** (or string constant) is a sequence of any number of characters surrounded by double quotation marks. Following are examples of string constants:

```
"This is a string constant."
"125"
"Is this John's car?"
```

In output statements string constants print without the enclosing double quotation marks. For example, the output statement

```
printf("This is a string constant.");
```

will simply print the string constant

```
This is a string constant.
```

String constants are especially useful in prompting users for input in interactive programs and in adding clarity to program output. In Figure 3.2 the output statement

```
printf("City tax is %f dollars.", city_tax);
```

contains a string constant, "City tax is %f dollars.". Because it is a part of the output statement and it controls the appearance of the output, this string constant is called a **format control string**. It consists of ordinary characters that are printed as they are and a format specifier `%f`. A **format specifier** for output converts the internal representation of data to readable characters. In this case the format specifier `%f` converts the internal representation for the value of the variable `city_tax` to readable characters. If the value of the variable `city_tax` is `450`, for example, this output statement will print

```
City tax is 450.000000 dollars.
```

Clearly, this is much better than printing only the value of the variable `city_tax` as `450`.

A string literal can contain any printable characters, including those that are not in the C character set (such as `@` and `$`). The only character that a string constant cannot contain is the double quotation mark, `"`. To include a double quotation mark in a string or print it, we have to use an escape sequence and precede it with a backslash as in

```
"Jim \"Mac\" MacDonald"
```

which will print out as `Jim "Mac" MacDonald`.

Two or more consecutive string constants can be combined into a single string constant during compilation. For example, the output statement

```
printf("THIS PROGRAM COMPUTES " "CITY INCOME TAX");
```

is equivalent to the statement

```
printf("THIS PROGRAM COMPUTES CITY INCOME TAX");
```

In a string constant the backslash character can be used as a continuation character to extend a string literal across line boundaries. For example, the output operation

```
        printf("THIS PROGRAM COMPUTES \
CITY INCOME TAX");
```

is equivalent to

```
printf("THIS PROGRAM COMPUTES CITY INCOME TAX");
```

provided the second line is typed beginning on the first column.

Appropriate escape sequences can be included in string constants to achieve any desired effect. For example, in Figure 3.2 the output statement

```
printf("A PROGRAM THAT COMPUTES CITY INCOME TAX\n");
```

will print the string

```
A PROGRAM THAT COMPUTES CITY INCOME TAX
```

on the current line on the standard output device, and then it will move the cursor down to the beginning of the next line.

## Punctuators

The punctuators (also known as separators) in C include the following symbols:

```
[ ] ( ) { } , ; : ... * #
```

For example, in Figure 3.2 the declaration

```
double gross_income;
```

contains the punctuator  ;. Essentially, punctuators in C are used to delimit various syntactical units. We will discuss each punctuator type when we come to the proper language feature in the book.

## Operators

**Operators** are tokens that result in some kind of computation or action when applied to variables or other elements in an expression. Some examples of operators in Figure 3.2 include the assignment operator = and the multiplication operator * in the statement

```
city_tax = CITY_TAX_RATE * gross_income;
```

Operators act on **operands**. For example, CITY_TAX_RATE and gross_income are operands for the multiplication operator in the preceding statement. An operator that requires one operand is a **unary operator**, one that requires two operands is **binary**, and an operator that acts on three operands is **ternary**. The arithmetic operator  -, which we use to indicate that a number is negative (for example,  -15), is a unary operator. The multiplication operator is binary.

There are many operators in the C language. Appendix B lists them with their classifications. We will study most of them in future chapters. At this point we mention the four familiar arithmetic operators: addition, represented by  +; subtraction,  -; multiplication, *; and division,  /. They all are binary operators, since each requires two operands. The symbols  + and  -  are also used to represent the unary plus and unary minus operators. The unary  +  essentially does nothing; the unary  -  changes the sign of its operand.

Note that some of the punctuators in C are also operators. Examples include the punctuator  *, which is also the multiplication operator, and  ( ), which is the function call operator that we will study soon.

---

## REVIEW QUESTIONS

**1.** Which of the following characters is *not* in the C character set?
   **a.** The left parenthesis,  (
   **b.** The left brace,  {
   **c.** The dollar sign,  $
   **d.** The quotation mark,  "
   **e.** The backslash,  \

**2.** Reserved words are keywords that identify language entities such as statements, data types, and language element attributes. (T or F)

**3.** Reserved words may be typed either in lowercase or uppercase. (T or F)

**4.** Which of the following is a C reserved word?
   **a.** `void`
   **b.** `double`
   **c.** `const`
   **d.** `return`
   **e.** All of the above
   **f.** None of the above

**5.** Identifiers in a program do not have to be unique within the same scope and the same name space. (T or F)

**6.** Which of the following is *not* a correct rule for constructing identifiers?
   **a.** The first character must be a decimal digit.
   **b.** An identifier can consist of letters, digits, and the underscore character.
   **c.** There can be no embedded blanks.
   **d.** Reserved words cannot be used as identifiers.

**7.** Which of the following is a legal C identifier?
   **a.** `1st_Place`
   **b.** `First-place`
   **c.** `First Place`
   **d.** `$FirstPlace`
   **e.** `FirstPlace`

**8.** Which of the following programmer-defined identifiers are illegal, and why?
   **a.** `Out-of-state-customers`
   **b.** `customer_checking_account`
   **c.** `student_on_dean's_list`
   **d.** `total_no_of_students_on_probation`
   **e.** `endOfFile Marker`
   **f.** `36th_row_occupant`
   **g.** `void`
   **h.** `continue`

**9.** Which of the following floating-point constants is legal?
   **a.** `.5678`
   **b.** `23e-1`
   **c.** `-3.7E4`
   **d.** `-.7e7`
   **e.** All of the above
   **f.** None of the above

**10.** Which of the following statements concerning character constants is correct?
   **a.** A character constant must be enclosed in double quotation marks.
   **b.** When used in an output statement, the character constant `'\''` causes a single quotation mark to be printed on the standard output device.

   **c.** When used in an output statement, the character constant `'\n'` causes a lowercase
   n to be printed on the standard output device.

   **d.** All of the above

   **e.** None of the above

**11.** Which of the following statements concerning string literals is correct?

   **a.** A string literal cannot contain characters such as `@` or `$`, because these characters
   are not in the C character set.

   **b.** A string literal can be empty, in which case it is written as `" "`.

   **c.** Escape sequences cannot be included in string literals.

   **d.** All of the above

   **e.** None of the above

**12.** Operators are tokens that result in some kind of computation or action when applied to
variables or other elements in an expression. (T or F)

# 3.4   THE STRUCTURE OF A C PROGRAM

Now that we have studied the basic language elements, the character set and tokens, we
will examine higher-level language constructs from a structural point of view. In general,
a C program consists of the following components:

1. Program comments

2. Preprocessor directives

3. Type declarations

4. Named constants

5. Statements

6. Function declarations (prototypes)

7. Function definitions

8. Function calls

## Program Comments

**Comments** are explanations or annotations that are included in a program for documentation and clarification purposes. Program comments describe the purpose of a program,
function, or statement. They are completely ignored by the compiler during compilation,
and they have no effect on program execution.

There are two ways to specify a comment in the C language. We can use `/*` and `*/` to surround comments, or `//` to begin comment lines. `//` type comments are known as **line comments**.

---

### Rules for Program Comments

1. The characters `/*` start a comment. Such a comment can run any number of lines and over line boundaries. A comment that starts with `/*` should be terminated by the characters `*/`.

2. A `/*` comment cannot contain the character combination `*/` unless this combination is intended to serve as comment terminator. In other words, `/*` comments cannot be nested.

3. The characters `//` start a line comment. Such a comment terminates at the end of the line on which it occurs. If a line comment runs several lines, each line must begin with `//`.

4. The comment characters `//`, `/*`, and `*/` are treated just like other characters in a `//` comment.

---

Some examples of comments follow.

```
// Variable declarations:
/* Purpose: Calculates city tax as 1.75 percent of gross income */
```

Following are some style considerations concerning the use of program comments:

1. Comments are valuable for enhancing the readability of a program. They should be meaningful, clear, pertinent, and up-to-date.

2. Comments should not be redundant. If something is clearly stated in the program, it should not be repeated in a comment. For example, the following comment is redundant:

```
/* Compute city tax as product of city tax rate and gross income: */
city_tax = CITY_TAX_RATE * gross_income;
```

3. Comments should be distinct and visually separated from the program code. It is a good practice to highlight comment lines by using blank lines before and after them.

## Preprocessor Directives

In Figure 3.2 the first program line after the initial blocks of comments is

```
#include <stdio.h>
```

Lines that begin with a pound sign,  #, are not C language statements. They are pre-processor directives.

A **preprocessor directive** (also called a compiler directive) is an instruction to the pre-processor. The **preprocessor** is part of the C compiler. It can perform three functions: (1) named file inclusion in a source program, (2) conditional compilation, and (3) macro substitution. We will discuss macro substitution later. Conditional compilation is outside the scope of this book. Named file inclusion is important at this point, and we will discuss it now.

Named file inclusion is concerned with adding the content of a header file to a source program file. A **header file** (also called an include file) is a file that contains some kind of appropriate C code. There are two types of header files: standard and programmer defined. **Standard header files** are supplied by the vendor of the C compiler system. They contain standard interface information expressed in C. Depending on the nature of an application program, the compiler needs several standard header files before it can compile the application program. Therefore, they must be included in the code using the pre-processor directive  #include. For example, in the preprocessor directive

```
#include <stdio.h>
```

we have the standard header file  stdio.h, which contains the declarations of the basic C input-output routines. When the compiler encounters this directive, it combines the content of the header file  stdio.h  and the source program code and proceeds with compilation. There are many useful standard C header files, and you will find them described in Appendix C.

Essentially, the  #include  directive is a text manipulation facility. It causes a header file to be copied into the code and compiled together with the rest of the program. Header file inclusion is conceptual; the source code itself is not changed, but the compiler generates the object code as if the source code actually includes the code that is in the header file. Standard header files are usually stored in the standard *include* directory of the C system, and they are given the file extension  .h, as in  stdio.h. To include a standard header file in a program, the name of the header file must be surrounded by angle brackets,  <  >.

On the other hand, a **programmer-defined header file** is a C code written by the programmer and stored in some directory. For programmer-defined header files, the #include  directive has a slightly different format. It requires the header file name to be surrounded by double quotation marks rather than angle brackets. The file name may optionally contain a path name. For example,

```
#include "d:header1.h"
```

causes the preprocessor to include the content of the header file  header1.h  that is in directory  d, whereas

```
#include "header2.h"
```

is a directive to the preprocessor to include the header file named  header2.h  that is in the current directory.

We can use programmer-defined header files to advantage in partitioning large programs into several files. We can, for example, store a sequence of declarations in a header file named `student.h`. If we need to use these declarations in our program, we will not have to type them. All we have to do is to have the preprocessor directive

```
#include "student.h"
```

in our source program file. This directive copies the content of the programmer-defined header file `student.h` into the current program before compilation.

The syntax rules for the preprocessor directives are different from those for the C language, and they are somewhat more rigid. Header file names and the surrounding angle brackets or double quotation marks must be typed without any space. For example,

```
#include < stdio.h >
```

will cause an error. You should also note that, unlike C statements, preprocessor directives do not terminate with semicolons.

## Data Types and Type Declarations

In Figure 3.2 following the program line

```
int main(void)
```

and the left brace  `{`, we have

```
double gross_income;
double city_tax;
```

These lines are type declarations for our program variables, telling the compiler that the program variables `gross_income` and `city_tax` are floating-point variables.

> A **declaration** is a syntactical element that associates a type with a program entity, such as a variable.

It is possible to combine declarations of more than one variable provided we use commas to separate them, as in the following example:

```
double gross_income, city_tax;
```

Section 3.3 introduced constants of different types. Because variables are symbolic names for memory locations that store constant values, it is not surprising that variables also have different types. The variable's type determines some very significant characteristics, which include the following:

1. How it is stored internally
2. What operations can be applied to it
3. How such operations are interpreted

We define data type as follows:

> A **data type** is a set of data values and a set of operations on those values.

Let us consider an example: If we declare a variable to be of type integer (designated by the reserved word `int`), the compiler allocates a memory location for that variable. The size of this memory location depends on the type of the compiler. For example, for some compilers that run on IBM PCs, it is 16 bits (or 2 bytes). We can include instructions in our program to store an integer value for such a variable. For integer values the computer uses binary representation. If the word length for variables of type `int` is 2 bytes, the left-most bit in the word is used for the sign and the remaining 15 bits for the value. Hence 16 bits are enough to represent decimal integer values in the range $-32,768$ through $32,767$ ($-2^{15}$ through $2^{15} - 1$). Therefore, if we declare a variable to be of type `int`, we know that any value assigned to it must be in this range. Because of its type, the compiler is designed to perform arithmetic operations (addition, subtraction, multiplication, and division) and assignment operations on an integer variable. The compiler will allow these operations and interpret them properly providing we specify them correctly in our program. Therefore, if we are using a C compiler that stores integers in 2 bytes, the data type `int` is the set of integer values in the range $-32,768$ through $32,767$ and the standard arithmetic operations and the assignment operation on such values.

It is possible to define many different data types, not all of which are supported by a programming language. C has two classes of data types:

1.  Built-in data types
2.  Programmer-defined data types

Those that are recognized by the C programming language are called **built-in data types** (or native data types). On the other hand, some data types can be defined by the programmer. Such data types are called **programmer-defined data types**. We discuss programmer-defined data types in Chapter 12.

In addition, the C language has two classes of built-in data types:

1.  Fundamental data types
2.  Derived data types

A **fundamental data type** corresponds to the most common, fundamental storage units of a computer and the most common, fundamental ways of using such data. The data type `int` is a fundamental data type in C. On the other hand, **derived data types** are types that are derived from fundamental and programmer-defined data types using some operators. Examples of derived data types are arrays, strings, and structures. In this chapter we focus on some simple fundamental data types; we also cover some elementary aspects of strings.

The C fundamental data types include `int`, `char`, `double`, `float`, and `void`. In addition, some of these data types have `short`, `long`, `signed`, and `unsigned` variants (for example, `short int, long int, long double, signed int, signed long int`). This chapter covers the first three fundamental types: `int`, `char`, and `double`. The other types are covered later in the book.

**Data Type `int`**   `int` is used to declare numeric program variables of integer type. For example, the declaration

```
int counter;
```

declares the program variable `counter` as an integer variable. In C compilers that use two bytes for integers, once the variable `counter` is declared this way, we can store only positive or negative integers in the range –32,768 through 32,767. Furthermore, we can perform arithmetic and assignment operations on the variable `counter` in the program. If the C compiler uses four bytes (32 bits) for the type `int`, the range of admissible values for variables of type `int` will be –2,147,483,648 through 2,147,483,647 (that is, $-2^{31}$ through $2^{31} - 1$).

**Data Type `char`**   The type specifier `char` is used to declare character variables. For example, the declaration

```
char more;
```

declares the variable `more` to be of type character.

A character variable stores any printable or nonprintable character in the computer's character set, including lowercase letters, uppercase letters, decimal digits, special characters, and escape sequences. Such characters are represented in one byte (eight bits) of the computer's memory. The internal representation for character values is determined by the character-coding system (ASCII, EBCDIC, and so on) that the computer uses.

**Data Type `double`**   To declare a floating-point variable, we use the type specifier `double`, as in the following example:

```
double gross_income;
```

A variable of type `double` can store floating-point values in the computer's memory. How such values are internally represented and the number of bits needed for their representation depend on the type of the computer you are using.

**Data Initialization**   When the compiler encounters a type declaration for a variable, it reserves a memory location for it. Although such a variable has a bit string in its memory location, it does not correspond to an intended value for the variable. In other words the variable, although declared, may not have been initialized yet.

In C, data may be initialized in two ways, by using:

1.  Compile-time initialization
2.  Run-time initialization

    For example, the construct

```
char more;
```

is a declaration for the variable `more`. If we write it as

```
char more = 'y';
```

the compiler reserves a memory location for `more`. At run time the operating system assigns the reserved location to the variable and places the value `'y'` in the memory location. A variable declaration combined with a value initialization as in the preceding example is also called **compile-time initialization**. On the other hand, the statement

```
more = 'y';
```

assigns the value `'y'` to the previously declared character variable `more` at run time. Therefore, such an assignment is called **run-time initialization**.

**Strings as a Derived Data Type**  A character variable can store only a single character or an escape sequence. Therefore, we cannot use character variables to represent a sequence of characters. For this purpose, we need string variables.

---

A **string** is a sequence of characters that is treated as a single data item. A **string variable** is a variable that stores a string constant.

---

In C a string variable is represented in a one-dimensional array of type `char`. The maximum length of the string constant that can be stored in a character array of size $n$ is $n - 1$ because a string declared as a one-dimensional character array is always terminated by the null character. The null character is represented by either the symbolic constant `NULL` or the escape sequence `'\0'`. Therefore, to declare a string variable that can store string constants of length 30, we must declare a character array of size 31, as follows:

```
char student_name [31];
```

In this declaration `student_name` is the name of the array, `char` is its type, and 31 is its size. If we intend to use this array to store string constants, we must remember that the length of the string constants must not exceed 30 characters.

You will learn about arrays in Chapter 11 and about string processing in Chapter 13. Until then, to enhance your problem-solving skills, you need to know about simple strings. At this point all you need to learn is how to declare string variables. It is as simple as this:

1.  Begin the declaration with the keyword `char`, follow it with a programmer-defined name to represent the string variable, and then write in rectangular brackets, `[ ]`, an unsigned integer constant, which must be one more than the maximum length of string constants that the string variable should store. Example:

    ```
    char report_header [41];
    ```

    This declaration is for a string variable named `report_header` to store string constants of up to 40 characters.

2. To initialize a string variable at compile time, we must follow its declaration by the assignment operator = and a string constant. Example:

```
char report_header [41] = "Annual Report";
```

This declaration causes the compiler to reserve a memory location for `report_header` at compile time. At run time the operating system allocates the reserved memory location to `report_header` and initializes it to the string constant of `"Annual Report"`. Note that the length of the string constant `"Annual Report"` is 13, whereas the size of the array is 41. This difference is all right, as long as the length of the string is no more than the size of the array minus one.

3. Finally, we should note that with string variables declared as character arrays, it is not possible to perform run-time initialization using a simple assignment statement. The assignment statement

```
report_header = "Annual Report";
```

will generate a syntax error. Chapter 4 explains how to assign values to such string variables at run time.

## Named Constants

Another component that we may encounter in a C program is a named constant. In Figure 3.2 the program statement

```
const double CITY_TAX_RATE = 0.0175;
```

is a named constant declaration. A **named constant** is an identifier whose value is fixed and does not change during the execution of a program in which it appears.

In C the declaration of a named constant begins with the keyword `const`, continues with a type specifier (for example, `double`) for the constant, and concludes with an initialization for the identifier that will be treated as a named constant. Once an identifier is declared as a named constant, its value cannot be changed. For the preceding example, an attempt to reinitialize `CITY_TAX_RATE` using a statement such as

```
CITY_TAX_RATE = 0.0185;
```

will result in an error.

After we declare a named constant in a program, we can use the corresponding identifier in any statement in the rest of the code in place of the constant value. During execution, the processor replaces every occurrence of the named constant by the constant value assigned to it and executes the code. For example, in Figure 3.2, having declared `CITY_TAX_RATE` as a named constant, instead of the statement

```
city_tax = 0.0175 * gross_income;
```

we can write equivalently

```
city_tax = CITY_TAX_RATE * gross_income;
```

Using named constants in a program has two advantages:

1. If a complex constant value occurs frequently in a program, declaring it as a named constant minimizes the risk of typing it incorrectly.

2. If it becomes necessary to use another value for a constant entity, providing it has been declared as a named constant, all we have to do is change the named constant declaration and recompile the program. This process is substantially less tedious and safer than changing every occurrence of the constant in the program.

A matter of programming style: use uppercase letters in assigning names to named constants, for example, CITY_TAX_RATE, rather than city_tax_rate. This convention helps you differentiate named constants from variables in a program.

## Statements

In Example Program 1, following type declarations, we have six program lines that terminate with semicolons:

```
printf("A PROGRAM THAT COMPUTES CITY INCOME TAX\n");
printf("Enter gross income: ");
scanf("%lf", &gross_income);
city_tax = CITY_TAX_RATE * gross_income;
printf("City tax is %f dollars.", city_tax);
return 0;
```

Each such line is a statement.

> A **statement** is a specification of an action to be taken by the computer as the program executes.

Each statement causes the processor to do something. The first statement is an output statement that prints the string value A PROGRAM THAT COMPUTES CITY INCOME TAX on the standard output device, the monitor, and drops the cursor to the beginning of the next line. The second statement is also an output statement that prints a prompt for the user to input data. The third statement is an input statement that allows us to input a value for the variable gross_income. The fourth statement computes a value for the expression CITY_TAX_RATE * gross_income and stores the result in the memory location called city_tax. The fifth statement prints the output of the program. Finally, the sixth statement returns the program control to the operating system.

Every statement in C, if correct, does what it is expected to do and then passes the program control to the next statement in the program. The next statement is ordinarily the statement that physically follows it. For some special statements (for example, some jump and selection statements), the next statement executed is not necessarily adjacent to its predecessor; in fact, the next statement may be located anywhere in the program.

There are several types of statements in the C language:

1.   Expression statements
2.   Selection statements
3.   Repetition statements
4.   Jump statements
5.   Labeled statements
6.   Compound statements

You will learn about all C statement types in this book. This chapter, however, covers only three variations of expression statements (input, output, and arithmetic statements), and compound statements.

### Compound Statements

A **compound statement** is a list of statements enclosed in braces, `{ }`. In Figure 3.2 a compound statement begins immediately after `int main(void)` and extends until the end of the program. In this case this compound statement is the body of the program.

A compound statement can contain any number of statements and declarations. The compound statement in Figure 3.2 contains two declarations and six statements. You should note that, although all C statements must end with semicolons, a compound statement does not need the semicolon delimiter after the right brace, `}`.

## 3.5   A FIRST LOOK AT FUNCTIONS

The concept of function is of paramount importance in C programming. The term **function** is synonymous with the term *procedure*, which is defined as a block of code that performs a specific task. Every algorithm, when translated into a program using a programming language, becomes a procedure. In C every procedure is known as a function.

### The Function `main()`

The simplest function is the function main. The simplest definition of the function `main` consists of these elements:

1.  A type specifier, which in standard C must be  `int`
2.  The word  `main`
3.  A null argument list  `(void)`
4.  A compound statement

and it looks like this:

```
int main(void) {
      Statement;
      Statement;
      ..........
      ..........
      return 0;
}
```

In general, a C function may accept some values as input, perform a particular task, and return some values as output. As we will see later, we can use parameters (also called arguments) to supply input to a function and return computed values from it. We can also use the function name to return a single computed value as its output. In Figure 3.2 the function  `main`  returns an integer value of 0 under its name. Such functions must have a  `return`  statement as the last executable statement in their bodies. In Figure 3.2 the `return`  statement ensures that the constant value 0, the program status code, is returned to the program or the operating system that has triggered the execution of this function `main`.

Each C program must have one main function. In addition, a program may contain any number of functions that perform specific tasks. The function  `main`  in a program marks the entry point of the program. The program execution begins with the first statement in the function  `main`  and ends with the last statement in it. In Figure 3.2 the first program statement that is executed is

```
printf("A PROGRAM THAT COMPUTES CITY INCOME TAX\n");
```

in the compound statement that comes after  `int main(void)`. The execution of the program terminates after the execution of the statement

```
return 0;
```

is completed.

The type specifier for functions can be  `int`, `double`, `char`, `void`, and so on, depending on the type of data that it returns. We discuss sending and receiving data to and from functions beginning in Chapter 6. Until then, you must use the type specifier `int`  for the function  `main`. If no type specifier is used for a function, the default specifier is  `int`. We suggest that you avoid the use of language defaults because they tend to detract from program readability.

## REVIEW QUESTIONS

1. Which of the following is *not* a component of C programs?
   a. Preprocessor directives
   b. Type declarations
   c. Statements
   d. Compilation errors
   e. Function declarations

2. Which of the following is *not* a function of preprocessor directives?
   a. Inclusion of named files in a source program
   b. Function declaration
   c. Conditional compilation
   d. Macro substitution

3. A header file is a file that contains some kind of appropriate C code. (T or F)

4. The *type* of a variable determines
   a. How it is stored internally.
   b. What operations can be applied to it.
   c. How such operations are interpreted.
   d. All of the above.

5. Data types that are recognized by a given programming language are called built-in data types. (T or F)

6. Concerning data types in C, which of the following statements is correct?
   a. A fundamental data type is derived from programmer-defined data types using some operations.
   b. The data type `double` is a derived data type based on `float`.
   c. The data type `char` is one of the fundamental data types.
   d. All of the above
   e. None of the above.

7. An attempt to change the value of a named constant in a program results in an error. (T or F)

8. Which of the following about string variables in C is correct?
   a. They are one-dimensional arrays of type `double`.
   b. The maximum length of the string constants that can be stored in them must be the same as the size of the array.
   c. It is possible to initialize string variables at compile time.
   d. Run-time initialization of string variables using an assignment expression is permitted.
   e. All of the above.
   f. None of the above.

9. Which of the following C statements dealing with string variables is correct?
   a. `char book_title [];`
   b. `char book_title [12] = "C Programming";`
   c. `int book_title [13] = "C Programming";`

**d.** `char book_title = "C Programming";`
**e.** All of the above.
**f.** None of the above.

**10.** A list of statements enclosed in braces is a
 **a.** Compound statement
 **b.** Selection statement
 **c.** Repetition statement
 **d.** Jump statement
 **e.** Null statement

**11.** Which of the following statements concerning the function `main` is *incorrect*?
 **a.** Each C program must have one main function.
 **b.** A main function may not have a type specifier.
 **c.** The body of the function `main` is a compound statement.
 **d.** The main function is identified by the word `main`.

**Answers:** 1. d; 2. b; 3. T; 4. d; 5. T; 6. c; 7. T; 8. c; 9. F; 10. f; 11. b.

## 3.6 BUILDING A MINIMUM LANGUAGE SUBSET

You have now learned about every element that we have used in the C program of Figure 3.2. You have also seen that the body of function `main` has an input statement, output statements, an arithmetic calculation statement, and a `return` statement. This section covers simple forms of these statements so that you can begin writing C programs. These statements can be used in forming sequence control structures in algorithm implementations.

### An Introduction to Arithmetic Assignment Expression Statements

An **expression** is a syntactically correct and meaningful combination of operators and operands. Following is an example of a simple expression from Figure 3.2:

    CITY_TAX_RATE * gross_income

This expression instructs the computer to multiply the value of the named constant `CITY_TAX_RATE` by the value of the variable `gross_income`. Here we have the operator `*` for multiplication, and `CITY_TAX_RATE` and `gross_income` are its operands. This expression, however, is not very useful by itself, as the computed value is not saved in the memory. Let us change it a bit and write it as follows:

    city_tax = CITY_TAX_RATE * gross_income

The symbol `=` is the **assignment operator**, and the variable `city_tax` to its left and the expression `CITY_TAX_RATE * gross_income` to its right are its operands. Therefore, this is also an expression. C uses the symbol `=` for the assignment operator; however, you should not confuse it with "equality." As we will see shortly, equality is represented by the symbol `==`. The assignment operator requires two operands; it is a binary operator. Its purpose is to store the value computed for its right operand, that is, the expression `CITY_TAX_RATE * gross_income`, in the variable `city_tax`.

This expression moves us closer to our objective of calculating a value for `city_tax` and storing it in memory. However, the C language requires that this expression be included in an expression statement.

An **expression statement** is any expression followed by a semicolon. If we rewrite the preceding expression once again, this time with a terminating semicolon, we get

```
city_tax = CITY_TAX_RATE * gross_income;
```

Now this statement is complete and will do its task properly. An expression statement that contains the assignment operator is referred to as an **assignment expression statement**. An assignment expression statement that involves arithmetic operations is called an **arithmetic assignment expression statement**. Arithmetic assignment expression statements are used to perform arithmetic calculations.

The simplest arithmetic assignment expression statement in C has the following form:

*Variable = ArithmeticExpression;*

Such a statement computes a value for the *ArithmeticExpression* and stores this result in the memory cell for the *Variable* after necessary type conversions. *ArithmeticExpression* may be as simple as a constant or a variable.

Let us consider some more examples.

***Example 3.1***    Let the variable `current_year` be declared as an integer:

```
int current_year;
```

The assignment expression statement

```
current_year = 1999;
```

stores the constant integer value of `1999` in the memory cell for the variable `current_year`. Because `current_year` is also an integer, no type conversion is necessary during this assignment. This assignment destroys the previous content of the variable `current_year`. Suppose before this assignment statement is executed, the content of the memory cell for `current_year` is `1998`, as shown here:

current_year

```
1998
```

After the assignment statement is executed, the content of `current_year` becomes `1999` and the previous value of `1998` is lost:

current_year

```
1999
```

As you can see, an arithmetic assignment statement in which the expression is a constant can be used to initialize program variables to appropriate values.

***Example 3.2***    Suppose that we declare the variables    area,    short_side, and long_side    in a program as shown here:

```
double area, long_side, short_side;
```

Assume that we have the following picture in the memory of the computer:

```
area                    short_side              long_side
      ┌──────────┐            ┌──────────┐            ┌──────────┐
      │    ?     │            │  10.50   │            │  20.00   │
      └──────────┘            └──────────┘            └──────────┘
```

In other words, the values currently in the memory cells for    short_side    and long_side    are    10.50    and    20.00, respectively. The question mark in the memory cell    area    means that there is no value stored in    area. The arithmetic assignment expression statement

```
area = short_side * long_side;
```

instructs the computer to multiply the value of    short_side    by the value of long_side. The computer calculates the value of the expression (10.50 * 20.00), comes up with    210.00, and because of the assignment operator, stores this value in the memory cell for    area. After the assignment statement is executed, the memory picture becomes

```
area                    short_side              long_side
      ┌──────────┐            ┌──────────┐            ┌──────────┐
      │ 210.00   │            │  10.50   │            │  20.00   │
      └──────────┘            └──────────┘            └──────────┘
```

Again, note that the value of the variable    area    has changed; that is, its previous content has been destroyed. However, the values of the variables that appear in the expression to the right of the assignment operator do not change;    short_side    is still    10.50, and    long_side    is still    20.00.

You will study arithmetic assignment expression statements in more detail in Chapter 5. What you have learned thus far is sufficient for many simple applications.

## The Standard Output Function `printf`

We have already seen that interactive output in C requires the use of    printf. Perhaps the simplest form of    printf    is a user prompt for input, such as

```
printf("Enter your age: ");
```

In fact, this statement is a function call to the standard library function    printf. A **function call** in C consists of the name of the function and a list of arguments enclosed in parentheses. The parentheses    ()    are known as the **function call operator**, and a statement that consists of a function call is considered an expression statement in C. Therefore, the preceding statement, which involves a call to the    printf    function, is a form of expression statement.

Standard library functions are programs that are written to perform some standard tasks, such as input and output. As a programmer, you don't have to worry about writing programs for standard library functions; their object codes are supplied with the C IDE. However, to use a standard library function, you should know the following:

1. Its name
2. Its purpose
3. The name of the header file in which its declaration is found
4. The input it requires
5. The output, if any, that it returns

Input to standard library functions is provided by its actual parameters (or arguments). Arguments are constants, variables, or expressions that are enclosed by parentheses after the function name. If a library function has two or more arguments, they must be separated from each other by commas. Output from library functions can be through arguments, or the functions can return a single value under their name.

Now let us reconsider the `printf` function. Its purpose is to print values using the standard output device, the monitor screen. Its declaration is found in the header file `stdio.h`. Therefore, the preprocessor directive

```
#include <stdio.h>
```

must appear earlier in your program. Following compilation, the linker fetches the object code corresponding to `printf` from the standard C library and combines it with your object program. The input required by the `printf` function are the values that we want to print. They are supplied by its argument list. The `printf` function can have any number of arguments, and it prints them all on the screen. The function returns the number of characters that it prints under its name.

There are two syntactical forms for the `printf` function call:

```
printf(FormatControlString);
```

```
printf(FormatControlString, PrintList);
```

An example of the first form is the statement

```
printf("Enter your age: ");
```

which contains a call to the function `printf` with a single argument. The argument is the string constant `"Enter your age:  "`. This statement simply prints the string

```
Enter your age:
```

on the monitor screen.

The second form of the `printf` function call can be used to print constant values, values stored in variables, and values computed for expressions. In this case the first argument of the `printf` function must be a string constant, called the *FormatControlString*, which contains format specifiers. The remaining arguments make up the *PrintList*; they should be constants, variables, or expressions that are to be printed. Earlier in this chapter, we introduced the concept of format specifiers and stated that their purpose is to convert internal representations for data to printable characters. A format control string must have one format specifier for each value to be printed in the *PrintList*. Also in this chapter, you learned about the format specifier `%lf` for quantities of type `double`. For quantities of type `double`, the format specifier `%f` can also be used. For integer quantities the format specifier is `%d`, and for quantities of type `char`, it is `%c`. The following table summarizes the format specifiers that you have learned so far for the `printf` function:

| Quantity Type | printf Format Specifier |
|---|---|
| int | %d |
| double | %f or %lf |
| char | %c |

Following are additional examples of the `printf` function calls conforming to the second form.

**Example 3.3**    Suppose the value of the variable `year_of_birth` has been calculated as 1974 and stored in its memory cell. Now we want to output this value. The output statement

```
printf("%d", year_of_birth);
```

will print 1974 on the screen. Note that the format control string in this example contains only the format specifier `%d` corresponding to the integer variable `year_of_birth`. Therefore, nothing but the value of `year_of_birth` is printed.

**Example 3.4**    Now suppose that we want to make this output easier to understand. The `printf` function call

```
printf("Your year of birth is %d", year_of_birth);
```

will first print the string value

```
Your year of birth is
```

Following this, the function will print on the same line the value of the variable `year_of_birth`. Thus the screen ends up with the output

```
Your year of birth is 1974
```

***Example 3.5***   Here is a somewhat more complex `printf` function call:

```
printf
("Your year of birth is %d, and in 2000 you will be %d years old.",
year_of_birth, 2000 - year_of_birth);
```

The format control string in this example has two format specifiers, `%d` and `%d`, corresponding to the variable `year_of_birth` and the expression `2000 - year_of_birth`. This statement will print `Your year of birth is 1974, and in 2000 you will be 26 years old.`

The `printf` function can be used to print string variables. To print strings, we use the format specifier `%s`, as shown in the next example.

***Example 3.6***   Suppose we have the following declaration for a string variable:

```
char favorite_book [31] = "The Lord of the Rings";
```

The statement

```
printf("My favorite book is %s", favorite_book);
```

will print

```
My favorite book is The Lord of the Rings.
```

You should note that the name of the string in a `printf` function call appears without a subscript as `favorite_book`, not as `favorite_book [31]`.


## The Standard Input Function `scanf`

In the program in Figure 3.2, we used a statement that involves `scanf` for interactive input. This statement is a function call to the standard library function `scanf`. The declaration of the standard library function `scanf` is contained in the header file `stdio.h`. Therefore, for interactive input you must have the preprocessor directive `#include <stdio.h>` in your source program file.

The syntax of the `scanf` function call is as follows:

```
scanf (FormatControlString, InputList) ;
```

An example `scanf` function call is

```
scanf("%d", &age);
```

In the syntax of the `scanf` function call, *FormatControlString* must consist of format specifiers only. There must be one format specifier for each variable in *InputList*. The *InputList* can contain one or more variables. Constants and expressions in the *InputList* are not allowed. If you have two or more variables in *InputList*, they must be separated by commas. Also, each element of the *InputList* in the `scanf` function call must be an address to a memory location. If it is not already an address, it must be made into an address by prefixing the variable name by the ampersand character, `&`. In this context the ampersand character is the **address operator** in C. The address operator tells the `scanf` function where to find the variables into which values are to be stored.

We can use the following format specifiers in the format control string of the `scanf` function:

| Variable Type | `scanf` Format Specifier |
|---------------|--------------------------|
| int           | %d                       |
| double        | %lf                      |
| char          | %c                       |

Now, let us return to the statement

```
scanf("%d", &age);
```

Assume that the variable `age` is of type `int`. When the computer encounters this statement, the program execution temporarily halts and you will be expected to type a value for the variable `age`. Suppose you type 19 and press the Enter key. Then the `scanf` function converts the value 19 to its internal representation, finds the memory cell for the variable `age`, and stores the converted value in it. Whatever existed in the memory cell for `age` is destroyed, and the value you typed becomes its new value.

Here are some additional examples of `scanf` function calls.

***Example 3.7***   Suppose that we have two variables in a program: `height_in_inches` and `weight_in_pounds`. They are both declared as integers:

```
int height_in_inches, weight_in_pounds;
```

We want the user to enter values for these variables. To make the program easier to use and to avoid possible errors, we decide to use prompts for input. The following program segment will do the job:

```
printf("Type your height in inches: ");
scanf("%d", &height_in_inches);
printf("Type your weight in pounds: ");
scanf("%d", &weight_in_pounds);
```

The first output statement will print the prompt

```
Type your height in inches:
```

Because of the `scanf` function call that follows, the program execution will halt and the computer will wait for us to enter a value. If we type 73 and press the Enter key, the value 73 will be stored in the memory cell `height_in_inches`. Next, the second `printf` function call will execute and will print the following prompt on a new line:

```
Type your weight in pounds:
```

The final statement is another `scanf` function call. It will freeze the cursor after the preceding prompt and wait for us to type a value. If we type 150 and press the Enter key, the value of 150 will be stored in the memory cell for the variable `weight_in_pounds`. The terminal session corresponding to these statements looks like this:

```
Type your height in inches: 73
Type your weight in pounds: 150
```

and the values of the variables `height_in_inches` and `weight_in_pounds` will be 73 and 150, respectively.

A `scanf` function call forces us to terminate what we type by pressing the Enter key, which is equivalent to the new-line character. Therefore, an interactive output statement that follows an interactive input statement begins printing on a new line.

In the preceding example, we used two `scanf` function calls to input values for two variables. It is possible to input values for two or more variables using a single `scanf` function call. Let us not do this, however, until we cover interactive input and output again in Chapter 7. For the time being we will use one `scanf` function call for inputting values for each variable in our programs.

An important difference between the `printf` function and the `scanf` function is that in a `printf` function call, *PrintList* can contain constants, variables, or expressions. However, in a `scanf` function call, *InputList* must consist of addresses of variables only. The following statements are illegal:

```
scanf("%d", 15);
scanf("%d", height_in_inches - 12);
```

The reason is that the value we must type every time a `scanf` function call is executed has to be a constant. A constant can be stored only in a variable; it cannot be stored in another constant or in an expression.

Another feature of the `scanf` function is that it ignores whitespace in the input stream during the input of numeric variables. **Whitespace** is defined as spaces, horizontal or vertical tabs, carriage returns, and line feeds. For example, if you want to input 72 for the variable `height_in_inches` using the statement

```
scanf("%d", &height_in_inches);
```

you may type the value 72 directly, precede it with whitespace, or follow it with whitespace. In any case you must finally press the Enter key. The three streams have the same effect, that of assigning the value `72` to the variable `height_in_inches`. In other words, the following input streams are equivalent:

```
72<Enter>
␣␣␣72<Enter>
72␣␣␣<Enter>
```

␣ represents a whitespace character, and <Enter> is the action of pressing the Enter key.

Using the `scanf` function together with the `%c` format specifier, we can input character values for character variables. We can also input a whitespace character, say, a space, for a character variable. Assuming we have

```
char character;
```

and the statement

```
scanf("%c", &character);
```

we can type any character and assign it to the variable `character`, including whitespace characters.

### Input of String Variables

There are several ways we can input strings interactively in C. We can use the `scanf` function for this purpose, provided the string value does not contain any whitespace. For example, for the string variable `string1` declared as

```
char string1 [31];
```

we can input values using the `scanf` call

```
scanf("%s", string1);
```

Note the absence of the address operator `&` before `string1` in this function call; we will explain the reason for this later in the book. If, in response to this statement, we type the string value `Programming` and press the Enter key, the value assigned to `string1` will be `Programming`. However, if we type the string value `Structured Programming` and then press the Enter key, the value of the variable `string1` will be the string `Structured`. The reason is that `scanf` skips whitespace during string input and picks string values delimited by whitespace.

To input string values that contain whitespace, we can use several techniques in C. We will explain one easy way, which requires the use of the `gets` function that is declared in the header file `stdio.h`. The format of the `gets` function call is

```
gets (StringVariable);
```

*StringVariable* is the string variable to which we want to assign a value through input. For the string variable `string1` declared earlier, we can read values using the statement

```
gets(string1);
```

When the computer executes this statement, it will pause and wait for us to enter a string value. The string value must be typed without enclosing double quotations; its length must not exceed the string variable's declared length, in this case, 30; and typing must be terminated by pressing the Enter key. The string value may contain any character, including whitespace. After we press the Enter key, the string value that is typed is assigned to the variable `string1`. You must remember to have the preprocessor directive that includes the content of the standard header file `stdio.h` in your source program.

We have now covered three useful forms of the C expression statements. They are the arithmetic assignment expression statement, which we can use for value assignments and simple arithmetic calculations; the interactive output statement that uses `printf`; and the interactive input statements that involve `scanf` and `gets`. We are definitely on a roll here! However, no matter how we combine arithmetic expression, input, and output statements in a program, we always end up with sequence control structures. As we saw in Chapter 2, sequence control structures consist of statements that are executed one after another. They are certainly useful in problem solving, but only when we use them together with selection and repetition control structures do we have the ability to solve more interesting and challenging problems. Chapter 4 introduces simple C implementations of the selection and repetitions structures.

## 3.7  PREPARING C SOURCE PROGRAM FILES

After you develop a program as a solution to a problem, you must prepare a source program file. A C source program file is a sequential file that contains browsable and printable C code in character format. If your computer uses the ASCII character set, such a file is an ASCII file; therefore, you will need an ASCII text editor to create it. Most likely, your C system includes an appropriate text editor. If not, you can use a separate text editor. However, you must make sure that the text editor for preparing your C source program file is compatible with your C system.

### Typing the Source Program

In general, there are very few rules that you must keep in mind when typing a C source program into a source file. The C language is almost fully free-form: you can begin typing a language construct anywhere in a line; you can type one or more statements on a line; you can run a statement over two or more lines; and you can place any number of blanks, tabs, or carriage returns between consecutive tokens. All this freedom is possible because the compiler ignores whitespace almost completely. All you have to remember is to insert some whitespace between consecutive tokens.

The only exceptions are preprocessor directives and string constants. These language elements must each be written on one line. For example, the preprocessor directive

```
#include <stdio.h>
```

must not be typed as

```
#include
<stdio.h>
```

and the string constant in the output statement

```
printf("A PROGRAM THAT COMPUTES CITY INCOME TAX.");
```

must not be written as

```
printf("A PROGRAM THAT COMPUTES
        CITY INCOME TAX.");
```

Typing these elements on more than one line generates syntax errors.

However, there is a method you can use to splice two or more lines over which pre-processor directives and string constants may have to run. You can type a backslash as the last character on a line and continue typing the rest of the construct on the next line. For a preprocessor directive the text on the second line can begin anywhere. For a string constant the rest of the string must begin at the first column of the next line; otherwise, you will have unwanted whitespace in the string. The following examples illustrate correct line splicing:

```
#include \
    <stdio.h>
```

```
        printf("A PROGRAM THAT COMPUTES \
CITY INCOME TAX.");
```

## Style Considerations in Typing Source Programs

Take a look at the following code. Would you believe that this code is a C program, in fact, the same C program as Example Program 1?

```
#include <stdio.h>
const
double CITY_TAX_RATE = 0.0175; int main(void) { double
gross_income; double city_tax; printf("A PROGRAM THAT \
COMPUTES CITY INCOME TAX\n"); printf("Enter gross income: ");
scanf("%lf", &gross_income); city_tax = CITY_TAX_RATE *
gross_income; printf("City tax is %f dollars.", city_tax);
return 0;}
```

It compiles correctly and runs flawlessly to produce exactly the same results as Example Program 1. However, in this version the comments have been removed, and the rest of the code has been retyped so that the program is almost completely devoid of style. The program sections run together, many lines have more than one statement, statements run over two or more lines, and unnecessary line splicing has been done. Because line indentation has not been used, the beginning and end of the compound statement are not clearly visible. In short, the program is a mess—not to the compiler, but to the human reader it is almost incomprehensible.

What is style in the context of programming? **Programming style** is a collection of conventions, rules, and techniques that enable us to write programs in an elegant yet simple and efficient manner. Techniques of style are highly personal and subjective and are mostly a matter of common sense. A program with style has aesthetic worth; it is a pleasure to read. In general, it is easier to understand and maintain such a program, even for someone other than the original developer.

In this book we emphasize programming style almost as much as program correctness and efficiency. After all, what is the value of a correct and efficient program if no one, not even the person who wrote it, can understand it and expand on it? You should make sure, (if not while you are developing the program, at least after you are sure that it is running correctly) that your program is readable, understandable, and visually appealing.

Here are some style conventions commonly used by experienced and good C programmers to produce readable code. You should always use these conventions, or their reasonable variations, in your programs.

1. Insert blank lines between consecutive program sections, as in this example from Program 1:

```
double gross_income;
double city_tax;

printf("A PROGRAM THAT COMPUTES CITY INCOME TAX\n");
printf("Enter gross income: ");
scanf("%lf", &gross_income);
```

2. Make liberal use of clear and helpful comments.

3. Keep your comments separate from the program statements.

4. Type each statement or declaration on a single line.

5. Avoid running a statement over multiple lines.

6. Avoid line splicing.

7. Indent all lines that form a compound statement by the same amount. (See Figure 3.2.)

8. Type the beginning and end braces, { }, for compound statements as shown in Figure 3.2; such conventions make C programs easy to read.

9.  Use whitespace in typing statements. The statement

```
city_tax = CITY_TAX_RATE * gross_income;
```

is easier to read than

```
city_tax=CITY_TAX_RATE*gross_income;
```

10. Conclude each function by a comment to mark its end, as in

```
/* end function main */
```

## REVIEW QUESTIONS

**1.** The meaning of the C assignment operator = is the same as equality in algebra. (T or F)

**2.** In an arithmetic assignment expression statement, the left operand of the assignment operator can be an arithmetic expression. (T or F)

**3.** For a `printf` function call, which of the following is correct?
**a.** The format control string can contain printable characters.
**b.** The variables in the *PrintList* must be prefixed by the address operator.
**c.** The *PrintList* cannot include constants or expressions.
**d.** The format specifier `%d` is used for quantities of type `double`.
**e.** All of the above.
**f.** None of the above.

**4.** Which of the following concerning the C interactive input statement that uses `scanf` is correct?
**a.** It is a form of the C expression statement.
**b.** During its execution, the program stops temporarily and waits for the user to enter values for variables.
**c.** It is possible to input values for more than one variable using a single `scanf` function call.
**d.** The elements of the *InputList* in a `scanf` function call cannot be constants or expressions; they must be variables.
**e.** All of the above.
**f.** None of the above.

**5.** The `gets` function
**a.** Is declared in the `stdio.h` standard header file.
**b.** Can be used to input values for string variables.
**c.** Can be used to input whitespace characters.
**d.** All of the above are correct.
**e.** None of the above is correct.

**6.** Whitespace is defined as spaces, horizontal or vertical tabs, carriage returns, and line feeds. (T or F)

**7.** C compilers ignore whitespace completely. (T or F)

**Answers:**  1. F; 2. F; 3. a; 4. e; 5. d; 6. T; 7. T.

## 3.8    EXAMPLE PROGRAM 2: A C Program that Converts Height and Weight to Metric Units

Before we conclude this chapter, we will solve one more problem and use the problem-solving skills that we developed thus far.

***Problem***    We want to develop a program that converts a person's height from inches to centimeters and also converts his or her weight from pounds to kilograms.

***Requirements Specification***    Design a program that does the following:

1. Prompts the user to enter his or her first and last names and reads them into two string variables.
2. Prompts the user to enter a value for his or her height in inches and reads it.
3. Converts the height from inches to centimeters.
4. Prompts the user to enter a value for his or her weight in pounds and reads it.
5. Converts the weight from pounds to kilograms.
6. Prints the user's name, his or her height in centimeters, and his or her weight in kilograms on the monitor screen.

***Analysis***

> **Inputs** Values for the string variables `first_name` and `last_name` and integer variables `height_in_inches` and `weight_in_pounds`.
>
> **Output**s Computed values of `height_in_centimeters` and `weight_in__kilograms`.
>
> **Formulas** The formula for converting inches to centimeters is
>
> $$height\_in\_centimeters = 2.54 \times height\_in\_inches$$
>
> The formula for converting pounds to kilograms is
>
> $$weight\_in\_kilograms = 0.45359 \times weight\_in\_pounds$$

***Design***    The solution of this problem is essentially a sequence structure, as shown in Figure 3.4.

---

*print "Enter your first name: "*
*read first_name*
*print "Enter your last name: "*

---

**Figure 3.4**    A pseudocode algorithm for converting height and weight to metric units *(continued)*    ▶

---

*read last_name*

*print "Enter your height in inches: "*
*read height_in_inches*
*compute height_in_centimeters = 2.54 × height_in_inches*

*print "Enter your weight in pounds: "*
*read weight_in_pounds*
*compute weight_in_kilograms = 0.45359 × weight_in_pounds*

*print first_name, " ", last_name, ", your height is ", height_in_centimeters, "centimeters,"*
   *" and your weight is ", weight_in_kilograms, " kilograms."*

---

**Figure 3.4**  ■

**Implementation**   The algorithm of Figure 3.4 consists of input, output, and arithmetic assignment statements. With our knowledge of the C statement types, we can easily translate this pseudocode into a program. Before we do that, let us decide on a few required program elements:

1.  We will use simple input-output streams for input and output operations. Therefore, we need the standard header file  stdio.h, and our program must begin with the preprocessor directive

    ```
    #include <stdio.h>
    ```

2.  Every variable in the program must be declared. Let us decide on using the type  int for the variables  height_in_inches  and  weight_in_pounds. The variables  height_in_centimeters  and  weight_in_kilograms  will be floating-point variables. Their declarations are

    ```
    int height_in_inches, weight_in_pounds;
    double height_in_centimeters, weight_in_kilograms;
    ```

3.  The string variable  first_name  must be large enough for first names that are 10 characters long, and the string variable  last_name  must be large enough for last names that are 20 characters long. Therefore, we have the following declarations:

    ```
    char first_name [11];
    char last_name [21];
    ```

   Now we can put all of these elements together with the set of statements that correspond to the pseudocode of Figure 3.4 and some appropriate comments. We end up with the code in Figure 3.5.

```
/*******************************************************************
Program Filename: prog03_2.c
Author           : Uckan
Purpose          : Converts height from inches to centimeters,
                   and weight from pounds to kilograms
Input from       : Terminal keyboard
Output to        : Screen
*******************************************************************/
#include <stdio.h>

int main(void) {
      /* Variable declarations: */
      char first_name [11], last_name [21];
      int height_in_inches, weight_in_pounds;
      double height_in_centimeters, weight_in_kilograms;

      /* Function body: */

      printf("Enter your first name: ");
      gets(first_name);

      printf("Enter your last name: ");
      gets(last_name);

      printf("Enter your height in \"inches\": ");
      scanf("%d", &height_in_inches);

      height_in_centimeters = 2.54 * height_in_inches;

      printf("Enter your weight in \"pounds\": ");
      scanf("%d", &weight_in_pounds);

      weight_in_kilograms = 0.45359 * weight_in_pounds;

      printf("%s %s, ", first_name, last_name);
      printf("your height is %lf centimeters, ", height_in_centimeters);
      printf("\nand your weight is %lf kilograms.", weight_in_kilograms);
      return 0;
} /* end function main */
```

**Figure 3.5**     C implementation of the algorithm in Figure 3.4

A few details about the program of Figure 3.5 need explanations:

1. The output statement

```
printf("Enter your height in \"inches\": ");
```

is meant to print the prompt

```
Enter your height in "inches":
```

Because the string constant in `printf` contains double quotations, we had to precede each double quotation with an escape character, `\`, in the string constant.

2. The arithmetic assignment expression statement

```
height_in_centimeters = 2.54 * height_in_inches;
```

contains the expression `2.54 * height_in_inches`, which consists of an integer variable, `height_in_inches`, and a floating-point constant, `2.54`. Such an expression is a **mixed-mode expression**. Mixed-mode expressions are permitted in C. We discuss mixed-mode expressions in detail in Chapter 5. At this point you should understand that if a mixed-mode expression consists of integer and floating-point quantities, the value computed for it will be floating-point. Thus the value of the preceding expression will be a floating-point quantity stored in the variable `height_in_centimeters`, also a floating-point variable.

3. The arithmetic assignment expression statement

```
weight_in_kilograms = 0.45359 * weight_in_pounds;
```

contains another mixed-mode expression that consists of a floating-point constant, `0.45359`, and an integer variable, `weight_in_pounds`; its result will be a floating-point value.

Figure 3.6 is an interactive program session for the program of Figure 3.5.

```
Enter your first name: Kelly
Enter your last name: Johnson
Enter your height in "inches": 64
Enter your weight in "pounds": 110
Kelly Johnson, your height is 162.560000 centimeters,
and your weight is 49.894900 kilograms.
```

**Figure 3.6**   An interactive terminal session for the program in Figure 3.5

## 3.9   PROGRAM DEBUGGING

Now that you have learned a few things about program design, let us return to debugging. In Chapter 2, while discussing program implementation, we mentioned that one of the major challenges in problem solving is program debugging. In general, program design and development are complicated activities, during which even experienced and professional programmers make a lot of mistakes. Depending on the nature of the errors in the program, detecting programming errors may be easy or very difficult.

## Debugging Syntax Errors

We know that programming errors are classified as design, syntax, and run-time errors. Debugging syntax errors is usually quite easy. Most compilers are designed to detect syntax errors and display helpful error diagnostic messages. Some error messages are straightforward and point precisely to the error source. Occasionally, they may be quite confusing. However, as you become more experienced in programming, your debugging skills will improve.

***Example 3.7***   Let us consider an example program that computes the inverse of a supplied number. We want this program to prompt the user to enter a number, read the input, compute its inverse, and print it.

```
1       #include <stdio.h>
2
3       int main(void) {
4             double number;
5
6             printf("Enter a number: ")
7             scanf("%lf", &number);
8             inverse = 1.0 / number;
9             printf("Inverse of %f is %f", number, inverse);
```

When we compile this program, we will see that the compilation will not be successful. The compiler will detect several errors and display some error diagnostic messages, as shown:

```
------------------Configuration: debug - Win32 Debug------------------
Compiling...
debug.c
D:\cprogs\debug.c(7) : error C2146: syntax error : missing ';' before
                      identifier 'scanf'
D:\cprogs\debug.c(8) : error C2065: 'inverse' : undeclared identifier
D:\cprogs\debug.c(8) : warning C4244: '=' : conversion from
                      'const double ' to 'int ', possible loss of data
D:\cprogs\debug.c(10) : fatal error C1004: unexpected end of file
                      found
Error executing cl.exe.
debug.exe - 3 error(s), 1 warning(s)
```

The way such messages are displayed depends on the compiler you are using. Some compilers display them in a message window, and others insert error messages into the source code. Regardless of how they are presented, compiler diagnostic messages are quite helpful. As you can see, the compiler produced four error messages in the preceding example. At the end of the messages, we also have summary statistics, indicating three errors and one warning.

1. The first error message is

```
D:\cprogs\debug.c(7)  :  error C2146:  syntax error  :  missing  ';'  before
                  identifier  'scanf'
```

The integer 7 in parentheses is the line number. Line 7 in our program contains the statement

```
scanf("%lf",  &number);
```

If we examine this statement closely, we will find no syntax errors and we would be right. In fact, as the error message is indicating, the error is actually in the preceding line:

```
printf("Enter  a  number:  ")
```

We notice that this output statement is missing the terminating semicolon. While the compiler was trying to compile this statement, it failed to find a semicolon after the string constant  `"Enter a number: "`. Therefore, assuming that we might have continued on the next line, the compiler looked at the first token on line 7. The compiler found  `scanf`  and concluded that there was an error.

Therefore, you should realize that the cause of a compilation error may not be in the line that the compiler indicates, but may lie elsewhere in a preceding line. In such cases, you should backtrack in the source code and examine the preceding statements carefully.

2. The second error message points to line 8, which has the arithmetic assignment statement

```
inverse = 1 / number;
```

The error message tells us that  `inverse`  is an undeclared identifier. When considered alone, there is nothing wrong with the statement in line 8. Again, the source of error is in the segment of the code that precedes the indicated line.

3. The third error is actually a warning and is again in line 8. It is warning us against possible loss of data during conversion of the result of the expression to the right of the assignment operator, which is of type  `double`, to the variable  `inverse`, which has not been declared. This compiler is assuming that the type of an undeclared variable is  `int`. Clearly, this warning is due to the fact that  `inverse`  is an undeclared variable. As you can see, a single error may cause the compiler to generate more than one message during compilation.

4.  The fourth error message indicates another error — in line 10. In this program, line 10 does not exist. However, the message is telling us that an unexpected end of file is found. We realize that this error is due to the fact that the compound statement, which is the function body, is missing the concluding brace, }. We can easily correct it.

### Debugging for Warning Diagnostics

Sometimes the compiler comes across situations that, although strange or questionable, do not force it to stop the compilation. The compiler decides that an executable load module can be generated and then proceeds, after issuing a warning diagnostic message.

***Example 3.8***   Having corrected the errors in the program of the previous example, we now have the following version:

```
1       #include <stdio.h>
2
3       int main(void) {
4               double number;
5               double inverse, result;
6
7               printf("Enter a number: ");
8               scanf("%lf", &number);
9               inverse = 1.0 / number;
10              printf("Inverse of %f is %f", number, inverse);
11              return 0;
12      } /* end function main */
```

If we attempt to compile this program, we will have success and a warning message:

```
------------------Configuration: debug - Win32 Debug------------------
Compiling...
debug.c
D:\cprogs\debug.c(12)  : warning C4101: 'result' : unreferenced local
                          variable
Linking...
debug.exe - 0 error(s), 1 warning(s)
```

The compiler is warning us that the variable `result` is an "unreferenced local variable"; that is, it is not being used in the rest of the program. This extraneous variable declaration, however, did not stop the compiler from generating an executable load module. In this case the program will execute and generate the desired output, but not all program flaws that generate warning messages are as innocuous; therefore, it is a good idea to treat them as if they are errors. We can correct this problem by getting rid of the declaration for `result`.

### Debugging Run-Time Errors

**Run-time errors** are errors that become apparent while a program is executed. Generally, they are substantially more difficult to debug and require a careful trace of the program logic. Certain run-time errors cause the operating system to produce reasonably helpful error messages; however, debugging them very often requires programmer's ingenuity.

***Example 3.9***   Again, we go back to the previous example, which now has become completely free of compilation errors and warnings:

```
1        #include <stdio.h>
2
3        int main(void) {
4              double number;
5              double inverse;
6
7              printf("Enter a number: ");
8              scanf("%lf", &number);
9              inverse = 1.0 / number;
10             printf("Inverse of %f is %f", number, inverse);
11             return 0;
12        } /* end function main */
```

If we run this program, we will get correct output for many values of the variable `number`. Consider, however, the following program run in which we typed 0 when prompted to enter a number.

```
Enter a number: 0
Floating point error: Divide by 0.
Abnormal program termination.
```

The arithmetic assignment statement on line 9 has an expression that divides 1.0 by `number` to compute a value for `inverse`. We cannot divide a number by zero; neither can the computer. More precisely, a number divided by zero gives infinity, and the computer cannot represent infinity. Therefore, when it comes to division by zero, it terminates the execution of the program and produces a run-time error message.

Since this program is very simple and contains only one division, we can detect the source of error without too much trouble. In more complex programs, however, debugging for run-time errors might be considerably more difficult. In this example we really cannot correct the problem. The only thing that we can do is remember that the number zero does not have a finite inverse, and we can avoid asking the computer to do the inverse computation for zero. On the other hand, we can protect ourselves against inadvertent zero division by using a selection structure in our program. In pseudocode we can replace the statement on line 9 by the *if* statement

---

*if number is equal to zero*
    *print "Zero does not have a finite inverse."*
*else*
    *compute inverse = 1 / number*
*end_if*

---

This way, if we enter zero for `number`, our program will not terminate; instead, it will remind us that we are doing something inappropriate. Chapter 4 explains how we can do something similar in C.

## Debugging Design Errors

Design errors originate during the analysis, design, and implementation phases of a program. Like run-time errors, they are quite difficult to debug. For example, using incorrect formulas in a program will produce erroneous results, and most of the time we will have no error diagnostics to help us find them. If we have the statement

```
inverse = 10.0 / number;
```

instead of the correct statement

```
inverse = 1.0 / number;
```

in the program of Example 3.9, while executing the program for nonzero values of `number`, we will not have any run-time errors. But, we will always get wrong output.

Another cause of design errors is the use of inappropriate input data. For example, if we run the program of Example 3.9 as follows:

---

```
Enter a number: 1e320
Inverse of 1.797693e+308 is 0
```

we see that we do not have a correct value computed for the inverse of `1e320`, which is the scientific notation for $10^{320}$, a very large value. This number is in excess of the largest floating-point value that our computer can store, which means that we should always know the largest and smallest values a computer can represent for arithmetic data types. We consider this issue in Chapter 5.

Debugging programs is one of the major concerns in this book. We will frequently return to this topic and examine additional examples of program debugging to further sharpen your program debugging skills.

## 3.10   SUMMARY

### This Chapter at a Glance

- This chapter was your formal exposure to the C language and C programming. You encountered your second complete C program. Using it as an example, you learned about the fundamental language elements.

- The fundamental language elements covered in this chapter are the C character set, reserved words, identifiers, constants, string constants, punctuators, and operators.

- We examined C programs from a structural point of view. We identified program comments, preprocessor directives, data types, type declarations, named constants, and statements.

- You learned that a function is a program designed to perform a specific task. In this respect, we observed that every C program contains a function called `main` and that program execution begins and terminates at this function.

- Keeping in mind that we are learning C in order to develop problem-solving skills, we focused on three simple expression statement types: arithmetic assignment, interactive input, and interactive output.

- For interactive input you studied the `scanf` and `gets` functions, and for interactive output you learned about the `printf` function.

- Now your bag of skills includes the ability to
  1. Write appropriate comments.
  2. Write the preprocessor directive to include declarations of the standard input and output functions in programs.
  3. Declare variables of type `int`, `double`, and `char`, and strings.
  4. Declare and use named constants.
  5. Initialize data in programs.
  6. Do simple arithmetic calculations using arithmetic assignment statements.
  7. Input values interactively using the `scanf` and the `gets` functions.
  8. Output results using the `printf` function.

- We learned how to prepare a C source program file and studied some program style considerations.

- We discussed program debugging and examined techniques for debugging syntax, run-time, and design errors. This discussion is the beginning point for developing program debugging skills. Program debugging is a very important element of problem solving, and we will continue to emphasize it in future chapters.

## Coming Attractions

- In Chapter 2 you learned that in addition to sequence structures, algorithms are also built on selection and repetition control structures. In fact, many interesting problems require the use of these control structures. In Chapter 4 we discuss the C `if` and `while` statements.
- The `if` statement is one of the selection statements in C that can be used for implementing selection control structures. The `while` statement is one of the three available repetition statements. These two statements enable programmers to solve many interesting and challenging problems.
- By the end of Chapter 4, you will have mastered a minimal subset of C statements and have become quite proficient in problem solving using C.

---

## STUDY GUIDE

### Test Your Comprehension

**1.** Which of the following is *not* a token in C?
   **a.** Reserved words
   **b.** Statements
   **c.** String literals
   **d.** Punctuators
   **e.** Operators

**2.** An identifier in C
   **a.** Cannot contain any uppercase or lowercase letters, decimal digits, or the underscore character.
   **b.** Can have no more than one embedded blank.
   **c.** Can begin with an underscore.
   **d.** Can be a reserved word.
   **e.** All of the above are correct.
   **f.** None of the above is correct.

**3.** Which of the following is *not* a legal identifier?
   **a.** `downPayment`
   **b.** `1st_Root`
   **c.** `end_of_month_report`
   **d.** `costPerPound`
   **e.** `HASH_TABLE`

**4.** For a floating-point constant, which statement is correct?
   **a.** If the sign is omitted for the entire constant, the computer assumes a negative value.
   **b.** The decimal integer cannot be omitted and must always be written, even if it is zero.

   **c.** In scientific notation, the decimal point may be omitted.

   **d.** Commas are allowed only in the integer exponent.

   **e.** All of the above.

   **f.** None of the above.

**5.** Which of the following statements concerning program comments is correct?

   **a.** Comments that begin with the characters `/*` terminate at the end of the line on which they occur.

   **b.** Comments that start with the characters `//` can run any number of lines and over line boundaries. They should be terminated by the characters `//`.

   **c.** The comment characters `//`, `/*`, and `*/` are treated just like other characters in a `//` comment.

   **d.** Comments are processed by the compiler just like any other program element.

**6.** Which of the following statements concerning header files is correct?

   **a.** Standard header files are supplied by vendors of C compilers and reside in the standard *include* directory.

   **b.** Programmer-defined header files can be stored in any directory.

   **c.** A preprocessor directive, such as `#include <stdio.h>`, causes a standard header file to be copied into the code.

   **d.** A preprocessor directive, such as `#include "myheader.h"`, causes a programmer-defined header file in the current directory to be copied into the code.

   **e.** All of the above.

   **f.** None of the above.

**7.** Strings in C

   **a.** Are a programmer-defined data type.

   **b.** Are represented as one-dimensional arrays of type `int`.

   **c.** Can be assigned values at run time using assignment expression statements.

   **d.** Can be assigned initial values at compile time.

   **e.** All of the above are correct.

   **f.** None of the above is correct.

**8.** Which of the following statements about C is correct?

   **a.** A statement does what it is expected to do and then passes the program control to the next statement in the program.

   **b.** The next statement for specific jump and selection statements is not necessarily adjacent to them; it may be located anywhere in the program.

   **c.** An expression statement is an expression followed by a semicolon.

   **d.** An assignment statement is an expression statement.

   **e.** All of the above.

   **f.** None of the above.

**9.** Which of the following concerning expression statements is *incorrect*?

   **a.** An expression statement is any expression followed by a semicolon.

   **b.** An expression statement that contains the assignment operator is called an assignment expression statement.

   **c.** An arithmetic assignment expression statement is a form of an expression statement.

   **d.** The C selection statements are forms of an expression statement.

   **e.** The output statement that involves a `printf` function call is a form of an expression statement.

**10.** Concerning the `printf` function:
   **a.** The names of variables to be printed by `printf` must be prefixed by the address operator, `&`.
   **b.** A statement that consists of a `printf` function call is a form of the C expression statement.
   **c.** We can print only values of variables, not constants or expressions.
   **d.** It is not possible to print more than one value by a single `printf` function call.
   **e.** All of the above are correct.
   **f.** None of the above is correct.

**11.** Choose the correct alternative.
   **a.** The standard library function `scanf` can be used for interactive input.
   **b.** The format control string for `scanf` must include only format specifiers and no printable characters.
   **c.** The `scanf` format specifier for integer variables is `%d`.
   **d.** The `scanf` format specifier for variables of type `double` is `%lf`.
   **e.** All of the above are correct.
   **f.** None of the above is correct.

**12.** The statement `gets(job_title);` can be used to input values for the variable `job_title` that is declared as
   **a.** `char job_title;`
   **b.** `char job_title [40];`
   **c.** `int job_title [40];`
   **d.** `char job_title [];`
   **e.** None of the above.

**Answers:** 1. b; 2. c; 3. b; 4. c; 5. c; 6. e; 7. d; 8. d; 9. e; 10. b; 11. e; 12. b.

## Improve Your Problem-Solving Ability

### *Debugging Exercises*

**13.** For each of the following C decimal constants, state whether they are legal or not, and if illegal, why.
   **a.** `12,000,000`
   **b.** `0934`
   **c.** `-11e11`
   **d.** `.05e+2.2`
   **e.** `'Hello!'`
   **f.** `"He said "Hi""`

**14.** For each of the following identifiers, specify whether they are legal or not, and if illegal, state your reason.
   **a.** `item-code`
   **b.** `$_amount`
   **c.** `#include`
   **d.** `class`
   **e.** `classOf85`

**f.** `return`

**g.** `purchase_price`

**15.** In each of the following C constructs, find the syntax errors, if any, and explain why they are errors.

**a.** `cost + profit = price;`

**b.** `25.0 = cost + profit;`

**c.** `current_balance == previous_balance + deposit;`

**d.** `scanf("Enter a value: ");`

**e.** `scanf("%d", 18);`

**f.** `printf("The result is: %d", &result);`

**g.** `scanf("%lf", x + z);`

**h.** `void function main()`

**i.** `gets(40, string);`

### *Programming Exercises*

**16.** Write a single C statement corresponding to each of the following tasks:

**a.** Declare the variables `weight` and `height` as floating-point variables.

**b.** Declare the variable `counter` as an integer variable with an initial value of 0.

**c.** Set the value of `weight` to `180.5`.

**d.** Add 1 to the value of `counter` and store the result in `counter`.

**e.** Declare the variables `weight_loss` and `new_weight` as floating-point variables.

**f.** Read a value for `weight_loss` using the terminal keyboard.

**g.** Compute the value of `new_weight` as the difference of the value of `weight` and the value of `weight_loss`.

**h.** Print the value of `new_weight` on the terminal screen, starting on a new line.

**i.** Print the message
   `"Congratulations!" to you; you are no longer overweight!`
   on the terminal screen starting on a new line.

**j.** Declare the variable `full_name` as a string variable of maximum length of 30.

**k.** Initialize `full_name` to your own name at compile time.

**l.** Print the content of the string variable `full_name` on the monitor screen.

### *Programming Projects*

**17.** Design and implement an interactive program that reads a temperature value in degrees centigrade and then converts and outputs its Fahrenheit equivalent. The conversion formula is

$$degrees\_in\_Fahrenheit = \tfrac{9}{5} \times degrees\_in\_centigrade + 32$$

**18.** Design and implement an interactive program that reads a temperature value in degrees Fahrenheit and then converts and outputs its centigrade equivalent. The conversion formula is

$$degrees\_in\_centigrade = \tfrac{5}{9} \times (degrees\_in\_Fahrenheit - 32)$$

**19.** Design and implement an interactive program that reads three floating-point values and computes and prints their arithmetic average.

**20.** Write an interactive program that reads values for three integers and computes and prints their sum and their product.

**21.** Write an interactive program that reads a floating-point value and computes and prints its inverse and its square.

**22.** Write an interactive program that reads values for string variables `first_name` and `last_name` and prints the value of `last_name`, a comma, and the value of `first_name`.

**23.** Design and implement an interactive program that prompts the user for his or her year of birth, month of birth, the current year, and the current month and then computes and prints the user's age in years and in months. The month values are integers in the range 1 through 12.

**24.** Design and implement an interactive program that prompts the user to enter and store in appropriately declared string variables values for a zip code, a two-letter state abbreviation, a town name, a street address, a last name, and a first name and then prints a standard address label.

**25.** Design and implement an interactive program that first prompts the user to enter values for the length of a car trip in miles, and the amount of gasoline (in gallons) in the car's tank at the beginning and end of the trip, and then computes and prints the average gasoline consumption in miles per gallon for the trip.

# 4

# Simple Selections and Repetitions

---

**CHAPTER OBJECTIVES**

In this chapter you will learn about:

- **Simple selection structures**
    Two-way selection using the `if` statement
    Relational C operators and simple predicates
    Precedence of arithmetic and relational operators
    Using strings in conditional expressions
    Multiway selections
    Using nested `if` statements for multiway selections

- **Controlled repetitions using the `while` statement**
    Counter-controlled loops
    Sentinel-controlled loops

- **Structured programming**

By the time you have completed this chapter, you will have acquired the ability to:

- **Solve problems that require two-way and multiway selections**

- **Solve problems using controlled repetition structures**

- **Solve problems using structured programs**

---

## 4.1   INTRODUCTION

Our discussions in the previous chapter concentrated on input, output, and arithmetic calculations, and the corresponding C statements. We saw that, with these statements, we can design only simple programs. Such programs will execute their statements beginning with the first, one after another, until their last statement is taken care of. Programs of this type are linear, and they are not very interesting.

The majority of challenging and interesting algorithms necessitate the ability to make decisions as to what code to execute and when (that is, selection) and the ability to execute certain portions of the code repeatedly (that is, repetition). The C language provides constructs for implementing selections and repetitions. In this chapter we examine some of them, specifically the `if` statement for selections and the `while` statement for repetitions. Also in this chapter we discuss structured programming, a programming discipline that simplifies program logic by using only the sequence, selection, and repetition control structures.

At the end of this chapter, you will have learned a minimum subset of C statements and be able to implement almost any algorithm in a well-structured C program.

## 4.2   PROGRAMMING FOR SIMPLE SELECTIONS

In Chapter 2 you learned that the selection control structure is one of the fundamental elements in algorithm design. Its purpose is to execute one of several possible alternatives using an appropriate selection criterion. Every programming language, including C, has some language constructs that correspond to the selection control structure. Let us begin our discussion by considering an example problem that requires the use of a selection control structure.

***Example 4.1***   We will reconsider Example Program 1 in chapter 3, which computes the city income tax for the city of Oxford, Ohio, as 1.75 percent of gross annual income. Suppose the tax laws change so that income above $10,000 is subject to city income tax and income up to and including $10,000 is exempt from it. We want to modify Example Program 1 to reflect this change.

The pseudocode algorithm for this problem is given in Figure 4.1.

---

*print "A PROGRAM THAT COMPUTES CITY INCOME TAX"*
*print "Enter gross income: "*
*read gross_income*

*if gross income is greater than $10,000*
    *compute city_tax = 0.0175 × gross_income*
*else*

---

**Figure 4.1**   Modified algorithm for computing city income tax (*continued*)   ▶

> *set city_tax to 0*
> *end_if*
>
> *print city_tax*

**Figure 4.1**                                                                                    ■

You should note that the only difference between this algorithm and the one given in Figure 3.1 is the selection structure:

> *if gross income is greater than $10,000*
>     *compute city_tax = 0.0175 × gross_income*
> *else*
>     *set city_tax to 0*
> *end_if*

The program corresponding to the algorithm of Figure 4.1 is given in Figure 4.2.

```c
#include <stdio.h>

const double CITY_TAX_RATE = 0.0175;

int main(void) {
        /* Variable declarations: */

        double gross_income;
        double city_tax;

        /* Function body: */

        printf("A PROGRAM THAT COMPUTES CITY INCOME TAX\n");
        printf("Enter gross income: ");
        scanf("%lf", &gross_income);

        if (gross_income > 10000.00)
                city_tax = CITY_TAX_RATE * gross_income;
        else
                city_tax = 0.0;
        /* end if */
```

**Figure 4.2**     A C implementation of the pseudocode of Figure 4.1 (*continued*)                          ▶

```
        printf("City tax is %f dollars.", city_tax);
        return 0;
} /* end function main */
```

**Figure 4.2**                                                                                                    ■

This program is almost exactly the same as the program of Figure 3.2. The only new statement in it is the `if` statement. This `if` statement uses a simple condition after the keyword `if`, `gross_income` > `10000.00`, which compares the value of the variable `gross_income` with `10000.00`. The symbol `>` is how we express "greater than" in C, and it is one of C's relational operators. If the value stored for the variable `gross_income` in the memory is greater than `10000.00`, this condition is true. In this case the statement

```
    city_tax = CITY_TAX_RATE * gross_income;
```

is executed and a value for `city_tax` is computed. However, if the value of `gross_income` is less than or equal to `10000.00`, the selection condition is false. The statement that computes `city_tax` as 1.75% of `gross_income` is bypassed, and the statement that comes after the keyword `else` is evaluated:

```
    city_tax = 0.0;
```

This statement sets `city_tax` to 0. Therefore, the `if` statement in Figure 4.2 is the proper implementation of the two-way selection control structure in Figure 4.1. Figure 4.3 is the flowchart representation of the logic of this `if` statement.

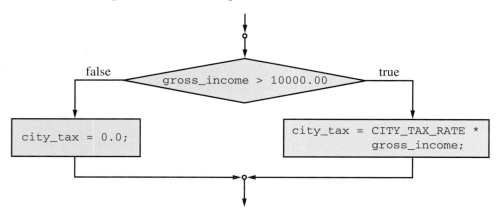

**Figure 4.3**    Flowchart for the `if` statement in Figure 4.2

## Selection Statements

The C language has two statements for implementing the selection control structure: `if` and `switch`. In this section we consider the `if` statement. The `if` statement can be used for two-way selection. In its nested forms this statement can also be used for

**multiway selections**. For this introduction to selection statements, the discussion of the `if` statement will be restricted to simple selection conditions. We examine the `if` statement based on complex conditions and the `switch` statement in Chapter 9.

## Two-Way Selection Using the `if` Statement

Essentially, the `if` statement implements two-way selection. It has the following general form:

```
if (Expression)
        Statement1;
else
        Statement2;
/* end if */
```

The keyword `if` identifies the statement type and is required. The *Expression* is called **selection expression** and is also required. It must be enclosed in parentheses. The selection expression can be any expression that produces numerical values. In this syntax *Statement1* is called the **then-part**, and *Statement2* is the **else-part**. Both *Statement1* and *Statement2* are any executable C statements that define the actions of each alternative. The keyword `else` is optional; however, if it is missing, *Statement2* should also be missing. Otherwise, we have a dangling `else` in the `if` statement. The comment `/* end if */` is a style convention that we adopt to show the termination point in an `if` statement.

As long as it is an expression that computes to a numerical value, the selection expression in an `if` statement can be any expression. It can also be a conditional expression. A **conditional expression**, also known as a **predicate**, is an expression that evaluates to a value of true or false, which brings us to a special data type, called Boolean. Data whose values can be only true or false are of the Boolean data type. Boolean variables are commonly used in selection and repetition structures. Some computer languages, such as Pascal, directly support the Boolean data type. In these languages, as you can declare variables to be of type `int` or `double`, you can also declare variables as of type Boolean. C does not directly support this data type. Instead, in C a nonzero value is assigned to a predicate if it is true; otherwise, its value will be zero.

At first glance, not supporting the Boolean data type appears as a deficiency of C; in fact, it is not. Because C considers any nonzero value computed for the selection expression in `if` statements to correspond to the Boolean true and the value zero to correspond to the Boolean false, it becomes possible to use any expression, instead of only conditional expressions, as selection expressions. Nevertheless, in many selection processes we rely on conditional expressions that in C evaluate to 1 or 0.

The flowchart of Figure 4.4 shows the logic of the `if` statement graphically. In executing an `if` statement, the computer goes through the following sequence of operations:

1.  Evaluate the parenthesized selection expression.
2.  If the computed value of the expression is nonzero, execute *Statement1* and bypass *Statement2*, dropping down to the statement that follows the entire `if` statement.
3.  If the expression evaluates to zero, bypass *Statement1*, execute *Statement2*, and continue with the statement that comes after the `if` statement.

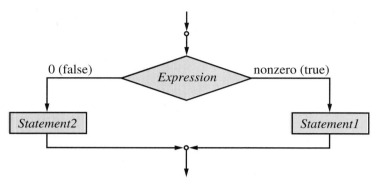

**Figure 4.4**     Flowchart for the logic of the `if` statement

## Using Relational Operators in Conditional Expressions

Conditional expressions are formed using relational and logical operators. (This chapter covers only relational operators.) **Relational operators** are used to compare values. An expression that compares two expressions using a relational operator is called a **simple predicate**. A simple predicate computes to either 1 (for true) or 0 (for false). C has six relational operators:

1.  Equal to, `==`
2.  Not equal to, `!=`
3.  Less than, `<`
4.  Less than or equal to, `<=`
5.  Greater than, `>`
6.  Greater than or equal to, `>=`

The following examples of `if` statements use relational operators in conditional expressions.

*Example 4.2*   Suppose a company uses full-time and part-time employees. Each employee is assigned a distinct `employee_number`. The character variable `employee_status` is used to distinguish between full- and part-time employees. If the value of `employee_status` is `'f'`, the employee is full-time; if it is `'p'`, the employee is part-time. We want to write a selection control structure to print the employee numbers of full- and part-time employees. The pseudocode algorithm for this selection structure follows.

---

*if employee_status is equal to 'f'*
    *print employee_number, " is full-time."*
*else*
    *print employee_number, " is part-time."*
*end_if*

---

In writing this pseudocode, we are assuming that the only two possible values for the variable `employee_status`, are `'f'` and `'p'`. Otherwise, the preceding pseudocode will be logically incomplete. In a C implementation the variables `employee_status` and `employee_number` must be declared as of type `char` and `int`, respectively:

```
char employee_status;
int employee_number;
```

The C implementation of this selection control structure is the following `if` statement:

```
if (employee_status == 'f')
      printf("%d is full-time.", employee_number);
else
      printf("%d is part-time.", employee_number);
/* end if */
```

In this statement the selection is based on the condition `employee_status == 'f'`. Here the symbol `==` is the equal-to relational operator. Whether or not this condition is true depends on the value of the variable `employee_status`. If the value of `employee_status` in the memory is `'f'`, the condition is logically true. In this case the value of the entire condition will be computed as 1, the program will execute the first output statement

```
printf("%d is full-time.", employee_number);
```

and skip the second output statement. If the value of the variable `employee_status` is `'p'`, the condition will evaluate to false. A condition that is false in C has the value of `0`. In this case the first output statement will be skipped, and the second output statement that comes after the `else` keyword

```
printf("%d is part-time.", employee_number);
```

will be executed. This `if` statement will carry out only one of the two possible actions, and hence it is a two-way selection structure.

**Example 4.3** Let us suppose that for the problem of the previous example, we want to print the employee number only if an employee is full-time. The pseudocode becomes simpler:

```
if employee_status is equal to 'f'
    print employee_number, " is full-time."
end_if
```

The corresponding `if` statement is also simpler and will be missing the keyword `else` and the statement that follows it:

```
if (employee_status == 'f')
      printf("%d is full-time.", employee_number);
/* end if */
```

In executing this statement, the computer will again begin with the condition `employee_status == 'f'`. If this condition turns out to be true, that is, its value is equal to `1`, the computer will execute the output statement and then drop down to the statement that follows the `if` statement in the program. Otherwise, it will bypass the output statement and consider the statement that follows the `if` statement.

You should realize that this `if` statement also defines two alternatives: the action of the first alternative is an output statement, and the action of the second alternative is "doing nothing."

## Using Multiple Operators in Conditional Expressions: Precedence of Arithmetic and Relational Operators

In addition to relational operators, conditional expressions may contain other types of operators, including arithmetic ones. Consider the following example.

***Example 4.4***  Suppose we are asked to solve the quadratic equation

$$a\,x^2 + b\,x + c = 0$$

where $a$, $b$, and $c$ are constant coefficients. We know that this equation has real roots if the following condition is satisfied:

$$b^2 - 4\,a\,c > = 0$$

The following `if` statement uses this condition:

```
if (b * b - 4 * a * c >= 0)
      printf("Roots are real");
else
      printf("Roots are complex");
/* end if */
```

The conditional expression in this `if` statement, `b * b - 4 * a * c >= 0`, involves multiple operators: we have three multiplications, one subtraction, and one comparison that uses the operator `>=`. How does the computer evaluate such an expression? Does it do multiplication first, and if so, which one? As you can see, we have an ambiguous situation here.

Such ambiguities are resolved by the computer's inherent knowledge of the precedence of operators, which determines a clear order in applying operators to their respective operands in expressions. For example, if an expression has an addition and a multiplication, the computer does the multiplication before the addition, because it knows that multiplication has higher precedence than addition. If, on the other hand, an expression has more than one addition, the computer uses the left-associativity rule in applying the expressions; that is, the computer evaluates the expressions from left to right.

---

A **precedence rule** states the order in which different operators are applied. An **associativity rule** specifies the order in which multiple occurrences of the same operator are applied.

---

Each operator in C has a specific precedence with respect to others, and either left or right associativity. **Left associativity** means from left to right, and **right associativity** implies from right to left.

It is possible, and sometimes even desirable, to alter the order of application of operators as determined by these rules. We can do this by using parentheses in an expression. For example, in the expression `a + b * c`, because multiplication has higher precedence compared to addition, first `b` will be multiplied by `c` and then the result will be added to `a`. If we use parentheses and write this expression as `(a + b) * c`, the computer will first add `a` and `b` and then multiply the result by `c`.

In summary, we have the following rules for evaluating expressions:

---

### Rules for Evaluation of Expressions

1.  Evaluate all parenthesized subexpressions, beginning with the innermost subexpressions in case they are nested.

2.  If there are two or more unnested parenthesized subexpressions in an expression, use the left-associativity rule: evaluate them left to right.

3.  Use the operator precedence rules in determining the order of application of operators in evaluating subexpressions.

4.  In case of two or more operators in the same subexpression at the same precedence level, use the appropriate associativity rules for these operators.

---

Figure 4.5 shows the precedence and associativity of all operators that we have covered so far, including the common unary and binary arithmetic operators, the assignment operator, the function call operator, and the relational operators. This table is a subset of the table presented in Appendix B.

| Precedence Level | Operator | Associativity |
|---|---|---|
| 1 (highest) | ( ) | left |
| 2 | Unary +, unary − | right |
| 3 | * / | left |
| 4 | + − | left |
| 5 | < <= > >= | left |
| 6 | == != | left |
| 7 (lowest) | = | right |

**Figure 4.5**    Precedence of a subset of C operators

Now that we know about operator precedence, let us return to Example 4.4.

***Example 4.4 (continued)***    We reconsider the expression

```
b * b - 4 * a * c >= 0
```

and apply the preceding rules. The order of application of the operators is shown here under the operators:

```
b * b - 4 * a * c >= 0
  1     4   2   3    5
```

Assuming that the values of the variables  a,  b, and  c  are 2, 9, and 5, respectively, this expression is evaluated in five steps:

**Step 1.** The multiplication operation in the subexpression  b * b  is carried out, yielding  81. The expression reduces to  81 - 4 * a * c >= 0.

**Step 2.** The multiplication operation in the subexpression  4 * a  is done. This produces  8, and the original expression reduces to  81 - 8 * c >= 0.

**Step 3.** The multiplication operation in the subexpression  8 * c  is executed. We have 40, and the expression reduces to  81 - 40 > 0.

**Step 4.** The subtraction operation is carried out, yielding the reduced expression  41 >= 0.

**Step 5.** The expression  41 >= 0  is evaluated as  1  (true).

Therefore, in the  if  statement of Example 4.4, the statement

```
printf("Roots are real");
```

will be executed to print  Roots are real  on the monitor screen.

***Example 4.5***    If the preceding rules are applied to the conditional expression

```
a + b >= 3 * c == a != 2 * c + b
```

the operations will be carried out in the order shown here under the operators:

```
a + b >= 3 * c == a != 2 * c + b
3   5   1   6   7   2   4
```

Let us assume that the variables a, b, and c have the values 10, 3, and 7, respectively. This conditional expression will be evaluated in seven steps:

| Step | Evaluated Subexpression | Reduced Expression |
|------|-------------------------|--------------------|
| 1 | 3 * c | a + b >= 21 == a != 2 * c + b |
| 2 | 2 * c | a + b >= 21 == a != 14 + b |
| 3 | a + b | 13 >= 21 == a != 14 + b |
| 4 | 14 + b | 13 >= 21 == a != 17 |
| 5 | 13 >= 21 | 0 == a != 17 |
| 6 | 0 == a | 0 != 17 |
| 7 | 0 != 17 | 1 |

***Example 4.6***   Now consider a parenthesized form of the expression in Example 4.5:

```
(a + b >= 3 * c) == (a != 2 * c + b)
```

The order of computations is

```
(a + b >= 3 * c) == (a != 2 * c + b)
   2    3   1       7    6   4   5
```

The expression evaluation process is shown in the following table for the same values of a, b, and c as in Example 4.5.

| Step | Evaluated Subexpression | Reduced Expression |
|------|-------------------------|--------------------|
| 1 | 3 * c | (a + b >= 21) == (a != 2 * c + b) |
| 2 | a + b | 13 >= 21 == (a != 2 * c + b) |
| 3 | 13 >= 21 | 0 == (a != 2 * c + b) |
| 4 | 2 * c | 0 == (a != 6 + b) |
| 5 | 6 + b | 0 == (10 != 13) |
| 6 | 10 != 13 | 0 == 1 |
| 7 | 0 == 1 | 0 |

## Using Arithmetic Expressions as Selection Criteria in **if** Statements

The selection expression in an if statement can also be any appropriate arithmetic expression. If the value computed for the selection expression is nonzero, the then-part of the if statement will be executed. If it is zero, the else-part will be selected. Examples follow.

***Example 4.7***   Consider the problem of determining whether a given integer variable, number, contains an even or an odd value. The following if statement is one possible solution:

```
if (number - number / 2 * 2)
      printf("Odd");
else
      printf("Even");
/* end if */
```

The selection expression `number - number / 2 * 2` computes the remainder of the division of `number` by 2; its value will be 0 if `number` is even, and 1 if it is odd. The reason this expression computes the remainder of the division of `number` by 2 correctly is because all operands in it are integers. Obviously, if the computed remainder is 0, the value stored in `number` is even; otherwise, it is odd. If, for a given value of `number`, the expression computes to 1, the predicate of the `if` statement will be logically true and its value will be 1. Thus, the first output statement will be executed, printing `Odd` on the screen, and the second output statement will be bypassed. On the other hand, if the value of `number` is even, the expression will compute to 0. Therefore, the predicate of the if statement will be logically false and its value will be 0. In this case the first output statement will be skipped, and the second will be executed, printing `Even`.

***Example 4.8***   The following `if` statement is a variation of the previous example. We want to know whether our `number` is odd, and we do not want to print anything if it is not.

```
if (number - number / 2 * 2)
      printf("Odd");
/* end if */
```

In this `if` statement the optional else-part is missing. The only statement in the then-part is an output statement. It will be executed if the predicate is computed as a nonzero value.

***Example 4.9***   In some selection situations we may opt to take no action if the selection expression evaluates to a nonzero value. However, we may want to do something if the selection expression is zero. In such cases, the `if` statement will have an empty then-part for which we should use the null statement. Consider the following example:

```
if (number - number / 2 * 2)
      ;
else
      printf("Even");
/* end if */
```

In this `if` statement we want a message to be printed if `number` contains an even integer value. The predicate associated with the `if` statement yields a value of `0` if the current value of the integer variable `number` is even. Because we are interested only in even integer values and do not want to do anything if they are odd, the then-part of the `if` statement can be written as the null statement `;`. In C a single semicolon is considered as the **null statement**; it is a statement that does not do anything.

You should note that, although this `if` statement is correct, the following equivalent form is more direct and is preferred:

```
if (number - number / 2 * 2 == 0)
      printf("Even");
/* end if */
```

***Example 4.10***   The next `if` statement determines whether the value of the variable *x* is the solution of the linear equation *3 x − 5 = 0.*

```
if (3 * x - 15) {
      printf("Your integer is not the solution of 3x - 15 = 0.\n");
      printf("The computed value of the expression 3x - 15 is: %d",
            (3 * number - 15));
}
else
      printf("Your integer is the solution of 3x - 15 = 0.");
/* end if */
```

For this statement the computer first calculates a value of the arithmetic expression `3 * x - 15`. If the value of this expression is not zero, the then-part of the `if` statement is executed. The then-part is a compound statement that consists of two output statements. Note the use of braces to mark the beginning and end of the compound statement. If the expression evaluates to zero, the compound statement is bypassed and the else-part is executed. In either case the next statement that is executed is the statement that physically follows the `if` statement.

## Using Strings in Conditional Expressions

In certain applications we may want to compare a string variable to another string variable or constant. It may also become necessary to copy a string constant or variable in another string variable. With C fundamental data types, the operations of copying and comparing are easy. For example, to copy an integer variable `first` in another integer variable `second`, we write

```
second = first;
```

To compare such variables in an `if` statement, we can use the relational operators, as in the predicate `first == second`.

Since strings are character arrays in C, we cannot operate on them in this manner. Suppose we have two strings declared as

```
char string1[21], string2[21];
```

A statement such as

```
string2 = string1;
```

intended to copy `string1` in `string2` will not work; neither will an attempt to compare `string1` and `string2` as in the predicate `string1 == string2`. The reason is that the names of string variables declared as character arrays are the addresses of the memory locations where they are stored.

All basic operations on strings require the use of the string manipulation functions of the standard string handling library. These functions are declared in the header file `string.h`. Therefore, if you are planning to use any of these functions, your program must contain the preprocessor directive `#include <string.h>`. Here we cover two important string operations, string copy and string compare, and the corresponding string handling functions.

We use the standard function `strcpy` to copy one string into another. The function `strcpy` has two string parameters. It copies the second parameter into the first and returns the first parameter.

**Example 4.11**    Suppose that we have two strings declared as

```
char string1[21], string2[21];
```

and suppose that `string1` has the value `"C programming"`. The statement

```
strcpy(string2, string1);
```

consists of a call to `strcpy`, which copies `string1` into `string2`. The content of `string2` becomes `"C programming"`, but the value of `string1` does not change. Thus both of the following output statements

```
printf("string1 contains: %s", string1);
printf("string2 contains: %s", string2);
```

print the same string, `"C programming"`.

The standard string library function `strcmp` can be used to compare two strings. This function has two string type parameters. It returns an integer that is less than zero, equal to zero, or greater than zero if the first string parameter is less than, equal to, or greater than the second string parameter.

In comparing two strings the computer considers the first characters in each. If the first characters match, it continues with the next characters until the two characters being compared do not match. In this case, depending on the character representation system used by the computer, it can conclude whether the first string is less than or greater than the second or whether they are equal. If all characters in both strings match and the two strings are of the same length, they are considered equal. For example, assuming an ASCII computer, the string

> "data"  is less than the string  "date"
> "data"  is greater than  " data"
> "data"  is less than  "data  "
> "125"  is greater than  "123"
> "A15"  is greater than  "15A"
> "data"  is equal to  "data"

***Example 4.12***   Given the declarations for two strings

    char string1[21], string2[21];

we may use the function  strcmp  in an  if  statement as shown:

```
if(strcmp(string1, string2) > 0)
      printf("%s is greater than %s", string1, string2);
else
      printf("%s is not greater than %s", string1, string2);
/* end if */
```

Assuming that the values of string1 and string2 are "data" and "date", respectively, the function call strcmp(string1, string2) returns a negative integer. Hence the second output statement in the code will be executed, and it will print data is not greater than date.

## Nested if Statements and Multiway Selection

Occasionally in a program, the programmer has to define multiway selection structures. This task can be accomplished in three ways:

1.  Using a series of consecutive  if  statements.

2.  Using an  if  statement such that its then-part and/or the else-part contains other if  statements. Such an  if  statement is called a **nested  if  statement**.

3.  Using a  switch  statement, which specifies multiple branches at a decision point. We cover the  switch  statement in Chapter 9.

This section focuses on multiway selections using the  if  and nested  if  statements. Let us study two examples.

***Example 4.13***    This example describes a multiway selection structure based on one variable. In a federal income tax computation problem, we have a variable called `filing_status` that may assume four integer values: `1` for single, `2` for married filing jointly, `3` for married filing separately, and `4` for head of household. Any other value for `filing_status` is considered an error. During output we would like to examine the value of `filing_status` and print a description that corresponds to its value. We can use the sequence of `if` statements in Figure 4.6 to accomplish this task.

```
if (filing_status == 1)
      printf("Single");
/* end if */

if (filing_status == 2)
      printf("Married filing jointly");
/* end if */

if (filing_status == 3)
      printf("Married filing separately");
/* end if */

if (filing_status == 4)
      printf("Head of household");
/* end if */

if (filing_status < 0)
      printf("Error in filing status");
/* end if */

if (filing_status > 4)
      printf("Error in filing status");
/* end if */
```

**Figure 4.6**    A multiway selection structure based on one variable: Use of unnested `if` statements

Although we are using six consecutive `if` statements, the last two indicate the same action. Therefore, this structure is a five-way selection structure. The logic of this sequence of `if` statements is shown graphically in the flowchart of Figure 4.7.

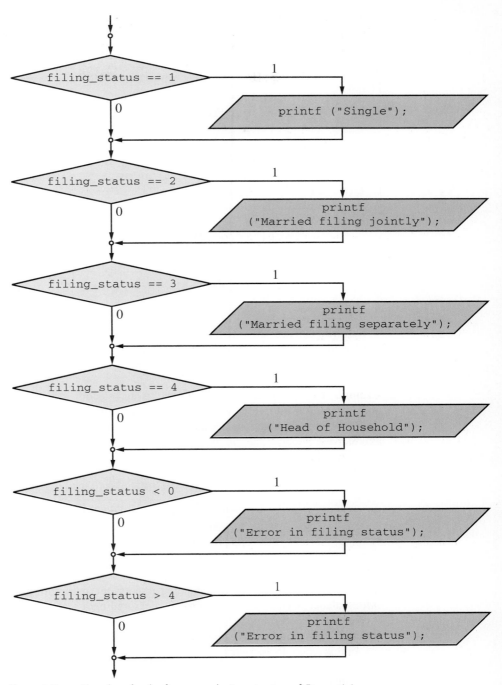

**Figure 4.7**    Flowchart for the five-way selection structure of Figure 4.6

For the same problem we can use a single nested if statement as shown in Figure 4.8. Figure 4.8 is also an implementation of a five-way selection structure. Its flowchart is given in Figure 4.9.

```
if (filing_status == 1)
      printf("Single");
else if (filing_status == 2)
      printf("Married filing jointly");
else if (filing_status == 3)
      printf("Married filing separately");
else if (filing_status == 4)
      printf("Head of household");
else
      printf("Error in filing status");
/* end if */
```

**Figure 4.8**   A multiway selection structure based on one variable: Use of a nested if statement

As you can see, these two techniques of multiway selection are logically equivalent, but not identical. You should note that the nested if selection structure is more efficient from a program execution point of view.

***Example 4.14***   This example shows multiway selection structures based on more than one variable. In the previous example the alternatives of the selection were based on a single variable. Let us consider an example in which two variables control the selection alternatives. Suppose the credit department of a retail outlet uses the following table to determine the minimum monthly payment for a revolving credit account for customers whose credit standing is good:

| Balance | Minimum Payment |
|---|---|
| $0–$20 | Balance |
| $20.01–$100 | $10 |
| Over $100 | 10% of Balance |

If, however, a customer's credit standing is poor, the minimum monthly payment is the entire balance. Customer credit rating is measured on a scale of 10, and a value above 6 is considered good standing. We want to write a nested if statement to implement this selection logic. Figure 4.10 gives a solution.

In this example the outer if statement has a selection condition based on the variable credit_standing. Its then-part is another if statement, with a selection condition that uses the variable balance. The inner if statement itself is nested, defining three alternatives. Together with the outer if statement, we have a total of four alternatives.

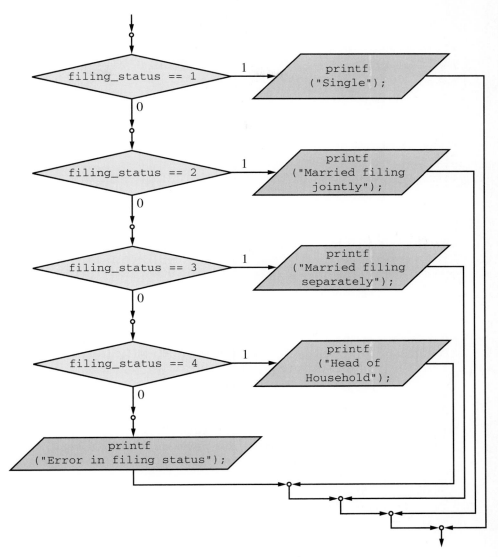

**Figure 4.9**    Flowchart for the five-way selection structure of Figure 4.8

In Figure 4.10 the inner nested `if` statement itself is nested. It is considered to be a single statement, and therefore we do not have to enclose it by braces to turn it into a compound statement. However, if we rewrite this nested `if` statement as a series of consecutive unnested `if` statements, we will have to treat them as a compound statement. Figure 4.11 gives this alternative formulation.

The selection structure of Figure 4.11 is also a four-alternative selection. It is equivalent to the nested selection structure of Figure 4.10

```
if (credit_standing > 6)
     if (balance <= 20.00)
          minimum_payment = balance;
     else
          if (balance <= 100.00)
               minimum_payment = 10.00;
          else
               minimum_payment = 0.1 * balance;
          /* end if */
     /* end if */
else
     minimum_payment = balance;
/* end if */
```

**Figure 4.10**    A multiway selection structure based on two variables: Use of a nested `if` statement

```
if (credit_standing > 6) {
     if (balance <= 20.00)
          minimum_payment = balance;
     else
          minimum_payment = 10.00;
     /* end if */

     if (balance > 100.00)
          minimum_payment = 0.1 * balance;
     /* end if */
}
else
     minimum_payment = balance;
/* end if */
```

**Figure 4.11**    A multiway selection structure based on two variables: Use of unnested `if` statements in the then-part of an outer `if`

## REVIEW QUESTIONS

1.  In the `if` statement syntax, the parenthesized expression is any valid C expression, including an arithmetic expression. (T or F)

2.  Which of the following statements concerning the semantics of the `if` statement is *incorrect*?

    **a.** The then-part is executed only if the parenthesized expression produces a nonzero value.

    **b.** After the then-part, the else-part is executed.

    **c.** The else-part is executed only if the parenthesized expression evaluates to a zero value.

    **d.** After the then-part or the else-part is executed, the program control drops down to the statement that follows the `if` statement.

3.  In general, a conditional expression is an expression that evaluates to a Boolean value of true or false. Because C does not support the Boolean data type, a conditional expression evaluates to integer `1` or integer `0`. (T or F)

4.  Which of the following operators is *not* a relational operator in C?

    **a.** `==`          **d.** `!=`

    **b.** `>=`          **e.** `>`

    **c.** `=<`

5.  Which of the following is *incorrect*? In evaluating conditional expressions,

    **a.** All parenthesized subexpressions are evaluated first.

    **b.** If there are two or more unnested parenthesized subexpressions, the left-associativity rule is used.

    **c.** The equal-to relational operator is applied before any arithmetic operator.

    **d.** The less-than operator is applied before the not-equal-to operator.

    **e.** The arithmetic operators are applied before the greater-than operator.

6.  The function call to `strcpy`

    ```
    strcpy(string2, string1);
    ```

    copies `string2` to `string1`. (T or F)

7.  Assume that your computer uses the ASCII character coding system. Which of the following statements concerning string comparison is correct?

    **a.** `strcmp("data", " data");` returns zero.

    **b.** The string `"A15"` is less than `"15A"`.

    **c.** The expression `string1 == "data"`, where `string1` is a string variable, is valid.

    **d.** All of the above.

    **e.** None of the above.

8.  Choose the *incorrect* statement. In C multiway selection can be implemented by

    **a.** A series of consecutive `if` statements

    **b.** Nested `if` statements

    **c.** The `switch` statement

    **d.** The `while` statement

**Answers:**   1. T; 2. b; 3. T; 4. c; 5. c; 6. F; 7. e; 8. d.

## 4.3    PROGRAMMING FOR CONTROLLED REPETITIONS

In a program we frequently want to execute a block of code repeatedly, a finite number of times, until a certain task is accomplished. For this purpose we use repetition statements. Let us begin our discussion with an example.

**Example 4.15**    We go back to the problem of city income tax computation for the city of Oxford, Ohio. As you will remember, at the beginning of Section 4.2 we enhanced our program by adding a selection control structure to it. Suppose that we now want to modify the code in Figure 4.2 to perform many tax computations in a single execution of the program. The pseudocode algorithm for this extended version is given in Figure 4.12.

```
while the user wants to continue
    begin
        print "Enter gross income: "
        read gross_income

        if gross income is greater than $10,000
            compute city_tax = 0.0175 × gross_income
        else
            set city_tax to 0
        end_if

        print city_tax
    end
end_while
```

**Figure 4.12**    Modified algorithm for computing city income tax repetitively

This pseudocode is somewhat ambiguous and needs to be refined. For this job, we introduce a program variable called *want_to_continue*, initialize it to 'y' for "yes", and use it for controlling the loop. The refined version is shown in Figure 4.13.

```
set want_to_continue to 'y'

while want_to_continue is equal to 'y'
    begin
        print "Enter gross income: "
        read gross_income

        if gross income is greater than $10,000
            compute city_tax = 0.0175 × gross_income
        else
```

**Figure 4.13**    Refinement of the algorithm of Figure 4.12 *(continued)*    ▶

```
              set city_tax to 0
          end_if

          print city_tax

          print "Do you want to continue? (y/n): "
          read want_to_continue
        end
    end_while
```

**Figure 4.13** ∎

Figure 4.14 shows a C program that corresponds to the algorithm of Figure 4.13.

```
#include <stdio.h>
const double CITY_TAX_RATE = 0.0175;

int main(void) {
      /* Variable declarations: */

      double gross_income;
      double city_tax;
      char want_to_continue = 'y';
      char new_line;

      /* Function body: */

      printf("A PROGRAM THAT COMPUTES CITY INCOME TAX\n");

      while (want_to_continue == 'y') {
            printf("Enter gross income: ");
            scanf("%lf", &gross_income);

            if (gross_income > 10000.00)
                  city_tax = CITY_TAX_RATE * gross_income;
            else
                  city_tax = 0.0;
            /* end if */

            printf("City tax is %f dollars.\n", city_tax);
```

**Figure 4.14**    A C implementation of the algorithm of Figure 4.13 (*continued*) ▶

```
              scanf("%c", &new_line);
              printf("Do you want to continue? Type y/n: ");
              scanf("%c", &want_to_continue);
       } /* end while */

       return 0;
} /* end function main */
```

Figure 4.14                                                                      ■

In this final version of the city income tax computation program, the following elements are new:

```
      ........................
      char want_to_continue = 'y';

      while (want_to_continue == 'y') {
             ........................
             ........................
             printf("Do you want to continue? Type y/n: ");
             scanf("%c", &want_to_continue);
      } /* end while */
```

The declaration

```
      char want_to_continue = 'y';
```

declares the loop control variable want_to_continue as a character variable and initializes it to the character value 'y'. The next statement is while, one of the repetition statements in C. It begins with the keyword while, continues with a simple condition enclosed in parentheses, and is followed by a compound statement. The compound statement is the loop body, containing the statements that will be executed repeatedly.

The loop control expression is the simple condition want_to_continue == 'y'. As long as this condition computes to the value of true, that is, the value of the variable want_to_continue remains 'y', the computer will execute the content of the loop body. Hence in the first cycle of repetition, we will compute a city income tax. Then the computer comes across the last two statements in the loop body, which are a prompt and an input statement. After the prompt the user should type a character value. The computer again checks the loop control expression. If the user has typed y for want_to_continue, the loop body is executed once again; otherwise, the execution of the loop terminates. This loop is a typical controlled repetition operation.

## Repetition Statements

Every programming language has some constructs that can be used to define controlled repetitions (or loops) on a program block. A program block that is executed repeatedly by a repetition statement is called its **loop body**. The repetition is controlled by a condition that is associated with the repetition statement.

There are two types of repetition statements:

1.   Pretest repetition statements
2.   Posttest repetition statements

A **pretest repetition statement** computes a value for its associated predicate before entering the loop body and will execute the loop body as long as the predicate is true. Once the predicate computes to false, repetition stops and the program control passes to the next statement that follows the repetition statement. The flowchart in Figure 4.15 depicts the logic of a typical pretest repetition statement.

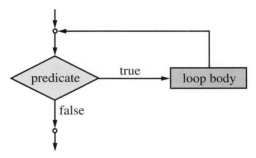

**Figure 4.15**      Logic of the pretest repetition statement

On the other hand, a **posttest repetition statement** first executes the loop body and then computes the predicate. If the predicate is true, the loop body is executed again; otherwise, the repetition terminates. The logic of a posttest repetition statement is shown in Figure 4.16.

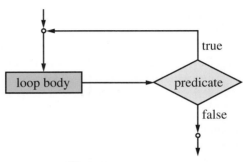

**Figure 4.16**      Logic of the posttest repetition statement

In C we have three statements for repetition:

1.  The `while` statement, which is a pretest repetition statement
2.  The `for` statement, which is also a pretest repetition statement
3.  The `do-while` statement, which is a posttest repetition statement

## Controlled Repetitions Using the `while` Statement

The `for` and `do-while` statements are discussed in Chapter 9. In this chapter we focus on the `while` statement. Its general form follows.

```
while (Expression)
       Statement
/* end while */
```

In this syntax the *Expression* that is enclosed in parentheses after the keyword `while` is called the **loop control expression**. It can be an arithmetic expression or a conditional expression that, when evaluated, produces a nonzero value that corresponds to true or a zero value that corresponds to false. Essentially, *Expression* here is the same as the *Expression* in the syntax of the `if` statement that we discussed in the previous section. The element *Statement* can be any valid statement, including a compound statement. It is, in fact, the loop body. The comment `/* end while */` is used as a style convention to show the end of a `while` statement.

A properly constructed `while` statement works as follows:

1.  The loop control expression in parentheses is evaluated.
2.  If the result of evaluation is a nonzero value (that is, the logical value of true), the loop body is executed. Then the program control goes back to the loop control expression, and the expression is evaluated again. This cycle continues until the expression computes to a value of zero.
3.  If the loop control expression produces a zero value (that is, the logical value of false), the loop body is bypassed and the program control drops down to the statement that follows the `while` statement.

Clearly, while the loop body is executed, something must be done so that, ultimately, the control expression evaluates to zero and the repetition stops. Otherwise, we get trapped in a **perpetual loop**.

Some examples of loop design using the `while` statement follow.

***Example 4.16***   We wish to compute the factorial of a given positive integer. By definition, the factorial of 0 is 1, and the factorial of an integer *n* is the product of all integers from 1 to *n*. The factorial can be expressed in algebra as

$$fact(n) = 1 \times 2 \times ... \times n$$

Because we have repetitive multiplication in this expression, it is easy to see that we will need a repetition statement to implement it. We observe that

$$fact(1) = 1$$

and that the factorial of 2 can be written as

$$fact(2) = 1 \times 2 = fact(1) \times 2$$

Generalizing, we can write

$$fact(n) = fact(n - 1) \times n$$

Therefore, to compute *fact(n)*, we should begin with *fact(1)*, which is 1, and multiply it by 2 to get *fact(2)*. Next, we should multiply *fact(2)* by 3 to get *fact(3)*, and so on, until at last we multiply *fact(n – 1)* by *n*. We should note that at each step, to calculate the factorial of an integer, we need only the factorial of the preceding integer, and not all the other factorials that we have computed previously. Therefore, the arithmetic assignment statement

$$fact = fact \times count$$

is appropriate for this purpose. Note that here the symbol = is the assignment operator, not equality. This statement will take the previously computed factorial value stored in the variable *fact*, multiply it by the value of *count*, and store the result in *fact* as the factorial of *count*. This operation should be repeated for all values of *count* from 2 to *n* to finally get the factorial of *n*. Hence we must initialize *count* to 2 before we get into the loop. In the loop body, after a new value for *fact* is computed, we must increment *count* by 1 to get ready for the next cycle. Finally, to terminate the loop when *count* becomes *(n+1)*, we must have an appropriate conditional statement. The predicate *count <= n*, when used with a *while* statement, will serve this purpose. For all values of *count* from 2 up to *n*, this predicate computes to true, and the loop body will be executed. As soon as *count* becomes *(n+1)*, the predicate will become integer 0 (false) and the loop will terminate. Here is a pseudocode for this loop logic:

---

*set fact to 1*
*set the counter variable count to 2*

*while count is less than or equal to n*
    *begin*
        *compute fact = fact × count*
        *increment count by 1*
    *end*

*end_while*

---

After the execution of the *while* statement, the variable *fact* contains the value for the factorial of *n*. The corresponding implementation in C makes use of the `while` statement:

```
fact = 1;
count = 2;

while (count <= n) {
        fact = fact * count;
        count = count + 1;
} /* end while */
```

In this example the variable  count  has been used to control the execution of the while loop. Such loops are called **counter-controlled loops**.

*Example 4.17*    We want to write a program that computes the square of an integer value that is entered interactively using the terminal keyboard. Our program should do this for all integer values, as many times as we wish, but should terminate when we enter a zero value. In other words, how many times the loop executes should depend on a sentinel value of the variable for which we supply values. Such loops are referred to as **sentinel-controlled loops**. The pseudocode algorithm for this problem follows.

> *print "Enter an integer to square; enter zero to stop: "*
> *read number*
>
> *while number is not equal to zero*
>    *begin*
>       *print "The square of ", number, " is: ", number × number*
>
>       *print "Enter an integer to square; enter zero to stop: "*
>       *read number*
>    *end*
> *end_while*

The corresponding C implementation of this algorithm is the following partial program, which uses the  while  statement.

```
int number;

printf("Enter an integer to square; enter zero to stop: ");
scanf("%d", &number);
```

```
while (number) {
      printf("The square of %d is: %d\n", number, number * number);

      printf("Enter an integer to square; enter zero to stop: ");
      scanf("%d", &number);
} /* end while */
```

Here, in the `while` statement, we have a simple arithmetic expression consisting of the variable `number`. If the value of `number` is a nonzero value, the loop control expression is considered to be equivalent to true and the loop body is executed. In the loop body the square of `number` is computed as `number * number` and printed on the screen. Next, the user is prompted to enter another value for `number`. If the user enters a zero value, the loop control expression is interpreted as false and the loop body is not executed anymore.

## 4.4   STYLE CONSIDERATIONS FOR `if` AND `while` STATEMENTS

There are some programming style rules that specifically apply to the `if` and `while` statements. Such rules are mostly conventions that help improve program readability and facilitate debugging and program maintenance.

1. Indent the then-part and the else-part of an `if` statement to improve program readability. If your `if` statement has an else-part, write the keyword `else` on a separate line and align it with the keyword `if`. If the then-part is a null statement, type it on a separate line. For example, the statement

```
if (employee_status_code == 1)
        no_of_full_time_emp = no_of_full_time_emp + 1;
else
        no_of_part_time_emp = no_of_part_time_emp + 1;
/* end if */
```

reflects good style, whereas the following variations are more difficult to read.

```
if (employee_status_code == 1)
no_of_full_time_emp = no_of_full_time_emp + 1;
else no_of_part_time_emp = no_of_part_time_emp + 1;

if (employee_status_code == 1) no_of_full_time_emp =
no_of_full_time_emp + 1; else
no_of_part_time_emp = no_of_part_time_emp + 1;
```

All of the preceding statements are syntactically correct. It really does not matter to the compiler how you type a statement. Style considerations are basically for the benefit of the readers of the program.

2. If nesting occurs in the then-part of the `if` statement in excess of three levels, the logic of nested `if` statements becomes difficult to understand. In such cases avoid deeply nested `if` statements; a series of simple `if` statements is preferable.

3. The loop body for a `while` statement should be indented to visually emphasize the syntactical elements. All statements in the loop body should be indented by the same amount. The `while` statement

```
while (count <= n) {
      fact = fact * count;
      count = count + 1;
} /* end while */
```

reflects good style, whereas the following variations do not.

```
while (count <= n) {fact = fact * count;
count = count + 1;}
```

```
while (count <= n)
{fact = fact * count; count = count + 1;}
```

4. Whenever possible, choose easy-to-understand selection and loop control expressions in `if` and `while` statements. For example, the predicate in

```
while (count <= n) {
      fact = fact * count;
      count = count + 1;
} /* end while */
```

is more natural and easier to comprehend than the expression in

```
while (n - count + 1) {
      fact = fact * count;
      count = count + 1;
} /* end while */
```

although both are correct for the computation of the factorial function.

5. In general, a negated predicate is more difficult to grasp than one that does not use negation. Therefore, if possible, avoid predicate negation. For example,

```
if (student_status == 5)
      printf("Graduate student");
else
      printf("Undergraduate student");
/ end if
```

is better than its following equivalent:

```
if (student_status != 5)
      printf("Undergraduate student");
else
      printf("Graduate student");
/* end if */
```

6. Use the comments `/* end if */` and `/* end while */` to mark the termination points of `if` and `while` statements.

## 4.5 STRUCTURED PROGRAMMING

We know that a computer, unless told otherwise, will execute instructions in a program in consecutive order. We also know that most algorithms require repeated or conditional execution of blocks of code at some point in a program. When translating such algorithms into programs, we must intentionally alter the tendency of computers to execute instructions consecutively. We do so by specifying branches to other instructions in our program.

There are two types of branches in a program structure: conditional and unconditional. A **conditional branch** creates a jump to a block of code if a certain condition is satisfied. The branches specified by the `if` and `while` statements are conditional in that they are determined by the value computed by a controlling expression. After branching, both the `if` and `while` statements return the program control either to the point of branching or to a predetermined point in the program.

On the other hand, **unconditional branches** take the program control to another point in the program without providing a return to the point of branching. Most programming languages implement unconditional branching through one form or another of the `goto` statement. The C language also has a `goto` statement. Its syntax is simple:

```
goto Label;
```

The element *Label* after the keyword `goto` is a name that is associated with a labeled statement. A **labeled statement** is any statement that conforms to the following form:

```
Label : Statement;
```

A *Label* is nothing but an identifier that serves as the name of a statement in the program. A labeled statement has a label, followed by a colon, which is followed by a statement. Here is an example of a labeled statement:

```
stmt1 : printf("Enter a value for a: ");
```

In forming labels for labeled statements, you can use the rules for identifiers as discussed in Section 3.3. Each label must be associated with one distinct labeled statement in a program.

The `goto` statement creates an unconditional jump to a labeled statement. Unless you use another jump statement, the program control does not come back to the point of the jump; it merely continues with the statements that follow the labeled statement.

Older high-level programming languages such as FORTRAN, PL/1 and COBOL have statements for unconditional branching that were used liberally in application programming. This tendency produced programs that are colloquially referred to as "spaghetti codes", or codes into which a large number of long, one-way, logical paths are incorporated. Such programs are usually very difficult to debug, read, and maintain.

At the same time, a number of computer scientists became increasingly concerned with the fact that programming languages, while growing naturally, borrowed too many features from one another and evolved into unnecessarily crowded and hard-to-learn tools. Clearly, leaner languages were needed. Computer scientists such as Dijkstra, Wirth, Hoare, Bohm, and Jacopini pioneered a new discipline called structured programming. They advocated and proved the following principles:

1.  Any program can be written using only three basic control structures: sequence, selection, and repetition.

2.  Unconditional branching and the `goto` statement are not essential control structures in programming.

3.  The three basic structures of structured programming are easy to understand. Also, from a practical standpoint, they result in programs that are easier to write, read, debug, and maintain compared to those that use `gotos` liberally.

---

**Structured programming** is the discipline of making a program's logic easy to follow by using only three primitive program structures: sequence, selection, and repetition. The use of structured programming primitives in the program development process helps ensure well-designed programs.

---

The objectives of structured programming are to

1.  Simplify the program design process
2.  Minimize program complexity
3.  Increase program readability
4.  Simplify program maintenance
5.  Define a disciplined programming methodology

The three primitive constructs of structured programming are the sequence, the selection, and the repetition structures. We examined these control structures in Chapters 2 and 3, as well as in the present chapter. We also know that C has language constructs for all primitives of structured programming. Consequently, in this sense C is a structured programming language.

In summary, a program that uses the three primitives of structured programming is a structured program. In its purest form structured programming is synonymous with "goto-less programming." Throughout this book we will write and study structured programs and avoid the use of `goto` statements.

## REVIEW QUESTIONS

1. The loop body is a program block executed repeatedly by a repetition statement. (T or F)

2. Which of the following statements concerning pretest repetition statements is *incorrect*?
   a. A pretest repetition statement computes a value for its loop control expression before entering the loop body.
   b. In pretest repetition, if the loop control expression computes to false, the iteration stops.
   c. If the loop control expression computes to true, the loop body is executed.
   d. The `do-while` statement in C is a pretest repetition statement.

3. In the C `while` statement, the parenthesized expression after the keyword `while` cannot be an arithmetic expression. (T or F)

4. Which of the following is *not* an underlying principle of structured programming?
   a. Any program can be written using only three basic structures: sequence, selection, and repetition.
   b. Unconditional branching is an essential control structure.
   c. The three basic control structures of structured programming are easy to comprehend and modify.
   d. Structured programs are easier to write, read, debug, and maintain compared to those which use `gotos` liberally.

**Answers:**  1. T; 2. d; 3. F; 4. b.

## 4.6   EXAMPLE PROGRAM 1: A C Program that Computes Federal Income Tax from Tax Rate Schedules

In this section we will solve another problem and develop a complete application program that computes federal income tax from tax rate schedules. This problem was analyzed in detail in Chapter 2, and we presented a pseudocode algorithm for it in Figure 2.3. All we have to do now is to implement this algorithm in C. One possible implementation, based on what you have learned so far, is given in Figure 4.17.

```
/****************************************************************
    Program Filename: Prog04_1.c
    Author           : Uckan
    Purpose          : Computes Federal Income Tax for 1991 from Tax Rate
                       Schedules
    Input from       : Keyboard
    Output to        : Screen
 ****************************************************************/
#include <stdio.h>
```

**Figure 4.17**   A C program that computes federal income tax from tax rate schedules *(continued)*   ▶

```c
#include <string.h>

const double LOWRATE  = 0.28;
const double HIGHRATE = 0.31;

int main(void) {
      /* Variable declarations: */

      int filing_status;
      double income, tax;
      char correctStatusInput[4];

      /* Function body: */

      printf("THIS PROGRAM COMPUTES FEDERAL INCOME TAX\n");
      printf("FROM TAX RATE SCHEDULES.\n");

      printf("Enter taxable income; ");
      printf("should be greater than or equal to $50,000: ");
      scanf("%lf", &income);

      while (income < 50000.00) {
            printf("Enter taxable income; ");
            printf("should be greater than or equal to $50,000: ");
            scanf("%lf", &income);
      } /* end while */

      printf("\n");
      printf("*************************************\n");
      printf("* FILING STATUS MENU:              *\n");
      printf("* Single                 ---- 1 *\n");
      printf("* Married filing jointly    ---- 2 *\n");
      printf("* Married filing separately ---- 3 *\n");
      printf("* Head of household         ---- 4 *\n");
      printf("*************************************\n");
      printf("\n");

      strcpy(correctStatusInput, "no");

      while (strcmp(correctStatusInput, "no") == 0) {
            printf("Enter filing status; should be between 1 and 4: ");
            scanf("%d", &filing_status);
```

**Figure 4.17** *(continued)*      ▶

```
                   if (filing_status > 0)
                        if (filing_status < 5)
                             strcpy(correctStatusInput, "yes");
                        /* end if */
               /* end if */
        } /* end while */

        if (filing_status == 1)
             tax = 11158.50 + HIGHRATE * (income - 49300.00);
        else if (filing_status == 2)
             if (income <= 82150)
                  tax = 5100.00 + LOWRATE * (income - 34000.00);
             else
                  tax = 18582.00 + HIGHRATE * (income - 82150.00);
             /* end if */
        else if (filing_status == 3)
             tax = 9291.00 + HIGHRATE * (income - 41075.00);
        else if (filing_status == 4)
             if (income <= 70450.00)
                  tax = 4095.00 + LOWRATE * (income - 27300.00);
             else
                  tax = 16177.00 + HIGHRATE * (income - 70450.00);
             /* end if */
        /* end if */

        printf("\n");
        printf("RESULTS OF COMPUTATIONS:\n");
        printf("   Taxable income: %f\n", income);
        printf("   Filing Status : ");

        if (filing_status == 1)
             printf("Single");
        else if (filing_status == 2)
             printf("Married filing jointly");
        else if (filing_status == 3)
             printf("Married filing separately");
        else if (filing_status == 4)
             printf("Head of household");
        /* end if */

        printf("\n");
        printf("   Tax           : %f", tax);
        return 0;
} /* end function main */
```

**Figure 4.17**

Let us go over this program and explain some of its features.

1. There are two problem constants in the tax schedule formulas, 0.28 and 0.31. Early in the program they are declared as two named constants, LOWRATE and HIGH-RATE, respectively.

2. The first two statements in the function body print a brief description of the purpose of the program. In interactive programs a short self-identification produced by the program may be helpful to the user.

3. We wish to incorporate into this program a data validation routine to make sure that the user enters a taxable income amount that is greater than or equal to $50,000. For this purpose we construct a while loop, the first while statement in the program, which uses income as the loop control variable.

4. The second while loop is used to input and verify the filing status. We resort to a different technique here; we declare correctStatusInput as a string variable and use it to control the loop.

5. The block of statements from after the second while loop to the output statements that print the results are the implementation of the tax schedule formulas. This block consists of a nested if statement, which defines six selection alternatives. Indeed, we have six formulas for tax schedules.

6. The remaining statements output the results of computations in terms of a header line (RESULTS OF COMPUTATIONS:), income, filing status, and tax. Note that filing status is reported verbally. To print filing status verbally, we need a nested if statement that converts a value of the variable filing_status to a verbal description. Finally, the last output statement is for the output of tax as a floating-point value.

A sample test run of the program of Figure 4.17 is given in Figure 4.18.

```
THIS PROGRAM COMPUTES FEDERAL INCOME TAX
FROM TAX RATE SCHEDULES.
Enter taxable income; should be greater than or equal to $50,000: 45000
Enter taxable income; should be greater than or equal to $50,000: 57000


***********************************
* FILING STATUS MENU:             *
* Single                   ---- 1 *
* Married filing jointly    ---- 2 *
* Married filing separately ---- 3 *
* Head of household         ---- 4 *
***********************************


Enter filing status; should be between 1 and 4: 0
Enter filing status; should be between 1 and 4: 5
Enter filing status; should be between 1 and 4: 1
```

**Figure 4.18**    A sample interactive session for the program of Figure 4.17 *(continued)*    ▶

```
RESULTS OF COMPUTATIONS:
   Taxable income: 57000.000000
   Filing Status : Single
   Tax           : 13545.500000
```

**Figure 4.18**

## 4.7 SUMMARY

### This Chapter at a Glance

- In this chapter we began our look at the selection control structures in C. Of the two available selection statements, `if` and `switch`, we discussed `if`. The `if` statement can be used for two-way selections.

- The `if` statement's ability to make selections depends on a selection expression. A selection expression that computes either true or false is called a predicate. We covered simple predicates, which compare quantities using relational operators.

- We discussed precedence and associativity rules for the C operators that have been covered so far, including arithmetic and relational operators. We saw that operator precedence can be changed by using parentheses in expressions.

- You added to your knowledge of string processing and learned about copying strings and using them in conditional expressions.

- You learned that the `if` statement can also be used for multiway selection in its nested form.

- We focused on the implementation of the repetition control structure. C has three repetition statements: `while`, `for`, and `do-while`. Of these, `while` and `for` are pretest repetition statements, and `do-while` is a posttest repetition statement.

- We considered the `while` statement in detail. We observed that the number of times a `while` statement executes its loop body depends on a loop control expression and that this expression is essentially similar to the selection expression that is associated with the `if` statement.

- To design controlled loops with the `while` statement, we noted that we must have some statements in the loop body that will eventually change the outcome of the loop control expression so that the loop terminates.

- We also discussed labels, labeled statements, and the unconditional transfer of control statement `goto`. We examined the `goto` statement and highlighted its disadvantages — that its excessive use in a program may unnecessarily complicate the program logic and make the program difficult to debug. In general, you should avoid using the `goto` statement.

- We concluded this chapter with a discussion of structured programming. Structured programming is a programming discipline that uses only the sequence, selection, and repetition control structures in a program. Structured programming simplifies program logic, program design, debugging, and maintenance. We noted that because the C language permits the design of structured programs, it is a structured programming language.

- With this chapter we have achieved our objective of building a minimum subset of C statements. The subset includes input, output, arithmetic assignment, `if`, and `while` statements. It is sufficient to implement any algorithm, no matter how complex.

## Coming Attractions

- Chapter 3 covered simple arithmetic assignment statements to perform arithmetic. In Chapter 5 we continue to study arithmetic calculations.

- You will learn about additional C arithmetic operators, which will enable you to deal with complex arithmetic formulas.

- We will discuss standard mathematical library functions. These functions are helpful in computing values for mathematical functions, such as the square root, exponentiation, logarithmic functions, and trigonometric functions.

- We will also explore additional C fundamental data types for numeric data, types of arithmetic errors and inaccuracies, and automatic conversion of numeric data types.

- In this manner, you will add to your skills for dealing with relatively complex mathematical problems.

## STUDY GUIDE

### Test Your Comprehension

1. Which of the following statements concerning the C `if` statement is correct?
   **a.** It is essentially used for the implementation of two-way selection processes.
   **b.** The else-part is executed only if the parenthesized expression that follows the keyword `if` evaluates to a nonzero value.
   **c.** The else-part is required; however, the then-part is optional.
   **d.** After the then-part is executed, the program control drops to the beginning of the else-part.
   **e.** All of the above.
   **f.** None of the above.

2. Which of the following operators is *not* a relational operator in C?
   **a.** `<>`
   **b.** `==`
   **c.** `>=`
   **d.** `<=`
   **e.** `>`

3. Which of the following statements concerning the evaluation of conditional expressions is correct?

**a.** All parenthesized subexpressions, beginning with the innermost subexpressions, are evaluated first.

**b.** Unary arithmetic operators have higher precedence than binary arithmetic operators.

**c.** All arithmetic operators are applied before all relational operators.

**d.** The relational operators less-than, less-than-or-equal-to, greater-than, and greater-than-or-equal-to are applied before the equal-to and not-equal-to operators.

**e.** All of the above.

**f.** None of the above.

**4.** The standard string handling function `strcmp`

**a.** Is declared in the `stdio.h` header file.

**b.** Requires a single argument.

**c.** Is used to make a copy of a string value in a string variable.

**d.** All of the above are correct.

**e.** None of the above is correct.

**5.** Concerning posttest repetition, choose the correct alternative.

**a.** A posttest repetition statement computes a value for its predicate before entering the loop body.

**b.** If the predicate computes to true, the repetition terminates.

**c.** If the predicate computes to false, the loop body is executed.

**d.** The `while` statement in C is a posttest repetition statement.

**e.** All of the above.

**f.** None of the above.

**6.** Which of the following is *not* an objective of structured programming?

**a.** Simplify the program design process

**b.** Minimize program complexity

**c.** Increase execution efficiency

**d.** Increase program readability

**e.** Simplify program maintenance

**7.** Suppose we have the following conditional expression in an `if` statement:

```
a * b / c + 4 > d != 3 * c ++ <= a
```

Which of the following is the correct order of computations for this expression?

**a.**
```
a * b / c + 4 > d != 3 * c ++ <= a
  1   2   3   4     8   5     6  7
```

**b.**
```
a * b / c + 4 > d != 3 * c ++ <= a
  2   3   5   6     7   4     1  8
```

**c.**
```
a * b / c + 4 > d != 3 * c ++ <= a
  3   2   5   6     8   4     1  7
```

**d.**
```
a * b / c + 4 > d != 3 * c ++ <= a
  2   3   5   6     8   4     1  7
```

**e.** None of these

## Improve Your Problem-Solving Ability

*Debugging Exercises*

**8.** Find and explain the errors, if any, in each of the following `if` statements.

**a.**
```
if (test_score >= 60)
        printf("%d passes.", student_idno);
        passing_students = passing_students + 1;
    else
        failing_students = failing_students + 1;
```

**b.**
```
if (filing_status == 1);
        printf("Single");
```

**c.**
```
if (b * b - 4 * a * c >= 0)
        then
                printf("Real roots");
        else
                printf("Complex roots");
```

**d.**
```
if (b * b - 4 * a * c >= 0)
        printf("Real roots")
    else
        printf("Complex roots");
```

**e.**
```
if (val1 <> val2)
        ;
    else
        c = val1;
```

**f.**
```
if (a >= 0) {
        printf("You have entered a positive value");
    else
        printf("You have entered a negative value");
}
```

**g.**
```
if(strcpy(string1, "yes") == 0)
        printf("The string value is yes");
```

**9.** What are the syntax errors in each of the following nested `if` statements?

**a.**
```
if (number - number / 2 * 2 == 0)
   printf("The number is divisible by 2")
   else
      if (number - number / 3 * 3 == 0)
         printf("The number is divisible by 3")
      else
         if (number - number / 5 * 5 == 0)
            printf("The number is divisible by 5")
         else
            printf("The number has no small factors");
```

**b.** 
```
if (year > 4) {
    grad_students = grad_students + 1;
    if (sex_code == 1)
        male_grad_students = male_grad_students + 1;
    else
        female_grad_students = female_grad_students + 1;
    else
        undergrad_students = undergrad_students + 1;
}
```

**c.** 
```
if (grade_point_average <= 1.99)
        printf("%d Probation", student_idno);
        students_on_probation = students_on_probation + 1;
    else
        printf("%d Satisfactory");
```

**10.** Find the errors, if any, in each of the following `while` statements.

**a.** 
```
while (a * a + b * b >= 0)
        printf("a = %d b = %d", a, b);
```

**b.** 
```
while (grade_point_average <= 1.99)
        printf("Probation");
    else
        printf("Satisfactory");
```

**c.** 
```
sum = 0.0;
denom = 1.0;
while (denom <= 10.0) {
        sum = sum + 1 / denom;
        denom = denom - 1;
}
```

**d.** 
```
odds = 0;
evens = 0;
printf("Enter an integer: ");
scanf("%d", &number);

while (number)
    if (number - number / 2 * 2) {
      printf("You have entered an odd integer.");
      odds++;
    }
    else {
      printf("You have entered an even integer.");
      evens++;
    }
    printf("Enter an integer: ");
```

```
scanf("%d", &number);
printf("Number of odd integers: %d", odds);
printf("Number of even integers: %d", evens);
```

### Programming Exercises

**11.** For each of the following values of the variables a, b, and c, compute the value of the given simple predicate.
**a.** 8, 5, and 7;    a + b == c
**b.** 1, 7, and 9;    a + b < c
**c.** 4, 5, and 3;    a <= b - c
**d.** 6, 1, and 2;    a > b + c
**e.** 6, 6, and 6;    a >= 3 * b - c

**12.** Write an if statement that computes and prints the circumference or the area of a square using the formulas:

```
circumference = 4 * side
```

and

```
area = side * side
```

Assume that there are values in the memory for the variables side and user_request. Also assume that if user_request is 1, we want the circumference; and if it is 2, we want the area.

**13.** Write an if statement that determines and prints the larger of two values, value1 and value2.

**14.** Express the following selection problem using an if statement: Compute and print the height of a person in feet if the value of the character variable height_unit is 'F'; do so in meters if the value is 'M'. Assume that the value of the variable height is expressed in inches. (One foot is 12 inches, and one inch is 0.0254 meter.)

**15.** The following table shows the letter grades corresponding to different ranges of test score:

| Test Score | Letter Grade |
| --- | --- |
| 90–100 | A |
| 80–89 | B |
| 70–79 | C |
| 60–69 | D |
| 0–59 | F |

Write a series of unnested if statements that print a correct letter grade for a supplied value of test score.

**16.** Solve exercise 15 so that your program incorporates data validation logic; that is, the program prints a warning message for values of test scores that are less than 0 or greater than 100.

**17.** Solve exercise 16 using a single nested if statement.

**18.** Suppose the following scheme is used for assigning grades in a course:

| Test Score | Letter Grade |
|---|---|
| 97–100 | A+ |
| 93–96 | A |
| 90–92 | A− |
| 87–89 | B+ |
| 83–86 | B |
| 80–82 | B− |
| 77–79 | C+ |
| 73–76 | C |
| 70–72 | C− |
| 67–69 | D+ |
| 63–66 | D |
| 60–62 | D− |
| 0–59 | F |

Write a nested `if` statement that prints the letter grade for a supplied value of test score.

**19.** For the grading scheme in exercise 18, write a nested `if` statement that prints the range of test scores for a given value of letter grade. Note that in this application, letter grade values are strings.

**20.** Suppose a company decides to raise the salaries of its employees according to the following table:

| employee_status | years_of_service | percent_raise |
|---|---|---|
| Full-time | Less than 5 years | 4.0 |
| Full-time | 5 years or more | 5.0 |
| Part-time | Less than 5 years | 2.5 |
| Part-time | 5 years or more | 3.0 |

If `employee_status` value is `'F'`, the employee is full-time; if it is `'P'`, he or she is part-time. Write a single nested `if` statement that computes the new salary of an employee given his or her `employee_status`, `years_of_service`, and `salary`.

**21.** Solve exercise 20 so that your `if` statement also validates `employee_status` and `years_of_service` data values. The variable `employee_status` can have only two values: `'F'` and `'P'`. On the other hand, `years_of_service` cannot be negative, nor can it be greater than 20.

**22.** Suppose we have the if statement

```
if (a - 3 * b > c * c != a + 3 * b < c + a)
      a = b * b;
else
      a = c * c;
/* end if */
```

Initially, the values of the integer variables `a`, `b`, and `c` are `5`, `4`, and `3`, respectively. What will be the value computed for `a` after this `if` statement is executed? Explain your answer.

**23.** Write a program code that uses a `while` statement to compute the sum of all integers between `first` and `second`, where `first` and `second` are integers and `first <= second`.

**24.** Solve exercise 23 so that your code prompts the user to enter new values for `first` and `second` if `first > second`.

**25.** Write a `while` loop that determines the number of digits in a given integer by repeatedly removing the least significant digit until the number becomes zero.

**26.** Design a `while` loop that interactively reads test score values until a test score value of zero is entered and then computes and outputs the average test score.

**27.** Solve exercise 26 so that the test score values entered by the user are validated to ensure that they are between 10 and 100.

**28.** We have the following program code:

```
sum = 0;
counter = 7;
while (counter <= 37) {
        sum = sum + counter;
        counter = counter + 3;
} /* end while */
```

How many times will the `while` loop body be executed? What will be the values computed for the variables `sum` and `counter` after the program code completes its execution?

**29.** The following program code is correct but written without any style considerations. Rewrite the code using program style rules so that it becomes easy to follow.

```
if (seq_number == 1) fib_number = first;
if (seq_number == 2) fib_number = second;
while (count <= seq_number) { fib_number = first + second;
first = second; second = fib_number; count = count + 1; }
```

### Programming Projects

**30.** Write a program that reads a positive single-digit integer and prints the word equivalent for it. For example, if the user enters 8, your program should print `You have entered eight`. The program should execute repeatedly until the user enters a negative digit.

**31.** Design and implement a program that reads a positive integer $n$ and then computes and prints the sum of all integers between 1 and $n$.

**32.** Write a program that accepts a positive integer $n$ as input and then computes and outputs the sum of all integers between 1 and $n$ that are evenly divisible by 3.

**33.** Design and implement a program that reads a positive integer $n$ and then computes and prints the factorial of $n$.

**34.** Design a program that accepts a positive integer and determines whether it is a numerical palindrome. A *numerical palindrome* is a number that is the same forward and backward, such as 13431.

**35.** Write a program that reads a positive integer and then determines and outputs the largest power of 2 that is less than or equal to the given integer.

**36.** Design and implement a program that reads floating-point numbers in a sentinel-controlled loop until the user terminates the program by entering zero. Your program should determine and print the smallest, largest, and average of the supplied numbers.

**37.** Solve project 36 using a counter-controlled loop so that the program determines the smallest, largest, and average of *n* numbers, where *n* is an integer supplied by the user.

**38.** Write a program that reads two positive integers corresponding to two year values, ensures that the first year value is less than the second, and then determines and outputs all year values for leap years. A leap year is one that can be evenly divided by 4, unless it is a centennial, in which case it must be evenly divisible by 400. For example, 1600 and 1992 are leap years, whereas 1700 and 1998 are not.

**39.** Write a program for the following problem. An instructor needs a program that accepts a student identification number and three test scores, `test1`, `test2`, and `final_test`, as input and then determines and outputs for each student the semester average and the final letter grade according to the following scheme:

| Semester Average | Final Letter Grade |
|:---:|:---:|
| 90–100 | A |
| 80–89 | B |
| 70–79 | C |
| 60–69 | D |
| 0–59 | F |

The semester average for students is computed using the following formula:

```
semester_average = 0.20 * test1 + 0.30 * test2 + 0.50 * final_test
```

Student identification numbers are nonzero integers. Input should terminate when the instructor types 0 for student identification number. The instructor also wants a distribution of letter grades and a class average. Class average is computed using the following formula:

```
class_average = (4 * number_of_A_grades + 3 * number_of_B_grades +
                2 * number_of_C_grades + 1 *  number_of_D_grades) /
                number_of_students
```

A typical interactive session is given below. Design your program accordingly.

```
***> Enter student idno: 1100
***> Enter test score 1: 70
***> Enter test score 2: 80
***> Enter final score : 100
     Semester average for student 1100: 88
     Letter grade for student 1100    : B

***> Enter student idno: 1200
***> Enter test score 1: 75
***> Enter test score 2: 65
***> Enter final score : 76
     Semester average for student 1200: 73
     Letter grade for student 1200    : C


     . . . . . . . . . . . . .
     . . . . . . . . . . . . .
***> Enter student idno: 0

     Grade distributions:
          A    4
          B    6
          C    7
          D    2
          F    0

     Class average: 2.63
```

# Arithmetic Calculations

---

**CHAPTER OBJECTIVES**

In this chapter you will learn about:

- **Arithmetic calculations in C**
    Basic arithmetic operators
    Increment and decrement operators
    Compound assignment operators

- **Type of arithmetic expressions**
    Explicit type conversions using the cast operator

- **Mathematical library functions**

- **Additional fundamental data types**
    Integer and floating-point data types

- **Arithmetic errors and inaccuracies**

- **Automatic conversion of numeric data types**
    Arithmetic conversions
    Assignment conversions

- **Random number generation in C**

By the time you have completed this chapter, you will have acquired the ability to:

- **Solve problems that require complex arithmetic calculations**

- **Use standard mathematical library functions in problem solving**

- **Use random number generators in simulating random events**

---

## 5.1    INTRODUCTION

Chapter 3 briefly introduced arithmetic assignment expression statements, and you learned that they perform calculations in C. In this chapter you learn more about numeric data types and arithmetic calculations. We will examine additional arithmetic operators, more complex forms of arithmetic assignment expression statements, and standard mathematical library functions. We will also consider variations of the integers and floating-point data types. We will explore several types of arithmetic errors and inaccuracies, as well as techniques to avoid them. Ultimately, you will acquire the ability to formulate complex mathematical formulas in C programs. Also, we will introduce the use of the C random-number generators in simulating random events.

## 5.2    BASIC ARITHMETIC OPERATORS

We can form arithmetic expressions by using arithmetic operators. You already know that there are two types of arithmetic operators in C: unary arithmetic operators and binary arithmetic operators.

**Unary arithmetic operators** require one operand. They include the unary plus  +, unary minus  -, increment operator  ++, and decrement operator  --. Unary plus has no effect on the result. Unary minus reverses the sign of the operand to which it applies. For example, if the value of the variable  first  is  100, the statements

```
second = + first;
third = - first;
```

result in a value of  100  for the variable  second  and a value of  -100  for the variable  third. The two increment operators  ++  and  --  are discussed later in this section.

**Binary arithmetic operators** require two operands. They are  +  for addition,  -  for subtraction,  *  for multiplication,  /  for division, and  %  for remainder (or modulus). You are already familiar with the first four binary arithmetic operators  +,  -,  *, and  /. Their operands can be integer or floating-point quantities. The fifth operator,  %, is called the **remainder** (or **modulus**) **operator**. Its operands must be integer quantities. It computes the remainder of the division of its first operand by its second operand. For example, the expression  17 % 3  computes to the value of 2 because the division of 17 by 3 yields an integer quotient of 5 with an integer remainder of 2. In this operation the quotient 5 is irrelevant; we are after the remainder 2.

The remainder operator has the same precedence and associativity as the multiplication and division operators. In fact, the multiplication, division, and remainder operators are collectively known as **multiplicative operators**. The addition and subtraction operators are called **additive operators**.

Chapter 4 covered the precedence and associativity rules for the arithmetic operators as well as the other operators that you learned previously. To develop a better understanding of arithmetic operators, we will look at some examples that deal with their functions and how they are handled by the computer in computing values for arithmetic expressions.

***Example 5.1*** The following table shows some examples of arithmetic assignment expression statements in which binary arithmetic operators are used. These examples are based on the following data declarations:

```
int first = 100, second = 7, third;
```

| No. | Statement | VALUE BEFORE EXECUTION | | | VALUE AFTER EXECUTION | | |
|-----|-----------|-------|--------|-------|-------|--------|-------|
| | | first | second | third | first | second | third |
| 1 | third = first + second; | 100 | 7 | ? | 100 | 7 | 107 |
| 2 | third = first - second; | 100 | 7 | ? | 100 | 7 | 93 |
| 3 | third = first * second; | 100 | 7 | ? | 100 | 7 | 700 |
| 4 | third = first / second; | 100 | 7 | ? | 100 | 7 | 14 |
| 5 | third = first % second; | 100 | 7 | ? | 100 | 7 | 2 |

The first three examples above are obvious. You should note that in each case, the statements compute and assign a value for the variable `third`. They do not change the values for the variables `first` and `second`.

The fourth statement concerns division of two integers. The result of the division of `first` by `second` with respective values of 100 and 7 is 14, not 14.285714 as you might have expected. The reason is that the operands in the arithmetic expression are of type `int`, and as a rule the computer computes an integer value for an expression in which all operands are integer. Therefore, the result of the expression is the integer value 14 obtained after 14.285714 is truncated to an integer. Therefore, this value will be stored in the variable `third`. Had the variables `first`, `second`, and `third` been of type `double`, the value 14.285714 would have been stored in `third`.

The fifth example uses the remainder operator `%`. The remainder operator, when applied on `first` and `second` with values 100 and 7, will result in 2, which is the remainder of the division of 100 by 7. You should note that the fifth example and the statement

```
third = first - first / second * second;
```

are equivalent; both will compute the remainder and store it in the variable `third`.

***Example 5.2*** Suppose our program has the following declarations:

```
int a, b, c, d, e;
```

Let us assume that at some point during program execution, the values of these variables are a = 10, b = 20, c = 15, d = 8, and e = 40. We are given the following arithmetic expression:

```
(a + b / (c - 5)) / ((d + 7) / (e - 37) % 3)
```

The evaluation of this expression proceeds as follows:

**Step 1.** Because the first innermost parenthesized subexpression is `(c - 5)`, the evaluation process begins with it. This subexpression becomes `(15 - 5)`, yielding `10`.

The original expression reduces to

```
(a + b / 10) / ((d + 7) / (e - 37) % 3)
```

**Step 2.** In the reduced expression, the first innermost parenthesized subexpression from the left is `(d + 7)`. When evaluated, `(8 + 7)` gives `15`, further reducing the expression to

```
(a + b / 10) / (15 / (e - 37) % 3)
```

**Step 3.** The second innermost parenthesized expression is `(e - 37)`. After evaluating `(40 - 37)`, the expression becomes

```
(a + b / 10) / (15 / 3 % 3)
```

**Step 4.** The higher precedence operator in the first parenthesized subexpression `(a + b / 10)` is division. As `20 / 10` is `2`, this step produces the expression

```
(a + 2) / ( 15 / 3 % 3)
```

**Step 5.** The evaluation of the first parenthesized subexpression `(a + 2)` is completed:

```
12 / ( 15 / 3 % 3)
```

**Step 6.** In the remaining parenthesized subexpression, `(15 / 3 % 3)`, we have two operators, `/` and `%`, of the same precedence level. In this case the left-associativity rule is used:

```
12 / (5 % 3)
```

**Step 7.** The parenthesized subexpression `(5 % 3)` is evaluated. This step yields:

```
12 / 2
```

**Step 8.** Division is performed to produce `6` as the result of the expression.

For the same expression in this example, we can show the order of computations more concisely as follows:

```
(a + b / (c - 5)) / ((d + 7) / (e - 37) % 3)
    5   4    1        8     2      6     3   7
```

The integers in the bottom line indicate the order in which each operation is performed in computing the expression. Suppose the same expression is written without any parentheses. Then the order of computations will be

```
a + b / c - 5 / d + 7 / e - 37 % 3
    5   1   6   2   7   3   8   4
```

and the expression will compute to `10`. As an exercise, go through the computations and verify that the computed value is indeed 10.

***Example 5.3***   Our last example is concerned with floating-point arithmetic. Suppose the variables are declared as

```
double a, b, c, d, e;
```

and their respective values are  a = 10.0, b = 20.0, c = 15.0, d = 8.0, and  e = 40.0. The expression to be evaluated is

```
(a + b / (c - 5.0)) / ((d + 7.0) / (e - 37.0) / 3.0)
```

The evaluation sequence is

```
(a + b / (c - 5.0)) / ((d + 7.0) / (e - 37.0) / 3.0)
     5    4    1           8        2        6   3        7
```

The following table shows the operators considered at each step and the reduced expression after the operators are applied, ultimately yielding  7.2  as the result.

| Step | Operator | Reduced Expression |
|------|----------|--------------------|
| 1 | - | (a + b / 10.0) / ((d + 7.0) / (e - 37.0) / 3.0) |
| 2 | + | (a + b / 10.0) / (15.0 / (e - 37.0) / 3.0) |
| 3 | - | (a + b / 10.0) / (15.0 / 3.0 / 3.0) |
| 4 | / | (a + 2.0) / (15.0 / 3.0 / 3.0) |
| 5 | + | 12.0 / (15.0 / 3.0 / 3.0) |
| 6 | / | 12.0 / (5.0 / 3.0) |
| 7 | / | 12.0 / 1.666667 |
| 8 | / | 7.2 |

## 5.3    INCREMENT AND DECREMENT OPERATORS

At first glance a statement such as

```
count = count + 1;
```

where the variable  count  is of type  int, may look strange. But when we remember that the operator  =  stands for assignment and not for equality, the statement makes sense; it is our instruction to the computer to increment the current value of  count  by  1 and store the new result in  count's memory location. Similarly, the statement

```
count = count - 1;
```

decrements the value of  count  by  1. If the previous value of  count  is  10, it becomes  9  after the statement is executed.

C has two special operators for incrementing or decrementing a variable by 1. They are the operators  ++  and  --, the unary **increment** and **decrement operators**. Instead of writing

```
count = count + 1;
```

we can more concisely write

```
count ++;
```

which is the postfix form of the increment operator. Also, we can write

```
++ count;
```

which is its prefix form. These operators are also called **postincrement** and **preincrement operators**, respectively.

The decrement operator is also unary and has postfix and prefix forms called **post-decrement** and **predecrement operators**. The statements

```
count --;
-- count;
```

are identical to the statement

```
count = count - 1;
```

Every statement in C has a main purpose — a task that it must accomplish. In addition, some statements have **side effects**. Side effects are mostly in the form of value assignments for variables, and they may or may not be desirable. The main purpose of an arithmetic assignment expression statement is to compute a value for the expression and assign that value to a variable. For example, the statement

```
count = count + 1;
```

adds  1  to the variable  count  and stores the new value in  count. If  count  is currently  3, the value computed for the expression is  4, and this value is assigned to count. This statement has no side effect. However, the statement

```
count ++;
```

returns the current value of the variable  count, which is  3. Also, the statement has a side effect; it adds  1  to  count, making it  4. In other words, if we have the following two consecutive output statements in a program

```
printf("%d", count ++);
printf("%d", count);
```

the first statement will print  3  and the second statement will print  4. The reason is that the postincrement operator increments the operand by 1 after the expression is evaluated.

The preincrement operator works differently; the operand is incremented by 1 before the expression is evaluated. For example, if the current value of  count  is  3  and we have the following two statements in our program:

```
printf("%d", ++ count);
printf("%d", count);
```

both statements print  4.

---

## Rules for Increment and Decrement Operators

1. All increment and decrement operators are unary operators and they require variables as their operands.

2. The postincrement operator has the side effect of incrementing its operand by one, after the expression in which it appears is evaluated using the operand's previous value. Similarly, the postdecrement operator does not change the value of the operand while the expression is being evaluated. After the post decrement operator is applied, the value of the operand is decremented by one.

> 3.  The preincrement and predecrement operators first generate their side effect; that is, they increment or decrement their operand by 1. Then, the expression in which they appear is evaluated.
> 4.  The precedence and associativity of the increment and decrement operators are the same as those of unary + and unary −.

***Example 5.4***   Suppose we have the following declarations:

```
int count, first, second;
```

Let us assume that the current values of the variables `count` and `first` are 5 and 10, respectively. The statement

```
second = 5 * -- count + first;
```

contains a predecrement operator applied to `count`. Therefore, the computer first decrements the value of `count` by 1 making it 4. This value is used in the expression to compute   30   for the variable   second. Following this statement, the output statement

```
printf("%d", count);
```

will print   4, and the statement

```
printf("%d", second);
```

will print   30.

## 5.4   COMPOUND ASSIGNMENT OPERATORS

You know by now that to compute a value for an expression and store it in a variable, you have to use the assignment operator   =. This assignment operator is also known as the **simple assignment operator**. C supports **compound assignment operators**, which are obtained by combining some operators with the simple assignment operator. For arithmetic assignment expression statements, the compound assignment operators are

1.  Assign sum,   +=
2.  Assign difference,   -=
3.  Assign product,   *=
4.  Assign division,   /=
5.  Assign remainder,   %=

The general form of all compound assignment operators is *op=*, where *op* stands for any one of the operators   +,   −,   *,   /, and   %. An arithmetic assignment expression statement such as

> *Variable op = Expression;*

is the same as the statement

> *Variable = Variable op Expression;*

For example, the statements

```
count += first;
count = count + first;
```

are equivalent. In both cases the current value of the variable `count` will be added to that of the variable `first`, and the result will be stored in `count`.

The precedence and associativity of the compound assignment operators are the same as those of the simple assignment operator.

The following examples clarify the semantics of arithmetic assignment expression statements that use compound assignment operators.

**Example 5.5**   Suppose we want to decrement the value of the variable `count` by `1`. All four of the following statements will do the job:

```
count = count - 1;
-- count;
count --;
count -= 1;
```

**Example 5.6**   Assume that we have the following declarations for two floating-point variables:

```
double first, second;
```

The following table contains four examples of assignment statements with four compound assignment operators. In each example we assume that the values of the variables `first` and `second` before the execution are `12.75` and `13.75`, respectively. The values of the variable `first` do not change after the execution of these statements. However, the values of `second` change and are shown in the table.

| No. | Statement | Value of `second` after Execution |
|---|---|---|
| 1 | `second += first;` | 26.5 |
| 2 | `second -= first;` | 1.0 |
| 3 | `second *= first;` | 175.3125 |
| 4 | `second /= first;` | 1.078431 |

**Example 5.7**   Now we consider two integer variables, `third` and `fourth`, declared as follows:

```
int third, fourth;
```

The following table shows ten assignment statements that use various compound assignment operators. In each example we assume that the values of `third` and `fourth` are `13` and `20`.

| No. | Statement | Value of `fourth` after Execution |
|-----|-----------|-----------------------------------|
| 1 | `fourth += third;` | 33 |
| 2 | `fourth -= third;` | 7 |
| 3 | `fourth *= third;` | 260 |
| 4 | `fourth /= third;` | 1 |
| 5 | `fourth %= third;` | 7 |
| 6 | `fourth += third + 4;` | 37 |
| 7 | `fourth -= third + 4;` | 3 |
| 8 | `fourth *= third + 4;` | 340 |
| 9 | `fourth /= third + 4;` | 1 |
| 10 | `fourth %= third + 4;` | 3 |

Note that the compound assignment operator `%=` requires integers as its operands. The fifth and tenth examples in the table above illustrate the use of `%=`.

## 5.5   TYPE OF ARITHMETIC EXPRESSIONS

You already know that each constant and variable in a C program is assigned a type. A constant such as `12` is of type integer. Variable types must be declared explicitly, using type declarations. If you want the variable `count` to be of type integer, then you must use the declaration

```
int count;
```

in your program. C supports quite a few data types. So far we have described three fundamental data types: `int`, `double`, and `char`. Of these `int` and `double` are arithmetic data types.

Because an arithmetic assignment expression statement generates a computed value, such a value must have a type, and so must the arithmetic expression in the statement. In assigning a type to an arithmetic expression with `int` and `double` types, the compiler uses the following rules.

---

**Rules for Assigning a Type to Arithmetic Expressions that Involve `int` and `double`**

1.   If one or more of the operands in an arithmetic expression are of type `double`, the result of the expression is also of type `double`.

2.   If all operands in an arithmetic expression are of type `int`, the result of the expression is also of type `int`.

> 3.  In an arithmetic assignment expression statement, the type of the entire statement and the type of the value stored in the variable to the left of the assignment operator are the same as the type of the variable itself.

Let us consider some examples based on the following declarations:

```
double first = 4.7, second;
int third = 27, fourth;
```

***Example 5.8***   The expression statement

```
first + third;
```

computes to `31.7`, which is of type `double` because `first` is of type `double`. Therefore, the value of the variable `third`, which is of type `int`, is converted to a floating-point value in temporary storage, and the expression is evaluated to yield a floating-point value.

***Example 5.9***   Now we consider the arithmetic assignment expression statement

```
first = first + third;
```

In evaluating this statement, the computer goes through the following steps:

**Step 1.** Because one of the operands in the expression, `first`, is of type `double`, the computer converts the value of the second operand, `third`, to type `double` (that is, `27.0`) in temporary storage and computes a floating-point value for the expression. This value is `31.7`.

**Step 2.** The computer assigns this value to the variable `first`. Because both the variable `first` and the computed expression are of type `double`, no conversion is necessary in performing the assignment operation. The value of the assignment statement expression is also `31.7`.

***Example 5.10***   A slightly different form of the statement in Example 5.9 is

```
third = first + third;
```

The first step of the expression evaluation process is the same in both examples; a value of `31.7` is computed. However, because the variable `third` is of type `int`, the value `31.7` is converted to the integer value of `31` during assignment. Note that such a conversion truncates the fractional part of the floating-point number. The value of the assignment expression statement is also `31`.

***Example 5.11***   Now consider an assignment statement with a mixed-mode expression:

```
x = a / 3 + b;
```

Let us assume that we have the following declarations:

```
    double x, b = 12.5;
    int a = 7;
```

The assignment statement is evaluated as follows:

**Step 1.** Because division has higher precedence than addition, the integer division expression `(a / 3)` is evaluated first. This expression becomes `(7 / 3)`, and the result is the integer value `2`.

**Step 2.** The expression `(2 + b)` is considered. Because the value of `b` is `12.5`, the result is the floating-point value `14.5`.

**Step 3.** The value computed for the expression is `14.5`, and it is assigned to the floating-point variable `x`.

## Explicit Type Conversions: The Cast Operator and Casting

We know that, once declared, the type of a variable cannot be changed. However, sometimes we may want to temporarily convert the types of the values of variables while computing expressions. For example, suppose we want to determine both the number of $50 bills in a dollar amount and the remaining amount after the $50 bills are deducted. A possible solution follows.

```
1    #include <stdio.h>

2    int main(void) {
3       double amount, remnant;
4       int no_of_fifties;

5       printf("Enter a dollar amount as a floating-point value: ");
6       scanf("%lf", &amount);

7       no_of_fifties = amount / 50;
8       remnant = ((amount * 100) % 5000) / 100.0;

9       printf("Number of fifties: %d\n", no_of_fifties);
10      printf("Remnant: %f", remnant);
11      return 0;
12   } /* end function main */
```

If we attempt to compile this program, we will have a warning and an error. The warning will be for the statement on line 7, and it will be to the effect that because of the assignment operation, there may be possible loss of value. The reason is that the variable `amount` is of type `double` and, when divided by 50, will compute to a value that is also of type `double`. The variable `no_of_fifties` is of type `int`, and during the assignment operation, the value computed by the expression will be converted to an integer, thus resulting in the loss of the fractional part. In this case this loss was intended; however, the warning message is a minor irritant.

The error is for the statement on line 8 and occurs because of the subexpression `(amount * 100) % 5000` in the expression to the right of the assignment operator. In this expression one of the operands of the remainder operator `%` is of type `double`, since the variable `amount` is of type `double`. We know that the remainder operator requires integer operands.

These problems can be resolved without having to change the type declaration for the variable `amount` by using explicit type conversion. In C explicit type conversion is possible through the use of the cast operator. We can rewrite the statements on lines 7 and 8 as follows:

```
no_of_fifties = (int) amount / 50;
remnant = ((int)(amount * 100) % 5000) / 100.0;
```

In these statements the type specifier enclosed in parentheses is known as the **cast operator**. The cast operator is a unary operator, and it requires an expression as its operand. It converts the type of the operand in temporary storage to the type specified by the cast operator. The operand of the cast operator can be a constant, a variable, or an expression. If it is a variable, you should note that the cast operator does not change the basic type of the variable itself; it changes only the type of its value in temporary storage and uses this value in computing the expression in which it appears.

Accordingly, in line 7 of the example the value of `amount` will be converted to an integer and, when divided by integer 50, will produce an integer. Therefore, during assignment there will be no possible loss of data, and the compiler will not generate a warning message. In line 8 the cast operator `(int)` will temporarily convert the value computed by the expression `(amount * 100)` to an integer, and the remainder operator will have two integer operands. Note that the use of the cast operator on `amount` in line 7 does not alter the data type of the variable `amount`; it is still of type `double` in the rest of the program.

The operation of explicitly converting the type of an expression in temporary storage to a specified type is called **casting**. The form of a cast expression is as follows:

*(Type) Expression*

where *Type* is a type specifier such as `int`, `double`, or `char`.

***Example 5.12***   The following table contains additional examples of the use of the cast operator. They are based on the declarations for the variables `first` and `second`:

```
double first = 4.7;
int second = 27;
```

| No. | Statement | Value after Execution Expression | first |
|-----|-----------|:-------------------------------:|:-----:|
| 1 | `(int) (first + second);` | 31 | 4.7 |
| 2 | `first = (int) first + second;` | 31.0 | 31.0 |
| 3 | `first = (int) first % second;` | 4.0 | 4.0 |
| 4 | `first = second % (int) first;` | 3.0 | 3.0 |

## 5.6   MATHEMATICAL LIBRARY FUNCTIONS

To perform arithmetic calculations in C, we have to use arithmetic assignment expression statements. However, the basic arithmetic operations recognized by the compiler appear to be limited to unary plus, unary minus, increment, decrement, multiplication, division, remainder, addition, and subtraction. What if we want to compute square roots, exponentiations, logarithms, and so on? For instance, how do we express the following formula in C?

$$distance = \quad \sqrt{(x1 - x2)^2 + (y1 - y2)^2}$$

The answer to these questions are found in standard C libraries, which are a collection of library functions that come with your C compiler. Standard libraries cover a broad range of areas, including input-output, string manipulation, mathematics, and interfacing with the operating system. In the preceding chapter we used the standard library *stdio* for interactive input and output. In this section we will examine some of the library functions useful for mathematical computations.

In the C programming environments, there are two categories of mathematical functions: those that accept as their arguments values of type `double` and return values of type `double`, and those that accept and return only values of type `int`. Just like input-output library functions, mathematical library functions are declared in standard header files. If you are planning to make use of them, you must have appropriate preprocessor directives in your program. The floating-point type function declarations are found in the `math.h` header file. Hence you need the directive `#include <math.h>`. On the other hand, the integer type mathematical functions require the preprocessor directive `#include <stdlib.h>`.

To use library functions, you do not have to know how they are programmed. All you have to do is to use the proper function and know about the purpose, number and type of arguments, and the type of values that are returned. Figure 5.1 summarizes some of the important mathematical functions available in C. All except `abs(x)` require floating-point arguments and return floating-point values. The function `abs(x)` is an integer type function; it requires one integer argument and returns an integer value. The pair of parentheses, `()`, in function calls is known as the **function call operator**.

You should note that if you supply arguments whose types are different from the type defined for the function you are using, the compiler will automatically attempt a type conversion, and if successful, will go ahead with the computations. To avoid possible errors, you must try to use correct argument types with library functions, instead of relying on the computer's ability to convert types.

| Function | Purpose |
|----------|---------|
| ceil(x) | Returns the smallest integer larger than or equal to x. |
| floor(x) | Returns the largest integer smaller than or equal to x. |
| abs(x) | Returns the absolute value of x, where x is an integer. |
| fabs(x) | Returns the absolute value of x, where x is a floating-point value. |
| sqrt(x) | Returns the square root of x, where x >= 0. |
| pow(x, y) | Returns x raised to the y power; if x is zero, y should be positive, and if x is negative, y should be an integer. |
| cos(x) | Returns the cosine of x, where x is in radians. |
| sin(x) | Returns the sine of x, where x is in radians. |
| tan(x) | Returns the tangent of x, where x is radians. |
| exp(x) | Returns the exponential of x with the base e, where e is 2.718282. |
| log(x) | Returns the natural logarithm of x. |
| log10(x) | Returns the base-10 logarithm of x. |

**Figure 5.1**    Some important mathematical library functions

**Example 5.13**    The following table contains examples of mathematical function calls and shows the value returned for each function call.

| Function Call | Value Returned |
|---------------|----------------|
| ceil(4.2) | 5 |
| ceil(4.0) | 4 |
| ceil(-5.7) | -5 |
| floor(4.2) | 4 |
| floor(4.0) | 4 |
| floor(-5.7) | -6 |
| abs(-12) | 12 |
| abs(-12.7) | 12 |
| fabs(-120) | 120 |
| fabs(-120.8) | 120.8 |
| sqrt(2.7) | 1.643168 |
| sqrt(2) | 1.414214 |
| pow(2, 3) | 8 |
| pow(2.0, -3.2) | 0.108819 |
| pow(0, -3) | Domain error |
| pow(-2.0, 3.2) | Domain error |
| cos(60 * 3.141593/180) | 0.5 |
| sin(60 * 3.141593/180) | 0.866025 |
| tan(45 * 3.141593/180) | 1 |
| exp(2.1) | 8.16617 |
| log(2) | 0.693147 |
| log10(2) | 0.30103 |

## REVIEW QUESTIONS

1. Which of the following statements concerning arithmetic operators is correct?
   **a.** The division operator is a unary operator.
   **b.** The division operator applies only to integer values.
   **c.** The operands of the remainder operator must be integers.
   **d.** The effects of the unary minus and the subtraction operators are identical.
   **e.** All of the above.

2. The expressions `(a % b)` and `(a - a / b * b)`, where `a` and `b` are integer variables, are equivalent. (T or F)

3. Which of the following statements concerning rules for evaluating arithmetic expressions is *incorrect*?
   **a.** In evaluating nested parenthesized subexpressions, the computer begins with the innermost subexpressions.
   **b.** If two or more unnested parenthesized subexpressions occur in an expression, the computer uses the left-associativity rule.
   **c.** The left-associativity rule says to evaluate from right to left.
   **d.** In arithmetic expressions multiplication is performed before addition.

4. Assume that we have the following variable declarations in a program:

   ```
   int a = 5, b = 8, c = 13, d = 15;
   ```

   What will be the value computed for the expression `(a + b % c * d)`?
   **a.** 13
   **b.** 125
   **c.** 5
   **d.** 195
   **e.** None of the above.

5. In computing the arithmetic expression

   ```
   (a * a - b * (d / a))
   ```

   the correct order of computations is shown by
   **a.** (a  *  a  -  b  *  (d  /  a))
          1        2        3        4
   **b.** (a  *  a  -  b  *  (d  /  a))
          2        4        3        1
   **c.** (a  *  a  -  b  *  (d  /  a))
          3        4        2        1
   **d.** (a  *  a  -  b  *  (d  /  a))
          3        4        1        2
   **e.** None of the above.

6. Concerning the C increment and decrement operators:
   **a.** They both are unary operators.

     **b.** They both have a postfix and a prefix form.
     **c.** The increment operator, ++, increments the value of its operand by one.
     **d.** The decrement operator, --, subtracts one from the value of its operand.
     **e.** All of the above are correct.
     **f.** None of the above is correct.

**7.** The side effect of a statement may be a value assignment not intended by that statement's main purpose. (T or F)

**8.** The precedence level of the increment and decrement operators are the same as that of unary plus and unary minus. (T or F)

**9.** Assume that we have the following variable declarations:

```
int counter = 4, a = 5, b = -7, c;
```

and the arithmetic assignment expression statement

```
c = a * ++ counter - b;
```

has just been executed. The values of the variables counter and c are
     **a.** 5 and 32
     **b.** 4 and 32
     **c.** 5 and 27
     **d.** 4 and 27
     **e.** None of the above.

**10.** Let the values of the integer variables a and b be 10 and 12, respectively. After the statement

```
a += (b -= 2);
```

is executed, the variables a and b will become
     **a.** 20 and 10
     **b.** 10 and 20
     **c.** 10 and 12
     **d.** 12 and 10
     **e.** None of the above.

**11.** If all operands in an arithmetic expression are of type int, the result of the expression is also of type int. (T or F)

**12.** The library function
     **a.** ceil(x) returns the largest integer that is smaller than or equal to x.
     **b.** floor(x) returns the smallest integer that is larger than or equal to x.
     **c.** abs(x) requires an integer argument and returns the absolute value of its argument.
     **d.** pow(x, y) returns y raised to the x power.
     **e.** All of the above are correct.
     **f.** None of the above is correct.

**13.** We want to translate the algebraic expression

$$\frac{1}{c} + \frac{1-a}{1+b}$$

into a C arithmetic expression. Which of the following is the correct form?

**a.** 1 / c + 1 - a / 1 + b
**b.** 1 / c + (1 - a / 1 + b)
**c.** (1 / c) + (1 - a / 1 + b)
**d.** 1 / c + (1 - a) / (1 + b)
**e.** None of the above.

**Answers:** 1. c; 2. T; 3. c; 4. b; 5. b; 6. e; 7. T; 8. T; 9. a; 10. a; 11. T; 12. c; 13. d.

---

## 5.7 EXAMPLE PROGRAM 1: A C Program that Solves Quadratic Equations

In this section we will develop a complete application program that uses the concepts and techniques covered so far in this chapter.

***Problem***   We are given a quadratic equation of the form

$$a x^2 + b x + c = 0$$

where $a$, $b$, and $c$ are constant coefficients. We want to develop a C program that solves as many quadratic equations as the user would like. We know that a quadratic equation has two roots, and they can be computed using the following formulas:

$$root1 = \frac{-b - \sqrt{b^2 - 4 \times a \times c}}{2 \times a}$$

$$root2 = \frac{-b + \sqrt{b^2 - 4 \times a \times c}}{2 \times a}$$

***Requirements Specification***   Develop a program that does the following:

1.  Prompts the user to enter values for the coefficients $a$, $b$, and $c$ using the terminal keyboard.

2.  Computes the discriminant of the quadratic equation using the formula

$$discriminant = b^2 - 4 \times a \times c$$

3.  Determines whether the roots of the equation are real by comparing the discriminant to zero. If the discriminant is less than zero, we know that the roots are complex. In this case we do not want to compute the roots; instead, we want to print a message on the screen that informs the user that the roots are complex.

4.  However, if the discriminant is greater than or equal to zero, we have two roots to be computed using the preceding formulas. We want the program to compute the roots and print them out on the screen.

5.  After a quadratic equation is solved, the user should be able to continue with others if desired. The program should ask the user whether to continue and prompt him or

her to respond by typing yes or no. If the user wishes to solve another equation, the preceding steps should be repeated. Otherwise, the program should terminate.

### Analysis

**Inputs.**    Values of the coefficients *a*, *b*, and *c* for each equation.

**Outputs.**    Values of the roots *root1* and *root2* or a message informing the user that the roots are complex.

**Formulas.**    The formulas given here for the computation of *root1* and *root2*.

***Design***    We begin with an initial pseudocode algorithm as given in Figure 5.2.

```
1   while there are more equations to solve
2       begin
3               prompt user to enter values for coefficients a, b, and c and read values for coefficients
4               solve the quadratic equation and print roots root1 and root2
5               ask user if there are more equations to solve
6       end
7   end_while
```

**Figure 5.2**    Algorithm for computing roots of quadratic equations (initial pseudocode)

Because this algorithm is not sufficiently detailed, it cannot be translated into a C program. We will again use the top-down stepwise refinement method to generate an algorithm that can be implemented directly from this initial version. Two steps in Figure 5.2 have to be refined — the steps in lines 3 and 4. We first consider line 3: *prompt user to enter values for coefficients a, b, and c and read values for coefficients*. The refinement of this step is quite straightforward and produces the following six statements:

```
print "Enter value for a:"
read a
print "Enter value for b:"
read b
print "Enter value for c:"
read c
```

Next, we focus on statement 4 in Figure 5.2: *solve the quadratic equation and print roots root1 and root2*. We note that in a quadratic equation the coefficient *a* cannot be equal to zero; if it is, then we do not have a quadratic equation. We incorporate this consideration into our algorithm by using a selection control structure:

> *if a is equal to zero*
>     *print "This is not a quadratic equation."*
> *else*
>     *compute and print the roots of the quadratic equation*
> *end_if*

So far, so good, but how do we *compute and print the roots of the quadratic equation?* We begin by computing the value of the discriminant and the value of the expression $2 \times a$, which appears as the denominator in the formulas for the roots. Following this step, we must check whether the roots are complex. If so, we do not attempt to compute them; otherwise, we use the formulas for the computation of the roots. Here is the final refinement of line 4:

> *if a is equal to zero*
>     *print "This is not a quadratic equation."*
> *else*
>     *begin*
>         *compute discriminant = b × b − 4 × a × c*
>         *compute denom = 2 × a*
>
>         *if discriminant is less than zero*
>             *print "The roots are complex."*
>         *else*
>             *begin*
>                 *compute root1 = (−b − sqrt(discriminant)) / denom*
>                 *compute root2 = (−b + sqrt(discriminant)) / denom*
>                 *print root1, root2*
>             *end*
>         *end_if*
>     *end*
> *end_if*

In this pseudocode *sqrt* is a function that computes and returns the square root of a given number. We already know that C indeed has a function for computing square root in its standard math library.

The final step in the algorithm design is the refinement of the elements associated with the *while* loop in Figure 5.2; they are the condition *there are more equations to solve* and the statement a*sk user if there are more equations to solve.* For this purpose we use a loop control variable called *more*, which is initialized to *'y'* outside the *while* loop. In the loop body, after an equation is solved, we prompt the user to type *y* if he or she wants to continue. Depending on what the user enters for *more*, the algorithm will either repeat or terminate. Following is the refined pseudocode for the *while* loop:

```
set more to 'y'

while more is equal to 'y'
    begin
        ..........
        ..........
        print "Do you want to continue? Type y/n:"
        read more
    end
end_while
```

This step concludes the design of the algorithm. All we have to do now is to combine the refinements according to the pattern in Figure 5.2. The final algorithm is given in Figure 5.3.

```
set more to 'y'

while more is equal to 'y'
    begin
        print "Enter value for a:"
        read a
        print "Enter value for b:"
        read b
        print "Enter value for c:"
        read c

        if a is equal to zero
            print "This is not a quadratic equation."
        else
            begin
                compute discriminant = b × b − 4 × a × c
                compute denom = 2 × a

                if discriminant is less than zero
                    print "The roots are complex."
                else
                    begin
                        compute root1 = (−b − sqrt(discriminant)) / denom
                        compute root2 = (−b + sqrt(discriminant)) / denom
                        print root1, root2
                    end
                end_if
```

**Figure 5.3**    Algorithm for computing roots of quadratic equations (final pseudocode)    ▶

> end
>      end_if
>
>      print "Do you want to continue? Type y/n:"
>      read more
>    end
>  end_while

**Figure 5.3**                                                                                    ∎

***Implementation***    A C implementation of the algorithm of Figure 5.3 is presented in Figure 5.4.

```
/******************************************************************
 Program Filename: prog05_2.c
 Author          : Uckan
 Purpose         : Solves quadratic equations.
 Input from      : Terminal keyboard
 Output to       : Screen
 *****************************************************************/
#include <stdio.h>
#include <math.h>

int main(void) {
      /* Variable declarations: */

      double coef1, coef2, coef3;
      double discriminant, denom;
      double root1, root2;
      char more = 'y', new_line;

      /* Function body: */

      printf("THIS PROGRAM COMPUTES THE ROOTS OF QUADRATIC EQUATIONS.\n");

      while (more == 'y') {
            printf("Enter value for a: ");
            scanf("%lf", &coef1);

            printf("Enter value for b: ");
            scanf("%lf", &coef2);
```

**Figure 5.4**    A C program that solves quadratic equations (*continued*)    ▶

```
              printf("Enter value for c: ");
              scanf("%lf", &coef3);

              if(coef1 == 0.00)
                   printf("This is not a quadratic equation.\n");
              else {
                   discriminant = coef2 * coef2 - 4 * coef1 * coef3;
                   denom = 2 * coef1;
                   if (discriminant < 0)
                        printf("The roots are complex.\n");
                   else {
                        root1 = (- coef2 - sqrt(discriminant)) / denom;
                        root2 = (- coef2 + sqrt(discriminant)) / denom;
                        printf("The roots are %f and %f.\n", root1, root2);
                   } /* end if */
              } /* end if */

              scanf("%c", &new_line);
              printf("Do you want to continue? Type y/n: ");
              scanf("%c", &more);
          } /* end while */

     printf("TERMINATING . . .");
        return 0;
  } /* end function main */
```

Figure 5.4                                                              ■

We note the following about the program of Figure 5.4:

1.  The header file  stdio.h  is needed because it contains the declarations of the C interactive input-output routines that we are planning to use in our program. The header file math.h contains the declarations for the standard mathematical functions, and we will need the standard square root function,  sqrt, in our computations.

2.  The first output statement in the function body prints on the screen a brief description of the purpose of the program early during its execution.

3.  The rest of the function body is a sentinel-controlled  while  loop for which the sentinel variable is the the character variable  more. This  while  loop enables the user to solve any number of quadratic equations in one execution of the program.

4.  Note the use of the standard mathematical function  sqrt  in the assignment statements that compute the roots  root1  and  root2.

Figure 5.5 shows a complete test run of the program of Figure 5.4.

```
THIS PROGRAM COMPUTES THE ROOTS OF QUADRATIC EQUATIONS.
Enter value for a: 0
Enter value for b: 1
Enter value for c: 3
This is not a quadratic equation.
Do you want to continue? Type y/n: y
Enter value for a: 1
Enter value for b: 1
Enter value for c: 3
The roots are complex.
Do you want to continue? Type y/n: y
Enter value for a: 1
Enter value for b: -3
Enter value for c: 2
The roots are 1.000000 and 2.000000.
Do you want to continue? Type y/n: n
TERMINATING . . .
```

**Figure 5.5**     A test run of the program of Figure 5.4

## 5.8   STYLE CONSIDERATIONS FOR ARITHMETIC ASSIGNMENT EXPRESSION STATEMENTS

The following are some important style rules for arithmetic assignment expression statements.

1.   Use parentheses only to change the order in which the operators are evaluated in an arithmetic expression. Avoid using unnecessary parentheses, since they may detract from the readability of your code. For example, in the assignment statement

```
c = (((a * 3) + (b / 2)) - 5);
```

all parentheses are superfluous. It is better to write this statement as

```
c = a * 3 + b / 2 - 5;
```

2.   If you can compute a value using simple expressions, avoid calls to mathematical functions that do the same thing. When you call a function, the program control passes to it. After the function is done with its task, it returns the control back to your program. These transfers take additional computer time. Therefore, unnecessary function calls result in less efficient programs. For example, instead of the statement

```
c = pow(a, 2) + 4;
```

it is better to write

```
c = a * a + 4;
```

since `pow(a, 2)` does the same thing as `a * a`.

3.   Avoid using the increment and decrement operators in complex expressions. These operators, although useful for some situations, tend to produce cryptic code. Also, they have side effects that may not be obvious at first glance, and thus excessive use of these operators may add to program maintenance difficulties. For example,

```
result = pow(a, b++) * -- c;
```

is equivalent to the three statements

```
c = c - 1;
result = pow(a, b) * c;
b = b + 1;
```

The first form enables you to achieve brevity; however, in this case brevity is at the expense of clarity — the second version is certainly easier to understand.

4.   Again, to improve the readability of your code, avoid using excessively long expressions; instead, split your expressions into two or more shorter statements. For example, the statement

```
root1 = ( -b + sqrt(b * b - 4 * a * c)) / (2 * a);
```

can be written as

```
discriminant = b * b - 4 * a * c;
root1 = (-b + sqrt(discriminant)) / (2 * a);
```

By splitting this statement we are introducing another variable, `discriminant`, that will use computer storage. However, with computer systems providing increasingly larger capacity internal memory at low costs, we really do not have to be excessively stingy with memory. Once again, program readability is a very important factor in software design.

---

## 5.9   ADDITIONAL FUNDAMENTAL DATA TYPES

So far in the book, we have worked with three fundamental data types: `int`, `double`, and `char`. C supports additional numeric data types as shown in Figure 5.6. Figure 5.6 lists all C fundamental data types with their type specifiers and the minimum standard number of bits used for their internal representation.

| Data Type | Number of Bits |
|---|---|
| Integer | |
|     Signed | |
|         Short integer (`short, short int, signed short, signed short int`) | 16 |
|         Integer (`int, signed, signed int`) | Word size of the machine |
|         Long integer (`long, long int, signed long, signed long int`) | 32 |
|     Unsigned | |
|         Short integer (`unsigned short, unsigned short int`) | 16 |
|         Integer (`unsigned, unsigned int`) | Word size of the machine |
|         Long integer (`unsigned long, unsigned long int`) | 32 |
| Floating-point | |
|     Floating-point (`float`) | 32 |
|     Double floating-point (`double`) | 64 |
|     Long double floating-point (`long double`) | Implementation dependent (usually 96 or 128) |
| Character (`char`) | 8 |

**Figure 5.6**    C fundamental data types

## Integer Data Types

Integer data types are classified as signed and unsigned. A signed integer variable can represent a negative or positive integer value, whereas an unsigned integer variable can store only integer values with no + or − sign. Therefore, we cannot assign a negative integer value to an unsigned integer variable.

Signed and unsigned integers are further classified as short integers, integers, and long integers. All integers are represented in binary notation in the main memory. For all signed integers the left-most bit is used to represent the sign of the quantity, and the remaining bits are used for the value. The second column in Figure 5.6 shows the minimum standard number of bits for the fundamental data types. For signed short integers, it is 16 bits, which leaves 15 bits for the representation of the value. Therefore, a quantity of type `short int` can store values in the range of $-2^{15}$ through $2^{15} - 1$ ($-32,768$ through $32,767$). A variable of type `int` has the same range if the word size of the machine is 16 bits. On 32-bit machines the range for `int` is $-2^{31}$ through $2^{31} - 1$ ($-2,147,483,648$ through $2,147,483,647$). Finally, signed long integer quantities use 32 bits and can store any integer in the range of $-2^{31}$ through $2^{31} - 1$ ($-2,147,483,648$ through $2,147,483,647$).

In some applications certain integer values need not have a sign, such as the weight of objects or square of integer values. For such quantities we may prefer to use unsigned integer types. Unsigned integers do not have a sign bit, and all available bits are used for the representation of the value. Unsigned integers can be short integers, integers, and long integers. A variable of type `unsigned short int` can store positive values in the range of 0 through $2^{16} - 1$ (0 through 65,535). The range for variables of type `unsigned int` depends on the word size of the machine: on systems that use 16 bits for integers, it is the same as unsigned short integers (that is, 0 through 65,535), and on 32-bit machines, it is 0 through $2^{32} - 1$ (0 through 4,294,967,295). A variable declared as of type `unsigned long int` can store integers in the same range as unsigned integer variables on 32-bit machines, that is, 0 through $2^{32} - 1$.

All integer fundamental data types have more than one alias for their type specifiers. For example, for signed short integers, you can use `short`, `short int`, `signed short`, and `signed short int`. As a matter of programming style, we suggest using the most explicit alias for each type. It is better to use `signed short int` rather than just `short` for signed short integers. This alias may be a bit verbose, but it makes the code more readable.

## Floating-Point Data Types

C supports three floating-point data types: `float`, `double`, and `long double`. We have used the data type `double` up to this point in our discussions. All floating-point data types use the same internal representation, which is similar to scientific notation. The memory location for a floating-point variable consists of a section to represent the mantissa and a section to represent the exponent. The mantissa is a signed fraction, and the exponent is a signed integer.

The differences among data types `float`, `double`, and `long double` are with respect to the range of values and the precision (that is, the number of decimal digits in the mantissa) of the values that can be represented. The minimum standards for the number of bits for floating-point words in the main memory are shown in Figure 5.6. For `float` it is 32 bits, for `double` it is 64 bits, and for `long double` it is implementation dependent (usually 96 or 128 bits). The precision and smallest and largest floating-point values for each type are also implementation dependent. For example, in Microsoft Visual C/C++ on IBM-compatible systems the range of positive values that a variable of type `float` can store is 1.175494e–38 and 3.402823e+38, and the precision is 6 digits; whereas for variables of type `long double` the range is 2.22507e–308 and 1.79769e+308, and the precision is 15 digits. Thus `long double` variables can store extremely small and extremely large floating-point values with very high precision and are therefore appropriate for some scientific and mathematical applications.

Note that a variable of any integer data type can represent all integers in its range, whereas a floating-point variable, even of type `long double`, cannot represent all possible floating-point values precisely in its range. The reason is that the computer word used for the variable and, therefore, the precision of the value stored in it are limited.

To determine the largest and smallest values for different numeric data types that your computer system can store, run the C program given in Figure 5.7.

```
#include <stdio.h>
#include <limits.h>
#include <float.h>

int main(void) {
      printf("Smallest short int SHRT_MIN          : %hd\n", SHRT_MIN);
      printf("Largest short int SHRT_MAX           : %hd\n\n",
             SHRT_MAX);
      printf("Smallest int INT_MIN                 : %d\n", INT_MIN);
      printf("Largest int INT_MAX                  : %d\n\n", INT_MAX);
      printf("Smallest long int LONG_MIN           : %ld\n", LONG_MIN);
      printf("Largest long int LONG_MAX            : %ld\n\n",
             LONG_MAX);
      printf("Largest unsigned short int: USHRT_MAX: %u\n", USHRT_MAX);
      printf("Largest unsigned int UINT_MAX        : %u\n", UINT_MAX);
      printf("Largest unsigned long int ULONG_MAX  : %lu\n\n",
             ULONG_MAX);
      printf("Smallest float FLT_MIN               : %e\n", FLT_MIN);
      printf("Largest float FLT_MAX                : %e\n", FLT_MAX);
      printf("Precision for float FLT_DIG          : %d\n\n", FLT_DIG);
      printf("Smallest double DBL_MIN              : %e\n", DBL_MIN);
      printf("Largest double DBL_MAX               : %e\n", DBL_MAX);
      printf("Precision for double DBL_DIG         : %d\n\n", DBL_DIG);
      printf("Smallest long double LDBL_MIN        : %Le\n", LDBL_MIN);
      printf("Largest long double LDBL_MAX         : %Le\n", LDBL_MAX);
      printf("Precision for long double LDBL_DIG   : %d", LDBL_DIG);
      return 0;
} /* end function main */
```

**Figure 5.7**    A C program that prints limits for numeric data types

The program in Figure 5.7 contains quite a few standard named constants. Two of them are `INT_MIN` and `INT_MAX`, which represent the smallest and largest values that can be stored in an integer variable of type `int`. The declarations of such named constants for integer data types are found in the standard header file `limits.h`, and those for floating-point data types are in the header file `float.h`. Hence we have the preprocessor directives `#include <limits.h>` and `#include <float.h>` in the program. Figure 5.8 shows the output produced by the program of Figure 5.7 when it is run on IBM-compatible computers using the Microsoft Visual C/C++ system. The output may be different when you run this program on your system.

```
Smallest short int SHRT_MIN          : -32768
Largest short int SHRT_MAX           : 32767

Smallest int INT_MIN                 : -2147483648
Largest int INT_MAX                  : 2147483647

Smallest long int LONG_MIN           : -2147483648
Largest long int LONG_MAX            : 2147483647

Largest unsigned short int: USHRT_MAX: 65535
Largest unsigned int UINT_MAX        : 4294967295
Largest unsigned long int ULONG_MAX  : 4294967295

Smallest float FLT_MIN               : 1.17549e-038
Largest float FLT_MAX                : 3.40282e+038
Precision for float FLT_DIG          : 6

Smallest double DBL_MIN              : 2.22507e-308
Largest double DBL_MAX               : 1.79769e+308
Precision for double DBL_DIG         : 15

Smallest long double LDBL_MIN        : 2.22507e-308
Largest long double LDBL_MAX         : 1.79769e+308
Precision for long double LDBL_DIG   : 15
```

**Figure 5.8**    Output of the program of Figure 5.7 for IBM-compatible systems and Microsoft Visual C/C++

The program in Figure 5.7 uses several `printf` format specifiers. You are familiar with some of them; the others are new. We covered the `printf` format specifiers `%d`, `%f`, and `%c`, and the `scanf` format specifiers `%d`, `%f`, and `%c` in Chapter 3. Figure 5.9 shows the format specifiers for `printf` and `scanf` corresponding to all C fundamental data types.

In Figure 5.9 the format specifiers `%f`, `%lf`, and `%Lf` are for data of type `float`, `double`, and `long double`, respectively, represented using conventional notation, whereas the format specifiers `%e`, `%le`, and `%Le` are their scientific notation counterparts.

Floating-point constants are numeric constant values that appear in program statements in either conventional or scientific floating-point notation. Like floating-point variables, floating-point constants can be of type `float`, `double`, or `long double`. A floating-point constant such as `1.25` is of type `double`. If the constant value has a suffix of `F` or `f`, it is of type `float`. Examples are `1.25F` and `2.3e-2f`. Finally, the suffix `L` or `l` indicates that the constant is of type `long double`, as in `5.5l` and `-78e+5L`.

| Data Type | printf<br>Format Specifier | scanf<br>Format Specifier |
|---|---|---|
| Integer | | |
|   Signed | | |
|     Short integer (`short, short int, signed short, signed short int`) | `%hd` | `%hd` |
|     Integer (`int, signed, signed int`) | `%d` | `%d` |
|     Long integer (`long, long int, signed long, signed long int`) | `%ld` | `%ld` |
|   Unsigned | | |
|     Short integer (`unsigned short, unsigned short int`) | `%u` | `%u` |
|     Integer (`unsigned, unsigned int`) | `%u` | `%u` |
|     Long integer (`unsigned long, unsigned long int`) | `%lu` | `%lu` |
| Floating-point | | |
|   Floating-point (`float`) | `%f, %e` | `%f, %e` |
|   Double floating-point (`double`) | `%f, %e` | `%lf, %le` |
|   Long double floating-point (`long double`) | `%Lf, %Le` | `%Lf, %Le` |
| Character (`char`) | `%c` | `%c` |

**Figure 5.9**   Format specifiers for fundamental data types

## 5.10   ARITHMETIC ERRORS AND INACCURACIES

As was discussed in this chapter, the arithmetic capabilities of the C language are extensive. Certain arithmetic operations, however, are critical, and they may easily lead to errors and inaccuracies. Important arithmetic errors are classified as follows:

1. Division by zero
2. Arithmetic overflow
3. Arithmetic underflow

On the other hand, some arithmetic operations may produce errors in the sense that the results are correct but not accurate. Typical arithmetic inaccuracies include

1. Integer division
2. Representational inaccuracies
3. Cancellation inaccuracies

## Division by Zero

If we divide any numeric value by zero, we get infinity. Because infinity cannot be represented in the computer's memory, division by zero will generally result in a run-time error and the program execution will stop. For example, in computing the value of the expression  a  /  b, where  a  and  b  are variables of any numeric data type, we have division by zero if the value of b ever becomes zero. In certain systems you don't get a run-time error; instead, the computer stores a special value to represent an impossibly large value, which, for example, in Microsoft Visual C/C++, prints as  1.#INF.

In any case you must be careful to avoid division by zero. If you suspect that the denominator in an expression involving division may become zero, you should program defensively and execute such expressions in an  if  statement, as in the following example:

```
int a, b, c;

if (b != 0)
      c = a / b;
else
      printf("Denominator expression is equal to zero.");
/* end if */
```

## Arithmetic Overflow

In an arithmetic assignment statement, when two numeric values are multiplied or added, the result of the operation may be a value that is in excess of the maximum value that can be stored in a word allocated for the target variable. In this case the computer does not generate an error message; it simply stores an incorrect value as the result. For example, in the following partial code

```
int x, y, z;
. . . . . . . . . . .
z = x * y;
```

if the values of the variables  x  and  y  are 28,775 and 15, respectively, the arithmetic assignment statement tries to compute a value for  z  by multiplying 28,775 and 15. The resulting value is 431,625. If we are running our program using a C compiler that stores integers in 16-bit words, this value is larger than the largest value that can be stored for signed integers, which is 32,767. Therefore, we will have an arithmetic overflow, and the computer will store an incorrect value for the variable  z.

Arithmetic overflow is also possible with floating-point quantities. For example, if we multiply two variables of type `float` and the product turns out to be greater than the largest `float`, `FLT_MAX`, we will have overflow. On some systems floating-point overflow may result in a run-time error; on others, you may have a special value (for example, `1.#INF` or `INFINITY`), which signifies an impossibly large value, printed during output.

To avoid arithmetic overflow, you should try to anticipate the magnitude of the result of arithmetic computations and use an appropriate data type. In the earlier example with integers, the type `long int` will do the job.

## Arithmetic Underflow

If an arithmetic operation results in a value that is less than the smallest value that can be stored for that data type, the computer stores zero instead for the result. For example, given the declarations

```
float a, b;
```

if the value of the variable `a` is `1e-25`, the statement

```
b = a * a;
```

which should compute `b` as `1e-50`, will cause an arithmetic underflow on an IBM PC running Microsoft Visual C/C++ (see Figure 5.9). The reason is that this value is less than the smallest value for a variable of type `float`, which is `1.17549e-38`. Hence the computer will store 0.0 for `b` without producing an error or a warning message.

## Integer Division

If an integer quantity is divided by an integer, the result of the division is also an integer. For example, in normal arithmetic the division `1 / 4` yields 0.25. In computer arithmetic this division yields zero, since the result is always truncated to an integer. In such a situation you will not get a run-time error or a warning message. You will simply get zero as the result of the division. If you want to avoid this situation, you should use a floating-point data type for one or both of the operands of the division operator. For example, in the following partial code

```
int a, b;
..........
printf("%d", (a / b));
```

the output statement will print 0 if the value of the variables `a` and `b` are 20 and 25, respectively. If you would rather have the value 0.8, you may use the cast operator as follows:

```
printf("%f", ((double) a / b));
```

The cast operator converts the type of the variable `a` to `double` during arithmetic without changing its representation in the memory and computes the value of 0.8 for the division.

### Representational Inaccuracies

We have already mentioned that, because of precision limitations for floating-point data types, it is not possible to represent all floating-point values accurately. For example, in the following partial code

```
float result, numerator, denominator;
.................
result = numerator / denominator;
```

if the values of the variables `numerator` and `denominator` turn out to be 4.0 and 3.0, respectively, the value computed for `result` will be 1.33333, which is obtained by rounding off the result of the division `4.0 / 3.0` to a floating-point number with a precision of 6. Such inaccuracies are also called **round-off errors**. If you wish to have higher accuracy in your computations, you should use the data type `double` or even `long double` for your floating-point variables.

### Cancellation Inaccuracies

In floating-point arithmetic the addition or subtraction of two values, one large and the other very small, may result in the cancellation of the value of the small operand in the result. Consider the following code:

```
float large_value, small_value, sum;
int k = 1;

sum = large_value;

while (k <= 10000) {
      sum = sum + small_value;
      k = k + 1;
} /* end while */
```

Suppose the value of `large_value` is `5.5` and the value of `small_value` is `1e-7`. We expect the `while` loop to compute 5.501 for `sum`. If you run a program containing this code on an IBM PC using Microsoft Visual C/C++, you will get 5.5 for `sum`. In other words, the contribution of the `small_value` to `sum`, although magnified by 10,000 times, is canceled out. The reason is that the value computed for `sum` in the first cycle of iteration by the statement

```
sum = sum + small_value;
```

in the `for` loop will produce 5.5000001, which can be stored only as 5.50000 with a precision of 6. Hence no matter how many times this loop is executed, the value of sum will remain the same as that of `large_value`.

## 5.11  AUTOMATIC CONVERSION OF NUMERIC DATA TYPES

Unless we resort to explicit type conversion through the use of the cast operator, C uses automatic conversion rules to determine the type of an expression. In this chapter we discussed the type of arithmetic expressions and arithmetic assignment statements in view of two numeric data types: `int` and `double`. With two numeric types the **automatic type conversion** rules that determine the type of an expression are few and simple. Basically, they can be summarized as follows: If one of the operands in an arithmetic operation is of type `double`, the result of the expression is also of type `double`. Otherwise, the type of the expression is `int`.

We have quite a few numeric types in our repertoire. We have to consider expressions with mixed-type operands, including `long double`, `double`, `float`, `unsigned long int`, `signed long int`, `unsigned int`, `signed int`, `unsigned short int`, and `signed short int`. There are three instances of type incompatibility:

1.   The operands in an arithmetic operation are of different types. If so, how does C compute the value of the expression and determine its type?

2.   In an arithmetic assignment statement, the type of the expression is different from the type of the variable to which the value of the expression is assigned. We know that, once declared, the type of a variable cannot be changed. Therefore, what happens to the value of the variable to the left of the assignment operator in an assignment expression?

3.   As you will see when we discuss functions in Chapter 6, a formal parameter of a function definition may have a type that is different from the type of the corresponding actual parameter, or the type of the return expression in a `return` statement may be different from the function's return type. How do such incompatibilities affect the inter-function data transfer process? In these cases C uses additional automatic type conversion rules. In evaluating arithmetic expressions the automatic conversion rules used are **arithmetic conversion rules**. In assignment expressions and function calls, type incompatibility is handled using **assignment conversion rules**.

### Arithmetic Conversions

The general rule C uses in determining the type of a mixed arithmetic expression is that the "shorter" type is converted to the "longer" type, the expression is evaluated, and the result of the expression is the longer type. The term *longer type* implies the type that requires a longer word, represents more values, or both. The numeric types from longer to shorter follow.

1. `long double`
2. `double`
3. `float`
4. `unsigned long int`
5. `signed long int`
6. `unsigned int`
7. `signed int`, `unsigned short int`, `signed short int`

You should note that an unsigned type is longer than its signed counterpart. For example, `unsigned long int` is longer than `signed long int` because the largest value that can be stored in a variable of type `unsigned long int` is greater than the largest value for the type `signed long int`. Also, although in some implementations the word length for the types `signed long int` and `signed int` are the same and both can represent the same number of values, C considers `signed long int` to be logically longer than `signed int`.

The main purpose of automatic type conversion rules is to avoid loss of data. Therefore, if in a mixed expression, the longest type is `long double`, the other operand will be converted (or promoted) to `long double` and the result of the expression will be `long double` and so on. This general rule applies until the type `unsigned int`. If the longest type is `unsigned int`, the other operand will be converted to `unsigned int` and the result of the expression will be `unsigned int`. For the remaining three types, `signed int`, `unsigned short int`, and `signed short int`, the rule C uses (called the **integral promotion rule**) is as follows:

> Unless both operands are of type `signed int`, convert any short operand to `signed int` if its value fits in a word of type `signed int`; if it doesn't fit, convert both to unsigned int. If both operands are of type `signed int`, no conversion takes place.

Figure 5.10 shows a pseudocode algorithm that expresses the automatic type conversion rules for arithmetic expressions in C. It should be noted that in all type conversions, the signs of the operands, plus or minus, will be preserved.

*if one of the operands is of type* `long double`
   *convert the other to* `long double` *and make the result* `long double`
*else if one of the operands is of type* `double`
   *convert the other to* `double` *and make the result* `double`
*else if one of the operands is of type* `float`
   *convert the other to* `float` *and make the result* `float`
*else if one of the operands is of type* `unsigned long int`
   *convert the other to unsigned* `long int` *and make the result* `unsigned long int`
*else if one of the operands is of type* `signed long int`
   *convert the other to* `signed long int` *and make the result* `signed long int`
*else if one of the operands is of type* `unsigned int`
   *convert the other to* `unsigned int` *and make the result* `unsigned int`
*else if one of the operands is of type* `signed int,` `unsigned short int,` *or* `signed short`
       `int`
  *begin*
    *convert both operands to* `signed int`

    *if each value of the converted operands fits in a* `signed int` *word*
      *make the result* `signed int`
    *else*
      *convert both arguments to* `unsigned int` *and make the result* `unsigned int`
    *end_if*
  *end*
*else*
  *no conversion is necessary; make the result* `signed int`
*end_if*

**Figure 5.10**    Automatic type conversion rules for C arithmetic expressions expressed as a pseudocode algorithm

***Example 5.14***   Let us study some examples based on the following declarations:

```
long double first;
unsigned int second;
signed int third;
signed short int fourth;
```

The expression `first + second` is a mixed-type expression. The longer type is `long double` for the variable `first`. Therefore, C converts the type of `second` from `unsigned int` to `long double` and performs the addition. The result of the expression is of type `long double`.

Now consider the expression `second * third`. The type of the first operand is `unsigned int`, which is longer than `signed int`, the type of the second operand. Therefore, the value of the variable `third` will be converted to `unsigned int`, and the multiplication will be carried out. The result of the expression is of type `unsigned int`. You should note that the sign of the converted operand is preserved.

Finally, we consider the expression `third + fourth`. Here the type of the variable `third` is `signed int`, and the type of `fourth` is `signed short int`. Therefore, the integral promotion rule is applied, and the value of `fourth` is converted to `signed int`. Let us assume that the current values of `third` and `fourth` are 20,000 and 25,000, respectively. The result will be 45,000, which is larger than the largest value for the type `signed int` if 16 bits are used for this data type. Consequently, the result is converted to `unsigned int`, for which the largest value is 65,535.

## Assignment Conversions

If the types of the operands in an assignment expression are different, if the return type for a function is different from the function's type, or if a formal parameter and a corresponding actual parameter of a function have incompatible types in parameter passing by value, C attempts to automatically convert the source value to the type of the receiving variable. Such conversions are **assignment conversions**. Assignment conversions between numeric data types are possible and problem free, provided they are from a shorter type to a longer type. However, the success of an automatic conversion from a longer type to a shorter type depends on the value being converted.

***Example 5.15***   Consider the following declarations:

```
double var1;
float var2;
```

The conversion involved in the assignment statement

```
var1 = var2;
```

is safe, since the type of the variable `var2` is `float`, which is shorter than `double`, the type of the variable `var1`. However, the success of the assignment statement

```
var2 = var1;
```

depends on the value of the variable `var1`. If that value is not in excess of the maximum value that can be stored in a variable of type `float`, there is no problem. Otherwise, we may have a run-time error indicating that an arithmetic overflow has occurred.

Now suppose we have the declarations

```
unsigned int var3;
int var4;
```

and the assignment expression

```
var3 = var4;
```

Again, the conversion due to this statement is safe because the type `unsigned int` is longer than the type `int`. The reverse conversion implied by

```
var4 = var3;
```

may be problematic. If the value of the variable `var3` is not greater than the maximum value that can be stored in a variable of type `int`, then this assignment statement will work. If not, the value stored in the variable `var4` will be incorrect. For example, when executed in a C environment that uses 16 bits for the type `int`, the value of 60,000 for the variable `var3` will be assigned as –5536 to the variable `var4`. This result occurs because, during an automatic assignment conversion from a longer to a shorter field, the excess most significant bits are truncated and only the least significant bits are assigned. Thus, depending on the C system in use, we get some incorrect value stored in the shorter field.

Some compilers produce warning messages in case there is an assignment conversion from a longer to a shorter field in the program; others don't. In general, you should avoid conversions from longer to shorter fields, or at least make sure that the assignment conversion does not result in a value loss or a run-time error. In other words, program defensively. Here is an example of defensive programming in the context of the present discussion:

```
unsigned int var3;
int var4;
. . . . . . . . . . . . . . . .
if (var3 > INT_MAX)
        printf("Unsafe conversion. var4 = var3; is not executed.");
else
        var4 = var3;
/* end if */
```

`INT_MAX` is the named constant that represents the largest value that can be stored in a field of type `int`, also used in the program of Figure 5.8.

Before we close this section, we should mention that C can also do automatic conversions between characters and integers. We discuss characters, their internal representations, and character-integer conversions in Chapter 13.

## 5.12    C FEATURES FOR RANDOM NUMBER GENERATION

Many events in life are random; they do not produce the same outcome every time they occur under identical circumstances. Examples of random events include coin flips, dice rolls, cars crossing a bridge, and atmospheric conditions that control the weather. In any such event it is not possible to predict exactly the outcome or the pattern.

Computer programs and their executions are not random. Every program we have designed so far has been predictable. Considering the input and the logic of the algorithm, you could always determine the output. Therefore, we can effectively use computers for solving deterministic problems. We can also use computers for solving probabilistic problems that require simulating random events. To do so, however, we need random number generators.

A **random number generator** is an algorithm that generates a sequence of numbers in a given range with no repeating cycles. If every element of a sequence of random numbers has the same likelihood of occurring, such a sequence is a **uniform random**

**number sequence**. A sequence of numbers obtained by throwing a proper six-sided die, such as the sequence {1, 3, 4, 2, 6, 1, 4, 2, 5} is a random sequence; furthermore, it is a uniform random sequence because the likelihood for each value occurring is the same.

In general, it is not easy to find a random number generator that produces truly random numbers with no repeating cycles. In fact, because all steps in an algorithm are deterministic, that is, you can always tell what it will produce if you know its input, computerized random number generators are not true random number generators. They tend to generate the same sequence of random numbers every time you execute them. A generated random number depends on the previous random number, and the first random number depends on an initial value, called the **seed**. Such random number generators are **pseudorandom number generators**. However, it is possible to obtain sequences of random numbers that appear to be quite random.

Random numbers and random number generators are important in many applications. C has two standard library functions that can be used for random number generation. They are `rand` and `srand` functions of the `stdlib` standard library, and their declarations are found in the `stdlib.h` header file.

## The Standard Function `rand` for Pseudorandom Number Generation

The function `rand` has no parameters. Each time it is called, it returns a uniform pseudorandom number in the range zero through RAND_MAX. RAND_MAX is a standard named constant whose value is implementation-dependent, with a minimum of 32,767. In most implementations of the C compilers, the initial seed value for `rand` is the same. The declaration of the standard named constant RAND_MAX is also found in the header file `stdlib.h`.

***Example 5.16***   The program in Figure 5.11 computes and prints a sequence of five pseudorandom numbers, simulating five throws of a six-faced die.

```c
#include <stdio.h>
#include <stdlib.h>

int main(void) {
      int i = 1;

      while (i <= 5) {
            printf("Throw #%d: %d\n", i, (rand() % 6 + 1));
            i++;
      } /* end while */

      return 0;
} /* end function main */
```

**Figure 5.11**   A C program that simulates throwing a six-faced die

To get a random integer in the range one through six, we generate a pseudorandom integer by calling the function `rand` in the output statement in the body of the `while` loop. We know that the value returned for `rand` is in the range zero through `RAND_MAX`. To convert such an integer to a proper die face value, we use the modulus operator in the expression `rand() % 6`. This expression, however, produces integers in the range zero through five. To get integer values in the range one through six, all we have to do is add one to the result; hence, the expression `rand() % 6 + 1` in the output statement.

If you run this program using a C IDE, you get something like this:

```
Throw #1:  6
Throw #2:  6
Throw #3:  5
Throw #4:  5
Throw #5:  6
```

In fact, every time you execute this program in the same environment, you get the same result because the function `rand` is a pseudorandom number generator. To get a somewhat more random sequence, you must use the function `srand` together with `rand`.

## The Standard Function `srand` for Random Number Generation

The function `srand` has one integer parameter, which must have a nonnegative value. The parameter is of type `unsigned int`, and it is the seed of the next random number that will be computed by an invocation of the function `rand`. Therefore, the purpose of the `srand` function is to provide a seed for the next generation of a pseudorandom number.

There are several ways of providing a seed value in generating sequences of random numbers. One obvious way is to let the user supply an appropriate seed value to be used by the function `srand` and then make calls to the function `rand`. An example follows.

***Example 5.17*** The program in Figure 5.12 is similar to that of Figure 5.11. However, in computing a sequence of five pseudorandom numbers to simulate five throws of a die, we let the user enter a value for the seed of the random sequence.

```
#include <stdio.h>
#include <stdlib.h>
```

**Figure 5.12**   A C program that simulates throwing a six-faced die (use of `srand` with a user-supplied seed value) (*continued*) ▶

```
int main(void) {
        int i = 1;
        unsigned int seed;

        printf("Enter a seed value for random-number generation: ");
        scanf("%u", &seed);

        srand(seed);

        while (i <= 5) {
            printf("Throw #%d: %d\n", i, (rand() % 6 + 1));
            i++;
        } /* end while */

        return 0;
} /* end function main */
```

**Figure 5.12**

In this program, the value entered by the user for the variable  seed  is used as the parameter of the function call  srand. Different executions of this program with different seed values produce sequences of random numbers that are not identical.

A common way to get a "more" random sequence of numbers is to use the current time as the parameter of the function  rand. The standard function time, declared in the header file  time.h, returns the current time if invoked with a parameter value of zero, as in  time(0). The value returned by  time(0)  is an implementation-dependent value of the current time. Here is an example of the use of the  time  function to provide a seed value.

***Example 5.18***    The program in Figure 5.13 uses the current time as the seed of the sequence of random numbers that simulate five throws of a die. The value returned by the function call  time(0)  is the parameter of the function  srand. Because current time keeps on changing, every execution of this program generates a different sequence of random numbers.

```
#include <stdio.h>
#include <stdlib.h>
#include <time.h>
```

**Figure 5.13**    A C program that simulates throwing a six-faced die (use of current time with  srand  as the seed value) (*continued*)

```
int main(void) {
      int i = 1;
      unsigned int seed;

      seed = time(0);
      srand(seed);

      while (i <= 5) {
          printf("Throw #%d: %d\n", i, (rand() % 6 + 1));
          i++;
      } /* end while */

      return 0;
} /* end function main */
```

Figure 5.13                                                                    ■

---

### REVIEW QUESTIONS

1.  A variable of type `short int` requires a word length that is the same as or smaller than the word length for variables of type `int`. (T or F)

2.  Choose the *incorrect* statement.
    a. Both unsigned and signed integers are classified as `short int`, `int`, and `long int`.
    b. The type specifier `signed short int` is an acceptable alias for the data type short integer.
    c. A variable of type `long int` is stored in two bytes if a variable of type `int` is stored in four bytes.
    d. The type `unsigned int` is longer than the type `signed int`.

3.  A floating-point variable of type `double` can store more values with greater precision than a variable of type `long double` can store. (T or F)

4.  Which of the following statements concerning arithmetic errors and inaccuracies is correct?
    a. Integer division in a program results in a run-time error.
    b. Division by zero is an error that is detected at compile time.
    c. If the result of an arithmetic operation is greater than the largest value that can be stored in a variable, we get an arithmetic underflow error.
    d. Adding a very large and a very small floating-point value causes a representational inaccuracy.
    e. All of the above.
    f. None of the above.

**5.** Suppose a mixed-mode arithmetic expression consists of variables of types `double`, `unsigned long int`, `unsigned int`, and `signed int`. After automatic arithmetic type conversions, the type of this expression becomes

  **a.** `long double`

  **b.** `double`

  **c.** `unsigned long int`

  **d.** `unsigned int`

  **e.** None of the above.

**6.** Concerning C features for random number generation,

  **a.** The standard function `srand` is used to generate a random integer in the range zero through `RAND_MAX`.

  **b.** The standard function `rand` is used to supply seed values for the random numbers generated by `srand`.

  **c.** The declarations of the functions `srand` and `rand` are found in the `stdio.h` header file.

  **d.** The declaration of the standard named constant `RAND_MAX` is in the `stdlib.h` header file.

  **e.** All of the above are correct.

  **f.** None of the above is correct.

**Answers:** 1. T; 2. c; 3. F; 4. f; 5. b; 6. d.

---

## 5.13   SUMMARY

### This Chapter at a Glance

- This chapter covered in detail the C features for arithmetic calculations. You learned about additional arithmetic operators and compound assignment operators.
- You studied the type of arithmetic expressions, casting, and the cast operator.
- You were exposed to standard mathematical library functions and learned how to use them.
- You learned about some new numeric fundamental data types that C supports. These include signed, unsigned, short, and long variations of integer data and `float`, `double`, and `long double` variations of floating-point data. Depending on the nature of an application, one of these variations may be better than the others. In this chapter one of the principal objectives was to develop your ability to choose the right data types for program entities.
- You studied types of arithmetic errors and inaccuracies in arithmetic expressions and thus enhanced your understanding of the arithmetic capabilities of the C language.
- In case an arithmetic or assignment operation deals with quantities of different types, C uses automatic type conversion rules. We discussed these rules.
- You are now able to write arithmetic assignment statements in C for relatively complex mathematical computations.
- You also studied the standard C library functions that can be used in generating sequences of random numbers.

## Coming Attractions

- Chapter 3 introduced functions in C and stated that functions are very important in C programming.
- In the next chapter you will study functions in greater detail. If a program is too long, it should be split into smaller units, called modules. Each module carries out a relatively simple task, may require data from other modules, and may communicate its output to other modules.
- A program that consists of two or more modules is a modular program. Modules in a modular program are implemented as C functions.
- Chapter 6 discusses the principles of modular program design and the implementation of such programs using C functions. It also considers the simple aspects of data communication among the modules of a modular program.

## STUDY GUIDE

### Test Your Comprehension

**1.** Which of the following statements concerning arithmetic operators is *incorrect*?
   **a.** The unary plus operator has no effect on the result.
   **b.** The multiplication operator is a binary operator.
   **c.** The operands of the multiplication operator may be integer or floating-point values.
   **d.** The remainder operator requires floating-point operands.

**2.** Suppose we have the arithmetic expression

$$(a * (b - (c * 11 / d) + (e \% f * 5)))$$

Which of the following is the correct order of computations for this expression?

```
a. (a  *  (b  -  (c  *  11  /  d)  +  (e  %  f  *  5)))
         7      6      1       2        5     3      4

b. (a  *  (b  -  (c  *  11  /  d)  +  (e  %  f  *  5)))
         5      6      1       2        7     3      4

c. (a  *  (b  -  (c  *  11  /  d)  +  (e  %  f  *  5)))
         1      2      3       4        5     6      7

d. (a  *  (b  -  (c  *  11  /  d)  +  (e  %  f  *  5)))
         7      5      1       2        6     3      4
```

   **e.** None of the above.

**3.** If the values of the integer variables `a`, `b`, and `d` are `5`, `8`, and `15`, respectively, the value computed for the expression `(a * a - b * (d / a))` will be
   **a.** `1`
   **b.** `-1`
   **c.** `-3.8`
   **d.** `3.8`
   **e.** None of the above.

**4.** Let us assume that $x$, $y$, and $z$ are three variables of type `double` and that their respective values in memory are $3.5$, $12.2$, and $4.0$. What will be the value calculated for the expression $(x + y * (x / y / z))$?
   **a.** $4.0$
   **b.** $4.375$
   **c.** $1.126$
   **d.** None of the above.

**5.** Which of the following statements concerning the C increment and decrement operators is *incorrect*?
   **a.** They both have a postfix and a prefix form.
   **b.** The increment operator ++ adds one to the value of its operand.
   **c.** The decrement operator $--$ subtracts one from the value of its operand.
   **d.** The operand of the increment and decrement operators may be a constant or a variable.

**6.** Concerning the increment and decrement operators:
   **a.** The postincrement operator has the side effect of incrementing its operand by one before the expression in which it appears is evaluated using the operand's value.
   **b.** The postdecrement operator changes the value of its operand before the expression in which it appears is evaluated.
   **c.** The preincrement and predecrement operators first generate their side effect.
   **d.** The precedence level of the increment and decrement operators is the same as that of multiplication.
   **e.** All of the above are correct.
   **f.** None of the above is correct.

**7.** Assume that we have the following variable declarations:

```
int counter = 4, a = 5, b = -7, c;
```

and the arithmetic assignment expression statement

```
c = a % counter ++ - b;
```

has just been executed. The values of the variables `counter` and `c` are
   **a.** 5 and 7.
   **b.** 4 and 7.
   **c.** 5 and 8.
   **d.** 4 and 8.
   **e.** None of the above.

**8.** We have the following declarations in our program:

```
int a, c, d, count = 4, x = 15, y = 18;
double b, w = -17.3;
```

Suppose we execute the statement:

```
d = (a = -- count, b = w ++, c = (x + count ++ - y));
```

What will be printed by the following statement?

```
printf("%d   %d   %f   %f   %d   %d", count, a, w, b, c, d);
```

**a.** 4   4   -17.3   -17.3   0   0
**b.** 4   3   -16.3   -17.3   0   0
**c.** 4   3   -16.3   -17.3   0   4
**d.** 4   4   -16.3   -17.3   0   4
**e.** None of the above.

9. Initially, the values of the integer variables  a  and  b  are  10  and  12, respectively. After the statement

```
    a *= (b %= 7);
```

is executed, the variables  a  and  b  will become
**a.** 5  and  50.
**b.** 50  and  5.
**c.** 10  and  12.
**d.** 12  and  10.
**e.** None of the above.

10. Which of the following statements concerning C standard mathematical library functions is *incorrect*?
**a.** `ceil(4.7)`  returns  4.
**b.** `floor(4.0)`  returns  4.
**c.** `abs(-15.5)`  returns  15.
**d.** `pow(2, 5)`  returns  32.

11. Given is the algebraic expression

$$\frac{a^3 + b^3}{c^2 - d^2}$$

Which of the following expressions in C is the correct translation of this expression?
**a.** `pow(a, 3) + pow (b, 3) / pow(c, 2) + pow(d, 2)`
**b.** `(pow(a, 3) + pow (b, 3)) / pow(c, 2) + pow(d, 2)`
**c.** `(pow(a, 3) + pow (b, 3)) / (pow(c, 2) + pow(d, 2))`
**d.** `pow(a, 3) + (pow (b, 3) / pow(c, 2)) + pow(d, 2)`
**e.** None of the above.

12. Which of the following statements concerning C integer data types is correct?
**a.** Signed integer variables can represent only positive integer values.
**b.** The largest value that can be stored in a variable of type  `unsigned int`  is greater than the largest value that a variable of type  `int`  can store.
**c.** The largest value that an unsigned integer variable can store in two bytes is 32,767.
**d.** All of the above.
**e.** None of the above.

13. If a mixed-type expression consists of variables of types  `signed int, unsigned int, unsigned long int,` and  `float`, its type, after automatic type conversions, will be

**a.** double
**b.** unsigned int
**c.** float
**d.** signed int
**e.** None of the above.

## Improve Your Problem-Solving Ability

### Debugging Exercises

**14.** Find and explain the errors, if any, in each of the following arithmetic assignment expression statements.

**a.** `25.0 = cost + profit;`
**b.** `second = first ++ ++ third;`
**c.** `first = 3 * ((second + 7) + (third + 8);`
**d.** `t = (a + b / ) * (c - 5) / (d + 7);`
**e.** `second - = first + 4;`
**f.** `a = b + ceil(b, 3);`
**g.** `x = abs (int fabs(y));`
**h.** `a = pow(log(b, 10), 3);`

**15.** Explain why the following code will not compute a correct value for sum.

```c
#include <stdio.h>

int main(void) {
      int i = 5;
      unsigned int sum = 0;

      while (i >= -10) {
            sum = sum + i;
            i--;
      } /* end while */

      printf("Sum: %d", sum);
      return 0;
} /* end function main */
```

**16.** Explain why the following program may result in a run-time error? What kind of error will it be?

```
#include <stdio.h>
#include <float.h>

int main(void) {
      float a;

      a = DBL_MAX;
      printf("%f", a);
      return 0;
} /* end function main */
```

### Programming Exercises

**17.** For each of the following algebraic expressions, write an equivalent C arithmetic expression.

**a.** $\dfrac{a^3 - b^3}{d^3 + 17}$

**b.** $\dfrac{1}{x} + \dfrac{1}{x^2} + \dfrac{1}{x^3} + \dfrac{1}{x^4}$

**c.** $x + y^2 + \dfrac{t}{z}$

**18.** Suppose we have the following variable declarations in our program:

```
int x, y, z;
double u, v, w;
```

Assume that the current values of these variables are x = 10, y = 3, z = 5, u = -3.7, v = 10.25, and w = 12.37. What values will be computed for each of the following arithmetic expressions or arithmetic assignment expression statements?

**a.** x % y * z
**b.** x++ % --y + 7 / z
**c.** ((x - 6) * (x - 6) + y * y) / (z * z)
**d.** x += y + z;
**e.** (int) v % (int) w - v
**f.** ceil(u) + floor(v - 2)
**g.** sqrt(pow(w, 2))

### Programming Projects

**19.** Design and implement an interactive program that reads a dollar amount as an integer and then determines and prints the minimum number of bills of $50, $20, $10, $5, and $1 denominations in it. For example, if the dollar amount is $179, your program should print that it consists of three $50, one $20, zero $10, one $5, and four $1 bills. Your program should execute for as long as the user wants to continue without exiting to the operating system.

**20.** Design and implement an interactive program that reads your yearly gross salary and then computes and prints your net monthly take-home income. Assume that your yearly gross salary is greater than or equal to $50,000 but less than $80,000 and that the following deductions are applicable:

a. Federal income tax: $5,100.00 plus 28 percent of gross income over $34,000.00.

b. State tax: 9 percent of gross income.

c. City tax: 1.75 percent of gross income.

d. Social security: 8.75 percent of the first $45,000 of gross income.

Your program should execute in a sentinel-controlled loop for as long as the user wants to continue. It should incorporate a data validation routine to ensure that the yearly gross salary value is in the range of $50,000 through $79,999.

**21.** The fixed monthly *payment* for an installment *loan* taken over $n$ monthly payments at an annual interest rate of $i$ can be computed using the following formula:

$$payment = \frac{\left[ 1 + \dfrac{i}{12} \right]^n}{\left[ 1 + \dfrac{i}{12} \right]^n - 1} \times loan \times \frac{i}{12}$$

Design and implement a program that interactively inputs values for *loan*, $n$, and $i$, and then computes and outputs monthly payment values for all values of annual interest rate from $i$ to $i + 3$ at increments of 0.5 (that is, if $i$ is 8.3 percent, your program should compute monthly payment values for annual interest rate values of 8.3, 8.8, 9.3, 9.8, 10.3, 10.8, and 11.3 percent). You must use a counter-controlled loop to generate and use different annual interest rate values.

**22.** The following series summation is an approximation for computing the natural logarithm of a floating-point value $x$:

$$\log x = (x - 1) - (x - 1)^2 / 2 + (x - 1)^3 / 3 - (x - 1)^4 / 4 + \dots + (-i)^{n+1} (x - 1)^n / n$$

where $2 >= x > 0$ and $n$ is a positive integer. Design and implement an interactive program that does the following:

**a.** Prompts the user to enter a floating-point value for $x$ and reads it.

**b.** Ensures that $x$ is in the proper range; if not, reprompts the user to enter another value.

**c.** Computes the natural logarithm of $x$ using the standard library function `log(x)` and prints it.

**d.** Computes the natural logarithm of $x$ using the preceding approximation and prints it. You should do your computations in a loop and terminate the loop if the absolute value of the last term computed in the series is less than 0.00001.

**23.** Write a program that reads a positive integer and prints all powers from 1 to $n$, where $n$ is the last power that can be computed without causing overflow. Recompile and execute your program several times by declaring the program output variable (that is, the power of the integer number) as `signed int, unsigned int, signed long int,` and `unsigned long int` and then note the value of $n$ for each data type.

**24.** A polynomial of degree $n$ is represented as

$$p_n(x) = a_0 + a_1 x + a_2 x^2 + \ldots + a_n x^n$$

where $a_0$, $a_1$, $a_2$, . . ., $a_n$ are constant coefficients. Evaluation of such polynomials may be important if $p_n(x)$ is to be computed many times for different values of $x$. Design and implement a program that asks the user to enter a value for the degree of a polynomial, $n$, and values for $n + 1$ coefficients. Your program should read these values, and then in a loop it should prompt the user to enter values for $x$ and compute and print values for the polynomial. Your program should terminate execution if the last two values read for $x$ are equal. Your program should be able to process polynomials of degree 6 or less.

**25.** Solve the problem of computing values for polynomials as in project 24 by using Horner's rule. According to Horner's rule, a polynomial is written as

$$p_n(x) = a_0 + x \, (a_1 + x \, (a_2 \ldots + x \, (a_{n-1} + x \, a_n) \ldots ))$$

Note that this is equivalent to the original form. The straightforward term-by-term computation of a polynomial for large values of $n$ is inefficient. Horner's rule is significantly more efficient because it requires only $n$ multiplications and $n$ additions.

**26.** Heron's formula for computing the area of a triangle with sides $a$, $b$, and $c$ is

$$Area = \sqrt{s \, (s - a) \, (s - b) \, (s - c)}$$

where $s = (a + b + c)/2$. Develop an interactive program that reads values for $a$, $b$, and $c$, and computes and prints the value of the area of the triangle using Heron's formula. Your program should do computations for as long as the user wants to continue.

**27.** Design and implement an interactive program that reads a *low* value, a *high* value, and an *increment* value, ensures that the *low* value is less than or equal to the *high* value, and computes and prints a table of square roots and cubic roots for all values from *low* to *high* at increments of *increment*. For example, if the values of *low*, *high*, and *increment* are 1, 1.55, and 0.1, respectively, then your table should look like this:

```
Value        Square Root      Cubic Root
 1.0         1.0              1.0
 1.1         1.04881          1.03228
 1.2         1.09545          1.06266
 1.3         1.14018          1.09139
 1.4         1.18322          1.11869
 1.5         1.22474          1.14471
```

**28.** Develop an interactive program that computes and prints a table of trigonometric functions sine, cosine, tangent, and cotangent, corresponding to angles from *low* to *high* at increments of 1 degree. The values for *low* and *high* are to be input by the user, and they are in degrees. The trigonometric function cotangent is the inverse of the function tangent. Be careful about very large values that the functions tangent and cotangent may yield. Also, make sure that your program forces the user to enter a *low* value that is less than or equal to the *high* value. Note that the conversion from degrees to radians is given by the formula:

$$radians = degrees \times \pi / 180$$

where $\pi$ is the constant 3.141593.

**29.** We can use the following formula in computing an approximate value for the square root of a floating-point quantity *number*:

$$next\_guess = 0.5 \times (last\_guess + number / last\_guess)$$

We can start with an initial value of 1.0 for *last_guess*, and using the formula compute *next_guess*. If the absolute value of the difference between *next_guess* and *last_guess* is less than *difference*, which is a small value, such as 0.0001, we accept the value of *next_guess* as an approximation for the square root of *number*.

Design and implement an interactive program that reads values for *number* and *difference* and then computes and prints an approximation for the square root of *number* using the method described here.

**30.** Design and implement an interactive program that does the following:
   **a.** Reads values for the variables called *lower* and *upper*, where *lower* and *upper* are integer variables representing a range of integers, such that *lower* <= *upper*.
   **b.** Reads a value for the variable called *size_of_sequence*.
   **c.** Generates *size_of_sequence* uniform random integers in the range *lower* through *upper*. Use the current time as the seed for random number generation.
   **d.** Computes and prints the number of odd and even random integers while they are being generated in the previous step.
   **e.** Computes and prints the percentage of odd and even random integers. (For large values of *size_of_sequence*, these percentages must be close to 0.5 each. Why?)

# 6

# Modular Programming and Functions

---

## CHAPTER OBJECTIVES

In this chapter you will learn about:

- **Modular programming**
    Top-down design of modular programs
    Bottom-up implementation of modular programs

- **C functions**
    Function definitions
    Function declarations
    Function calls

- **Program structure and structure charts**

- **C functions that return values**

- **C functions with parameters**
    Formal and actual parameters
    Defining and declaring functions with parameters
    Calling functions with parameters
    Parameter passing by value

- **Storage classes, scope, visibility, and duration of variables**

By the time you have completed this chapter, you will have acquired the ability to:

- **Design modular programs using top-down design**

- **Implement modular programs using bottom-up development**

- **Draw structure charts for modular programs**

- **Develop C functions that return values under their name**

- **Develop C functions that receive values using parameters**

---

## 6.1    INTRODUCTION

For most software development projects in business and industry, thousands of lines of code are written. If all statements in such a project are gathered in a single program, we may end up with a huge and complex monster. Such a monolithic program would be quite difficult to develop, debug, and test. Also, generally, in order to expedite the software development process, several programmers work together in teams on the same project. If our goal is to develop a large program, how do we divide the programming task among team members? Even if we can do that, it would be extremely hard to integrate different code segments developed by different programmers into one program.

In addition, there is the problem of software maintenance. Assuming we could develop a software system in the form of a huge, single program, it would be difficult for the software maintenance personnel to understand the intricacies of our product and repair or expand it when needed.

This problem is common to the development of all large-scale artificial systems. For example, a car is not manufactured as a single task. The process is divided into smaller, more manageable tasks of manufacturing individual engine and chassis components. These components are assembled into larger components such as the distributor, battery, transmission, and so on. The parts are separately tested and are eventually integrated into the final product, the car.

In general, a software system is a just another complex artificial system. In developing it we use a similar strategy, namely, the divide-and-conquer approach. We discussed divide-and-conquer as a problem-solving strategy in Chapter 2. While designing an algorithm for a problem, we divide it into simpler subproblems. We proceed in this manner until all subproblems are of manageable size, and then we develop algorithms for them. During the programming phase each such algorithm can be regarded as a functional unit that can be implemented easily in a programming language. These units are called **modules**. Initially, each one is developed, debugged, and tested as an independent program. Then they are integrated and combined to work under the supervision of a main module. The finished software system is capable of performing its assigned task because each module does its task correctly and at the right time. This design and development strategy is referred to as modular programming.

---

**Modular programming** is defined as organizing a program into small, independent modules that are separately named and individually invokeable program elements. These modules are integrated to become a software system that satisfies the problem requirements.

---

This chapter introduces modular programming and modular program design. We examine design strategies for modular program systems and discuss C features that enable us to implement these strategies.

## 6.2    EXAMPLE PROGRAM 1: A Modular C Program that Draws Geometrical Figures (Use of Functions that Do Not Receive or Send Data)

Let us consider a relatively simple problem that we can solve using C.

***Problem***   We want to design and implement a program that draws a rectangle or a triangle, depending on what the user requests.

***Requirements Specifications***   Develop a program that does the following until the user decides to terminate its execution:

1.   Displays a menu of choices to print either a rectangle or a triangle.
2.   Inputs a user request code value and ensures that it is valid. If the request code value is 1, the program will print a rectangle; if the request value is 2, the program will print a triangle.
3.   Prints either a rectangle or a triangle on the screen.

***Analysis***

>   **Input.** A value for user request code.
>   **Output.** A rectangle or a triangle.

***Design***   Figure 6.1 is a somewhat refined pseudocode for an algorithm to solve this problem.

---

> *set want_to_continue to 'y'*
>
> *while want_to_continue is equal to 'y'*
>     *begin*
>         *set correct_request to 'n'*
>         *while correct_request is equal to 'n'*
>             *begin*
>                 *print menu*
>                 *read request*
>
>                 *if request is equal to 1*
>                     *begin*
>                         *draw rectangle*

---

**Figure 6.1**    Initial algorithm to print geometrical figures (*continued*)    ▶

```
                        set correct_request to 'y'
                end
        else if request is equal to 2
                begin
                        draw triangle
                        set correct_request to 'y'
                end
            end_if
        end
    end_while

    print "Do you want to continue? (y/n): "
    read want_to_continue
end
end_while
```

Figure 6.1                                                                        ■

This algorithm contains three subproblems that need further refinement: *print menu*, *draw rectangle*, and *draw triangle*. In applying top-down stepwise refinement, we devise algorithms for these subproblems, refine them, and combine them into one pseudocode. We will do the same thing here with one exception: after the final refinement of each subproblem, we will leave them as separate modules. We will assign a name to each module and combine the named modules in a program structure under the control of a main program. Such a program structure consists of a set of modules and an order of execution.

This strategy is essentially based on the divide-and-conquer approach to problem solving and has many advantages over developing a monolithic program for the entire problem.

1.    When we modularize a problem, we end up with a set of smaller and simpler problems, which can be assigned to different teams. If the teams work in parallel, we can reduce the program development time considerably.

2.    Converting simple problems to individual programs facilitates programming, program debugging, testing, expansion, repair, and maintenance.

3.    If our modular program has features that are specific to a particular computer system and we want to run the program on another system, we can change the modules easily because they are relatively small. Thus modular programs improve program portability.

4.    Some general-purpose modules of a modular program can be used without any change in other software development projects. This feature greatly improves the efficiency of program development.

Let us now apply this design approach to the problem of printing geometrical figures. In Figure 6.1, instead of describing a subproblem as in *print menu*, we assume that there is a module called *print_menu* and replace the preceding pseudocode statement with *call print_menu*. We do the same thing for *draw rectangle* and *draw triangle*; we replace them with *call draw_rectangle* and *call draw_triangle*, respectively. Here *print_menu*, *draw_rectangle*, and *draw_triangle* are the names of three modules corresponding to three subproblems. Their simple pseudocode algorithms are given in Figure 6.2 together with the modified pseudocode algorithm of Figure 6.1.

---

*main program:*
    *set want_to_continue to 'y'*

    *while want_to_continue is equal to 'y'*
      *begin*
        *set correct_request to 'n'*

        *while correct_request is equal to 'n'*
          *begin*
            *call print_menu*
            *read request*

            *if request is equal to 1*
              *begin*
                *call draw_rectangle*
                *set correct_request to 'y'*
              *end*
            *else if request is equal to 2*
              *begin*
                *call draw_triangle*
                *set correct_request to 'y'*
              *end*
            *end_if*
          *end*
        *end_while*

        *print "Do you want to continue? (y/n): "*
        *read want_to_continue*
      *end*
    *end_while*

---

*print_menu:*
    *print "This program draws a rectangle or a triangle on the screen."*
    *print "Enter 1 to draw a rectangle."*
    *print "Enter 2 to draw a triangle: "*

---

**Figure 6.2**   Final algorithm to print geometrical figures (*continued*)   ▶

```
draw_rectangle:
    print "+---------------+"
    print "|               |"
    print "|               |"
    print "|               |"
    print "+---------------+"
-----------------------------------------------------------------------------
draw_triangle:
    print "     / \"
    print "    /   \"
    print "   /     \"
    print "  /       \"
    print "+-------------+"
```

**Figure 6.2**                                                                      ■

Now we have a main program and three subprograms. Together, they make up a modular program. The program execution begins with the first statement in the main program and ultimately terminates in the main program. When a *call* statement is encountered, the program control passes to the called module. Its content is executed, and the control goes back to the main program. Clearly, if we proceed this way, the problem will be solved.

The main program and the three subprogram modules constitute a program structure. Figure 6.3 is a structure chart that shows the structure of our modular program. In this figure each module is represented by a rectangle. The main program appears at the top of the chart, and all three modules that the main program calls are shown at a lower level. A line connecting a module to a module below it means that the top module calls the one that is at a lower level of hierarchy. Also, that the modules *print_menu*, *draw_rectangle*, and *draw_triangle* are drawn in this order, from left to right, means that the main program calls them in this order. Therefore, a structure chart such as the one in Figure 6.3 shows all the modules in a modular program, all module invocations, and the order of module invocations.

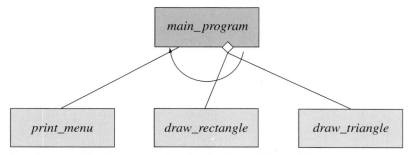

**Figure 6.3**    Structure chart for the pseudocode algorithm of Figure 6.2

The modular program that we have designed contains four modules to be implemented. Suppose we have a team of four C programmers. We can assign one module to each team member, supply him or her with a copy of Figure 6.3 and the pseudocode of the module, and ask him or her to implement it. This way, each member has a simple program to develop. Alternatively, if there is only one programmer, he or she may develop the entire program, one module at a time, starting with the modules at the lowest level of hierarchy in the structure chart of Figure 6.3 and moving up from there. This implementation strategy is referred to as **bottom-up implementation**.

*Implementation*    Figure 6.4 shows the C implementations of the pseudocode algorithms of Figures 6.1 and 6.2. Together they form a program that solves our problem correctly.

```
/*******************************************************************
   Program Filename: Prog06_1.c
   Author          : Uckan
   Purpose         : Draws either a rectangle or a triangle on
                     the screen.
   Input from      : Keyboard
   Output to       : Screen
 *******************************************************************/
#include <stdio.h>

/* Function prototypes: */

void print_menu(void);
void draw_rectangle(void);
void draw_triangle(void);

int main(void) {
      /* Variable declarations: */

      int request;
      char want_to_continue = 'y', correct_request, new_line;

      /* Function body: */

      while (want_to_continue == 'y') {
          correct_request = 'n';

          while (correct_request == 'n') {
                print_menu();
                scanf("%d", &request);
```

**Figure 6.4**    A C implementation of the pseudocode algorithms of Figures 6.1 and 6.2 (*continued*)    ▶

```
                          if (request == 1) {
                                  draw_rectangle();
                                  correct_request = 'y';
                          }
                          else if (request == 2) {
                                  draw_triangle();
                                  correct_request = 'y';
                          } /* end if */
                  } /* end while */

                  scanf("%c", &new_line);
                  printf("Do you want to continue? (y/n): ");
                  scanf("%c", &want_to_continue);
          } /* end while */
          return 0;
  } /* end function main */

  /*...................................................*/
  /* Purpose: prints a menu of options on the screen. */
  void print_menu(void) {
          printf("THIS PROGRAM DRAWS A RECTANGLE OR A TRIANGLE ON THE ");
          printf("SCREEN.\n");
          printf("Enter 1 to draw a rectangle.\n");
          printf("Enter 2 to draw a triangle: ");
  } /* end function print_menu */

  /*...................................................*/
  /* Purpose: draws a rectangle on the screen. */
  void draw_rectangle(void) {
          printf("+---------------+\n");
          printf("|               |\n");
          printf("|               |\n");
          printf("|               |\n");
          printf("+---------------+\n");
  } /* end function draw_rectangle */
```

Figure 6.4

▶

```
/*..............................................*/
/* Purpose: draws a triangle on the screen. */
void draw_triangle(void) {
      printf("         /\\\n");
      printf("       /    \\\n");
      printf("     /        \\\n");
      printf("   /            \\\n");
      printf("+--------------+\n");
} /* end function draw_triangle */
```

Figure 6.4                                                                 ∎

If you examine this program, you will see that most of it is familiar. The new aspect is the existence of functions. In Chapter 3 we discussed the function `main`. Here, in addition, we have three functions, each corresponding to a module in the program. These functions require three elements:

1.   Function definitions

2.   Function calls

3.   Function declarations (also called prototypes)

Function definitions are C implementations of the logic of subalgorithms designed as modules. The program in Figure 6.4 has three function definitions. Function calls such as

```
draw_triangle();
```

in Figure 6.4 are counterparts of the *call* statements in our pseudocode, which appear as *call draw_triangle*. Function prototypes are declarations of functions in the program that uses them. Figure 6.4, has three function prototypes, one of which is

```
void draw_triangle(void);
```

The next section discusses these three important elements of modular programs in C.

## 6.3   ELEMENTS OF MODULAR PROGRAMS

In C programs each module of a modular program is implemented as a programmer-defined function. Functions must be identified by programmer-defined names. To avoid ambiguities, C requires that function names be unique in a source program file.

In all modular programs one of the modules is the main function. The main function is identified by the word `main`. Program execution always begins and eventually terminates in the main function.

In modular C programs we have three elements that are related to functions: function definitions, function calls, and function declarations.

## Function Definitions

A **function definition** (also called **function implementation**) consists of these elements:

1. A function type
2. A function name
3. An optional list of formal parameters enclosed in parentheses
4. A compound statement.

Figure 6.5 is an example of function definition for a programmer-defined function. This function is the first function after the function `main` in Figure 6.4. The first line in it is the function header, and it specifies the type of the function as `void`. This type of function will not return a value under its name. If a function is designed such that it does not return any value under its name, its type must be `void`.

```
void print_menu(void) {
     printf("THIS PROGRAM DRAWS A RECTANGLE OR A TRIANGLE ON THE ");
     printf("SCREEN.\n");
     printf("Enter 1 to draw a rectangle.\n");
     printf("Enter 2 to draw a triangle: ");
} /* end function print_menu */
```

**Figure 6.5**    A programmer-defined C function

In Figure 6.5 the name of the function, `print_menu`, follows the function type. Next to the function name, we have a pair of parentheses that enclose the keyword `void`, `(void)`. In function definitions parentheses enclose the formal parameters. We cover formal parameters later in this chapter; they are used to send values to and receive value from functions. Because the function `print_menu` does not need to receive values from or send values to its calling functions, it has no formal parameters. To indicate that the formal parameter list is empty, we use the keyword `void` between parentheses, as in `void print_menu(void)`. Alternatively, some compilers accept a left and a right parentheses with nothing written in between, as in `void print_menu()`.

Following the function header we have a compound statement, which is the function body. The **function body** is the expression of the algorithm for the module in C. The function body consists of variable declarations and statements.

## Function Calls

Functions for which a definition exists in a program can be called by any function, including the function `main`. However, the reverse is not true: programmer-defined functions may not call the function `main`. A **function call** requires the name of the function followed by a list of actual parameters (or arguments), if any, enclosed in parentheses. We will discuss actual parameters later. If a function has no formal parameters in its definition, it cannot have any actual parameters in calls to it. In this case, in a function call, the name of the function must be followed by the function call operator, ( ), to indicate that it has no parameters. For example, to call the function `print_menu` of Figure 6.5, we must use the statement

```
print_menu();
```

When a function call is encountered, the program control passes to the called function. Next, the code corresponding to the called function is executed. The function code is kept in a separate area of the main memory during program execution. After the function body completes its execution, the program control goes back to the calling function.

## Function Declarations

In general, all functions in a C program must be declared. The only exception is the function `main`, which must not be declared. A **function declaration** (also called **function prototype**) consists of a function type, a function name, a list of function parameter types enclosed in parentheses, and a terminating semicolon. If the function has no formal parameters, the list of function parameter types is written as `(void)` or `()`. If the function has more than one formal parameter, the parameter types in the list must be separated by commas. For example, the prototype for the function `print_menu` in Figure 6.5 is

```
void print_menu(void);
```

Before a function can be called, it must be either defined or declared by a prototype in the source file. A function prototype informs the compiler that, even if no function definition has yet been encountered in the source file, the called function will have a definition elsewhere in the file and that this definition will be consistent with its prototype. You can place your function prototypes in the source file outside function definitions. Such prototypes are **global prototypes**. You can also place function prototypes in a function definition, providing you have calls to the declared functions in it. In this case the prototypes are **local prototypes** with respect to the function in which they appear. In the program of Figure 6.4, the prototypes for functions `print_menu`, `draw_rectangle`, and `draw_triangle` are all global.

The declaration of a function defines a region in a program in which that function may be used by other functions. This region is the **scope** of the function. The scope of a function declared using a global prototype begins at the point where its prototype is placed and extends until the end of the source file. The scope of a function declared by a local prototype, on the other hand, begins at the point where its prototype is placed and extends until the end of the function in which it appears. In the program of Figure 6.4, the scope of the three functions is the entire source program file.

If a function prototype is global, any function in the program may use it; because of this flexibility, and other considerations that will eventually become clear, we will use global function prototypes in this book. In general, in single source file programs, we will place function prototypes right after the preprocessor directives and before the definition of function `main`.

## 6.4   STRUCTURE OF MODULAR PROGRAMS

We know that every program has a logic that is defined by its algorithm. A modular program consists of many modules, each corresponding to a simpler problem and implemented as a function, and each module has its own logic. Program logic is one of the important aspects of computer programs. Another aspect of modular programs is program structure. In section 6.2 we used the top-down design strategy to solve the problem of drawing geometrical figures, and we ended up with a structure chart, as shown in Figure 6.3. Such a structure chart depicts the program structure.

### Program Structure and Structure Charts

The modules in a modular program are related to one another, and they define a relationship. This relationship is the "invoked by" relationship. The modules, together with the invoked-by relationship, define the program structure.

> A **program structure** is a collection of logical program modules and the invoked-by relationship existing among the modules.

We can represent the structure of any modular program in the form of a graph. Such a graph is called a **structure chart**. Figure 6.3 is an example of a structure chart in which each module is shown as a labeled node using a rectangular box. Node labels are the module names, and nodes are connected to other nodes by lines. All such lines stand for the invoked-by relationship. The line from *main_function to print_menu,* for example, implies that the module *print_menu* is invoked by the module *main_function* sometime during program execution.

In structure charts, different modules invoked by the same module are shown on the same level. Thus a structure chart always shows a hierarchical organization of a collection of modules. In fact, another name for a structure chart is a **hierarchy chart**. Modules on the same level of hierarchy are understood to be executed in left-to-right order. In Figure 6.3 the module *main_function* calls on the modules *print_menu, draw_rectangle,* and *draw_triangle*, in that order.

In a structure chart a module may call on many other modules. In other words, a module may have more than one subordinate. Any hierarchical structure in which the number of superordinates for a module is restricted to a maximum of one is called a **tree**. Thus a structure chart can be a tree. Trees are very important structures in computer science, and they have many applications.

Although all structure charts are hierarchical, they are not always trees. For example, the structure chart of Figure 6.6 is not a tree structure because module G is invoked twice —once by module B at level 2 and once more by module F at level 3. In other words, module G is being used more than once, a commendable strategy if the problem is amenable

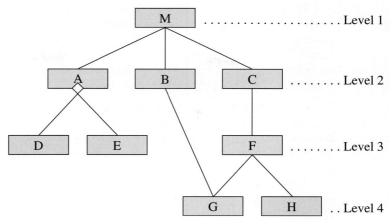

**Figure 6.6**   A hierarchical program structure

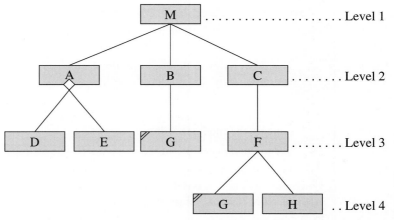

**Figure 6.7**   The hierarchical program structure of Figure 6.6 converted to a tree structure

to it. Even in such cases, it is possible to convert a nontree structure chart to an equivalent tree structure chart by repeating the modules that are used by more than one module. Figure 6.7 shows a tree structure chart that is equivalent to the structure of Figure 6.6. In general, you should use tree structure charts because they are easier to understand.

A *complete* structure chart shows the following elements:

1.   Program modules
2.   Module invocations
3.   Data transfers, if any, between modules
4.   Order of module invocations
5.   Nature of module invocations (simple, conditional, and repetitive)

There are three types of module invocations: simple, conditional, and repetitive. A **simple module invocation** is a single module call within a calling module. A **conditional module invocation** is made in a selection structure (for example, an `if` statement). To show that a module invocation is conditional, we draw a small diamond-shaped block on the bottom edge of the box for the calling module. For example, in Figures 6.6 and 6.7, the invocation of module D by module A is conditional.

A **repetitive module invocation** is made within a repetition structure (for example, a `while` statement) in a calling module. Repetitive module invocations are shown by drawing a clockwise arc over the line connecting the modules. In Figure 6.3, for example, the module *main_function* calls on the modules *print_menu, draw_rectangle*, and *draw_triangle* repetitively.

A structure chart also indicates data transfers between modules. A data transfer is shown by drawing a small arrow parallel to the line connecting the modules and writing the data names next to the arrow. We will examine data transfers between modules beginning with the next section.

## Conventions Used in Drawing Structure Charts

1. Represent each module by a rectangular box. Write the names assigned to program modules inside the rectangular boxes.

2. Assign descriptive names to program modules. If necessary, write a brief description of the module inside its box.

3. If a module invokes another module, place the box for the invoking module above that of the subordinate module to properly reflect the hierarchy and connect the modules with a line.

4. For unconditional or simple invocations, use a simple connecting line.

5. For conditional invocations, draw a small diamond-shaped block on the bottom edge of the box for the calling module and connect the diamond to one or more lower-level modules.

6. For repetitive module invocations, draw a clockwise arc over the line connecting the modules.

7. When the program control passes from one module to another during invocation or after the called module completes its execution, data are sometimes also transferred in either direction. If data transfers are to be shown on the structure chart, draw a small arrow (——>) parallel to the line connecting the modules and write the data names next to the arrow to identify the data that are passed.

8. In the program structures of hierarchical type, certain modules may have more than one calling module. Drawing the lines to represent all invocations may produce a cluttered and confusing diagram. As a matter of convention, replicate the common module so that the resulting structure is a simple tree. The replicated common module boxes are highlighted by drawing wedges at the upper-left corner.

A structure chart is a natural outcome of the top-down design process and an important element of program documentation. A good programming practice is to supplement every modular program system with its corresponding structure chart.

## REVIEW QUESTIONS

1. Choose the correct statement.
   a. In a modular program each module performs a specific and relatively simple task that can be expressed in one or two sentences.
   b. In modular programming we organize a program into small, independent modules that are separately named and individually invokeable program elements. Then we integrate them to become a software system that satisfies the problem requirements.
   c. A modular program is obtained as a result of top-down design.
   d. A modular program is a set of modules and an order of execution for them.
   e. All of the above are correct.
   f. None of the above is correct.

2. Modular programming enables programmers to work in teams and reduces the program development time. (T or F)

3. Which of the following concerning C functions is correct?
   a. All functions, including the main function, must be assigned programmer-defined names.
   b. Function names do not have to be distinct in a source file.
   c. Program execution always begins in the main function.
   d. All of the above.
   e. None of the above.

4. A function call consists of the name of the called function and a list of actual parameters enclosed in parentheses. (T or F)

5. Choose the *incorrect* statement. A structure chart for a modular program represents
   a. All modules in the program.
   b. Module invocations.
   c. Data transfers between modules.
   d. Order of module invocations.
   e. Program logic.

6. In bottom-up development we begin program development at the lowest level of hierarchy in the structure chart and proceed in a left-to-right, bottom-to-top manner. (T or F)

**Answers:** 1. e; 2. T; 3. c; 4. T; 5. e; 6. T.

## 6.5     EXAMPLE PROGRAM 2: A Modular C Program that Draws Geometrical Figures (Use of Functions that Return a Single Value)

In Figure 6.4 we have the main function of the modular program that draws geometrical figures. In that version the main function performs the tasks of printing a menu of choices and ascertaining that the value entered by the user is correct. Then it calls on the modules `draw_rectangle` or `draw_triangle`.

Let us now adopt a different modularization scheme for the same problem. This time we will have a module called *user_request* that does the following:

1.  Displays a menu of choices by calling on the module *print_menu*.
2.  Reads a value for *request*.
3.  Verifies that the value entered for *request* is correct (that is, 1 or 2).
4.  Returns that value to the calling program.

The pseudocode algorithm for the module *user_request* is given in Figure 6.8.

---

*user_request:*
   *set correct_request to 'n'*

   *while correct_request is equal to 'n'*
      *begin*
         *call print_menu*
         *read request*

         *if request is equal to 1*
            *set correct_request to 'y'*
         *else if request is equal to 2*
            *set correct_request to 'y'*
         *end_if*

      *end*
   *end_while*
   *return request*

---

**Figure 6.8**     Pseudocode algorithm for module *user_request*

The logic of this algorithm is somewhat similar to that of Figure 6.1 except here the module *user_request* does not call the modules *draw_rectangle* and *draw_triangle*; it leaves these tasks to the main program. The pseudocode statement *return request* simply makes the value of the variable *request* available to the calling program if the calling program refers to it using the name of the module *user_request*. Figure 6.9 shows the pseudocode algorithm for the main program.

> *set want_to_continue to 'y'*
>
> *while want_to_continue is equal to 'y'*
>    *begin*
>
>        *set request_code to user_request*
>
>        *if request_code is equal to 1*
>            *call draw_rectangle*
>        *else if request_code is equal to 2*
>            *call draw_triangle*
>        *end_if*
>
>        *print "Do you want to continue? (y/n): "*
>        *read want_to_continue*
>
>    *end*
> *end_while*

**Figure 6.9**    Pseudocode algorithm for the main program that calls *user_request*

The logic of the modules *print_menu*, *draw_rectangle*, and *draw_triangle* do not change; they are given in Figure 6.2. The structure of this version of the pseudocode is shown in the structure chart of Figure 6.10.

The C implementation of the pseudocode algorithms of Figure 6.8 and 6.9, together with the algorithms of the modules *print_menu*, *draw_rectangle*, and *draw_triangle*, is presented in Figure 6.11.

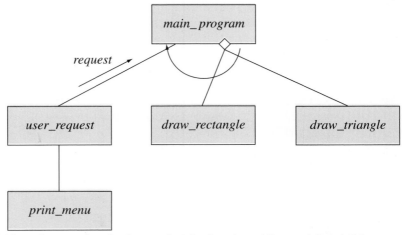

**Figure 6.10**    Structure chart for the pseudocode algorithms of Figures 6.8 and 6.9

```
/******************************************************************
   Program Filename: Prog06_2.c
   Author          : Uckan
   Purpose         : Draws either a rectangle or a triangle on
                     the screen.
   Input from      : Keyboard
   Output to       : Screen
 ******************************************************************/
#include <stdio.h>

/* Function prototypes: */

void draw_rectangle(void);
void draw_triangle(void);
void print_menu(void);
int user_request(void);

int main(void) {
     /* Variable declarations: */

     int request_code;
     char want_to_continue = 'y', new_line;

     /* Function body: */

     while (want_to_continue == 'y') {
          request_code = user_request();

          if (request_code == 1)
               draw_rectangle();
          else if (request_code == 2)
               draw_triangle();
          /* end if */

          scanf("%c", &new_line);
          printf("Do you want to continue? (y/n): ");
          scanf("%c", &want_to_continue);
     } /* end while */

     return 0;
```

**Figure 6.11**    A C implementation of the pseudocode algorithms of Figures 6.8 and 6.9 *(continued)*    ▶

```
} /* end function main */

/*...........................................................*/
/* Purpose: ensures that the user types a correct request code
   value and returns that value to the calling function. */
int user_request(void) {
      /* Local variable declarations: */

      char correct_request = 'n';
      int request;

      /* Function body: */

      while (correct_request == 'n') {
            print_menu();
            scanf("%d", &request);

            if (request == 1)
                  correct_request = 'y';
            else if (request == 2)
                  correct_request = 'y';
            /* end if */

      } /* end while */

      return request;
} /* end function user_request */

/*...........................................................*/
/* Purpose: prints a menu of options on the screen. */
void print_menu(void) {
      printf("THIS PROGRAM DRAWS A RECTANGLE OR A TRIANGLE ON THE ");
      printf("SCREEN.\n");
      printf("Enter 1 to draw a rectangle.\n");
      printf("Enter 2 to draw a triangle: ");
```

Figure 6.11                                                              ▶

```
} /* end function print_menu */

/*..............................................................*/
/* Purpose: draws a rectangle on the screen. */
void draw_rectangle(void) {

        printf("+---------------+\n");
        printf("|               |\n");
        printf("|               |\n");
        printf("|               |\n");
        printf("+---------------+\n");
} /* end function draw_rectangle */

/*..............................................................*/
/* Purpose: draws a triangle on the screen. */
void draw_triangle(void) {
        printf("        /\\\n");
        printf("       /   \\\n");
        printf("      /     \\\n");
        printf("     /       \\\n");
        printf("+---------------+\n");
} /* end function draw_triangle */
```

**Figure 6.11**

Figure 6.11 has one new element: the fact that the function user_request must return a value. This feature results in some differences in the definition, declaration, and calls for the function:

1.  Because the function user_request is expected to return a value—in this case, an integer value—its definition must begin with the function type specifier int as shown in Figure 6.11:

        int user_request(void)

2.  To ensure that the function user_request returns a value to the calling program, we must place at least one return statement somewhere in its body. This return statement must be placed at an appropriate point in the function, just when it is ready to return the program control to the calling function. The return statement in Figure 6.11

        return request;

ensures that the value of the integer variable request is returned under the name of the function user_request. Note that both the value that is returned, request, and the function that returns it, user_request, are of the same data type, int. Their data types must be at least convertible, if not the same.

3.  The function prototype for `user_request` is

    ```
    int user_request(void);
    ```

Consistent with the function definition, this prototype specifies the function type as `int`.

4.  We have a call to this function in Figure 6.11:

    ```
    request_code = user_request();
    ```

The function call is the expression `user_request()`. This call does two things:

a.  Transfers the program control to the first statement in the body of `user_request` and ensures that the control is returned when a `return` statement is executed.

b.  Brings an integer value that replaces the function call upon its return. To preserve the returned value for further processing, we store it in the integer variable `request_code`, which is a variable declared in the function `main`, in Figure 6.11.

Now that we have reviewed an example, we are ready to discuss the principles of C functions that return values under their names.

## 6.6   FUNCTIONS THAT RETURN VALUES UNDER THEIR NAMES

If the function that we are designing is expected to produce and return only one value, we can use the function name for this purpose. Such functions are also referred to as **valued functions**. In this case the function name must have a return type other than `void`. The return type is any data type, such as `int`, `double`, or `char`, that C supports. For example, the header of the function definition, `int user_request(void)`, in Figure 6.11 has `int` as its return type. This return type implies that the function will return to the calling function an integer value under the name `user_request`, its own name.

### The `return` Statement

A valued function must contain at least one `return` statement in its body. We have been using the `return` statement since Chapter 1. The syntax is simple: the keyword `return` followed by a return expression. The return expression must produce a value consistent with the type of the function in which the `return` statement appears because this value is returned under the function name to the calling program. Also, the `return` statement terminates the execution of the function and takes the program control back to the calling program.

If the return type of a function definition is missing, the default is `int`. However, if a function is not intended to return a value under its name, its return type must be `void`. For void functions the `return` statement must not have a return expression, and it can simply be written as

```
return;
```

If we want a void function to go back to the calling program after it completes its execution and encounters the final closing brace of the function body, then the `return` statement may be completely missing.

## 6.7     EXAMPLE PROGRAM 3: A Modular C Program that Draws Geometrical Figures (Use of Functions that Receive Data Values)

Once again, we will consider the problem of drawing geometrical figures. We will begin with the pseudocode in Figure 6.9 and introduce a variation. In the main program we have the following pseudocode segment:

> if request_code is equal to 1
>     call draw_rectangle
> else if request_code is equal to 2
>     call draw_triangle
> end_if

We will turn this into a module called *process_request*. However, before we do that, we observe that such a module will have to receive the value of the variable *request_code* in order to carry out its task of calling on either *draw_rectangle* or *draw_triangle*. Therefore, we will rewrite its pseudocode as shown in Figure 6.12.

> process_request( request_code ):
>     if request_code is equal to 1
>         call draw_rectangle
>     else if request_code is equal to 2
>         call draw_triangle
>     end_if

**Figure 6.12**     Pseudocode algorithm for module *process_request*

We can then replace the extracted segment in Figure 6.9 by a call to the module *process_request*:

> call process_request( request_code )

The pseudocode algorithm for the main program is now shown in Figure 6.13.

*set want_to_continue to 'y'*

*while want_to_continue is equal to 'y'*
    *begin*
        *set request_code to user_request*
        *call process_request(request_code)*

        *print "Do you want to continue? (y/n): "*
        *read want_to_continue*
    *end*
*end_while*

**Figure 6.13**   Pseudocode algorithm for the main program that calls *user_request* and *process_request*

In this new modularization scheme the logic of the modules *print_menu*, *draw_rectangle*, *draw_triangle*, and *user_request* remains the same; the modules appear in Figures 6.2 and 6.8. Figure 6.14 is the structure chart of this version of the pseudocode.

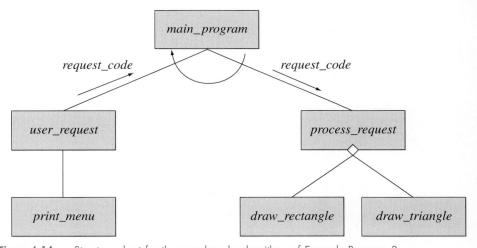

**Figure 6.14**   Structure chart for the pseudocode algorithms of Example Program 3

The C program that is the implementation of the pseudocode algorithms for the modules *print_menu*, *draw_rectangle*, and *draw_triangle* (as given in Figure 6.2), the module *user_request* of Figure 6.8, and the pseudocode algorithms of Figures 6.12 and 6.13 is given in Figure 6.15.

```
/********************************************************************
   Program Filename: Prog06_3.c
   Author          : Uckan
   Purpose         : Draws either a rectangle or a triangle on
                     the screen.
   Input from      : Keyboard
   Output to       : Screen

 *********************************************************************/
#include <stdio.h>

/* Function prototypes: */

void draw_rectangle(void);
void draw_triangle(void);
void print_menu(void);
int user_request(void);
void process_request(int r);

int main(void) {
      /* Variable declarations: */

      int request_code;
      char want_to_continue = 'y', new_line;

      /* Function body: */

      while (want_to_continue == 'y') {
            request_code = user_request();

            process_request(request_code);

            scanf("%c", &new_line);
            printf("Do you want to continue? (y/n): ");
            scanf("%c", &want_to_continue);
      } /* end while */

      return 0;
} /* end function main */
```

**Figure 6.15**     A C implementation of the pseudocode algorithms of Figures 6.12 and 6.13 *(continued)*     ▶

```
/*..........................................................*/
/* Purpose : ensures that the user types a correct request code value
             and returns that value to the calling function.

   Receives: None
   Returns : request
*/
int user_request(void) {
     /* Local variable declarations: */

     char correct_request = 'n';
     int request;

     /* Function body: */

     while (correct_request == 'n') {
          print_menu();
          scanf("%d", &request);

          if (request == 1)
               correct_request = 'y';
          else if (request == 2)
               correct_request = 'y';
          /* end if */

     } /* end while */

     return request;
} /* end function user_request */
```

Figure 6.15                                                                    ▶

```
/*............................................................*/
/* Purpose: prints a menu of options on the screen. */
void print_menu(void) {
    printf("THIS PROGRAM DRAWS A RECTANGLE OR A TRIANGLE ON THE ");
    printf("SCREEN.\n");
    printf("Enter 1 to draw a rectangle.\n");
    printf("Enter 2 to draw a triangle: ");
} /* end function print_menu */


/*............................................................*/
/* Purpose: draws a rectangle on the screen. */
void draw_rectangle(void) {

    printf("+---------------+\n");
    printf("|               |\n");
    printf("|               |\n");
    printf("|               |\n");
    printf("+---------------+\n");
} /* end function draw_rectangle */


/*.........................................................*/
/* Purpose: draws a triangle on the screen. */
void draw_triangle(void) {
    printf("        /\\\n");
    printf("       /    \\\n");
    printf("     /        \\\n");
    printf("   /            \\\n");
    printf("+--------------+\n");
} /* end function draw_triangle */


/*..............................................................*/
/* Purpose : Depending on the request value, calls draw_rectangle
             or draw_triangle.
   Receives: request_code
   Returns : None
*/
void process_request(int request_value) {
    if (request_value == 1)
        draw_rectangle();
    else if (request_value == 2)
        draw_triangle();
    /* end if */
} /* end function process_request */
```

Figure 6.15

In this version of the program, we have introduced a function that requires the calling function to send a value to it. One way—actually, the best way—of sending a value to a function is through its parameter list. In defining the function `process_request` in the program of Figure 6.15, we have associated a formal parameter with it:

```
void process_request(int request_code)
```

This header defines the function `process_request` as one that does not return a value because its return type is `void`, but requires an integer value sent to it to be stored in its integer formal parameter `request_code`. Accordingly, the function prototype for `process_request` in Figure 6.15 looks like this:

```
void process_request(int request_code);
```

This prototype informs the compiler that the function `main` will be using the function `process_request`, which does not return any values but has an integer formal parameter. Now that we have defined and declared the function `process_request` properly, we can let the function `main` call it, which is done as follows:

```
process_request(request_code);
```

This function call uses the name of the function and a variable, `request_code`, as the actual parameter. The variable `request_code` is declared in the function `main`. As a result of this function call, the following events take place:

1. The program control passes to the first statement in the function `process_request`.

2. A copy of the content of the variable `request_code` in the function `main` is made in the memory location for the formal parameter `request_code` of the function `process_request`. You should note that the variable `request_code` that appears as the formal parameter of the function `process_request` is not the same variable as its namesake, `request_code`, which is declared in the function `main`. We cover this point in detail in the following sections.

3. The function `process_request` is executed using the value of `request_code`. After its task is completed, the program control is returned to the statement that follows the function call in the function `main`.

The parameter passing process that we have used in this application is known as parameter passing by value. The following two sections consider the principles of functions with parameters and parameter passing by value.

## 6.8 FUNCTIONS WITH PARAMETERS

When a function calls another function to perform a task, the calling function may also send data to the called function. After completing its task, the called function may pass data that it has generated back to the calling function. There are three ways through which functions can communicate data:

1. Through global variables, which are variables declared in the source file outside and before function definitions

```
/* Global variables: */

int i; double j; int k;

/* Function prototype: */

void function_1(void);

int main(void)  {
      . . . . . . . . . . . . . . . . .
      . . . . . . . . . . . . . . . . .
      /* Function call; */
      function_1();
      . . . . . . . . . . . . . . . . .
      . . . . . . . . . . . . . . . . .
}   /* end function main*/
```

Global variables:    i        j        k

Global variables:    i        j        k

```
void function_1(void) {
      . . . . . . . . . . . . . . . . .
      . . . . . . . . . . . . . . . . .
}   /* end function function_1*/
```

**Figure 6.16**    Data communication between functions using global variables

2.  By returning a value under a function name

3.  By using parameters

Data communication between two functions is possible if they can both access some common variables. Figure 6.16 shows a main function and another function named function_1 that the main function invokes. Three global variables, i, j, and k, are declared in the source file and act like channels of communication between the two functions. Any change made in the value of a global variable by one function will be "felt" by the other as well. All functions in a source file can access global variables. Therefore, we can use global variables for passing values to a function and returning values from it.

However, using global variables for data communication purposes has certain drawbacks:

1.  The reader of the program does not immediately know which values are being received by the called function and which values are being returned by it.

2.  Values that are sent to the called function are not protected against changes inadvertently made in the called function.

3.  One of the most important advantages of functions is that they can be used to implement the concept of isolated and independent modules. If they are allowed to access global variables, this independence is largely compromised.

4.  A function based on global variables is not generally reusable. In other words, it becomes difficult to use such a function in other programs even if it appears to be suitable.

Therefore, you should avoid using global variables in passing values to functions in modular programs. Instead, you should use parameters to send values to a called function and use the function name to return a value from it.

We have already seen that a nonvoid function can return a value under its name to a function that calls it. If a function requires data to be passed to it by the calling function and if we are not to use global variables for this purpose, then we must resort to function parameters. To use function parameters for data communication, you must learn how to define and declare functions with parameters and how to call functions with parameters.

## Defining Functions with Parameters

In section 6.3 we mentioned that a function definition consists of a function type, a function name, a list of formal parameters enclosed in parentheses, and a compound statement, which is the function body. Following is its format:

> *TypeSpecifier FunctionName* ( *FormalParameterList* ) *CompoundStatement*

You already know about function type specifiers, function name, and function body. The new element here is the formal parameter list.

> **Formal parameters** of a function are variables declared in the formal parameter list of the function header. They are used to send values to the function, return values from it, or both.

An example of a function with a formal parameter was given in Figure 6.15. Its definition begins with `void process_request(int request_code)`. Here the variable `request_code` is a formal parameter for the function `process_request`. The declaration of `request_code` is made in the function header inside the parentheses, whereas the declarations of other variables that the function may use must be inside the function body.

A function may have any number of parameters. If it has more than one, the declarations must be separated by commas in the formal parameter list. For example, `double` `expo(double x, double y)` is the header in a function definition for a function called `expo` with two formal parameters, `x` and `y`, both of type `double`. In this example the function itself has a type specifier `double`, meaning that it must return a floating-point value to the calling function.

C supports two types of formal parameters:

1. **Value parameters**, which are used only to send values to functions
2. **Pointer parameters**, which are suitable for sending values to and/or returning values from functions

Accordingly, in C, parameters may be passed by value or by pointers. In this chapter you will learn about parameter passing by value. Parameter passing by pointers is explored in Chapter 10.

## Declaring Functions with Parameters

We know that, in general, all functions in a C program except the function `main` must be declared using function prototypes. If the declared function has formal parameters in its definition, its prototype must also have parameter declarations. For example, in Figure 6.15 the function prototype

```
void process_request(int request_code);
```

is the declaration of the function `process_request`. This declaration informs the compiler that the function `process_request` is a `void` function and that it has one integer parameter. The variable `request_code` in this prototype is optional. Instead, we could have written

```
void process_request(int r);
```

or simply

```
void process_request(int);
```

However, it is better—from a program readability point of view—to use descriptive identifiers for parameters in function prototypes, since they may tell the reader more about the nature of the parameters.

If a function has more than one formal parameter, this information must be reflected in its prototype by including appropriate type specifiers in parentheses. For example, for the function `expo` in the preceding section, the prototype can be written as

```
double expo(double x, double y);
```

## Calling Functions with Parameters

We have used function calls before, and we know that if the function being called has no parameters, a call to it consists of the name of the function followed by the function call operator `()`. If the function has formal parameters, then its call must have actual parameters.

> **Actual parameters** (or **arguments**) are constants, variables, or expressions in a function call that correspond to its formal parameters.

For example, in Figure 6.15 we have a call to the function `process_request`:

```
process_request(request_code);
```

This call will pass the program control to `process_request`. At the same time it will make a copy of the content of `request_code` in the formal parameter `request_code`. We can use a constant value as an actual parameter in a function call:

```
process_request(1);
```

Also, an expression may be a legitimate actual parameter:

```
process_request(request_code - 1);
```

In this case the value passed to the function `process_request` is the value of `request_code` less 1.

If we call a function that has more than one formal parameter, we must supply the same number of actual parameters whose types are compatible with those of formal parameters. For example, to call the function `expo` with the header `double expo(double x, double y)`, we may write

```
t = expo(1.2, a + 5.5);
```

While this call passes the program control to the function `expo`, it makes a copy of the constant value `1.2`, the first actual parameter, in `x`, the first formal parameter. Also, the computer computes the value of the expression `a + 5.5`, which is the second actual parameter, and sends this value to the second formal parameter, `y`. The function then completes its task and returns a floating-point value, which is stored in the variable `t` in the calling function.

## Correspondence of Actual and Formal Parameters

Three important points concerning functions with parameters are the number, order, and type of actual parameters in function calls.

1.   The number of actual parameters in a function call must be the same as the number of formal parameters in the function definition.

2.   A one-to-one correspondence must occur among the actual and formal parameters. The first actual parameter must correspond to the first formal parameter, the second to the second formal parameter, and so on.

3.   The type of each actual parameter must be either the same as that of the corresponding formal parameter or a type that the compiler can convert to the type of the latter.

For example, if the header for a function definition is `void print_logos(char logo_type, int size)`, the function call

```
print_logos('c', 44);
```

is correct. However, the function call

```
print_logos(12.5, 44);
```

is incorrect, since the first actual parameter is a floating-point constant instead of a character value.

## 6.9   PARAMETER PASSING BY VALUE

If the formal parameters in a function are declared as regular variables, and not as pointer variables (which you will study in Chapter 10), then the compiler understands that you intend to pass parameters by value. As we have seen, pass by value has certain implications:

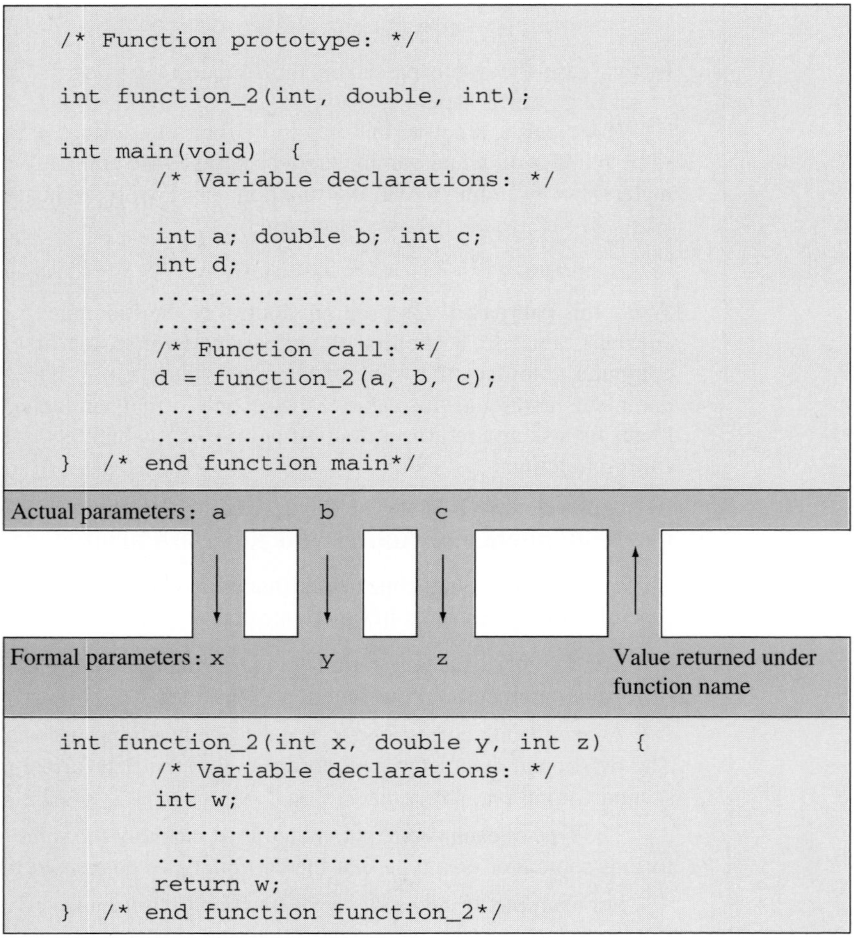

**Figure 6.17**    Data communication between functions using function name and function parameters

1.   A function call passes the program control to the function.

2.   During this process, the values of the actual parameters are copied to the memory locations of the corresponding formal parameters in the called function's data area.

3.   After the function completes its task, the program control is returned to the calling function. At the same time, if the function is intended to return a value to the calling function under its name, this process also occurs. However, the values of the formal parameters are not copied back to their corresponding actual parameters.

This last point is important. It means that even if the called function makes changes in the values of its formal parameters, these changes will not be reflected in the actual parameters in the calling function. Therefore, they are protected against changes. It also means that we can use value parameters only to send values to functions, and not to receive values from them.

Figure 6.17 shows two partial C functions, a function `main` and a function `function_2` defined with the header `int function_2(int x, double y, int z)`. A function call such as

```
d = function_2(a, b, c);
```

in the main program is conceptually equivalent to establishing three communication channels among the actual and formal parameters as shown in the figure. The first channel enables the function call to send a value of the variable `a` to the formal parameter `x`, the second is for the pair `b` and `y`, and the third is for `c` and `z`. These channels are all one-way, from the calling to the called function. Therefore, they are input channels for the function `function_2`. In addition, there is one output channel from `function_2` to the function `main`, which is used to return a value under the function name.

Let us now summarize what you have learned about parameter passing by value.

---

### Rules for Parameter Passing by Value

1.   In parameter passing by value, the actual and formal parameters must be of similar types.

2.   The formal parameters must be declared in the function definition as regular variables, not as pointer variables.

3.   The actual parameters in function calls can be constants, variables, or expressions.

4.   At the time the program control passes to the called function, a copy of the value of each actual parameter is made in the memory location for the corresponding formal parameter. Any changes made by the called function on this copy will not be reflected in the corresponding actual parameter. Therefore, parameter passing by value can be used only for sending values to a called function.

5.   Because the called function cannot access the memory location of the actual parameters in the data area of the calling function, the actual parameters are protected against inadvertent alterations. Hence, to send data to functions, parameter passing by value should be preferred to other methods of parameter passing.

We conclude this section with an example that deals with Fibonacci numbers. Our task is to write a main function and a programmer-defined function called fibonacci. The purpose of fibonacci is to compute and return a requested member of the Fibonacci sequence. The **Fibonacci sequence** is a sequence of positive integers in which the first member is 0, the second is 1, and all other members are computed by adding the previous two members. Therefore, the first 10 members of the sequence are 0, 1, 1, 2, 3, 5, 8, 13, 21, and 34. Fibonacci numbers are important in many applications in computer science.

In the program of Figure 6.18, we have a function fibonacci, which receives a value through a formal parameter and returns the computed Fibonacci number under the function's name.

```c
#include <stdio.h>

/* Function prototypes: */

int fibonacci(int sequence_number);

int main(void) {
      int sequence_number;
      printf("What Fibonacci number? Enter a positive integer: ");
      scanf("%d", &sequence_number);

      printf("The %dth Fibonacci number is: %d", sequence_number,
            fibonacci(sequence_number));
      return 0;
} /* end function main */

/*.............................................................
Purpose : Computes the Fibonacci number corresponding to a given
          sequence number.
Receives: seq_number
Returns : Fibonacci number under function name
*/
int fibonacci(int seq_number) {
      int first = 0, second = 1, count = 3, fib_number;

      /* Function body: */

      if (seq_number == 1)
            fib_number = first;
      else if (seq_number == 2)
            fib_number = second;
      /* end if */
```

**Figure 6.18**    A program that computes Fibonacci numbers (*continued*)    ▶

```
        while (count <= seq_number) {
                fib_number = first + second;
                first = second;
                second = fib_number;
                count = count + 1;
        } /* end while */

        return fib_number;
} /* end function fibonacci */
```

Figure 6.18                                                                    ■

Let us briefly explain the logic of `fibonacci`. It has one value parameter, the integer variable `seq_number`. The calling function passes a value to `fibonacci` through its actual parameter, and that value is available to `fibonacci` in `seq_number`. In the function we declare four integer variables, `first`, `second`, `count`, and `fib_number`. The variable called `first` is intended initially to stand for the first element of the Fibonacci sequence and is assigned the value of 0. The variable `second` is the second element of the Fibonacci sequence and is initialized to 1. The variable `count` is a loop control variable. The `if` statement in the function sets `fib_number` to `first` (that is, 0) if `seq_number` is equal to 1 and to `second` (that is 1) if `seq_number` is equal to 2. In either of these cases, because `count` is greater than `seq_number`, the `while` loop that comes next will not be executed and the program control will go back to the function `main`. At that point we have the correct value stored in the variable `fib_number`, and the function will return the value of this variable under the function's name.

On the other hand, if the value of `seq_number` is greater than 2, the `if` statement will have no effect and we get into the `while` loop. In this loop the assignment statement

```
        fib_number = first + second;
```

will compute the next number in the Fibonacci sequence. The statements

```
        first = second;
        second = fib_number;
```

will store the previous member of the sequence (that is, the value in `second`) in the variable `first` and the current value of `fib_number` in the variable `second`. With these assignments we are getting prepared for the next cycle of repetition of the `while` loop. Following this step, we increment the loop control variable `count` by 1:

```
        count = count + 1;
```

Now, if the value of `count` is still less than or equal to the value of `seq_number`, the `while` loop will execute once again; otherwise, the loop will terminate and the program control will go back to the function `main`. At the same time the function will return the value of `fib_number`, using the `return` statement

```
        return fib_number;
```

## Passing Strings to Functions Through Parameters

You began learning about strings in Chapter 3, and since then, we have been using them in some simple applications. Soon we will need to communicate strings to functions through function parameters. In this chapter we have studied passing fundamental data types to functions as value parameters. Strings can also be passed to functions as parameters. In this section we will introduce the subject in a simple form and discuss it in greater detail in Chapter 13.

Suppose we have a string variable declared as a character array in our program:

```
char student_name[31];
```

Further, suppose we have a simple function called `print_name` with one string parameter, `stu_name`. Here is how such a function can be defined:

```
void print_name(char stu_name[]) {
      printf("%s", stu_name);
} /* end function print_name */
```

The prototype for this function can be

```
void print_name(char stu_name[]);
```

and a typical function call is

```
print_name(student_name);
```

In this example the parameter declaration for the string variable `stu_name`, `char stu_name[]`, is similar to the declaration of the string `student_name` except for its name and the lack of the array size in brackets. We already know that the name of the formal parameter can be different from that of the corresponding actual parameter. As a rule, in C, when a string that is represented as a character array is declared as a formal parameter, the left and right brackets must follow the name of the string; however, the array size information must be missing. The same rule applies to the declaration of string parameters in function prototypes.

In calls to functions with string parameters, the actual parameter, if it is a string variable, must be the name of the string variable with no brackets and size information, as in the preceding example.

It must be stated here that strings in C cannot be passed by value to functions. The only way they can be passed is by pointers. We will have more to say about this subject in Chapters 10 and 13. For the time being, that much will suffice for our applications.

## 6.10   STORAGE CLASSES, SCOPE, VISIBILITY, AND DURATION OF VARIABLES

So far in this chapter, we have seen that, depending on where they are declared, variables in a modular program can be global, local, or formal parameter variables. **Global variables** are variables that are declared outside function definitions; **local variables** are declared in function definitions, and **formal parameter variables** are declared in the formal parameter list of function definitions. Also, no matter where a variable is declared, it is associated with a data type.

Where a variable is declared in a program provides information about

1.   The region in the program in which it can be used legitimately, that is, its scope.

2.   A program's ability to access that variable's memory location, that is, its visibility.

3.   The time during which a memory location exists for that variable, that is, its duration.

4.   Where it is located in the main memory at run time.

### Storage Classes of Variables

In addition to type, each variable in C also has a storage class. The **storage class** of a variable determines its visibility, duration, and location. There are several storage classes for variables, identified by the keywords auto, register, static, and extern. The storage classes register and extern are outside the scope of this book. Variables with storage class specifiers static and auto are referred to as **static variables** and **automatic variables,** respectively.

Storage classes for variables can be explicitly specified in their declarations by preceding the type specifier by one of these storage class specifiers, as in

```
static int a;
```

which declares the variable a as a static variable of type int. Variables of storage class static are allocated memory locations that exist during the execution of the program in which they are declared. On the other hand, automatic variables are reserved memory locations that exist only during the execution of the function in which they are declared. All global variables are static, and all local variables and function formal parameters are automatic by default. For example, in the function fibonacci of Figure 6.18, the local variables first, second, count, and fib_number and the function parameter seq_number are all automatic variables. Storage locations for them are in existence only while the function fibonacci is being executed. When the program control is in the function main, these variables do not exist in the memory.

Since all global variables are static by default, in general, it is not necessary to use the storage class specifier static in their declarations. Static variables are automatically initialized at the time they are allocated storage. Numeric static variables (of types int, double, float, and so on) are initialized to zero; and character static variables are initialized to null. Although static variables are initialized automatically, we recommend that you initialize your variables explicitly in the program, and not rely on the compiler to do automatic initializations. Also, you should note that global variables cannot be declared as automatic variables.

Because local function variables and function formal parameters are automatic by default, in their declarations the use of the storage class specifier auto is redundant. Automatic variables are not automatically initialized by the compiler. You must assign initial values to them using either compile-time or run-time initialization.

It is possible to declare local function variables (but not function formal parameters) as variables of static storage class. In this case the keyword static must be explicit in the declarations. Just like static global variables, a static local variable is allocated a memory location that is in existence during the execution of the entire program, and such a variable is automatically initialized. An application that uses a static local variable could be one in which we are interested in the number of times a programmer-defined function is executed. For example, we can modify the function draw_rectangle of Figure 6.4 as shown in Figure 6.19.

```
void draw_rectangle(void) {
        static int no_of_execs = 0;

        printf("+---------------+\n");
        printf("|               |\n");
        printf("|               |\n");
        printf("|               |\n");
        printf("+---------------+\n");

        no_of_execs++;
        printf("This is the %dth rectangle drawn.\n", no_of_execs);
} /* end function draw_rectangle */
```

**Figure 6.19**     A function that keeps track of the number of times it is called

The version of draw_rectangle shown in Figure 6.19 contains a local variable, no_of_execs of type int, declared as a static variable. Because this variable is static, it is allocated a memory location that exists even when the program control is outside the function draw_rectangle. The variable no_of_execs is initialized to zero at compile-time. Every time the function is called, the variable is incremented by one because of the expression no_of_execs++ in the function body. With an automatic local variable, the value of no_of_execs printed by the last output statement in Figure 6.19 would always be 1.

## Scope of Variables

In C, before we can use a program variable, we must declare it. By declaring a variable we define a certain region in the program. This region is known as that variable's scope.

> The **scope** of a variable is the region in which it can be used legitimately.

The scope of any variable begins at the point of its declaration. Where it ends depends on where and how it is declared. In block-structured languages the end of the scope for a variable is the end of the block in which it is declared. C is a block-structured language in that programs written in it consist of blocks. A block in C is essentially a compound statement defined by braces, { }.

A global variable's scope begins at the point of its declaration and terminates at the end of the file. Hence global variables are said to have **file scope**. On the other hand, the scope of a local variable, whether static or automatic, begins at the point of its declaration and extends until the end of the block that contains it. Such a scope is called **block** (or **local**) **scope**.

Formal function parameters are local to the function in which they are declared. In fact, the only difference between formal function parameters and local function variables is that the former are declared in the function parameter list and the latter in the function body. Therefore, the scope of formal function parameters is the same as the scope of local variables, beginning at the point where they are declared and extending until the end of the function. This scope is called **parameter scope**. For example, in Figure 6.18 the local variables `first`, `second`, `count`, and `fib_number` in the function `fibonacci` have local scope, which is the function `fibonacci`; that means they can be used only in the function `fibonacci`. The scope of the formal parameter `seq_number` is also the function `fibonacci`.

## Multiple Declarations of Variables and Visibility

Another consideration that is closely related to scope is visibility.

> **Visibility** of a variable is a program's ability to access that variable's memory location.

To better understand scope and visibility, let us consider the program of Figure 6.20, which computes the sum of odd and even integers between one and an integer `limit` entered by the user. This program also computes the sum of all integers between one and `limit`. Note that the program consists of a single function `main`, and it contains a block defined by a compound statement between lines 13 and 23.

```
1   #include <stdio.h>

2   int main(void) {
3       int limit, count = 1, sum_of_odd = 0, sum_of_all;

4       printf("Enter an integer: ");
5       scanf("%d", &limit);

6       while (count <= limit) {
7               if (count % 2)
8                       sum_of_odd += count;
9               /* end if */

10              count++;
11      } /* end while */

12      printf("%d\n", sum_of_odd);

13      {
14              int count = 1, sum_of_even = 0;

15              while (count <= limit) {
16                      if (count %2 == 0)
17                              sum_of_even += count;
18                      /* end if */

19                      count++;
20              } /* end while */

21              printf("%d\n", sum_of_even);

22              sum_of_all = sum_of_odd + sum_of_even;
23      }

24      printf("%d\n", sum_of_all);

25      return 0;
26  } /* end function main */
```

**Figure 6.20**    A C program that contains a block

The table of Figure 6.21 shows the scope and visibility of the variables in the program of Figure 6.20. In Figure 6.20 all variables are automatic local variables. The variables limit, count, sum_of_odd, and sum_of_all, declared in line 3, are local to the function `main`. The variables `count` and `sum_of_even`, declared in line 14, are local to the block in lines 13 through 23. As you can see, we can have multiple declarations for variables in a function; the variable `count` is declared once in line 3 and once again in line 14. However, such variables must have different **name spaces;** that is, they must be declared in different blocks. Multiple declarations in the same name space are invalid and produce compilation errors. The variable `count`, declared in line 3, is in the name space defined by the body of the function `main`; but this name space excludes the name spaces defined by other compound statements in the function `main`. The name space of the variable `count`, declared in line 14, is the compound statement in lines 13 through 23. It is important to realize that such variables are allocated different memory locations, and although they have the same name and even the same type, they are treated as different variables. In other words, the memory locations for a variable with multiple declarations are distinct, and the computer will access the appropriate location depending on where your program is trying to access it.

| Variable | Declared at Line | Scope | Visibility Zone | Invisibility Zone in Variable's Scope |
|---|---|---|---|---|
| `limit` | 3 | Lines 3 – 26 | Lines 3 – 26 | None |
| `count` | 3 | Lines 3 – 26 | Lines 3 – 12, 24 – 26 | Lines 14 – 23 |
| `sum_of_odd` | 3 | Lines 3 – 26 | Lines 3 – 26 | None |
| `sum_of_all` | 3 | Lines 3 – 26 | Lines 3 – 26 | None |
| `count` | 14 | Lines 14 – 23 | Lines 14 – 23 | None |
| `sum_of_even` | 14 | Lines 14 – 23 | Lines 14 – 23 | None |

**Figure 6.21**   Scope and visibility of the variables in the program of Figure 6.20

Provided there is only one declaration for a variable, it is always visible in its scope. For example, in Figure 6.20 the variables `limit`, `sum_of_odd`, and `sum_of_all` are visible in their scope, which is lines 3 through 26. Also, the variable `sum_of_even` is visible in its scope, lines 14 through 23.

If we include a declaration for a variable in a block that is contained in the scope of another variable of the same name, the latter loses its visibility and becomes hidden inside the scope of the former. After exiting this scope, the hidden variable becomes visible again. For example, in Figure 6.20 declaring `count` in line 14 renders the variable `count` declared in line 3 invisible in lines 14 through 23. After line 23 the variable `count`, declared in line 3, becomes visible until the end of its own scope.

Now let us consider a modular version of the program of Figure 6.20, as shown in Figure 6.22. We artificially introduce a global variable, `count`, into this program in line 4, but never use it. It will help us illustrate the concept of visibility in this example.

```
1    #include <stdio.h>

2    int sum_of_odd_values(int limit);
3    int sum_of_even_values(int limit);

4    int count;

5    int main(void) {
6        int limit, sum_of_odd, sum_of_even, sum_of_all;

7        printf("Enter an integer: ");
8        scanf("%d", &limit);

9        sum_of_odd = sum_of_odd_values(limit);
10       printf("%d\n", sum_of_odd);

11       sum_of_even = sum_of_even_values(limit);
12       printf("%d\n", sum_of_even);

13       sum_of_all = sum_of_odd + sum_of_even;
14       printf("%d\n", sum_of_all);

15       return 0;
16   } /* end function main */


17   int sum_of_odd_values(int limit) {
18       int count = 1, sum_of_odd = 0;

19       while (count <= limit) {
20           if (count % 2)
21               sum_of_odd += count;
22           /* end if */

23           count++;
24       } /* end while */

25       return sum_of_odd;
26       } /* end function sum_of_odd_values */

27   int sum_of_even_values(int limit) {
28       int count = 1, sum_of_even = 0;
```

**Figure 6.22**    A modular version of the program of Figure 6.20 (*continued*) ▶

```
29        while (count <= limit) {
30              if (count %2 == 0)
31                    sum_of_even += count;
32              /* end if */

33              count++;
34        } /* end while */

35        return sum_of_even;
36  } /* end function sum_of_even_values */
```

Figure 6.22

Figure 6.23 describes the scope and visibility of the variables in the program of Figure 6.22. We have multiple declarations for the variable count, once in line 4 as a global variable, once in line 18 as a local variable of the function sum_of_odd_values, and once more in line 28 as a local variable of the function sum_of_even_values. Therefore, although the scope of the global count extends until line 36, it becomes invisible in the scopes of the other two variables of the same name. The variable limit also has multiple declarations in lines 6, 17, and 27. However, these declarations are for three distinct variables of the same name with nonoverlapping scopes, and therefore, they are visible in their own scopes. Similarly, the variables sum_of_odd and sum_of_even are also declared twice as variables with nonoverlapping scopes.

| Variable | Declared at Line | Scope | Visibility Zone | Invisibility Zone in Variable's Scope |
| --- | --- | --- | --- | --- |
| count | 4 | Lines 4 – 36 | Lines 4 – 17, 26 – 27 | Lines 18 – 25, 28 – 36 |
| limit | 6 | Lines 6 – 16 | Lines 6 – 16 | None |
| sum_of_odd | 6 | Lines 6 – 16 | Lines 6 – 16 | None |
| sum_of_even | 6 | Lines 6 – 16 | Lines 6 – 16 | None |
| sum_of_all | 6 | Lines 6 – 16 | Lines 6 – 16 | None |
| limit | 17 | Lines 17 – 26 | Lines 17 – 26 | None |
| count | 18 | Lines 18 – 26 | Lines 18 – 26 | None |
| sum_of_odd | 18 | Lines 18 – 26 | Lines 18 – 26 | None |
| limit | 27 | Lines 27 – 36 | Lines 27 – 36 | None |
| count | 28 | Lines 28 – 36 | Lines 28 – 36 | None |
| sum_of_odd | 28 | Lines 28 – 36 | Lines 28 – 36 | None |

Figure 6.23      Scope and visibility of the variables in the program of Figure 6.22

## Duration of Variables

In addition to scope and visibility of variables, another related consideration deals with what happens at run time to the memory locations allocated to variables. We know that at run time a memory location is reserved for each declared variable. Depending on how declarations are made, such memory locations exist for a certain period. That period is known as a variable's duration.

> **Duration** (or **lifetime**) of a variable is the time during which a memory location exists for that variable at run time.

C, supports three kinds of duration: static, local, and dynamic. We know that global variables are of storage class `static` by default, and they are reserved memory locations as soon as the program execution begins. These locations exist in the memory in fixed data segments until the termination of the program. Therefore, global variables are said to have **static duration**.

On the other hand, variables with local scope, which are variables of `automatic` storage class by default, are allocated memory locations when the object code corresponding to the enclosing block or function is encountered during execution. The memory locations for such variables are in existence until the end of that block or function; afterward, they cease to exist. These variables have **local duration**. If local variables are declared to be of storage class `static`, as in the function of Figure 6.19, like global variables, they will have static duration.

Finally, there are variables that are created and destroyed by using special functions at run time. These variables are called **dynamic variables**, and they are said to have **dynamic duration**. We cover dynamic variables in Chapter 11.

> ### Summary of Scope, Visibility, and Duration Rules
>
> 1. A global variable is of storage class `static` by default. The scope of such a variable begins at the point of its declaration and extends until the end of the source program file. Therefore, a global variable has file scope and static duration.
>
> 2. The scope of a local variable begins at the point it is declared and extends until the end of the block in which it is declared. The scope of a formal parameter is the function for which it is declared. Local variables and function formal parameters have block scope and local duration.
>
> 3. If a local variable is declared to be of storage class `static`, although its scope is confined to the block in which it is declared, it will have static duration.
>
> 4. All variables are visible in their scope, provided they are declared only once.
>
> 5. If a global variable is declared again in a function as a local variable, it loses its visibility in the scope of the local variable. Similarly, if a variable that has a declaration in a block is declared again in a nested inner block, the original variable becomes invisible in the scope of the redeclared variable.

## REVIEW QUESTIONS

**1.** Data communication between two functions is possible if there are some variables that can be accessed by both. (T or F)

**2.** Functions can communicate data
   **a.** Through global variables.
   **b.** By returning a value under a function name.
   **c.** By using parameters.
   **d.** All of the above.
   **e.** None of the above.

**3.** One of the disadvantages of letting functions communicate through global variables is that values sent to functions are not protected against changes by called functions. (T or F)

**4.** Which of the following concerning function formal parameters is *incorrect*?
   **a.** They are used to send data to the function and/or to return values from it.
   **b.** They may be constants, variables, or expressions.
   **c.** They have the same scope as variables that are local to the function.
   **d.** They are visible only in the function body.

**5.** In parameter passing by value,
   **a.** Actual and formal parameters must be of similar types.
   **b.** Formal parameters must be declared in the function definition as pointer variables.
   **c.** Actual parameters in a function call cannot be constants or expressions; they must be variables.

**d.** Parameter passing by value can be used both for sending data to and receiving data from functions.

**e.** All of the above are correct.

**f.** None of the above is correct.

**6.** Choose the *incorrect* statement.

**a.** When the compiler comes across a function call, it generates a jump to the main memory segment that is used to store the executable load module for that function.

**b.** After the function is executed, there is another jump back to the load module of the calling function.

**c.** The executable load module of the called function is stored only once and is not duplicated in the main memory.

**d.** The number of function calls has no negative effect on the execution time of a program.

**7.** Global variables

**a.** Are of storage class `static` by default.

**b.** Are automatically initialized at the time they are allocated storage.

**c.** Cannot be declared as automatic variables.

**d.** All of the above are correct.

**e.** None of the above is correct.

**8.** Which of the following statements is *incorrect*?

**a.** The scope of a global variable begins at the point of its declaration and terminates at the end of the source program file.

**b.** Global variables are visible in all blocks in the source program file that follow their declarations.

**c.** A variable that is declared in a block is a local variable, and its scope is called local scope.

**d.** If there is only one declaration for a variable, it is always visible in its scope.

**e.** The time during which a memory location exists for a variable at run time is called its duration.

**Answers:**    1. T; 2. d; 3. T; 4. b; 5. a; 6. d; 7. d; 8. b.

---

## 6.11    EXAMPLE PROGRAM 4: A Modular C Program that Computes Federal Income Tax Using Tax Rate Schedules

In Chapter 2 you learned about top-down stepwise refinement as an algorithm design technique. We applied this technique to the problem of computing income tax from the tax rate schedules and finally ended up with the pseudocode algorithm of Figure 2.10. At that time, since you did not yet know enough C, you could not implement this algorithm as a C program. We had to wait until Chapter 4, where we developed Example Program 1 as its implementation. This program, which is given in Figure 4.17, is fine, but it is monolithic. It is somewhat lengthy and therefore hard to read. Had this been an even more complex application, we would have had an unacceptably long program in our hands.

In this section we will consider the same problem and design it as a modular program. Essentially, we will do the same thing and apply top-down stepwise refinement in designing its algorithm. However, after the final refinement of each subproblem, instead of combining them in one pseudocode, we will leave them as separate modules. We will assign a name to each module and identify the data it should receive and the data it should generate and return. Finally, we will combine all the modules in a program structure under the control of a main program.

### Designing a Modular Program Using Top-Down Stepwise Refinement

We begin with an initial pseudocode algorithm that is slightly different from that given in Figure 2.5. The differences are as follows:

1.  In this pseudocode algorithm, instead of describing a subproblem as in *read and verify income*, we assume that there is a module called *entered_gross_income*, whose task is to read and verify the value typed by the user for *income*, and replace the preceding pseudocode statement with *set income to entered_gross_income*.

2.  Similarly, instead of the subproblem *read and verify filing status*, we write *set status to entered_filing_status*, where *entered_filing_status* is a module that reads and verifies the value provided for the variable *filing_status*.

3.  The pseudocode statement *compute tax* of Figure 2.5 is replaced by *set tax to computed_tax*, where *computed_tax* is a module that computes the federal income tax using values for *income* and *filing_status* and returns it to be saved in the variable *tax*.

4.  The pseudocode statement *print income, filing status, and tax* is replaced by *call output_results*. Here, *output_results* is a module that requires values for *income, filing_status*, and *tax* and prints them on the monitor screen.

Hence the initial pseudocode becomes

*set income to entered_gross_income*
*call print_status_menu*
*set filing_status to entered_ filing_status*
*set tax to computed_tax*
*call output_results*

Here, in addition to the modules *entered_gross_income*, *entered_ filing_status*, *computed_tax*, and *output_results*, we have the module *print_status_menu*, which prints the filing status menu.

Let us concentrate on the module *output_results*. We can write the following pseudocode:

*output_results(income, filing_status, tax):*
  *print income*
  *call print_status*
  *print tax*

In this algorithm the first and last *print* statements are straightforward steps. The second statement, *call print_status*, is a call to a module *print_status* whose task is to print a verbal description of the filing status.

What do we have so far? We have six modules, each with a distinct task: *entered_gross_income*, *print_status_menu*, *entered_filing_status*, *computed_tax*, *output_results*, and *print_status*. Also, there has to be a main module that executes these modules in a specific order and ultimately produces the solution of the problem. Let us call this module *main_program*. The logic of the *main_program* is actually the initial pseudocode given earlier. Figure 6.24 is a structure chart that shows these seven modules, the order in which they are executed, and the nature of module invocations. In view of this chart, we will refine the modules in six steps. Because these refinements are similar to those given in Chapter 2, we will not explain them in detail; you are already familiar with them. In each case we will also specify data to be received and returned by each module.

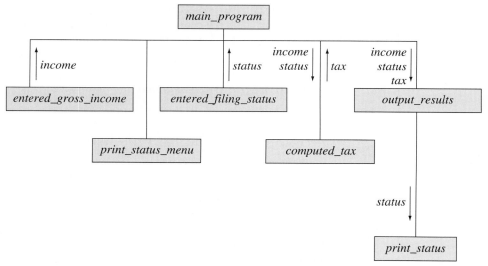

**Figure 6.24**   Structure chart for the modular program to compute federal income tax using rate schedules

**Step 1.** The final pseudocode for the module *entered_gross_income* is given in Figure 6.25. This module does not need any data. It should, however, return the value of the variable *income* to the main module that calls it.

---

*entered_gross_income:*
    *print "Enter taxable income; "*
    *print "should be greater than or equal to $50,000:"*
    *read gross_income*

---

**Figure 6.25**   Pseudocode algorithm for module *entered_gross_income* (continued)   ▶

```
while gross_income is less than $50,000
    begin
        print "Enter taxable income; "
        print "should be greater than or equal to $50,000:"
        read gross_income
    end
end_while

return gross_income
```

Figure 6.25

**Step 2.** Figure 6.26 is the pseudocode algorithm for the module *print_status_menu*. It does not receive or return any data. All it does is print the filing status menu.

```
print_status_menu:
    print "FILING STATUS MENU:"
    print "Single                      ---- 1"
    print "Married filing jointly      ---- 2"
    print "Married filing separately   ---- 3"
    print "Head of household           ---- 4"
```

Figure 6.26    Pseudocode algorithm for module *print_status_menu*

**Step 3.** The pseudocode algorithm for the module *entered_filing_status* is given in Figure 6.27. It does not receive any data, but should return *filing_status* to a calling module.

```
entered_filing_status:
    set correctStatusInput to "no"

    while correctStatusInput is equal to "no"
        begin
            print "Enter filing status; should be between 1 and 4:"
            read filing_status
```

Figure 6.27    Pseudocode algorithm for module *entered_filing_status* (continued)

*if filing_status is greater than 0*
  *if filing_status is less than 5*
   *set correctStatusInput to "yes"*
  *end_if*
 *end_if*

 *end*
*end_while*

*return filing_status*

Figure 6.27

&#9632;

**Step 4**.  Figure 6.28 is the pseudocode algorithm for the module *computed_tax*. This module receives the values of *income* and *filing_status* and then computes and returns *tax* to a calling function.

*computed_tax(income, filing_status):*
 *if filing_status is 1*
  *compute tax = 11158.50 + 0.31 × (income − 49300.00)*
 *else if filing_status is 2*
  *if income is less than or equal to 82,150*
   *compute tax = 5100.00 + 0.28 × (income − 34000.00)*
  *else*
   *compute tax = 18582.00 + 0.31 × (income − 82150.00)*
  *end_if*
 *else if filing_status is 3*
  *compute tax = 9291.00 + 0.31 × (income − 41075.00)*
 *else if filing_status is 4*
  *if income is less than or equal to 70450.00*
   *compute tax = 4095.00 + 0.28 × (income − 27300.00)*
  *else*
   *compute tax = 16177.00 + 0.31 × (income − 70450.00)*
  *end_if*
 *end_if*

 *return tax*

Figure 6.28 Pseudocode algorithm for module *computed_tax*

**Step 5.** The pseudocode algorithm for the module *output_results* was given before early in this section, during our analysis of the required modules, and is shown again in Figure 6.29. Its receives values for *income*, *status*, and *tax* and does not return any data.

---

*output_results(income, filing_status, tax):*
    *print income*
    *call print_status*
    *print tax*

---

**Figure 6.29**     Pseudocode algorithm for module *output_results*

**Step 6.** The next module is *print_status*. Its pseudocode is given in Figure 6.30. It receives the value of *filing_status* and does not return any data.

---

*print_status(filing_status):*
    *if filing_status is equal to 1*
        *print "Single"*
    *else if filing_status is equal to 2*
        *print "Married filing jointly"*
    *else if filing_status is equal to 3*
        *print "Married filing separately"*
    *else if filing_status is equal to 4*
        *print "Head of household"*
    *end_if*

---

**Figure 6.30**     Pseudocode algorithm for module *print_status*

## Implementing a Modular Program in C Using Bottom-Up Development

Because you have acquired a sufficient background about C functions, we are now in a position to implement the modular system that we designed in the previous section. In the implementation we will start with the modules at the lowest level of hierarchy in the structure chart of Figure 6.24 and proceed in a left-to-right, bottom-to-top manner; hence the term bottom-up development.

**Step 1.** The implementation of the pseudocode of Figure 6.30 for the module *print_status* is shown in Figure 6.31. Here the function `print_status` is not expected to return a value under its name. Therefore, its type is `void`. It needs the value of the variable `status` to perform its task and has one formal parameter. Its body consists of an output statement and a nested `if` statement.

```
/*******************************************************************
  Function Name     : print_status
  Purpose           : Prints a verbal description of the filing status
                      for a given status value on the screen.
  Called by         : output_results
  Receives          : status
  Returns           : None
 *******************************************************************/
void print_status(int status) {
     printf("   Filing Status : ");

     if (status == 1)
          printf("Single");
     else if (status == 2)
          printf("Married filing jointly");
     else if (status == 3)
          printf("Married filing separately");
     else if (status == 4)
          printf("Head of household");
     /* end if */
} /* end function print_status */
```

**Figure 6.31**    C implementation of the function `print_status`

**Step 2.** The C version of `output_results` is given in Figure 6.32. This function does not return any data. Therefore, its type is `void`. All data that it receives are through its parameter list, which consists of `income`, `status`, and `tax`. In its body there is a function call to `print_status` with an actual parameter of `status`.

```
/*******************************************************************
  Function Name     : output_results
  Purpose           : Prints the values of income, status, and
                      computed tax on the screen.
  Called by         : main
  Receives          : income, status, tax
  Returns           : None
 *******************************************************************/
void output_results(double income, int status, double tax) {
     printf("\n");
     printf("RESULTS OF COMPUTATIONS:\n");
     printf("   Taxable income: %f\n", income);
```

**Figure 6.32**    C implementation of the function `output_results` (continued)  ▶

```
      print_status(status);

      printf("\n");
      printf("   Tax             : %f", tax);
} /* end function output_results */
```

Figure 6.32                                                                                      ■

> **Step 3.** Next we consider the pseudocode of Figure 6.25 for *entered_gross_income*.
> Because this module is expected to return the value of income to a calling function,
> its type must be the same as the type of income (that is, double). This module does
> not need to receive any data, and has no formal parameters. The C function correspond-
> ing to this module is in Figure 6.33. Its logic was explained in detail in Chapter 4.

```
/**********************************************************************
  Function Name    : entered_gross_income
  Purpose          : Prompts the user to enter a gross annual income
                     value that is not less than $50,000, reads it,
                     and sends it to the calling program.
  Called by        : main
  Receives         : None
  Returns          : gross_income under function name
**********************************************************************/
double entered_gross_income(void) {
      /* Local variable declarations: */

      double gross_income;

      /* Function body: */

      printf("Enter taxable income; ");
      printf("should be greater than or equal to $50,000: ");
      scanf("%lf", &gross_income);

      while (gross_income < 50000.00) {
            printf("Enter taxable income; ");
            printf("should be greater than or equal to $50,000: ");
            scanf("%lf", &gross_income);
      } /* end while */

      return gross_income;
} /* end function entered_gross_income */
```

**Figure 6.33**   C implementation of the function entered_gross_income

**Step 4.** The implementation of the module *print_status_menu* given in Figure 6.26 is shown in Figure 6.34. Because the module does not receive and return any data, the function type is `void` and its parameter list is empty. Its body consists of a single output statement that displays the menu.

```
/************************************************************
  Function Name    : print_status_menu
  Purpose          : Displays a menu of filing status
                     values on the screen.
  Called by        : main
  Receives         : None
  Returns          : None
 *************************************************************/
void print_status_menu(void) {
     printf("\n");
     printf("************************************\n");
     printf("* FILING STATUS MENU:              *\n");
     printf("* Single                  ---- 1 *\n");
     printf("* Married filing jointly    ---- 2 *\n");
     printf("* Married filing separately ---- 3 *\n");
     printf("* Head of household         ---- 4 *\n");
     printf("************************************\n");
     printf("\n");
} /* end function print_status_menu */
```

**Figure 6.34**    C implementation of the function `print_status_menu`

**Step 5.** Similar to the module `entered_gross_income`, the module `entered_filing_status` requires no data and must return `status` as its only output. The C function corresponding to it (Figure 6.35) is of type `int` because the value that it returns, `filing_status`, is an integer. This function has no formal parameters. Its logic was previously explained in Chapter 4.

```
/**************************************************************************
  Function Name    : entered_filing_status
  Purpose          : Prompts the user to enter a value for filing
                     status, ensures that it is in the correct range
                     of 1 - 4, reads it, and sends it to the calling
                     program.
  Called by        : main
  Receives         : None
  Returns          : filing_status under function name
***************************************************************************/
int entered_filing_status(void) {
     /* Local variable declarations: */

     char correctStatusInput[4] = "no";
     int filing_status;

     /* Function body: */

     while (strcmp(correctStatusInput, "no") == 0) {
         printf("Enter filing status; should be between 1 and 4: ");
         scanf("%d", &filing_status);

         if (filing_status > 0)
               if (filing_status < 5)
                      strcpy(correctStatusInput, "yes");
               /* end if */
         /* end if */
     } /* end while */

     return filing_status;
} /* end function entered_filing_status */
```

**Figure 6.35**   C implementation of the function `entered_filing_status`

**Step 6.** The program of Figure 6.36 is an implementation of *computed_tax*. We have designed this function to receive data through its parameters, `income` and `status`, and to return `tax` under its name. Hence the function type is `double`, same as that of the variable `tax`. The parameter list is `(double income, int status)`, and both `income` and `status` are data received by the function. This function will not change the values of `income` and `status`; it will use them to compute a value for `tax`. Therefore, `income` and `status` are passed by value.

```
/************************************************************************
  Function Name    : computed_tax
  Purpose          : Computes the federal income tax according to
                     the tax rate schedules for a supplied income
                     and status values and then sends the computed tax
                     value to the calling program.
  Called by        : main
  Receives         : income, status
  Returns          : tax under function name
 ************************************************************************/
double computed_tax(double income, int status) {
      /* Local variable declarations: */

      double tax;

      /* Function body: */

      if (status == 1)
           tax = 11158.50 + HIGHRATE * (income - 49300.00);
      else if (status == 2)
           if (income <= 82150.00)
                tax = 5100.00 + LOWRATE * (income - 34000.00);
           else
                tax = 18582.00 + HIGHRATE * (income - 82150.00);
      /* end if */
      else if (status == 3)
           tax = 9291.00 + HIGHRATE * (income - 41075.00);
      else if (status == 4)
           if (income <= 70450.00)
                tax = 4095.00 + LOWRATE * (income - 27300.00);
           else
                tax = 16177.00 + HIGHRATE * (income - 70450.00);
           /* end if */
      /* end if */

      return tax;
} /* end function computed_tax */
```

Figure 6.36    C implementation of the function `computed_tax`

**Step 7.** The implementation of the module `main_program` consists of the necessary preprocessor directives, the function prototypes, and the function `main` as shown in Figure 6.37. The body of the function `main` contains declarations for three program variables: `status`, `income`, and `tax`. The variable `income` is used in the statement

```
income = entered_gross_income();
```

to capture the value returned by the function `entered_gross_income`. The variable `status` appears in the statement

```
status = entered_filing_status();
```

and it stores the value returned by the function `entered_filing_status`. Next, the variables `income` and `status` are used as the actual arguments of the function call to `computed_tax`:

```
tax = computed_tax(income, status);
```

and the returned value is saved in the variable `tax`.

The rest of the function body is a simplified version of the corresponding code in Chapter 4. The main difference is that five function calls replace a major portion of the body of the program in Chapter 4. Function calls not only simplify the implementation of the function `main`, but also make it more understandable.

```
/******************************************************
   Program Filename: Prog06_4.c
   Author          : Uckan
   Purpose         : Computes Federal Income Tax for 1991
                     from Tax Rate Schedules.
   Input from      : Keyboard
   Output to       : Screen
*******************************************************/
#include <stdio.h>
#include <string.h>

const double LOWRATE  = 0.28;
const double HIGHRATE = 0.31;

/* Function prototypes: */

double entered_gross_income(void);
void print_status_menu(void);
int entered_filing_status(void);
double computed_tax(double income, int status);
void output_results(double income, int status, double tax);
void print_status(int status);


int main(void) {
      /* Variable declarations: */
```

**Figure 6.37**    The C main function for the income tax computations software system (*continued*) ▶

```
        int status;
        double income, tax;

        /* Function body: */

        printf("THIS PROGRAM COMPUTES FEDERAL INCOME TAX\n");
        printf("FROM TAX RATE SCHEDULES.\n");

        income = entered_gross_income();
        print_status_menu();
        status = entered_filing_status();
        tax = computed_tax(income, status);
        output_results(income, status, tax);
        return 0;
} /* end function main */
```

Figure 6.37                                                              ■

Now we have a complete modular program that consists of the code of Figure 6.37 followed by the functions of Figures 6.31 through 6.36. It is equivalent to Example Program 4.1, and when compiled and executed, will solve the same problem.

## 6.12   USING DRIVER FUNCTIONS TO TEST MODULES

In Chapter 2 we defined program testing as the process of executing a program to demonstrate its correctness. To test a module or a group of modules during bottom-up development, we should write a test driver. A **test driver** is a C program that calls on the module whose development is completed to verify that it does what it is expected to do properly.

Let us consider an example. A test driver for testing the module print_status of Figure 6.31 must include a function prototype for print_status and four calls to it to verify that it operates properly for every possible value of its formal parameter status. In other words, we should demonstrate that every logical path in print_status is traversed and that it behaves as expected. Here is a C function that is a test driver for the module print_status:

```
/* Test driver for the module print_status: */

#include <stdio.h>
```

```
int main(void) {
     /* Function prototype: */

     void print_status(int status);

     /* Local variables: */

     int status = 1;

     /* Function body: */

     while (status <= 4) {
          printf("Value of status: %d\n", status);
          print_status(status);
          status = status + 1;
     } /* end while */

     return 0;
} /* end function main */
```

If you compile and execute this driver program with the function `print_status`, you get the following result:

```
Value of status: 1
   Filing status : Single
Value of status: 2
   Filing status : Married filing jointly
Value of status: 3
   Filing status : Married filing separately
Value of status: 4
   Filing status : Head of household
```

This output indicates that the module `print_status` has been tested thoroughly and does its job correctly. After you complete the development of each module in your modular program, you should write a test module and ensure the correctness of your program.

## 6.13    STYLE CONSIDERATIONS IN MODULAR PROGRAM DESIGN AND IMPLEMENTATION

In our discussions in this chapter, we have occasionally touched on programming style considerations for modular systems. Now we bring them all together.

1.  In designing modular programs, carry out the stepwise refinement process until each module's task becomes expressible in one or two short English sentences. A task description such as "Module X computes a student's semester grade point average and formats and prints the student's semester grade report" should be further refined and split into two modules, such as "Module X computes a student's semester grade point average" and "Module Y formats and prints a student's semester grade report."

2.  In implementing modules in C as functions, optimize the module size, that is, the number of lines in it. There is no rule about the optimum module size. A good guideline is that it should be in the range of 2 to 50 lines. A function of 50 lines or less can be printed on a single page, which enables the reader of the program to see the content of the module at a glance and thus facilitates visual code inspection and debugging. On the other hand, modules that are too small produce a program structure with too many nodes (that is, functions) and increase structural complexity. In general, very small modules should be avoided.

3.  The number of functions that a function calls should not be excessive. Otherwise, the structure of the program becomes difficult to understand. Because the capacity of human short-term memory is about five to nine items of information, an average designer can probably handle about seven function calls for a given function, without confusion and possible error. Therefore, in our designs, we should restrict the number of functions that a function calls to about seven.

4.  Assign descriptive names to functions; the names should reflect the purpose of the function as much as possible. A name such as `compute_values` is not clear, whereas `compute_tax` is sufficiently descriptive. If a function returns a value under its name, assign a name that is descriptive of the nature of the quantity the function returns. For example, `computed_tax` is an appropriate name for a function that returns a value for `tax` to a calling program. If the return type for a function is `void`, name such functions using a verb, as in `print_status`.

5.  While implementing a module as a function, clearly identify data that it receives and data that it returns. All data received by a function and most of what it returns should be through parameters, and not through global variables. Chapter 10 explains how parameters can be used to return values from functions.

6.  In the source code, to clarify the data that a function receives and returns, use comments before the function header in its definition. Example:

```
/* Receives: first, second
   Returns : largest of first and second under its name */
int largest_of_two(int first, int second) {
       ..........
       ..........
} /* end function largest_of_two */
```

7.  For all data to be received by functions, use parameter passing by value to avoid inadvertent alterations of variables of the calling function by the called function.

8.  If a function has one value to return, you may return it under its name using the `return` statement. To avoid confusion, if a functions returns two or more data values, use parameter passing by pointers—a method we discuss in Chapter 10—for all values to be returned.

9.  As you know, function prototypes are not strictly necessary in some cases. Despite that, we encourage you to use them uniformly. Function prototypes provide useful information about functions in a modular program system and about the program structure.

10.  To the extent possible, try to design functions that can be used in other programs. A function that has been debugged and tested and can be used in solving other problems is called a **reusable function**. **Software reusability** is important in developing software systems.

11.  Along the same theme, whenever possible, try to use functions that are already available for solving new problems. Such functions may be library functions that C supports or functions that you may have developed in the past for other problems. You should never attempt to "reinvent the wheel" in program design, such as writing a function to compute the square root of numbers rather than using the library function `sqrt`; you certainly have better things to do with your time.

## 6.14   SUMMARY

### This Chapter at a Glance

- In this chapter we began the study of modular programming. We defined modular programming as organizing a program into small, independent modules that are integrated to become a software system that satisfies the problem requirements.
- A modular program is designed using top-down stepwise refinement. We refine each subproblem, which we identify in steps. However, instead of combining the refined subalgorithms in one pseudocode algorithm as we did previously, we leave them as separate modules.
- Modular programming facilitates teamwork in software development; reduces program development time; makes program debugging, testing, expansion, repair, and maintenance easier; improves program portability; and enhances software reusability.

- You learned that a modular program has a structure that consists of its modules and the "called by" relationships among them. This structure can be represented in a structure chart.

- A modular program design can be implemented using the bottom-up approach. In this process each module becomes a C function. In a modular program one of the functions is the function `main`. The function `main` monitors the execution of the other functions in the program.

- We discussed the elements of C functions. Each function must be defined, appropriately declared, and called by other functions.

- You studied valued functions, which return a value under their name, and learned to use the `return` statement.

- We saw that in many instances modules have to communicate data to each other. Although we can use global variables to pass data to modules, this method has its drawbacks and is not recommended.

- The usual way in which modules communicate data is through function parameters. In a function definition we may have formal parameters, which must be variables. In calling a function with parameters, we must use actual parameters, which may be constants, variables, or expressions.

- In parameter passing by value, copies of actual parameters are made in the data area of the called function, and the actual parameters are protected against changes by the called function. Therefore, parameter passing by value is the best way to send data to functions.

- We covered the concepts of storage classes, scope, visibility, and duration of variables. The scope of a variable is the region in which it can be accessed; its visibility is a program's ability to access that variable's memory location; and its duration is the time during which a memory location exists for that variable at run time.

- With what you have learned in this chapter, you have added significantly to your problem-solving skills. Now you can design modular programs using top-down stepwise refinement, implement them by bottom-up development, use C valued functions, and use parameter passing by value to supply data to functions.

## Coming Attractions

- In the next two chapters, we examine input and output in more detail. First, in Chapter 7, we consider formatted input and output in C. Formatting will give us the ability to exercise control over the input and output of our programs. Next, in Chapter 8, we discuss file-oriented input and output, and you will learn how to do batch applications.

# STUDY GUIDE

## Test Your Comprehension

1. Which of the following is *not* an advantage of modular programming?
   a. Modularizing a program improves its execution efficiency.
   b. Modular programming enables programmers to work in teams and reduces the program development time.
   c. In modular programs converting simple problems to programs becomes easier, and consequently, program debugging, testing, expansion, repair, and maintenance are all expedited.
   d. In modular programs machine-dependent functions are easy to separate. This feature improves program portability.
   e. Some general purpose modules of a modular program can be used without any change in other software development projects. This feature improves the efficiency of program development.

2. Which of the following statements concerning C function calls is *incorrect*?
   a. When a function call is encountered, the program control passes to the called function.
   b. During a function call, values for the actual parameters are also passed to the function.
   c. After the function body is executed, the program control goes to the next function in the source file.
   d. The number and type of actual parameters in a function call must be consistent with those of the formal parameters in its definition.

3. Which of the following is *not* depicted in a complete structure chart?
   a. Module invocations
   b. Data transfers between modules
   c. Order of module invocations
   d. Nature of module invocations
   e. Program statements

4. Choose the correct statement.
   a. A function prototype is global if it is placed outside function definitions in the source file.
   b. A function prototype is local if it is placed in a function definition.
   c. The scope of a global prototype begins at the point it is placed and extends until the end of the source file.
   d. The scope of a local prototype begins at the point it is placed and extends until the end of the function in which it appears.
   e. All of the above.
   f. None of the above.

5. Choose the correct statement.
   a. A variable of storage class `static` exists as long as the function in which it is declared is being executed.
   b. A variable of storage class `automatic` exists throughout the execution of the program in which it is declared.

**c.** All function formal parameters are static variables by default.
**d.** All global variables are automatic variables by default.
**e.** All of the above.
**f.** None of the above.

6. Which of the following rules concerning scope of variables is correct?
   **a.** The scope of a global variable begins at the point of its declaration and terminates at the end of the first program block that follows it.
   **b.** The scope of a local variable begins at the beginning of the block in which it is declared and terminates at the end of the block that contains it.
   **c.** The scope of formal parameters is the body of their associated function definition.
   **d.** All of the above.
   **e.** None of the above.

7. Which of the following statements concerning multiple declarations is correct?
   **a.** Provided they are made in different blocks, a variable can be declared more than once in a C program.
   **b.** The memory locations for a variable with multiple declarations are distinct.
   **c.** If there is a declaration for a variable in a block that is contained in the scope of another variable of the same name, the latter loses its visibility and becomes hidden inside the scope of the former.
   **d.** All of the above.
   **e.** None of the above.

8. Which of the following statements about parameter passing by value is *incorrect*?
   **a.** The actual parameters in a function call may be constants, variables, or expressions.
   **b.** The actual and formal parameters must be of similar types.
   **c.** At the time the program control passes to the called function, a copy of the value of each actual parameter is made in the memory location for the corresponding formal parameter.
   **d.** Changes made by the called function on formal parameters will be reflected on the corresponding actual parameters.

9. Which of the following statements about a valued function is *incorrect*?
   **a.** It must have a nonvoid type specifier in its declaration.
   **b.** It must contain at least one `return` statement in its body.
   **c.** The `return` statement must have a return expression.
   **d.** Its parameters must all be value parameters.

**Answers:** 1. a; 2. c; 3. e; 4. e; 5. f; 6. c; 7. d; 8. d; 9. d.

## Improve Your Problem-Solving Ability

### *Debugging Exercises*

**10.** We are given the following C modular program. Identify all the errors, explain why they are errors, and suggest ways to correct them.

```c
#include <stdio.h>

double void area_of_circle(float rad);
double void area_of_rectangle(float s1, float s2);

int main(void) {
      double radius;
      double side1, side2;

      printf("Enter radius: ");
      scanf("%lf", &radius);

      printf("Area of circle with radius %f is %f.\n", radius,
            area_of_circle(radius));

      printf("Enter first side for rectangle : ");
      scanf("%lf", &side1);

      printf("Enter second side for rectangle: ");
      scanf("%lf", &side2);

      printf("Area of rectangle with sides %f and %f is %f.",
            side1, side2, area_of_rectangle(side1, side2));
      return 0;
} /* end function main */

double area_of_circle(void) {
      return 3.141594 * square_of(R);
} /* end function area_of_circle */


double area_of_rectangle(x, y) {
      return x * y;
} /* end function area_of_rectangle */
```

```
double square_of(t) {
      return t * t;
} /* end function square_of */
```

**11.** In each of the following function definitions, declarations, or calls, identify and correct any errors. Explain your answer.

**a.** The function definition for `sum_of_digits`, which computes the sum of all digits of a given integer:

```
int sum_of_digits(int value) {
      int sum = 0;

      while (value) {
            sum = sum + (value % 10);
            value = value / 10;
      }
} /* end function sum_of_digits */
```

**b.** The function definition for `sum_of_square_of_digits`:

```
int sum_of_square_of_digits(int val) {
      int digit, result = 0;

      while (val) {
            digit = val % 10;

            result = result + digit * digit;
            val = val / 10;
      }
      return sum_of_digits;
} /* end function sum_of_square_of_digits */
```

**c.** The prototype for the function `sum_of_digits` of part (a) :

```
int sum_of_digits(int x, int y);
```

**d.** The prototype for the function `sum_of_square_of_digits` of part (b) :

```
void sum_of_square_of_digits(int a);
```

**e.** The function call to `sum_of_digits` of part (a) :

```
sum_of_digits(12345, result);
```

**f.** The function call to `sum_of_square_of_digits` of part (b) :

```
sum_of_square_of_digits(12345);
```

### Programming Exercises

**12.** Suppose the function F1 is coded as follows:

```
int F1(int value) {
      int d, num = 0;

      while (value) {
            d = value % 10;

            if (d % 2)
                  num = num + 1;
            /* end if */

            value = value / 10;
      } /* end while */
      return num;
} /* end function F1 */
```

**a.** Write an appropriate function prototype for the function `F1`.
**b.** Which value will be computed for the variable `result` after the function call in the statement

```
result = F1(1334);
```

is executed? Explain why.

**13.** We are given the following rather cryptically coded function `F2`:

```
int F2(int val) {
      int d, p, c, result = 0;

      while (val) {
            d = val % 10;
            c = 2;
            p = 1;
```

```
            while (c < d) {
                    if(d % c == 0)
                            p = 0;
                    c = c + 1;
            }

            if (p)
                    result = result + 1;

            val = val / 10;
        }
        return result;
}
```

**a.** Write a prototype for  F2.

**b.** Trace this function and compute the value that it will return for the function call F2(7589).

**14.** We want a function that receives a positive integer and computes and returns its factorial. Write a version of this function using value return under function name to return data and parameter passing by value to receive data.

**15.** Suppose we have *n* items, and we want to form groups by choosing *r* items from *n* items. Order of items in groups is unimportant. The number of different groups of *r* items each (that is, the number of different combinations) can be computed using the following formula from the probability theory:

$$C(n, r) = \frac{n!}{r! \ (n - r)!}$$

where *n!* is the factorial of *n*. For example, if we want to know the number of different soccer teams that we can form from a class of 14 students, assuming all can play soccer, we can use the fact that a soccer team has 11 players and the above formula, and find

$$C(14, 11) = \frac{14!}{11! \ (14 - 11)!} = 364$$

different teams.

Write a function that receives values for *n* and *r* such that *r* <= *n* and then computes and returns *C(n, r)*. Your function should use the factorial function of Exercise 14, and should include its prototype as a local declaration. Use parameter passing by value to receive data and value return under function name to return data.

*Programming Projects*

In each of the following problems, use top-down design to produce a modular C program. In refining your solutions, make use of the style rules discussed for modular programs in this chapter. Design your modules so that each is about 3 to 15 lines of code after implementation, given that most of the problems are simple. Make sure that you can express the purpose of each module in one or two short sentences. After the design, draw a detailed structure chart for each and implement it using the bottom-up approach. Debug and test your solutions thoroughly.

**16.** Solve Programming Project 38 of Chapter 4.

**17.** Solve Programming Project 39 of Chapter 4.

**18.** Solve Programming Project 20 of Chapter 5.

**19.** Solve Programming Project 21 of Chapter 5.

**20.** Solve Programming Project 27 of Chapter 5.

**21.** Redesign and implement the solution of the problem of quadratic equations of Example Program 1 of Chapter 5 as a modular program.

**22.** Develop an interactive program that accepts values for loan amount, yearly interest rate, and monthly payment amount from the terminal and then computes and displays on the monitor screen a loan repayment table. Your program execution session should have the same layout as the following sample terminal run:

```
Enter loan amount: 10000.00
Enter yearly interest rate: 0.1790
Enter monthly payment: 50.00
***> Monthly payment too small.
Enter monthly payment: 1000.00

Beginning     Payment    Interest    Principal    Ending
Balance                                           Balance
----------    --------   --------    ---------    --------
10000.00      1000.00    149.17      850.83       9149.16
9149.16       1000.00    136.47      863.52       8285.64
8285.64       1000.00    123.59      876.41       7409.23
7409.23       1000.00    110.52      889.48       6519.75
. . . . . . . . . . . . . . . . . . . . . . . . .
. . . . . . . . . . . . . . . . . . . . . . . . .
1869.33       1000.00     27.88      972.12       897.21
 897.21        897.21      0.00      897.21         0.00
```

You should note the following:

**a.** Monthly interest is computed on the beginning balance as

*(beginning balance)* × *(interest rate) / 12*

**b.** Principal is obtained by subtracting monthly interest from monthly payment.

**c.** Ending balance is beginning balance minus principal paid.

**d.** The beginning balance for a month is the same as the ending balance for the previous month.

**e.** When the beginning balance for a month becomes less than or equal to the monthly payment amount, no interest is charged and the monthly payment is considered as the principal amount. In this case the monthly payment will be the final payment on the loan.

**f.** If the entered value for monthly payment is less than the computed monthly interest, the loan will never be repaid. Therefore, your program should print a message telling the user that the monthly payment is too small and asking the user to enter a larger value.

**23.** Develop an interactive program that accepts for each faculty member of a small college two data values: faculty salary (a dollar amount) and a character value for faculty performance level. The performance-level data item can have the values S, G, and A for superior, good, and average, respectively. We want the program to compute and display on the terminal screen the cost of a proposed pay increase scheme. The pay increase scheme assumes a 3.5 percent across-the-board increase for all faculty members, plus a merit raise. Merit raise percentages depend on the performance level; for superior performance it is 2.5 percent, for good performance it is 1.5 percent, and for average performance no merit raise is given. Test your program on the following data set:

| Faculty Salary | Performance Level |
|---|---|
| 40000.00 | S |
| 42500.00 | S |
| 33500.00 | A |
| 36700.00 | G |
| 55000.00 | S |
| 31000.00 | A |

**24.** Design and implement a program that does the following:

**a.** Gives the user a choice of determining whether a supplied positive integer number is a perfect number or of determining and printing all perfect numbers in a range of *low* through *high*, where *low* and *high* are positive integers such that *low* <= *high*. A positive integer is a *perfect number* if it is equal to the sum of all of its factors, including one but excluding itself. For example, 6 is a perfect number, since 6 = 1 + 2 + 3, and 1, 2, and 3 are factors of 6.

**b.** If the user wants to determine whether a supplied number is a perfect number, the program reads an integer, verifies that it is positive, and determines and prints whether it is a perfect number.

**c.** If the user wants to determine all perfect numbers in a range, the program reads values for *low* and *high*, verifies that they are positive and that *low* <= *high*, and then determines and prints all perfect numbers in the range.

**d.** Executes the program in a loop until the user wants to stop.

**25.** Develop a program that is capable of playing a game of dice according to the following specifications:

**a.** One of the players is the computer; the other is the user. Each player has a six-sided die.

**b.** The scores are computed by computing the sum of the face value of the die for 10 consecutive throws.

**c.** The computer is the first player. It uses the time of day, obtained by the function call `time(0)`, as the seed for the `srand` function and generates 10 random integers in the range one through six, using the `rand` function. The computer's score is the sum of face values of the 10 die throws.

**d.** The user is the second player. The program prompts the player to enter an integer to be used as the seed in simulating 10 die throws.

**e.** The computer should compare the total scores and announce the winner as, for example, in `My score is 55 and yours is 49. I am the winner.`

**f.** Your program should allow the user to play as long as desired.

## chapter

# 7

# Formatted Input and Output

---

**CHAPTER OBJECTIVES**

In this chapter you will learn about:

- **The standard output function** `printf`
- **Output formatting in C**
  Formatting integer values
  Formatting floating-point values
  Formatting character values and strings
- **The standard input function** `scanf`
- **Formatting input data**

By the time you have completed this chapter, you will have acquired the ability to:

- **Get formatted output from C programs**
- **Input data values to C programs in a variety of ways**

## 7.1   INTRODUCTION

In Chapter 3 you learned about simple forms of interactive C input and output statements. You learned to use the `printf` function for interactive output and the `scanf` function for interactive input. Chapter 3 also mentioned that we need the standard C header file `stdio.h` because the input and output functions are declared in it.

We have been using the simple forms of `scanf` and `printf` in our programs since Chapter 1. In most cases they have been adequate for our purposes. Occasionally, however, they fail to fully satisfy our output requirements. For example, the program of Figure 4.23, which computes federal income tax from tax rate schedules, contains the output statement

```
printf("Tax: %f", tax);
```

which prints

```
Tax: 13545.500000
```

as shown in Figure 4.24. For the input data supplied, this result is correct; but it would clearly be better to have it printed as `13545.50`, or maybe even as `$13,545.50`. The reason this value is printed as `13545.500000` is that the `printf` function we have used is for unformatted output. Had we made use of the formatting capabilities of C, we would have better output.

The purpose of this chapter is to study formatted output and input in C. We will still use the `scanf` and `printf` functions for formatted input-output. Therefore, we will examine these functions in greater detail and learn about their features that make formatting of input and output possible.

## 7.2   INTERACTIVE VERSUS BATCH PROGRAMS

Before we are ready to discuss formatted input and output facilities in C, you should understand the following important aspects of input and output for programs.

1.   Input for a program can come from the **standard input device**, which is usually the terminal keyboard. We may design a program such that it allows user interaction; that is, while the program is executing, we may enter data values for program variables. Such a program is said to have **interactive input**. All programs that we have studied so far are programs that do interactive input.

2.   Input can also come from data files. A **data file** consists of lines into which we type data values. It is possible to create a data file by using a text editor—exactly as we do to create a program source file. After a data file is created and saved on a magnetic storage medium such as a disk, we may link it to a program. The program will then get its data values from the data file. A computer program that operates in this manner is said to have **batch input**.

3.   The output of a computer program can be directed to the **standard output device**. The monitor screen is the usual standard output device. A program that is sending its output to the standard output device is doing **interactive output**. In interactive output it is also possible to send messages to the screen by using output statements to prompt the user for interactive input.

4.   If the output of our program is a report, it can be generated by sending the output to the printer. If we want to save the output of a program in a file, we can direct it to a computer file. In this case the program has **batch output.** The output of a computer program, if saved in a file, can be the input of another program. Therefore, another way of creating a data file is through the use of a computer program written for that purpose.

5.   As you can see, a program may be designed to do interactive input and interactive output. Such a program is **fully interactive**. If a program does batch input and batch output, it is said to be a **batch application**. Naturally, we may have programs with interactive input and batch output, as well as programs with batch input and interactive output.

## 7.3    STANDARD INPUT-OUTPUT FUNCTIONS IN C

Standard input and output in C are stream oriented.

> A **stream** is an abstraction for a flow of data from a source that produces data to a sink that uses them.

To understand streams, you should visualize their sources and sinks. Figure 7.1 shows input and output streams and their sources and sinks. In interactive input, the source is the standard input device, and the sink is the program itself. Therefore, an input stream is a flow

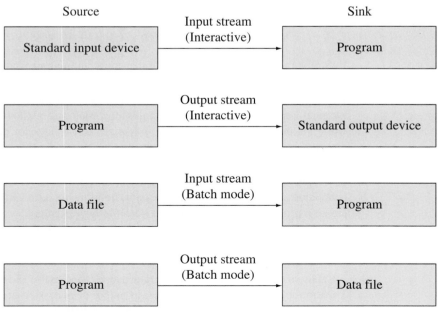

**Figure 7.1**    Input and output streams and their sources and sinks

of data from the standard input device to the program. If we use an input file in batch mode, the source is that file and the sink is the program. In output the source is the program, and the sink is either the standard output device or the printer, or a file that is produced by the program. Inputting data from a source is also referred to as **extracting** or getting data from a source. Outputting data to a sink is known as **inserting** or putting data to a sink.

## 7.4   THE OUTPUT FUNCTION `printf`

In C we use the `printf` function for interactive output. You had a brief exposure to `printf` in Chapter 3, and since then we have used it in our programs. Let us briefly review what you already know about the `printf` function.

The `printf` function call has the following general syntax:

> `printf` (*FormatControlString, PrintList*) ;

*FormatControlString* is a string that may consist of ordinary characters, escape sequences, and format specifiers. *PrintList* is any number of constants, variables, expressions, and function calls separated by commas. Output format specifiers convert internal representations for data to readable characters. They begin with the character `%`. For example, in the output statement

```
printf("The sum of integers between %d and %d is %d",
       first, second, sum);
```

the string `"The sum of integers between %d and %d is %d"` is a format control string, and `%d` is a format specifier that converts an internal representation for an integer field to a readable integer value. For each format specifier in the format control string, we must have an actual parameter in the `printf` function call that is either a constant, a variable, an expression, or a function call. In the above `printf` function call, we have three format specifiers corresponding to the variables `first`, `second`, and `sum`.

The result of the execution of a `printf` function call is a string printed on the standard output device. This string includes every ordinary character in the format control string, with each format specifier replaced by the value of the corresponding constant, variable, or expression. For example, assuming that the values of the variables `first`, `second`, and `sum` are 1, 3, and 6, respectively, the preceding `printf` function call will print on the screen

```
The sum of integers between 1 and 3 is 6
```

Previously, we have worked with five types of format specifiers. They are `%d` for integers, `%c` for characters, `%f` or `%lf` for floating-point values in conventional notation, and `%s` for strings. In this section we consider one more format specifier in detail: `%e` for floating-point values represented in scientific notation. Thus we will have the following list of format specifiers for output:

1.  %d  for integers
2.  %c  for characters
3.  %f  and  %lf  for floating-point values in conventional notation
4.  %e  for floating-point values in scientific notation
5.  %s  for strings

In Chapter 5, Figure 5.9, we gave variations of the format specifiers  %d  and  %f, which are %hd, %ld, %u, %lu, and  %Lf. The uses of these variations in formatted output are based on principles similar to those for %d and %f. We will not discuss them here.

## The Format Specifier %e for Floating-Point Values

The format specifier  %e  is used to print floating-point values in scientific notation. Let us consider an example of its use.

***Example 7.1***    In the following partial C code, the printf function call contains the format specifiers  %f  and  %e for printing the value of the variable  height  twice.

```
double height = 147.2578;
printf("The value of %f printed in scientific notation is
        %e.", height, height);
```

As a result, we get the output

```
The value of 147.257800 printed in scientific notation is
        1.472578e+02.
```

The first specifier %f prints the value in conventional notation, whereas the second, %e, prints it in scientific notation.

## Additional Examples of printf

Now, let us assume that the variables  number, response, and  root1  are declared as follows:

```
int number = 10;
char response = 'y';
double root1 = 3.25;
char str[21] = "Normal termination";
```

The following are all legal examples of stream-oriented output statements using the printf function.

| Output Statement | Prints on the Screen |
|---|---|
| `printf("%d", 15);` | 15 |
| `printf("%d", number);` | 10 |
| `printf("%d", number + 5);` | 15 |
| | |
| `printf("Enter value for a: ");` | Enter value for a: |
| `printf("%s", "Enter value for a: ");` | Enter value for a: |
| | |
| `printf("%c", 'a');` | a |
| `printf("%c", response);` | y |
| | |
| `printf("%f", 1.25);` | 1.250000 |
| `printf("%f", 1.2500);` | 1.250000 |
| `printf("%f", -1.0000);` | -1.000000 |
| `printf("%f", 1.2500e1);` | 12.500000 |
| `printf("%f", root1);` | 3.250000 |
| | |
| `printf("%lf", root1);` | 3.250000 |
| | |
| `printf("%e", root1);` | 3.250000e+00 |
| | |
| `printf("%s", str);` | Normal |
| `termination` | |

As you can see, in all cases the values generated for the elements of the print list are printed on the screen without formatting. Each such value is printed in a field of minimum length, beginning on the current position on the current line. For example, the constant value typed as  `1.25`  is printed using only eight positions as  `1.250000`. The floating-point constant  `1.2500e1`, expressed in scientific notation, is printed in a field of minimum length as `12.500000`. Character constants, variables, and strings are printed fully without the surrounding quotation marks.

Consecutive unformatted output statements result in the printing of values one after another. For example, if the output statements

```
printf("%s", "VALUE OF VARIABLE ");
printf("%c", 'a');
printf("%s", " IS: ");
printf("%f", 1.25);
```

appear in this order in a program, they will produce the following on the screen:

```
VALUE OF VARIABLE a IS: 1.250000
```

The same effect can be obtained by combining the format specifiers and the elements of the print list in an output statement as follows:

```
printf("%s%c%s%f", "VALUE OF VARIABLE ", 'a', " IS: ", 1.25);
```

## 7.5 OUTPUT FORMATTING

While discussing stream-oriented output, we mentioned that the computer would print the value of an element of the print list of the `printf` function call in a minimum amount of space, beginning at the current position of the cursor. In some applications this type of output is sufficient. However, there are many applications in which we would like to have more control over the appearance, or format, of our output.

### Common Output Formatting Requirements for Fundamental Data Types and Strings

Output formatting requirements depend on the type of data to be printed. So far we have learned about all C fundamental data types and string variables and literals. For string variables and literals and all fundamental data types, there are some common formatting requirements. We may want to print such data

1. Right-adjusted in a fixed-width field.
2. Left-adjusted in a fixed-width field.
3. In a fixed-width field with a specified fill character.

Figure 7.2 shows examples of data printed right-adjusted in a field of width 10.

| Data Type | Value to Be Printed | Formatted Output |
|-----------|---------------------|------------------|
| | | 1   2   3   4   5   6   7   8   9   10 |
| Character | X |                   X |
| | | 1   2   3   4   5   6   7   8   9   10 |
| Integer | -120 |             −   1   2   0 |
| | | 1   2   3   4   5   6   7   8   9   10 |
| Floating-point | -15.578 |       −   1   5   .   5   7   8 |
| | | 1   2   3   4   5   6   7   8   9   10 |
| String | Hello |           H   e   l   l   o |

**Figure 7.2**   Data printed right-adjusted in a fixed-width field

Figure 7.3 shows the same data printed left-adjusted in a field of width 10.

| Data Type | Value to Be Printed | Formatted Output | | | | | | | | | |
|-----------|--------------------|--------|---|---|---|---|---|---|---|---|---|

| | | 1 | 2 | 3 | 4 | 5 | 6 | 7 | 8 | 9 | 10 |
|---|---|---|---|---|---|---|---|---|---|---|---|
| Character | X | X | | | | | | | | | |

| | | 1 | 2 | 3 | 4 | 5 | 6 | 7 | 8 | 9 | 10 |
|---|---|---|---|---|---|---|---|---|---|---|---|
| Integer | -120 | − | 1 | 2 | 0 | | | | | | |

| | | 1 | 2 | 3 | 4 | 5 | 6 | 7 | 8 | 9 | 10 |
|---|---|---|---|---|---|---|---|---|---|---|---|
| Floating-point | -15.578 | − | 1 | 5 | . | 5 | 7 | 8 | | | |

| | | 1 | 2 | 3 | 4 | 5 | 6 | 7 | 8 | 9 | 10 |
|---|---|---|---|---|---|---|---|---|---|---|---|
| String | Hello | H | e | l | l | o | | | | | |

**Figure 7.3**  Data printed left-adjusted in a fixed-width field

Finally, Figure 7.4 displays data printed right-adjusted in a field of width 10 with a fill character of  *. A **fill character** is any character that replaces the leading or trailing blanks in an output field.

| Data Type | Value to Be Printed | Formatted Output | | | | | | | | | |
|-----------|--------------------|--------|---|---|---|---|---|---|---|---|---|

| | | 1 | 2 | 3 | 4 | 5 | 6 | 7 | 8 | 9 | 10 |
|---|---|---|---|---|---|---|---|---|---|---|---|
| Character | X | * | * | * | * | * | * | * | * | * | X |

| | | 1 | 2 | 3 | 4 | 5 | 6 | 7 | 8 | 9 | 10 |
|---|---|---|---|---|---|---|---|---|---|---|---|
| Integer | -120 | * | * | * | * | * | * | − | 1 | 2 | 0 |

| | | 1 | 2 | 3 | 4 | 5 | 6 | 7 | 8 | 9 | 10 |
|---|---|---|---|---|---|---|---|---|---|---|---|
| Floating-point | -15.578 | * | * | * | − | 1 | 5 | . | 5 | 7 | 8 |

| | | 1 | 2 | 3 | 4 | 5 | 6 | 7 | 8 | 9 | 10 |
|---|---|---|---|---|---|---|---|---|---|---|---|
| String | Hello | * | * | * | * | * | H | e | l | l | o |

**Figure 7.4**  Data printed right-adjusted in a fixed-width field with a fill character

## Output Formatting for Numeric Data

For integer and floating-point numeric data, in addition to printing them in a field of fixed width, left- or right-adjusted, and with or without a fill character, there may be another requirement: printing them with a plus sign if they are positive. Examples are shown in Figure 7.5.

| Data Type | Value to Be Printed | Formatted Output |
|---|---|---|

| | | 1 | 2 | 3 | 4 | 5 | 6 | 7 | 8 | 9 | 10 |
|---|---|---|---|---|---|---|---|---|---|---|---|
| Integer | 150 | | | | | | | + | 1 | 5 | 0 |

| | | 1 | 2 | 3 | 4 | 5 | 6 | 7 | 8 | 9 | 10 |
|---|---|---|---|---|---|---|---|---|---|---|---|
| Floating-point | 7.566 | | | | 1 | 7 | 5 | . | 5 | 6 | 6 |

**Figure 7.5**   Numeric data printed right-adjusted with a plus sign in a fixed-width field

## Output Formatting for Floating-Point Data

A floating-point value with a zero fractional part may be printed in conventional notation with or without a decimal point. Figure 7.6 has two examples of right-adjusted printing in a field of width 10, with and without a decimal point.

| Data Type | Value to Be Printed | Formatted Output |
|---|---|---|

Without a decimal point

| | | 1 | 2 | 3 | 4 | 5 | 6 | 7 | 8 | 9 | 10 |
|---|---|---|---|---|---|---|---|---|---|---|---|
| Floating-point | 15.00 | | | | | | | | | 1 | 5 |

With a decimal point

| | | 1 | 2 | 3 | 4 | 5 | 6 | 7 | 8 | 9 | 10 |
|---|---|---|---|---|---|---|---|---|---|---|---|
| Floating-point | 15.00 | | 1 | 5 | . | 0 | 0 | 0 | 0 | 0 | 0 |

**Figure 7.6**   Floating-point data printed right-adjusted in conventional notation in a fixed-width field with and without a decimal point

Floating-point data can be printed with a specified precision for their fractional part. In Figure 7.7 we have examples of floating-point values printed in conventional notation right-adjusted in a field of width 10 and a precision of 2 (that is, two decimal places after the decimal point). As you can see, a value such as 15.7525 is truncated to 15.75 during printing, whereas the value 15.7586 is rounded to 15.76.

| Data Type | Value to Be Printed | Formatted Output | | | | | | | | | |
|-----------|---------------------|---|---|---|---|---|---|---|---|---|---|
| | | 1 | 2 | 3 | 4 | 5 | 6 | 7 | 8 | 9 | 10 |
| Floating-point | 15.7525 | | | | | | 1 | 5 | . | 7 | 5 |
| | | 1 | 2 | 3 | 4 | 5 | 6 | 7 | 8 | 9 | 10 |
| Floating-point | 15.7586 | | | | | | 1 | 5 | . | 7 | 6 |

**Figure 7.7**  Floating-point data printed right-adjusted in conventional notation in a fixed-width field with a precision of 2

It is possible to print floating-point values in scientific notation. Examples are shown in Figure 7.8.

| Data Type | Value to Be Printed | Formatted Output | | | | | | | | | |
|-----------|---------------------|---|---|---|---|---|---|---|---|---|---|
| | | Without a decimal point | | | | | | | | | |
| | | 1 | 2 | 3 | 4 | 5 | 6 | 7 | 8 | 9 | 10 |
| Floating-point | 50.00 | | | | | | 5 | e | + | 0 | 1 |
| | | With a decimal point | | | | | | | | | |
| | | 1 | 2 | 3 | 4 | 5 | 6 | 7 | 8 | 9 | 10 |
| Floating-point | 50.00 | | | 5 | . | 0 | 0 | e | + | 0 | 1 |

**Figure 7.8**  Floating-point data printed right-adjusted in scientific notation in a fixed-width field with and without a decimal point and a precision of 2

## Use of Format Specifiers in Output Formatting

Output formatting in C can be accomplished using various forms of the basic format specifiers in `printf` function calls. In fact, in standard C the suffix `f` in `printf` connotes formatted output, and there is no special statement for unformatted output. If we use the format specifiers without any variations, we get unformatted output. Output formatting possibilities in C include specifying

1. A print field of fixed width
2. Right-adjusted printing
3. Left-adjusted printing
4. Right-adjusted printing with a fill character of zero
5. Printing numeric values with a + sign, if positive.
6. Printing floating-point values with a specified precision

7. Printing floating-point values in conventional notation

8. Printing floating-point values in scientific notation

**Specifying a Print Field of Fixed Width**     In any format specifier it is possible to define a fixed-width field into which the value is printed. In this case the format specifier must include an unsigned, nonzero, positive constant after the % symbol that represents the field width. Some examples are %6d, which specifies an integer for a field of width 6; %10c, which causes printing of a character in a field of width 10; and %8f, which prints a floating-point value in conventional notation in a field of width 8.

    If the specified field width is insufficient to print the entire value, the compiler ignores it and prints the value according to the corresponding specifier with no field width. If the actual width of the value to be printed is less than the specified width in the format specifier, the value is printed right-adjusted in the field, with spaces for padding on the left.

***Example 7.2***    Consider the output statement

```
printf("%10d", number);
```

Let us assume that the current value of the variable  number  is 20. This statement prints the following:

| 1 | 2 | 3 | 4 | 5 | 6 | 7 | 8 | 9 | 10 |
|---|---|---|---|---|---|---|---|---|----|
|   |   |   |   |   |   |   |   | 2 | 0  |

As you can see, printing is right-adjusted in its field of specified width. Left-adjusted printing is also possible.

**Specifying Left-Adjusted Printing in a Fixed-Width Field**     To print a value left-adjusted in a fixed-width field, we must have a minus after the symbol  %  in the format specifier. Examples are  %-6d,  %-10c, and  %-8f.

***Example 7.3***    The printf function call

```
printf("%-10d", number);
```

uses the format specifier  %-10d  to print an integer left-adjusted in a field of width 10. If the value of the variable  number  is 20, this statement prints

| 1 | 2 | 3 | 4 | 5 | 6 | 7 | 8 | 9 | 10 |
|---|---|---|---|---|---|---|---|---|----|
| 2 | 0 |   |   |   |   |   |   |   |    |

**Specifying Right-Adjusted Printing with a Fill Character**     Standard C does not support any fill characters except space for fields of all types and leading zeros for numeric fields. The default padding fill character is space. If a numeric value is right-adjusted in a fixed-width field, it is possible to have it padded with zeros on the left. This padding requires that the field width start with a zero in the format specifier, as in `%06d`, `%010f`, and `%08e`. With character data and strings, zero padding is not possible; that is, `%06c`, for example, has the same effect as `%6c`, and `%025s` is the same as `%25s`.

**Example 7.4**   The format specifier `%010d` in the statement

```
printf("%010d", number);
```

will print

| 1 | 2 | 3 | 4 | 5 | 6 | 7 | 8 | 9 | 10 |
|---|---|---|---|---|---|---|---|---|----|
| 0 | 0 | 0 | 0 | 0 | 0 | 0 | 0 | 2 | 0 |

if the value of the variable `number` is 20.

**Printing Numeric Values with a Plus Sign**     If an integer or a floating-point value is negative, the printed value is preceded by a minus sign. If the numeric value is positive, no sign is printed. However, it is possible to print a plus sign for a positive numeric value by inserting a `+` after the symbol `%` in the format specifier. Examples: `%+6d`, `%+f`, and `%+10e`.

**Example 7.5**   Let us assume that the value of the variable `number` is 35. The function call

```
printf("%+10d", number);
```

will produce the following output:

| 1 | 2 | 3 | 4 | 5 | 6 | 7 | 8 | 9 | 10 |
|---|---|---|---|---|---|---|---|---|----|
|   |   |   |   |   |   |   | + | 3 | 5 |

**Printing Floating-Point Values with a Specified Precision**     For floating-point values, we can specify precision using the form *w.d* in the format specifier. Here, *w* is the field width and *d* is the precision. For example, `%10.3f` will print a floating-point value in conventional notation, right-adjusted in a field of width 10, with a precision of three decimal digits after rounding.

**Example 7.6**   Consider the `printf` function call

```
printf("%15.3f", number);
```

Assume that the variable `number` is of type `double`, and its value is 34.5678. This output statement will print the following:

| 1 | 2 | 3 | 4 | 5 | 6 | 7 | 8 | 9 | 10 | 11 | 12 | 13 | 14 | 15 |
|---|---|---|---|---|---|---|---|---|----|----|----|----|----|----|
|   |   |   |   |   |   |   |   |   | 3  | 4  | .  | 5  | 6  | 8  |

As you can see, the value 34.5678 has been rounded to 34.568. Had it been something like 34.5672, the printed value with the same format specifier would be truncated to 34.567.

With integer and character values, precision specification has no effect. In other words, %15.3d and %15.3c are the same as %15d and %15c, respectively. For strings a format specifier such as %15.3s results in a truncation of the string, and only the first three characters will be printed.

**Example 7.7**   The output statement

```
printf("%15s", "Greetings!");
```

will produce the line

| 1 | 2 | 3 | 4 | 5 | 6 | 7 | 8 | 9 | 10 | 11 | 12 | 13 | 14 | 15 |
|---|---|---|---|---|---|---|---|---|----|----|----|----|----|----|
|   |   |   |   |   | G | r | e | e | t  | i  | n  | g  | s  | !  |

whereas the printf function call

```
printf("%15.3s", "Greetings!");
```

will print

| 1 | 2 | 3 | 4 | 5 | 6 | 7 | 8 | 9 | 10 | 11 | 12 | 13 | 14 | 15 |
|---|---|---|---|---|---|---|---|---|----|----|----|----|----|----|
|   |   |   |   |   |   |   |   |   |    |    |    | G  | r  | e  |

**Printing Floating-Point Values in Conventional or Scientific Notation**   We know that to print a floating-point value in conventional notation we must use the format specifier %f or %lf. Printing in scientific notation requires %e.

**Example 7.8**   Let us assume that the value of the variable number of type double is 155.56788. The output statement

```
printf("%15.3f", number);
```

prints the value of number in conventional notation, right-adjusted in a field of width 15 with a precision of 3 as follows:

| 1 | 2 | 3 | 4 | 5 | 6 | 7 | 8 | 9 | 10 | 11 | 12 | 13 | 14 | 15 |
|---|---|---|---|---|---|---|---|---|----|----|----|----|----|----|
|   |   |   |   |   |   |   |   | 1 | 5  | 5  | .  | 5  | 6  | 8  |

It is possible to specify a precision of 0 using a specifier such as %15.0f or %15.f. In this case a statement such as

```
printf("%15.0f", number);
```

prints the floating-point value with no fractional part and no decimal point after truncating it if the fractional part is less than 0.5. Otherwise, the printed value will be rounded as shown here:

| 1 | 2 | 3 | 4 | 5 | 6 | 7 | 8 | 9 | 10 | 11 | 12 | 13 | 14 | 15 |
|---|---|---|---|---|---|---|---|---|----|----|----|----|----|----|
|   |   |   |   |   |   |   |   |   |    |    |    | 1  | 5  | 6  |

If we want to print a floating-point value in scientific notation, with a precision of 3 in a field of width 15, we use the specifier %15.3e. For example, the printf function call

```
printf("%15.3e", number);
```

produces

| 1 | 2 | 3 | 4 | 5 | 6 | 7 | 8 | 9 | 10 | 11 | 12 | 13 | 14 | 15 |
|---|---|---|---|---|---|---|---|---|----|----|----|----|----|----|
|   |   |   |   |   |   | 1 | . | 5 | 5  | 6  | e  | +  | 0  | 2  |

This last example needs explanation. You already know that a floating-point value can be expressed in scientific notation in many different but equivalent ways. For example, the floating-point value 155.56788 can be represented as 155.56788e+00, 15.556788e+01, 1.5556788e+02, and so on. Of these forms 1.5556788e+02 is the **normalized scientific notation** for this floating-point value. The value preceding the letter e in this notation is called the **mantissa**, and the value after the letter e is the **exponent**. In the representation 1.5556788e+02, 1.5556788 is the mantissa, and +02 is the exponent. In C, before a floating-point value is printed in scientific notation, it is normalized. Following this step, if a precision has been specified, it is applied to the mantissa. Therefore, in the preceding example the mantissa becomes 1.556, and the value is printed as 1.556e+02. Note that this format may be unacceptable in your application because the accuracy of the result is less than what you expect. If so, you should specify higher precision in the format specifier.

**Specifying Variables for Field Width and Precision**     Occasionally, it is useful to specify a variable value for field width and, in case of floating-point quantities, a variable value for precision in output formatting. In other words, we may want to design a program that can print a value in a field of width *w*, where *w* is a variable for which a value is available at run time. While printing a floating-point quantity, it may be desirable to specify a variable field width of *w* and a variable precision of *d* and then to supply values for *w* and *d* at run time.

Suppose we want to print the value of an integer variable number in a field of width 15. We know that the function call

```
printf("%15d", number);
```

that uses the format specifier %15d will do it. Let us assume that width is an integer variable, and we want to print number in a field of width width. A format specifier such as `%widthd` is not legal in C. However, standard C has a special feature to solve this problem. The `printf` function call

```
printf("%*d", width, number);
```

containing the format specifier `%*d` is legal. At run time this format specifier is converted to one in which the symbol `*` is replaced by the integer value of the variable `width`. Therefore, if the value of `width` is 15, at run time the above `printf` function call acts the same way as the statement

```
printf("%15d", number);
```

which prints the value of the variable `number` in a field of width 15. In other words, to print an integer in a field of width `width`, we can use the partial code

```
int number, width;
. . . . . . . . . . . . . . .
. . . . . . . . . . . . . . .
printf("%*d", width, number);
```

Similarly, to print a floating-point quantity, say, `weight`, in conventional notation, in a field of width `width`, and with a precision of `precision`, we must first declare the variables `width` and `precision` as integers and then use the following `printf` function call:

```
printf("%*.*f", width, precision, weight);
```

Because of the format specifier `%*.*f`, the first asterisk will be replaced by the value of the second parameter and the second asterisk by the value of the third parameter at run time; the format specifier thus generated will be used to print the fourth parameter, `weight`. If the values of `width` and `precision` are 15 and 3, respectively, the format specifier `%*.*f` will be translated into `%15.3f`.

**Combining Special Characters in Format Specifiers**    The special characters that can be used in format specifiers are `-`, `+`, and `0`, for left-adjusted printing, plus-sign printing, and left zero padding, respectively. Provided the combinations are meaningful, these characters can be combined in format specifiers. For example, the specifier `%+-15d` is a legal request to print an integer left-adjusted in a field of width 15 with a plus sign if the value is positive. This specifier is the same as `%-+15d`. Another meaningful combination is using `+` and `0` together, as in `%+015d`. On the other hand, the combination of `-` and `0` is not effective, since `0` is for padding on the left with zeros and `-` is for left-adjusted printing. Therefore, a specifier such as `%-015d` is treated the same as `%-15d`.

***Example 7.9***    The combination format specifier `%+015.3f` can be used to print a floating-point value in conventional notation in a field of width 15 with a precision of 3, left zero padding, and a plus sign. Thus the `printf` function call

```
printf("%+015.3f", number);
```

will print

| 1 | 2 | 3 | 4 | 5 | 6 | 7 | 8 | 9 | 10 | 11 | 12 | 13 | 14 | 15 |
|---|---|---|---|---|---|---|---|---|----|----|----|----|----|----|
|   |   |   |   |   |   |   |   | 1 | 5  | 5  | .  | 5  | 6  | 8  |

if the value of the floating-point variable `number` is 155.56788.

## REVIEW QUESTIONS

**1.** Choose the correct statement.
  **a.** In interactive input the source is the terminal keyboard, and the sink is the program that uses the input.
  **b.** In output the source is the program, and the sink can be a data file produced by the program.
  **c.** Inputting data from a source is called extracting data.
  **d.** Outputting data to a sink is called inserting data.
  **e.** All of the above.
  **f.** None of the above.

**2.** Which of the following is *not* a legal element of the format control string in a `printf` function call?
  **a.** Ordinary characters
  **b.** Escape sequences
  **c.** Format specifiers
  **d.** Variables

**3.** Which of the following statements concerning the output library function `printf` is correct?
  **a.** In a program `printf` is a function call with a variable number of parameters.
  **b.** The first parameter is a format control string.
  **c.** The rest of the parameters are constants, variables, or expressions that are output using the standard output device.
  **d.** All of the above.
  **e.** None of the above.

**4.** Format specifiers for output convert internal representations for data to readable characters. (T or F)

**5.** The format specifiers for output are
  **a.** `%d`  for integers.
  **b.** `%c`  for characters.
  **c.** `%f`  and  `%e`  for floating-point values.
  **d.** `%s`  for strings.
  **e.** All of the above are correct.
  **f.** None of the above is correct.

**6.** Identify the following `printf` function calls as legal or illegal. If illegal, state the reason. Assume that  `number`  is an integer variable.
  **a.** `printf("%s", "\n%s");`

    **b.** `printf("%d%d%d", number, number, number);`
    **c.** `printf(number, "%d");`
    **d.** `printf(number);`
    **e.** `printf('%d', number);`

**7.** Which of the following statements concerning printing into a fixed-width field is correct?

    **a.** If the field width in a format specifier is larger than the actual width of the value, the value is printed right-adjusted in the field.

    **b.** To print a value left-adjusted in a fixed-width field, we must have a minus sign after the symbol `%` in the format specifier, as in `%-10d`.

    **c.** To print a plus sign for a positive numeric value, we must insert a plus sign after the symbol `%` in the format specifier, as in `%+10d`.

    **d.** Standard C does not support any fill characters except space for padding and leading zeros for numeric values.

    **e.** All of the above.

    **f.** None of the above.

**8.** The format specifier `%+-15d` prints an integer left-adjusted in a field of width 15 with a plus sign if the value is positive. (T or F)

**9.** The `printf` function call

    `printf("%-*d", 5, 6);`

prints the integer 5 left-adjusted in a field of width 6. (T or F)

**Answers:** 1. e; 2. d; 3. d; 4. T; 5. e; 6. a. Legal, b. Legal, c. Illegal because the first parameter of `printf` must be a string, d. Illegal because the first parameter must be a string, e. Illegal because the first parameter is a character constant, not a string; 7. e; 8. T; 9. F.

---

## 7.6    EXAMPLE PROGRAM 1: A C Program that Demonstrates Output Formatting for Integer Values

Let us design a C application program that can be used to demonstrate formatted output capabilities for integers to its users. We want the program to be flexible and allow the user to try several integers and different print field width values. We know that by default integer values are printed right-adjusted in a field of fixed width with a fill character of blank. We can change these defaults and print an integer in a fixed-width field in various ways. In our program we will have integers printed

1. Right-adjusted in a fixed-width field.
2. Left-adjusted in a fixed-width field.
3. Right-adjusted with a plus sign, if it is positive.
4. Right-adjusted with leading zeros.

With your present knowledge of C, this task should not be difficult. Figure 7.9 shows a C program that can be used as a teaching aid for formatted output of integer values.

```c
/*******************************************************************
   Program Filename: Prog07_1.c
   Author           : Uckan
   Purpose          : Demonstrates C formatted output features for
                      integers.
   Input from       : Keyboard
   Output to        : Screen
 *******************************************************************/
#include <stdio.h>

/* Function prototypes: */

void print_integer(int number);


int main(void) {
      /* Local variables: */

      int integer_number;
      char do_more = 'y', new_line;

      /* Function body: */

      printf("THIS PROGRAM DEMONSTRATES OUTPUT FORMATTING FEATURES\n");
      printf("FOR INTEGER VALUES IN C.\n");

      while (do_more == 'y') {
            printf("Enter an integer: ");
            scanf("%d", &integer_number);

            print_integer(integer_number);

            scanf("%c", &new_line);
            printf("Do you want to continue? (y/n): ");
            scanf("%c", &do_more);
      } /* end while */


      return 0;
} /* end function main */
```

**Figure 7.9**    A C program that demonstrates formatted output for integers *(continued)*    ▶

```
/*****************************************************
   Function Name   : print_integer
   Purpose         : Prints integers in a variety of ways.
   Called by       : main
   Receives        : number
   Returns         : None
*****************************************************/
void print_integer(int number) {
      /* Local variables: */

      int width;

      /* Function body: */

      printf("What is the field width? ");
      scanf("%d", &width);
      printf("\n");

      printf("===> Printing right-adjusted in a field of width %d:\n",
             width);
      printf("     5   10   15   20   25   30   35   40\n");
      printf("----+----+----+----+----+----+----+----+\n");
      printf("%*d\n\n", width, number);

      printf("===> Printing left-adjusted in a field of width %d:\n",
             width);
      printf("     5   10   15   20   25   30   35   40\n");
      printf("----+----+----+----+----+----+----+----+\n");
      printf("%-*d\n\n", width, number);

      printf("===> Printing with a plus sign in a field of width %d:\n",
             width);
      printf("     5   10   15   20   25   30   35   40\n");
      printf("----+----+----+----+----+----+----+----+\n");
      printf("%+*d\n\n", width, number);

      printf("===> Printing with leading zeros in a field of width %d:\n",
             width);
      printf("     5   10   15   20   25   30   35   40\n");
      printf("----+----+----+----+----+----+----+----+\n");
      printf("%0*d\n", width, number);
} /* end function print_integer */
```

Figure 7.9

A sample interactive session obtained by running the program of Figure 7.9 is shown in Figure 7.10. We suggest that you run this program on your system and use it to reinforce your knowledge of formatted output of integers in C.

```
THIS PROGRAM DEMONSTRATES OUTPUT FORMATTING FEATURES
FOR INTEGER VALUES IN C.
Enter an integer: 145
What is the field width? 25

===> Printing right-adjusted in a field of width 25:
     5    10    15    20    25    30    35    40
----+----+----+----+----+----+----+----+
                         145

===> Printing left-adjusted in a field of width 25:
     5    10    15    20    25    30    35    40
----+----+----+----+----+----+----+----+
145

===> Printing with a plus sign in a field of width 25:
     5    10    15    20    25    30    35    40
----+----+----+----+----+----+----+----+
                        +145

===> Printing with leading zeros in a field of width 25:
     5    10    15    20    25    30    35    40
----+----+----+----+----+----+----+----+
0000000000000000000000145
Do you want to continue? (y/n): n
```

**Figure 7.10**    A sample interactive session for the program of Figure 7.9

## 7.7    MORE ON INTERACTIVE INPUT

In Chapter 3 we introduced the `scanf` function for interactive input and used that function in all the programs that we have designed until now. In this section you will learn more about interactive input in C.

### The Standard Input Function `scanf`

In standard C interactive input requires the use of the library function `scanf`. This function is declared in the standard header file `stdio.h`. To use it for interactive input, our program must contain the preprocessor directive `#include <stdio.h>`.

The syntax of the  scanf  function call follows.

---

scanf (*FormatControlString, InputList*);

---

The *FormatControlString* contains one or more format specifiers, escape sequences, and possibly other ordinary characters. The format specifiers for interactive input are

1.  %hd, %d, %ld, %u, and %lu  for integers
2.  %f, %lf, %Lf, %e, %le, and %Le  for floating-point values
3.  %c  for characters

The *InputList* consists of one or more variable addresses, each corresponding to a format specifier in the *FormatControlString*. Therefore, unless they are pointers themselves, the variable names in the input list must be prefixed by the character &, which is the address operator. For example, for variables of fundamental data types (such as int, double, and char)  we must use the address operator and provide their addresses in the *InputList*. However, for string variables, we don't use the address operator, since the name of a string is a pointer to the memory location (that is, the address of the memory location) where the string value is stored.

Let us study examples of  scanf  invocations.

***Example 7.10***   Let  number  be an integer variable declared as

```
int number;
```

To input a value for number interactively, we execute the statement

```
scanf("%d", &number);
```

When this statement is encountered, the program execution comes to a temporary halt and waits for the user to type a value for the variable  number. Since the format control string "%d"  contains one format specifier, %d, for an integer variable, the value that is typed must be an integer. This value is ordinarily typed beginning at the current cursor position. However, if you want, you may type it anywhere to the right of the current position or below it on any line. You have this flexibility because whitespace (that is, blanks, tabs, and the new-line character, which is the carriage return or the Enter key on most terminal keyboards) is completely ignored during input. Whatever you type will be converted to its appropriate internal representation and assigned as the value of the variable  number. For example, in an interactive program an appropriate prompt should come before an input statement, reminding the user of the action to be taken next. An output statement can be used for this purpose:

```
printf("Enter an integer: ");
scanf("%d", &number);
```

In this example the  printf  function call will print the message  Enter an integer:  on the screen. Now, if we type 21, for example, and subsequently press Enter, the value 21 will be assigned to the variable  number.

After we type an integer value, we must press the Enter key so that program execution can continue. In the preceding example the integer value and the new-line character are pushed into the input stream. At that instant the computer scans the input stream and looks for an integer value. If found, this integer value is converted to an internal representation and is assigned to the integer variable  number.

What if we type a floating-point value for an integer variable? For example, if we enter the floating-point value  125.56  in conventional notation for  number  using the statement

```
scanf("%d", &number);
```

this value is truncated to  125  and is assigned to the variable number. On the other hand, if we enter a floating-point value in scientific notation such as  14.56e-2, we will have only the first integer value that can be extracted from the input stream, that is, 14, assigned to the variable.

As you can see, in interactive input the computer takes any value typed into the input stream and converts it, if it can, to a value that is compatible with the type of the variable to which this value is to be assigned. Therefore, the user of the program should be aware of the type of the value to be entered. If we enter a value that cannot be converted to the target type, depending on the way the compiler is designed, either we will get an error message or an incorrect value assignment will occur. Although most C compilers are capable of type conversion in many instances, entering values that are consistent with the types of input variables is better programming practice than relying on the compiler's ability to convert types.

**Example 7.11**   Suppose we have the declaration

```
double weight;
```

and the code

```
printf("Enter a value for weight: ");
scanf("%lf", &weight);
```

If the value that we would like to input for  weight  is 15.2, we can type it in many different ways. For example, we can type it as  15.2 and then press Enter, or we can use whitespace before 15.2 and type it as ⎵⎵⎵⎵⎵⎵⎵⎵15.2  followed by an Enter. Also, we can type this value with a plus sign and in scientific notation as  +0.152e+2  and press the Enter key. All of these variations are equivalent. Again, the computer scans the input stream, ignores whitespace, and picks the first value it comes across to assign to the variable  weight. This value is 15.2 in all of the preceding cases.

On the other hand, if we enter an integer value such as 15 for  weight, it is converted to its floating-point representation and stored as 15.0. In this case we have not lost anything because of the conversion.

**Example 7.12**   Let response be a character variable declared as

```
char response;
```

The scanf function call in the following partial code

```
printf("Enter a character: ");
scanf("%c", &response);
```

will bring the program execution to a temporary halt. If you want to store the value 'X' in the variable `response` through input, you may type X and subsequently press the Enter key. You may also type ⊔⊔⊔⊔⊔⊔ X and then press the Enter key. Here ⊔⊔⊔⊔⊔ stands for whitespace of arbitrary length. In assigning a value to the variable `response`, the computer ignores whitespace and processes the content of the input stream until it encounters a nonblank character. Then it assigns that character to the variable. In this example, if you type 5 instead of X, the value 5 will be assigned to `response` in character format.

## Formatting Input Data

In general, as we can format output, we can also format input data. For example, we could type an integer value such as 25, right-adjusted in a field of width 10 as follows:

| 1 | 2 | 3 | 4 | 5 | 6 | 7 | 8 | 9 | 10 |
|---|---|---|---|---|---|---|---|---|----|
|   |   |   |   |   |   |   |   | 2 | 5  |

and then instruct the computer to read it into a variable. So that the computer could read this value correctly, we would have to somehow specify the field width and that the value is right-adjusted in the field.

However, in stream-oriented input all blanks are skipped. During data conversion whitespace in the string typed by the user is ignored. Therefore, if we specify fixed-width fields in format specifiers, for example, as `%10d`, the specified width is considered to be the number of characters in the typed value. Let us study an example.

***Example 7.13***   Assuming `number` is an integer variable and that we are using the statement

```
scanf("%4d", &number);
```

to input a value for it, if we enter the value such as 1150 with or without leading whitespace, the value assignment will be correct and the variable number will be assigned 1150. Therefore, for an integer value of up to four digits, this statement has the same effect as the statement

```
scanf("%d", &number);
```

However, if the value of number is meant to be 11556, the statement

```
scanf("%4d", &number);
```

will convert the first four digits to an internal representation and assign the value 1155 to `number`. The last digit, which is 6, will be left in the input stream for the next value assignment.

Similar considerations are valid for input of floating-point and string values. More examples follow.

***Example 7.14***   Suppose we have

```
double coefficient;
```

and the input statement

```
scanf("%3lf", &coefficient);
```

The following table shows some values entered by the user and, in each case, the value assigned to the variable `coefficient`:

| Value Entered | Value Assigned |
|:---:|:---:|
| 1234.5 | 123.0 |
| 2456.8e+1 | 245.0 |
| 1.3e-4 | 1.3 |
| 17889 | 178.0 |
| -347.5 | -34.0 |
| 3e+3 | 3.0 |
| 3e3 | 3000.0 |

**Example 7.15**   Let `string` be a string variable declared as

```
char string[11];
```

The `scanf` invocation

```
scanf("%5s", string);
```

will read the first five characters of the string value we type and assign it to the variable `string`, provided the first five characters do not contain whitespace. Therefore, if we type `flamenco` in response to this `scanf` function call, the value that is stored in `string` will be `flame`. Note that the variable `string` in this example is not prefixed by the address operator in the input list of the `scanf` function call, because the variable `string` itself is an address.

Apart from the possibility of specifying the width of the value to be converted, the format specifiers for `scanf` do not permit the use of special characters such as `+`, `-`, decimal point, and `0` that we can use for output formatting purposes. A format specifier such as `%10c` for character data has the same effect as `%c`. Format specifiers such as `%10.3lf`, `%+10d`, `%-10d`, and `%010d`, if used in `scanf` function calls, will not cause any compilation errors, but they will result in execution errors. Therefore, they should be avoided.

## Inputting Multiple Values with a Single `scanf` Function Call

It is possible to input values for several variables using one `scanf` function call. Let us study some examples.

**Example 7.16**   Assume that we have the declarations

```
int height;
char response;
double weight;
```

and the statement

```
scanf("%d%c%lf", &height, &response, &weight);
```

The format control string has three specifiers, `%d`, `%c`, and `%lf`, for the variables `height`, `response`, and `weight`, respectively. However, because the format control string does not contain any whitespace, the values must be typed without any whitespace. In other words, if we want to assign the values 100, 't', and 1.2e2 to `height`, `response`, and `weight`, we must type these values as `100t1.2e2`. If we enter these values with delimiting whitespace as

```
100 t 1.2e2
```

the first integer value, 100, will be correctly assigned to the variable `height`. The values that are picked for `response` and `weight` will be incorrect; they will be a space for `response` and 0.000000 for `weight`.

Even if we agree not to use any whitespace in typing values for several variables, we may encounter another problem. Suppose we wish to assign the values 100, '5', and 1.2e2 to `height`, `response`, and `weight`, respectively. The value '5' represents 5 in character code—not numeric 5. If we type these values as `10051.2e2`, the values assigned to the variables will be 10051, '.', and 200.0, respectively.

In such cases we clearly need the ability to use whitespace as separators, which can be achieved by introducing some whitespace into the format control string to separate the specifiers.

**Example 7.17**    The following statement

```
scanf("%d %c %lf", &weight, &response, &height);
```

will permit us to separate the three values with whitespace. Therefore, the string 100⎵⎵⎵⎵5⎵⎵⎵⎵1.2e2, where ⎵⎵⎵⎵ represents whitespace of arbitrary length, will result in the intended value assignments for our variables.

In general, in the interactive mode of processing, instead of using `scanf` function calls that input multiple values, you should try to use `scanf` function calls that read a single value. This way you can avoid unnecessary complications. However, as you will see in Chapter 8, if input data is coming from a file, then you will need `scanf` function calls with multiple input variables. We return to this topic again in the next chapter.

## REVIEW QUESTIONS

**1.** For the standard input function `scanf`, the source is the program, and the sink is the standard input device. (T or F)

**2.** The input list in a `scanf` function call can contain one or more variables. (T or F)

**3.** Which of the following `scanf` function calls is syntactically legal?
   **a.** scanf("%d", number + 5);
   **b.** scanf("%d%c%d", &number, &response, 15);
   **c.** scanf("%lf%lf%lf", &par_a, &par_b, &par_c);

**d.** `scanf(&number, "%d");`

**e.** None of the above.

**4.** Consider the following partial code:

```
int a, c;
char b;
scanf("%d%c%d", &a, &b, &c);
```

If the input stream entered for the `scanf` function call is `0.67  7  8`, which values will be assigned to the variables `a`, `b`, and `c`?

**a.** `0,  '.',  67`           **c.** `0,  '.',  7`

**b.** `0,  '7',  8`           **d.** None of the above.

**5.** Which value is assigned to the variable `var` by the `scanf` function call

```
scanf("%3lf", &var);
```

if we enter `-12.567` for it?

**a.** `-12.567`          **d.** `-12.6`

**b.** `-12.0`             **e.** None of the above.

**c.** `-12.5`

**6.** Assume that we have the following declarations:

```
int var1, var2, var3;
```

The input stream contains `333445555`. Which of the following `scanf` function calls will read this input stream and assign the values 333, 44, and 5555 to the variables `var1`, `var2`, and `var3`, respectively?

**a.** `scanf("%3d%2d%4d", &var1, &var2, &var3);`

**b.** `scanf("%3d %2d%4d", &var1, &var2, &var3);`

**c.** `scanf("%3d%2d %4d", &var1, &var2, &var3);`

**d.** `scanf("%3d %2d %4d", &var1, &var2, &var3);`

**e.** All of the above.

**f.** None of the above.

**7.** If an input stream contains more values than can be assigned by a `scanf` function call, the unused values in the stream will remain in it and will be used by another `scanf` execution in the program. (T or F)

**Answers:** 1. F; 2. T; 3. c; 4. a; 5. b; 6. e; 7. T.

## 7.8 EXAMPLE PROGRAM 2: A C Program that Prints Checks

The following application enables you to apply what you have learned in this chapter.

***Problem*** We want to design and implement a program that reads the name of a person, who is the payee, and a check amount and then prints the main line of a check that bears the payee's name and the check amount.

***Requirements Specification*** Develop a program that does the following for as long as the user wants to continue:

1.  Interactively reads the first name, middle initial, and last name of the payee.
2.  Reads a check amount, which must be less than $25,000, and validates this value.
3.  Prints the main line of the check as shown:

```
PAY TO THE ORDER OF John J. Smith           $****1,256.87
```

Here the string literal PAY TO THE ORDER OF should be printed beginning at print position 1. The name of the payee should be printed left-adjusted in the print position defined by columns 21 through 52. Next, we should have a dollar sign, $, on column 53, followed by four asterisks (for check protection) and the check amount. The check amount should be printed with a precision of 2, and a comma should separate thousands from hundreds if the amount is greater than or equal to $1000.

***Analysis***

**Inputs** Payee's first name, middle initial, and last name, and a check amount.

**Output** The main line of a check.

**Constraints** Check amount should be less than $25,000.

***Design*** Figure 7.11 shows an initial pseudocode algorithm for this problem.

*while there are more checks to print*
  *begin*
      *print "Enter payee's name: "*
      *read payee_ name*
      *read and validate check amount*
      *print check*
  *end*
*end_while*

**Figure 7.11** Initial pseudocode algorithm to print a check

In this pseudocode, corresponding to the step *read and validate check amount*, we will design and implement a function called *validated_check_value*, which will read a check amount, ensure that it is less than $25,000, and return the read amount to the calling program. We will leave the design of this function to the reader as an exercise.

The step *print check* is the punchline in this application. We will design and implement a function called *print_check* that will receive the payee's name and the check amount through its parameters and then print the check. As you will see, the logic of this function is simple. Therefore, rather than describing its pseudocode algorithm, we will present its implementation.

Figure 7.12 shows the refined pseudocode algorithm for the main function of the program that prints a check.

---

*set more_checks_to_print to 'y'*

*while more_checks_to_print is equal to 'y'*
  *begin*
    *print "Enter payee's name: "*
    *read payee_ name*
    *set check_amount to validated_check_value*
    *call print_check(payee_name, check_amount)*

    *print "More checks to print? (y/n): "*
    *read more_checks_to_print*
  *end*
*end_while*

---

**Figure 7.12**    Refined pseudocode algorithm of the main function to print a check

**Implementation**    Figure 7.13 is a C implementation of the design presented above, and Figure 7.14 shows a complete test run of the program.

```
/ * * * * * * * * * * * * * * * * * * * * * * * * * * * * * * * * * * * * * * * * * * * * * * * *
  Program Filename: prog07_2.c
  Author           : Uckan
  Purpose          : Partially prints a check.
  Input from       : terminal keyboard
  Output to        : screen
* * * * * * * * * * * * * * * * * * * * * * * * * * * * * * * * * * * * * * * * * * * * * * * * * /
#include <stdio.h>
#include <string.h>

// Function prototypes:

void print_check(char payee_name[], double check_amount);
double validated_check_value(void);


int main(void) {
      /* Local variables: */
```

**Figure 7.13**    A C program that prints the main line of a check (*continued*)    ▶

```
      double check_amount;
      char more_checks_to_print = 'y', new_line;
      char payee_name[31];

      /* Function body: */

      while (more_checks_to_print == 'y') {
            printf("===> Enter payee's name: ");
            gets(payee_name);

            check_amount = validated_check_value();
            print_check(payee_name, check_amount);

            scanf("%c", &new_line);
            printf("===> More checks to print? (y/n): ");
            scanf("%c", &more_checks_to_print);
            scanf("%c", &new_line);
      } /* end while */

      return 0;
} /* end function main */

/*****************************************************************
 Function Name    : validated_check_value
 Purpose          : Reads the face value of a check, ensures that
                    it is less than $25,000, and returns the
                    value to the calling function.
 Called by        : main
 Receives         : None
 Returns          : check_value under function name
 *****************************************************************/
double validated_check_value(void) {
      /* Local variables: */

      double check_value;

      /* Function body: */

      printf("===> Enter check amount; should be less than");
      printf("$25,000: ");
      scanf("%lf", &check_value);
```

**Figure 7.13**    A C program that prints the main line of a check (*continued*)    ▶

```
        while (check_value >= 25000.00) {
             printf("===> Enter check amount; should be less than ");
             printf("$25,000: ");
             scanf("%lf", &check_value);
        } /* end while */

        return check_value;
} /* end function validated_check_value */

/*****************************************************************
 Function Name    : print_check
 Purpose          : Prints the main line of a check.
 Called by        : main
 Receives         : payee_name, check_value
 Returns          : None
 *****************************************************************/
1  void print_check(char payee_name[], double check_value) {
2      /* Local variables: */

3      int thousands;
4      double rest;

5      /* Function body: */

6      printf("PAY TO THE ORDER OF ");
7      printf("%-32s$****", payee_name);
8
9      if (check_value < 1000.00)
10          printf("%.2f\n", check_value);
11     else {
12          thousands = (int) (check_value / 1000);
13          rest = check_value - 1000 * thousands;
14          printf("%d,%06.2f\n", thousands, rest);
15     } /* end if */
16  } /* end function print_check */
```

Figure 7.13

```
===> Enter payee's name: John J. Smith
===> Enter check amount; should be less than $25,000: 127.65
PAY TO THE ORDER OF John J. Smith                  $****127.65
===> More checks to print? (y/n): y
===> Enter payee's name: Karen H. Hollis
===> Enter check amount; should be less than $25,000:  27000
===> Enter check amount; should be less than $25,000:  21700
PAY TO THE ORDER OF Karen H. Hollis                $****21,700.00
===> More checks to print? (y/n): y
===> Enter payee's name: William Q. Sullivan
===> Enter check amount; should be less than $25,000: 1000.33
PAY TO THE ORDER OF William Q. Sullivan            $****1,000.33
===> More checks to print? (y/n): n
```

**Figure 7.14**    A test run of the program of Figure 7.13

We ask the reader to study this program, focus on the function `print_check`, and answer the following questions:

1.  What is the purpose of the format control string `"%-32s$****"` on line 7?
2.  Why do we have an `if` statement between lines 9 and 15?
3.  What do the then-part and the else-part of this `if` statement accomplish?
4.  Why have we used the format specifier `%06.2f` on line 14?

## 7.9   SUMMARY

### This Chapter at a Glance

*   Chapter 3 briefly introduced the C interactive input and output functions. This chapter returned to this important topic and described stream-oriented input-output in detail.
*   We discussed output formatting requirements for integers, floating-point values, character data, and strings. You learned about the C format specifiers and their use in output formatting.
*   You learned more about the input function `scanf` and saw that it can be used to input values for more than one variable.
*   The information in this chapter enables you to exercise precise control over the format of a program's output and to input data to C programs in a variety of ways.

### Coming Attractions

*   Up to this point all of our applications have been interactive. It is time to start learning about tools and techniques that make batch applications possible.

- The next chapter considers simple aspects of data files and file-oriented input and output and discusses file-processing features of the C language. You will learn about reading data from text files sequentially and writing data to text files.

- At the end of the next chapter, you will have the knowledge and problem-solving ability to design and implement programs that read data from files, write the program output to files, or both.

---

## STUDY GUIDE

### Test Your Comprehension

**1.** Which of the following statements concerning input-output is correct?
   **a.** In fully interactive programs input comes from the standard input device, which is usually the disk drive.
   **b.** A data file consists of lines into which we type program statements.
   **c.** If a program gets its input data values from a data file, it is said to have interactive input.
   **d.** The output of a computer program can be directed to the standard output device, which is usually the monitor screen.
   **e.** All of the above.
   **f.** None of the above.

**2.** Which of the following statements concerning stream-oriented input-output in C is correct?
   **a.** A stream is an abstraction for a flow of data from a sink to a source.
   **b.** In interactive input the source is the standard output device.
   **c.** In batch mode the source for an input stream is the program that uses data.
   **d.** Inputting data from a source is called inserting.
   **e.** All of the above.
   **f.** None of the above.

**3.** The print list in a `printf` function call can contain
   **a.** Constants           **d.** Expressions
   **b.** Variables           **e.** All of the above
   **c.** Function calls

**4.** Which of the following `printf` function calls is syntactically legal?
   **a.** `printf(%d, %d, %d, a, b, c);`
   **b.** `printf("3%d", a, b, c);`
   **c.** `printf("%d", a + b + c);`
   **d.** `printf("%d%d" a; b);`
   **e.** All of them are legal.
   **f.** None of them is legal.

**5.** For left-adjusted printing of an integer in an output field of width 10, we use the following format specifier:
   **a.** `%10d`
   **b.** `%010d`
   **c.** `%+10d`
   **d.** `%-10d`
   **e.** None of the above.

6. Choose the correct statement.
   a. The format specifier `%20d` ensures left-adjusted printing of an integer in a field of width 20.
   b. The format specifier `%10s` prints floating-point values in conventional notation.
   c. The specifier `%10e` prints floating-point values in scientific notation.
   d. The specifier `%010d` prints a plus sign for positive numeric integer values.
   e. None of the above is correct.

7. What will the following `printf` function call print?

   ```
   printf("%015e", 1e1);
   ```

   a. `0001.000000e+01`
   b. `1e+01`
   c. `000000001.0e+01`
   d. `00000000001.0e1`
   e. None of the above.

8. Which of the following `printf` function calls will print `000100.887`?
   a. `printf("%10f", 100.88678);`
   b. `printf("%-10.3f", 100.88678);`
   c. `printf("%010f", 100.88678);`
   d. `printf("%010.3f", 100.88678);`
   e. None of the above.

9. Which of the following `scanf` function calls is syntactically legal?
   a. `scanf(%d, &number);`
   b. `scanf("%dc"; &number, &response);`
   c. `scanf("%d%c%lf", &number, &response, &coef1);`
   d. `scanf(&number, &response, &coef1);`
   e. None of the above.

10. We have the following partial code:

    ```
    char x, y;
    int z;
    scanf("%c%c%d", &x, &y, &z);
    ```

    If the input stream contains `1235`, which values will be assigned to the variables `x`, `y`, and `z`?
    a. ' ', ' ', 1235
    b. '1', '2', 35
    c. 0, 0, 1235
    d. None of the above.

Answers:  1. d; 2. f; 3. e; 4. c; 5. d; 6. c; 7. a; 8. d; 9. c; 10. b.

## Improve Your Problem-Solving Ability

### Debugging Exercises

11. Identify the errors, if any, in each of the following `printf` function calls. The variables `c1`, `c2`, and `c3` are declared as follows:

```
int c1;
char c2;
double c3;
```

**a.** `printf("The value of c1 is: %d, c1");`
**b.** `printf(c1, c2, c3);`
**c.** `printf(%d, %c, %f, c1, c2, c3);`
**d.** `printf("%d, %c, %f", c1, c2, c3);`
**e.** `printf("%-+15d %f", c1);`
**f.** `printf("%e", c2);`
**g.** `printf("%e", &c3);`

**12.** Find the errors, if any, in each of the following `scanf` function calls. The variable declarations are given as follows:

```
int c1;
char c2;
double c3;
```

**a.** `scanf("Enter a value for x: ", c1);`
**b.** `scanf("%d", c1 + 5);`
**c.** `scanf("%e", c2);`
**d.** `scanf(%e, &c3);`
**e.** `scanf("%c", 'x');`

### *Programming Exercises*

**13.** Suppose we have the variable declarations

```
int part1;
char part2;
double part3;
```

Write the appropriate `printf` function call to print
**a.** The values of `part1`, `part2`, and `part3` with four blanks separating them.
**b.** The value of `part1`, left-adjusted in a field of width 10.
**c.** The value of `part1`, left-adjusted in a field of width 10, with a plus sign if the value is positive.
**d.** The value of `part3`, left-adjusted in a field of width 15 in conventional notation.
**e.** The value of `part3`, left-adjusted in a field of width 15 in scientific notation.
**f.** The value of `part3`, left-adjusted in a field of width 15 in conventional notation with a precision of 3.
**g.** The value of `part3`, right-adjusted in a field of width 15 in conventional notation with a fill character of zero.

**14.** Suppose we have the variable declarations:

```
int c1;
char c2;
double c3;
```

Assume that the values that are stored in the memory for c1, c2, and c3 are 125, 'T', and −5.23456, respectively. What will be printed by each of the following `printf` function calls?

**a.** `printf("%d     %f     %c", c1, c3, c2);`
**b.** `printf("%-10d", c1);`
**c.** `printf("%+10d%-10s", c1, "END");`
**d.** `printf("%15.3f", c3);`
**e.** `printf("%-15.3f%10c", c3, c2);`
**f.** `printf("%015.2f", c3);`

**15.** We have the following variable declarations:

```
int list_size;
double first_member, last_member;
char title[16];
char check;
```

For each of the following `scanf` function calls and the associated input streams, what are the value assignments for the variables in the input list of the `scanf` function?
**a.** `scanf("%d%lf%lf", &list_size, &first_member, &last_member);`
Input stream: `130   14.75   -16.42`
**b.** `scanf("%2d%3lf%3lf", &list_size, &first_member,`
`&last_member);`
Input stream: `13014.75-16.42`
**c.** `scanf("%s", title);`
Input stream: `Plant Manager`
**d.** `scanf("%4s", title);`
Input stream: `Plant Manager`
**e.** `scanf("%s%c", title, &check);`
Input stream: `Plant Manager`

### Programming Projects

**16.** Design and implement a modular C program that is similar to Example Program 1 in this chapter except it should demonstrate all C output formatting capabilities on floating-point values instead of integer values.

**17.** Design and implement a modular program that demonstrates all C output formatting capabilities for string values.

**18.** Solve Programming Project 21 in Chapter 5 that computes the fixed monthly payment for an installment loan using appropriate C output formatting capabilities. In particular, monetary values should be printed properly, as in 2,850.56, with inserted commas, decimal points, and a precision of 2.

**19.** If you solved the Programming Project 22 of Chapter 6, you were probably unhappy with the way the loan repayment table was printed on the monitor screen. Recall that the problem did not require the use of the output formatting features of the language. Now that you know about them, modify your program to produce a better looking table.

**20.** Develop a program that reads
   **a.** A date as three integers: the first representing the month, the second the day, and the third the year
   **b.** A check number, as a character string of length 4
   **c.** A name, which is the name of the payer, into a string of length 30
   **d.** A street address, which is the address of the payer, into a string of length 35
   **e.** City, state, and zip code, treated as a single string, into a string of length 35

These input operations should be done in the function `main`. Then, again in the function `main`, your program should read another name, which is the name of the payee, into a character string of length 30 and should ensure that the payee and the payer are not the same person.

Next, your program should read a dollar amount, representing the face value of a check, in a function named `read_and_verify_check_amount`. The function should verify that the face value of the check is not more than $25,000 and return this value to the function `main`.

Finally, your program should call a function named `print_check`, which prints a check according to the following format:

```
John J. Smith                          Check No: 4295
31 Poplar Street                       Date: 03-12-1998
Oxford, OH 45056


PAY TO THE
ORDER OF        Joseph J. Thunder            $*****2,340.68


                                        John J. Smith
```

(Hint: Refer to Example Program 2 in this chapter.)

21. Develop a program that reads *n* integers, one at a time, in the range 0 through 30, and prints a horizontal bar chart using a specified fill character. For example, if the fill character is `*`, *n* is 4, and the four integers read are 3, 17, 12, and 30, your bar chart should look like this:

```
      |* * *
   3  |* * *
      |* * *
      |
      |* * * * * * * * * * * * * * * * *
  17  |* * * * * * * * * * * * * * * * *
      |* * * * * * * * * * * * * * * * *
      |
      |* * * * * * * * * * * *
  12  |* * * * * * * * * * * *
      |* * * * * * * * * * * *
      |
      |* * * * * * * * * * * * * * * * * * * * * * * * * * * * * *
  30  |* * * * * * * * * * * * * * * * * * * * * * * * * * * * * *
      |* * * * * * * * * * * * * * * * * * * * * * * * * * * * * *
```

22. Develop an interactive modular program that can be used to teach multiplication to grade school students. The program should prompt the user to enter two three-digit integers, verify that they are indeed three-digit integers, and then print the product of the integers according to the following format:

```
                              435
                    x         148
                         --------
        8 times 435 is       3480
        4 times 435 is       1740
        1 times 435 is       435
                         --------
        Add the products to get   64380
```

23. Develop a modular program that reads two integers, *beginning* and *end*, as the beginning and end of a range, such that *beginning* is less than or equal to *end*, and computes and prints all prime integers in this range in a nicely formatted table, containing no more than six prime numbers on a row. Your program output should resemble the following sample. (Hint: An integer $n$ that cannot be divided evenly by any integer between 1 and $n$, except 1 and $n$, is prime. An efficient algorithm to determine whether a given integer $n$ is prime tests for even division of $n$ by integers between 2 and the integer obtained by converting the square root of $n$ to an integer.)

```
    ****> Enter beginning of range: 10
    ****> Enter end of range: 6
    Incorrect range specification
    ****> Enter beginning of range: 10
    ****> Enter end of range: 60
    Prime numbers between 10 and 60:
        11       13       17       19       23       29
        31       37       41       43       47       53
        59
```

# 8

# File-Oriented Input and Output

---

**CHAPTER OBJECTIVES**

In this chapter you will learn about:

- **Data files**

- **C data files and streams**
  Declaring files
  Naming data files
  Opening files
  File open verification
  Closing files
  Testing for end-of-file

- **Processing C text files**
  Writing data to text files
  Reading data from text files
  Copying files

By the time you have completed this chapter, you will have acquired the ability to:

- **Design batch programs that do file input-output**

---

## 8.1     INTRODUCTION

All the programs we have developed up to this point have been interactive. In the interactive processing mode, input for a program comes from the terminal keyboard, output goes to the monitor screen, or both. In Chapter 7 we briefly mentioned batch processing, and you learned that in this mode input for a program comes from a data file, and its output may be directed to another file. There are many applications for which input-output may involve or require files.

At this point you know that a file is a named block of external storage. In contrast to what is stored in the internal memory, files are permanent until we decide to delete them. Once a file is created, we can keep it for as long as we want, for example, on disk storage. Our file may contain program code; in this case we have a source program file, an object program file, or an executable load module.

A file can also be designed to store data. Data files have significant advantages in application programming. They provide an inexpensive way to store large volumes of data permanently. We can easily update files, that is, make changes on the data stored in a file to keep them up-to-date. We can use a data file as input for the same program for as many program runs as we want without having to retype data. We can also use it as input for many programs. In other words, data files facilitate sharing of data by many applications. Because of these characteristics, files are important data structures.

We can create a data file using a text editor in pretty much the same way we create a C program. We can also create a data file by designing a program for this purpose and running it. In this chapter we examine the C file-processing features that we can use to create data files or access data stored in them. C has extensive file-processing capabilities. In this chapter we will limit our coverage to simple text files; in Chapter 14, you will learn more about C binary and random-access files.

## 8.2     FUNDAMENTALS OF C DATA FILES

Let us recall the definitions for a data file and a record:

> A **data file** is a named collection of records, normally kept in external storage. A **record** is the collection of related data values in a file.

Depending on how data are stored in it, a file may be a text file or a binary file. A **text file** stores data as readable and printable characters, whereas a **binary file** consists of nonreadable characters in binary code or control code. A C program prepared using a text editor is a text file. Similarly, a data file created by using a text editor or the output redirection feature of an operating system is a text file. You can browse a text file and read its content, and if you wish, you can get a hard copy of its content by printing it. On the other hand, an object program file consists of binary representations of program instructions, and its content is neither printable nor readable by humans. Computer programs, however, can read and process binary files. Some data files created using computer programs can be binary files. C has features for creating and processing both text and binary data files.

In a text file each record may be thought of as a collection of data values terminated by a new-line character, which is not visible. All records in a text file are terminated by an end-of-file marker placed by the operating system to mark the physical end of the file. For example, we may have a text file in which data are stored as follows:

---

```
1000 John Carlos⏎2000 Kim Trout⏎3000 Steven MacDonald⏎◆
```

---

In this file ⏎ represents the new-line character and ◆ represents the end-of-file marker. The file has three records. If we print it, we get the following, more readable, tabular representation:

```
1000 John Carlos
2000 Kim Trout
3000 Steven MacDonald
```

In a binary data file, records are not separated by special markers. If it is a C binary data file, during processing the C system relies on length information provided by the programmer to extract that portion of data stored in the file that we visualize as a record. A binary data file also ends with an end-of-file marker.

## C Files and Streams

We have seen that C uses streams in interactive processing. A stream is a series of bytes associated with a file. We have used two streams in interactive processing: the standard input stream and the standard output stream. In fact, there is another stream, called the standard error stream, in the interactive mode. When a program begins to execute, the three standard streams for input, output, and error are automatically established, and we can use them for input and output whenever we need them. There are many functions in the standard library for input and output, such as `scanf` and `printf`, and they are all declared in the `stdio.h` header file.

The **standard input stream** establishes a communication channel between the standard input device and a C program. In this channel the standard input device is the source, and the program is the sink. The standard input device is regarded as a file, and its name is `stdin`.

The **standard output stream**, on the other hand, links the program to the standard output device such that the program is the source and the standard output device is the sink. In this linkage the standard output device is also regarded as a file, and its name is `stdout`.

Finally, there is the standard error stream established between the program and the standard error device. The **standard error stream** is essentially an output stream in which the program is the source and the standard error device is the sink. Usually, the standard error device is the same as the standard output device, but it has a different file name, `stderr`. Since there is only one standard input, one standard output, and one standard error device, we don't declare the files `stdin`, `stdout`, and `stderr` in our programs; we use them directly.

In batch processing C also relies on stream-oriented input-output. The fundamental operations on file streams are carried out by some functions that are also declared in the `stdio.h` header file. The most commonly used functions are

1.  The function `fopen` to open files, that is, to establish a stream between a program and a file
2.  The functions `fscanf`, `fgetc`, `fgets`, and `fread` for input of data from files
3.  The functions `fprintf`, `fputc`, `fputs`, and `fwrite` for output of data to a file
4.  The function `feof` to check for the end-of-file marker during input
5.  The function `fclose` to close a file, or detach it from the program

This chapter covers most of these functions; the functions not covered here, `fread` and `fwrite`, are considered in Chapter 14. Among these functions, we recognize the input functions `fscanf` and `fgets` and the output function `fprintf` from our knowledge of interactive input and output. The functions `fscanf` and `fgets` are the counterparts of the functions `scanf` and `gets`, respectively. The `fprintf` function corresponds to `printf` interactive output function. In fact, for example, the statement

        scanf("%d", &test_score);

is equivalent to the statement

        fscanf(stdin, "%d", &test_score);

They both read an integer value from the standard input stream, `stdin`, and store the value in the integer variable `test_score`. The difference is that in `scanf` we do not have to specify the name of the standard input stream, `stdin`. However, if we want the input to come from a file other than `stdin`, we must use the second form, which requires the explicit specification of the name of the file, as in

        fscanf(student_file, "%d", &test_score);

The prefix `f` in the name of `fscanf` and the other functions in the list is a reminder that they all operate on files. We will discuss these functions in detail in the following sections.


## Declaring Files

A program may work on many files. So that they can be differentiated, you must declare them as appropriate file streams. For example, the declaration

        FILE *personnel_file;

declares `personnel_file` as a file, and establishes a stream between your program and the file `personnel_file`. Note that `personnel_file` is prefixed by the symbol `*`, and is, therefore, declared as a pointer. You will learn about pointers in Chapter 10. For the time being, it is sufficient to know that a pointer is a variable that contains the address of another variable or program entity in the main memory. The preceding declaration creates a pointer to a file structure called `personnel_file`. This file structure is defined in `stdio.h` and will be available when we open the file. The structure contains information that the operating system uses to manage the file. You should note that the keyword `FILE` in a file declaration must be all uppercase.

## Naming Data Files

We defined a data file as a named collection of records. This definition implies that a data file must have a name so that it can be identified and distinguished from many other files that we may have in our applications. In fact, in C, each data file must have two names: an internal name and an external name.

An **internal file name** is the name that the C system uses to identify a file among others that a program might process. File declarations assign internal names to data files. For example, in the declaration for the file

```
FILE *personnel_file;
```

`personnel_file` is an internal file name.

An **external file name** is the name that the operating system uses to identify a file in a disk directory. The conventions used in forming external file names depend on the operating system. For example, in MS-DOS, the name `A:\PRSONNEL.TXT` identifies a file in directory A whose name is `PRSONNEL` with an extension of `TXT`. You must be familiar with file-naming conventions inherent in your operating system.

## Opening Files and the `fopen` Function

Before we can process a file, we must open it. In other words, we must properly associate the external and internal names for a file so that whenever our C program references the file, the operating system can understand which external file it should access for input or output purposes. For this purpose we use the `fopen` function.

A call to the function `fopen` has the following format:

---

*InternalFileName* = fopen(*ExternalFileName, OpenMode*);

---

Here *InternalFileName* is the name of the file pointer declared in the program. *ExternalFileName* is a string literal, which is the external name of the file, or a string variable that stores the external name of the file as a character string.

The second parameter of the `fopen` function, *OpenMode*, indicates the mode in which the file is to be opened. The more commonly used **file open modes** are

1.   `"r"`, if the file is to be opened in input mode so that we can read data from it

2.   `"w"`, if the file is intended to be an output file and we are planning to write data to it

3.   `"a"`, if we are planning to append data to the end of an already existing file

4.   `"r+"`, which opens a file for update (that is, the file is both an input and an output file). If the file already exists, its content is not destroyed

5.   `"w+"`, which destroys the file if it already exists and opens a new file for update

6.   `"a+"`, which opens the file for update such that writing is done at the end of the file

Opening files in the proper file open mode is important. When opening files, you should keep in mind the following:

1.   The *OpenMode* parameter in the `fopen` statement is required. It can be any permissible open mode provided it is followed by an appropriate input or output statement in the program. If a file is opened in output mode, an input statement referencing it will have no effect at run time. Similarly, a file that is opened in input mode must be used in an input statement; if it is used in an output statement, such a statement will not be executed.

2.   The file open modes `"w"` and `"w+"` are destructive; an `fopen` function call for an existing file in one of these modes will destroy that file and begin creating a new file.

3.   The file open modes `"a"` and `"a+"` are nondestructive. A subsequent output statement will append new data to the end of an existing file without destroying the data already in it. You can read data from a file that has been opened in `"a+"` mode, but not from one that has the `"a"` open mode.

4.   For a file open mode of input (that is, `"r"`) to work, the file must exist physically in external storage; otherwise, the `fopen` statement will fail.

Let us study some examples.

***Example 8.1***   We assume that we have the following declaration for a named string constant:

```
#define in_file_name "A:INPUT.TXT"
```

where `A:INPUT.TXT` is the external name of a file in an MS-DOS environment. The file declaration

```
FILE *indata;
```

is for a file with an internal name of `indata`. We can open the file `indata` as follows:

```
indata = fopen(in_file_name, "r");
```

This statement will associate `indata` with its external counterpart `A:INPUT.TXT` and open it for input.

***Example 8.2***   Now consider the declaration for a file called `outdata`:

```
FILE *outdata;
```

This file can be opened for output as follows:

```
outdata = fopen("A:OUTPUT.TXT", "w");
```

With this `fopen` function call, we establish `outdata` as an output stream between our program and the external file `A:OUTPUT.TXT`.

As we saw in Example 8.1, we can have a named constant declaration for a string variable, and we can assign an external file name to it. Subsequently, we can use the string variable wherever a reference to the external file name is required. So we have

```
#define in_file_name "A:INPUT.TXT"
```

***Example 8.3***    Suppose we have the following partial code that deals with two files:

```
1    char in_file_name[15];
2    char out_file_name[15];
3    FILE *indata;
4    FILE *outdata;
5    ...................
6    ...................
7    printf("Enter external file name for output file: ");
8    gets(out_file_name);
9    ...................
10   ...................
11   printf("Enter external file name for input file: ");
12   gets(in_file_name);
13   ...................
14   ...................
15   outdata = fopen(out_file_name, "w");
16   ...................
17   ...................
18   indata = fopen(in_file_name, "r");
```

The internal names of the files are `indata` and `outdata`, respectively, and they are declared on lines 3 and 4. Their external names are provided by the user of the program. To make this possible, we declare `in_file_name` and `out_file_name` as two character string variables on lines 1 and 2. The interactive prompts and input statements on lines 7 through 12 enable the user to enter external file names and store them in these character variables.

The `fopen` function call on line 15 associates the stream `outdata` with the external file name stored in the variable `out_file_name` and opens this file in output mode. Following this statement we must have one or more appropriate output statements. Since the file open mode is output, if this file already exists, the `fopen` function call in the program will destroy its previous content. Had the file open mode been append instead of output, an existing file with the same external name would not be destroyed, and the new data would be appended to the end of the file. If we have some input statements attempting to read data from this file in the program, they will have no effect.

On the other hand, the `fopen` function call on line 18 establishes an association between `indata` and the external file whose name is stored in the variable `in_file_name`. Also, this function call opens `indata` in input mode so that we can read data from it.

## File Open Verification

Under certain circumstances, an attempt to open a file may fail. For example, we may have an `fopen` function call that is intended to ready a file for input, and that file may not exist in the indicated file directory, or we may not have a disk in the appropriate drive. In this case the `fopen` function call cannot execute successfully. Whether an `fopen` call is successful or not is reflected by the result that it returns. If an `fopen` function call returns a `NULL` pointer value, then the call has failed. `NULL` is a special named constant that is used as a value for pointer variables. It is declared in the standard header file `stdio.h`.

If an `fopen` call on a file is not successful, your program will probably not execute properly, and you may even have run-time errors or be caught in an infinite loop. To avoid such situations, it is good programming practice to verify the success of `fopen` calls and, in case of failure, terminate the execution of the program.

A C program execution may be terminated if we use the `exit` function, which is declared in the `stdlib.h` header file. The form of the `exit` function is simple; it has one integer argument, which is returned to the operating system upon program termination. For example, the function call

```
exit(-1);
```

will terminate the program execution and return the control to the operating system with a termination status value of −1. In common practice a negative argument value is taken as indication of abnormal program termination.

Thus we can use the value returned by the `fopen` function and a call to `exit` in an `if` statement to verify the success of an `fopen` call and to terminate the program in case of failure. The partial code in the following example contains such an `if` statement.

*Example 8.4*

```
#include <stdlib.h>
.......................
.......................
if((indata = fopen(file_name, "r")) == NULL) {
      printf("File open error on %s", file_name);
      exit(-1);
} /* end if */
.......................
.......................
```

In this example we have the preprocessor directive `#include <stdlib.h>` because we have decided to use the `exit` function in the `if` statement. The predicate of the `if` statement compares the pointer value returned by the `fopen` call to `NULL`. In case the file `indata` cannot be opened successfully, the then-part of the `if` statement will be executed. It contains a `printf` function call that prints on the screen a message informing us of a file open failure and the file on which the failure occurred. Following the `printf` function call, we have a call to `exit` that terminates the program execution.

The approach of Example 8.4 will work. However, instead of using the standard interactive output function `printf` to print a message on the standard output device, `stdout`, it is preferable to use the function `fprintf` to print it on the standard error device `stderr`. The use of `fprintf` is very similar to that of `printf`, as shown below. We will discuss the function `fprintf` in further detail in the next section.

```
if((indata = fopen(file_name, "r")) == NULL) {
      fprintf(stderr, "File open error on %s", file_name);
      exit(-1);
} /* end if */
```

As you can see, the difference between `fprintf` and `printf` is that `fprintf` requires the name of the file to which output will be sent as its first argument. The rest is similar to `printf`. As a matter of programming style, you should prefer sending messages to `stderr`, rather than to `stdout`, whenever your intention is to print on the screen an alert to an error or an exception condition. There are two reasons for this advice. First, an output to `stderr` states the purpose of your program quite explicitly to the reader. Second, printing to `stderr` is faster than printing to `stdout` because the message appears on the screen without any delay or intermediate character buffering.

## Closing Files and the `fclose` Function

After we open a file and process it for input and/or output, we must close it. For this purpose we use the `fclose` function with the following call format:

```
fclose(InternalFileName);
```

The `fclose` function has one argument, the *InternalFileName*. If the file has been opened in output or append mode, depending on the operating system you are using, a call to `fclose` may cause the operating system to place an end-of-file marker in the file and cuts the connection between the program and the file. For a file that has been opened in input mode, the `fclose` function simply disconnects it from the program. When a file is closed, the file pointer no longer exists. Therefore, we cannot use any input-output statements on that file in our program unless we reopen it. Here is an fclose function call that closes an open file called indata:

        fclose(indata);

The use of the fclose function to disconnect an open file from your program is optional. If you don't close a file, the operating system will close it when your program terminates either normally or abnormally. However, it is good programming practice to close all your files when you are done with them for two reasons:

1.   If your file is an output file and you want to change it to input, you must first close the file and then reopen it in input mode, as in the following partial code:

```
. . . . . . . . . . . . . . . . . .
. . . . . . . . . . . . . . . . . .
FILE *student_file;
. . . . . . . . . . . . . . . . . .
. . . . . . . . . . . . . . . . . .
student_file = fopen("A:STU.DAT", "w");
. . . . . . . . . . . . . . . . .  /* Output statements to create file: */
fclose(student_file);
. . . . . . . . . . . . . . . . . .
. . . . . . . . . . . . . . . . . .
student_file = fopen("A:STU.DAT", "r");
. . . . . . . . . . . . . . . . .  /* Input statements to read file: */
fclose(student_file);
. . . . . . . . . . . . . . . . . .
. . . . . . . . . . . . . . . . . .
```

2.   For most operating systems, the number of files that can be open simultaneously is limited. If in an application you are working with a large number of files and the number of files open at a given time exceeds the limit inherent in your operating system, you will have an error. Therefore, you should close every file explicitly as soon as you are done with it in your program.

## Checking for End-of-File and the feof Function

Another useful function when reading data from files is the feof function. It can be used to detect the end-of-file marker at the end of a data file. A call to this function has the following format:

        feof (*InternalFileName*)

The `feof` function returns a nonzero integer (true) if the most recent input operation on the file *InternalFileName* has detected the end-of-file marker; otherwise, it returns zero (false). We commonly use the `feof` function in a loop while reading data from a file that has been opened in input mode. For example, for a file whose internal name is `student_file`, a `while` loop that checks to see whether the end of the file has been reached begins with `while (! feof(student_file))`. In this loop control expression, we have the symbol `!`, which is the C logical *not* operator. The logical *not* operator is one of the logical operators that C supports. You will learn about logical operators in Chapter 9. Here we examine the logical *not* operator briefly so that we can use it in checking for end-of-file markers in file processing.

The **logical *not* operator** is unary, that is, it requires one operand, and is represented by the symbol `!`. The operand must be an expression that computes to a numeric value. If the value of the operand is nonzero (true), the logical *not* operator returns zero (false). If, however, the value of its operand is zero (false), the logical *not* operator returns 1 (true). Therefore, in the expression `! feof(student_file)`, if the end of the file has not been reached, the value returned by the `feof` function is 0 (false) and the operator `!` negates it to 1 (true) so that the loop body can be executed.

Now we can turn to an example that uses the `feof` function.

***Example 8.5***    In the following skeleton code, we have a file called `student_file` that we open in input mode.

```
. . . . . . . . . . . . . . . . . .
. . . . . . . . . . . . . . . . . .
FILE *student_file;
. . . . . . . . . . . . . . . . . .
. . . . . . . . . . . . . . . . . .
student_file = fopen("A:STU.DAT", "r");
. . . . . . . . . . . . . . . . . . /* Input statements to read data from
                                       file */
while(! feof(student_file)) {
. . . . . . . . . . . . . . . . . . /* Statements to process data */
. . . . . . . . . . . . . . . . . . /* Statements to read data from file */
} /* end while */
. . . . . . . . . . . . . . . . . .
. . . . . . . . . . . . . . . . . .
fclose(student_file);
. . . . . . . . . . . . . . . . . .
. . . . . . . . . . . . . . . . . .
```

Before the `while` statement we have appropriate file input statements that read data from `student_file`. The `while` statement has the predicate `! feof(student_file)`, which returns a nonzero integer if the previous input statement has indeed read data, that is, if it has not yet encountered the end-of-file marker. In this case, the body of the `while` statement is executed. The body contains both statements that process the data according to problem requirements and other file input statements. Processing continues until the last input statement detects the end-of-file marker. In this case the predicate returns zero, and the loop is appropriately terminated.

## REVIEW QUESTIONS

**1.** Files are important because
   **a.** they provide an inexpensive way to store large volumes of data.
   **b.** they can be easily updated and kept up-to-date.
   **c.** they facilitate sharing of data by many applications.
   **d.** All of the above are correct.
   **e.** None of the above is correct.

**2.** In a binary data file,
   **a.** records are represented as readable collection of characters.
   **b.** each record ends with a new-line character.
   **c.** a binary data file is terminated by an end-of-file marker.
   **d.** All of the above are correct.
   **e.** None of the above is correct.

**3.** Choose the *incorrect* statement: The most commonly used file processing functions in C include
   **a.** `fopen`, which establishes a stream between a file and a program.
   **b.** `feof`, which can be used to check for the end-of-file marker during input from a file.
   **c.** `close`, which detaches a file from a program.
   **d.** the functions `fscanf`, `fgetc`, `fgets`, and `fread` for input of data from files.
   **e.** the functions `fprintf`, `fputc`, `fputs`, and `fwrite` for output of data to a file.

**4.** In C a file is declared as a pointer to a file structure defined in `stdio.h`. (T or F)

**5.** Concerning C file names:
   **a.** Each C file must have an internal and an external name.
   **b.** The internal name is the name of the file pointer declared in the program.
   **c.** The external name is the directory name of the file that the operating system uses to identify it.
   **d.** Internal and external file names are associated in calls to the `fopen` function.
   **e.** All of the above are correct.
   **f.** None of the above is correct.

**6.** The file open mode
   **a.** `"r"` opens a file in input mode, even if the file does not exist physically.
   **b.** `"w"` opens an existing file for output without destroying its content.
   **c.** `"a"` destroys the file if it exists and starts a new file to which we can append data.
   **d.** `"r+"` opens a data file for update.
   **e.** All of the above are correct.
   **f.** None of the above is correct.

**7.** The standard error device `stderr` is normally used to print error and warning messages, and it is faster than printing on `stdout` because messages are printed without any delay or character buffering. (T or F)

**8.** It is possible to reopen in input mode a file that has been opened in output mode without closing it. (T or F)

**Answers:** 1. d; 2. c; 3. c; 4. T; 5. e; 6. d; 7. T; 8. F.

## 8.3   PROCESSING TEXT FILES

As we mentioned earlier, a text data file contains readable and printable characters. In this sense the output of a program on the terminal screen is a text file. The data that we type using the keyboard in interactive input are readable and, therefore, also constitute a text file.

In a text file a sequence of characters ending with the new-line character, `\n`, is a record. A line printed on the terminal screen in interactive output is the equivalent of a record in file-oriented output. In interactive input whatever we type using the terminal keyboard and terminate by depressing the Enter key is also a record.

Therefore, in creating a text file to write a record, we must use output statements that can write values of a list of expressions to the file and terminate this series by a new-line character. In reading records from an existing file, we must use input statements that transfer values from a record in the file to a series of variables in the program.

As you can see, the basic principles of file input-output are quite the same as those for interactive input-output. What we need are some functions, similar to those used for interactive input-output, except they should work for declared files instead of the standard `stdin` and `stdout` files. We will consider the more common file input-output functions in this section.

### Writing Data to Text Files

We can use the function `fprintf` to write to files any expression of fundamental data types (that is, `int`, `double`, `float`, and `char`) and strings. Also, we have the functions `fputc` and `fputs` that we can use to output character values and string values, respectively. The `fprintf` function is a variation of the `printf` function. The main difference is that the call to file output functions must include the name of the file to which data are to be sent.

The format of the call to the functions `fprintf`, `fputc`, and `fputs` follow:

```
fprintf(InternalFileName, FormatControlString, WriteList);
```

```
fputc (CharacterExpression, InternalFileName);
```

```
fputs (StringExpression, InternalFileName);
```

The function `fputc` writes a character value to a file whose name is *InternalFile-Name*. Similarly, the function `fputs` writes its first argument, a string value, to a file whose name is *InternalFileName*. Here are some examples.

***Example 8.6***    Let us assume that we declare `outdata` as

```
FILE *outdata;
```

and open it in output mode:

```
outdata = fopen("A:OUT.TXT", "w");
```

Further, let us assume that we have the following declarations for several variables:

```
int value1 = 10, value2 = 20;
double value3 = 15.75;
char value4 = 'x', value5 = 'y';
char value6[15] = "C programming";
```

The following table shows different output statements and the records that are written to the file `outdata` when they are executed.

| Output Statements | Record Written |
|---|---|
| `fprintf(outdata, "%d\n",`<br>`value1);` | `10↵` |
| `fprintf(outdata, "%d%d\n",`<br>`      value1, value2);` | `1020↵` |
| `fprintf(outdata, "%f\n",`<br>`      value3);` | `15.750000↵` |
| `fprintf(outdata, "%15e\n",`<br>`      value3);` | `      1.575000e+01↵` |
| `fprintf(outdata, "%c%c\n",`<br>`      value4, value5);` | `xy↵` |
| `fputc(value4, outdata);`<br>`fputc(value5, outdata);`<br>`fputc('\n', outdata);` | `xy↵` |
| `fputs(value6, outdata);`<br>`fputs("\n", outdata);` | `C programming↵` |
| `fprintf(outdata,`<br>`      "%d %d %f %c %c %s\n",`<br>`      value1, value2, value3,`<br>`      value4, value5, value6);` | `10 20 15.750000 x y C programming↵` |

You will notice that almost nothing in these statements is new. We used similar output statements many times in the past for formatted or unformatted output of different data types. The only difference here is that the file name `outdata` appears in the output statements. Also, we made sure that the statements ended with `"\n"` or `'\n'` so that each output statement or group of statements creates a record that ends with the newline character shown by the symbol ↵ in the table.

During file output the manner in which we format the records to be written to a file depends on the requirements of the problem. To illustrate this concept, we will design several C functions that create text files with different record formats.

***Example 8.7***   The C function in Figure 8.1 creates a text file of integers in which each record consists of a single integer value for the variable `test_score`.

```
void create_integer_file(char file_name[]) {
      /* Local variable declarations: */

      FILE *out;
      int test_score;

      /* Function body: */

      if ((out = fopen(file_name, "w")) == NULL) {
            fprintf(stderr, "***> Open error on output file %s",
                  file_name);
            exit(-1);
      } /* end if */

      printf("Enter a test score (0 terminates input): ");
      scanf("%d", &test_score);

      while (test_score != 0) {
            fprintf(out, "%d\n", test_score);

            printf("Enter a test score (0 terminates input): ");
            scanf("%d", &test_score);
      } /* end while */

      fclose(out);
} /* end function create_integer_file */
```

**Figure 8.1**      A C function that creates a text file of integers

In designing the function `create_integer_file`, we have gone through the following basic steps:

1. We declared a file as a local variable:

     `FILE *out;`

where `out` is the internal name of the file we will create.

2. We chose an external name for the file `out`. It is `file_name`, a string variable, which is the only parameter of the function `create_integer_file`. This approach enables us to pass an external file name to the function.

3. We opened the file using the `fopen` function call in the expression `out = fopen(file_name, "w")`, which is in the predicate of the `if` statement. This call associates the external name of the file, the value of `file_name`, with its internal name,

out. At the same time, it opens the file in output mode. Because we are expected to create a nonexistent file, its open mode must be output.

4.   We used an `if` statement to do file open verification. Note the use of `stderr` and the function `exit`. If the file open operation fails, the program will abort. Otherwise, the rest of the function will be executed.

5.   We have performed appropriate file input-output operations. In this case we have an interactive input statement followed by a `while` loop, which contains the file output statement:

```
fprintf(out, "%d\n", test_score);
```

This is very much like a regular `printf` function call except we have the name of the file, `out`, as the first parameter of the `fprintf` function call. Therefore, it writes the value of the variable `test_score` to the file `out` and begins a new line, thus forming a record in the file.

6.   We closed the file; the last statement in the function is

```
fclose(out);
```

This statement instructs the operating system to place an end-of-file marker at the end of the file and detaches the file from the program.

A call to the function `create_integer_file` can be as follows:

```
create_integer_file("A:\OUTINT.TXT");
```

This call will result in the creation of a text file whose external name is `A:\OUTINT.TXT`.

As you see, there is a pattern in the function `create_integer_file`, which consists of assigning internal and external names to a file, opening it in the right mode, doing file open verification, performing output operations, and closing the file. This pattern is present in all file processing applications where we create files.

***Example 8.8***   Because a text file consists of printable characters, we can create one by using file output statements and functions that write characters. The function `create_character_file` of Figure 8.2 can be used to produce a text file of characters in which a record can contain any number of characters and is terminated by a new-line character.

```
1   void create_character_file(char file_name[]) {
2       /* Local variable declarations: */

3       FILE *out;
4       char ch;
5
```

**Figure 8.2**   A C function that creates a text file of characters (*continued*)   ▶

```
6        /* Function body: */

7        if ((out = fopen(file_name, "w")) == NULL) {
8              fprintf(stderr, "***> Open error on output file %s",
9                      file_name);
10             exit(-1);
11       } /* end if */

12       printf("Enter a record (\\ terminates input): ");
13       scanf("%c", &ch);

14       while (ch != '\\') {
15             fputc(ch, out);

16             if (ch == '\n')
17                   printf("Enter a record (\\ terminates input): ");
18             /* end if */

19             scanf("%c", &ch);
20       } /* end while */

21       fclose(out);
22  } /* end function create_character_file */
```

**Figure 8.2**                                                              ■

In this application the user interactively types a record when prompted and terminates the record by pressing the Enter key. The `scanf("%c", &ch)` function calls on lines 13 and 19 read a character at a time from the standard input device, and the `fputc(ch, out);` statement on line 15 writes the most recently entered character to the file. If the value of the variable `ch` is the new-line character, the `if` statement in lines 16 through 18 prints a prompt to enter another record. Interactive input concludes when the user types a backslash character, \. In this case the file is closed, and the program control passes to the calling function.

Figure 8.3 is a C program that uses the function `create_character_file`.

```
#include <stdio.h>
#include <stdlib.h>

/* Function prototypes: */
```

**Figure 8.3**     A C program that uses the function `create_character_file` of Figure 8.2
*(continued)*                                                              ▶

```
void create_character_file(char file_name[]);

int main(void) {
        /* Local variable declarations: */

        char file_name[15];

        /* Function body: */

        printf("Assign an external name to the file: ");
        gets(file_name);

        printf("Creating output file %s. . .\n", file_name);

        create_character_file(file_name);

        printf("%s has been created.\n", file_name);

        return 0;
} /* end function main */
```

Figure 8.3                                                               ■

We can compile and execute the program of Figure 8.3 together with the function definition of Figure 8.2. A typical test run for this program is shown in the following box.

```
Assign an external name to the file: A:CHAROUT.TXT
Creating output file A:CHAROUT.TXT. . .
Enter a record (\ terminates input): 1000 Kimberly Brown 3.50
Enter a record (\ terminates input): 2000 John Doe       2.00
Enter a record (\ terminates input): 3000 Sharon Willow  3.45
Enter a record (\ terminates input): \
A:CHAROUT.TXT has been created.
```

Now, if we get a printout of the external file A:CHAROUT.TXT, it will look like this:

```
1000 Kimberly Brown 3.50
2000 John Doe       2.00
3000 Sharon Willow  3.45
```

The content of the records in the created file appears to be structured. The structure is a function of the manner in which we typed the records during creation; it was not imposed by the C programs of Figures 8.2 and 8.3.

***Example 8.9***    Finally, we can create a text file by storing records in string variables and writing them to the file as strings. Figure 8.4 shows a C function named `create_string_file`, which creates a text file of strings.

```c
void create_string_file(char file_name[]) {
    /* Local variable declarations: */

    FILE *out;
    char student_record[81];

    /* Function body: */

    if ((out = fopen(file_name, "w")) == NULL) {
        fprintf(stderr, "***> Open error on output file %s",
                file_name);
        exit(-1);
    } /* end if */

    printf("Enter student record (0000 terminates input): ");
    gets(student_record);

    while (strcmp(student_record, "0000") != 0) {
        fputs(student_record, out);
        fputc('\n', out);

        printf("Enter student record (0000 terminates input): ");
        gets(student_record);
    } /* end while */

    fclose(out);
} /* end function create_string_file */
```

**Figure 8.4**    A C function that creates a text file of strings

The main thing to note about this program is the file output statements:

```c
fputs(student_record, out);
fputc('\n', out);
```

which write to the file `out` the content of the string `student_record` and a newline character. Again, the records of the file created by this function will be structured if you type them in a structured manner during interactive input; the program does not impose any structure on them.

## Reading Data from Text Files

In C reading records from text files is as easy as writing records to text files. To read the records we must declare a file pointer, open the corresponding file in input or input-output mode, and use file input statements. File input statements are calls to appropriate file input functions such as `fscanf`, `fgetc`, and `fgets`. These functions are the counterparts of the functions `scanf`, `getchar`, and `gets` that we use for interactive input. You know about `scanf` and `gets`; you will study `getchar` in Chapter 13. The call formats of `fscanf`, `fgetc`, and `fgets` follows.

---

fscanf (*InternalFileName*, *FormatControlString*, *InputList*) ;

---

fgetc (*InternalFileName*) ;

---

fgets (*StringVariable*, *Size*, *InternalFileName*) ;

---

The function `fscanf` is just like `scanf` except the first parameter of `fscanf` is the internal name of the file from which data are read.

The function `fgetc` returns a character that we usually store in a program variable, as in the statement

```
ch = fgetc(infile);
```

where `ch` is a character variable and `infile` is the name of the file from which data are being read.

The second parameter, *Size*, in the format for the function call `fgets` is an integer. The function `fgets` reads a string of at most *Size* − 1 characters into *StringVariable* from the file *InternalFileName*. If the input operation is successful, `fgets` returns the string value that is read into *StringVariable*; otherwise, it returns NULL.

The variables into which we read values from a file must be declared appropriately, and how they are declared depends on the content of the file being read. If the records of the input file consist of single integers, then we may want to read each such integer into an integer variable. For example, assuming we have the declaration for the file `indata`

```
FILE *indata;
```

and that it has been successfully opened in input mode, the input statement

```
fscanf(indata, "%d", &test_score);
```

will read a record from the file  indata  and store the integer value in the variable test_score.

***Example 8.10***   Let A:OUTINT.TXT be the external name of a text file created by the program of Figure 8.1. This file contains records of a single integer, each corresponding to a test score. Suppose the file's current content is as shown in Figure 8.5.

```
100
98
77
65
45
89
43
100
64
88
```

**Figure 8.5**     Content of file  A:OUTINT.TXT

Let us develop a function named  compute_avg_test_score, which reads test score values from a file whose external name is supplied by the calling function and then computes and prints on the monitor screen the number of test score values and their arithmetic average. This function is given in the program of Figure 8.6.

```
1    void compute_avg_test_score(char file_name[]) {
2       /* Local variable declarations: */

3       FILE *indata;
4       int test_score, sum_of_test_scores = 0;
5       int avg_test_score, number_of_records = 0;

6       /* Function body: */

7       if ((indata = fopen(file_name, "r")) == NULL) {
8           fprintf(stderr, "***> Open error reading input file %s",
9                   file_name);
10          exit(-1);
11      } /* end if */
```

**Figure 8.6**     A C function that processes a text file of integers (*continued*)   ▶

```
12          fscanf(indata, "%d", &test_score);

13      while(! feof(indata)) {
14          printf("Echo-printing test score read: %d\n",
                   test_score);

15          sum_of_test_scores = sum_of_test_scores + test_score;
16          number_of_records++;

17          fscanf(indata, "%d", &test_score);
18      } /* end while */

19      fclose(indata);

20      if (number_of_records == 0)
21          avg_test_score = 0;
22      else
23          avg_test_score = sum_of_test_scores / number_of_records;
24      /* end if */

25      printf("Number of records: %d\n", number_of_records);
26      printf("Average test score: %d\n", avg_test_score);
27  } /* end function compute_avg_test_score */
```

Figure 8.6                                                                    ■

We note the following about the function `compute_avg_test_score`:

1.   It has one formal parameter, `file_name`. The value of `file_name` is the external name of the file that contains the input data.

2.   The expression `indata = fopen(file_name, "r")` in the predicate of the `if` statement on line 7 opens the file in input mode.

3.   The `if` statement in lines 7 through 11 checks to see whether the file is opened correctly.

4.   The input statement on line 12

```
    fscanf(indata, "%d", &test_score);
```

reads a record and stores its content, an integer, in the variable `test_score`.

5.   The while loop in lines 13 through 18 contains a `printf` function call:

```
    printf("Echo-printing test score read: %d\n",
        test_score);
```

It prints the value read from the file on the terminal screen. Printing a value read from a file immediately after a file input statement is executed is called **echo-printing**. Echo-printing of data in batch processing is a useful technique in program debugging and testing. It shows that the input operation has been executed successfully as intended or, if not, may help us detect the error that has caused unsuccessful input.

The rest of the program of Figure 8.6 is straightforward. Ultimately, it computes and prints the average test score and the number of records read. A main program that uses the function `compute_avg_test_score`, as well as the function `create_integer_file` of Figure 8.1, is given in Figure 8.7.

```c
#include <stdio.h>
#include <stdlib.h>

/* Function prototypes: */

void create_integer_file(char file_name[]);
void compute_avg_test_score(char file_name[]);

int main(void) {
        /* Variable declarations: */

        char file_name[15];

        /* Function body: */

        printf("Enter the external name of the file: ");
        gets(file_name);

        printf("Creating output file %s. . .\n", file_name);

        create_integer_file(file_name);

        printf("%s has been created.\n", file_name);

        printf("Processing file %s. . .\n", file_name);

        compute_avg_test_score(file_name);
        return 0;
} /* end function main */
```

**Figure 8.7**     A C program that uses the function `compute_avg_test_score` of Figure 8.6

If we compile and execute the programs of Figures 8.1, 8.6, and 8.7 together, we get the interactive output shown in Figure 8.8.

```
Enter the external name of the file: A:OUTINT.TXT
Creating output file A:OUTINT.TXT. . .
Enter a test score (0 terminates input): 100
Enter a test score (0 terminates input): 98
Enter a test score (0 terminates input): 77
Enter a test score (0 terminates input): 65
Enter a test score (0 terminates input): 45
Enter a test score (0 terminates input): 89
Enter a test score (0 terminates input): 43
Enter a test score (0 terminates input): 100
Enter a test score (0 terminates input): 64
Enter a test score (0 terminates input): 88
Enter a test score (0 terminates input): 0
A:OUTINT.TXT has been created.
Processing file A:OUTINT.TXT. . .
Echo-printing test score read: 100
Echo-printing test score read: 98
Echo-printing test score read: 77
Echo-printing test score read: 65
Echo-printing test score read: 45
Echo-printing test score read: 89
Echo-printing test score read: 43
Echo-printing test score read: 100
Echo-printing test score read: 64
Echo-printing test score read: 88
Number of records: 10
Average test score: 76
```

**Figure 8.8**    A test run of the program of Figure 8.7

***Example 8.11***   As another example of file input, we will design a C function that can read a text file and print its content on the terminal screen. We will consider the text file to consist of character data. A record in such a file is a sequence of characters terminated by the new-line character. The function named `print_character_file` is given in Figure 8.9.

```
1     void print_character_file(char file_name[]) {
2         /* Local variable declarations: */

3         FILE *in;
4         char ch;

5         /* Function body: */

6         if ((in = fopen(file_name, "r")) == NULL) {

7                 fprintf(stderr, "***> Open error reading input file %s",
8                         file_name);
9                 exit(-1);
10        } /* end if */

11        ch = fgetc(in);

12        while (! feof(in)) {
13                printf("%c", ch);
14                ch = fgetc(in);
15        } /* end while */

16        fclose(in);
17    } /* end function print_character_file */
```

**Figure 8.9**    A C function that prints a text file of characters

The function `print_character_file` has one formal parameter, a string variable, `file_name`, which stores an external file name for the file we want to print. We declare an internal file name, `in`, in line 3. To print its content, we must open the file in input mode; we do this with the `fopen` function call of line 6. Then, for input of character values, we use the input statement `ch = fgetc(in);` once on line 11 outside the `while` loop beginning on line 12 and once again on line 14 in the loop body. The `printf` function call on line 13 will print the character read, whether it is the end-of-record new-line character or any other character, on the terminal screen. Finally, upon exiting the loop, we close the file using an `fclose` function call on line 16. We can use this program to print the content of any text file, regardless of how its records are structured and how it has been prepared.

Let us summarize the fundamental steps that must be followed in reading data from files. These steps define a pattern that you may use in batch applications that require reading data from files.

1. Declare a file.

2. Assign an external name to the file, which must correspond to an existing data file.

3.  Using an `fopen` function call, associate the internal and external names for the file and open the file in either input or input-output mode.

4.  Do file open verification in an `if` statement.

5.  Read data from the file using an appropriate input statement or function.

6.  Construct a controlled loop in which you continue reading and processing data coming from the file. Use the `feof` function to control the loop.

7.  Close the file.

## Input of Preformatted Data from Files

Data in input files may be preformatted; for example, they may be typed into fixed-width fields with no separators, or they may be typed with separator characters, such as comma. In reading such data, we must use appropriate format specifiers.

**Scanning the Input Stream for Fixed-Width Data Fields**    If, in a preformatted input file, we have records consisting of values typed into fields of specified widths, we can use format specifiers with **width factors** for correct value assignments. An example follows.

*Example 8.12*    Suppose we have an input file, and each record contains values for three variables called `height`, `depth`, and `width`, all of type `double`. A typical record is

```
12.6517.2521.50
```

where the three values `12.65`, `17.25`, and `21.50` for `height`, `depth`, and `width` are typed without any separating characters. The field width for all data is 5. Therefore, we can use the format specifier `%5lf` to correctly scan the input stream as shown here:

```
fscanf(input_file, "%5lf%5lf%5lf", &height, &depth,
        &width);
```

Here, `input_file` is the internal name of the file from which we read data. In the format specifier `%5lf`, 5 is the width factor.

**Skipping Specific Characters in the Input Stream**    Suppose we have a preformatted input data file in which each record consists of a four-character student identification number, and three integer test score values, separated by commas, as shown:

```
1000, 90, 90, 90
1200, 100, 100, 90
1300, 45, 55, 78
1400, 67, 77, 48
```

From each preformatted record we would like to read a string into `stu_idno` and three integers into each score, `score1`, `score2`, and `score3`. Since the values are separated by commas, how do we ascertain correct value assignments? How do we make C discard the unnecessary commas?

C has several ways of skipping specific characters in the input stream. We mention three methods:

1.  Read the character to be skipped into a variable.

2.  Include the characters to be skipped in the format control string in a `scanf` function call.

3.  Use the assignment suppression character, `*`, to suppress value assignment.

***Example 8.13***   We can solve the problem of skipping the separator commas by declaring a character variable called `separator` as

```
char separator;
```

and by using it in an appropriate input function call, such as `fscanf`, as shown:

```
fscanf(test_file, "%4s%c%d%c%d%c%d", stu_idno, &separator,
       &score1, &separator, &score2, &separator, &score3);
```

`test_file` is the internal name of the input data file.

***Example 8.14***   Alternatively, we can use a format string that contains the characters to be skipped, as in the following `fscanf`:

```
fscanf(test_file, "%4s,%d,%d,%d", stu_idno, &score1,
       &score2, &score3);
```

Here, in the format string `"%4s,%d,%d,%d"`, we have the format specifier `%4s` for `stu_idno` and three occurrences of the format specifier `%d` corresponding to `score1`, `score2`, and `score3`. These format specifiers are separated by commas, ensuring that the comma characters between integers are skipped.

***Example 8.15***   A third way of suppressing characters in the input stream requires the use of the **assignment suppression character**, `*`, as in the following `fscanf` call:

```
fscanf(test_file, "%4s%*c%d%*c%d%*c%d", stu_idno,
       &score1, &score2, &score3);
```

In the format control string `%4s%*c%d%*c%d%*c%d"` of this `fscanf` call, we have the format specifier `%*c`. In this format specifier the character `*` is the assignment suppression character. It enables the `fscanf` function to read a character value and skip it without assigning it to a variable. Accordingly, this `fscanf` function uses the format specifier `%4s` to read a value into `stu_idno`, skips a character, uses `%d` to read a value into `score1`, skips a character, uses `%d` to read a value into `score2`, skips another character, and finally reads a value into `score3`.

## Copying Files

Given that we invest substantial amounts of time and money in creating data files, we do not want, and cannot afford, to lose them. For security reasons a common practice is to make backup copies of files. Therefore, file copying is a frequently performed operation.

Most operating systems have features that can be used to make copies of program or data files. It is also possible to write C programs that can make copies of files easily. Now that you are familiar with file operations, the logic of the **file copy** algorithm is relatively simple. Suppose we want to make a copy of the text file *source_file* to another text file *copy_file*. Clearly, we want to read data from *source_file*. Therefore, we must open it in input mode. As we want to write to *copy_file*, its open mode must be output. Next, we must copy a character at a time from *source_file* to *copy_file* until we come to the end of *source_file*. Finally, we must close both files. Hence we have the pseudocode algorithm in Figure 8.10.

---

*open source_file in input mode*
*open copy_file in output mode*

*read a character from source_file into ch*

*while it is not the end of source_file*
   *begin*
      *write ch to copy_file*
      *read a character from source_file into ch*
   *end*
*end_while*

*close source_file*
*close copy_file*

---

**Figure 8.10**    A pseudocode algorithm for file copying

The main logical element in the pseudocode of Figure 8.10 is file input and output operations. As we have shown in this chapter, there are several different ways to do file input-output. For example, if the records consist of single integers, we can read an integer from *source_file* and immediately write it to *copy_file*. Alternatively, we may decide to read a record into a string variable and then write the content of that string variable to *copy_file*. However, because a text file is composed of characters, probably the best procedure is to copy the file character by character. We followed this approach in the pseudocode algorithm of Figure 8.10. Note that the *while* loop is a sentinel-controlled loop, and the sentinel is the end-of-file character in *source_file*.

In Example Program 1, we present a C implementation of the preceding file copy logic.

## REVIEW QUESTIONS

**1.** Concerning text files,
   **a.** A C source program is a text file.
   **b.** A text data file can be prepared using a text editor.
   **c.** The data typed during interactive input constitute a text file.
   **d.** The interactive output of a program on the terminal screen is a text file.
   **e.** All of the above are correct.
   **f.** None of the above is correct.

**2.** To write data to a text file, we can use the `fprintf` function on a declared file that has been opened in output or append mode. (T or F)

**3.** Which of the following statements will write a record to a file named `test_scores` that has been opened in output mode?
   **a.** `fprintf(test_scores, "%d\n", test_score);`
   **b.** `fprintf(stdout, "%d\n", test_score);`
   **c.** `fprintf(test_scores, "%d", test_score);`
   **d.** `fputs(test_score, test_scores);`
   **e.** None of the above is correct.

**4.** Which of the following file input statements will read a record from a file that is named `indata` and opened in input mode? Assume that each record in the file consists of three integer values separated by blanks, the record length does not exceed 40 bytes, and the variable `record` is declared as a string.
   **a.** `fscanf(indata, "%d %d %d", &record);`
   **b.** `fgetc(indata);`
   **c.** `fgets(record, 80, indata);`
   **d.** `fgets(record, 40, indata);`
   **e.** None of the above

**5.** Consider the following partial code:

```
int a, c;
char b;
FILE *input_file;
fscanf(input_file, "%d%c%d", &a, &b, &c);
```

If the input stream being scanned by the `fscanf` function is 0.67 7 8, which values will be assigned to the variables a, b, and c?
   **a.** 0, '.', 67
   **b.** 0, '7', 8
   **c.** 0, '.', 7
   **d.** None of the above.

**6.** Which value is assigned to the variable `var` by the `fscanf` function call

```
fscanf(input_file, "%3lf", &var);
```

if the input stream being scanned contains $-12.567$?
**a.** -12.567
**b.** -12.0
**c.** -12.5
**d.** -12.6
**e.** None of the above.

**7.** Assume that we have the following declarations:

```
int var1, var2, var3;
```

A preformatted data file, whose internal name is infile, contains the record

```
333445555
```

Which of the following fscanf function calls will read this record and assign the values 333, 44, and 5555 to the variables var1, var2, and var3, respectively?
**a.** fscanf(infile, "%3d%2d%4d", &var1, &var2, &var3);
**b.** fscanf(infile, "%3d %2d%4d", &var1, &var2, &var3);
**c.** fscanf(infile, "%3d%2d %4d", &var1, &var2, &var3);
**d.** fscanf(infile, "%3d %2d %4d", &var1, &var2, &var3);
**e.** All of the above.
**f.** None of the above.

**Answers:** 1. e; 2. T; 3. a; 4. c; 5. a; 6. b; 7. e.

## 8.4 EXAMPLE PROGRAM 1: A C Program that Copies a Text File

In Figure 8.11 we have a C program that can be used to copy text files. It consists of a function main that uses the function copy_file, which is an implementation of the pseudocode algorithm of Figure 8.10, and the function print_character_file of Figure 8.9. The definition of the function print_character_file is not repeated here.

```
/*********************************************************************
 Program Filename: prog08_1.c
 Author          : Uckan
 Purpose         : Copies a specified file to another file and
                   prints their contents.
 Input from      : A data file
 Output to       : A data file
 *********************************************************************/
```

**Figure 8.11**    A C program that copies a text file (*continued*)    ▶

```c
#include <stdio.h>
#include <stdlib.h>

/* Function prototypes: */

void copy_file(char input_file_name[], char output_file_name[]);
void print_character_file(char file_name[]);


int main(void) {
      /* Variable declarations: */

      char in_file_name[15];
      char out_file_name[15];

      /* Function body: */

      printf("Enter name of file to copy from: ");
      gets(in_file_name);

      printf("Enter name of file to copy to  : ");
      gets(out_file_name);

      printf("Copying from %s to %s. . .\n", in_file_name,
             out_file_name);

      copy_file(in_file_name, out_file_name);

      printf("Copy operation completed. . .\n");

      printf("Content of input file %s:\n", in_file_name);
      print_character_file(in_file_name);

      printf("Content of copy file %s:\n", out_file_name);
      print_character_file(out_file_name);
      return 0;
} /* end function main */
```

**Figure 8.11**    A C program that copies a text file (*continued*)    ▶

```
/*...............................................................*/
/****************************************************************
 Function Name    : copy_file
 Purpose          : Copies a file to another file
 Called by        : main
 Receives         : in_file_name, out_file_name
 Returns          : None
 ****************************************************************/
void copy_file(char in_file_name[], char out_file_name[]) {
      /* Local variable declarations: */

      FILE *indata;
      FILE *outdata;
      int number_of_records;
      char ch;

      /* Function body: */

      if ((indata = fopen(in_file_name, "r")) == NULL) {
          fprintf(stderr, "***> Open error while opening file %s",
                  in_file_name);
          exit(-1);
      } /* end if */

      if ((outdata = fopen(out_file_name, "w")) == NULL) {
          fprintf(stderr, "***> Open error while opening file %s",
                  out_file_name);
          exit(-1);
      } /* end if */

      ch = fgetc(indata);

      if (! feof(indata))
          number_of_records = 1;
      else
          number_of_records = 0;
      /* end if */

      while (! feof(indata)) {
          fputc(ch, outdata);
```

**Figure 8.11**     A C program that copies a text file (*continued*)                                      ▶

```
            if (ch == '\n')
                    number_of_records++;
            /* end if */

            ch = fgetc(indata);
      } /* end while */

      fclose(indata);
      fclose(outdata);

      printf("%d records copied.\n", number_of_records);
} /* end function copy_file */
```

**Figure 8.11**                                                                 ■

The interactive dialogue created by the input-output statements in the function `main` of Figure 8.11 and the logic of the program enable the user to specify the external name of the source file as well as the external name of the copy file. Therefore, this program is quite general. You can use it to copy any text file, whether it contains data or a C source program.

In the function `copy_file` of Figure 8.11, we have an integer variable, number_of_records. In the `if` statement placed in the body of the `while` loop, the value of the variable `number_of_records` is incremented by one every time the last character read into `ch` is the new-line character. However, this logic will not compute the correct number of records in a text file. Remember, we have defined a record in a text file as a string of characters ending with the new-line character. The last string of characters that comes just before the end-of-file character is also a record. Also, in a text file with no new-line characters, if there is any data, then we have one record. To take these into account in computing the number of records copied during the file copy process, we have an `if` statement placed right after the first `ch = fgetc(indata);` statement:

```
if (! feof(indata))
        number_of_records = 1;
else
        number_of_records = 0;
/* end if */
```

This `if` statement initializes `number_of_records` to one if the first character read is not the end-of-file character, that is, if the file contains data. Otherwise, the variable `number_of_records` is initialized to zero.

We suggest that you generate the load module for the program that consists of Figures 8.9 and 8.11, and run it to copy a text file, such as any C program that you have developed this semester.

## 8.5    EXAMPLE PROGRAM 2: A C Program that Computes Federal Income Tax Using Tax Rate Schedules (Batch Version)

Let us work on an example program that is in batch mode with its input coming from a data file and output going to a text file. Our problem will be similar to that solved in Example Program 4 of Chapter 6, which required a program that computed federal income tax from the tax rate schedules. Here we will take the same problem and alter it such that it is in batch mode.

***Problem***   We have a file called   A:TAXPAYER.TXT   containing data on taxpayers. It is a text file, prepared using a text editor, and its records consist of a taxpayer identification number, a value for annual gross income, and a single-digit status code. Taxpayer identification number is actually the nine-digit Social Security number. Status code values are 1, 2, 3, and 4, corresponding to single, married filing jointly, married filing separately, and head of household, respectively. Figure 8.12 shows an instance of the taxpayer data file. In each data record of this file, data values are delimited by one blank.

```
111111111 120788.50 1
222222222 89670.00 2
333333333 57775.99 3
444444444 65500.00 4
```

**Figure 8.12**    An instance of the taxpayer data file

We would like to design and implement a C program that validates annual gross income, which should not be less than $50,000.00, and status values in the input data file. If the input data file is correct, the program should compute federal income tax for each taxpayer using tax rate schedules, write them to another text file called   A:RE-SULTS.TXT, and also compute and print on the monitor screen the sum of taxes to be collected from the taxpayers in the input file.

***Requirements Specification***   Develop a C program that does the following:

1.   Reads the records in the file   A:TAXPAYER.TXT   sequentially, and, for each record validates the gross income and the status values. If gross income is less than $50,000.00 and/or status is not 1, 2, 3, or 4, the program should print on the monitor screen the

records that are in error. If any record is in error, the program should terminate processing.

2. If the input data file is correct, the program reads the records in the file A:TAX-PAYER.TXT sequentially and, for each taxpayer, computes the federal income tax. Then the program constructs a record that includes taxpayer identification number, gross income, status code, and the computed federal income tax, and writes it to the file A:RESULTS.TXT.

3. Also, the program computes the sum of income tax values and prints it on the monitor screen.

### Analysis

**Inputs** Data from the file A:TAXPAYER.TXT.

**Outputs** Error messages printed on the monitor screen if the input data file contains erroneous data. If not, the output file A:RESULTS.TXT and the sum of taxes printed on the monitor screen.

***Design*** We begin with the initial pseudocode algorithm of Figure 8.13.

---

*validate input data file*

*if input data file contains no errors*
    *compute and output taxes and sum of taxes*
*end_if*

---

**Figure 8.13**     Initial pseudocode algorithm to compute federal income tax from tax rate schedules (batch version)

The first refinement is for the step *validate input data file*. Figure 8.14 shows one way of doing it.

---

*error_free_input_file:*
    *set error_free to 'y'*

    *open input data file*
    *do file open validation on input data file*
    *read a record from input data file*

---

**Figure 8.14**     A pseudocode algorithm for *error_free_input_file* (continued)     ▶

*while the end of input data file has not yet been encountered*
   *begin*
      *echo-print the current record*

      *if gross_income is less than 50000.00*
         *begin*
            *set error_free to 'n'*
            *print error message*
         *end*
      *end_if*

      *if status is less than 1*
         *begin*
            *set error_free to 'n'*
            *print error message*
         *end*
      *else if status is greater than 4*
         *begin*
            *set error_free to 'n'*
            *print error message*
         *end*

      *end_if*

      *read a record from input data file*
   *end*
*end_while*

*close input data file*
*return error_free*

**Figure 8.14**                                                                     ■

Because we have designed the module *error_free_input_file* to return the character value *'n'* if the input file is in error, we modify the initial pseudocode algorithm slightly and write it as shown in Figure 8.15.

*if value returned by error_free_input_file is equal to 'y'*
   *compute and output taxes and sum of taxes*
*end_if*

**Figure 8.15**    Modified pseudocode algorithm to compute federal income tax from tax rate schedules (batch version)

It is time to refine the body of the *if* statement, *compute and output taxes and sum of taxes*. For this purpose we will use a module named *do_taxes*. Its logic is described in the pseudocode of Figure 8.16.

---

*do_taxes:*
    *set sum_of_taxes to 0.00*

    *open input data file*
    *open output file*

    *read a record from input data file*

    *while the end of input data file has not yet been encountered*
        *begin*
            *compute federal income tax*
            *add tax to sum_of_taxes*
            *write taxpayer id, income, status, and tax to output file*

            *read a record from input data file*
        *end*
    *end_while*

    *close input data file*
    *close output file*
    *print sum_of_taxes on the monitor screen*

---

**Figure 8.16**    A pseudocode algorithm for the module *do_taxes*

In Figure 8.16 the step *compute federal income tax* needs further refinement. However, we remember that we have a module called *computed_tax* in Figure 6.28 designed exactly for this purpose. We will use it in our implementation.

Now, in the pseudocode algorithms of Figures 8.14, 8.15, 8.16, and 6.28, we have the solution of the problem as a modular system. The structure chart of the designed program is given in Figure 8.17.

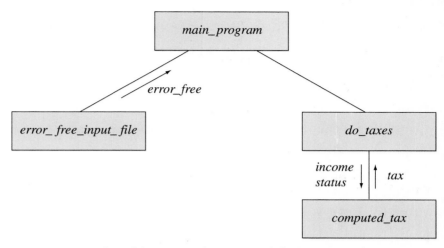

**Figure 8.17**    Structure chart of the program that computes federal income tax from tax rate schedules (batch version)

*Implementation*    Let us do the bottom-up implementation in four steps.

**Step 1.** The implementation of the module *computed_tax* already exists and was given in Figure 6.36. We will use it as is.

**Step 2.** Figure 8.18 is a C implementation of the module *error_free_input_file*.

```
/*******************************************************************
 Function Name    : error_free_input_file
 Purpose          : Reads records from the taxpayer file and
                    validates gross income and status values.
 Called by        : main
 Receives         : None
 Returns          : error_free
********************************************************************/
char error_free_input_file(void) {
     /* Variable declarations: */

     char taxpayer_idno[10];
     double gross_income;
     int status;
     char error_free = 'y';
     FILE *tax_file;
```

**Figure 8.18**    A C implementation of module *error_free_input_file* (continued)    ▶

```
       /* Function body: */

       if ((tax_file = fopen("A:TAXPAYER.TXT", "r"))== NULL) {
           fprintf(stderr, "***> Open error reading taxpayer file.");
           exit(-1);
       } /* end if */

       fscanf(tax_file, "%s%lf%d", taxpayer_idno, &gross_income,
           &status);

       while (! feof(tax_file)) {
           printf("Echo-printing: %s %.2f %d\n", taxpayer_idno,
                   gross_income, status);

           if (gross_income < 50000.00) {
               error_free = 'n';
               printf("Error in gross income of %s: %.2f\n",
                   taxpayer_idno, gross_income);
               } /* end if */

           if (status < 1) {
               error_free = 'n';
               printf("Error in status code of %s: %d\n",
                   taxpayer_idno, status);
               }


           else if (status > 4) {
               error_free = 'n';
               printf("Error in status code of %s: %d\n",
                   taxpayer_idno, status);
           } /* end if */

           fscanf(tax_file, "%s%lf%d", taxpayer_idno, &gross_income,
                   &status);
       } /* end while */

       fclose(tax_file);
       return error_free;
} /* end function error_free_input_file */
```

Figure 8.18

The function `error_free_input_file` is a typical input file processing function. It has a declaration for the file `tax_file`, opens it in input mode, and performs file open verification on it. The important element is the input statement

```
fscanf(tax_file, "%s%lf%d", taxpayer_idno, &gross_income,
        &status);
```

This statement reads a string from the input stream `tax_file` and assigns it to `taxpayer_idno`, reads and assigns a value to `gross_income`, and finally, reads and assigns a value to `status`. The input file records are preformatted such that each record has three appropriate values in it. If the input file happens to be empty, the end-of-file marker will be encountered during this input operation. In this case, the program control will not get into the `while` loop that follows. Otherwise, the body of the `while` loop will be executed.

Note that in the body of the `while` loop, following the `if` statements that validate data, the same formatted input statement reads the next record.

**Step 3.** Figure 8.19 is a C function for the module *do_taxes*.

```
/************************************************************************
  Function Name    : do_taxes
  Purpose          : Reads data from taxpayer file, computes
                     income tax, writes results to the file
                     a:results.txt. Also, computes sum of taxes
                     and prints it on the monitor screen.
  Called by        : main

  Receives         : None
  Returns          : None
 ************************************************************************/
void do_taxes(void) {
      /* Local variable declarations: */

      char idno[10];
      double income, tax, sum_of_taxes = 0.0;
      int status;
      FILE *tax_file;
      FILE *result;

      /* Function body: */

      tax_file = fopen("A:TAXPAYER.TXT", "r");
```

**Figure 8.19**    A C implementation of module *do_taxes* (*continued*)    ▶

```
    result = fopen("A:RESULTS.TXT", "w");

    fscanf(tax_file, "%s%lf%d", idno, &income, &status);

    while (! feof(tax_file)) {
        tax = computed_tax(income, status);

        sum_of_taxes += tax;

        fprintf(result, "%s %.2f %d %.2f\n", idno, income,
            status, tax);

        fscanf(tax_file, "%s%lf%d", idno, &income, &status);
    } /* end while */

    fclose(tax_file);
    fclose(result);

    printf("\nSum of taxes: %.2f", sum_of_taxes);
} /* end function do_taxes */
```

**Figure 8.19**                                                                    ■

The function `do_taxes` uses the function `computed_tax`. The first thing that we do in its body is to open the file `tax_file` in input mode and the file `result` in output mode. The input statement

```
    fscanf(tax_file, "%s%lf%d", idno, &income, &status);
```

reads values from the preformatted input file `tax_file`. If the end-of-file marker if not encountered during input, the program control gets into the `while` loop. In the body of the `while` loop, income tax is computed by using the function `computed_tax` and stored in the variable `tax`, the computed tax value is added to `sum_of_taxes`, and the output statement

```
    fprintf(result, "%s %.2f %d %.2f\n", idno, income,
        status, tax);
```

is executed. This statement writes a record to the output file `result`. Note that upon exit from the `while` loop, both `tax_file` and `result` are closed.

**Step 4.** Finally, we have the function `main` for the soluton of this problem in Figure 8.20.

```
/*******************************************************
Program Filename: prog08_2.c
Author          : Uckan
Purpose         : Computes federal income tax from tax rate
                  schedules.
Input from      : Taxpayer data file a:taxpayer.txt
Output to       : a:results.txt
*******************************************************/
#include <stdio.h>
#include <stdlib.h>

/* Named constant declarations: */

const double LOWRATE  = 0.28;
const double HIGHRATE = 0.31;

/* Function prototypes: */

char error_free_input_file(void);
void do_taxes(void);
double computed_tax(double income, int status);


int main(void) {
      /* Function body: */

      if (error_free_input_file() == 'y')
            do_taxes();
      /* end if */

         return 0;
  } /* end function main */
```

**Figure 8.20**                                                                  ∎

The code in Figure 8.20 is simple, and it needs no explanation. Because the function `computed_tax` uses the global named constants `LOWRATE` and `HIGHRATE` (see Figure 6.37), their declarations must also be included in the source program file.

Let us test this program once with an erroneous input file and once again with a data file that has no errors. First, we will consider the following instance for  A:TAX-PAYER.TXT:

```
111111111  15000.00  0
222222222  55000.78  1
333333333  56789.99  6
444444444  89999.99  2
555555555  12008.88  4
```

As you can see, the first, third, and fifth records in this file are in error. If we run our program on this data file, we get the following console output:

```
Echo-printing: 111111111 15000.00 0
Error in gross income of 111111111: 15000.00
Error in status code of 111111111: 0
Echo-printing: 222222222 55000.78 1
Echo-printing: 333333333 56789.99 6
Error in status code of 333333333: 6
Echo-printing: 444444444 89999.99 2
Echo-printing: 555555555 12008.88 4
Error in gross income of 555555555: 12008.88
```

Now we correct the errors in the input data file such that it becomes:

```
111111111  75000.00  2
222222222  55000.78  1
333333333  56789.99  3
444444444  89999.99  2
555555555  112008.88  4
```

The program that we have developed, when run on this data file, produces the output file A:RESULTS.TXT:

```
111111111  75000.00  2  16580.00
222222222  55000.78  1  12925.74
333333333  56789.99  3  14162.65
444444444  89999.99  2  21015.50
555555555  112008.88  4  29060.25
```

Also, the following console output is obtained during the same run:

```
Echo-printing: 111111111 75000.00 2
Echo-printing: 222222222 55000.78 1
Echo-printing: 333333333 56789.99 3
Echo-printing: 444444444 89999.99 2
Echo-printing: 555555555 112008.88 4

Sum of taxes: 93744.14
```

## 8.6 SUMMARY

### This Chapter at a Glance

- This chapter covered batch-mode processing, in which input for a program comes from a file or the program's output may be directed to a file.

- In batch processing we use C file-processing functions. C has extensive file-processing capabilities for text and binary files. In this chapter we focused on text files.

- We discussed the standard C functions for file processing and considered how to declare, name, open, and close files; check for end-of-file; and verify opening files.

- You studied the operations of input from text files, output to text files, and copying files. Now, in addition to knowing how to design interactive applications, you have the skills to design batch applications.

### Coming Attractions

- In Chapter 5, you studied simple C selection and repetition statements. You learned about the `if` statement, relational operators and simple predicates, and controlled repetitions using the `while` statement.

- The next chapter returns to the `if` statement and explains how to use it for multi-way selections and in situations where complex predicates are indicated.

- You will learn a new selection statement in C, the `switch` statement, which can be used for multiway selection.

- You will also study two additional C repetition statements: the pretest `for` and the posttest `do-while`. These statements will enhance your ability to implement repetition structures in problem solving.

## STUDY GUIDE

### Test Your Comprehension

**1.** In a text file:
   **a.** Data are stored as nonreadable characters in binary code or control code.
   **b.** Each record is separated from the next by an end-of-file marker.
   **c.** The file is terminated by a new-line character.
   **d.** The terminating new-line character is placed at the end of the file by the operating system.
   **e.** All of the above are correct.
   **f.** None of the above is correct.

**2.** Which of the following statements opens a file named `empfile` for update without destroying it if it already exists?
   **a.** `empfile = fopen("A:EMPFILE.TXT", "w");`
   **b.** `empfile = fopen("A:EMPFILE.TXT", "r");`
   **c.** `empfile = fopen("A:EMPFILE.TXT", "u");`
   **d.** `empfile = fopen("A:EMPFILE.TXT", "r+");`
   **e.** None of the above

**3.** If the file open mode for a data file is
   **a.** `"w"`, an input statement referencing the file will read a record from it.
   **b.** `"w+"`, we can write data to such a file and read data from it without closing it.
   **c.** `"a"`, the existing file is destroyed.
   **d.** `"w"`, we can add new data to the end of the file.
   **e.** All of the above are correct.
   **f.** None of the above is correct.

**4.** A C file-processing program contains the following `if` statement:

```
if((input_file = fopen(file_name, "r")) == NULL) {
        fprintf("File open error on %s", file_name);
        exit(-1);
/* end if */
```

This program must include the standard header file
   **a.** `string.h`
   **b.** `math.h`
   **c.** `conio.h`
   **d.** `stdlib.h`
   **e.** All of the above.
   **f.** None of the above.

**5.** Which of the following statements concerning writing data to text files is correct?
   **a.** A declared file must be opened in output, input-output, or append mode.
   **b.** To write data of fundamental types, we can use the `fprintf` function on the declared file.
   **c.** Strings can also be written using the `fprintf` function on the declared file.

**d.** The function `fputc` can be used to write character expressions to a file.

**e.** All of the above.

**f.** None of the above.

**6.** Which of the following statements is a correct file output statement to write a record to a file named `results` and opened in input mode?

**a.** `fputc(record, results); fputc('\n', results);`

**b.** `fprintf(results, "%s\n", record);`

**c.** `fscanf(results, "%s\n", &record);`

**d.** None of the above.

**7.** Which of the following `fscanf` function calls is correct? Assume that `value` is a variable of type `int`.

**a.** `fscanf(stdin, "%d", &value);`

**b.** `fscanf(stdout, "%d", &value);`

**c.** `fscanf(stderr, "%d", &value);`

**d.** `fscanf("%d", &value);`

**e.** All of the above.

**f.** None of the above.

**Answers:** 1. f; 2. d; 3. b; 4. d; 5. e; 6. d; 7. a.

## Improve Your Problem-Solving Ability

### *Debugging Exercises*

Examine each of the following C code segments carefully, find all compilation and execution errors that they contain, explain why they are errors, and describe how you would correct them.

**8.**
```
FILE *first_file;
int value;
first_file = fopen("A:OUTINT.TXT", "r");
fscanf(first_file, "%d", &value);

while (! feof(first_file)) {
        printf("%d\n", value);
        fclose(first_file);

        first_file = fopen("A:OUTINT.TXT", "r");
        fscanf(first_file, "%d", &value);
} /* end while */
```

**9.**
```
FILE *my_file;
int value;
my_file = fopen("A:OUTINT.TXT", "r");
```

```
    while (! feof(my_file)) {
          fscanf(my_file, "%d", &value);
          printf("%d\n", value);
    } /* end while */
    fclose(my_file);
```

10.
```
    FILE *input;
    int value;
    input = fopen("A:OUTINT.TXT", "w");
    fscanf(input, "%d", &value);

    while (! feof(input)) {
          printf("%d\n", value);
          fscanf(input, "%d", &value);
    } /* end while */
    fclose(input);
```

11.
```
    FILE *output;
    char ch;
    output = fopen("A:OUTPUT.TXT", "r");
    printf("Enter a string: ");
    scanf("%c", &ch);

    while (ch != '\n') {
          fprintf(output, "%c", ch);
          scanf("%c", &ch);
    } /* end while */
    fclose(output);
```

12.
```
    FILE *char_file;
    char ch;
    char_file = fopen("A:OUTPUT.TXT", "w");
    printf("Enter a string: ");
    scanf("%c", &ch);

    while (! feof(char_file)) {
          fprintf(char_file, "%c", ch);

          scanf("%c", &ch);
    } /* end while */
    fclose(char_file);
```

### Programming Exercises

We have `faculty_file`, which is a text file. Each record in `faculty_file` consists of the following data items:

• A five-digit faculty identification number

- A faculty name whose maximum length is 25 bytes
- A single-digit faculty rank code (1 for full professor, 2 for associate professor, 3 for assistant professor, and 4 for instructor)
- An annual salary value typed in conventional notation as DDDDD.CC where DDDDD represents the dollar amount and CC stands for cents.

  Typical faculty records are exemplified below:

  ```
  12000 James Brick 147000.00
  13000 Janice Frederick 254300.00
  ```

  As you can see, data fields in the records are delimited by blanks, and the faculty name field can contain blanks separating first and last names.

**13.** Write a function that prints on the monitor screen the content of `faculty_file` according to the following format:

| Data Item | Columns |
|---|---|
| Faculty idno | 1 – 5 |
| Faculty name | 7 – 31 |
| Faculty rank | 33 |
| Faculty salary | 35 – 42 |

Your printed list should look like this:

```
12000  James Brick                    1 47000.00
13000  Janice Frederick               2 54300.00
```

**14.** Write a function that copies `faculty_file` to another text file named `fixed_faculty_file`, which contains fixed-length faculty records formatted as explained in Programming Exercise 13.

**15.** Examine the following function, named `mystery`, and explain what it does.

```
void mystery(void) {
      fstream first, second, third;
      int number;

      first = fopen("A:OUTINT.TXT", "r");
      second = fopen("A:ONE.TXT", "w");
      third = fopen("A:TWO.TXT", "w");
      fscanf(first, "%d", &number);

      while (! feof(first)) {
            if (number % 2 == 0)
                  fprintf(second, "%d\n", number);
            else
                  fprintf(third, "%d\n", number);
            /* end if */

            fscanf(first, "%d", &number);
      } /* end while */

      fclose(first);
      fclose(second);
      fclose(third);
} /* end function mystery */
```

### Programming Projects

**16.** Solve Programming Project 39 of Chapter 4, assuming that the input data, which consists of a student identification number and three test scores, `test1`, `test2`, and `final_test`, come from a text file. In the input file, the data values in each record are separated by blanks. The output of the program should be printed on the monitor screen.

**17.** Convert Programming Project 23 of Chapter 6 to a batch application. Assume that faculty data are in a text file and that each record of the data file consists of two data values–a faculty salary and a performance level code—separated by a blank.

**18.** You are given a text data file, called `STUDENTS.TXT`, which consists of records with a four-digit student identification number and a student name, separated by a blank. Develop a program that processes this file to determine whether it is sorted in ascending or descending order by student identification number or whether it is unsorted.

**19.** Assume that you have two text files, `male_students` and `female_students`, both containing records that consist of a four-digit student identification number and a student name, separated from the identification number field by a blank. Further assume that records in both files are in increasing order by student identification number. Develop a program that reads `male_students` and `female_students` and creates a new file named `all_students`, which contains all records in the two source files merged together in increasing order by student identification number. The student identification numbers are distinct for each student.

**20.** Develop a program that reads a text file and prints its records in blocks of 10 lines on the terminal screen. After printing each block, the user should have the option to terminate the program or to request printing of the next block.

**21.** Our department has the policy of evaluating all courses and instructors at the end of each academic semester. For this purpose we use a standard form with five questions that aim to measure the students' evaluation of the instructor's knowledge of subject matter, organization, effectiveness, helpfulness, and so on. The response to each question may be excellent (E), good (G), average (A), poor (P), or unsatisfactory (U).

Student responses for each instructor and course are coded and stored in a disk file. The record of this file consists of the following fields:

**a.** Instructor number: three-digit integer

**b.** Course number: three-digit integer

**c.** Question 1: E, G, A, P, or U

**d.** Question 2: E, G, A, P, or U

**e.** Question 3: E, G, A, P, or U

**f.** Question 4: E, G, A, P, or U

**g.** Question 5: E, G, A, P, or U

Here is a sample course evaluation file:

```
500   200   E E G E E
500   200   E G G G E
500   200   G G G E E
500   200   G G A G A
500   200   A G G A E
500   200   G G G A E
500   200   G G G A A
500   200   E E E E E
500   200   E E E G E
500   200   G E E E E
```

Each record in this file corresponds to one evaluation form completed by a student for a class. For example, the record

```
500   200   E E G E E
```

is the evaluation of a student for instructor 500 and course 200; the student's evaluations are E, E, G, E, and E, respectively, for the five questions included in the evaluation form. Note that each field is separated from the next by some blanks.

First, using a text editor, type the preceding records into a text data file. Next, design a modular C program that reads this file and produces a summary evaluation report to be returned to the instructor. The format and content of the report are shown in the following example. The output should be printed on the screen.

```
COURSE/INSTRUCTOR EVALUATION SUMMARY

INSTRUCTOR NUMBER: 500
COURSE NUMBER    : 200

NUMBER OF PARTICIPANTS: 10
AVERAGES:
    QUESTION 1        3.50
    QUESTION 2        3.60
    QUESTION 3        3.80
    QUESTION 4        3.75
    QUESTION 5        3.40

INSTRUCTOR AVERAGE    : 3.75
```

In computing averages for the questions, use a numeric weight of 4 for E, 3 for G, 2 for A, 1 for P, and 0 for U. The final instructor average should be computed using the formula:

$$instructor\_average = 0.15 \times average\_of\_Q1 + 0.23 \times average\_of\_Q2 + \\ 0.08 \times average\_of\_Q3 + 0.32 \times average\_of\_Q4 + \\ 0.22 \times average\_of\_Q5$$

**22.** Suppose we have a text file of student data in which each record consists of an identification number, a first name, a last name, an age, and a major code value. A typical student file follows.

```
1000  John Carlos 21 BUS
2000  Kim Trout 20 MTH
3000  Tom Burns 19 PHY
4000  Ellen McDonald 22 BUS
5000  Timothy Daniels 18 BUS
```

Develop a program that interactively reads a student major code value as the search key, processes the student file sequentially, and prints on the monitor screen a list of student records for students whose majors match the search key value.

**23.** Develop a modular program that consists of a function `main` and two programmer-defined functions named `create_student_file` and `process_student_file`. The function `main` should first call `create_student_file` and then `process_student_file`. The function `create_student_file` should interactively read values for `student_idno`, `student_first_name`, `student_last_name`, and `final_average`, where `student_idno` is a 4-digit integer, `student_first_name`, and `student_last_name` are character strings of length 15 each, and `final_average` is an integer between 0 and 100, and create a text file, whose internal name is `student_file`. The external name of `student_file` should be provided interactively by the user in the function `main`. The process of writing data to `student_file` should stop when the user enters 0 for `student_idno`. The `student_file` that is created by the function `create_student_file` should look like this:

```
1000  John McDonald 87
2000  Kimberly Johnson 100
3000  Jeanne Whiteoak 59
4000  Thomas Blake 69
5000  Steven Erin 89
6000  Christine Jones 90
```

The function `process_student_file` should read the records in `student_file` sequentially, determine the letter grade for each student, and print on the monitor screen a table of `student_idno`, `student_first_name`, `student_last_name`, `final_average`, and `letter_grade`. It should also print the maximum, minimum, and average of final student averages. The output should look like this:

```
STUDENT IDNO    FIRST NAME    LAST NAME    FINAL AVG    GRADE
1000            John          McDonald     87           B
2000            Kimberly      Johnson      100          A
3000            Jeanne        Whiteoak     59           F
4000            Thomas        Blake        69           D
5000            Steven        Erin         89           B
6000            Christine     Jones        90           A

MAXIMUM FINAL AVERAGE      : 100
MINIMUM FINAL AVERAGE      : 59
AVERAGE OF FINAL AVERAGES  : 82
```

In determining the final letter grades, use the following conversion rules:

| Final Average | Letter Grade |
| --- | --- |
| 90 – 100 | A |
| 80 – 89 | B |
| 70 – 79 | C |
| 60 – 69 | D |
| 0 – 59 | F |

# Complex Selections and Repetitions

---

In this chapter you will learn about:

- **Formulating multiway selections in C**
  C logical operators and complex predicates
  Multiway selection using the `if` statement with complex predicates
  The `switch` and `break` statements

- **The pretest repetition structures and the `for` statement**

- **The posttest repetition structures and the `do-while` statement**

- **Counter- and sentinel-controlled loops and nested loops**

By the time you have completed this chapter, you will have acquired the ability to design and implement:

- **Multiway selection structures**

- **Counter-controlled loops**

- **Sentinel-controlled loops**

- **Nested loops**

---

## 9.1     INTRODUCTION

Chapter 4 covered the  if  statement as the C implementation of the two-way selection control structure. You also learned that multiway selection structures can be formed using a series of consecutive  if  statements or a nested  if  statement. Since then, you have been liberally using these language constructs in problem solving.

In this chapter we investigate relatively more complex selection problems for which simple predicates are occasionally inadequate. Instead, we have to use complex predicates in  if  statements. Complex predicates are formed using logical operators. First, we examine three logical operators that C supports: logical *and*, logical *or*, and logical *not*. Then we introduce the  switch  statement, which can also be used for multiway selection.

Chapter 4 also discussed the  while  statement as one of the C implementations of the pretest repetition structure. The second half of this chapter covers the  for  statement, which is another pretest repetition structure. Next, we consider the  do-while  statement. The  do-while  statement is the C implementation of the posttest repetition structure. By the end of the chapter, you will know how to design counter- and sentinel-controlled loops and nested loops using the  for  and  do-while  statements.

## 9.2     COMPLEX PREDICATES

So far in our discussion of selection structures, we have considered only simple predicates. Simple predicates compare two expressions using relational operators and produce either 1 (for true) or 0 (for false). A simple predicate such as  semester_average >= 90  can be used to test only one condition. When there are several conditions to be tested, simple predicates may not do the job satisfactorily. Consider the following cases.

***Case 1***   How do we check to see whether, for example, the value of the variable semester_average  is in the range of 80 through 89? We cannot use one simple predicate. However, we can use a nested if statement such as

```
if (semester_average <= 89)
    if (semester_average >= 80)
        printf("%d", student_idno);
    /* end if */
/* end if */
```

***Case 2***   Suppose we have two variables, student_status  and grade_point_average, and we want to identify those students who are undergraduate high honor students, that is, student_status  is 'u' for undergraduate and grade_point_average  is 3.50 or above. Again, we cannot write a single simple predicate to cover both conditions, but we can use a nested  if  statement:

```
if (student_status == 'u')
      if (grade_point_average >= 3.50)
            printf("%d", student_idno);
      /* end if */
/* end if */
```

*Case 3*  Finally, suppose we want to identify those students who are either undergraduates or high honor students. This task cannot be done by a single simple predicate; we need a nested  if  as shown here:

```
if (student_status == 'u')
      printf("%d", student_idno);
else if (grade_point_average >= 3.50)
      printf("%d", student_idno);
/* end if */
```

As you can see, in all these cases we must use nested  if  statements if we cannot combine simple predicates appropriately in a single  if  statement.

### Logical Expressions and Logical Operators

To cope with complex selection problems such as those in the preceding cases, C allows us to use complex logical expressions (or predicates) in selection structures. Before we discuss how we can form complex predicates in C, let us consider the fundamentals of complex logical expressions.

In general, a **logical expression** is one that computes to either true or false. A simple predicate is a logical expression because it produces either a true or false result; similarly, a complex predicate is a logical expression.

> A **complex predicate** is an expression that is formed using simple predicates and logical operators.

Three logical operators can be used in forming complex predicates:

1. Logical *and* (conjunction)
2. Logical *or* (disjunction)
3. Logical *not* (negation)

**Logical *and*** is a binary operator that requires two operands that are logical expressions. It yields true if and only if both of its operands evaluate to true. Otherwise, it computes to false. Following is the truth table for logical *and*:

| operand_1 | operand_2 | operand_1 *and* operand_2 |
|-----------|-----------|---------------------------|
| true | true | true |
| true | false | false |
| false | true | false |
| false | false | false |

As an example, the complex predicate formed using a logical *and*

*(student_status is equal to 'u') and (grade_point_average >= 3.50)*

will return true for students who are undergraduates and high honor students.

**Logical *or*** is also a binary operator requiring two operands that are logical expressions. It returns false if and only if both of its operands are false; otherwise, it returns true. Here is the truth table for logical *or*:

| operand_1 | operand_2 | operand_1 *or* operand_2 |
|-----------|-----------|--------------------------|
| true | true | true |
| true | false | true |
| false | true | true |
| false | false | false |

As an example, consider the predicate

*(student_status is equal to 'u') or (grade_point_average >= 3.50)*

This predicate evaluates to true for students who are undergraduates or high honor students or undergraduate high honor students.

The third logical operator is logical *not*. We briefly introduced this operator in the previous chapter. **Logical *not*** is a unary operator, applying on a single logical expression. If its operand computes to true, logical *not* returns false; otherwise, it returns true. Here is the truth table for logical *not*:

| operand_1 | *not* operand_1 |
|-----------|-----------------|
| true | false |
| false | true |

For example, the expression *not (student_status is equal to 'u')* evaluates to false for undergraduates and to true for any other *student_status* value.

## The C Logical Operators

In C the symbols used for the three logical operators and their semantics are somewhat different from the usual notation and interpretation.

1.   Logical *and* is represented by `&&`. Its truth table is

| operand_1 | operand_2 | operand_1 && operand_2 |
|-----------|-----------|------------------------|
| nonzero   | nonzero   | 1                      |
| nonzero   | 0         | 0                      |
| 0         | nonzero   | 0                      |
| 0         | 0         | 0                      |

Accordingly, `&&` returns 1 (for true) if and only if both of its operands are expressions that produce nonzero values; otherwise, it returns 0 for false.

2.   The symbol `||` stands for logical *or*. It returns 0 (for false) if and only if both of its operands are expressions with zero values; otherwise, it evaluates to 1 (true). The truth table for the `||` operator is

| operand_1 | operand_2 | operand_1 \|\| operand_2 |
|-----------|-----------|--------------------------|
| nonzero   | nonzero   | 1                        |
| nonzero   | 0         | 1                        |
| 0         | nonzero   | 1                        |
| 0         | 0         | 0                        |

3.   The C logical *not* operator is `!`. It evaluates to 0 (for false) if its operand expression has a nonzero value; otherwise, it evaluates to 1 (for true). The truth table for the `!` operator is

| operand_1 | ! operand_1 |
|-----------|-------------|
| nonzero   | 0           |
| 0         | 1           |

Some examples of complex predicates follow.

*Example 9.1*   The predicate

```
(semester_average >= 80) && (semester_average <= 89)
```

returns 1 for any value of the variable `semester_average` in the range of 80 through 89. Essentially, the predicate tests for a range of values. For any value of the `semester_average` outside this range, the predicate returns 0.

*Example 9.2*   The predicate

```
(student_status == 'u') || (grade_point_average >= 3.50)
```

evaluates to 1 if the variable `student_status` is equal to 'u' or if the variable `grade_point_average` is greater than or equal to 3.50 or if both conditions are satisfied. In other words, this predicate can identify students who are either undergraduates or high honor students or both.

**Example 9.3**   The following predicate involves negation:

```
! (student_status == 'u')
```

It returns 1 if the value of the variable `student_status` is not equal to 'u'. Clearly, this predicate is equivalent to the simple predicate `(student_status != 'u')`.

## Simplifying Complex Predicates

Example 9.3 shows that in some selection problems there are several forms for expressing the same condition. In constructing predicates we should choose the form that is simplest and easiest to understand. The human mind does not react well to negated statements. For example, the statement *All books on this table belong to me* is logically the same as the statement *There is not a single book on this table that does not belong to me*. However, because the second form involves negation, it is more difficult to understand than the first.

In forming predicates, especially if we have a complex predicate that contains negation, we should try to get rid of the negation and find the simplest form in order to enhance the readability of the code. Figure 9.1 shows some basic predicate forms and the corresponding simpler forms.

| Predicate | Equivalent Simple Form |
|---|---|
| ! (a == b) | a != b |
| ! (a != b) | a == b |
| ! (a < b) | a >= b |
| ! (a <= b) | a > b |
| ! (a > b) | a <= b |
| ! (a >= b) | a < b |
| ! (*Expression_1* && *Expression_2*) | (! *Expression_1*) \|\| (! *Expression_2*) |
| ! (*Expression_1* \|\| *Expression_2*) | (! *Expression_1*) && (! *Expression_2*) |

**Figure 9.1**   Equivalent forms for predicates involving negation

The first six forms in Figure 9.1 are for negated simple predicates. For example, the negated simple predicate `! (a < b)` is the same as the simple predicate `a >= b`, and in general, the latter form should be preferred to the former. This statement is true of all negated simple predicates; using the equivalent simple predicates (those given in the second column of Figure 9.1) makes the program code more readable.

The last two entries in Figure 9.1 are the **DeMorgan's laws**. We can use these laws to change the form of a negated complex predicate to one that contains few or no negations. Here are two examples.

**Example 9.4**   Suppose we want to test a variable called `time` for the range of values of 9 through 11. The complex predicate

```
(time >= 9) && (time <= 11)
```

can be used for this purpose. If `time` is in the range of 9 through 11, this predicate will return 1; otherwise, it will return 0. Now let us assume that we want to test for the values of `time` outside this range. We can negate the above predicate and get

```
! ((time >= 9) && (time <= 11))
```

Using the first DeMorgan's law, we can transform this form into the predicate

```
(! (time >= 9)) || (! (time <= 11))
```

Now, if we eliminate the negated simple predicates by replacing them by their equivalent simple predicates, we get

```
(time < 9) || (time > 11)
```

This form reads as *time is less than 9 or greater than 11,* and it is easier to understand than the original negated form.

**Example 9.5**   Suppose we want to identify undergraduate, high honor students in a selection problem. The negated complex predicate

```
! ((student_status != 'u') || (grade_point_average < 3.50))
```

is, by virtue of the second deMorgan's law, equivalent to the predicate

```
(student_status == 'u') && (grade_point_average >= 3.50)
```

The first form can be expressed as *students who are neither not undergraduates nor with a grade point average of less than 3.50.* Clearly, although this form is correct, it is somewhat difficult to grasp. The second form is more natural and can be expressed as *students who are undergraduates and have a grade point average of 3.50 or higher.*

## Precedence of Logical Operators

In the examples of complex predicates given above, we have made liberal use of parentheses. The reason is that we have not yet explained the precedence of logical operators, and we want to make sure that the operators are applied so that the results are consistent with our expectations. For example, in the predicate `! (time < 9)`, if the current value of the variable `time` is 8, the predicate returns 0, because the simple predicate in parentheses, `(time < 9)`, is computed first as 1 and its negation is 0. If we do not use parentheses, we have `! time < 9` and if the operator `!` has higher precedence than the operator `<` (and it indeed does, as you will soon see) we will have `! time` evaluated as 0. Because 0 `<` 9, the predicate will return 1. Clearly, this value is not the expected result.

In order to understand how complex predicates and expressions are evaluated, and to decide whether or not we should use parentheses, we must know about the precedence of logical, arithmetic, and relational operators. Their precedence, from highest to lowest, is as follows:

Logical *not*, unary arithmetic operators

Binary arithmetic operators

Relational operators

Logical *and*

Logical *or*

Unless we use parentheses to change the precedence of operators, these precedence rules will be applied in evaluating complex predicates. Let us study some examples.

**Example 9.6**   Suppose we have the complex predicate

```
x + y >= 13 && ! (x - y) || x * y - 16 == 4
```

in an `if` statement. In evaluating this expression, the computer will carry out the operations in the order shown on the bottom line:

```
x + y >= 13 && ! (x - y) || x * y - 16 == 4
    4  6       8   2    1     9   3    5    7
```

If the current values for the variables `x` and `y` are 20 and 4, respectively, this complex predicate will be computed in nine steps as follows:

| Step | Operator | Reduced Expression |
|------|----------|---------------------|
| 1 | – | x + y >= 13 && ! 16 \|\| x * y - 16 == 4 |
| 2 | ! | x + y >= 13 && 0 \|\| x * y - 16 == 4 |
| 3 | * | x + y >= 13 && 0 \|\| 80 - 16 == 4 |
| 4 | + | 24 >= 13 && 0 \|\| 80 - 16 == 4 |
| 5 | – | 24 >= 13 && 0 \|\| 64 == 4 |
| 6 | >= | 1 && 0 \|\| 64 == 4 |
| 7 | == | 1 && 0 \|\| 0 |
| 8 | && | 0 \|\| 0 |
| 9 | \|\| | 0 |

**Example 9.7**   Additional examples of predicates are listed in the following table. They are based on the variable declarations:

```
int var1 = 15, var2 = 5, is_done = 1;
double var3 = 3.5;
char var4 = 'c';
```

The table shows several predicates and the values that will be computed for them.

| No. | Predicate | Value of Predicate |
|-----|-----------|--------------------|
| 1 | (var1 <= 10) && (var2 == 5) | 0 |
| 2 | (var1 <= 10) \|\| (var2 == 5) | 1 |
| 3 | ! var1 \|\| ! (! var2) | 1 |
| 4 | ! var1 \|\| var2 | 1 |
| 5 | var1 && var2 && var3 | 1 |
| 6 | var1 && (var2 - 5) && var3 | 0 |
| 7 | (var3 == 3.5) \|\| (var4 == 'c') | 1 |
| 8 | ! is_done | 0 |
| 9 | is_done \|\| (var4 != 'c') | 1 |
| 10 | ! var3 && ! var2 | 0 |
| 11 | ! (var3 \|\| var2) | 0 |

## Multiway Selection Using the `if` Statement with Complex Predicates

Now that you know about logical operators and can use complex predicates, many selection problems will become easier to formulate. The use of complex predicates makes it possible to avoid deeply nested `if` statements.

***Example 9.8***  The five-way selection problem for the letter grade assignment scheme

| Semester Average | Letter Grade |
|------------------|--------------|
| >= 90 | A |
| 80 – 89 | B |
| 70 – 79 | C |
| 60 – 69 | D |
| < 60 | F |

can be implemented using a sequence of five unnested `if` statements and complex predicates:

```
if (semester_average >= 90)
     letter_grade = 'A';
/* end if */

if (semester_average < 90 && semester_average >= 80)
     letter_grade = 'B';
/* end if */
```

```
if (semester_average < 80 && semester_average >= 70)
     letter_grade = 'C';
/* end if */

if (semester_average < 70 && semester_average >= 60)
     letter_grade = 'D';
/* end if */

if (semester_average < 60)
     letter_grade = 'F';
/* end if */
```

By using complex predicates, we can more easily test for incorrect values of variables. Consider the following example.

***Example 9.9***   Instead of writing

```
if (semester_average > 100)
     printf("Incorrect test score.");
/* end if */

if (semester_average < 0)
     printf("Incorrect test score.");
/* end if */
```

we can use a single  if  statement to accomplish the same objective:

```
if (semester_average > 100 || semester_average < 0)
     printf("Incorrect test score.");
/* end if */
```

Selection problems based on two or more variables are easier to solve using complex predicates.

***Example 9.10***   Suppose we want to print the identification numbers of high honor students majoring in computer science or computer engineering. Let us assume that the variable  major_code  has a value of 1 for computer science students and a value of 7 for computer engineering majors. If we do not use complex predicates, the solution of this problem requires two consecutive nested  if  statements:

```
if (grade_point_average >= 3.50)
      if (major_code == 1)
            printf("%d", student_idno);
      /* end if */
/* end if */

if (grade_point_average >= 3.50)
      if (major_code == 7)
            printf("%d", student_idno);
      /* end if */
/* end if */
```

If we use complex predicates instead, a single unnested `if` statement will suffice:

```
if (grade_point_average >= 3.50 && (major_code == 1 || major_code == 7))
      printf("%d", student_idno);
/* end if */
```

## 9.3   MULTIWAY SELECTION USING THE `switch` AND `break` STATEMENTS

If the alternatives in a multiway selection structure are based on a variable or an expression that computes to an integral value (such as integer or character values), we may use the `switch` statement instead of a nested `if` statement. The syntax of the `switch` statement follows.

```
switch (ControllingExpression) {
      CaseClause-1
      CaseClause-2
         .
         .
      CaseClause-n
      DefaultClause
} /* end switch */
```

where each *CaseClause* is defined as

```
case Constant-1 :
case Constant-2 :
      .

      .
case Constant-m :
         Statement
```

and the *DefaultClause* is defined as

```
default :
         Statement
```

As you can see, a `switch` statement consists of the following elements:

1. The keyword `switch`
2. An expression, called the controlling expression, enclosed in parentheses
3. Enclosed in braces

   a. Any number of case clauses consisting of the keyword `case` followed by a constant, a colon, and any number of statements

   b. An optional default clause consisting of the keyword `default` followed by a colon and any number of statements

In the `switch` statement the controlling expression is evaluated first. The controlling expression must compute to an integral value and must be of type `int` or `char`; it cannot be `double` or `float`. If the `switch` statement contains a `case` clause with a constant value that matches the value of the controlling expression, the statements in that `case` clause are executed until the end of the `switch` statement is reached. The end of a `switch` statement is the right brace, }, that is associated with it. If the value of the controlling expression does not match any of the constant values in the `case` clauses, the content of the `default` clause is executed. If there is no `default` clause, the program control exits the `switch` statement.

We consider an example:

```
switch (major_code) {
     case 1 :
           printf("Student major is computer science.");
     case 7 :
           printf("Student major is computer engineering.");
     default :
           printf("Student major is a noncomputer field.");
} /* end switch */
```

This statement is syntactically correct. Semantically, it is equivalent to the following nested `if` statement:

```
if (major_code == 1) {
      printf("Student major is computer science.");
      printf("Student major is computer engineering.");
      printf("Student major is a noncomputer field.");
}
else if (major_code == 7) {
      printf("Student major is computer engineering.");
      printf("Student major is a noncomputer field.");
}
else
      printf("Student major is a noncomputer field.");
/* end if */
```

Clearly, this is not what we want to achieve. We do not want, for example, to print the messages

```
Student major is computer science.
Student major is computer engineering.
Student major is a noncomputer field.
```

if the `major_code` is equal to 1. This action, however, is what will happen unless we create in each `case` clause a jump to the statement that follows the `switch` statement.

To force an exit from inside a `switch` statement, we can use the `break` statement. The syntax of the `break` statement is simple—just the keyword `break`. It should be used only in the `switch` and repetition statements. The `break` statement causes a jump from inside a `switch` or repetition statement to whatever follows.

Using the `break` statement, we rewrite the preceding example as follows:

```
switch (major_code) {
      case 1 :
            printf("Student major is computer science.");
            break;
      case 7 :
            printf("Student major is computer engineering.");
            break;
      default :
            printf("Student major is a noncomputer field.");
} /* end switch */
```

Now this multiway selection structure becomes equivalent to the following nested `if`:

```
if (major_code == 1)
        printf("Student major is computer science.");
else if (major_code == 7)
        printf("Student major is computer engineering.");
else
        printf("Student major is a non computer field.");
/* end if */
```

As you can see, the `switch` statement almost always goes with one or more `break` statements, but not every `case` or `default` clause requires a `break` statement. Clearly, we do not need a `break` statement in the last clause. Also, if the actions of two or more consecutive cases are identical, all we have to do is list the cases with empty statements and specify the action and a `break` statement in the final case. An example follows.

```
switch (major_code) {
        case 1 :
        case 7 :
                printf("Student major is a computer field.");
                break;
        default :
                printf("Student major is a non computer field.");
} /* end switch */
```

Let us study a few more examples of multiway selection using the `switch` statement.

***Example 9.11*** Again we consider the five-way selection problem of Example 9.8 and recall the letter grade assignment scheme. If we use the variable `semester_average` as the controlling expression in a `switch` statement, since there are 101 legitimate `semester_average` values, we will end up with too many cases. However, we note that the preceding scheme can be reformulated on the basis of the controlling expression `semester_average / 10`, provided the variable `semester_average` is of type `int`, as follows:

| semester_average / 10 | letter_grade |
| :---: | :---: |
| >= 9 | A |
| 8 | B |
| 7 | C |
| 6 | D |
| < 6 | F |

We conclude that a switch statement with five case clauses and one default can be used to implement this five-way selection structure:

```
switch (semester_average / 10) {
    case 10 :
    case 9  :
         letter_grade = 'A';
         break;
    case 8 :
         letter_grade = 'B';
         break;
    case 7 :
         letter_grade = 'C';
         break;
    case 6 :
         letter_grade = 'D';
         break;
    default :
         letter_grade = 'F';
} /* end switch */
```

***Example 9.12***   Suppose that the variable character is of type char and it can be used to store any printable character on the keyboard. We want to determine whether its content is a decimal integer, 0 through 9. Because there are ten decimal integers, we have an 11-way decision problem, the 11th alternative corresponding to any nondecimal character.

First, we will implement this selection problem using a switch statement:

```
switch (character) {
    case '0': case '1': case '2': case '3': case '4':
    case '5': case '6': case '7': case '8': case '9':
         printf("The content is a decimal integer.");
         break;
    default :
         printf("The content is a nondecimal character.");
} /* end switch */
```

The ten case clauses corresponding to the values '0' through '9' of character indicate the same action. Therefore, the cases for '0' through '8' contain no statements, and only the case for '9' has an output and a break statement.

The same decision problem can be formulated using a nested if statement as follows:

```
if (character == '0')
        printf("The content is a decimal integer.");
else if (character == '1')
        printf("The content is a decimal integer.");
else if (character == '2')
        printf("The content is a decimal integer.");
else if (character == '3')
        printf("The content is a decimal integer.");
else if (character == '4')
        printf("The content is a decimal integer.");
else if (character == '5')
        printf("The content is a decimal integer.");
else if (character == '6')
        printf("The content is a decimal integer.");
else if (character == '7')
        printf("The content is a decimal integer.");
else if (character == '8')
        printf("The content is a decimal integer.");
else if (character == '9')
        printf("The content is a decimal integer.");
else
        printf("The content is a nondecimal character.");
/* end if */
```

As you can see, the resulting formulation is longer than the preceding `switch` statement and also contains repetitions of the common action. We can avoid this situation by using a single `if` statement in which the logical *or* operators combine the ten simple conditions into a complex predicate:

```
if (character == '0' || character == '1' || character == '2' ||
    character == '3' || character == '4' || character == '5' ||
    character == '6' || character == '7' || character == '8' ||
    character == '9')
      printf("The content is a decimal integer.");
else
      printf("The content is a nondecimal character.");
/* end if */
```

## 9.4   STYLE CONSIDERATIONS FOR MULTIWAY SELECTION STRUCTURES

In software design our objective is always to create clear and readable code. Complex and multiway selection structures require special care. Otherwise, the reader of the program may have trouble understanding its logic. In addition to the style considerations in section 4.4, we suggest the following:

1.   Keep the use of logical negation to a minimum in forming complex predicates. For predicates requiring negation, use the simple forms provided in Figure 9.1.

2.   Keep logical expressions simple by using nested selection structures if necessary. For example, instead of

```
if ((major_code == 1 || major_code == 7) &&
     grade_point_average >= 3.50)
        . . . . . . . . .
```

write the nested `if` statement

```
if (major_code == 1 || major_code == 7)
      if (grade_point_average >= 3.50)
           . . . . . . . . .
```

3.   Remember that a nested `if` statement is more general than a `switch` statement. However, you should prefer the `switch` statement whenever the alternatives in a selection structure are based on a reasonably small number of values of a variable or an expression. A good rule of thumb is to use the `switch` statement for three to ten alternative selection structures.

4.   Use proper indentations in forming `switch` statements. Indent the keyword `case` for each case clause with respect to the left brace of the `switch` statement by an equal amount. Also, indent the statements in each case clause with respect to the `case` keyword. Example:

```
switch (letter_grade) {
    case 'A' :
            number_of_As++;
            break;
    case 'B' :
            number_of_Bs++;
            break;
    case 'C' :
            number_of_Cs++;
            break;
    case 'D' :
            number_of_Ds++;
            break;
```

```
        case 'F' :
                number_of_Fs++;
                break;
        default :
                printf("Incorrect letter grade.");
} /* end switch */
```

5. Whenever possible, use a `default` clause in your `switch` statements. This convention will force you to consider all alternatives, including those that are not defined by your `case` clauses.

6. Arrange your `case` clauses in `switch` statements in a way that avoids duplication of similar actions to several alternatives. For example, the following `switch` statement has duplicate actions:

```
switch (major_code) {
    case 1 :
        printf("Science student");
        break;
    case 2 :
        printf("Art student");
        break;
    case 3 :
        printf("Science student");
        break;
    case 4 :
        printf("Art student");
        break;
    case 5 :
        printf("Science student");
} /* end switch */
```

On the other hand, the following `switch` statement eliminates duplications by arranging cases with similar actions in groups:

```
switch (major_code) {
    case 1 :
    case 3 :
    case 5 :
            printf("Science student");
            break;
```

```
      case 2 :
      case 4 :
            printf("Art student");
} /* end switch */
```

## REVIEW QUESTIONS

**1.** Concerning logical expressions:
   **a.** They compute to either true or false.
   **b.** A simple predicate is not a logical expression.
   **c.** Logical expressions are operands for relational operators.
   **d.** All of the above are correct.
   **e.** None of the above is correct.

**2.** Which of the following statements about the C logical operators is correct?
   **a.** Logical *and* is represented by `||`.
   **b.** Logical *or* is represented by `&&`.
   **c.** Logical *not* evaluates to 0 if its operand expression has a nonzero value.
   **d.** Logical *and* evaluates to 0 if its operands are both nonzero values.
   **e.** All of the above.
   **f.** None of the above.

**3.** The predicate `!((a < c) && (b == d))` is equivalent to
   **a.** `(a >= c) || (b != d)`
   **b.** `(a < c) || (b == d)`
   **c.** `(a >= c) || (b == d)`
   **d.** `(a < c) || (b != d)`
   **e.** None of the above.

**4.** The precedence of logical operators in C from highest to lowest is
   **a.** `!, ||, &&`
   **b.** `!, &&, ||`
   **c.** `&&, ||, !`
   **d.** `||, &&, !`
   **e.** None of the above.

**5.** The controlling expression in a `switch` statement can be of type `double`. (T or F)

**Answers:** 1. a; 2. c; 3. a; 4. b; 5. F.

## 9.5    THE PRETEST REPETITION STRUCTURE

Chapter 2 briefly introduced the pretest and posttest repetition structures. In a **pretest repetition structure** the loop body is executed after the loop control expression is tested, whereas in a **posttest repetition structure**, the loop control expression is executed before it is tested. In Chapter 4 you learned that the `while` statement is an implementation of the pretest repetition structure. C has another repetition statement that can be used in implementing pretest repetition; it is the `for` statement.

### The `for` Statement for Pretest Repetition

The syntax of the `for` statement is as follows:

```
for (InitializationExpression; LoopControlExpression; UpdateExpression)
        LoopBody
/* end for */
```

In this syntax *InitializationExpression* is a C expression that may assign an initial value to a loop control variable, and *UpdateExpression* is one that may change its value. The *LoopControlExpression* is an expression that computes to zero (for false) or a nonzero value (for true). It can be a predicate that is based on the loop control variable. Finally, *LoopBody* can be a single statement or a compound statement.

Figure 9.2 gives the semantics of the `for` statement. In executing a `for` statement, the computer does the following:

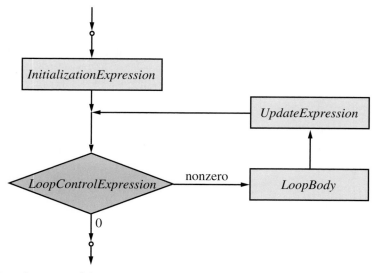

**Figure 9.2**    Semantics of the `for` statement

1. Executes the *InitializationExpression.*
2. Evaluates the *LoopControlExpression.* If it computes to zero, the loop is exited.
3. If the *LoopControlExpression* yields a nonzero value, the *LoopBody* is executed and then the *UpdateExpression* is evaluated.
4. Tests the *LoopControlExpression* again. Thus the *LoopBody* is repeated until the *LoopControlExpression* computes to a zero value.

Some examples of the `for` statement follow.

***Example 9.13*** The `while` statement in the following code

```
int number, sum = 0, counter = 1;
. . . . . . . . . . . . . . . . .
. . . . . . . . . . . . . . . . .
while (counter <= number) {
      sum = sum + counter;
      counter = counter + 1;
} /* end while */
```

computes the sum of integers from 1 to `number`. In this process, in every cycle of repetition, the `while` checks whether the loop control expression `counter <= num-ber` evaluates to a nonzero integer (i.e., true); if so, the `while` executes the loop body.

The preceding `while` loop can be reformulated using a `for` statement as follows:

```
int number, sum, counter;
. . . . . . . . . . . . . . . . .
. . . . . . . . . . . . . . . . .
sum = 0;

for (counter = 1; counter <= number; counter = counter + 1)
      sum = sum + counter;
/* end for */
```

Here the integer variable `counter` is a loop control variable. The initialization expression `counter = 1` in the `for` statement header assigns the initial value of 1 to it. The loop control expression `counter <= number` is evaluated before the loop body is executed. If the loop control expression yields a nonzero value, the loop body, in this case the statement

```
sum = sum + counter;
```

is executed; otherwise, the loop is exited. After each execution of the loop body, the update expression `counter = counter + 1` is evaluated. The update expression here is an arithmetic assignment statement that increments `counter` by 1.

To better understand the behavior of the  for  statement, let us draw a trace table. The columns in a **trace table** show the expression evaluated at each step of the program execution and the affected program variables. Each row shows the expression considered by the computer and the current values of the variables after the execution of that expression. A trace table is also a valuable program debugging tool. You can use it to find the logical errors in programs that do not produce expected results. Naturally, the columns in a trace table depend on the program code that you are tracing.

In the following trace table, we will assume that the current value of the variable number is 3. The variables of interest to us are  sum  and  counter, and they are shown as columns of the table.

| Step | Expression Evaluated | sum | counter |
|------|---------------------|-----|---------|
| 1 | The statement:  sum  =  0 | 0 | – |
| 2 | The initialization expression:  counter  =  1 | 0 | 1 |
| 3 | The loop control expression:  counter  <=  number  <br> 1  <=  3  yields true. | 0 | 1 |
| 4 | The loop body:  sum  =  sum  +  counter | 1 | 1 |
| 5 | The update expression:  counter  =  counter  +  1 | 1 | 2 |
| 6 | The loop control expression:  counter  <=  number  <br> 2  <=  3  yields true. | 1 | 2 |
| 7 | The loop body:  sum  =  sum  +  counter. | 3 | 2 |
| 8 | The update expression: counter  =  counter  +  1 | 3 | 3 |
| 9 | The loop control expression:  counter  <=  number  <br> 3  <=  3  yields true. | 3 | 3 |
| 10 | The loop body:  sum  =  sum  +  counter | 6 | 3 |
| 11 | The update expression:  counter  =  counter  +  1 | 6 | 4 |
| 12 | The loop control expression:  counter  <=  number  <br> 4  <=  3  yields false, <br> and the loop is exited. | 6 | 4 |

***Example 9.14***   The problem of Example 9.13 can be solved using a  for  statement that initializes its loop control variable to  number  and decrements it by 1 until its value is less than 1.

```
int number, sum, counter;
. . . . . . . . . . . . . . . . .
. . . . . . . . . . . . . . . . .
sum = 0;

for (counter = number; counter >= 1; counter = counter - 1)
      sum = sum + counter;
/* end for */
```

In this formulation the initialization expression is `counter = number`, and it sets `counter` to the current value of `number`. The loop control expression has changed to `counter >= 1`, since the last integer that we want to add to `sum` is 1. Accordingly, the update expression has also changed to `counter = counter - 1`. If we use the previous update expression, `counter = counter + 1`, the value of `counter` will keep on increasing and the loop control expression, `counter >= 1`, will never become false. Thus we will be trapped in an infinite loop. To avoid infinite loops, we must exercise special care in the specification of the initialization, loop control, and update expressions in `for` statements.

**Example 9.15**    Let us assume that we have the declarations

```
int number, sum = 0, counter, number1, number2;
```

The `for` statement

```
for (counter = 1; counter <= number; counter = counter + 2)
    sum = sum + counter;
/* end for */
```

computes the sum of every second integer from 1 to `number`. The values that will be assigned to `counter` are 1, 3, 5, 7, 9, and so on.

On the other hand, the `for` statement

```
for (counter = number1; counter <= number2; counter = counter + 1)
    sum = sum + counter;
/* end for */
```

determines the sum of integers from `number1` to `number2`.

### Equivalence of `for` and `while` Statements

Both the `while` and `for` statements are implementations of the pretest repetition structure. Example 9.13 demonstrated that the same repetition problem can be expressed equivalently using either a `while` or a `for` statement. This equivalence is true in general. Let us remember the format of the `for` statement:

```
for  (InitializationExpression; LoopControlExpression; UpdateExpression)
        LoopBody
/* end for */
```

The four elements of this format, that is, the *InitializationExpression*, *LoopControl Expression*, *UpdateExpression*, and *LoopBody*, can be placed in the structure of a `while` statement as follows:

```
InitializationExpression

while (LoopControlExpression) {
   LoopBody
   UpdateExpression;
} /* end while */
```

As you can see, you can directly convert a `for` statement to a `while` statement that accomplishes the same function, and vice versa. Here is an example.

**Example 9.16**   Given the declarations

```
int number, factorial, counter;
```

the following program code computes the factorial of an integer number using a `while` statement:

```
counter = 1;
factorial = 1;

while (counter <= number) {
      factorial = factorial * counter;
      counter = counter + 1;
} /* end while */
```

The same effect can be achieved using a `for` statement,:

```
factorial = 1;

for (counter = 1; counter <= number; counter = counter + 1)
     factorial = factorial * counter;
/* end for */
```

## Using the `for` Statement for Counter-Controlled Loops

Depending on whether or not we know how many times it will be executed, a repetition structure may be counter- or sentinel-controlled. Counter- and sentinel-controlled repetition structures were introduced in Chapter 4. To review, the number of times a **counter-controlled loop** is executed is determined by the variation of a loop control variable. On the other hand, in a **sentinel-controlled loop**, we use certain values of a loop control variable to terminate the loop; therefore, we do not know in advance how many times the loop will be repeated.

The examples of the  for  statement so far in this chapter are counter-controlled repetitions. In counter-controlled repetition you must

1.   Declare a loop control variable.

2.   Assign an initial value to the variable.

3.   Test the loop control variable in a loop control expression by comparing the variable to a final value.

4.   Update the loop control variable by incrementing or decrementing it by a certain value.

The  while  and  for  loops of Example 9.16 use  counter  as their loop control variable. It is assigned the initial value of 1 and compared to the value of the variable  number, using the comparison operator  <=. Therefore, the final value of  counter  for which the loop is executed is the value of the variable  number. The loop control variable  counter  is incremented by 1 before each repetition.

### Using the `for` Statement for Sentinel-Controlled Loops

The  for  statement can also be used for sentinel-controlled loops. In this case you must

1.   Declare a sentinel variable and decide on the values that will terminate the loop.

2.   Use an initialization expression to assign a value to the sentinel variable.

3.   Design a loop control expression that uses the sentinel variable.

4.   Include an update expression that changes the value of the sentinel variable so that eventually the loop is exited.

Let us study some examples.

***Example 9.17***    Suppose we want to design a loop that prompts the user to type a character value for the variable  answer. Further, suppose only uppercase and lowercase values for the letters  y  and  n  are considered legitimate for  answer, and for any other value the user is reminded to enter a correct value. The following  for  loop will do the job:

```
char answer;

printf("Do you want to continue? (y/n): ");

for (scanf("%c", &answer);
     answer != 'y' && answer != 'Y' && answer != 'n' && answer != 'N';
     scanf("%c", &answer))
      printf("Please type y or n: ");
/* end for */
```

In this loop  answer  is the sentinel variable. The initialization expression is
scanf("%c", &answer)  for which the user must type a character value and initialize the variable  answer. The loop control expression is

```
answer != 'y' && answer != 'Y' && answer != 'n' &&
answer != 'N'
```

which is based on the sentinel variable answer and computes to true for any value of
answer  other than  y,  Y,  n, and  N. If the user types a value other than these four
values, the loop control expression will be true and the loop body will be executed. The
loop body is the statement

```
printf("Please type y or n: ");
```

which warns the user to type a correct value. The update expression is again the expression
scanf("%c", &answer), which allows the user to enter another value for  answer.
      This  for  loop repeats for as long as the user enters an inappropriate value for  an-
swer. Therefore, the number of times the loop repeats depends on the input. Not knowing
beforehand how many repetitions will occur is a characteristic of sentinel-controlled loops.

***Example 9.18***    We want to develop a program that lets the user enter the beginning checking account balance and any subsequent number of transactions. If the transaction is a de-
posit, the user should enter a positive floating-point number. For a withdrawal the amount
should be entered as a negative floating-point number. Each transaction should be used
to update the checking account balance. The computations should stop if the user types
0.0 for a transaction. In this case the program should print the ending account balance.
      The C program of Figure 9.3 uses a  for  statement to update the account balance.

```
#include <stdio.h>

int main(void) {
      double balance, transaction;

      printf("Enter beginning account balance: ");
      scanf("%lf", &balance);
      printf("Enter transaction amount: ");

      for (scanf("%lf", &transaction); transaction != 0.0;
            scanf("%lf", &transaction)) {
            balance = balance + transaction;
            printf("Enter transaction amount: ");
      } /* end for */

      printf("Ending account balance is: %8.2f", balance);
      return 0;
} /* end function main */
```

**Figure 9.3**    A C program that uses a sentinel-controlled  for  loop

We will focus on the `for` statement that forms a sentinel-controlled loop. Here the initialization expression is `scanf("%lf", &transaction)` that reads a value of `transaction`, which is the sentinel variable. The loop control expression `transaction != 0.0` ensures that the loop is exited if the user enters zero for `transaction`. Otherwise, the loop body is executed. The loop body updates `balance` by adding to its previous value the value of the variable `transaction`, and then prompts the user to enter another `transaction` amount. The update expression is once again the expression `scanf("%lf", &transaction)`, which allows the user to input another value.

In a sentinel-controlled `for` loop, we have to decide on a sentinel variable and a value or range of values that will terminate the repetition of the loop body. In Example 9.18 the sentinel variable is the variable `transaction`, and the execution of the `for` loop ends when the value of `transaction` is 0.0. This approach is necessary because the input for the program is provided interactively.

In batch programs, where input comes from a data file, we can use the end-of-file marker as a sentinel value. In fact, we did so in the program of Figure 8.6, which has the following `while` loop:

```
fscanf(indata, "%d", &test_score);

while(! feof(indata)) {
      printf("Echo-printing test score read: %d\n", test_score);

      sum_of_test_scores = sum_of_test_scores + test_score;
      number_of_records++;

      fscanf(indata, "%d", &test_score);
} /* end while */
```

We can easily rewrite this sentinel-controlled loop using the `for` statement:

```
for (fscanf(indata, "%d", &test_score); ! feof(indata);
fscanf(indata, "%d", &test_score)) {
      printf("Echo-printing test score read: %d\n", test_score);
      sum_of_test_scores = sum_of_test_scores + test_score;
      number_of_records++;
} /* end for */
```

Here the expression `fscanf(indata, "%d", &test_score)` is the initialization expression, which reads a `test_score` value from the file `indata`. The expression `! feof(indata)` serves as the loop control expression, and it will return 0 (false) if the end of the `indata` file has been encountered during the most recent `fscanf` invocation, thus terminating the loop. The update expression, `fscanf(indata, "%d", &test_score)`, reads another record from the file.

### Checking for Incorrect Data in a Loop and the `continue` Statement

In certain applications we may have an input statement in the body of a loop that causes the reading of an incorrect value for a program variable. Rather than using a `break` statement to exit the loop, we may prefer to warn the user and skip the rest of the loop body. We can do so with the `continue` statement.

The `continue` statement has a simple syntax—just the keyword `continue`. It causes the program control to skip the rest of the loop body and execute the loop again. The following example uses the `continue` statement.

***Example 9.19***   Suppose we want to write a program that allows its user to enter test score values and compute and output the class average and the number of students who took the test. Legitimate test score values are integers in the range 1 through 100. If the user enters a test score value outside this range, the program should warn the user to enter a correct value, disregard the incorrect test score in computing the class average, but continue with the processing. The program should terminate when the user enters a zero for test score.

The C program of Figure 9.4 is one correct solution to this problem. It initializes the variables `sum` and `number_of_students` to 0 and prompts the user to enter a test score value. Then it gets into a `for` loop.

```c
#include <stdio.h>

int main(void) {
        int test_score, number_of_students = 0, sum = 0;
        double class_average;

        printf("Enter a test score. Enter 0 to stop: ");

        for (scanf("%d", &test_score); test_score != 0;
                scanf("%d", &test_score)) {
                if (test_score < 0 || test_score > 100) {
                    printf("Incorrect test score! Enter a correct value: ");
                    continue;
                } /* end if */

                sum = sum + test_score;
                number_of_students = number_of_students + 1;

                printf("Enter a test score. Enter 0 to stop: ");
        } /* end for */
```

**Figure 9.4**    A C program that uses the `continue` statement in a loop (*continued*)    ▶

```
        if (number_of_students != 0)
             class_average = (double) sum / number_of_students;
        else
             class_average = 0.0;
        /* end if */

        printf("Number of students : %d\n", number_of_students);
        printf("Class average      : %6.1f", class_average);
        return 0;
    } /* end function main */
```

**Figure 9.4**                                                                  ∎

Let us focus on the  `for`  loop. Its initialization expression is  `scanf("%d",
&test_score)`, which reads a value for  `test_score`. The loop control expression
is  `test_score != 0`, which terminates the execution of the loop in case the value
of  `test_score`  is zero.

In the body of the  `for`  loop, we have an  `if`  statement. This statement checks
whether if the current value of  `test_score`  is in the correct range. If not, it prints
the message

`Incorrect test score! Enter a correct value:`

on the screen and, because of the  `continue` statement, skips the rest of the loop body.
Next, the update expression  `scanf("%d", &test_score)`  is executed, thus giving the user a chance to enter a correct  `test_score`  value. If, however, the
`test_score`  value is correct, the rest of the loop body is executed to add the value of
`test_score`  to  `sum`  and to increment  `number_of_students`  by one.

The  `if`  statement after the  `for`  loop avoids division by zero in case no test score
is entered. The use of the cast operator  `(double)`  in the statement

`class_average = (double) sum / number_of_students;`

is necessary because both  `sum`  and  `number_of_students`  have been declared as
type  `int`. To retain the fractional part of the class average, the type of  `sum`  has to be
converted to  `double`  before division.

## 9.6   THE POSTTEST REPETITION STRUCTURE

In a posttest repetition structure, the loop body is executed before the loop control expression is tested. After the first execution of the loop body, if the loop control expression evaluates to a nonzero value (that is, true), the loop body is executed again; otherwise, the loop is exited.

## The `do-while` Statement

In C the posttest repetition structure finds an implementation in the `do-while` statement. The syntax of the `do-while` statement follows.

```
do
        LoopBody
while (LoopControlExpression);
/* end do-while */
```

Here the *LoopControlExpression* is a C expression that evaluates to the value of zero (for false) or a nonzero value (for true). The *LoopBody* can be a single statement or a compound statement.

The flowchart of Figure 9.5 shows the semantics of the `do-while` statement. The computer goes through the following steps in executing a `do-while` statement:

1. It executes the *LoopBody*.
2. It evaluates the *LoopControlExpression*. If the value of the *LoopControlExpression* is 0, the computer exits the loop; otherwise, it does the *LoopBody* again.

The following example illustrates the `do-while` statement.

***Example 9.20*** We again consider Example 9.13 in which a `while` statement computes the sum of integers from 1 to `number`. We can solve this problem using a `do-while` loop as follows:

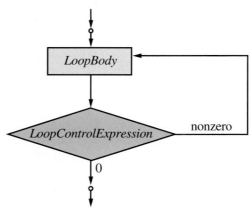

**Figure 9.5** Semantics of the `do-while` statement

```
int number, sum = 0, counter = 0;
. . . . . . . . . . . . . . . . .
. . . . . . . . . . . . . . . . .
do {
     sum = sum + counter;
     counter = counter + 1;
} while (counter <= number);
/* end do-while */
```

In this version of the solution, we initialize the variable `counter` before the `do-while` loop to 0. We set it to 0 instead of to 1 because the `do-while` statement executes its loop body once without considering the loop control expression. If we initialize `counter` to 1, when the variable `number` is 0, the loop computes `sum` as 1, which is clearly wrong.

The following trace table for this code assumes the value of the variable `number` is 3. You should study it and compare it to the trace table for the `for` statement of Example 9.13.

| Step | Expression Evaluated | sum | counter |
|------|---------------------|-----|---------|
| 1 | The statement: `sum = 0;` | 0 | – |
| 2 | The statement: `sum = 0;` | 0 | 0 |
| 3 | The statement in the loop body:<br>`sum = sum + counter;` | 0 | 0 |
| 4 | The statement in the loop body:<br>`counter = counter + 1;` | 0 | 1 |
| 5 | The loop control expression: `counter <= number`<br>`1 <= 3` yields true. | 0 | 1 |
| 6 | The statement in the loop body:<br>`sum = sum + counter;` | 1 | 1 |
| 7 | The statement in the loop body:<br>`counter = counter + 1;` | 1 | 2 |
| 8 | The loop control expression: `counter <= number`<br>`2 <= 3` yields true. | 1 | 2 |
| 9 | The statement in the loop body:<br>`sum = sum + counter;` | 3 | 2 |
| 10 | The statement in the loop body:<br>`counter = counter + 1;` | 3 | 3 |
| 11 | The loop control expression: `counter <= number`<br>`3 <= 3` yields true. | 3 | 3 |
| 12 | The statement in the loop body:<br>`sum = sum + counter;` | 6 | 3 |
| 13 | The statement in the loop body:<br>`counter = counter + 1;` | 6 | 4 |
| 14 | The loop control expression: `counter <= number`<br>`4 <= 3` yields false,<br>and the loop is exited. | 6 | 4 |

## Use of `do-while` for Counter- and Sentinel-Controlled Loops

The `do-while` statement can be used both for counter-controlled and sentinel-controlled loops. In Example 9.20 the `do-while` loop is a counter-controlled loop. We will discuss one more example in which this statement is used to form a sentinel-controlled loop.

***Example 9.21*** We consider the problem of Example 9.18, where we developed a program to compute the ending balance for a checking account. In that program we used a `for` statement to construct a sentinel-controlled loop. The sentinel variable was `transaction`, and the sentinel value was 0.0 for `transaction`, which terminated the repetition. The program given in Figure 9.6 solves the same problem using a sentinel-controlled `do-while` loop.

```c
#include <stdio.h>

int main(void) {
        double balance, transaction;

        printf("Enter beginning account balance: ");
        scanf("%lf", &balance);

        do {
                printf("Enter transaction amount: ");
                scanf("%lf", &transaction);
                balance = balance + transaction;
        } while (transaction != 0.0);
        /* end do-while */

        printf("Ending account balance is: %8.2f", balance);
        return 0;
} /* end function main */
```

**Figure 9.6**   A C program that uses a sentinel-controlled `do-while` loop

Compared to the solution presented in Example 9.18, we note one difference: the initialization and update expressions for the `for` loop of Example 9.18 are the expression `scanf("%lf", &transaction)`. We use the same expression here, but only once in the `do-while` loop body. In the first cycle of repetition, this expression serves as the initialization expression; afterwards, it is used as an update expression. The loop control expression `transaction != 0.0` is the same in both versions.

It has been possible to use the `do-while` statement in this application in constructing a sentinel-controlled loop because the sentinel value of the variable `transaction` is 0. Because a `do-while` loop is a posttest repetition structure, when the user enters the sentinel value of 0.0, it is added to the `balance` by the statement

```
balance = balance + transaction;
```

However, adding 0 to a value does not change anything, and hence the result is correct. If the sentinel value is other than 0, this loop will not work. For example, assuming a limit of $500.00 on a check that a bank customer may write, we may have decided to use any value less than −500.00 (remember, withdrawals are negative values) as the sentinel value to control this loop. In this case the `do-while` loop would look like this:

```
do {
        printf("Enter transaction amount: ");
        scanf("%lf", &transaction);
        balance = balance + transaction;
} while (transaction >= -500.00);
/* end do-while */
```

And a transaction value of, say, −600 to terminate the repetition would be incorrectly subtracted from `balance`. To avoid this possibility, we have to write the loop with an `if` statement:

```
do {
        printf("Enter transaction amount: ");
        scanf("%lf", &transaction);

        if (transaction >= -500.00)
                balance = balance + transaction;
        /* end if */

} while (transaction >= -500.00);
/* end do-while */
```

The necessity of the `if` statement here is obvious; however, it complicates the code. In such cases a pretest repetition statement is more appropriate, and you should choose either a `while` or a `for` loop.

### Use of the `break` and `continue` Statements in `do-while` Loops

The `break` and `continue` statements can also be used in posttest repetition loops based on the `do-while` statement. The `break` statement interrupts the execution of the loop and creates a forced exit to the statement that follows the `do-while`. The `continue` statement, on the other hand, skips the rest of the loop body and proceeds with the next repetition of the loop. The following program illustrates their use in a `do-while` loop.

*Example 9.22*   We will develop a calculator program that allows the user to enter an arithmetic expression as

   *Constant Operator Constant*

where *Constant* is a numeric value and *Operator* can be +, –, *, and / for addition, subtraction, multiplication, and division. We want the program to compute the value of the expression and print it in a loop for as long as the user wants to continue. Division by zero is to be avoided by exiting the loop, printing a message, and terminating the program execution. If the user enters an incorrect symbol for *Operator*, the program should print a warning message and prompt the user to enter a new expression. The C program that functions as a simple calculator is given in Figure 9.7.

```c
#include <stdio.h>

int main(void) {
        double operand1, operand2, result;
        char oper, zero_division = 'n', another_expression = 'y';
        char newline_char;

        do {
                printf("Type an arithmetic expression as ");
                printf("Constant Operator Constant");
                printf("\nand press Enter.");
                printf("  Operator can be +, -, * or /.\n");
                scanf("%lf %c %lf", &operand1, &oper, &operand2);
                scanf("%c", &newline_char);

                if (oper != '+' && oper != '-' && oper != '*' &&
                    oper != '/') {
                    printf("Incorrect operator!\n");
                    continue;
                } /* end if */

                if (oper == '/' && operand2 == 0.0) {
                        zero_division = 'y';
                        break;
                } /* end if */

                switch (oper) {
                        case '+' :
                                result = operand1 + operand2;
                                break;
```

**Figure 9.7**    A C program that simulates a simple calculator *(continued)*    ▶

```
                  case '-' :
                        result = operand1 - operand2;
                        break;
                  case '*' :
                        result = operand1 * operand2;
                        break;
                  case '/' :
                        result = operand1 / operand2;
            } /* end switch */

            printf("%f %c %f = %f\n", operand1, oper, operand2,
                  result);

            printf("Another expression? (y/n): ");
            scanf("%c", &another_expression);
      } while (another_expression == 'y' || another_expression == 'Y');
      /* end do-while */

      if (zero_division == 'y')
            printf("Division by zero. Program terminating . . .");
      else
            printf("Normal program termination . . .");
      /* end if */
      return 0;
} /* end function main */
```

Figure 9.7                                                                   ◼

This program contains a `do-while` statement. The `if` statement in the loop body checks whether the operator entered by the user is `+`, `-`, `*`, or `/`. If not, it prints the message `Incorrect operator!`, and because of the `continue` statement in the then-part of this `if` statement, it skips the rest of the loop, evaluates the loop control condition, and proceeds with the next cycle of repetition.

The next `if` statement tests for the possibility of division by zero; that is, whether the operator is `/` and the second operand is zero. If so, it sets the character variable `zero_division` to `'y'` and executes the `break` statement placed in the then-part of the `if` statement. The `break` statement forces an exit from the loop to the `if` statement that comes after the `do-while` loop.

## 9.7   NESTED LOOPS

As we can have nested `if` statements, we can also have nested loops. A **nested loop** is a repetition structure that contains one or more loops in its body. In a nested loop structure, in every repetition of the outer loop the inner loops are completely executed.

A loop contained in another loop forms a **doubly nested loop**. A doubly nested loop can be placed inside another loop—in which case we have a **triply nested loop**, and so on. In C the loops in a nested loop structure may be formed using `while`, `for`, and `do-while` statements.

We will look at two examples of nested loops.

***Example 9.23***   Consider the partial code:

```
int control_var1, control_var2;

for (control_var1 = 1; control_var1 <= 8; control_var1 += 2)
    for (control_var2 = control_var1; control_var2 <= 10;
        control_var2 += 3)
        printf("control_var1 = %d  control_var2 = %d\n",
            control_var1, control_var2);
    /* end for */
/* end for */
```

The outer `for` loop, controlled by the integer variable `control_var1`, contains a nested `for` loop, which in turn is controlled by the variable `control_var2`. In the first cycle of repetition of the outer loop, the value of `control_var1` is 1. The initialization expression for the inner `for` loop is `control_var2` = `control_var1`. Therefore, `control_var2` is also initialized to 1, and the loop body of the inner `for` statement is executed four times with 1, 4, 7, and 10 as the values of `control_var2`.

In the second cycle of repetition of the outer `for` loop, the variable `control_var1` is incremented by 2 and becomes 3. This time the inner loop is executed three times, with 3, 6, and 9 as the values of the variable `control_var2`. The execution continues in this manner until the outer loop terminates. The following result is produced by this nested loop when we run it in a proper C function. As you can see, the body of the inner loop is executed a total of 11 times.

```
control_var1 = 1   control_var2 = 1
control_var1 = 1   control_var2 = 4
control_var1 = 1   control_var2 = 7
control_var1 = 1   control_var2 = 10
control_var1 = 3   control_var2 = 3
control_var1 = 3   control_var2 = 6
control_var1 = 3   control_var2 = 9
control_var1 = 5   control_var2 = 5
control_var1 = 5   control_var2 = 8
control_var1 = 7   control_var2 = 7
control_var1 = 7   control_var2 = 10
```

***Example 9.24***   Suppose we want to write a function that prints the capital letter E in a grid of 17 rows and 20 columns, consisting of the characters blank and   * as follows:

```
* * * * * * * * * * * * * * * * * * * *
* * * * * * * * * * * * * * * * * * * *
* * * * * * * * * * * * * * * * * * * *
* * * *
* * * *
* * * *
* * * *
* * * * * * * * * * * *
* * * * * * * * * * * *
* * * * * * * * * * * *
* * * *
* * * *
* * * *
* * * *
* * * * * * * * * * * * * * * * * * * *
* * * * * * * * * * * * * * * * * * * *
* * * * * * * * * * * * * * * * * * * *
```

As you can see, the block consists of

1.   Twenty asterisks on rows 1 through 3 and 15 through 17
2.   Four asterisks on rows 4 through 7 and 11 through 14
3.   Thirteen asterisks on rows 8 through 10.

The C function shown in Figure 9.8 will generate the block letter E.

```
void print_E(void) {
      int i, j;

      for (i = 1; i <= 17; i += 1) {
           if (i <= 3 || i >= 15)
                for (j = 1; j <= 20; j += 1)
                     printf("*");
                /* end for */
           /* end if */
```

**Figure 9.8**   A C function that prints the block letter E (*continued*)   ▶

```
                    if (i > 3 && i <= 7 || i > 10 && i <= 14)
                        for (j = 1; j <= 4; j += 1)
                            printf("*");
                        /* end for */
                    /* end if */

                    if (i > 7 && i <= 10)
                        for (j = 1; j <= 13; j += 1)
                            printf("*");
                        /* end for */
                    /* end if */

                    printf("\n");
                }/* end for */
            } /* end function print_E */
```

Figure 9.8                                                                    ∎

The body of this function consists of a `for` loop controlled by the variable `i`. Each execution of this loop will generate one row of the grid. Therefore, the variation of the variable `i` is from 1 to 17 at increments of one. In the outer `for` loop body, we have three `if` statements to print the necessary number of asterisks. Each `if` statement contains a `for` loop. Therefore, we have a nested repetition structure in this example.

The first `if` statement in Figure 9.8 executes the `for` loop in its body if the condition `i <= 3 || i >= 15` is satisfied. In other words, this statement prints rows 1 through 3 and 15 through 17 of the grid. The `for` statement uses `j` as its loop control variable and prints the character `*` 20 times. Hence this `if` statement properly generates the first three and the last three lines of the grid. The other `if` statements will take care of the remaining elements of the block letter.

We will have more challenging and meaningful applications of nested loops in Chapter 11 when we cover arrays.

## 9.8    STYLE CONSIDERATIONS FOR REPETITION STATEMENTS

Before we conclude this chapter, we will once again emphasize programming style, this time in connection with the `for` and `do-while` repetition statements. Now that you can design loops, you should do so with style and produce code that is easy to understand.

1.   Indent the loop body of `for` statements to visually emphasize the syntactical elements. Example:

```
for (count = 3; count <= sequence_number; count++) {
      fibonacci_number = first + second;
      first = second;
      second = fibonacci_number;
} /* end for */
```

2.   Avoid the following permitted syntax elements of the `for` statement: missing initialization, update, and/or loop control expressions in the header, especially in designing counter-controlled loops. The statement

```
for (counter = 1; counter <= number; counter = counter + 1)
      sum = sum + counter;
/* end for */
```

is easier to understand than the following version:

```
counter = 1;

for (; ;) {
      if (counter <= number) {
            sum = sum + counter;
            counter = counter + 1;
      }
      else
            break;
      /* end if */
} /* end for */
```

3.   Avoid using `while` and `for` statements for the implementation of posttest repetition structures; instead, use the `do-while` statement. Similarly, use the `do-while` statement only for the implementation of posttest repetition structures and not for pretest repetitions.

4.   Indent the loop body of `do-while` loops as follows:

```
do {
      sum = sum + counter;
      counter = counter + 1;
} while (counter <= number);
/* end do-while */
```

5.    Place blank lines before and after `while`, `for`, and `do-while` loops to visually separate them from the rest of the code.

6.    Note the use of the terminating comments `/* end for */` and `/* end do-while */`. They are highly recommended.

---

## REVIEW QUESTIONS

**1.**    The C `for` statement is an implementation of the pretest repetition structure. (T or F)

**2.**    In executing a `for` statement:
  **a.** The computer first evaluates the loop control expression.
  **b.** If the loop control expression yields a nonzero value, the loop body is executed.
  **c.** The initialization expression is evaluated after the loop control expression is tested.
  **d.** The update expression is executed before the loop control expression is evaluated.
  **e.** All of the above are correct.
  **f.** None of the above is correct.

**3.**    If a `for` statement is used for a sentinel-controlled loop, the loop control expression must be based on the sentinel variable. (T or F)

**4.**    In a sentinel-controlled loop using a `for` statement, if we don't have an update expression that changes the value of the sentinel variable, we have an infinite loop. (T or F)

**5.**    The `do-while` statement first executes the loop body and then evaluates the loop control expression. (T or F)

**6.**    A `break` statement in the loop body of a repetition statement forces an exit from the loop. (T or F)

**7.**    To skip the rest of the loop body in a repetition statement and proceed with the next cycle of repetition, we must use
  **a.** A `continue` statement.
  **b.** A `break` statement.
  **c.** A `goto` statement.
  **d.** An `if` statement.
  **e.** None of the above.

**Answers:**  1. T; 2. b; 3. T; 4. T; 5. T; 6. T; 7. a.

---

## 9.9    EXAMPLE PROGRAM 1: A C Program that Computes Distribution of Letter Grades

We will design and implement a complete C program that uses the new language constructs introduced in this chapter.

***Problem***   Your instructor needs a program that can input student letter grades and compute and output a letter grade distribution, class grade point average, and a bar chart of letter grade distribution. She wants this program to be general and work for any class size.

***Requirements Specification***   Develop a program that does the following:

1.   Interactively reads student grade values (A, B, C, D, or F) for any number of students until the user decides to terminate input.

2.   Computes and outputs on the monitor screen a letter grade distribution table, such as

```
Number of A grades: XX
Number of B grades: XX
Number of C grades: XX
Number of D grades: XX
Number of F grades: XX
Total number of grades: XX
```

where  XX  represents integer values.

3.   Computes and outputs a class grade point average using the formula

$$class\_grade\_point\_average = (4 \times number\_of\_A\_grades + 3 \times number\_of\_B\_grades + 2 \times number\_of\_C\_grades + 1 \times number\_of\_D\_grades) / total\_number\_of\_grades$$

4.   Generates and prints on the monitor screen a vertical bar chart of grade distribution that looks like this:

```
BAR CHART:

       |* * *
   A   |* * *
       |* * *
       |
       |* * * * *
   B   |* * * * *
       |* * * * *
       |
       |* * * * * * * *
   C   |* * * * * * * *
       |* * * * * * * *
       |
       |* * *
   D   |* * *
       |* * *
```

```
        |
        | *
F       | *
        | *
        |
```

*Analysis*

**Inputs.** Values for the `char` variable `letter_grade`. The legal values for `letter_grade` are A, B, C, D, and F, uppercase or lowercase. To terminate input, the user should type Z or z. Therefore, Z and z are also legal values for `letter_grade`. For any other value the user should be warned and asked to enter a legal value.

**Outputs.** `number_of_As`, `number_of_Bs`, `number_of_Cs`, `number_of_Ds`, `number_of_Fs`, `total_number_of_grades`, `class_GPA`, and a vertical bar chart of grade distribution.

**Formulas.** The formula for computing the class grade point average is given in the requirements specification.

*Design*    We should note that a more proper bar chart would have been a horizontal chart of grade distribution. With your present knowledge of programming, however, you would have a hard time generating such a chart. Therefore, we will be satisfied with a vertical one and leave a horizontal version as a future challenge.

We begin with an initial pseudocode algorithm, given in Figure 9.9.

```
while there are more letter grades
    begin
        input letter_grade values
        compute number_of_As, number_of_Bs, number_of_Cs, number_of_Ds, number_of_Fs
        compute total_number_of_grades
    end
end_while

output results
generate and print bar chart
```

**Figure 9.9**    An initial pseudocode for computing distribution of letter grades

At this point let us decide on having three modules for outputting the results and generating and printing the bar chart. Let us call them:

1. *output_results*, which prints the number of different letter grades and the total number of grades

2. *computed_GPA*, which computes the class grade point average

3. *print_chart*, which generates and prints the bar chart.

The activities in the *while* loop will be handled by the function `main`. Accordingly, we refine the pseudocode of Figure 9.9 and present it in Figure 9.10.

---

*set more_data to 'y'*
*initialize number_of_As, number_of_Bs, number_of_Cs, number_of_Ds, number_of_Fs, and*
    *total_number_of_grades to zero*

*print "Enter letter grade. Type Z to terminate data input: "*
*read letter_grade*

*while more_data is equal to 'y'*
    *begin*
        *if letter_grade is equal to 'A' or 'a'*
            *add 1 to number_of_As and total_number_of_grades*
        *else if letter_grade is equal to 'B' or 'b'*
            *add 1 to number_of_Bs and total_number_of_grades*
        *else if letter_grade is equal to 'C' or 'c'*
            *add 1 to number_of_Cs and total_number_of_grades*
        *else if letter_grade is equal to 'D' or 'd'*
            *add 1 to number_of_Ds and total_number_of_grades*
        *else if letter_grade is equal to 'F' or 'f'*
            *add 1 to number_of_Fs and total_number_of_grades*
        *else if letter_grade is equal to 'Z' or 'z'*
            *set more_data to 'n'*
        *else*
            *print "Incorrect letter grade."*
        *end_if*

        *if more_data is equal to 'y'*
            *begin*
                *print "Enter letter grade: "*
                *read letter_grade*
            *end*
        *end_if*
    *end*
*end_while*

*call output_results*
*print "Class average: ", computed_GPA*

---

**Figure 9.10**    Refined pseudocode for the main program (*continued*)    ▶

*print "BAR CHART: "*
*call print_chart to print chart segment for grade A*
*call print_chart to print chart segment for grade B*
*call print_chart to print chart segment for grade C*
*call print_chart to print chart segment for grade D*
*call print_chart to print chart segment for grade F*

**Figure 9.10**                                                                                       ■

Now let us work on the modules. The module *output_results* and *computed_GPA* are simple, and their pseudocodes are given in Figures 9.11 and 9.12.

*output_results(number_of_As, number_of_Bs, number_of_Cs, number_of_Ds, number_of_Fs,*
*        total_number_of_grades):*
  *print "Number of A grades: ", number_of_As*
  *print "Number of B grades: ", number_of_Bs*
  *print "Number of C grades: ", number_of_Cs*
  *print "Number of D grades: ", number_of_Ds*
  *print "Number of F grades: ", number_of_Fs*
  *print "Total number of grades: ", total_number_of_grades*

**Figure 9.11**     Pseudocode for the module *output_results*

*computed_GPA(number_of_As, number_of_Bs, number_of_Cs, number_of_Ds,*
    *total_number_of_grades):*
  *if total_number_of_grades is not equal to 0*
    *compute GPA = (4.0 * number_of_As + 3.0 * number_of_Bs +*
    *               2.0 * number_of_Cs + number_of_Ds) / total_number_of_grades*
  *else*
    *set GPA to 0.0*
  *end_if*

  *return GPA*

**Figure 9.12**     Pseudocode for the module *computed_GPA*

Our final task is to design the module that will print the segment of the bar chart corresponding to a letter grade. Clearly, the inputs for this module must be a letter grade value and the number of this letter grade value. Let us call them *grade* and *number*, respectively. A typical segment of the bar chart is shown here:

```
        | * * * * * * * *
  C     | * * * * * * * *
        | * * * * * * * *
```

Such a segment consists of three lines. On the first and third lines, we want to print the symbol   |   and as many *s as the value of number. On the second line, in addition, we want to print the letter grade itself. Figure 9.13 shows the pseudocode to print a typical line of the segment, with the exception of the letter grade and the symbol   |.

*set counter2 to 0*

*while counter2 is less than number*
    *begin*
        *print on the current line the symbol *
        *add 1 to counter2*
    *end*
*end_while*

**Figure 9.13**    Pseudocode to print a typical line of the bar chart

The pseudocode to print a three-line segment appears in Figure 9.14.

*set counter1 to 1*

*while counter1 is less than or equal to 3*
    *begin*
        *if counter1 is equal to 2*
            *print " ", grade, " |"*
        *else*
            *print "   |"*
        *end_if*

        *print a typical line of the bar chart*
        *add 1 to counter1*
    *end*
*end_while*

**Figure 9.14**    Pseudocode to print three lines of a bar chart segment

We are ready to combine the pseudocodes of Figures 9.13 and 9.14 to get the algorithm for *print_chart*. It is given in Figure 9.15.

```
print_chart(grade, number):
    set counter1 to 1

    while counter1 is less than or equal to 3
        begin
            if counter1 is equal to 2
                print " ", grade, " |"
            else
                print "    |"
            end_if

            set counter2 to 0

            while counter2 is less than number
                begin
                    print on the current line the symbol ' * '
                    add 1 to counter2
                end
            end_while

            add 1 to counter1
        end
    end_while

    print "    |"
```

**Figure 9.15**    Pseudocode algorithm for the module *print_chart*

***Implementation***    A C implementation of this design is presented in the program of Figure 9.16.

```
/****************************************************************************
Program Filename: prog09_1.c
Author          : Uckan
Purpose         : Inputs student letter grades, computes and
                  prints letter grade distribution and class
                  grade point average, and prints a bar chart
                  of grade distribution.
Input from      : terminal keyboard
Output to       : screen
```

**Figure 9.16**    A C program that computes distribution of letter grades *(continued)*  ▶

```
* * * * * * * * * * * * * * * * * * * * * * * * * * * * * * * * * * * * * * * * * * * * * * * * * * * * * * * * * * * * * * * * * * /
#include <stdio.h>

/* Function prototypes: */

void output_results(int A, int B, int C, int D, int F, int total);
double computed_GPA(int A, int B, int C, int D, int total);
void print_chart(char grade, int number);


int main(void) {
        /* Variable declarations: */

        int number_of_As = 0, number_of_Bs = 0, number_of_Cs = 0,
            number_of_Ds = 0, number_of_Fs = 0,
            total_number_of_grades = 0;
        char letter_grade, more_data = 'y', return_char;

        /* Function body: */

        printf("Enter letter grade. Type Z to terminate data input: ");
        scanf("%c", &letter_grade);
        scanf("%c", &return_char);

        while (more_data == 'y') {
                switch (letter_grade) {
                        case 'A' :  case 'a' :
                                number_of_As++;
                                total_number_of_grades++;
                                break;
                        case 'B' :  case 'b' :
                                number_of_Bs++;
                                total_number_of_grades++;
                                break;
                        case 'C' :  case 'c' :
                                number_of_Cs++;
                                total_number_of_grades++;
                                break;
                        case 'D' :  case 'd' :
                                number_of_Ds++;
                                total_number_of_grades++;
                                break;
```

**Figure 9.16**    (continued)    ▶

```
                        case 'F' :  case 'f':
                                number_of_Fs++;
                                total_number_of_grades++;
                                break;
                        case 'Z' :  case 'z' :
                                more_data = 'n';
                                break;
                        default :
                                printf("Incorrect letter grade.\n");
                } /* end switch */

                if (more_data == 'y') {
                        printf("Enter letter grade: ");
                        scanf("%c", &letter_grade);
                        scanf("%c", &return_char);
                } /* end if */
        } /* end while */

        output_results(number_of_As, number_of_Bs, number_of_Cs,
                number_of_Ds, number_of_Fs, total_number_of_grades);
        printf("\n");
        printf("Class average: %4.2f\n\n", computed_GPA(number_of_As,
                number_of_Bs, number_of_Cs, number_of_Ds,
                total_number_of_grades));

        printf("BAR CHART:\n");
        print_chart('A', number_of_As);
        print_chart('B', number_of_Bs);
        print_chart('C', number_of_Cs);
        print_chart('D', number_of_Ds);
        print_chart('F', number_of_Fs);

        return 0;
} /* end function main */


/*********************************************************************
  Function Name    : output_results
  Purpose          : Prints distribution of grades and total number
                     of grades on the screen.
  Called by        : main
  Receives         : number_of_As, number_of_Bs, number_of_Cs,
```

**Figure 9.16**      (continued)                                                            ▶

```
                       number_of_Ds, number_of_Fs, total_number_of_grades
 Returns           : None
************************************************************************/
void output_results(int number_of_As, int number_of_Bs,
                    int number_of_Cs, int number_of_Ds,
                    int number_of_Fs, int total_number_of_grades) {
     printf("\n");
     printf("Number of A grades: %d\n", number_of_As);
     printf("Number of B grades: %d\n", number_of_Bs);
     printf("Number of C grades: %d\n", number_of_Cs);
     printf("Number of D grades: %d\n", number_of_Ds);
     printf("Number of F grades: %d\n", number_of_Fs);
     printf("Total number of grades: %d\n", total_number_of_grades);
} /* end function output_results */


/*************************************************************
 Function Name     : computed_GPA
 Purpose           : Computes the class grade point average.
 Called by         : main
 Receives          : number_of_As, number_of_Bs, number_of_Cs,
                     number_of_Ds, number_of_Fs, total_number_of_grades
 Returns           : GPA
************************************************************/
double computed_GPA(int number_of_As, int number_of_Bs,
                    int number_of_Cs, int number_of_Ds,
                    int total_number_of_grades) {
     /* Local variables: */

     double GPA;

     /* Function body: */
     if (total_number_of_grades != 0)
         GPA = (4.0 * number_of_As + 3.0 * number_of_Bs +
                2.0 * number_of_Cs + number_of_Ds) /
                  total_number_of_grades;
     else
         GPA = 0.0;
     /* end if */

     return GPA;
} /* end function computed_GPA */
```

Figure 9.16      (continued)

```
/*****************************************************************
Function Name    : print_chart
Purpose          : Prints a bar chart for the distribution of grades.
Called by        : main
Receives         : grade, number_of_grades
Returns          : None
*****************************************************************/
void print_chart(char grade, int number_of_grades) {
        /* Local variable declarations: */

        int counter1, counter2;

        /* Function body: */

        for (counter1 = 1; counter1 <= 3; counter1++) {
            if (counter1 == 2)
                printf("\n  %c  |", grade);
            else
                printf("\n     |");
            /* end if */

            for (counter2 = 0; counter2 < number_of_grades;
                counter2++)
                printf("*");
            /* end for */
        } /* end for */

        printf("\n     |");
} /* end function print_chart */
```

Figure 9.16                                                                 ■

The program of Figure 9.16 is an almost statement-by-statement translation of the pseudocode algorithms of Figures 9.10, 9.11, 9.12, and 9.15 and any further explanation is redundant. We note only the use of the  switch  statement in the function  main and the use of the  break  statements in its body in implementing the seven-way selection structure of Figure 9.10. Also, the *while* loop in the function  main  and the doubly-nested *while* loops in the function  print_chart  are implemented using the  for statement.

Figure 9.17 is a sample interactive session of the program of Figure 9.16.

```
Enter letter grade. Type Z to terminate data input: g
Incorrect letter grade.
Enter letter grade: A
Enter letter grade: B
.....................
.....................
Enter letter grade: Z

Number of A grades: 3
Number of B grades: 5
Number of C grades: 9
Number of D grades: 1
Number of F grades: 1
Total number of grades: 19

Class average: 2.42

BAR CHART:

        |***
    A   |***
        |***
        |
        |*****
    B   |*****
        |*****
        |
        |********
    C   |********
        |********
        |
        |*
    D   |*
        |*
        |
        |*
    F   |*
        |*
        |
```

**Figure 9.17**    A sample interactive session for the program of Figure 9.16

## 9.10     SUMMARY

### This Chapter at a Glance

- In this chapter we continued the discussion of selection and repetition structures that we started in Chapter 4.

- We focused on multiway selection structures and their implementations in C. We considered the logical operators, which are logical *and*, *or*, and *not*, and how to construct complex predicates to be used in selection and repetition structures. We also covered the `switch` statement for multiway selection.

- Next we returned to repetition structures. We discussed the `for` statement and how it can be used to design pretest counter- and sentinel-controlled loops. Both the `for` and `while` statements are pretest repetition statements, and they are equivalent.

- The only posttest repetition statement in C is the `do-while` statement. It can also be used for counter- and sentinel-controlled loops.

- We covered two C jump statements: `break` and `continue`. The `break` statement creates a forced exit from within a selection or a repetition structure. The `continue` statement causes a skip of the rest of a cycle of repetition in a loop and continues with the next cycle.

- Finally, we discussed nested loops and how we can construct them using the C repetition statements.

- This chapter has added a lot to your problem-solving skills. Now you can design complex predicates, multiway selection structures, pretest and posttest loops, counter- and sentinel-controlled loops, and nested loops.

### Coming Attractions

- Chapter 6 introduced functions that return a single value under their name and functions that use value parameters to get values from calling functions. This background has enabled you to do a lot with functions. However, you still do not know how to design functions that can return multiple values using parameters.

- In the next chapter we return to our discussion of functions and consider a technique, parameter passing by pointers, to return values from functions.

- You will first learn about pointer variables in C. Then, you will study parameter passing by pointers.

- Finally, in Chapter 10, you will study program modularization using the preprocessor.

## STUDY GUIDE

### Test Your Comprehension

**1.** Multiway selection structures can be implemented in C using
 **a.** Nested `if` statements
 **b.** Consecutive unnested `if` statements
 **c.** `switch` statements
 **d.** All of the above
 **e.** None of the above

**2.** The predicate `!((a >= 5) || (b == 7))` is equivalent to
 **a.** `(a >= 5) && (b == 7)`
 **b.** `(a < 5) && (b == 7)`
 **c.** `(a >= 5) && (b != 7)`
 **d.** `(a < 5) && (b != 7)`
 **e.** None of the above.

**3.** Which of the following statements concerning the C `switch` statement is *incorrect*?
 **a.** The controlling expression can be of type `double`, `int`, or `char`.
 **b.** The `default` clause is optional.
 **c.** A `case` clause may be empty.
 **d.** If the value of the controlling expression does not match any of the constant values in the `case` clauses, the content of the `default` clause is executed.

**4.** Which of the following concerning the `for` statement is *incorrect*?
 **a.** It can be used for counter-controlled loops.
 **b.** It can also be used in designing sentinel-controlled loops.
 **c.** The initialization, loop control, and update expressions may be missing in a `for` statement header.
 **d.** The update expression is used to initialize the loop control variable.

**5.** Choose the *incorrect* statement: In designing a counter-controlled loop, we must
 **a.** Declare a loop control variable.
 **b.** Assign an initial value to it.
 **c.** Test the loop control variable in a loop control expression.
 **d.** Reinitialize the loop control variable every time it has to be updated.

**6.** Concerning the `do-while` statement:
 **a.** It is a posttest repetition statement.
 **b.** It first executes the loop body and then evaluates the loop control expression.
 **c.** Its loop body must contain an update expression.
 **d.** When used for counter-controlled loops, an initialization expression must precede the `do-while` statement.
 **e.** All of the above are correct.
 **f.** None of the above is correct.

**Answers:** 1. d; 2. d; 3. a; 4. d; 5. d; 6. e.

## Improve Your Problem-Solving Ability

### *Debugging Exercises*

**7.** Find and explain the errors, if any, in each of the following C selection statements.

**a.**
```c
if (radius <= 1)
    printf("Great shot; you earn 10 points.");
else if (radius > 1 && radius <= 2)
    printf("Good shot; you earn 5 points.");
else if (radius > 2 && radius <= 3)
    printf("Not bad; you earn 2 points.")
else
    printf("You missed.");
/* end if */
```

**b.**
```c
if (major_code = 1 || major_code = 3 || major_code = 5)
    printf("Science student");
else if (major_code = 2 || major_code = 4)
    printf("Art student");
else
    printf("Error in major code");
/* end if */
```

**c.**
```c
switch major_code {
    case 1 :
        printf("Science student");
        break
    case 2 :
        printf("Art student");
        break
    case 3 :
        printf("Science student");
        break
    case 4 :
        printf("Art student");
        break
    case 5 :
        printf("Science student");
        break
    default :
        printf("Error in major code");
} /* end switch */
```

**d.**
```c
switch (major_code) {
    case 1, 3, 5 :
        printf("Science student");
        break;
    case 2, 4 :
```

```
        printf("Art student");
        break;
     default :
        printf("Error in major code");
  }/* end switch */
```

**8.** Find and explain the errors, if any, in each of the following C repetition statements.

**a.** 
```
for (counter <= limit; counter = 1; counter += 2)
    product = product * counter;
/* end for */
```

**b.** 
```
for (counter = 1; counter <= limit; counter += 2) {
    product = product * counter;
    counter = counter + 2;
} /* end for */
```

**c.** 
```
do
    product = product * counter;
    counter += 2;
while (counter <= limit);
/* end do-while */
```

**d.** 
```
for (counter2 = 2; counter1 <= 5; counter1++)
    for (counter1 = counter2 + 2; counter2 <= 7; counter2++)
        printf("\n%d   %d", counter1, counter2);
    /* end for */
/* end for */
```

**9.** Each of the following `for` loops is an infinite loop. Examine them carefully and explain why.

**a.** 
```
for (counter = 1; counter != 10; counter += 2)
    sum = sum + counter;
/* end for */
```

**b.** 
```
for (counter = -10; counter <= number; counter -= 1)
    sum = sum + counter;
/* end for */
```

**c.** 
```
for (counter = 1; counter <= 10;)
    sum = sum + counter;
/* end for */
```

**d.** 
```
for (counter = 1;  ; counter += 1)
    sum = sum + counter;
/* end for */
```

*Programming Exercises*

**10.** A video rental shop uses the following type classification scheme for movie video cassettes:

| Type Code | Movie Category |
|-----------|----------------|
| A | Action and adventure |
| C | Comedy |
| D | Drama |
| F | Family |
| H | Horror and science fiction |
| M | Musicals |

Any other type code value is considered an error. Write a nested `if` statement that tests the value of type code, increments the number of videos of the appropriate category by one, and computes the total number of videos in the inventory. Your code should print a warning message if the type code value is in error.

**11.** Solve Programming Exercise 10 using a `switch` statement instead of a nested `if` statement.

**12.** Write a nested `if` statement that determines the largest of three integer variables `first`, `second`, and `third`.

**13.** Write a complex predicate to determine whether
  **a.** `x_coordinate` is in the range of −5 through 10.
  **b.** `x_coordinate` is outside the range of −5 through 10.
  **c.** Both `x_coordinate` and `y_coordinate` are positive.
  **d.** Either or both of `x_coordinate` and `y_coordinate` are positive.
  **e.** `x_coordinate` is negative and also equal to `y_coordinate`.

**14.** Suppose the character variable `employee_status` may have the value of `'f'` for full-time and `'p'` for part-time employees. The values of the integer variable `department_code` are 1 for sales, 2 for marketing, and 3 for accounting. The integer variable `years_with_us` indicates the number of years an employee has been working for the company.

Write a complex predicate to test for
  **a.** Part-time employees who have been working for the company for less than three years.
  **b.** Part-time employees in the sales department who have been working for the company for less than three years.
  **c.** Full-time employees in the accounting department or part-time accounting department employees who have been with the company for more than 10 years.
  **d.** Full-time employees in the marketing department who have been working for the company for 10 to 15 years.

**15.** Parenthesize each of the following complex predicates completely to explicitly show the precedence of operators.
  **a.** `x - y <= 3 || x * y == z && x + y > 10`
  **b.** `!x + !y == !z && x + y > z`
  **c.** `x || y || z && x - y - 5`
  **d.** `!x + 3 == y || z && y`

**16.** Assume that the current values of the integer variables x, y, and z are 10, 5, and 8, respectively. What will be computed for each predicate of Programming Exercise 15? Show your computations in a step-by-step manner.

**17.** Simplify each of the following complex predicates using the identities given in the table of Figure 9.1. Show your steps clearly.

**a.** ! (a >= 5)
**b.** ! (a != 5) || ! ((b == 3) || (c > 10))
**c.** ! ((a + b == c) || ! (c > 10))
**d.** ! ((a >= 10) && (b == 8) && (c < 15))

**18.** Write a `switch` statement to determine if the variable `digit` is an octal digit. An octal digit has a value in the range 0 through 7.

**19.** Solve Programming Exercise 18, using a single `if` statement with a complex predicate instead of a `switch` statement.

**20.** Write a `for` loop that computes the number of integer values that can be divided evenly by 11 or by 13 in the range of `start` through `end`, where `start` and `end` are integer variables.

**21.** Design a sentinel-controlled `for` loop that forces the user to enter an octal digit for a variable called `octal_digit`. (Hint: Programming Exercise 18.)

**22.** Write a `for` statement to print the indicated sequence of integers:

**a.** −15, −10, −5, 0, 5, 10, 15
**b.** −100, −109, −118, −127, −136, −145
**c.** 1, 2, 4, 8, 16, 32
**d.** 5, 15, 45, 135, 405

**23.** Solve Programming Exercise 20, using a `do-while` loop instead of a `for` loop.

**24.** Solve Programming Exercise 21, using a sentinel-controlled `do-while` loop.

**25.** Solve Programming Exercise 22, using the `do-while` statement.

**26.** Write a function that is similar to the function `print_E` of Figure 9.8 that can be used to print the block letter H.

**27.** Consider the following C code:

```
int i, r = 0;

for (i = 0; i < 5; i++) {
      if (i == 3) {
            r = r + i;
            break;
      }
      else
            continue;
      /* end if */
```

```
        printf("%d\n", r);
} /* end for */

printf("%d\n", r);
```

What will be printed on the screen as a result of execution of this code in a function? Explain your answer.

### Programming Projects

**28.** Write an interactive, modular program that reads an integer in the range of 0 through 99 and prints the word equivalent for it. For example, if the user enters 78, the program should respond by printing `You have entered seventy-eight`. Use `switch` statements in your program with a minimum number of cases, not one `switch` statement with 100 cases. Validate the input data to ensure that the entered integer is in the proper range.

**29.** Develop a C program that first reads an integer value for $n$; then reads $n$ floating-point values; and lastly computes and outputs the smallest, the largest, and the average of $n$ floating-point values.

**30.** Develop a C program that first reads an integer value for $n$ and then reads $n$ floating-point values and computes and outputs their standard deviation using the formula

$$s = \sqrt{\frac{(x_1^2 + x_2^2 + x_3^2 + \cdots x_n^2) - n \cdot m^2}{n - 1}}$$

where $m$ is the average (or mean) of n numbers, and $x_1, x_2, x_3, \ldots x_n$ represent the floating-point values. The standard deviation is a measure of how scattered $n$ numbers are around their mean and is frequently used in statistical computations.

**31.** Solve Programming Project 22 of Chapter 6 using the control structures studied in this chapter.

**32.** Design a modular C program that interactively reads values for floating-point constants $a$ and $b$, and computes and generates a plot of the function

$$y = a \cdot x + b$$

as shown in the following figure.

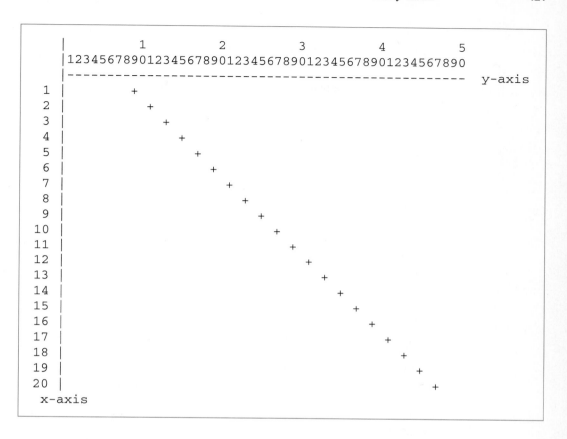

33. Revise your program of Programming Project 32 such that it works for the quadratic function

$$y = a \cdot x^2 + b \cdot x + c$$

where $a$, $b$, and $c$ are floating-point constants.

34. Suppose you are the manager of a retail store that carries eight types of items. You maintain an inventory file as a text file, such that each record in the inventory file consists of an item number and the number of that item in stock at the beginning of a business day. Your inventory file looks like this:

```
1    356
2    56
3    35
. . . . . . . . . .
. . . . . . . . .
8    112
```

All sales are recorded in a sales file in terms of item number and quantity sold. The inventory file is sorted in increasing order of item number. The daily sales file, also a text file, is not sorted. Here is an instance of the sales file:

```
1    3
2    1
1    6
4    8
5    10
. . . . . . . . . .
. . . . . . . . . .
```

Design and implement a modular batch program that can be used at the end of a business day to compute a new inventory file. Your program should read records from the old inventory file and, for each inventory item, should read the sales file in its entirety to generate a new inventory record and write it to a new inventory file. You can assume that you have a computerized inventory control system that prevents sales below existing inventory levels.

**35.** A popular form of fitness aerobics makes use of an adjustable-height bench that increases the intensity of aerobics workout without making it high impact. One of the important safety factors in bench exercises is the bench height. The bench should not be too high for you; otherwise, there is a danger of developing "chondromalacia patellae," a degenerative knee condition caused by the grinding of the cartilage between the patella and the femur. The safe bench height depends on your femur length and is determined by the knee angle formed when you stand in front of the bench with one foot on the bench.

Develop a menu-driven interactive program that does the following for as long as the user wants to continue:

**a.** Displays a menu of three choices.

**b.** If the user choice is 1, reads interactively a femur length in inches and then computes and prints the safe bench height, as well as the maximum allowable bench height that is not considered dangerous.

**c.** If the user choice is 2, computes and prints a table of knee angles for all femur lengths and bench heights. A typical table of knee angles follows.

```
                           TABLE OF ANGLES
FEMUR LENGTH:          10    11  . . . . . . . . . . . . . . . . . . . . . . . . . . . . . . . . .    21
BENCH HEIGHT:   2    143   144  . . . . . . . . . . . . . . . . . . . . . . . . . . . . . . .   154
BENCH HEIGHT:   4    126   129  . . . . . . . . . . . . . . . . . . . . . . . . . . . . . . .   144
. . . . . . . . . . .            . . . . . . . . . . . . . . . . . . . . . . . . . . . . . . . . . . . . . .
. . . . . . . . . . .            . . . . . . . . . . . . . . . . . . . . . . . . . . . . . . . . . . . . . .
BENCH HEIGHT:  12    78    84  . . . . . . . . . . . . . . . . . . . . . . . . . . . . . . .   115
```

▶

```
SAFE ZONE    : >= 140
CAUTION ZONE : 125 - 139
DANGER ZONE  : <= 124
```

**d.** If the user choice is 3, terminates the program.

The formula for knee angle in terms of bench_height and femur_length is

$$angle = 180 - \frac{180}{PI} * arccos\left(1 - \frac{bench\_height}{femur\_length}\right)$$

where *PI = 3.1415936*, *angle* is in degrees, and *arccos* is the "arc cosine" function. Values for *bench_height* can be 2, 4, 6, 8, 10, and 12 inches. Values for *femur_length* can be integers in the range of 10 to 21 inches. Safe, risky, and dangerous zones are defined as follows:

Safe zone            : *angle >= 140*

Risky zone          : *124 < angle < 140*

Dangerous zone   : angle <= *124*

36. Expand Programming Project 35 by incorporating modules into the design such that, in addition to what it already does, the program should compute and print a table of safe, risky, and dangerous zones for all values of femur length and bench height. Here is a sample table of zones:

```
                    TABLE OF SAFE ZONES
FEMUR LENGTH:      10   11 ....................................... 21
BENCH HEIGHT:  2 SSSS SSSS ...................................... SSSS
BENCH HEIGHT:  4 CCCC CCCC ...................................... SSSS
.............  ................................................. .....
.............  ................................................. .....
BENCH HEIGHT: 12 DDDD DDDD ...................................... DDDD

LEGENDS:  SSSS = SAFE, CCCC = CAUTION, DDDD = DANGER
```

# More on Modular Programming and Functions

---

**CHAPTER OBJECTIVES**

In this chapter you will learn about:

- **Use of pointer variables to return values from functions**
  Pointer variables
  Assigning values to pointer variables
  Pointer parameters and pass by pointers

- **Libraries**
  Standard C libraries
  Programmer-defined libraries
  Modularization through the use of libraries
  Constructing and using libraries

By the time you have completed this chapter, you will have acquired the ability to design and implement:

- **Functions that return values through pointer parameters**

- **Programmer-defined libraries**

---

## 10.1    INTRODUCTION

In Chapter 6 we saw that the preferred way to pass data between functions is to use function parameters. C supports two types of parameters: value and pointer. We have covered value parameters extensively. They are useful in supplying input to a called function. However, they cannot be used to return values to the calling function.

If a function must return a single value, we can define the function such that it returns the value under its name. Yet, for a function that must return multiple values, this method falls short. In this case we use parameter passing by pointers. In this chapter we will first consider pointer variables. Next, we will discuss parameter passing by pointers. We will then be in a position to design functions that can freely communicate data through parameters.

Also in this chapter you will learn more about standard libraries in C. Then you will study programmer-defined libraries, their advantages, how they enhance program modularization, and the rules for constructing and using programmer-defined libraries.

## 10.2    POINTER VARIABLES

A method in C that allows a function to return multiple values through its parameter list is parameter passing by pointers. In addition to parameter passing by pointers, pointer variables have other uses in C programming. In this section we discuss pointer variables and assigning values to pointer variables. After you develop a good understanding of pointer variables, you will study parameter passing by pointers.

It should be noted here that certain arithmetic operations can be performed on pointer variables. These, however, are significant when dealing with arrays. Therefore, the discussion of pointer variables in this section is restricted to those features that are important in designing functions. We will return to pointer variables later in the book on several occasions.

We know that a variable name is the symbolic address of a memory location, which contains a value that is consistent with the declared type of that variable. A declaration such as

```
int margaret = 20;
```

causes the compiler to allocate a memory location for the variable `margaret` and store in it the integer value 20. The absolute address of the memory location for `margaret` is readily available to our program at run time. The computer uses this address to access its content.

C allows us to declare variables that contain as their values, memory addresses rather than integers, floating-point values, or characters. Such variables are called pointer variables.

**Pointer variables** are variables whose values are memory addresses.

## Declaring Pointer Variables

All variables, including pointer variables, must be declared in a C program. To declare a pointer variable, we must associate it with a data type such as `int`, `char`, or `double` and use the symbol `*` as its prefix. Here is an example:

```
int *pointer_to_margaret;
```

This declares the variable `pointer_to_margaret` as a pointer variable to a memory location that can store a value of type `int`. You should not confuse such a declaration with a regular declaration of an integer variable. The declaration

```
int margaret;
```

declares `margaret` as an integer variable, whereas

```
int *pointer_to_margaret;
```

declares `pointer_to_margaret` as a variable that points to an integer variable. Its content is not an integer; it is a memory address.

Figure 10.1a shows what happens in the memory because of the series of declarations

```
int margaret;
int *pointer_to_margaret;
int *another_pointer;
```

These declarations cause the compiler to allocate memory locations for the integer variable `margaret` and for the pointer variables `pointer_to_margaret` and `another_pointer`. Since the memory locations have not been assigned any values, the locations do not store anything meaningful; this status is indicated by the symbol `?` in Figure 10.1a.

## Initializing Pointer Variables

After a pointer variable has been declared we can use the assignment operator to initialize the variable to any of the following:

1. The value `NULL`
2. An address
3. The value of another pointer variable

For example, the statement

```
pointer_to_margaret = NULL;
```

stores a special address value in the pointer variable `pointer_to_margaret`, as shown in Figure 10.1b. This address does not belong to any variable in the main memory. As we know, `NULL` is a symbolic constant defined in the `stdio.h` header file. It is used only as a special value for pointer variables. You can think of a pointer variable that contains the value `NULL` as an empty pointer variable.

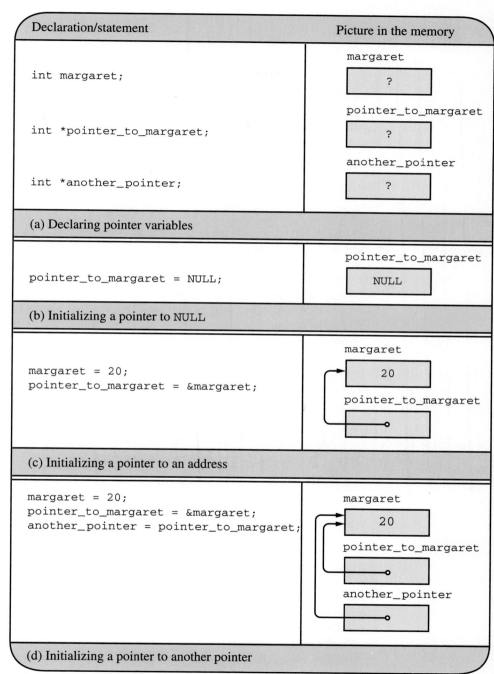

**Figure 10.1**    Declaring and initializing pointer variables

Another constant that can be assigned to pointer variables is the integer 0. The assignment

```
pointer_to_margaret = 0;
```

is legal, and in most cases it is precisely the same thing as assigning  NULL  to the pointer variable. In this book we will prefer  NULL  to  0. With the exception of  NULL  and 0, no other constant value can be assigned to pointer variables.

It is possible to store the address of a memory location in a pointer variable. Let us assume that we have the statement

```
margaret = 20;
```

which assigns the value of  20  to  margaret. The statement

```
pointer_to_margaret = &margaret;
```

stores the address of the memory location  margaret  in the pointer variable pointer_to_margaret. The symbol  &, as we know, is the address operator. Now the value of  pointer_to_margaret  is the absolute address of the memory location  margaret. This status is shown in Figure 10.1c by a directional line, drawn from the middle of the box representing  pointer_to_margaret to the box representing margaret. When dealing with pointer variables, drawing figures such as those in Figure 10.1 is very helpful.

You should note that the declaration

```
int *pointer_to_margaret;
```

and the assignment

```
pointer_to_margaret = &margaret;
```

can be combined and written as

```
int *pointer_to_margaret = &margaret;
```

In either case now we have two ways of referencing the variable  margaret. We can either do it directly, as in

```
printf("%d", margaret);
```

which prints the content of  margaret, or indirectly, as in

```
printf("%d", *pointer_to_margaret);
```

Here we are using the pointer variable  pointer_to_margaret  to indirectly reference the memory location  margaret. Hence the symbol  *  in this context is an operator, known as the **indirection operator**. Another name for the indirection operator is the **dereferencing operator**.

We can assign the value of another pointer variable to a pointer variable provided both are of the same type. In Figure 10.1d, on top of the situation corresponding to Figure 10.1c, we have the assignment

```
another_pointer = pointer_to_margaret;
```

This assignment copies the content of `pointer_to_margaret`, the address of the memory location `margaret`, in the pointer variable `another_pointer`. Now both `pointer_to_margaret` and `another_pointer` point to `margaret`, and the memory location `margaret` can be accessed using any of the three names for it, `margaret`, `*pointer_to_margaret`, and `*another_pointer`.

To better understand pointer variables and their operations, let us consider the C program of Figure 10.2.

```
1    #include <stdio.h>

2    int main(void) {
3        int margaret = 20;
4        int *pointer_to_margaret = NULL;
5        int *another_pointer;

6        if (pointer_to_margaret == NULL)
7            printf("The value of pointer_to_margaret is NULL.\n");
8        else
9            printf("The value of pointer_to_margaret is not NULL.\n");
10       /* end if */

11       pointer_to_margaret = &margaret;

12       if (pointer_to_margaret == NULL)
13           printf("The value of pointer_to_margaret is NULL.\n");
14       else
15           printf("The value of pointer_to_margaret is not NULL.\n");
16       /* end if */

17       another_pointer = pointer_to_margaret;

18       /* Block 1 -- Print contents of variables: */

19       printf("\n");
20       printf("CONTENT OF VARIABLE MARGARET:\n");
21       printf("Content using margaret        : %d\n", margaret);
22       printf("Content pointer_to_margaret  : %d\n",
                 *pointer_to_margaret);
23       printf("Content using another_pointer: %d\n\n",
                 *another_pointer);

24       /* Block 2 -- Print addresses of variables: */
```

**Figure 10.2**    Use of pointer variables (*continued*)    ▶

```
25      printf("ADDRESS OF VARIABLE MARGARET:\n");
26      printf("Address using &margaret          : %x\n", &margaret);
27      printf("Address using pointer_to_margaret: %x\n",
28          &*pointer_to_margaret);
29      printf("Address using another_pointer    : %x\n\n",
            &*another_pointer);

30      /* Block 3 -- Print contents of pointer variables: */

31      printf("CONTENTS OF POINTER VARIABLES:\n");
32      printf("Content of pointer_to_margaret: %x\n",
33          pointer_to_margaret);
34      printf("Content of another_pointer    : %x\n\n",
35          pointer_to_margaret);

36      /* Block 4 -- Print addresses of pointer variables: */

37      printf("ADDRESSES OF POINTER VARIABLES:\n");
38      printf("Address of pointer_to_margaret: %x\n",
            &pointer_to_margaret);
39      printf("Address of another_pointer    : %x\n",
            &another_pointer);

40      return 0;
41  } /* end function main */
```

**Figure 10.2**    ■

Figure 10.3 is the output of the program of Figure 10.2. Let us review the important elements of this program.

1.  Lines 3 through 5 declare an integer variable `margaret` and two pointer variables to integers, `pointer_to_margaret` and `another_pointer`. The declaration on line 4 initializes `pointer_to_margaret` to `NULL`.

2.  The `if` statement in lines 6 through 10 has the predicate `pointer_to_margaret == NULL`. As you can see, we can compare the content of a pointer variable to `NULL`.

3.  Line 11 assigns the address of `margaret` to `pointer_to_margaret`. Now the value of the pointer variable `pointer_to_margaret` is no longer `NULL`, as is demonstrated by the `if` statement in lines 12 through 16.

4.  The statement on line 17 assigns the value of `pointer_to_margaret` to `another_pointer`. Now both pointer variables point to the variable `margaret`. This situation appears in Figure 10.1d.

5.  The `printf` function calls in lines 20 through 23 print the content of the memory location using its three names: `margaret`, `*pointer_to_margaret`, and `*another_pointer`. Figure 10.3 shows that all three print the same value, 20.

6.   The `printf` function calls in lines 26 through 29 print the address of the memory location `margaret`, again using its three names. (The format specifier `%x` prints values in hexadecimal notation.) Note that each name is preceded by the address operator `&`, as in `&*pointer_to_margaret`. The address turns out to be `64fdec`, a hexadecimal number, which depends on the computer system you are using.

7.   The two `printf` function calls in lines 32 through 35 print the contents of the pointer variables `pointer_to_margaret` and `another_pointer`. They are the same address, `64fdec`, which is the address of the memory location `margaret`.

8.   The `printf` function calls in lines 38 and 39 print the addresses of the pointer variables `pointer_to_margaret` and `another_pointer`. To print the address of `pointer_to_margaret`, you must precede it by the address operator `&` and write it as `&pointer_to_margaret`. The addresses turn out to be `64fdf4` and `64fdf0`, respectively, as determined by the compiler for the specific computer system on which the program was run.

```
The value of pointer_to_margaret is NULL.
The value of pointer_to_margaret is not NULL.

CONTENT OF VARIABLE MARGARET:
Content using margaret        : 20
Content pointer_to_margaret   : 20
Content using another_pointer: 20

ADDRESS OF VARIABLE MARGARET:
Address using &margaret              : 64fdec
Address using pointer_to_margaret: 64fdec
Address using another_pointer     : 64fdec

CONTENTS OF POINTER VARIABLES:
Content of pointer_to_margaret: 64fdec
Content of another_pointer     : 64fdec

ADDRESSES OF POINTER VARIABLES:
Address of pointer_to_margaret: 64fdf4
Address of another_pointer     : 64fdf0
```

**Figure 10.3**    Output of the program of Figure 10.2

> **Rules for Pointer Variables**
>
> 1. A pointer variable must be declared for another variable of a specific type, as in
>
>    ```
>    int *pointer_to_margaret;
>    ```
>
>    In the declaration of a pointer variable, the variable name must be prefixed by the symbol *.
>
> 2. A pointer variable may be initialized to 0 or NULL, an address, or the content of another pointer variable of the same type.
>
> 3. If a pointer variable contains the address of the memory location of another variable, the name of the pointer variable prefixed by the indirection operator * can be used as another name for the variable to which it points.

## 10.3    PARAMETER PASSING BY POINTERS

We may design functions that can return multiple values by declaring their formal parameters as pointer variables. This way of communicating data between functions is called **parameter passing by pointers**. Actually, parameter passing by pointers is somewhat similar to passing by value in that, although a copy of the variable that we want to pass to a function is not made in that function's data area, the address of the variable is copied in a pointer variable in the data area of the function.

To pass the value of a variable by pointers between two functions, we must do the following:

1. Declare the variable that is meant to return a value to the calling function as a pointer variable in the formal parameter list of the function. For example, if there is only one formal parameter called result in the function whose name is called_function and if the variable is of type int, the header of the called_function must be written as

```
void called_function(int *result)
```

2. In calling the function called_function, use a variable of the same type as the corresponding formal parameter in the called function and, unless that variable itself is a pointer variable, precede the name of that variable by the address operator, &. A function call to called_function may be

```
called_function(&value_returned);
```

The actual parameters in a function call that correspond to pointer parameters in the function must be variables; they may not be constants or expressions. The effect of the above actions is the same as the effect of the declarations

```
int value_returned;
int *result = &value_returned;
```

except that the scope of the variable `value_returned` is the calling function and the variable `result` has a parameter scope in the function `called_function`. Therefore, we can reference the memory location for the variable `value_returned` using the name `value_returned` in the calling function and the name `*result` in the function `called_function`. Any change in the value of `*result` is reflected in the value of `value_returned`, and vice versa. Therefore, we can use the pointer variable `result` to return values to the calling function. We can also use the actual parameter `value_returned` to send a value to `called_function`.

3.  We must declare the function with pointer parameters appropriately in a function prototype by using the symbol * as a prefix for pointer parameters. For example, the function `called_function` must be declared as

```
void called_function(int *x);
```

Let us study two examples of parameter passing by pointers.

***Example 10.1***  In Figure 6.18 we designed a function called `fibonacci` with one value parameter `seq_number`, which could compute and return a Fibonacci number corresponding to the supplied value of `seq_number`. The Fibonacci number was returned under the name of the function `fibonacci`. In Figure 10.4 we reformulate the same problem such that the computed Fibonacci number is returned through a pointer parameter.

```
void fibonacci(int seq_number, int *fib_number) {
        int first = 0, second = 1, count = 3;

        if (seq_number == 1)
            *fib_number = first;
        else if (seq_number == 2)
            *fib_number = second;
        /* end if */

        while (count <= seq_number) {
            *fib_number = first + second;
            first = second;
            second = *fib_number;
            count = count + 1;
        } /* end while */
} /* end function fibonacci */
```

**Figure 10.4**  A function that computes Fibonacci numbers (use of a `void` function with one value parameter and one pointer parameter)

The important aspects of the program of Figure 10.4 are the function header that declares `seq_number` as a value parameter and `*fib_number` as a pointer parameter and the references to `fib_number` in `fibonacci`, which are all prefixed by the indirection operator and written as `*fib_number`. The function prototype for `fibonacci` can be written as

```
void fibonacci(int x, int *y);
```

which informs the compiler that the first parameter is a value parameter and the second is a pointer parameter.

**Example 10.2**   We will design a function called `get_day` that reads and validates the day part of a date. The input for this function consists of a year and a month value, both supplied through its parameters. The function should prompt the user to enter a day value, read it, validate it, and return the day value through a parameter. Because year and month values are input for the function, they should be value parameters, and its only output, day, will be a pointer parameter. The function `get_day` is given in Figure 10.5.

```
/*******************************************************************
 Function Name   : get_day
 Purpose         : Reads a day and validates input.
 Called by       : get_data
 Receives        : month, year
 Returns         : day
 *******************************************************************/
void get_day(int *day, int month, int year) {
       /* Local variables: */

       char correct_data = 'n';

       /* Function body: */

       do {
              printf("***> Enter day as an integer: ");
              scanf("%d", &(*day));

              switch (month) {
                     case 1 : case 3 : case 5 : case 7 : case 8 :
                     case 10 : case 12 :
                            if (*day >= 1 && *day <= 31)
                                   correct_data = 'y';
                            /* end if */
                            break;
                     case 4 : case 6 : case 9 : case 11 :
                            if (*day >= 1 && *day <= 30)
```

**Figure 10.5**     A C implementation of the function `get_day` *(continued)*     ▶

```
                                    correct_data = 'y';
                          /* end if */
                          break;
                   case 2 :
                          if (*day >= 1 && *day <= 28)
                                  correct_data = 'y';
                          else if ((year % 100) != 0 && (year % 4) == 0
                                    && *day >= 1 && *day <= 29)
                                  correct_data = 'y';
                          else if ((year % 100) == 0 && (year % 400) == 0
                                    && *day >= 1 && *day <= 29)
                                  correct_data = 'y';
                          /* end if */
             } /* end switch */

             if (correct_data == 'n')
                   printf("Incorrect day. Please try again.\n");
             /* end if */
      } while (correct_data == 'n');
      /* end do-while */
} /* end function get_day */
```

Figure 10.5                                                                          ■

In Figure 10.5 the do-while loop reads a value for day and makes sure that
the value is correct. The data validation process for day is handled by the switch
statement in the loop body. If the value of month is 1, 3, 5, 7, 8, 10, or 12 (that is, the
month is January, March, May, July, August, October, or December), all we have to do is
to make sure that day is in the range 1 through 31. This test is done by the if statement that has the predicate day >= 1 && day <= 31. The corresponding test for
April, June, September, and November (that is, month values of 4, 6, 9, and 11) is in
the if statement with the predicate day >= 1 && day <= 30.

The test for the month of February, that is, if month is 2, is more complicated and
depends on whether the year is a leap year. By definition, every year that is divisible by
4 is a leap year, with the exception of centennial numbers (that is, those that are divisible
by 100), which are leap years only if they are divisible by 400. Therefore, the test for
days in February can be expressed as follows:

1.  Any day in the range 1 through 28 is legitimate.

2.  For a year that is not centennial and is divisible by 4 (that is, a leap year), any day
    in the range 1 through 29 is legitimate.

3.  For a year that is centennial and is divisible by 400 (that is, also a leap year), any day
    in the range 1 through 29 is legitimate.

Test 1 is expressed by the first predicate of the nested  if  in  case  2  of the switch statement: day >= 1 && day <= 28. Test 2 is the second predicate of the nested  if: (year % 100) != 0 && (year % 4) == 0 && day >= 1 && day <= 29. Finally, test 3 is the third predicate of the nested if statement: (year % 100) == 0 && (year % 400) == 0 && day >= 1 && day <= 29.

**Example 10.3**   We want to design a function called  compute_number_of_days, which receives a date as a four-digit  year, a two-digit  month, and a two-digit day value through its parameters and then computes and returns the number of days from the beginning of that year to the given date. The function will receive values for  year, month, and  day, which are its value parameters, and it will return the value of no_of_days, which is a pointer parameter.

One possible solution that uses a  switch  statement instead of a loop is given in Figure 10.6.

```
/*************************************************************
 Function Name   : compute_number_of_days
 Purpose         : Computes the number of days from the beginning
                   of the year to a given date.
 Called by       : main
 Receives        : year, month, day
 Returns         : no_of_days
*************************************************************/
void compute_number_of_days(int year, int month, int day,
                            int *no_of_days) {
        *no_of_days = 0;

        switch (month) {
                case 12 : *no_of_days += 30;
                case 11 : *no_of_days += 31;
                case 10 : *no_of_days += 30;
                case 9 : *no_of_days += 31;
                case 8 : *no_of_days += 31;
                case 7 : *no_of_days += 30;
                case 6 : *no_of_days += 31;
                case 5 : *no_of_days += 30;
                case 4 : *no_of_days += 31;
                case 3 :
                    if (((year % 4) == 0 && (year % 100) != 0) ||
                        ((year % 100) == 0 && (year % 400) == 0))
                        *no_of_days += 29;
```

**Figure 10.6**   A C function that computes number of days to a date *(continued)*   ▶

```
            else
                *no_of_days += 28;
            /* end if */
        case 2 : *no_of_days += 31;
        case 1 : *no_of_days += day;
    } /* end switch */
} /* end function compute_number_of_days */
```

**Figure 10.6**                                                                    ■

The following should be noted about the program of Figure 10.6:

1. The function header specifies `year`, `month`, and `day` as value parameters and `no_of_days` as a pointer parameter.

2. The `switch` statement in the function body is controlled by the variable `month` and has 12 cases, written in descending order from 12 to 1. Note that there is no `default` for the `switch` statement; we are assuming that `month` has been previously validated and cannot have an incorrect value. Also note that the cases of the `switch` statement do not contain any `break` statements, which makes it possible to compute the number of days to the given date without using a loop. Each case except cases 1 and 3 has a statement that increments `no_of_days` by the number of days in the preceding month. For example, case 12 contains the statement

```
no_of_days += 30;
```

which adds 30, the number of days in the 11th month (November), to the current value of `no_of_days`.

3. Case 3 is different. Its function is to increment `no_of_days` by the number of days in the month of February. Since February has 29 days in leap years and 28 days otherwise, we use an `if` statement to test for leap years and accordingly add to `no_of_years`.

4. Case 1 simply adds to `no_of_days` the value of the variable `day`.

It would be useful for the reader to draw a trace table and verify that this program will correctly compute `no_of_days` for any given date.

***Example 10.4*** Suppose we want to design a function called `determine_week_day`, which receives three data values:

1. `day_of_year1`, which is an integer value representing the day number for a day in a year.

2. `week_day1`, an integer that represents the day of the week such that 1 stands for Sunday, 2 for Monday, and so on.

3. `day_of_year2`, which is also an integer value for the day number for another day in the same year.

The function `determine_week_day` should compute and return the day of the week corresponding to `day_of_year2`. In other words, this function should provide the solution to a problem, such as "If the 100th day of a year is a Tuesday, what is the day of the week for the 185th day?" When expressed in terms of the parameters of the function, this problem becomes "If `day_of_year1` is 100, `week_day1` is 3, and `day_of_year2` is 185, what is the value of `week_day2`?"

Let us try to devise a solution for this problem.

1.  Trivially, if `day_of_year2` is equal to `day_of_year1`, `week_day2` will be the same as `week_day1`.

2.  If `day_of_year2` is greater than `day_of_year1`, then we note that the expression

```
d = day_of_year1 - week_day1
```

gives the day of the year corresponding to the seventh day of the week before `day_of_year1`. Therefore, the difference `day_of_year2` - `d` is the number of days from day `d` to day `day_of_year2`. The value of `week_day2` can be obtained by computing the remainder of the division of `day_of_year2` - `d` by 7. We also note that this remainder can be 0, and as 0 is not a legal value for `week_day2`, it must be made 7. Combining our observations, we conclude that the C statement

```
week_day2 = (day_of_year2 - day_of_year1 + week_day1) % 7;
```

will compute `week_day2` correctly except when `week_day2` turns out to be 0; in this case we change it to 7.

3.  If `day_of_year2` is less than `day_of_year1`, the C statement that computes `week_day2` is

```
week_day2 = 7 + (day_of_year2 - day_of_year1 + week_day1) % 7;
```

provided `week_day2` is assigned the value 7 if it is computed as 0. We will leave the derivation of this expression as an exercise for the reader. The variable `week_day2` computed using this expression may produce a value that is larger than 7; in this case we must subtract 7 from it.

The function `determine_week_day`, coded in C, is shown in Figure 10.7. In this function, the formal parameters `day_of_year1`, `day_of_year2`, and `week_day1` are for sending data to the function, and are therefore value parameters. The fourth parameter, `week_day2`, is for returning a value from the function, and it is declared as a pointer parameter. The function body consists of three `if` statements that implement the solution explained above. Note the use of the indirection operator for the variable `week_day2` in the body of the function.

```
/*******************************************************************
 Function Name     : determine_week_day
 Purpose           : Computes the day of week for a date, given
                     another date and the corresponding day of week.
 Called by         : main
 Receives          : day_of_year1, day_of_year2, week_day1
 Returns           : week_day2
 *******************************************************************/
void determine_week_day(int day_of_year1, int day_of_year2,
                        int week_day1, int *week_day2) {
     if (day_of_year2 == day_of_year1)
          *week_day2 = week_day1;
     else if (day_of_year2 > day_of_year1)
          *week_day2 = (day_of_year2 - day_of_year1 + week_day1) % 7;
        else
              *week_day2 = 7 + (day_of_year2 - day_of_year1 +
                           week_day1) % 7;
     /* end if */

     if (*week_day2 == 0)
          *week_day2 = 7;
     /* end if */

     if (*week_day2 > 7)
          *week_day2 = *week_day2 - 7;
     /* end if */
} /* end function determine_week_day */
```

**Figure 10.7**    A C function that determines week day

---

## Rules for Parameter Passing by Pointers

1. In parameter passing by pointers, the types of the actual and formal parameters must be similar.
2. The actual parameters must be the addresses of variables that are local to the calling function; in function calls, if they are not already pointers, they must be prefixed by the address operator, &.
3. In the formal parameter declaration list, the formal parameters must be prefixed by the symbol *.
4. In the function prototype, pointer parameters must be prefixed by the symbol *.
5. To access the content of the memory location for an actual parameter in the called function, we must use the name of the corresponding formal parameter prefixed by the indirection operator, *.

## REVIEW QUESTIONS

**1.** A pointer variable is a variable that contains a memory address. (T or F)

**2.** Choose the correct statement:
  **a.** A pointer variable may be declared in reference to another previously declared variable.
  **b.** In its declaration a pointer variable is prefixed by the symbol  *.
  **c.** If a pointer variable  x  is defined in reference to another variable  y, then the content of  x  is the address of the variable  y.
  **d.** All of the above are correct.
  **e.** None of the above is correct.

**3.** Suppose we have the following declarations:

```
int weight;
int *my_pointer;
```

Which of the following assignments is legal?
  **a.** weight = &my_pointer;
  **b.** my_pointer = NULL;
  **c.** &my_pointer = 0;
  **d.** weight = NULL;
  **e.** All of the above are legal.
  **f.** None of the above is legal.

**4.** In parameter passing by pointers, the formal parameters must be prefixed by the symbol * in their declarations. (T or F)

**5.** In parameter passing by pointers,
  **a.** The actual parameters in the function call corresponding to pointer parameters must be variables, not constants or expressions.
  **b.** The actual parameters corresponding to pointer parameters must be prefixed by the indirection operator,  *.
  **c.** The formal parameters in the called function must be prefixed by the address operator,  &.
  **d.** The function prototype must indicate the pointer parameters by prefixing them by the address operator,  &.
  **e.** All of the above are correct.
  **f.** None of the above is correct.

**Answers:**  1. T; 2. d; 3. b; 4. T; 5. a.

## 10.4    ADDITIONAL STYLE CONSIDERATIONS FOR MODULAR PROGRAMS

We discussed some style issues in connection with modular programming in Chapter 6. Now that we know more about functions and modular programs, we can add the following guidelines to our list.

1.   While implementing a module as a function, clearly identify data that it must receive and data that it must return. All data that a function must receive, and most data that it must return, should be through parameters, not through global variables.

2.   To send data to functions, use parameter passing by value to avoid inadvertent alterations of variables local to the calling function.

3.   If a function has one value to return, you may return it under its name using the return statement. For functions with two or more return values, it is better to use parameter passing by pointers for all such parameters to avoid confusion.

4.   In the source code use comments to clarify data to be received and returned by functions. Example:

```
/* Receives: first, second */
/* Returns : largest */
void find_largest(int first, int second, int *largest) {
        . . . . . . . . . . . . . .
        . . . . . . . . . . . . . .
} /* end function find_largest
```

## 10.5   EXAMPLE PROGRAM 1: A C Program that Generates Calendars

In this application we will develop a C program that can be used to generate and print a monthly calendar for a specified year and month.

***Problem***   Develop an interactive C program that can

1.   Input a year and a month for which a calendar is requested.

2.   Input base information about any day in that year. This information should consist of a day, a month, and a day of week for that day. In other words, to generate a calendar for August 1998, in addition to this information we must supply data as to the fact that, for example, February 2, 1998, is a Monday.

3.   Generate and print the calendar for the specified month and year.

***Requirements Specification***   Develop a program that does the following:

1.   Prompts the user to enter an integer for year and an integer for month for which a calendar is requested. The program should validate the values entered for year and month.

2.   Prompts the user to enter base data about any day in that year. The base data consist of an integer for month, an integer for day, and an integer representing the day of week for that day (for example, 1 for Sunday, 2 for Monday, and so on). The month, day, and day of week values entered by the user should be validated.

3. Generates and prints a monthly calendar for this month, as shown in the following example:

```
            DECEMBER 1998

       S    M    T    W    T    F    S

                 1    2    3    4    5
       6    7    8    9   10   11   12
      13   14   15   16   17   18   19
      20   21   22   23   24   25   26
      27   28   29   30   31
```

### Analysis

**Inputs.** Year and month for which a calendar is requested and for any date in that year, month, day, and day of week corresponding to that day.

**Output.** A monthly calendar.

### Design

We begin by observing the following:

1. We can generate a calendar for a month if we know the *calendar_year* and the *calendar_month* values, and *week_day_of_first_day*, the day of week for the first day of the calendar month. The *calendar_year* and *calendar_month* values will come through input. The value of *week_day_of_first_day* must be computed. If this task is to be carried out by a function called `generate_calendar`, its prototype may be

```
void generate_calendar(int calendar_year,
        int calendar_month, int week_day_of_first_day);
```

Note that because the variables `calendar_year`, `calendar_month`, and `week_day_of_first_day` are data to be sent to `generate_calendar`, they are all value parameters.

2. To compute the *week_day_of_first_day* of the calendar month, we must know the number of days from the beginning of the year to the first day of the calendar month (*no_of_days_to_calendar_month*), the day of week for any day in the year (*week_day_of_base_day*), and the number of days from the first day of the year to the base day (*no_of_days_to_base_day*). The value of *week_day_of_base_day* is provided through input. The values for *no_of_days_to_calendar_month* and *no_of_days_to_base_day* must be computed. The prototype of the function `determine_week_day` may be

```
void determine_week_day(int no_of_days_to_base_day,
        int no_of_days_to_calendar_month,
        int week_day_of_base_day,
        int *week_day_of_first_day);
```

For this function the data to be received consists of `no_of_days_to_base_day`, `no_of_days_to_calendar_month`, and `week_day_of_base_day`. Therefore, they are value parameters. It must return `week_day_of_first_day`, which is a pointer parameter.

3.   We can design a function that computes the number of days from the beginning of a year to any day in that year and use it in determining *no_of_days_to_calendar_month* and *no_of_days_to_base_day*. Let that function be `compute_number_of_days`. Here is its prototype:

```
void compute_number_of_days(int year, int month,
        int day, int *day_of_year);
```

In our problem-solving exercises, we have always used the top-down design coupled with bottom-up implementation. In this application we will take a different approach. We will assume that the structure of the program—obtained by applying top-down stepwise refinement—is as given in Figure 10.8. We will further assume that we have at our disposal the following C functions:

1.   A function called `get_day`, which receives a year and a month value. This function prompts the user to enter a day value, reads it, validates the day value, and returns it to the calling function. It is the function that we developed in Example 10.2.

2.   A function called `compute_number_of_days`, which receives values for a year, a month, and a day, and computes and returns the number of days from the beginning of that year to the given date. This function is given in Example 10.3.

3.   A function called `determine_week_day`, which receives values of a day number for a day in a year, the corresponding day of week for it, and another day number for another day in the same year. This function computes and returns the day of week of the second date. This function was designed and presented in Example 10.4.

Now all we have to do is to design and implement five additional functions to satisfy the structure of the chart of Figure 10.8. These functions are

1.   `get_year`, which prompts the user to enter a year value, reads it, validates it, and returns it to the calling function.

2.   `get_month`, which inputs, validates, and returns a month value.

3.   `get_week_day`, which inputs, validates, and returns a day of week.

4.   `get_data`, which calls on the functions `get_year`, `get_month`, `get_day`, and `get_week_day` to obtain validated values for `calendar_year`, `calendar_month`, `base_month`, `base_day`, and `base_week_day` and returns them to the calling function.

5.   `print_year_and_month`, which prints the header of a monthly calendar as, for example, `DECEMBER 1998`, given a year value of 1998 and a month value of 12.

6.   `print_calendar`, which prints the calendar for the requested month, given the number of days in the month and the week day of the first day of the month.

7.   `generate_calendar`, which generates and prints a monthly calendar given a year, a month, and the week day of the first day of the month. The function `generate_cal-`

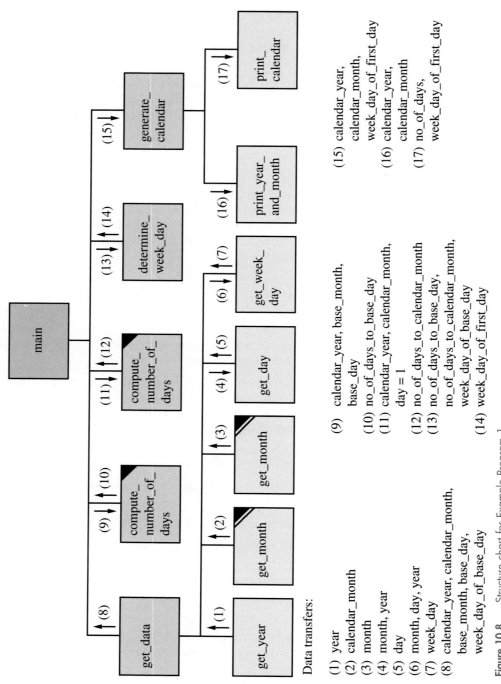

Data transfers:

(1) year
(2) calendar_month
(3) month
(4) month, year
(5) day
(6) month, day, year
(7) week_day
(8) calendar_year, calendar_month,
    base_month, base_day,
    week_day_of_base_day

(9) calendar_year, base_month,
    base_day
(10) no_of_days_to_base_day
(11) calendar_year, calendar_month,
    day = 1
(12) no_of_days_to_calendar_month
(13) no_of_days_to_base_day,
    no_of_days_to_calendar_month,
    week_day_of_base_day
(14) week_day_of_first_day

(15) calendar_year,
    calendar_month,
    week_day_of_first_day
(16) calendar_year,
    calendar_month
(17) no_of_days,
    week_day_of_first_day

**Figure 10.8**  Structure chart for Example Program 1

endar uses `print_year_and_month` and `print_calendar` while printing the calendar for the month.

8.   The function `main` that coordinates four modules at the second level of hierarchy in the structure chart of Figure 10.8.

The design of all modules, except the functions `main` and `get_data`, will be carried out using the top-down-design and bottom-up-implementation strategy. The functions `main` and `get_data`, however, are influenced by the existing modules that we have decided to use. Therefore, for their design we will resort to the design strategy called **bottom-up design**. We will complete the design and implementation in eight steps.

### Implementation

**Step 1.** Figure 10.9 shows a C implementation for the module `get_year`. This function is straightforward. Its only formal parameter is a pointer parameter through which it returns a value for year.

```
/*******************************************************************
 Function Name     : get_year
 Purpose           : Reads a year and validates input.
 Called by         : get_data
 Receives          : None
 Returns           : year
 ******************************************************************/
void get_year(int *year) {
      /* Local variables: */

      char correct_data = 'n';

      /* Function body: */

      do {
            printf("***> Enter calendar year as a four-digit
                  integer: ");
            scanf("%d", &(*year));

            if (*year < 1)
                  printf("Incorrect year. Please try again.\n");
            else
                  correct_data = 'y';
            /* end if */
      } while (correct_data == 'n');
      /* end do-while */
} /* end function get_year */
```

**Figure 10.9**   A C implementation of module `get_year`

**Step 2.** We implement the function get_month as shown in Figure 10.10.

```
/*********************************************************************
  Function Name   : get_month
  Purpose         : Reads a month and validates input.
  Called by       : get_data
  Receives        : None
  Returns         : month
*********************************************************************/
void get_month(int *month) {
        /* Local variables: */

        char correct_data = 'n';

        /* Function body: */

        do {
                printf("***> Enter month as an integer: ");
                scanf("%d", &(*month));

                if (*month < 1 || *month > 12)
                        printf("Incorrect month. Please try again.\n");
                else
                        correct_data = 'y';
                /* end if */
        } while (correct_data == 'n');
        /* end do-while */
} /* end function get_month */
```

**Figure 10.10**     A C implementation of module get_month

**Step 3.** The next function to be implemented is get_week_day, as shown in Figure 10.11. Note that this function has three value parameters, used for sending month, day, and year values to it. It has one pointer parameter, week_day. Obviously, to input and return week_day, we don't need the values for month, day, and year. We use them in the function get_week_day in the first printf call of the do-while loop to enhance the user interface.

```
/****************************************************************
  Function Name    : get_week_day
  Purpose          : Reads a day of week and validates input.
  Called by        : get_data
  Receives         : month, day, year
  Returns          : week_day
 ****************************************************************/
void get_week_day(int *week_day, int month, int day, int year) {
       /* Local variables: */

       char correct_data = 'n';

       /* Function body: */

       printf("\n");
       printf("***> For day of week, please use:\n");
       printf("      1 for SUN   2 for MON   3 for TUE   4 for WED\n");
       printf("      5 for THU   6 for FRI   7 for SAT\n\n");

       do {
              printf("***> Enter day of week for %d/%d/%d: ",
                       month, day, year);
              scanf("%d", &(*week_day));

              if (*week_day < 1 || *week_day > 7)
                 printf("Incorrect day of week. Please try again.\n");
              else
                 correct_data = 'y';
              /* end if */
       } while (correct_data == 'n');
       /* end do-while */
} /* end function get_week_day */
```

**Figure 10.11**   A C implementation of module `get_week_day`

**Step 4.** Now that all the functions needed by the module `get_data` are available, we can implement it, as shown in Figure 10.12. The function `get_data` has five pointer parameters: `year`, `calendar_month`, `month`, `day`, and `week_day`. These parameters return values to the calling function.

```
/*******************************************************************
 Function Name    : get_data
 Purpose          : Reads and validates input.
 Called by        : main
 Receives         : None
 Returns          : year, calendar_month, month, day, week_day
 ******************************************************************/
void get_data(int *year, int *calendar_month, int *month,
                   int *day, int *week_day) {
      /* Function body: */

      printf("TO GENERATE A CALENDAR, I NEED TO KNOW THE YEAR\n");
      printf("AND THE MONTH FOR WHICH YOU WANT THE CALENDAR.\n\n");
      get_year(&(*year));
      get_month(&(*calendar_month));

      printf("\n");
      printf("NOW, I NEED TO KNOW DAY, MONTH, AND\n");
      printf("DAY-OF-WEEK INFORMATION FOR \"ANY\" DAY IN %d.\n\n",
            *year);
      get_month(&(*month));
      get_day(&(*day), *month, *year);
      get_week_day(&(*week_day), *month, *day, *year);
} /* end function get_data */
```

**Figure 10.12**   A C implementation of module `get_data`

**Step 5.** We focus on the module `print_year_and_month`. The C code is given in Figure 10.13. This function has two value parameters, `year` and `month`. Its body contains a nested `if` statement that has 12 alternatives, one for each month. Each alternative copies the name of a month as a string literal to the string variable `month_name`. The `printf` function call that comes after the nested `if` prints the value of `month_name` and an integer `year` value.

```
/*******************************************************
 Function Name    : print_year_and_month
 Purpose          : Prints the header for the calendar.
 Called by        : generate_calendar
 Receives         : year, month
 Returns          : None
 *******************************************************/
```

**Figure 10.13**   A C implementation of module `print_year_and_month`  (continued)  ▶

```
void print_year_and_month(int year, int month) {
      /* Local variables: */

      char month_name[9];

      /* Function body: */

      if (month == 1)
            strcpy(month_name, "JANUARY");
      else if (month == 2)
            strcpy(month_name, "FEBRUARY");
      else if (month == 3)
            strcpy(month_name, "MARCH");
      else if (month == 4)
            strcpy(month_name, "APRIL");
      else if (month == 5)
            strcpy(month_name, "MAY");
      else if (month == 6)
            strcpy(month_name, "JUNE");
      else if (month == 7)
            strcpy(month_name, "JULY");
      else if (month == 8)
            strcpy(month_name, "AUGUST");
      else if (month == 9)
            strcpy(month_name, "SEPTEMBER");
      else if (month == 10)
            strcpy(month_name, "OCTOBER");
      else if (month == 11)
            strcpy(month_name, "NOVEMBER");
      else
            strcpy(month_name, "DECEMBER");
      /* end if */

      printf("\n");
      printf("%16s %d\n", month_name, year);
} /* end function print_year_and_month */
```

Figure 10.13

**Step 6.** The implementation of the function  print_calendar  is given in Figure
10.14. It has two value parameters,  no_of_days, which is the number of days in the
month for which the calendar is to be generated, and  first_day, the day of the week
value for the first day of that month.

```
/*********************************************************
 Function Name    : print_calendar
 Purpose          : Prints the body of the calendar.
 Called by        : generate_calendar
 Receives         : no_of_days, first_day
 Returns          : None
 *********************************************************/
void print_calendar(int no_of_days, int first_day) {
        /* Local variables: */

        int no_of_empties, count = 1, days = 1;

        /* Function body: */

        printf("\n");
        printf("   S   M   T   W   T   F   S\n\n");
        no_of_empties = first_day - 1;

        while (count <= 7) {
              if (no_of_empties > 0) {
                     printf("    ");
                     no_of_empties = no_of_empties - 1;
                     count = count + 1;
              }
              else {
                     printf("%4d", days);
                     days = days + 1;
                     count = count + 1;
              } /* end if */
        } /* end while */

        while (days <= no_of_days) {
              printf("\n");
              count = 1;

              while (count <= 7) {
                     printf("%4d", days);
                     days = days + 1;
                     count = count + 1;

                     if (days > no_of_days)
                            break;
```

**Figure 10.14**     A C implementation of module `print_calendar` *(continued)*     ▶

```
                          /* end if */
                } /* end while */
          } /* end while */
   } /* end function print_calendar */
```

Figure 10.14

Printing the first week of the monthly calendar is somewhat complicated in that, depending on the day of week for the first day of the month, we have to print blank fields for up to six days. For example, if the first day is Sunday (that is, `first_day` is equal to 1), we don't need to print blank fields for the first week; if, however, the first day is Monday, we have to print a blank field corresponding to Sunday. The number of blank fields to be printed is the value of `first_day` minus 1, as reflected by the statement

```
no_of_empties = first_day - 1;
```

which assigns a value to the variable `no_of_empties`. The first `while` loop in the function body prints an appropriate number of blank fields on the line for the first week and prints for the remaining days integers stored in the variable `days` beginning with 1. The last value assigned to `days` in the `while` statement is the value of the first day of the second week of the month.

The second `while` loop prints the remaining weeks of the month. Note that the `break` statement in the then-part of the `if` statement stops the print operation after the last day of the month is printed on the line corresponding to the last week.

**Step 7.** Now that we have the implementations of `print_year_and_month` and `print_calendar`, we can complete the implementation of the module `generate_calendar`, as given in Figure 10.15. This function has three value parameters, `year`, `month`, and `first_day`, which is the day of week value for the first day of the month for which a calendar will be generated.

```
/* * * * * * * * * * * * * * * * * * * * * * * * * * * * * * * * * * * * * * * * * * * * * * * * * * * * * * * * * * *
   Function Name    : generate_calendar
   Purpose          : Generates and prints the calendar for a month,
                      given the month and the day of week for its
                      first day.
   Called by        : main
   Receives         : year, month, first_day
   Returns          : None
   * * * * * * * * * * * * * * * * * * * * * * * * * * * * * * * * * * * * * * * * * * * * * * * * * * * * * * * * * * */
void generate_calendar(int year, int month, int first_day) {
      /* Local variables: */
```

Figure 10.15    A C implementation of module  `generate_calendar`  (*continued*)    ▶

```
        int no_of_days;

        /* Function body: */

        switch (month) {
                case 1 : case 3 : case 5 : case 7 : case 8 :
                case 10 : case 12 :
                        no_of_days = 31;
                        break;
                case 4 : case 6 : case 9 : case 11 :
                        no_of_days = 30;
                        break;
                case 2 :
                        if (((year % 4) == 0 && (year % 100) != 0) ||
                                ((year % 100) == 0 && (year % 400) == 0))
                                no_of_days = 29;
                        else
                                no_of_days = 28;
                        /* end if */
        } /* end switch */

        print_year_and_month(year, month);
        print_calendar(no_of_days, first_day);
} /* end function generate_calendar */
```

**Figure 10.15**                                                                                    ■

The body of `generate_calendar` consists of a `switch` statement and function calls to `print_year_and_month` and `print_calendar`. The `switch` statement determines the number of days in the given month, needed by the function `print_calendar`. Cases 1, 3, 5, 7, 8, 10, and 12 correspond to months that have 31 days. Cases 4, 6, 9, and 11 are for 30-day months. Case 2 is for February. The `if` statement in case 2 tests for leap year and accordingly determines the number of days as 28 or 29.

**Step 8.** We implement the function `main`, shown in Figure 10.16.

```
/*****************************************************************
  Program Filename: prog10_1.c
  Author           : Uckan
  Purpose          : Computes and prints the calendar for any month
                     of a year, given the date of any day in that
                     year and its day of week.
```

**Figure 10.16**    A C implementation of function `main` *(continued)*    ▶

```
 Input from       : terminal keyboard
 Output to        : screen
*****************************************************************/
#include <stdio.h>
#include <string.h>

/* Function prototypes: */

void get_data(int *calendar_year, int *calendar_month, int *month,
      int *day, int *week_day);
void compute_number_of_days(int year, int month, int day,
      int *day_of_year);
void determine_week_day(int no_of_days_to_base_day,
      int no_of_days_to_calendar_month, int week_day_of_base_day,
      int *week_day_of_first_day);
void generate_calendar(int calendar_year, int calendar_month,
      int week_day_of_first_day);
void get_year(int *year);
void get_month(int *month);
void get_day(int *day, int month, int year);
void get_week_day(int *week_day, int month, int day, int year);
void print_year_and_month(int year, int month);
void print_calendar(int no_of_days, int first_day);

int main(void) {
        /* Local variables: */

        int calendar_year, calendar_month;
        int base_month, base_day, week_day_of_base_day;
        int no_of_days_to_base_day, no_of_days_to_calendar_month;
        int week_day_of_first_day;

        // Function body:

        get_data(&calendar_year, &calendar_month, &base_month,
              &base_day, &week_day_of_base_day);
        compute_number_of_days(calendar_year, base_month, base_day,
              &no_of_days_to_base_day);
        compute_number_of_days(calendar_year, calendar_month, 1,
              &no_of_days_to_calendar_month);
        determine_week_day(no_of_days_to_base_day,
              no_of_days_to_calendar_month, week_day_of_base_day,
              &week_day_of_first_day);
```

**Figure 10.16**    A C implementation of function `main` (*continued*)    ▶

```
        printf("\n");
        printf("HERE IS YOUR CALENDAR:\n");
        generate_calendar(calendar_year, calendar_month,
              week_day_of_first_day);
        return 0;
} /* end function main */
```

**Figure 10.16**   ■

We note the following about the function  main  of Figure 10.16.

1.   The function call

```
compute_number_of_days(calendar_year, base_month,
        base_day, &no_of_days_to_base_day);
```

triggers the execution of  compute_number_of_days, which returns in no_of_ days_to_base_day  the number of days from the beginning of the calendar year to the date defined by  calendar_year,  base_month, and  base_day.

2.   Similarly, the function call

```
compute_number_of_days(calendar_year, calendar_month,
          1, &no_of_days_to_calendar_month);
```

causes the function  compute_number_of_days  to return in  no_of_days_to_ calendar_month  the number of days from the first day of the calendar year to the first day of the calendar month for which we want to generate a calendar.

3.   The function call

```
determine_week_day(no_of_days_to_base_day,
          no_of_days_to_calendar_month, week_day_of_base_day,
          &week_day_of_first_day);
```

executes  determine_week_day, which returns in  week_day_of_first_day the day of week for the first day of the calendar month. In order to determine the week day, the function  determine_week_day  needs values for the day of year and the corresponding week day for a base date (that is,  no_of_days_to_base_day  and week_day_of_base_day) and the day of year for the first day of the calendar month, no_of_days_to_calendar_month.

Figure 10.17 is a sample interactive session of the program of Figure 10.16 and all other related modules.

```
TO GENERATE A CALENDAR, I NEED TO KNOW THE YEAR
AND THE MONTH FOR WHICH YOU WANT THE CALENDAR.

***> Enter calendar year as a four-digit integer: 0000
Incorrect year. Please try again.
***> Enter calendar year as a four-digit integer: 1998
***> Enter month as an integer: 13
Incorrect month. Please try again.
***> Enter month as an integer: 9

NOW, I NEED TO KNOW DAY, MONTH, AND
DAY-OF-WEEK INFORMATION FOR "ANY" DAY IN 1998.

***> Enter month as an integer: 1
***> Enter day as an integer: 32
Incorrect day. Please try again.
***> Enter day as an integer: 31

***> For day of week, please use:
     1 for SUN   2 for MON   3 for TUE   4 for WED
     5 for THU   6 for FRI   7 for SAT

***> Enter day of week for 1/31/1998: 8
Incorrect day of week. Please try again.
***> Enter day of week for 1/31/1998: 7

HERE IS YOUR CALENDAR:

       SEPTEMBER 1998

   S   M   T   W   T   F   S

               1   2   3   4   5
   6   7   8   9  10  11  12
  13  14  15  16  17  18  19
  20  21  22  23  24  25  26
  27  28  29  30
```

**Figure 10.17**    A sample interactive session for the program of Figure 10.16

## 10.6    MODULAR PROGRAMMING WITH PROGRAMMER-DEFINED LIBRARIES

The concept of libraries is important in C. We already know that

> A **library** in C is a collection of reasonably general-purpose and related functions.

There are two types of libraries:

1. Standard libraries
2. Programmer-defined libraries

### Standard C Libraries

We have been using standard libraries for quite some time now. A **standard library** is a collection of functions provided by the vendor of the C integrated development environment (IDE) as an integral part of it. Examples of standard C libraries that we are familiar with include `stdio`, `math`, `stdlib`, and `string`. Of these, the `stdio` library contains functions for input-output; `math` consists of some standard mathematical functions, such as `sqrt`, and so on.

Each standard library comprises two elements:

1. A **header file**, stored in the standard include directory of the C IDE, containing declarations of the standard functions in the library and declarations of related constants and data types

2. An **implementation file**, which is a compiled version of a C program that contains the implementations of the standard functions declared in the header file

For example, the declarations of the functions of the standard library `stdio` are found in the standard header file `stdio.h`. For any standard library you may browse the standard header file; in fact, it is very useful and instructive to read the contents of the standard header files. However, you must refrain from making changes to standard header files; if you do, you may inadvertently destroy your copy of the C IDE.

As you already know, if we need some standard functions for our program, we must use the `include` preprocessor directive for the library that contains these functions. For example, to be able to use the standard functions for input-output, we must have the preprocessor directive `#include <stdio.h>` in our program. After we design a program that contains one or more `include` preprocessor directives, the following events take place during compilation and linking, as shown in Figure 10.18:

1. A project workspace is created. A **project** is a collection of one or more related C source or object files, treated as a whole. The C IDE allows you to create a new project and assign a name to it, or in case you have only one C file and you choose not to create a project explicitly, the IDE creates a default project for your program. After you

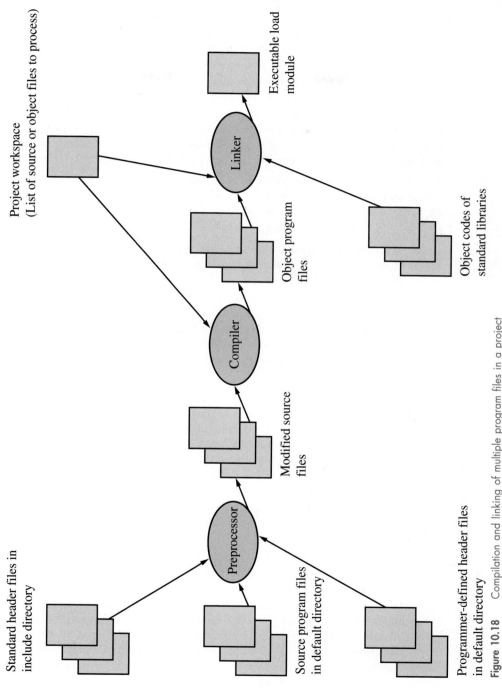

**Figure 10.18**   Compilation and linking of multiple program files in a project

Project workspace
(List of source or object files to process)

Executable load module

Linker

Object program files

Object codes of standard libraries

Compiler

Modified source files

Preprocessor

Standard header files in include directory

Source program files in default directory

Programmer-defined header files in default directory

create a project workspace, you are expected to insert source or object files into the project using the project management feature of the C IDE. A list of files to be compiled and linked is maintained in the project workspace.

2.   The next step is to compile your source files in the project workspace. If the source files contain `include` preprocessor directives in reference to standard or programmer-defined libraries, the compiler activates the preprocessor.

3.   The preprocessor combines the contents of the indicated standard and/or programmer-defined header files and your source program files—without making any changes in your source program files—and produces a temporary modified source program file for each source file. Then the preprocessor passes the control back to the compiler.

4.   The compiler compiles the modified source program files to generate object files. Of course, this step happens if you have no compilation errors in your programs. The object files are stored in your project workspace in the default directory.

5.   The linker does the following:

   a. It verifies the programmer-defined function prototypes against function definitions. If function prototypes do not match function definitions, you get errors. Such errors are called **linker errors**.

   b. If no linker errors occur, the linker combines the object programs corresponding to the programmer-defined functions in the source programs with those for the standard functions being used by the programs and comes up with an executable load module. The executable load module is also saved in your project workspace in the default directory, to be used when you are ready to run the program.

As you can see, a C program ultimately is a combination of the programs that you write and some standard functions that are at your disposal. By using standard libraries, you are introducing some modules into your application. Therefore, even if your own source program is not modular, the whole program is, since you are making use of some modules in some standard libraries. In fact, the only truly nonmodular program that you can write would be a program that has no input or output and uses operations that are intrinsic to the C language on some constants or variables with preassigned constant values. Such a program is probably worthless, and you wouldn't write it.

We conclude that a modular program is modular because it contains two or more programmer-defined functions, because it uses some standard or programmer-defined libraries, or both.

## Program Modularization through Programmer-Defined Libraries

As you can use standard libraries to develop a modular program, you can use your own programmer-defined libraries to further modularize your program and improve the software development and maintenance processes. Before we discuss how to develop programmer-defined libraries, let us recall the main motivation behind doing so: that a library contains some general-purpose functions—functions we expect to use in future applications. If we can collect such functions in libraries and implement them, then we may use them in other projects, just as we use standard library functions in many programs, thereby avoiding "reinventing the wheel" and enhancing software reusability.

Here is how we can develop programmer-defined libraries and use them:

**Step 1.** In a software development process, after the design phase is completed, identify the reusable modules, those that you expect to use in the future because they are somewhat general-purpose. For example, in Example Program 1, of the 11 functions that make up the final program, the functions compute_number_of_days, determine_week_day, get_year, get_month, get_day, and get_week_day appear to be reusable, and the others are application specific. Let us decide to include these six functions in a programmer-defined library named calendar. Of course, determining which functions are candidates for inclusion in a library is significantly difficult and requires experience and use of common sense. You want useful libraries; you must avoid libraries just for the sake of having libraries.

**Step 2.** A programmer-defined library, like a standard library, consists of one or more header files and one or more implementation files. Header and implementation files are C source files, and they can contain any type of C code, provided a program entity, such as a function or a declaration, is not split between two or more files. However, the usual practice, consistent with the development and implementation of standard C libraries, is to have *only* declarations (of functions, global variables, named constants, typedefs, and programmer-defined data types) in header files, and *only* the definitions of the functions that we have decided to include in our library in the implementation file. You already know about function declarations, global variable declarations, and named constants; you will learn about typedefs and programmer-defined data types in the future chapters.

A programmer-defined header file has an extension that is different from the extension of an implementation file. In DOS-based systems the extension for header files is h, and for implementation files it is c. Returning to our sample calendar library, we prepare a header file, named calendar.h, and store it in our default directory. This header file contains only the prototypes of the six functions and some explanatory comments. The content of the header file calendar.h is shown in Figure 10.19.

```
/* Header file calendar.h */

/******************************************************************
  Function Name     : compute_number_of_days
  Purpose           : Computes the number of days from the beginning
                      of the year to a given date.
  Receives          : year, month, day
  Returns           : no_of_days
 ******************************************************************/
void compute_number_of_days(int year, int month, int day,
                            int *day_of_year);


/******************************************************************
  Function Name     : determine_week_day
```

**Figure 10.19**   The header file calendar.h for the calendar library *(continued)*   ▶

```
  Purpose           : Computes the day of week for a date, given
                      another date and the corresponding day of week.
  Receives          : day_of_year1, day_of_year2, week_day1
  Returns           : week_day2
  **********************************************************************/
void determine_week_day(int base_day_of_year, int calendar_day_of_year,
                        int base_week_day, int *week_day_of_first_day);


/***********************************************************************
  Function Name     : get_year
  Purpose           : Reads a year and validates input.
  Receives          : None
  Returns           : year
  **********************************************************************/
void get_year(int *year);


/***********************************************************************
  Function Name     : get_month
  Purpose           : Reads a month and validates input.
  Receives          : None
  Returns           : month
  **********************************************************************/
void get_month(int *month);


/***********************************************************************
  Function Name     : get_day
  Purpose           : Reads a day and validates input.
  Receives          : month, year
  Returns           : day
  **********************************************************************/
void get_day(int *day, int month, int year);


/***********************************************************************
  Function Name     : get_week_day
  Purpose           : Reads a day of week and validates input.
  Receives          : month, day, year
  Returns           : week_day
  **********************************************************************/
void get_week_day(int *week_day, int month, int day, int year);
```

Figure 10.19   ■

**Step 3.** Next, we prepare an implementation file. The name of the implementation file can be anything. As a matter of convention, we will use the name of the library, in this case `calendar`, as the name of the implementation file and the extension `c`. So, the implementation file is `calendar.c`. The implementation file, stored in the default directory, contains the following items:

1.  The preprocessor directive `#include "calendar.h"`, for the programmer-defined header file `calendar.h`. Note that the name of the file is enclosed by double quotations, not triangular brackets.

2.  `include` preprocessor directives for all standard libraries needed by the functions in the `calendar` library. If you examine the six functions, you will see that they use some library functions in the standard library `stdio`. Therefore, we must have `#include <stdio.h>` in the implementation file.

3.  The definitions for the six functions, as we have them in Figures 10.5, 10.6, 10.7, 10.9, 10.10, and 10.11.

**Step 4.** Now it is time to prepare what is commonly termed the application file. The **application file** is our source program. It must have a function `main` and any other related function that is not in the implementation file. In our example the application file will consist of these items:

1.  The preprocessor directive `#include "calendar.h"`, so that we can use the functions in our `calendar` library.

2.  The `include` preprocessor directives for the standard libraries `stdio` and `string` because these libraries are needed by the functions that make up the rest of our application file.

3.  The function definitions for the application-specific modules, which are `get_data`, `generate_calendar`, `print_year_and_month`, `print_calendar`, and the function `main`. These functions are given in Figures 10.12 through 10.15.

You should note that the application file does not contain the prototypes for the functions `compute_number_of_days`, `determine_week_day`, `get_year`, `get_month`, `get_day`, and `get_week_day`, because these prototypes are already in the `calendar.h` header file.

**Step 5.** Next, we open a new project and insert into it the application file and the implementation files. The header files must not be inserted into the project. Opening a new project, inserting files into it, deleting files from it, and closing it are system-specific issues. In most standard C environments, they can be done easily. We refer the reader to the online Help of the C IDE or the accompanying hard-copy documentation. If you experience difficulties, ask your instructor; undoubtedly, he or she will gladly help.

After you insert the application and implementation files into the project, you can go ahead and compile, link, and execute the programs. If the files in the project are all source files, they will be compiled by the compiler one at a time. Some or all of the implementation files in the project may be object program files, obtained by compiling their source files separately. In other words, you may make object program files available to a project, as is the case with standard libraries. This approach allows you to hide the source code for the implementation of your programmer-defined libraries from the users to whom you may give the privilege of using them. You provide the users only with the header files, thus making their content *public*, and object versions of the implementation files, rendering them *private*. Distinguishing between public and private information is an important issue in software design.

Libraries developed by programmers can be referenced for future use by creating a **library archive**. The creation and maintenance of a library archive is a specific environment-dependent issue; you should consult the C IDE documentation.

Obviously, programmer-defined libraries constitute a strategy for software modularization. Their advantages, listed below, are quite similar to the advantages of modular program design and implementation:

1. Libraries enhance module reusability.

2. Libraries make independent coding easier in large-scale software development projects. Once the header files for libraries are constructed, their contents can be partitioned into tasks assigned to different teams of programmers, whose charge would be to design the implementation files.

3. Libraries simplify program testing and ensure reliable functions.

4. Libraries facilitate program maintenance. If a more efficient algorithm is discovered for a library function, the only component that is affected is the implementation file that contains it. The header file and the application files that use the library will not have to be modified.

5. Libraries facilitate procedural abstraction and information hiding. In this context **procedural abstraction** means hiding the details of the implementation of modules in the implementation files from the modules that use them in the application files. To use a library, all a programmer needs to know is the content of the library's header file.

6. Implementation files can be compiled separately and can be used in their object form in large-scale projects. Compiling implementation files separately speeds up the compilation time of application programs.

Let us summarize the rules for constructing and using libraries:

---

### Rules for Constructing Programmer-Defined Libraries

1. In a software development project, identify modules that have the promise of reusability and group them.

2. For each group of modules, prepare a header file that consists of declarations of functions and other global program elements.

3. Corresponding to each header file, prepare one or more implementation files, each containing the implementations of the functions declared in the header file. The implementation files must have an `include` preprocessor directive for the header file of the library.

4. Present the header file and the associated implementation files as the library to users. The library may consist of the source form for the header file and either the source or the object form for the implementation files.

---

**Rules for Using Programmer-Defined Libraries**

1. Study the header file for the library and make sure that the file contains functions that you can use in your application. Note the declarations in the header file.

2. Make sure that the header and implementation files for the library are in your default directory.

3. Design your application and prepare an application file. The application file *must* contain an `include` preprocessor directive for the header file of the library. Do *not* include the global declarations that are in the header file in your application file. Make sure that you use the functions and the type declarations in the header file correctly in your application file.

4. Open a new project, using the project management feature of your C IDE, and insert into it your application file and the implementation files for the library. Do *not* insert the header file of the library into the project. Compile, link, and execute the project. The source of any and all errors is probably in your application file.

---

## 10.7    SUMMARY

### This Chapter at a Glance

- In this chapter we continued the discussion of modular programming and functions that we started in Chapter 6.

- We discussed pointer variables and parameter passing by pointers. Passing by pointers is a technique in C that allows us to return values from functions through parameters.

- You learned more about C standard libraries. Then you studied the principles of programmer-defined libraries, their advantages, how they can be used to enhance program modularization, and how to construct and use them in applications.

- This chapter introduced new problem-solving skills. These new skills include the design and implementation of functions that pass parameters by pointers and the design and use of programmer-defined libraries.

### Coming Attractions

- Data and techniques for structuring data are important aspects of programming. In the next four chapters we cover data design.

- In Chapter 11 we consider arrays, a structured data type that C supports. Arrays are useful in problems that deal with a large number of data of the same type.

- Chapters 12, 13, and 14 examine additional programmer-defined and structured data types: structures, enumerations, strings, and files.

## STUDY GUIDE

### Test Your Comprehension

1. Which of the following statements concerning C pointer variables is *incorrect*?
   a. The content of a pointer variable is a memory address.
   b. In declaring a pointer variable, its name must be prefixed by the address operator.
   c. A pointer variable must have a type that is compatible with that of the variable with respect to which it is declared.
   d. In accessing a variable to which a pointer variable points, the name of the pointer variable must be prefixed by the indirection operator.

2. Which of the following operations on a pointer variable is illegal?
   a. Assigning the value of another pointer variable of a different data type
   b. Assigning the value NULL
   c. Assigning an address
   d. Comparing its content to zero

3. Given are the declarations

   ```
   double total_cost;
   double *cost_ptr = &total_cost;
   double *general_ptr;
   ```

   which of the following statements is legal?
   a. `*cost_ptr = 1.05 * total_cost;`
   b. `general_ptr = cost_ptr;`
   c. `general_ptr = &cost_ptr;`
   d. `general_ptr = &*cost_ptr;`
   e. All of the above are legal.
   f. None of the above is legal.

4. Which of the following is *incorrect* as a rule for parameter passing by pointers?
   a. The types of actual and formal parameters must be similar.
   b. The actual parameters must be variable names and must be prefixed by the indirection operator, `*`.
   c. The formal parameters must be prefixed by the symbol `*`.
   d. To access the content of the memory location for an actual parameter in the called function, we must use the name of the corresponding formal parameter prefixed by the indirection operator, `*`.

5. A standard C library
   a. Has a header file that is stored in the *include* directory of the C system.
   b. Includes an implementation file that contains a compiled version of the implementations of the standard functions declared in the header file.
   c. Is part of the C integrated development environment.
   d. All of the above are correct.
   e. None of the above is correct.

6. Which of the following statements concerning programmer-defined libraries is *incorrect*?
   a. A programmer-defined library must have a header file that consists of declarations of the functions included in the library.

**b.** One or more implementation files must contain the implementations of the functions in the library.

**c.** The implementation file does not need to have an `include` preprocessor directive for the library's header file.

**d.** An application file that uses the library must have an `include` preprocessor directive for the library's header file.

## Improve Your Problem-Solving Ability

### *Debugging Exercises*

**7.** In each of the following function definitions, declarations, or calls, identify and correct any errors. Explain your answer.

**a.** The function definition for `divisible_by_11` that checks whether a given integer `value` is divisible by 11:

```
void divisible_by_11(int value, char *result) {
    result = 'n';

    if (value % 11 == 0)
        &result = 'y';
    /* end if */
} /* end function divisible_by_11 */
```

**b.** The prototype for the function `divisible_by_11` of part (a):

```
int divisible_by_11(int a, char b);
```

**c.** The function call to `divisible_by_11` of part (a):

```
void divisible_by_11(number, &result);
```

**d.** The function definition `product_or_sum_of_odd_integers` that computes either the product or the sum of odd integers between `lower` and `higher`:

```
void product_or_sum_of_odd_integers(int lower, int upper,
                                    char what_operation,
                                    int *result) {
    int i;
```

```
        if (lower % 2 == 0)
            lower = lower + 1;
        /* end if */

        if (what_operation == 'p') {
            result = 1;
            for (i = lower; i <= upper; i = i + 2)
                *result = result * i;
            /* end for */
        }
        else {
            result = 0;
            for (i = lower; i <= upper; i = i + 2)
                *result = result + i;
            /* end for */
        } /* end if */
} /* end function product_or_sum_of_integers */
```

**e.** The prototype for the function  `product_or_sum_of_integers`  of part (d):
>  `void product_or_sum_of_odd_integers(int *a, int *b,`
>      `char *c, int &d);`

**f.** The function call to  `product_or_sum_of_integers`  of part (d):
>  `int product_or_sum_of_odd_integers(low_value,`
>      `high_value, &opr);`

### Programming Exercises

**8.** Write a prototype and a call for each of the following functions.

   **a.** A function named  `compute_area_and_perimeter`  that receives  `radius`  of type  `float`  and returns  `area`  and  `perimeter`, both of type  `double`, as parameters.

   **b.** A function named  `compute_length`  that receives x- and y-coordinates of two points in a plane, all of type  `double`, and returns the length of the line joining the two points as a parameter of type  `double`.

   **c.** A function named  `get_values_and_find_average`  that interactively reads values for three variables  `x`,  `y`, and  `z`, all of type  `float`, computes their arithmetic average, and returns  `x`,  `y`,  `z`, and their arithmetic average.

   **d.** A function named  `compute_deviations`  that receives three floating-point values, computes their respective deviations from their arithmetic average, and returns these deviations. Your function must have no more than three parameters.

   **e.** A function named  `pinpoint_largest`  that receives three pointers to three integers, determines the largest, and returns a pointer to the largest.

**9.** Redesign the function  `entered_gross_income`  of Figure 6.33, using pointer parameters to return the gross income.

**10.** Redesign the function  `computed_tax`  of Figure 6.36, using pointer parameters to return the computed tax.

**11.** Write a `void` function with one value parameter and one pointer parameter that computes and returns the largest of two supplied floating-point values. After making sure that your function does its task correctly, analyze it and state why this solution is not ideal. What do you suggest to turn it into a better design?

**12.** Write a function that receives two integers and determines whether one of the integers is evenly divisible by the other. If yes, your function should return in a string parameter the value of `"yes"`; otherwise, it should return the value of `"no"`. Use a driver function to test your function.

**13.** Write a function that receives two integers and then computes and returns as a parameter the greatest common divisor of the two integers. The greatest common divisor of two integers is the largest integer that evenly divides both integers. For example, the greatest common divisor of 12 and 28 is 4. Test your function thoroughly.

### Programming Projects

**14.** Design an interactive, modular program that reads a floating-point value for the variable *number* and verifies that it is nonnegative, reads a floating-point value for the variable *difference* and verifies that it is smaller than 0.01, and computes and prints the square root of the floating-point value *number* using the following approximation:

$$next\_guess = 0.5 \times \left( last\_guess + \frac{number}{last\_guess} \right)$$

Your module that computes the square root should start with an initial value of 1.0 for *last_guess*, and using this formula, it should compute *next_guess*. If the absolute value of the difference between *next_guess* and *last_guess* is less than *difference*, the value of *next_guess* should be accepted and returned to your main module so that it can be reported to the user. Otherwise, *last_guess* should be set to *next_guess*, and the calculations should be repeated in a loop.

**15.** Example Program 1 of this chapter can generate a monthly calendar for a month in a year if we supply the date and week day for any day in that same year. Modify this application to generate a monthly calendar for a month in any year, and not necessarily only for a month in the year for which we supply information. Your input should consist of the year and month for which you want the calendar. Test your program thoroughly.

Hint: Use the following formula (from *A Collection of Programming Problems and Techniques*, by H. A. Maurer and M. R. Williams, Prentice Hall, Englewood Cliffs, New Jersey, 1972):

If *year* is a positive integer and *y* is an integer, the day of week for the first day of the year, *day_of_week_of_first_day*, can be computed as follows:

$y = year - 1$
$day\_of\_week\_of\_first\_day = (36 + y + (y / 4) - (y / 100) + (y / 400)) \% 7 + 1$

The value of *day_of_week_of_first_day* will be an integer in the range of 1 through 7, such that 1 corresponds to Sunday, 2 to Monday, and so on. Note that divisions involved in the formula are integer divisions, and % is the remainder operator.

In Programming Projects 16 through 22, redesign the indicated application so that, in the modular design, your functions can return values, where necessary, through parameters, instead of under function names. In each case draw a structure chart, implement your design, and test the resulting program thoroughly.

**16.** Example Program 2 of Chapter 8, which computes federal income tax using tax rate schedules.

**17.** Programming Project 22 of Chapter 6.

**18.** Programming Project 23 of Chapter 6.

**19.** Programming Project 24 of Chapter 6.

**20.** Programming Project 25 of Chapter 6.

**21.** Programming Project 20 of Chapter 7.

**22.** Programming Project 21 of Chapter 8.

**23.** Design and implement an interactive, modular program that prompts the user to enter a positive integer, *limit*, and computes and prints on the monitor screen all prime Fibonacci numbers that are less than or equal to *limit*.

**24.** Construct a programmer-defined library named `areas` containing functions that can be used to compute areas of the following geometrical figures. Then write a driver program to test your library.
   **a.** Square: *Area* = $s \times s$, where s is the length of the side of the square.
   **b.** Rectangle: *Area* = $a \times b$, where $a$ and $b$ are the sides of the rectangle.
   **c.** Triangle: *Area* = $sqrt(s \times (s - a) \times (s - b) \times (s - c))$, where $a$, $b$, and $c$ are the sides of the triangle and $s = (a + b + c)/2$.
   **d.** Trapezoid: *Area* = $h \times (a + b)/2$, where $a$ and $b$ are the two parallel sides and $h$ is the distance between the two parallel sides of the trapezoid.

**25.** Construct a library named `volumes` containing functions that can be used to compute volumes of the following regular geometrical shapes. Write a driver program and test your library thoroughly.
   **a.** Right circular cylinder: *Volume* = $\pi r^2 h$, where $r$ is the radius of the base and $h$ is the height.
   **b.** Right circular cone: *Volume* = $\pi r^2 h/3$, where $r$ is the radius of the base and $h$ is the height.
   **c.** Sphere: *Volume* = $4 \pi r^3/3$, where $r$ is the radius of the sphere.
   **d.** Ellipsoid: *Volume* = $4 \pi a b c/3$, where $a$, $b$, and $c$ are the lengths of the semiaxes of the ellipsoid.

**26.** Construct a library named `sumOfPow` containing functions that compute the sums of powers of the first $n$ integers, where $n$ is a parameter of each function. Your library should include four functions, `sum_of_1st_power`, `sum_of_2nd_power`, `sum_of_3rd_power`, and `sum_of_4th_power`. Use the following identities in your functions:
   **a.** $1 + 2 + 3 + ... + n = n (n + 1)/2$
   **b.** $1^2 + 2^2 + 3^2 + ... + n^2 = n (n + 1) (2n + 1)/6$
   **c.** $1^3 + 2^3 + 3^3 + ... + n^3 = n^2 (n + 1)^2/4$
   **d.** $1^4 + 2^4 + 3^4 + ... + n^4 = n (n + 1) (2n + 1) (3n^2 + 3n - 1)/30$

Write a driver program and test your library. Suggest other and better ways of constructing such a library.

# chapter

# 11

# Arrays

---

**CHAPTER OBJECTIVES**

In this chapter you will learn about:

- **Lists and arrays**
  Arrays as a derived, structured data type
  One-dimensional arrays
  Close relationship between arrays and pointers
  Passing arrays to functions
  Dynamic variables and dynamic arrays

- **Sorting arrays**

- **Searching arrays**

- **Higher dimensional arrays**

By the time you have completed this chapter, you will have acquired the ability to:

- **Use arrays to structure data of the same type**

- **Use arrays in solving problems that require operations on lists**

---

## 11.1    INTRODUCTION

In Chapter 3 we defined a data type as a set of data values and a set of operations on those values. We classified them as built-in data types and programmer-defined data types. Built-in data types are recognized by the C compiler without any effort on the part of the programmer. Programmer-defined data types can be defined by the programmer and must be declared in a program. Built-in data types are further classified as fundamental and derived data types.

So far we have considered all C fundamental data types. They include `char`, `int`, `double`, `float`, `void`, and variations of `double` and `int`. If we declare a variable as one of these types, the compiler reserves a memory location for the variable. An important characteristic for variables of fundamental data types is that only one value is stored for each at any given time. In some applications, however, it is convenient to store related data values under a common name. For such applications we use derived data types.

As the term implies, a **derived data type** is derived from other data types. The important C derived data types are pointers to data of any type, arrays, structures, and unions. We have already begun our discussion of pointers, and we will continue with it. In this chapter you will learn about arrays. In the next chapter you will study structures and briefly touch on unions. You will see that arrays are a built-in type, whereas structures and unions are programmer defined. Also, you will see that some of the derived data types are referred to as **structured data types** because they can be used to represent data values that have a structure of some sort. The structured data types that the C language supports include arrays, structures, and unions. Therefore, arrays, the subject of this chapter, are a built-in, structured, derived data type.

## 11.2    LISTS AND ARRAYS

Many applications contain sets of related data items of the same type. For instance, in an application in which we want to compute the average of test scores for a class of 30 students, we have to come up with 30 identifiers from `test_score1` to `test_score30` just to store the test score values in the memory, and we have to keep track of each identifier during program development. It would be definitely better if we could use one identifier, such as `test_score`, to represent all 30 test scores and an index to specify the student to whom the test score belongs. For example, `test_score[1]` would represent the test score of the first student, `test_score[2]` that of the second, and so on. The good news is that we can do this in C by using arrays.

Actually, a collection of test score values for 30 students has to be ordered such that the first value is the first student's score, the second value belongs to the second student, and so on. Such a collection is called a list, and it can be represented as *test_score = (89, 79, 88, 100, ..., 67)*.

> A **list** is a variable-size collection of data items of the same type, which are arranged in a linear fashion.

The linear arrangement in a list implies that each list element except the first has a predecessor that immediately precedes it and that each list element except the last has a successor that immediately follows it. For example, in the list *test_score = (89, 79, 88, 100, ..., 67)*, the list element 79 has 89 as its predecessor and 88 as its successor.

To store a list in the computer's memory, we use an array.

---

An **array** (or a one-dimensional array) is a fixed-size collection of consecutive memory locations. Each memory location in an array is accessed by a relative address called an **index** (or a **subscript**).

---

Each element of an array is of the same data type. An array consists of a fixed number of elements. The array `test_score` in Figure 11.1 has 30 elements. In C the first element of an array has an index value of 0, not 1. Therefore, the index of the last element of an array of 30 elements is 29.

```
index ———>   0   1   2   3   4  ....  27  28  29
test_score | ? | ? | ? | ? | ? | ? | ? | ? | ? |
```

**Figure 11.1**    An array of 30 elements with no values

We can store a list in an array. Figure 11.2 shows a list of size 4 in an array of size 30.

```
index ———>    0   1   2   3    4  ....  27  28  29
test_score | 89| 79| 88|100| ? | ? | ? | ? | ? |
```

**Figure 11.2**    A list of size 4 in an array of 30 elements

In Figure 11.2 the first array element has the name `test_score[0]`, and it contains the integer value of 89; the second array element is `test_score[1]` storing the value 79; and so on. Because we have only four list elements in 30 array elements, we can add more elements to the list and can go up to 30 elements.

## Declaring Arrays

We can declare an array variable directly using the following format:

---

*TypeSpecifier Identifier[ArraySize]* ;

---

Here *TypeSpecifier* is any legal C data type specifier, and *ArraySize* is either a constant or a named constant. The symbol `[]` is an operator in C; it is called the **subscripting array reference operator**.

For example, the array `test_score` can be declared as

```
int test_score[30];
```

This declaration causes the compiler to reserve 30 consecutive memory locations, each of type `int`. The first array element has the index (or subscript) of 0, and the 30th array element has the subscript 29.

**Example 11.1**   To store and organize in the memory the salaries of the employees of a company, we can declare an array as

```
double salary[50];
```

This declaration instructs the compiler to reserve 50 consecutive memory locations for the array `salary`. Each element of this array is of type `double`. The same can be achieved by the declaration

```
double salary[ARRAY_SIZE];
```

where `ARRAY_SIZE` is the named constant declared by the `#define` preprocessor directive

```
#define ARRAY_SIZE 50
```

The declaration of the named constant `ARRAY_SIZE` must precede the declaration of the array `salary`. Before program compilation the preprocessor replaces all occurrences of the named constant ARRAY_SIZE in the program by 50. You should note that, like all other preprocessor directives, the `#define` directive does not terminate with a semicolon.

To reference an array element, we use the name of the array and follow it with a subscript expression enclosed by brackets. For example, `test_score[4]` references the fifth array element. Subscript expressions may be constants, variables, or expressions; in all cases they must be integers or quantities that can be converted to integers.

**Example 11.2**   The following entries are valid examples of array element references based on the declarations in Example 11.1. Let us assume that the value of the integer variable `j` is 4.

| | |
|---|---|
| `salary[24]` | References the 25th element of salary. |
| `salary[j]` | References the 5th element of salary. |
| `salary[j*j+1]` | References the 18th element of salary. |
| `salary[j-1]` | References the 4th element of salary. |

As you can see, it is possible to use expressions for array subscripts in array element references. What happens if the value computed for a subscript expression turns out to be larger than the maximum allowable value? For example, what if we have the array element reference `salary[j*j*j-14]`, and the current value of the variable `j` is 4? At run time the expression `j*j*j-14` computes to 50, and this array element reference is interpreted as `salary[50]`. However, because salary has been declared as an array of size 50, its subscripts can be in the range 0 through 49. The subscript value of 50 is illegal. Any subscript value that is less than zero is also illegal. C has no array bounds checking. Therefore, if your program uses illegal subscript values at run time, you may have an error message; alternatively, the array element reference may be to a location with unknown content and may result in incorrect computed values, or your system may crash. To prevent illegal references to array elements, you should program defensively.

***Example 11.3***   If our array declaration is

```
double salary[50];
```

and we want to execute the statement

```
final_salary = 1.05 * salary[j + 5];
```

then a safer method follows.

```
if (j + 5 > 49)
      printf("Warning: out of bounds reference to salary.");
else
      final_salary = 1.05 * salary[j + 5];
/* end if */
```

## Initialization of Arrays

After an array is declared, its elements must be initialized. Otherwise, they will contain unknown data (that is, "garbage"). An array can be initialized at run time or at compile time.

**Run-Time Initialization of Arrays**   An array can be initialized explicitly at run time. Array initialization can be full or partial. For example, the `for` statement

```
for (i = 0; i < 50; i++)
      salary[i] = 0.0;
/* end for */
```

initializes all 50 elements of the array `salary` to 0.0. On the other hand, the `for` statement

```
for (i = 0; i < 10; i++)
      salary[i] = 0.0;
/* end for */
```

initializes the first 10 elements of the array `salary` to 0.0.

**Compile-Time Initialization of Arrays**   It is possible to initialize arrays at compile time while declaring them. This approach requires a list of initializers separated by commas, all enclosed by braces, and placed after the array declaration and an equal sign. An initializer must be a constant value. For example, the declaration

```
int test_score[5] = {88, 99, 100, 90, 70};
```

will create an array of five elements such that `test_score[0]` is initialized to 88, `test_score[1]` is initialized to 99, and so on.

We can declare and initialize an array without explicitly indicating the array size. For example, the declaration

```
int test_score[] = {88, 99, 100, 90, 70};
```

is valid. It declares `test_score` as an array of size 5 because we have five initializers in the list. At the same time this declaration initializes the array elements to the values of the initializers.

If we have more initializers than the number of elements in an array, we will have a compilation error. For example, the declaration

```
int test_score[5] = {88, 99, 100, 90, 70, 85};
```

will not work, since we have six initializers and only five array elements.

A compile-time array initialization can be partial. In other words, the number of initializers may be less than the number of array elements. In this case the remaining array elements are initialized to 0 if the array type is numeric and to `NULL` if the array type is `char`. For example,

```
int test_score[5] = {80, 90};
```

will initialize the first two elements of the array `test_score` to 80 and 90, respectively, and the remaining three elements to 0. On the other hand, the declaration

```
char sym[5] = {'a'};
```

will initialize `sym[0]` to `'a'` and the remaining four elements to `NULL`.

## Operations on Arrays

The operations that we can perform on array elements are defined by those that we can perform on any variable that is of the same type as the array itself. For example, if an array is of type `int` as in

```
int test_score[30];
```

then we can input values into array elements, output their values, perform arithmetic on them, use them in conditional expressions, and pass them to functions. Therefore, all of the following statements are valid:

```
scanf("%d", &test_score[2]);
printf("%d", test_score[2]);
test_score[3] = 1.05 * test_score[3];
```

```
        if (test_score[i] > largest)
               largest = test_score[i];
        /* end if */

        print_test_score(test_score[i]);
```

The last example assumes that `print_test_score` is a programmer-defined function with one integer parameter.

Is it possible to reference an array without using a subscript? What happens if we execute the following statement?

```
        printf("%x", test_score);
```

Instead of displaying a value stored in the array `test_score`, this statement will print an address on the screen because in C, the name of an array without a subscript is a pointer to the first element of the array. Here the format specifier `%x` prints a hexadecimal value.

***Example 11.4*** Consider the following simple program:

```
 1   #include <stdio.h>

 2   int main(void) {
 3       int test_score[4] = {80, 100, 95, 78};
 4       int *pointer_to_test_score = &test_score[0];

 5       printf("%x\n", pointer_to_test_score);
 6       printf("%x\n", test_score);

 7       printf("%d\n", *pointer_to_test_score);
 8       printf("%d\n", *test_score);
 9       printf("%d\n", test_score[0]);
10       return 0;
11   } /* end function main */
```

In this program the declaration on line 3 declares `test_score` as an integer array of size 4 and initializes its elements to the values shown. The declaration on line 4 is for `pointer_to_test_score`, a pointer variable that points to the first element of the array, `test_score[0]`. The next two `printf` function calls will print the same address of the memory location that belongs to the first array element. This address is system-dependent. The last three statements with `printf` calls are identical in effect and will all print the content of the array element `test_score[0]`, which is 80.

The fact that in C the name of an array is a pointer to its first element is useful in two situations: in processing arrays by using pointers and in passing arrays to functions by pointers. We discuss both situations in the following sections.

## Arrays, Pointers, and Pointer Arithmetic

We can reference the first element of an array using the array name with a zero subscript as in `test_score[0]` for the array `test_score`. This notation is called the **array subscript notation**. Because the name of an array used without a subscript is a pointer to its first element, we have another way to reference its first element. For the array `test_score`, `*test_score` is also a reference to its first element.

Let us assume that we have the following declarations:

```
int test_score[4] = {80, 100, 95, 78};
int *ptr = test_score;
```

The second declaration is for a pointer variable `ptr`, pointing to the first element of the array. Now the first element of the array has three names: `test_score[0]`, `*test_score`, and `*ptr`. Figure 11.3a shows the situation in the memory at this point. In this figure we are assuming that the address of the first element of the array is 5000 and that the word length for integer type data is two bytes.

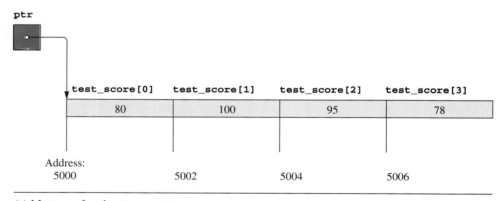

(a) Memory after the statement: **int \*ptr = test_score;**

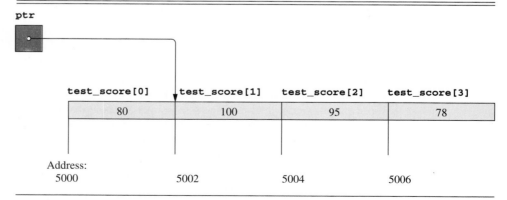

(b) Memory after the statement: **ptr = ptr + 1;**

**Figure 11.3**     Pointer arithmetic on a pointer to an array

We know that we can use the form `test_score[1]` to reference the second element of the array. On the other hand, we can change the value of the pointer variable `ptr` as

```
ptr = ptr + 1;
```

This statement involves an arithmetic operation, +, on the operand `ptr`, which is a pointer containing an address. Had this been conventional arithmetic, the result of the expression would be 5001. However, because `ptr` is a pointer, the computer performs pointer arithmetic. In **pointer arithmetic** the result of the preceding expression will be another address obtained by adding to the address value in `ptr` the number of bytes the machine uses to store an integer variable in the memory, which we have assumed to be 2. Therefore, the new value of `ptr` will be the address 5002. As 5002 is the address of the second element of the array `test_score`, `*ptr` will be a reference to the array element `test_score[1]` and the statement

```
printf("%d", *ptr);
```

will print its value, 100. Figure 11.3b shows `ptr` pointing to the second array element after it has been incremented by 1.

Therefore, we can process an array conventionally using subscripted variables or using pointers and pointer arithmetic. For example, the effect of the `for` statement

```
for (i = 0; i < 4; i++)
      printf("%d   ", test_score[i]);
/* end for */
```

is exactly the same as that of

```
for (j = 0; j < 4; j++)
      printf("%d   ", *(ptr + j));
/* end for */
```

They both print the full content of the array on a line. The second form uses pointer arithmetic. The integer value of the variable `j` in the expression `*(ptr + j)` is called the **offset** to the pointer. Note that parentheses are necessary in this expression because the operator + has a lower precedence than the indirection operator, *. The notation used in this expression is called the **pointer/offset notation**.

Pointer arithmetic in C is limited to only two operations: addition and subtraction.

1. We can add an integer constant to a pointer variable, using the +, ++, and += operators.

2. We can subtract an integer constant from a pointer variable, using the -, --, and -= operators.

3. We can subtract a pointer variable from another pointer variable.

***Example 11.5*** Suppose we have the following declarations for the array `test_score` and the pointers `ptr1` and `ptr2`:

```
int test_score[4] = {80, 100, 95, 78};
int *ptr1 = test_score;
```

```
int *ptr2 = test_score;
```

At this point in the program, both pointers `ptr1` and `ptr2` point to the first element of `test_score`. Now consider the statement

```
ptr2 = ptr2 + 3;
```

which involves pointer arithmetic. This statement adds an offset of 3 to the address stored in `ptr2`. Now, `ptr2` points to `test_score[3]`, the fourth element of the array. The output statement

```
printf("%d", ptr2 - ptr1);
```

involves an expression with pointer arithmetic, `ptr2 - ptr1`. This statement will print 3, which is the number of array elements from the first to the fourth.

Finally, the statement

```
ptr2 = ptr2 - 1;
```

subtracts an offset of 1 from `ptr2`, placing in it the address of the third element of `test_score`. The statement

```
printf("%d", *ptr2);
```

will print 95, the value of `test_score[2]`.

Pointer arithmetic is meaningless unless it is done on an array. Only if a pointer is declared in reference to an array will additions and subtractions produce pointer values that can be used to access array elements. We must be careful not to create addresses in pointer variables that are outside array bounds. In other words, a pointer for an array must not be permitted to point to an address before the first array element or to one that is after the last element. Finally, in subtracting one pointer variable from another, we must ensure that both pointers are declared for the same array.

The C compilers are designed to convert all array element references in the subscript notation to pointer notation during compilation. Accordingly, one advantage of using the pointer notation for arrays is a reduction in the program compilation time. On the other hand, compared to subscript notation, pointer notation is less clear for many people. Therefore, unless you have a very good reason for using the pointer notation in array manipulations, we suggest that you use subscript notation.

## Passing Arrays to Functions

We can pass individual array elements between functions by treating them as variables. In this respect, you have nothing new to learn. However, to pass a complete array to a function as a parameter, keep the following points in mind:

1.   The array must be declared as a formal parameter of the function. In such a declaration the array name must be followed by a right and a left bracket with no array size information. For example, in the function definition header

```
void input_test_scores(int *list_size, int test_scores[])
```

the second parameter is an integer type array, called `test_scores`. Since the name of an array is a pointer to its first element, we can use `int *test_scores` instead of `int test_scores[]` in the pointer/offset notation and, equivalently, write this function header as

`void input_test_scores(int *list_size, int *test_scores)`

2.   The function prototype must also indicate that the parameter is an array, as in

`void input_test_scores(int *list_size, int test_scores[]);`

which is equivalent to the following prototype, written using the pointer/offset notation:

`void input_test_scores(int *list_size, int *test_scores);`

3.   A call to such a function must include an array name as the corresponding actual parameter. Example:

`input_test_scores(&list_size, test_scores);`

In this function call the second parameter `test_scores` must be the name of an array that is properly declared before the function call.

Note that the actual argument corresponding to an array in a function call appears as the name of the array without any subscripts. Therefore, it is a pointer to the array. In other words, what is passed to the called function is a pointer to the array. Despite that, if we plan to use the subscript notation for the array in the called function, we do not need and must not use the indirection operator as a prefix to array element references.

If we pass arrays to functions this way, we are using parameter passing by pointers. In fact, in C, arrays can be passed to functions only by pointers; pass by value is not permitted. The called function can access elements of the array using this pointer, and hence a copy of the entire array is not made in the called function's data area. When duplicated, a large array eats up a lot of memory space. Therefore, passing arrays by pointers is significantly more efficient than passing arrays by value. You should also note that an array cannot be returned under a function name.

This way of passing arrays to functions is fine, provided the function makes changes in the elements of the passed array. However, if we want to use the inherent advantage of pass by value to write-protect array elements, then we may declare the passed array in the function declaration with the `const` qualifier, as shown in the following function definition header:

`void print_array(int list_size, const int test_scores[])`

The qualifier `const` is the qualifier we use in declaring named constants; it does the same thing here. If the called function attempts to access and modify an element of the passed array, the compiler generates a syntax error. This qualifier enables us to eliminate attempts in the called function to alter the contents of the array elements. When we use this technique, we must indicate the const qualifier also in the function prototype:

`void print_array(int list_size, const int test_scores[]);`

You should realize that even when you use the `const` qualifier, the array is being passed by pointers, and not by value. You should also remember that currently not all C compilers can enforce the semantics of the `const` qualifier properly. It is a good idea to test it on your system.

## Using `typedef` to Facilitate Program Modifiability

We are now able to appreciate the benefits of developing programs that are easy to modify. Because we may have to modify a program during its useful life, it is definitely to our advantage to design a program in which we can implement future changes without difficulty. Three techniques in C facilitate program modifiability:

1.  Modular design
2.  Use of named constants
3.  Use of `typedefs`

We know that one of the major benefits of modular program design is program modifiability; if a module needs to be rewritten, only that module will be replaced by the updated version. We don't have to worry about the rest of the program.

We also know about named constants. If we use a named constant, instead of a constant value that repeats itself in a program, and that constant value changes in the future, rather than pinpointing all occurrences of that constant and changing them, all we have to do is change the value of the named constant and recompile the program.

The third technique is the use of `typedefs`. In C `typedef` declarations declare synonyms for data types. The syntax of the `typedef` declarations follows.

---

typedef *TypeSpecifier SynonymList*;

---

*TypeSpecifier* is any type specifier, and *SynonymList* is a list of synonyms that we plan to use in our program instead of *TypeSpecifier*. For example, the declaration

```
typedef int project_score, test_score;
```

creates two synonyms, `project_score` and `test_score`, for the type specifier `int`. You should note that by this `typedef` declaration, we have not created new data types; we have simply assigned new names to one of the existing data types, `int`. Now our program can have variable declarations such as

```
project_score project1_score, project2_score;
test_score test1_score, test2_score, final_exam_score;
```

These declarations are equivalent to

```
int project1_score, project2_score;
int test1_score, test2_score, final_exam_score;
```

Clearly, `typedef` can be useful in enhancing the readability of a program; `test_score` may make more sense than `int` to a novice reader of the program. However, the most important advantage of `typedef` arises when a set of identifiers of a given type in a program will probably have to undergo a type change in the future. For example, suppose we have an application that involves some arrays and associated variables, all of type `int`, and we develop the application to our satisfaction. Say in a few weeks, we learn that the same application needs to be developed for arrays of type `double`. What to do? Well, we can always find the declarations for the the identifiers to be re-typed, change their type specifiers from `int` to `double`, and recompile the source program. Had we been wise, however, and used a `typedef` declaration such as

```
typedef int list_item_type;
```

and declared all our identifiers using the synonym `list_item_type` instead of `int`, as in

```
list_item_type array1[ARRAY_SIZE];
```

we would be able to modify the program just by replacing the `typedef` declaration, at only one point in the program, by

```
typedef double list_item_type;
```

In sections 11.5 and 11.6, we will use `typedefs` in connection with two applications while developing a sort and a search library.

## REVIEW QUESTIONS

**1.**  Which of the following statements concerning arrays in C is *incorrect*?
**a.** They can be used to store lists.
**b.** Each element of an array can be accessed using a relative address called an index.
**c.** The index of the first element of an array is always 1.
**d.** The index of the last element of a one-dimensional array of size 30 is 29.

**2.**  Which of the following array declarations is correct? Assume that `ARRAY_SIZE` is a named constant.
**a.** `double array salary[30];`
**b.** `double salary[];`
**c.** `double salary[i + 1];`
**d.** `double salary[ARRAY_SIZE];`
**e.** All of the above.
**f.** None of the above.

**3.**  The declaration `int array1[] = {0};`
**a.** Is illegal.
**b.** Declares a one-dimensional array of size 1 and initializes the only element to 0.
**c.** Declares a one-dimensional array of variable size and initializes all elements to 0.
**d.** Declares a one-dimensional array of variable size and initializes the first element to 0.
**e.** All of the above are correct.
**f.** None of the above is correct.

**4.**  In C the name of an array without a subscript is a pointer to the first element of the array. (T or F)

**5.**  Given the array declaration `int degree[5] = {15, 17, 19, 21, 23};`
The statement `printf("%d", *(degree + 2));`
**a.** Is illegal.
**b.** Will print the address of the first element of `degree`.

    **c.** Will print 19.

    **d.** Will print 15.

    **e.** Will print 23.

**6.** A pointer variable can be subtracted from another pointer variable only if both are declared for the same array. (T or F)

**7.** Choose the *incorrect* statement. In passing arrays to functions:

    **a.** The function call must have an actual parameter, which is the name of the array to be passed without brackets.

    **b.** What is actually passed to the called function is a pointer to the array. Hence in C arrays are passed only by pointers.

    **c.** In the called function we must use the indirection operator to precede array elements when they are expressed in the subscript notation.

    **d.** To write-protect array elements, the passed array declaration must have the `const` qualifier.

**8.** Which of the following is *not* a technique in C that can be used to facilitate program modifiability?

    **a.** Use of `typedefs`

    **b.** Modular program design

    **c.** Use of arrays

    **d.** Use of named constants

**Answers:**  1. c; 2. d; 3. b; 4. T; 5. c; 6. T; 7. c; 8. c.

---

## 11.3    EXAMPLE PROGRAM 1: A C Program that Computes Distribution of Letter Grades

Our first application program in this chapter is the problem that we solved in Example Program 1 in Chapter 9. In that problem we developed a program to let an instructor enter letter grades and then compute and print on the screen a letter grade distribution table, the class grade point average, and a vertical bar chart of grade distribution. We will solve the same problem here using arrays. However, we will omit the generation of the bar chart until later in this chapter, after we cover two-dimensional arrays.

    Basically, the requirements specification, analysis, and design steps for this problem are unchanged from those given in Chapter 9. Our modularization scheme is slightly different, however. We will have a main program and three functions:

1.  `input_grades`, which reads letter grades and stores them in an array.

2.  `compute_grade_distribution`, which has the array of letter grades as its input and then computes and returns in another array the distribution of letter grades.

3.  `computed_GPA`, which computes and returns the class grade point average, given the class size and the distribution of letter grades.

    The C program for this design is given in Figure 11.4.

```c
/*******************************************************************
  Program Filename: prog11_1.c
  Author           : Uckan
  Purpose          : Computes the distribution of letter grades.
  Input from       : terminal keyboard
  Output to        : screen
 *******************************************************************/
#include <stdio.h>

#define ARRAY_SIZE 60

/* Function prototypes: */

void input_grades(int *list_size, char letter_grades[]);
void compute_grade_distribution(int list_size,
     const char letter_grades[], int distribution[]);
double computed_GPA(int list_size, const int distribution[]);


int main(void) {
     /* Local variables: */

     char letter_grades[ARRAY_SIZE];
     int distribution[5] = {0};
     int list_size;

     /* Function body: */

     input_grades(&list_size, letter_grades);
     compute_grade_distribution(list_size, letter_grades,
          distribution);

     printf("\nRESULTS:\n");
     printf("Number of A grades: %d\n", distribution[0]);
     printf("Number of B grades: %d\n", distribution[1]);
     printf("Number of C grades: %d\n", distribution[2]);
     printf("Number of D grades: %d\n", distribution[3]);
     printf("Number of F grades: %d\n", distribution[4]);
     printf("Total number of grades: %d\n", list_size);

     printf("Class average: %.2f",
          computed_GPA(list_size, distribution));
     return 0;
} /* end function main */
```

Figure 11.4    A C program that computes distribution of letter grades (*continued*)

```
/*****************************************************************
  Function Name    : input_grades
  Purpose          : Reads letter grades into an array until the user
                     types 'Z'.
  Called by        : main
  Receives         : None
  Returns          : list_size, letter_grades
 *****************************************************************/
void input_grades(int *list_size, char letter_grades[]) {
     // Local variables:

     char grade, new_line;

     /* Function body: */

     *list_size = 0;

     printf("Enter letter grade. Type Z to terminate data input: ");
     scanf("%c", &grade);
     scanf("%c", &new_line);

     while (grade != 'Z' && grade != 'z') {
          if (grade == 'A' || grade == 'B' || grade == 'C' ||
                 grade == 'D' || grade == 'F' ||
                 grade == 'a' || grade == 'b' || grade == 'c' ||
                 grade == 'd' || grade == 'f') {
                 letter_grades[*list_size] = grade;
                 *list_size = *list_size + 1;
          }
          else
                 printf("Incorrect letter grade.\n");
          /* end if */

          printf("Enter letter grade: ");
          scanf("%c", &grade);
          scanf("%c", &new_line);
     } /* end while */
} /* end function input_grades */
```

Figure 11.4                                                              ▶

```
/***************************************************************
  Function Name    : compute_grade_distribution
  Purpose          : Computes the distribution of letter grades
                     stored in an array.
  Called by        : main
  Receives         : list_size, letter_grades, distribution
  Returns          : distribution
 ***************************************************************/
void compute_grade_distribution(int list_size,
                                const char letter_grades[],
                                int distribution[]) {

       /* Local variables: */

       int i;

       /* Function body: */

       for (i = 0; i < list_size; i++)
            switch (letter_grades[i]) {
                  case 'A' : case 'a' :
                        distribution[0]++; break;
                  case 'B' : case 'b' :
                        distribution[1]++; break;
                  case 'C' : case 'c' :
                        distribution[2]++; break;
                  case 'D' : case 'd' :
                        distribution[3]++; break;
                  case 'F' : case 'f' :
                        distribution[4]++;
            } /* end switch */
       /* end for */
} /* end function compute_grade_distribution */


/***************************************************************
  Function Name    : computed_GPA
  Purpose          : Computes and returns the class GPA using
                     the letter grades stored in an array.
  Called by        : main
  Receives         : list_size, distribution
  Returns          : GPA under function name
 ***************************************************************/
```

Figure 11.4

```
double computed_GPA(int list_size, const int distribution[]) {
      /* Local variables: */

      double GPA;

      /* Function body: */

      if (list_size != 0)
            GPA = (4.0 * distribution[0] + 3.0 * distribution[1] +
                     2.0 * distribution[2] + distribution[3]) /
                     list_size;
      else
            GPA = 0.0;
      /* end if */

      return GPA;
} /* end function computed_GPA */
```

**Figure 11.4**                                                                        ■

We note the following points about this program:

1.  We have a named constant declaration for `ARRAY_SIZE` through a `#define` preprocessor directive and a one-dimensional array declaration local to the function `main` for a character array, called `letter_grade`, of a maximum size of `ARRAY_SIZE` (in this case, 60).

2.  The function `input_grades` has a pointer parameter, `list_size`, and an array parameter, `letter_grades`, passed to it by a pointer. Its body is essentially similar to a code segment in the main program of Example 9.1. It prompts the user to type letter grade values, either in lowercase or in capital letters, validates the typed values, and stores them in the array `letter_grades`. It terminates the input of letter grades when the user enters z or Z, and returns the array `letter_grades` and its actual size, as `list_size`, to the calling program.

3.  The second function in our design is `compute_grade_distribution`. It receives two data values, `list_size` and `letter_grades`, and returns the array `distribution`. Note the use of the qualifier `const` with the declaration of the array parameter `letter_grades`. This qualifier ensures that the function does not alter the values of the element of `letter_grades`. The function computes a letter grade distribution, stores it in the array `distribution` such that the number of As is in `distribution[0]`, the number of Bs is in `distribution[1]`, and so on, and returns this array to the calling function.

4.  In the function `main`, we have

```
int distribution[5] = {0};
```

which declares `distribution` as an integer array of size 5 and initializes its elements to 0. Therefore, we don't have to initialize these elements in the function `compute_grade_distribution`.

5. The output statement

```
printf("Class average: %.2f",
       computed_GPA(list_size, distribution));
```

in the main function contains a call to the function `computed_GPA`. This function has a value parameter, `list_size`, and an array parameter, `distribution`, protected against alterations by the `const` qualifier. It simply computes the class grade point average and returns it under its name.

The output of this program is exactly the same as that of Example Program 1 of Chapter 9, as shown in Figure 9.17, except for the bar chart.

## 11.4   DYNAMIC VARIABLES AND DYNAMIC ARRAYS

So far, in every program that we wrote, we created variables by declaring them as global, local, or parameter variables. In Chapter 6 you learned that global variables have static duration (that is, their locations in the memory exists until the program terminates) and that local and parameter variables have local duration (that is, their storage locations exist while the block in which they are declared is being executed). Variables and arrays may also be created dynamically at run time.

### Dynamic Variables

In C it is possible to create variables at run time, use them, and destroy them when we no longer need them. Such variables are called **dynamic variables**, and after their creation they exist until they are destroyed. Dynamic variables are said to have **dynamic duration**.

To create a dynamic variable, we must take the following actions:

1. Decide about the type of the data to be stored in such a variable.
2. Declare a pointer variable of that data type.
3. Assign to the pointer variable the address created by the standard library function `malloc`.

Suppose we want to create a dynamic variable of type `int`. We first declare a pointer variable of type `int` (see Figure 11.5):

```
int *ptr;
```

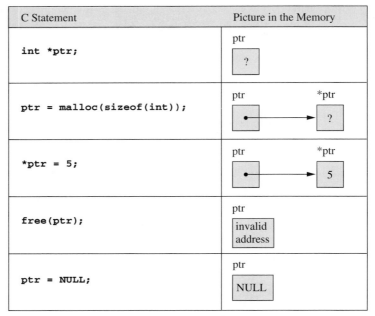

| C Statement | Picture in the Memory |
|---|---|
| `int *ptr;` | ptr<br>? |
| `ptr = malloc(sizeof(int));` | ptr    *ptr<br>●———→ ? |
| `*ptr = 5;` | ptr    *ptr<br>●———→ 5 |
| `free(ptr);` | ptr<br>invalid address |
| `ptr = NULL;` | ptr<br>NULL |

**Figure 11.5**    Creation and deletion of a dynamic variable

This declaration creates a memory location without any value assignment for the variable ptr, with the understanding that ptr may store a memory address to a location that is suitable for integer values. Next, we use the function malloc as follows:

        ptr = malloc(sizeof(int));

The function malloc is declared in the standard header file stdlib.h. Therefore, to use it, we need the preprocessor directive #include <stdlib.h> in our program. The argument of malloc is the number of bytes to be allocated for the dynamic variable that it creates. Normally, we use the sizeof operator on a data type to specify the number of bytes as the argument of malloc. A call to malloc causes the operating system to allocate from the free store a memory location that can store a value in the indicated number of bytes. **Free store** (or **heap**) is the collection of unallocated memory locations maintained by the operating system during the execution of a program. In this example the call to malloc instructs the operating system to allocate a memory location of sizeof(int) bytes (that is, either 2 or 4 bytes, depending on the implementation of the language). If there is enough space in the free store, the operating system removes a memory location from the free store, presents it to the program, and makes its address available to malloc. In this case the function malloc returns the address of the dynamically allocated memory location. The preceding statement stores this address in the pointer variable ptr. In Figure 11.5 the directional line from the box for ptr to the dynamically created variable is the pictorial representation of the address placed in ptr. If there is no available space in the free store, malloc returns NULL.

It should be noted that the declaration

```
int *ptr;
```

and the assignment statement

```
ptr = malloc(sizeof(int));
```

can be combined and written as

```
int *ptr = malloc(sizeof(int));
```

Assuming the function `malloc` succeeds in returning an address, we have a pointer variable, `ptr`, pointing to a memory location. Chapter 9 explained that we may prefix the name of a pointer variable by the indirection operator, `*`, to reference the memory location pointed to by the pointer variable. Therefore, the name of the dynamic variable becomes `*ptr`. Now that we have a name for the dynamic variable, we may use it any way we want, for example, as follows:

```
*ptr = 5;
```

If, later in the program, we decide that we no longer need the variable `*ptr`, we may destroy it by using the `free` function on the pointer variable `ptr`:

```
free(ptr);
```

The `free` function, also declared in the header file `stdlib.h`, causes the operating system to reclaim the memory location pointed to by the pointer variable, which is the argument of `free`, and return this memory location to the free store. However, the memory location for the variable `ptr` is not deallocated, and its content is not changed. It still contains an address, which can no longer be used to access a part of the memory legally. Now if we use the variable `ptr` in an expression, we will definitely have serious problems during program execution. To avoid such an incidence, it is advisable to assign the value `NULL` to `ptr` immediately after the application of the `free` function:

```
ptr = NULL;
```

Dynamic variables are useful in applications that use data structures such as linked lists, trees, and graphs. These topics are outside the scope of this book. However, in this chapter we are interested in dynamically allocated arrays, for which we use similar principles.

## Dynamic Arrays

To create a dynamic array at run time, we first declare a pointer variable of the same type as the type of the array and then use the standard function `malloc` as follows:

```
int *arr = malloc(array_size * sizeof(int));
```

Here `array_size` must be a previously declared integer variable that contains an integer value. This statement does the following:

1. It causes the operating system to allocate a memory location to the pointer variable `arr`, with the understanding that it may contain an address to an array that is suitable to store integer values.

2. It instructs the operating system to allocate `array_size * sizeof(int)` bytes from the free store and present the address of the first byte to the function `malloc`.

3. This address is returned by `malloc` and is stored in the pointer variable `arr`. If the operating system is not successful in creating the array, the value returned by `malloc` is NULL.

Roughly the same effect can be achieved using another standard memory function, `calloc`, which is also declared in the header file `stdlib.h`, as follows:

```
int *arr = calloc(array_size, sizeof(int));
```

This function causes the operating system to allocate from the free store `array_size` memory locations, the size of each being `sizeof(int)` bytes, and present the address of the first memory location to `calloc`. Again, this address is stored in the pointer variable `arr`, and again, if the memory allocation operation fails, the value that is returned by `calloc` is NULL. The main difference between `malloc` and `calloc` in creating dynamic arrays is that `calloc` automatically initializes the created array to appropriate values (0 if the array is of numeric type, NULL if it is of type char), whereas `malloc` doesn't do automatic initialization.

Therefore, if successfully executed, either of the preceding statements will create a dynamic array of size `array_size` in the memory, as shown in Figure 11.6. The pointer variable `arr` will be pointing to the first element of the array. Since the name of a one-dimensional array is a pointer to its first element, the name of the pointer `arr` can be used as the name of the array. In array/subscript notation, the first element of the array is `arr[0]`, the second is `arr[1]`, and so on.

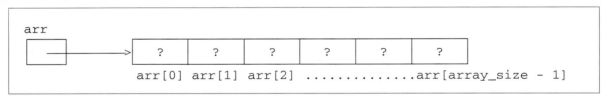

**Figure 11.6**     A dynamic array pointed to by a pointer variable `arr`

A dynamically created array can be destroyed by using the `free` function on the pointer to the array, as follows:

```
free(arr);
```

As the result of this operation, the elements of the dynamic array are reclaimed by the operating system and added to the free store. Again, it is good programming practice to set the pointer `arr` to NULL after the use of the function `free`:

```
arr = NULL;
```

***Example 11.6***   Figure 11.7 shows a function named `analyze_test_scores`, which performs these actions:

1. Creates a dynamic array called `test_scores` of size `array_size` using the function `calloc`.

2. Reads integers from a text file, whose external name is `A:TEST.TXT` and containing integer values separated by spaces from each other, and stores them in the array `test_scores`.

3. Processes the array `test_scores` to determine the maximum, minimum, and average of test score values and returns them to the calling program.

4. Deallocates the memory space reserved for the dynamic array using the function `free`.

```c
void analyze_test_scores(int array_size, int *maximum, int *minimum,
                         int *average) {
    /* Local variable declarations: */

    FILE *test_file;
    int *test_scores;
    int list_size = 0, count = 1, sum;

    /* Function body: */

    test_scores = calloc(array_size, sizeof(int));

    if ((test_file = fopen("A:TEST.TXT", "r")) == NULL) {
        fprintf(stderr, "***> Open error reading input file.");
        exit(-1);
    } /* end if */

    fscanf(test_file, "%d", &test_scores[list_size]);

    while (! feof(test_file)) {
        list_size++;
        fscanf(test_file, "%d", &test_scores[list_size]);
    } /* end while */

    fclose(test_file);

    *maximum = test_scores[0];
    *minimum = test_scores[0];
    sum = test_scores[0];
```

**Figure 11.7**    A C function that uses a dynamic array (*continued*)    ▶

```
        while (count < list_size) {
                if(*maximum < test_scores[count])
                        *maximum = test_scores[count];
                /* end if */

                if(*minimum > test_scores[count])
                        *minimum = test_scores[count];
                /* end if */

                sum = sum + test_scores[count];
                count++;
        } /* end while */

        free(test_scores);
        test_scores = NULL;

        *average = sum / list_size;
} /* end function analyze_test_scores */
```

Figure 11.7                                                                    ■

## 11.5  SORTING ARRAYS

In computer applications one of the most commonly performed operations on a list is sorting.

> **Sorting** is the process of transforming a list into an equivalent list, in which the elements are arranged in ascending or descending order.

A sorted list is called an **ordered list**. If an ordered list is stored in an array, the array is said to be sorted. In a sorted array *arr*, containing a list of *size n* in ascending order, we have

*arr[0] <= arr[1] <= ... <= arr[n–2] <= arr[n–1]*

Sorting is a frequent operation performed on lists. In general, we want to keep lists ordered in the computer's memory. Sorted lists are especially important in list searching because they facilitate search operations. We will discuss list searching in section 11.6. Because of the importance of sorting in practical applications, many sorting techniques have been developed. Some of these techniques are relatively simple; others are more complicated. In general, simple sorting techniques, although easier to program and debug, are significantly less efficient compared to complex sorting algorithms. However, if your list is not excessively large or if your application uses a sorting technique only a few times, simple sorting algorithms are useful. This section describes three simple sorting techniques that can be used to order lists stored in arrays.

## Bubble Sort

Suppose we have an array of five elements, called `array_to_sort`, as shown in Figure 11.8. This array is not ordered. It contains the integer value of 43 in its first element, followed by 22, 17, 36, and 16. Let us try comparing two consecutive array elements and swapping them if the first is greater than the second. For this array we go through the following steps:

**Step 1.** Compare `array_to_sort[0]` and `array_to_sort[1]`, (that is, 43 and 22). Because the first element is greater than the second, swap them so that we have 22 in `array_to_sort[0]` and 43 in `array_to_sort[1]`.

**Step 2.** Compare `array_to_sort[1]` and `array_to_sort[2]` and swap them. Now we have 17 in `array_to_sort[2]` and 43 in `array_to_sort[3]`.

**Step 3.** Compare `array_to_sort[2]` and `array_to_sort[3]` and swap them again. This produces 36 in `array_to_sort[2]` and 43 in `array_to_sort[3]`.

**Step 4.** Compare `array_to_sort[3]` and `array_to_sort[4]` and swap them. We end up with 16 in `array_to_sort[3]` and 43 in `array_to_sort[4]`.

Together, these steps are referred as a **pass**. At the end of the first pass, although the first four elements of the array are not yet in order, we have succeeded in pushing the largest value in the array to its end. In a sense the largest value has "bubbled" to the right because of four comparisons and exchanges. If this technique ultimately proves to be a working sorting algorithm — and you will see that it will — we can call it the **bubble sort** algorithm. In fact, the bubble sort algorithm is a variation of many sorting algorithms, collectively known as **exchange sort algorithms**.

Let us code the "swap" operation involved in the preceding steps. Assuming `temp` is a variable of the same type as the array `array_to_sort`, we can write:

```
temp = array_to_sort[i];
array_to_sort[i] = array_to_sort[i+1];
array_to_sort[i+1] = temp;
```

These statements will swap `array_to_sort[i]` and `array_to_sort[i+1]`.

The first pass of this algorithm can be generalized for an array containing a list, whose size is stored in the variable `list_size`. The C code follows figure 11.8.

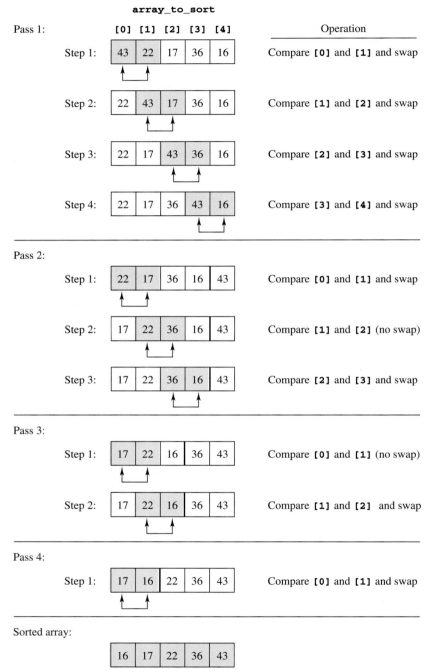

**Figure 11.8**    Bubble sort illustrated

```
for (i = 0; i < list_size - 1; i++) {
        if (array_to_sort[i] > array_to_sort[i+1]) {
                temp = array_to_sort[i];
                array_to_sort[i] = array_to_sort[i+1];
                array_to_sort[i+1] = temp;
        } /* end if */
} /* end for */
```

You should note that in this `for` statement, the loop control variable `i` is not permitted to assume the value `list_size - 1` to avoid an illegal array element reference in `array_to_sort[i+1]`.

Now let us continue applying the same technique to the first four elements of the array in Figure 11.8. In the second pass we go through three steps of comparisons and swaps and push the largest value in the first four elements of the array, which is 36, to the end of the list. At the conclusion of the second pass, we have an unordered list of three elements early in the array, followed by a sorted list of two elements. The third pass is applied on the first three elements, and it requires two steps to "bubble" the largest element to the right. Finally, the fourth pass will complete the job, and we have a sorted array.

We needed four passes to sort a list of five elements. Now we can refine our code as follows:

```
pass = 1;
while (pass < list_size) {
        for (i = 0; i < list_size - pass; i++) {
                if (array_to_sort[i] > array_to_sort[i+1]) {
                        temp = array_to_sort[i];
                        array_to_sort[i] = array_to_sort[i+1];
                        array_to_sort[i+1] = temp;
                } /* end if */
        } /* end for */
        pass = pass + 1;
} /* end while */
```

To improve the efficiency of this algorithm, we make the following observation. In any pass if no comparison results in a swap, then the list is already in order and we don't need to continue. We introduce into the preceding code a character variable called `exchanges`. Thus we obtain the following function shown in Figure 11.9 that sorts an array using the bubble sort algorithm.

```
void bubble_sort(int list_size, list_item_type array_to_sort[]) {
      /* Local variables: */

      int pass = 1, temp, i;
      char exchanges = 'y';

      /* Function body: */

      while (pass < list_size && exchanges == 'y') {
            exchanges = 'n';
            for (i = 0; i < list_size - pass; i++) {
                  if (array_to_sort[i] > array_to_sort[i+1]) {
                        temp = array_to_sort[i];
                        array_to_sort[i] = array_to_sort[i+1];
                        array_to_sort[i+1] = temp;
                        exchanges = 'y';
                  } /* end if   */
            } /* end for */

            pass = pass + 1;
      } /* end while */
} /* end function bubble_sort */
```

**Figure 11.9**    A C function that sorts an array using bubble sort

Note that the function presented in Figure 11.9 uses the formal parameter declaration, `list_item_type array_to_sort[]`, for the array `array_to_sort`. Here `list_item_type` is a synonym for the type of the data in `array_to_sort`. If we use this function to sort an integer array, then our program should include the `typedef` declaration

```
typedef int list_item_type;
```

### Selection Sort

Another simple sorting technique is based on the idea of selecting the largest array element and swapping it with the last array element. The result is an unsorted list whose size is 1 less than the size of the original list, which is followed by a sorted list of size 1. (Remember, a single value is a sorted list of size 1.) If we do this step again on the unsorted list, we will have an ordered list of size 2 at the end, and the size of the unordered list will be reduced by 1. Repetitive application of this process will give us a sorted list when the size of the unsorted list becomes one. This technique is known as simple **selection sort**.

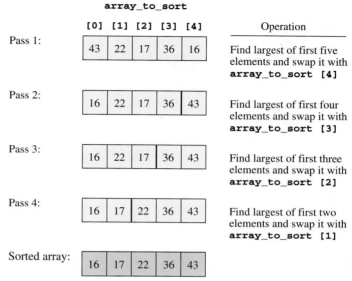

**Figure 11.10** Selection sort illustrated

To illustrate selection sort, consider Figure 11.10, which begins with an unsorted array of size 5. In the first pass we determine the largest element and swap it with the last array element. The largest array element is 43, found to be in `array_to_sort[0]`. Thus we exchange `array_to_sort[0]` and `array_to_sort[4]`. This exchange produces an unsorted list of size 4 in the array, followed by a sorted list of size 1. The operation of finding the largest element in a list of size `list_size` and swapping it with the last array element can be coded as follows:

```
index_of_largest = 0;

for (i = 1; i <= last; i++)
     if (array_to_sort[i] > array_to_sort[index_of_largest])
          index_of_largest = i;
     /* end if */
/* end for */

temp = array_to_sort[last];
array_to_sort[last] = array_to_sort[index_of_largest];
array_to_sort[index_of_largest] = temp;
```

The  for  statement determines the index of the largest element in a list of size list_size, and the next three statements do the exchange. Figure 11.10 shows that for an array of size 5, this process has to be repeated four times. Consequently, a C code for selection sort is as shown in Figure 11.11.

```c
void selection_sort(int list_size, list_item_type array_to_sort[]) {
    /* Local variables: */

    int i;
    int index_of_largest, last, temp;

    /* Function body: */

    for (last = list_size - 1; last >= 1; last--) {
        index_of_largest = 0;

        for (i = 1; i <= last; i++)
            if (array_to_sort[i] >
                array_to_sort[index_of_largest])
                    index_of_largest = i;
            /* end if */
        /* end for */

        temp = array_to_sort[last];
        array_to_sort[last] = array_to_sort[index_of_largest];
        array_to_sort[index_of_largest] = temp;
    } /* end for */
} /* end function selection_sort */
```

**Figure 11.11**    A C function that sorts an array using selection sort

### Insertion Sort

We will present another sorting algorithm that is based on the simple concept of inserting a new item into a list of ordered items of the same type. This algorithm uses operations that are similar to what we might do to order a hand of cards in a card game; take the second card and place it relative to the first such that the first two cards are ordered. Next, take the third card and insert it into the ordered set of two cards to end up with an ordered set of three cards, and so on. For the simple reason that we keep on inserting new items, this sorting algorithm is referred to as **insertion sort**.

Consider an unsorted array of five integers,  array_to_sort, shown in Figure 11.12. A list in a one-dimensional array may be perceived as consisting of two regions: a sorted region, followed by an unsorted one. Initially, the first list element, 43 in Figure 11.12, is an ordered list of size 1. The variable  unsorted  is the index of the first element of the unsorted region. We set  unsorted  to 1.

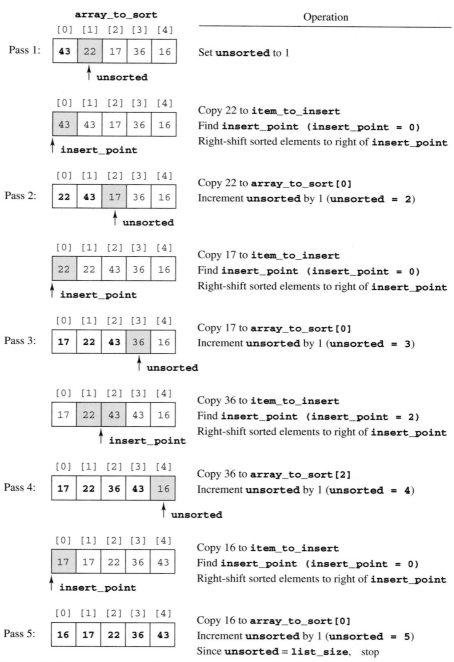

**Figure 11.12**   Insertion sort illustrated

In the first pass we want to insert the list element whose index is `unsorted` into the sorted region. To do so, we copy `array_to_sort[unsorted]` to a variable called `item_to_insert` using the statement

```
item_to_insert = array_to_sort[unsorted];
```

Next, we find the point of insertion, `insert_point`, in the sorted region, that is, the index of the list element that will be used to store `item_to_insert`, and right-shift all sorted list elements to its right. This can be done with the following code:

```
insert_point = unsorted;

while (insert_point > 0 &&
        array_to_sort[insert_point - 1] > item_to_insert) {
        array_to_sort[insert_point] = array_to_sort[insert_point - 1];
        insert_point--;
} /* end while */
```

Having determined the point of insertion, we insert `item_to_insert` into the sorted region using the statement

```
array_to_sort[insert_point] = item_to_insert;
```

This is the logic of a typical pass. At the end of each pass, the size of the sorted region is increased by 1 and the size of the unsorted region is decreased by 1. Clearly, for a list of size `list_size`, we need `list_size - 1` passes to fully sort the array. The function `insertion_sort` is given in Figure 11.13.

```
void insertion_sort(int list_size, list_item_type array_to_sort[]) {
        /* Local variables:    */

        list_item_type item_to_insert;
        int unsorted, insert_point;

        /* Function body: */

        for (unsorted = 1; unsorted < list_size; unsorted++) {
                item_to_insert = array_to_sort[unsorted];
                insert_point = unsorted;

                while (insert_point > 0 &&
                        array_to_sort[insert_point - 1] > item_to_insert) {
```

**Figure 11.13**    A C function that sorts an array using insertion sort *(continued)*    ▶

```
                    array_to_sort[insert_point] =
                        array_to_sort[insert_point - 1];
                    insert_point-;
            } /* end while */

            array_to_sort[insert_point] = item_to_insert;
        } /* end for */
} /* end function insertion_sort */
```

**Figure 11.13**                                                                  ■

## Constructing a Sort Library

Having described three basic sorting algorithms, we are at a good point to construct a pro-grammer-defined sort library. Sorting algorithms are general purpose, and once we have them in a library, we can use them in many applications without having to rewrite their implementations.

To construct a sort library, we must have a header file and an implementation file. We will call the header file `sort.h`. It will contain the declarations of the three sort functions, `bubble_sort`, `selection_sort`, and `insertion_sort`, that we have developed, plus the `typedef` declaration for `list_item_type`. The header file `sort.h` is given in Figure 11.14.

```
typedef int list_item_type;

/**************************************************************
  Function Name  : bubble_sort
  Purpose        : Sorts a one-dimensional array in increasing
                   order using the bubble sort algorithm.
  Receives       : list_size, array_to_sort
  Returns        : array_to_sort
 **************************************************************/
void bubble_sort(int list_size, list_item_type array_to_sort[]);

/**************************************************************
  Function Name  : selection_sort
  Purpose        : Sorts a one-dimensional array in increasing
                   order using the selection sort algorithm.
  Receives       : list_size, array_to_sort
  Returns        : array_to_sort
 **************************************************************/
void selection_sort(int list_size, list_item_type array_to_sort[]);
```

**Figure 11.14**    The header file `sort.h` for the programmer-defined sort library (*continued*)    ▶

```
/****************************************************************
Function Name    : insertion_sort
Purpose          : Sorts a one-dimensional array in increasing
                   order using the insertion sort algorithm.
Receives         : list_size, array_to_sort
Returns          : array_to_sort
****************************************************************/
void insertion_sort(int list_size, list_item_type array_to_sort[]);
```

**Figure 11.14**                                                                                 ■

The implementation file, which we will call sort.c, contains the preprocessor directive #include "sort.h", and the implementations of the functions bubble_sort, selection_sort, and insertion_sort, as given in Figures 11.9, 11.11, and 11.13. We will use this sort library in Example Program 2 in this chapter.

## 11.6   SEARCHING ARRAYS

Another common operation on arrays is the search operation. We search a list stored in an array to determine whether it contains an element that matches a given search key value. The **search key** is a data element of the same type as the list elements. If the process of searching finds a match of the search key value with a list element value, the search is said to be successful; otherwise, it is unsuccessful.

### Sequential Search

The simplest method of searching a list in an array is **sequential** (or **linear**) **search**. In sequential search, we access list elements, starting with the first, and compare each element with the search key. If we find a match, the search is successful. In this case we return the index of the list element that matches the search key. If we access and compare the last list element and still have no match, then the search is unsuccessful.

Figure 11.15 illustrates the logic of sequential search on an unordered list in an array. The list contains five integer elements, and it is unordered. In Figure 11.15a the search key is 25. In the first step we compare search_key with array_to_search[0]. We have no match, so in the second step we compare search_key with array_to_search[1], and so on. After the fifth step we conclude that the search is unsuccessful.

In Figure 11.15b the search key is 17. We apply the same logic; after three comparisons we find a match in array_to_search[2] and return 2 as the index of that list element.

We can easily convert this logic to a C function. Figure 11.16 is the function sequential_search_unordered with three input parameters, which are search_key, list_size, and the integer array array_to_search, and two output parameters, which are success and index. The variable success is a string

variable that returns the string  TRUE  if the search is successful; otherwise, it returns
FALSE. The variable  index  is used to return the index of the array element that matches
the search key if the search is successful; for an unsuccessful search, the value of  index  will be –1.

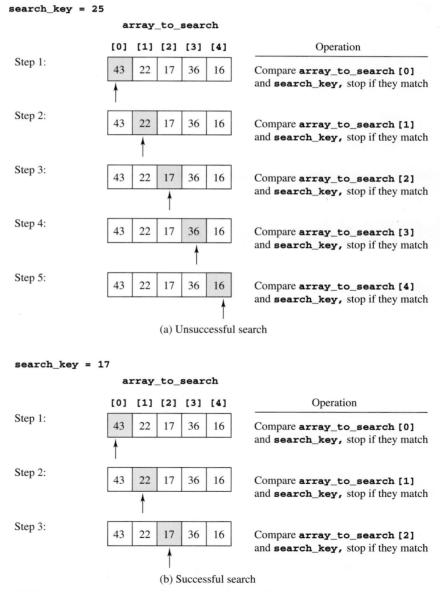

(a) Unsuccessful search

(b) Successful search

**Figure 11.15**   Sequential search of an unordered array illustrated

```
/*****************************************************************
  Function Name    : sequential_search_unordered
  Purpose          : Searches a one-dimensional unsorted array of
                     integers using the sequential search algorithm.
  Receives         : search_key, list_size, array_to_search
  Returns          : success, index
 *****************************************************************/
void sequential_search_unordered(list_item_type search_key,
                                 int list_size,
                                 const list_item_type
                                         array_to_search[],
                                 char success[], int *index) {
    /* Local variables: */

    int i;

    /* Function body: */

    strcpy(success, "FALSE");
    *index = -1;

    for (i = 0; i < list_size; i++)
        if (search_key == array_to_search[i]) {
            *index = i;
            strcpy(success, "TRUE");
            break;
        } /* end if */
    /* end for */
} /* end function sequential_search_unordered */
```

**Figure 11.16**    A C function that searches an unordered array sequentially

In the program of Figure 11.16, the integer array `array_to_search` is declared with a `const` qualifier as

```
const int array_to_search[]
```

because the sequential search logic does not need to and should not alter the array elements. Also, note the use of the `break` statement in the `if` statement; its purpose is to stop the search if a match for the search key is found.

The sequential search algorithm works well on small arrays. However, it is not very efficient for larger arrays because in the worst case it compares all elements of the array with the given search key before it can conclude that the search is unsuccessful. We can improve the efficiency of this algorithm by running it on an ordered list. In this case the algorithm terminates if the search key value turns out to be less than an array element. Figure 11.17 illustrates the sequential search technique on a sorted list. In Figure 11.17a the search key value is 25. After three unsuccessful comparisons, we find in the fourth step that the search key value is less than the list element value, which is 36. At this point we conclude that the list does not contain the search key value and terminate the algorithm without processing the rest of the list. In case the search is successful, as illustrated in Figure 11.17b, we really don't gain anything. However, for an unsuccessful search, especially if the search key is less than the majority of list elements, the gain in efficiency may be substantial.

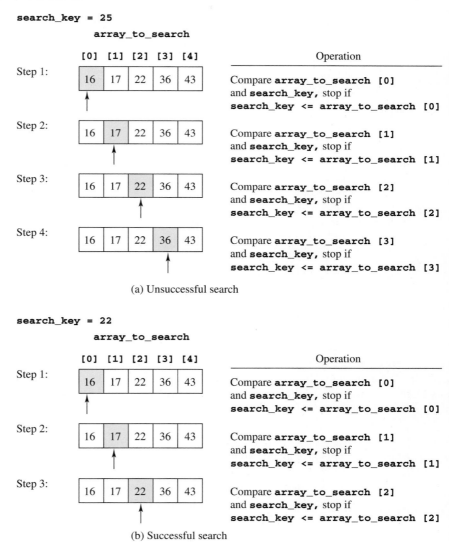

Figure 11.17    Sequential search of an ordered array illustrated

Figure 11.18 is a C function that implements the sequential search algorithm on an ordered list.

```
/****************************************************************
 Function Name    : sequential_search_ordered
 Purpose          : Searches a one-dimensional sorted array of
                    integers using the sequential search algorithm.
 Receives         : search_key, list_size, array_to_search
 Returns          : success, index
 ****************************************************************/
void sequential_search_ordered(list_item_type search_key,
                               int list_size,
                               const list_item_type array_to_search[],
                               char success[], int *index) {
      /* Local variables: */

      int i;

      /* Function body: */

      strcpy(success, "FALSE");
      *index = -1;

      for (i = 0; i < list_size; i++)
            if (search_key < array_to_search[i])
                  break;
            else if (search_key == array_to_search[i]) {
                  *index = i;
                  strcpy(success, "TRUE");
                  break;
            } /* end if */
      /* end for */
} /* end function sequential_search_ordered */
```

**Figure 11.18**    A C function that searches an ordered array sequentially

Once again, we note that two of the parameters of the functions in Figures 11.16 and 11.18, search_key and array_to_sort, are of type list_item_type, which is a synonym for whatever type the data in the list are. Therefore, we have a typedef declaration in our program, used to facilitate program modifiability.

## Binary Search

A very efficient list search algorithm is based on the application of the divide-and-conquer strategy to ordered lists. This technique, known as the **binary search** algorithm, compares the search key value with the value of the list element that is midway in the list. At this point we have three possibilities:

1. We have a match, in which case the search is successful and is terminated.

2. The search key value is less than the value of the middle element. In this case the second half of the list cannot possibly contain the search key value, and so we concentrate on the first half of the list.

3. The search key value may be greater than the value of the middle element. If so, we eliminate the first half of the list and concentrate on the second half.

Now, we have a smaller list to search; it is either the first or the second half. We apply the same logic on the half we have not eliminated and continue this way until we have a match or until the list size is reduced to one nonmatching element, which implies an unsuccessful search.

Figure 11.19 illustrates this technique. In Figure 11.19a the search key value is 17, and we have an ordered list of 10 elements stored in an array. We declare two variables, `first` and `last`, and set them to 0 and 9, respectively, to indicate the beginning and end of the list to be searched. The index of the middle element can be computed as

```
mid = (first + last) / 2;
```

This index, `mid`, must be an integer. If `first`, `last`, and `mid` are variables of type `int`, the preceding statement will compute 4 for `mid`. Thus we compare `search_key` with `array_to_search[4]` and find that `search_key` is less than `array_to_search[4]`, which is 26. Therefore, in the next step we apply the same technique on the sublist for which `first` remains the same, (that is, 0), and `last` becomes

```
last = mid - 1;
```

Had `search_key` been greater than `array_to_search[4]`, the value of `last` would not have changed, but `first` would have become

```
first = mid + 1;
```

so that we could search the second half of the list. In Figure 11.19a, after the fourth step, `last` becomes less than `first`, which is the termination condition for an unsuccessful search.

Figure 11.19b illustrates the binary search algorithm on the same list, this time with a search key value of 37. In three steps we find a match. In these steps we compare the `search_key` value with `array_to_search[4]`, `array_to_search[7]`, and finally `array_to_search[5]`.

Figure 11.20 is a C function that implements the binary search algorithm. This program uses the string parameter `success`, which returns the string value `TRUE` if the search is successful and `FALSE` if otherwise, and the integer parameter `index`, which returns a legal index value if the search is successful and −1 if otherwise.

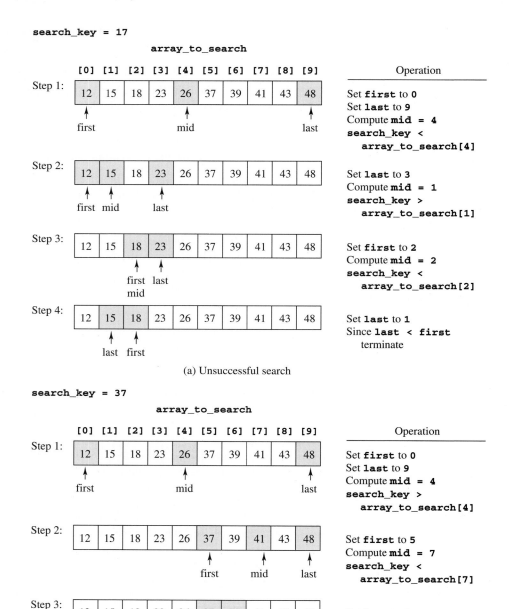

(a) Unsuccessful search

**Figure 11.19**  Binary search illustrated

```
/********************************************************************
 Function Name    : binary_search
 Purpose          : Searches a one-dimensional sorted array of
                    integers using the binary search algorithm.
 Receives         : search_key, list_size, array_to_search
 Returns          : success, index
 ********************************************************************/
void binary_search(list_item_type search_key, int list_size,
                   const list_item_type array_to_search[],
                   char success[], int *index) {
     /* Local variables: */

     int first, last, mid;

     /* Function body: */

     strcpy(success, "FALSE");
     *index = -1;

     first = 0;
     last = list_size - 1;

     while (first <= last && strcmp(success, "FALSE") == 0) {
          mid = (first + last) / 2;

          if (array_to_search[mid] == search_key) {
               *index = mid;
               strcpy(success, "TRUE");
          }
          else if (array_to_search[mid] > search_key)
               last = mid - 1;
          else
               first = mid + 1;
          /* end if */
     } /* end while */
} /* end function binary_search */
```

**Figure 11.20**    A C function that searches an array using binary search

Let us try to understand why the binary search algorithm is efficient. The worst case for any search algorithm is if the list does not contain a match for the search key value. If we have a list of seven elements in an array, the first step compares the search key with the array element that has index 3; the second step compares the search key with the array element that has either index 1 or 5; and the third step compares the search key with the array element that has index 0, 2, 4, or 6. In other words, we have a maximum of three comparisons. If we have a list with 15 elements, the maximum number of comparisons will be four. In general, the maximum number of comparisons for a list of size list_size is equal to the first power of 2 that is greater than list_size. On the other hand, the maximum number of comparisons made using the sequential search algorithm to search an unordered list is equal to list_size. Figure 11.21 compares sequential search and binary search algorithms for different values of list_size in terms of the maximum number of comparisons in the worst case.

| list_size | Maximum Number of Comparisons | |
|---|---|---|
| | **Sequential Search** | **Binary Search** |
| 100 | 100 | 7 |
| 1,000 | 1,000 | 10 |
| 10,000 | 10,000 | 14 |
| 100,000 | 100,000 | 17 |
| 1,000,000 | 1,000,000 | 20 |
| 10,000,000 | 10,000,000 | 24 |
| 100,000,000 | 100,000,000 | 27 |
| 1,000,000,000 | 1,000,000,000 | 30 |

**Figure 11.21**    Comparing efficiencies of sequential and binary search

As you can see, the difference is dramatic, especially for large lists. A list of 1,000,000,000 elements, for example, requires a maximum of 30 comparisons in binary search. Assuming we have a computer that performs 1,000,000 comparisons per second, and ignoring all other necessary operations, this list will take about 30 milliseconds with binary search and about 16.7 minutes with sequential search.

## Constructing a Search Library

Searching arrays is an operation that is quite common to many applications. In practice, it makes sense to construct a search library that includes several search algorithms. We have covered three of them, so we can construct our own search library. The header file search.h is given in Figure 11.22. It contains the typedef declaration for list_item_type and the prototypes of the functions sequential_search_unordered, sequential_search_ordered, and binary_search.

```
typedef int list_item_type;

/*****************************************************************
  Function Name    : sequential_search_unordered
  Purpose          : Searches a one-dimensional unsorted array of
                     integers using the sequential search algorithm.
  Receives         : search_key, list_size, array_to_search
  Returns          : success, index
 *****************************************************************/
void sequential_search_unordered(list_item_type search_key,
                                 int list_size,
                                 const list_item_type
                                        array_to_search[],
                                 char success[], int *index);


/*****************************************************************
  Function Name    : sequential_search_ordered
  Purpose          : Searches a one-dimensional sorted array of
                     integers using the sequential search algorithm.
  Receives         : search_key, list_size, array_to_search
  Returns          : success, index
 *****************************************************************/
void sequential_search_ordered(list_item_type search_key,
                               int list_size,
                               const list_item_type array_to_search[],
                               char success[], int *index);


/*****************************************************************
  Function Name    : binary_search
  Purpose          : Searches a one-dimensional sorted array of
                     integers using the binary search algorithm.
  Receives         : search_key, list_size, array_to_search
  Returns          : success, index
 *****************************************************************/
void binary_search(list_item_type search_key, int list_size,
                   const list_item_type array_to_search[],
                   char success[], int *index);
```

**Figure 11.22**    The header file `search.h` for the programmer-defined search library

The implementation file that we will name `search.cpp` contains two preprocessor directives, #include "search.h" and #include <string.h>, and the implementations of the three search functions `sequential_search_unordered`, `sequential_search_ordered`, and `binary_search`, as given in Figures 11.16, 11.18, and 11.20. We will also use this library in Example Program 2 in this chapter.

## REVIEW QUESTIONS

**1.** Dynamic variables
   **a.** Are declared as pointer variables.
   **b.** Are created at run time using the `malloc` function on a size value.
   **c.** Have static duration.
   **d.** Are destroyed using the `free` function on a size value.
   **e.** All of the above are correct.
   **f.** None of the above is correct.

**2.** Assume that we have the variable declaration

```
char *answer;
```

Which of the following statements will create a dynamic array of size 10?
   **a.** `answer = malloc(10 * sizeof(char));`
   **b.** `*answer = malloc(10 * sizeof(char));`
   **c.** `answer = malloc(sizeof(char)[10]);`
   **d.** `*answer = malloc(sizeof(char)[10]);`
   **e.** All of the above.
   **f.** None of the above.

**3.** Simple sorting techniques are easier to program than complex sorting algorithms; however, in general, the simple techniques are less execution efficient. (T or F)

**4.** Which of the following statements concerning the bubble sort algorithm is *incorrect*?
   **a.** The fundamental operations in bubble sort are the comparison of two consecutive list elements and a swap of them if necessary.
   **b.** To sort a list of $n$ elements, we need to make $n - 1$ passes.
   **c.** In the first pass we make $n - 1$ comparisons; in the second pass we make $n - 2$ comparisons, and so on.
   **d.** Even if there are no swap operations in any pass, there is no guarantee that the list is ordered; therefore, we must complete all $n - 1$ passes.

**5.** In the selection sort algorithm, in each pass we determine the largest element and exchange it with the last list element. This way, we have an unordered list, the size of which decreases in each pass, followed by an ordered list, whose size increases by 1 in each pass. (T or F)

**6.** In insertion sort:
   **a.** An array of size $n$ requires $n - 1$ passes.
   **b.** In the first pass the second element of the array is inserted into a sublist of size 1, which consists of the first element of the array.
   **c.** In the last pass the last element of the array is inserted into a sorted sublist of $n - 1$ elements.
   **d.** All of the above are correct.
   **e.** None of the above is correct.

**7.** In a C function that sorts an array, to ensure that the passed array is a read-only array, we must use the qualifier `const` in its declaration in the list of formal parameters. (T or F)

**8.** In searching a list of $n$ elements using the sequential search algorithm:
  **a.** If the list is unordered, a successful search requires $n$ comparisons of the search key and the list elements.
  **b.** If the list is ordered, a successful search takes less time compared to the case in which the list is unordered.
  **c.** In case the search is unsuccessful, the efficiency of sequential search cannot be improved by ordering the list before searching it.
  **d.** All of the above are correct.
  **e.** None of the above is correct.

**9.** In binary search, assuming that the list is sorted in increasing order:
  **a.** We compare the search key value with the value of the middle list element.
  **b.** If the search key value is less than the value of the middle list element, we focus on the second half of the list.
  **c.** If the search key value is greater than the value of the middle list element, we consider the first half of the list.
  **d.** All of the above are correct.
  **e.** None of the above is correct.

**10.** In binary search the maximum number of comparisons for a list of size $n$ is equal to the first power of 2 that is greater than $n$. (T or F)

**Answers:**   1. b; 2. a; 3. T; 4. d; 5. T; 6. d; 7. F; 8. e; 9. a; 10. T.

## 11.7   EXAMPLE PROGRAM 2: A C Program that Creates, Sorts, and Searches a One-Dimensional Array of Integers

In this section we will develop an application program that creates a list of integer test score values in an array, sorts the array in increasing order using bubble sort, and searches it for a test score value using the sequential search algorithm. We assume that the size of the list is a variable, for which the user inputs a value.

The design of this application is simple. It consists of a function `main` and three programmer-defined functions. They are `input_array`, which is used to create the list in an array; the function `bubble_sort` of Figure 11.9 for bubble sort; and the function `sequential_search_ordered` of Figure 11.18 for sequential search. As you remember, the function `bubble_sort` is in our sort library, and the function `sequential_search_ordered` is part of our search library. Therefore, all we have to do is to develop a program that uses our sort and search libraries and includes the implementation of the function `input_array`. The application file for this problem is presented in Figure 11.23.

```
/*****************************************************************
 Program Filename: prog11_2.c
 Author           : Uckan
 Purpose          : Inputs, sorts, and searches a one-dimensional
                    array of integers.
 Input from       : terminal keyboard
 Output to        : screen
 *****************************************************************/

#include <stdio.h>
#include <string.h>

#include "sort.h"
#include "search.h"

#define ARRAY_SIZE 60

/* Function prototypes:   */

void input_array(int *list_size, list_item_type test_scores[]);


int main(void) {
     /* Local variables:  */

     int list_size, search_key, index, i;
     list_item_type test_scores[ARRAY_SIZE];
     char success[6];

     /* Function body: */

     input_array(&list_size, test_scores);

     printf("Unsorted array: \n");

     for (i = 0; i < list_size; i++)
          printf("%d  %d\n", i, test_scores[i]);
     /* end for */

     bubble_sort(list_size, test_scores);

     printf("Sorted array: \n");
```

Figure 11.23      A C program that creates, sorts, and searches an array (*continued*)  ▶

```
        for (i = 0; i < list_size; i++)
              printf("%d  %d\n", i, test_scores[i]);
        /* end for */

        printf("Enter search key, an integer: ");
        scanf("%d", &search_key);

        sequential_search_ordered(search_key, list_size, test_scores,
              success, &index);

        if (strcmp(success, "TRUE") == 0)
          printf("Search is successful. %d is the %dth list element.\n",
                search_key, index + 1);
        else
          printf("Search is unsuccessful.\n");
        /* end if */

        return 0;
} /* end function main */


/*******************************************************************
  Function Name   : input_array
  Purpose         : Inputs a one-dimensional array of integers and
                    returns it and its size to the calling program.
  Called by       : main
  Receives        : None
  Returns         : list_size, test_scores
  *****************************************************************/
void input_array(int *list_size, list_item_type test_scores[]) {
        /* Local variables: */

        int i;

        /* Function body: */

        printf("How many test scores? Enter an integer: ");
        scanf("%d", &*list_size);

        for (i = 0; i < *list_size; i++) {
              printf("Enter a test score: ");
              scanf("%d", &test_scores[i]);
        } /* end for */
} /* end function input_array */
```

Figure 11.23

The following elements of the program of Figure 11.23 should be noted:

1. To use the sort and search libraries, we have the preprocessor directives `#include "sort.h"` and `#include "search.h"`.

2. Note the absence of the prototypes for the `bubble_sort` and `sequential_search_ordered` functions; they are in the header files `sort.h` and `search.h`, respectively.

3. The function `input_array` has a pointer parameter, `list_size`, and an array parameter `test_scores`. Both parameters are for returning values. This function prompts the user to enter an integer value for `list_size` and the test score values, stored in the array `test_scores`, to form a list of size `list_size`. Both `list_size` and `test_scores` are returned to the calling function.

4. The function `main` is simple. It calls on `input_array` and prints the content of `test_scores` using a `for` statement. Then it calls the function `bubble_sort`, which sorts the list, using bubble sort. After the execution of `bubble_sort`, the array `test_scores` contains the ordered list. This list is printed by another `for` statement. Finally, the user is prompted to enter a search key value. A subsequent call to `sequential_search_ordered` triggers the execution of that function, which does sequential search. The result of the search is printed in the final `if` statement.

Figure 11.24 shows a sample terminal session obtained by running the program of Figure 11.23.

```
How many test scores? Enter an integer: 5
Enter a test score: 89
Enter a test score: 77
Enter a test score: 100
Enter a test score: 67
Enter a test score: 85
Unsorted array:
0   89
1   77
2   100
3   67
4   85
Sorted array:
0   67
1   77
2   85
3   89
4   100
Enter search key, an integer: 89
Search is successful. 89 is the 4th list element.
```

**Figure 11.24**   A sample run of the program of Figure 11.23

## 11.8   HIGHER-DIMENSIONAL ARRAYS

We mentioned earlier that a C array can be of any type. Just as we can have arrays of integers, floating-point values, and characters, we can also have arrays of arrays.

> An array of one-dimensional arrays is called a **two-dimensional array**; an array of two-dimensional arrays is a called a **three-dimensional array**, and so on.

In most implementations of the C language, especially those based on standard C, we can go up to 12-dimensional arrays. In this section we will limit our coverage to two-dimensional arrays. Concepts and techniques for higher-dimensional arrays are extensions of those for two-dimensional ones.

An array of one-dimensional arrays (or a two-dimensional array) is equivalent to a table of a fixed number of rows and a fixed number of columns. Figure 11.25 shows the

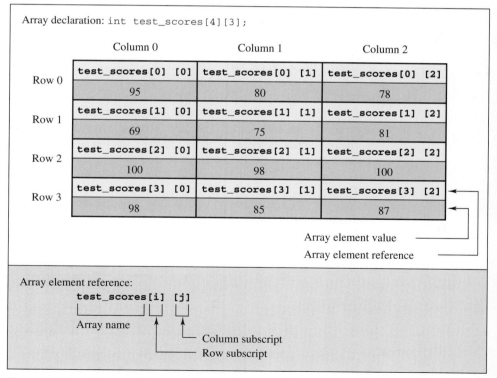

**Figure 11.25**    Conceptual structure of a two-dimensional array of four rows and three columns

conceptual structure for a two-dimensional array, called `test_scores`, which consists of four rows and three columns. In other words, the `test_scores` array of Figure 11.25 is a four-by-three array. Such an array can be used to depict three test scores for four students; each row would then represent a student, and the three values on each row would be the three test scores for that student.

## Declaring Two-Dimensional Arrays

The declaration of a two-dimensional array is similar to that of a one-dimensional array except we must have two subscripts showing the number of rows and the number of columns. The array `test_scores` is declared as

```
int test_scores[4][3];
```

The first subscript is the number of rows, and the second is the number of columns. Both row and column subscript values start with 0. Therefore, the first row of a two-dimensional array is called row 0, the second row is called row 1, and so on. Similarly, the first column is referred to as column 0, and so on.

To reference an element of a two-dimensional array, we use the array name and follow it with a row subscript and a column subscript. Hence `test_scores[0][0]` is the name of the first element on row 0; in Figure 11.25, its value is 95.

When the compiler encounters the declaration for a two-dimensional array, it allocates memory locations for its elements in a linear fashion. The memory locations for the elements on row 0 are followed by the memory locations for the elements on row 1; the allocation process continues until all elements on all rows are handled. Figure 11.26 shows a three-by-three integer array declared as

```
int a[3][3];
```

and the conceptual structure for this array as a table. Figure 11.27 shows the memory structure for the same array. The three elements on row 0 are reserved for three integer words. After the element `a[0][2]`, the compiler allocates memory locations for the three elements on row 1, and these are followed by three integer words for the three elements on row 2. Thus memory allocation for two-dimensional arrays is by row.

Array declaration: `int a[3][3];`

|  | Column 0 | Column 1 | Column 2 |
|---|---|---|---|
| Row 0 | a[0] [0] | a[0] [1] | a[0] [2] |
|  | 50 | 55 | 58 |
| Row 1 | a[1] [0] | a[1] [1] | a[1] [2] |
|  | 60 | 65 | 68 |
| Row 2 | a[2] [0] | a[2] [1] | a[2] [2] |
|  | 70 | 75 | 78 |

**Figure 11.26**    Conceptual structure of a 3×3 two-dimensional array

Array declaration: `int a[3][3];`

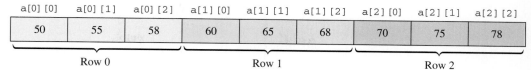

**Figure 11.27**   Storage structure of a 3×3 two-dimensional array

## Initialization of Two-Dimensional Arrays

We can initialize two-dimensional arrays explicitly at run time. For example, the array `test_scores` declared as

```
int test_scores[4][3];
```

can be initialized by row by a nested `for` loop:

```
for (i = 0; i < 4; i++)
    for (j = 0; j < 3; j++)
        test_scores[i][j] = 0;
    /* end for */
/* end for */
```

This `for` loop first sets the three elements on row 0 to 0, then it initializes the three elements on row 1 to 0, and continues until all elements are set to 0. The same can be accomplished by processing the array by column:

```
for (j = 0; j < 3; j++)
    for (i = 0; i < 4; i++)
        test_scores[i][j] = 0;
    /* end for */
/* end for */
```

Two-dimensional arrays can also be initialized at compile time by using constant initializers. The rules are simply extensions of those for one-dimensional arrays. For example, the declaration

```
int test_scores[4][3] = {{95, 80, 78}, {69, 75, 81},
                         {100, 98, 100}, {98, 85, 87}};
```

declares the four-by-three integer array `test_scores` and initializes its elements to values, as shown in Figure 11.25. After this initialization, if we print the content of the array using the loop

```
int i, j;

for (i = 0; i < 4; i++) {
    printf("ROW %d OF test_scores: ", i);

    for (j = 0; j < 3; j++)
        printf("%d  ", test_scores[i][j]);
    /* end for */

    printf("\n");
} /* end for */
```

we get the following output:

```
ROW 0 OF test_scores: 95   80   78
ROW 1 OF test_scores: 69   75   81
ROW 2 OF test_scores: 100  98   100
ROW 3 OF test_scores: 98   85   87
```

You should note that the first three values in the list of initializers are assigned to the three array elements on row 0, the next three initializers belong to the elements on row 1, and so on. In other words, compile-time initialization of two-dimensional arrays is by row.

The nesting in the list of initializers is optional. The preceding initialization can also be achieved with the declaration

```
int test_scores[4][3] = {95, 80, 78, 69, 75, 81,
                         100, 98, 100, 98, 85, 87};
```

The nested form is preferred, however, since it gives a better picture of the structure of the array.

It is possible to declare and initialize a two-dimensional array without explicitly declaring the number of rows. As we know, a two-dimensional array is a one-dimensional array of one-dimensional arrays. The number of these one-dimensional arrays is the number of rows in the two-dimensional array. Therefore, the number or rows in the declaration may be missing. However, so that the compiler can allocate storage for each row, the number of columns must be supplied. For example, the declaration

```
int test_scores[][3] = {{95, 80, 78}, {69, 75, 81},
                        {100, 98, 100}, {98, 85, 87}};
```

is acceptable; it declares the array as a two-dimensional array of four rows and three columns, since four groups of initializers occur in the initializer list. The following declaration, in which the number of columns is missing, is incorrect and will result in a compilation error:

```
int test_scores[4][] = {{95, 80, 78}, {69, 75, 81},
                        {100, 98, 100}, {98, 85, 87}};
```

Because of the ambiguity involved with respect to the number of rows and columns, the following declaration, where both row and column numbers are missing, will not work either and we will get a syntax error:

```
int test_scores[][] = {{95, 80, 78}, {69, 75, 81},
                       {100, 98, 100}, {98, 85, 87}};
```

If the number of initializers is larger than the number of array elements, we will have a compilation error, as in the following example that has 13 initializers and 12 array elements:

```
int test_scores[4][3] = {95, 80, 78, 69, 75, 81,
                         100, 98, 100, 98, 85, 87, 65};
```

On the other hand, if the number of initializers is less than the number of array elements, the explicit initializers will be assigned to the array elements, beginning with the first element on row 0, and continuing by row until the initializers are exhausted. The remaining array elements are automatically initialized to 0 if the type of the array is numeric; if the array type is char, they are assigned to NULL. Examples of partial initializations follow. The declaration

```
int test_scores[4][3] = {95};
```

initializes test_scores[0][0] to 95 and all remaining elements to 0. The declaration

```
int test_scores[4][3] = {95, 80, 78, 69};
```

sets the first three elements on row 0 to 95, 80, and 78 and sets the first element on row 1 to 69. The remaining elements are initialized to 0. Finally, the declaration

```
int test_scores[4][3] = {{95}, {69}, {100}, {98}};
```

initializes the four elements on column 0 to 95, 69, 100, and 98, respectively, and all remaining elements of the array to 0.

## Operations on Two-Dimensional Arrays

As in one-dimensional arrays, the operations that we can perform on the elements of a two-dimensional array are defined by those that can be applied on data elements of the array type. Thus if we have an integer type two-dimensional array, we can read values for its elements, output them, and use them anywhere we can use integer values. We can also pass two-dimensional arrays to functions.

**Passing Two-Dimensional Arrays to Functions**   The rules for passing two-dimensional arrays to functions are only slightly different from those for one-dimensional arrays. We know that in passing a one-dimensional array to a function, we are actually passing a pointer to its first element and that the pointer is the name of the array without a subscript. In the case of a two-dimensional array, the name of the array being passed without subscripts is also a pointer to the first element of the one-dimensional array. However, the first element of the array in an array of arrays (that is, a two-dimensional array) is itself an array. Therefore, the name of an array in the actual argument of a function call is a pointer to the first row of the two-dimensional array, and not to its first element.

We also know that even if we use the array subscript notation in our program, the compiler relies on pointer notation and uses offsets to access array elements. Because we provide the compiler with information about the data type of a one-dimensional array in the declaration of a formal parameter, the compiler will be able to compute the offsets and addresses for all elements of the array in the called function. It is sufficient to declare a one-dimensional array in the formal parameter list as `int a[]`, for example. The compiler can then use the pointer to the first element, and an offset of 2 bytes (assuming the type `int` requires 2-byte words) to determine the addresses of the following elements and access them.

If we declare a two-dimensional array in the formal parameter list as `int b[][]`, the compiler will need to know the size of each element of the one-dimensional array. But each element of the one-dimensional array is a one-dimensional array, and the compiler has no way of telling what the offset is, for example, for the first element of the second row. That each element is of type `int` is not enough; we must also tell the compiler about the number of elements in each row of the two-dimensional array. Therefore in the formal parameter list the proper declaration must be as `int b[][20]`, thus enabling the compiler to compute the offset for the first element of the second row as $2 \times 20 = 40$.

Here are, then, the rules for passing two-dimensional arrays to functions:

1. The array must be declared in the list of formal parameters with its type, a name, and no information for its rows, but with a constant column number information, as in the following function definition header:

```
void input_table(int *no_of_rows, int *no_of_columns,
                 int arr[][COLUMN_SIZE])
```

2. The function must similarly be declared in its prototype. Example:

```
void input_table(int *no_of_rows, int *no_of_columns,
                 int arr[][COLUMN_SIZE]);
```

3. In a call to the function, the corresponding actual argument must be the name of the array that we want to pass without any subscripts, as in

```
input_table(&rows, &columns, test_scores);
```

where the array `test_scores` might be declared as

```
int test_scores[ROW_SIZE][COLUMN_SIZE];
```

with `ROW_SIZE` and `COLUMN_SIZE` being two named constants.

***Example 11.7***   The function `input_table` of Figure 11.28 reads values for the number of rows and number of columns of a two-dimensional integer array, inputs values for its elements, and returns the number of rows, number of columns, and the two-dimensional array to the calling program.

```
void input_table(int *no_of_rows, int *no_of_columns,
                 int arr[][COLUMN_SIZE]) {
     int i, j;

     printf("Enter number of rows    : ");
     scanf("%d", &(*no_of_rows));
     printf("Enter number of columns: ");
     scanf("%d", &(*no_of_columns));

     for (i = 0; i < *no_of_rows; i++)
          for (j = 0; j < *no_of_columns; j++) {
               printf("Enter value of array element [%d][%d]: ",
                      i, j);
               scanf("%d", &arr[i][j]);
          } /* end for */
     /* end for */
} /* end function input_table */
```

**Figure 11.28**    A C function that interactively creates a two-dimensional array

In the program of Figure 11.28, you should note the array declaration,   `int arr[][COLUMN_SIZE]`, in the formal parameters list with only column number information. You should also note the references to array elements using two subscripts, as in  `arr[i][j]`, and the use of a nested  `for`  loop to read values for array elements. Nested  `for`  loops are quite common in applications that make use of two- or higher-dimensional arrays.

***Example 11.8***   The function  `output_table`  of Figure 11.29 has three parameters, `rows`, `columns`, and `arr[][COLUMN_SIZE]`. The first and the second parameters are value parameters, and the third is declared with the  `const`  qualifier, to render it a read-only parameter. This function prints a two-dimensional array by row.

```
void output_table(int rows, int columns,
                  const int arr[][COLUMN_SIZE]) {
     int i, j;

     printf("\n     ");

     for (j = 0; j < columns; j++)
          printf("[%d]   ", j);
     /* end for */
```

**Figure 11.29**    A C function that prints a two-dimensional array by row (*continued*)    ▶

```
          for (i = 0; i < rows; i++) {
                printf("\n[%d]   ", i);

                for (j = 0; j < columns; j++)
                      printf("%3d  ", arr[i][j]);
                /* end for */
          } /* end for */
    } /* end function output_table */
```

**Figure 11.29**                                                                    ■

***Example 11.9***   The function `computed_average` of Figure 11.30 computes the average of integers stored in an integer array `arr`. It receives values for `rows`, `columns`, and `arr[][COLUMN_SIZE]`. It returns the average of array elements under its name. The parameters `rows` and `columns` are value parameters. The third parameter `arr[][COLUMN_SIZE]` has the qualifier `const`, so it is treated as a read-only parameter by the function.

```
int computed_average(int rows, int columns,
                                    const int arr[][COLUMN_SIZE]) {
     int average, total = 0, i, j;

     for (i = 0; i < rows; i++)
          for (j = 0; j < columns; j++)
                total = total + arr[i][j];
          /* end for */
     /* end for */

     if (total != 0)
          average = total / (rows * columns);
     else
          average = 0;
     /* end if */

     return average;
} /* end function computed_average */
```

**Figure 11.30**     A C function that computes the average of integers in a two-dimensional array

We can write a main program (as shown in Figure 11.31) to use the functions `input_table`, `output_table`, and `computed_average` of the last three examples to build a table of `test_scores`, to print the table, and to compute the average of all test scores. In such a table each row might correspond to a student, and the number of columns might be the number of tests given in a class.

```c
#include <stdio.h>

/* Named constant declarations: */

#define ROW_SIZE 20
#define COLUMN_SIZE 30

/* Function prototypes: */

void input_table(int *rows, int *columns, int arr[][COLUMN_SIZE]);
void output_table(int rows, int columns,
                  const int arr[][COLUMN_SIZE]);
int computed_average(int rows, int columns,
                     const int arr[][COLUMN_SIZE]);

int main(void) {
        int test_scores[ROW_SIZE][COLUMN_SIZE];
        int rows, columns;

        input_table(&rows, &columns, test_scores);
        output_table(rows, columns, test_scores);

        printf("\n\nAverage test score: %d",
            computed_average(rows, columns, test_scores));
        return 0;
} /* end function main */
```

**Figure 11.31**    A C program that builds and prints a two-dimensional array of student test scores and computes the average score

A sample run of the programs of Figures 11.28 through 11.31 is given in Figure 11.32.

```
Enter number of rows    : 4
Enter number of columns: 3
Enter value of array element [0][0]: 100
Enter value of array element [0][1]: 90
Enter value of array element [0][2]: 95
Enter value of array element [1][0]: 67
Enter value of array element [1][1]: 78
```

**Figure 11.32**    A sample run of the programs of Figures 11.28 through 11.31 (*continued*)    ▶

```
Enter value of array element [1][2]: 77
Enter value of array element [2][0]: 87
Enter value of array element [2][1]: 85
Enter value of array element [2][2]: 80
Enter value of array element [3][0]: 100
Enter value of array element [3][1]: 75
Enter value of array element [3][2]: 95


       [0]   [1]   [2]
[0]    100    90    95
[1]     67    78    77
[2]     87    85    80
[3]    100    75    95

Average test score: 85
```

**Figure 11.32**    ■

**Two-Dimensional Arrays and Pointers**    In C the name of a two-dimensional array used without a subscript is a pointer to the array's first row. Thus if we declare an array  t  as

```
int t[4][3] = {{95, 80, 78}, {69, 75, 81},
               {100, 98, 100}, {98, 85, 87}};
```

we can use the identifier  t  as a pointer to row 0. However, row 0 itself is an array of three elements, not a memory location that stores a single value. We need a pointer to the first element in row 0, which we obtain by applying the indirection operator to  t,  making  *t  a pointer to  t[0][0].  Now that we have a pointer to  t[0][0], we can access its content by again applying the indirection operator as  *(*t).

We can use pointer arithmetic at this point to get a pointer to the second element in row 0. It is  *t  +  1, and the reference to  t[0][1]  in pointer/offset notation is  *(*t  +  1).  Similarly, the third element in row 0,  t[0][2], can be referenced in pointer/offset notation by  *(*t  +  2).

To access the elements in row 1 in a two-dimensional array, we need a pointer to row 1. If the pointer to row 0 is  t, the pointer to row 1 is  t  +  1.  Therefore, for example, the pointer to the third element in row 1 is  *(t  +  1)  +  2, and the name of that element is  *(*(t  +  1)  +  2).  This situation is shown in Figure 11.33.

Now we can generalize and note that the pointer expression  *(*(t  +  i)  +  j)  is the name of the array element  t[i][j]  in pointer/offset notation. If we use subscript notation for a two-dimensional array, at compile time the C compiler converts all array element references in subscript notation to their counterparts in pointer/offset notation. If we use pointer/offset notation in our program, this conversion will not be necessary and the program will be more efficient during compilation. For example, the following  for  loop prints the array  t  by row:

Array declaration: **int t[4][3]** = { {95, 80, 78}, {69, 75, 81}, {100, 98, 100}, {98, 85, 87} };

|  | Column 0 | Column 1 | Column 2 |
|---|---|---|---|
| t ○──────→ Row 0 | *(*(t)) | *(*(t) + 1) | *(*(t) + 2) |
|  | 95 | 80 | 78 |
| t + 1 ○──────→ Row 1 | *(*(t + 1)) | *(*(t + 1) + 1) | *(*(t + 1) + 2) |
|  | 69 | 75 | 81 |
| t + 2 ○──────→ Row 2 | *(*(t + 2)) | *(*(t + 2) + 1) | *(*(t + 2) + 2) |
|  | 100 | 98 | 100 |
| t + 3 ○──────→ Row 3 | *(*(t + 3)) | *(*(t + 3) + 1) | *(*(t + 3) + 2) |
|  | 98 | 85 | 87 |

**Figure 11.33**   Two-dimensional arrays and pointers

```
for (i = 0; i < 4; i++) {
     printf("\nROW %d OF array t: ", i);

     for (j = 0; j < 3; j++)
          printf("%d  ", t[i][j]);
     /* end for */
} /* end for */
```

The preceding code uses subscript notation. We can also use pointer/offset notation as in the following code, which does the same thing:

```
for (i = 0; i < 4; i++) {
     printf("\nROW %d OF array t: ", i);

     for (j = 0; j < 3; j++)
          printf("%d  ", *(*(t + i) + j));
     /* end for */
} /* end for */
```

This second version is more efficient than the first. However, pointer/offset notation is less natural than subscript notation, and we suggest that you avoid using pointer/offset notation unless program efficiency for compilation turns out to be very important in your applications.

## 11.9   EXAMPLE PROGRAM 3: A C Function that Generates a Bar Chart

Before we conclude this study of two-dimensional arrays, we will consider another application. If you recall, we have a promise pending from Example Program 1 in Chapter 9, where we developed a program to compute the distribution of letter grades. In that program we had a programmer-defined function called `print_chart`, which generated and printed a vertical bar chart. The bar chart was vertical because you did not know how to use arrays in Chapter 9. In this chapter Example Program 1 solves the same problem and computes letter grade distributions using arrays. Now, we will complement this application by developing a function called `print_chart`, which generates and prints a more conventional horizontal bar chart. Because you know how to use arrays, you can do this easily.

The function `print_chart` requires as its input the array `distribution`, which is computed by the function `compute_grade_distribution` of Figure 11.4. It has nothing to return. We need a two-dimensional array to store the image of the horizontal bar chart. In the program of Figure 11.34, it is the character array `bar_chart` declared as a local variable:

```
char bar_chart[13][25];
```

```
void print_chart(const int distribution[]) {
     /* Local variables: */

     int vertical_start, horizontal_start;
     char bar_chart[13][25];
     int i, j, k;

     /* Function body: */

     for (i = 0; i < 13; i++)
         for (j = 0; j < 25; j++)
             bar_chart[i][j] = ' ';
         /* end for */
     /* end for */

     horizontal_start = 1;

     for (k = 0; k < 5; k++) {
         vertical_start = 13 - distribution[k];

         for (i = vertical_start; i < 13; i++)
             for (j = horizontal_start; j < horizontal_start +
                 3; j++)
```

**Figure 11.34**   A C function that generates and prints a horizontal bar chart (*continued*)   ▶

```
                          bar_chart[i][j] = '*';
                 /* end for */
           /* end for */

           horizontal_start = horizontal_start + 5;
      } /* end for */

   for (i = 0; i < 13; i++) {
        printf("\n");

        for (j = 0; j < 25; j++)
             printf("%c", bar_chart[i][j]);
        /* end for */
   } /* end for */

   printf("\n");
   printf("-----------------------\n");
   printf("  A     B     C     D     F   ");
} /* end function print_chart */
```

**Figure 11.34**                                                                               ∎

Let us explain the program of Figure 11.34:

1.   The first nested `for` loop initializes the elements of the character array `bar_chart` to the blank character.

2.   Corresponding to each element of the array `distribution`, we will use a region in the two-dimensional array `bar_chart` consisting of five columns and 13 rows. This region is shown in Figure 11.35 for the bar for letter grade A, assuming the value of `distribution[0]` is 5, that is, we have five As in the distribution.

The first and fifth columns of each region contain blanks to separate a bar for a letter grade from the next bar. For the bar representing the letter grade A, the second, third, and fourth columns contain the character `*` in each array element, beginning with row `13 - distribution[0]` and extending until row 12. To mark the beginning of the starred region horizontally and vertically, we need two variables, `horizontal_start` and `vertical_start`. Initially, the variable `horizontal_start` should be set to 1. For each following value of `distribution`, `horizontal_start` should be incremented by 5.

The variable `vertical_start` marks the row at and below which we must have asterisks, until row 12. Its value is obtained by subtracting the value of the element of `distribution` from 13. If we have five As in the distribution of letter grades, the value of `vertical_start` will be 8.

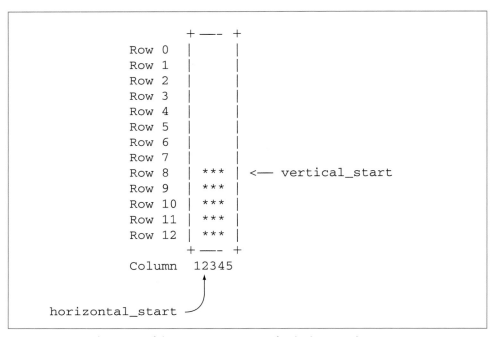

**Figure 11.35**    The region of the array `bar_chart` for the letter grade A

3.   Now that we know what the variables `horizontal_start` and `vertical_start` are for, we focus on the second nested `for` loop. The loop control variable k is assigned the values 0, 1, 2, 3, and 4 during the execution of the outer `for` statement. Each value of k corresponds to a letter grade distribution value in the array `distribution`.

4.   This `for` loop contains in its body another nested `for` loop, which generates the region in the array `bar_chart` for each element of `distribution`. Note that before the next element of `distribution` is considered by the outer `for` statement, the value of `horizontal_start` is incremented by 5. This way, when the outer `for` statement completes its execution, we have the bar chart generated in the array `bar_chart`.

5.   All we have to do now is to print the array, which is done using the last `for` loop in the function body. The following two `printf` function calls print the scale and labels for the bar chart.

6.   To use this function, we must have a call to it in the function `main` of the program of Figure 11.4. Also, we must include the following function prototype:

```
void print_chart(const int distribution[]);
```

Note that the `const` qualifier is used with the function parameter `distribution` to protect it against alterations in the function. Also, note that we have declared the array `bar_chart` as a two-dimensional array of 13 rows and 25 columns. This declaration imposes a limit of 13 on any element of the array `distribution`; in other words, this program cannot cope with a grade distribution in which the number of any letter grade is in excess of 13. If you want to use this program for a larger class size, you should rede-clare `bar_chart` and recompile the program.

Figure 11.36 shows a sample run with a horizontal bar chart obtained by using the function `print_chart` in the program of Figure 11.4.

```
Enter letter grade. Type Z to terminate data input: a
Enter letter grade: a
Enter letter grade: b
.........................
.........................

Number of A grades: 5
Number of B grades: 1
Number of C grades: 5
Number of D grades: 2
Number of F grades: 2
Total number of grades: 15
Class average: 2.33

BAR CHART:




    ***       ***
    ***       ***
    ***       ***
    ***       ***   ***   ***
    ***   ***   ***   ***   ***
    -------------------------
     A     B     C     D     F
```

**Figure 11.36**    A partial sample run of the program of Figure 11.4 with the function `print_chart` of Figure 11.34

## REVIEW QUESTIONS

1. Which of the following statements concerning the declaration below is correct?

   ```
   int table[3][5];
   ```

   **a.** This declaration declares a two-dimensional array of five rows and three columns.
   **b.** The reference `table[1][1]` is to the first array element on the first row.
   **c.** In the main memory the elements on column 0 are stored consecutively, and they are followed by the elements on column 1, and so on.
   **d.** The array element reference `table[0][0]` is illegal.
   **e.** All of the above.
   **f.** None of the above.

2. Which of the following two-dimensional array declarations is correct?
   **a.** `int t[2][3] = {{1, 2, 3}, {4, 5, 6}};`
   **b.** `int t[2][3] = {1, 2, 3, 4, 5, 6};`
   **c.** `int t[][3] = {1, 2, 3};`
   **d.** `int t[2][3] = {1};`
   **e.** All of the above.
   **f.** None of the above.

3. Let `tmax` be an integer two-dimensional array of 10 rows and 15 columns. In a function formal parameter list, it must be declared as
   **a.** `int tmax[][]`
   **b.** `int tmax[10][]`
   **c.** `int tmax[][15]`
   **d.** None of the above.

4. Assume that `mval` is the name of a two-dimensional array declared properly in the formal parameter list of a function definition. Inside that function:
   **a.** `mval` is a pointer to the first row of the array.
   **b.** `*mval` is a pointer to `mval[0][0]`.
   **c.** `*(*mval)` is a reference in pointer/offset notation to `mval[0][0]`.
   **d.** `*mval + 1` is a pointer to `mval[0][1]`.
   **e.** All of the above are correct.
   **f.** None of the above is correct.

**Answers:** 1. f; 2. e; 3. c; 4. e.

## 11.10 SUMMARY

### This Chapter at a Glance

- In this chapter you learned about lists, which are variable-size collections of ordered data items of the same type, and arrays, which are fixed-size storage structures that can be used to store lists.

- You studied one-dimensional arrays and arrays of arrays (also called higher-dimensional arrays).

- In C, arrays are a built-in, derived, structured data type. You studied the rules to declare arrays, to initialize them, to access array elements, and to pass arrays to functions.

- In C there is a close relationship between arrays and pointers. You learned about pointer/offset notation, which can be used as an alternative technique to process arrays.

- Next, you were introduced to dynamic variables, dynamic arrays, and the standard functions `malloc`, `calloc`, and `free`.

- Two common operations on lists stored in arrays are sorting and searching. You studied some fundamental sorting and searching algorithms.

- Now you are in a position to structure data as arrays and to use various types of arrays in solving problems that involve lists.

## Coming Attractions

- Arrays are useful if we have a collection of data of the same type. In case we have a collection of related data, such as data to describe an employee in a company (employee identification number, employee name, address, salary, marital status, and so on), we need another tool to structure them. This tool in C is a structure.

- A structure is a programmer-defined, derived, structured data type that brings together data of different types. In the next chapter you will learn about structures and use them in your problem-solving endeavors.

- The next chapter also covers a special programmer-defined data type, called enumerations.

## STUDY GUIDE

### Test Your Comprehension

1. Choose the correct statement.
   a. An array in C is a built-in, derived, structured data type.
   b. In declaring an array, the array size can be a constant, a variable, or an expression.
   c. An array can contain data of different types.
   d. All of the above.
   e. None of the above.

2. The declaration `int test_score[4] = {100, 90, 95, 97, 98};`
   a. Is illegal.
   b. Declares `test_score` as a one-dimensional integer array of size 4 and initializes its five elements to the values shown in the list of initializers.

  **c.** Declares `test_score` as a one-dimensional integer array of size 5, since we have five initializers in the initializer list.

  **d.** Declares `test_scores` as a one-dimensional integer array of size 4 and initializes its four elements to the first four values in the list of initializers, ignoring the last value.

  **e.** None of the above is correct.

**3.** Choose the *incorrect* statement. Suppose we have the declaration `int length[10];`
  **a.** `length` is a pointer to the first element of this array.
  **b.** `*length` and `length[0]` both refer to the first element of the array.
  **c.** `*length + 1` and `length[1]` both refer to the second element of the array.
  **d.** The reference `*(length + j)` is illegal if `j` is greater than 9.

**4.** In C
  **a.** Arrays can be passed by value.
  **b.** They can be passed only by pointers.
  **c.** It is possible to define functions that return arrays under their names.
  **d.** All of the above are correct.
  **e.** None of the above is correct.

**5.** Suppose we have declared the following array in our program:

```
double length[100];
```

  Which of the following statements can be used to deallocate the array `length`?
  **a.** `free([] length);`
  **b.** `free(length []);`
  **c.** `free([100] length);`
  **d.** `free(length [100]);`
  **e.** None of the above.

**6.** In sorting a list in decreasing order by selection sort:
  **a.** The first pass determines the largest list element and exchanges it with the last element.
  **b.** The first pass requires $n$ comparisons to find the largest element of a list of $n$ elements.
  **c.** We must go through $n$ passes to sort a list of $n$ elements.
  **d.** All of the above are correct.
  **e.** None of the above is correct.

**7.** Let `first` and `last` be the index values pointing to the beginning and end of the sublist to be searched at a given time while doing binary search on a list. For an unsuccessful search, the termination condition is
  **a.** `last == first`
  **b.** `last < first`
  **c.** `last > first`
  **d.** None of the above.

**8.** We want to declare a two-dimensional `double` array called `matrix` of 10 rows and 20 columns. Which of the following declarations is correct?

**a.** `double matrix[20][10];`
**b.** `double matrix[10][20];`
**c.** `double matrix[9][19];`
**d.** `double matrix[10, 20];`
**e.** None of the above.

9. In C a two-dimensional array can be
   **a.** Passed by value to a function.
   **b.** Passed by pointers to a function.
   **c.** Returned under a function name.
   **d.** All of the above.
   **e.** None of the above.

10. Which of the following is *not* a correct rule for passing two-dimensional arrays to functions?
    **a.** The array must be declared in the list of formal parameters with its type, name, and no information for its rows, but with a constant column number information.
    **b.** The corresponding function prototype must include the type and name of the two-dimensional array with no row or column number information.
    **c.** In a call to the function, the corresponding actual parameter must be the name of the array to be passed without any subscripts.
    **d.** In the called function, the names of array elements must not be prefixed by the indirection operator.

11. If `mat` is a two-dimensional array declared in the list of formal parameters of a function, the reference in pointer/offset notation `*(*(mat + i) + j)` is equivalent to
    **a.** A pointer to `mat[0][0]`.
    **b.** A pointer to `mat[i][j]`.
    **c.** The array element reference `mat[i][j]`.
    **d.** None of the above is correct.

**Answers:** 1. a; 2. a; 3. c; 4. b; 5. e; 6. e; 7. b; 8. b; 9. b; 10. b; 11. c.

## Improve Your Problem-Solving Ability

### *Debugging Exercises*

12. Identify and correct the errors, if any, in the following partial C program.

```
int i;
int tmin[5] = {1, 2, 3, 4, 5, 5};
int tmax[5];

tmax = tmin;
printf("\n");

for (i = 0; i <= 5; i++)
     printf("%d  ", tmax[i]);
/* end for */
```

**13.** In the following C program, identify and correct the errors, if any, and explain why they are errors.

```c
#include <stdio.h>
#define ARRAY_SIZE 10

int main(void) {
      int i;
      int squares[5];

      for (i = 0; i < ARRAY_SIZE; i++)
            squares[i] = i * i;
      /* end for */

      printf("\n");

      for (i = 0; i < ARRAY_SIZE; i++)
            printf("%d  ", squares[i]);
      /* end for */
      return 0;
} /* end function main */
```

**14.** Debug the following partial C program.

```c
int i, j;
int table[3][4] = { {1}, {2}, {3}, {4} };

for (i = 0; i < 3; i++) {
      printf("\n");
      for (j = 0; j < i - 2; j++)
            printf("%d  ", table[i][j]);
      /* end for */
} /* end for */
```

### Programming Exercises

**15.** Write a function that computes and returns the average of values stored in a one-dimensional floating-point array.

**16.** Write a function that determines whether an integer one-dimensional array is sorted in increasing order, in decreasing order, or is unordered. Your function should return 0 if the array is unordered, 1 if sorted in increasing order, and 2 if sorted in decreasing order.

**17.** Write a function that computes the sum of two integer arrays containing two lists of the same size and returns the result in another array. If *arr1* and *arr2* are the input to your function, the output array *result* can be computed using the formula *result[i]* = *arr1[i]* + *arr2[i]* for all legal values of *i*.

**18.** Write a function that sorts a list stored in a one-dimensional array in decreasing order using the bubble sort algorithm.

**19.** Write a function that implements the insertion sort algorithm using two one-dimensional arrays of the same size. Your function should have list size and two arrays as its parameters. One of the arrays should be used to bring into the function the unordered array. In each pass of the sort algorithm, you should insert an element from the unordered array into the second array. When the sort is over, the second array will contain a sorted list that should be returned to the calling function.

**20.** Modify the binary search algorithm given in Figure 11.20 so that it can be used to search an array that is sorted in descending order.

**21.** Another name for a two-dimensional array is a **matrix**. A matrix is called a **square matrix** if its number of rows is the same as the number of columns. Write a function that determines whether a given square matrix is symmetric and then returns 1 under its name if it is and 0 if it is not. A matrix *mat* is **symmetric** if *mat[i][j]* = *mat[j][i]* for all legal values of *i* and *j* except when *i* = *j*.

**22.** Write a function that reverses a list stored in a one-dimensional array and returns the reversed list in the same array. For example, if the list is {1, 2, 3}, you should end up with {3, 2, 1} after the function is executed.

**23.** Write a `void` function that computes the first *n* elements of the Fibonacci sequence and stores them in a one-dimensional array. The function should receive the value of *n* and return the array containing the first *n* elements of the Fibonacci sequence.

**24.** Write a `void` function that uses the standard function `rand` to generate and store *n* random integers in the range of 1 through 6 to simulate *n* throws of a six-sided die. The function should receive the value of *n* and return the array containing the result of *n* throws of a die.

### Programming Projects

**25.** Solve Programming Project 39 of Chapter 4, using arrays.

**26.** Solve Programming Project 23 of Chapter 6, using arrays.

**27.** Solve Programming Project 32 of Chapter 9, using a two-dimensional array.

**28.** In the mathematical theory of sets, a **set** is defined as a collection of distinct items of the same type. In some programming languages, sets are a built-in data type; unfortunately, this is not the case in C. However, we can simulate a set using a one-dimensional array.

Some operations can be performed on sets. We will consider only three of them: union, intersection, and difference. These are binary operations requiring two sets as operands. The **union** of two sets, A and B, is a set that contains elements that are in A or B or both. The **intersection** of two sets A and B is a set that contains elements common to both A and B. Finally, the **difference** of two sets A and B is a set that contains only the elements in A but not in B. For example, if A and B are two sets of integers defined as A = {5, 7, 8, 10} and B = {3, 9, 10}, then their union is the set {3, 5, 7, 8, 9, 10}, their intersection is the set {10}, and the difference of A and B is the set {5, 7, 8}.

Construct a programmer-defined library, named set, that includes functions that can compute the union, intersection, and difference of two sets stored in two one-dimensional arrays.

**29.** Develop a program that does the following:
   **a.** Generates a set of random integers in the range 0 through 50, using the standard library function rand (see Programming Exercise 24), and stores them in an array.
   **b.** Generates another set of random integers in the same range and stores them in another array.
   **c.** Makes sure that both arrays contain proper sets by eliminating recurring values in each.
   **d.** Depending on what the user wants, computes and prints on the screen the union, the intersection, or the difference of the two sets.

In your program use the set library that you developed for the preceding project.

**30.** Develop a program that allows the user to interactively create and load two one-dimensional arrays of floating-point values. Then have your program sort the two arrays in increasing order, using any of the sorting techniques discussed in this chapter. Finally, your program should merge the two arrays into one such that the result is an array that contains all values in the two input arrays in increasing order. Print the merged array on the screen.

**31.** Construct a sort library that is similar to the one in section 11.5 in that it includes the three sort algorithms (bubble, selection, and insertion) covered in this chapter. However, your library functions should be modified to sort a one-dimensional array of character strings in increasing order. Test your library thoroughly using a properly designed driver function.

**32.** Construct a search library, similar to the one presented in section 11.6, that includes functions that can do sequential search of unordered lists, sequential search of ordered lists, and binary search. In all cases the lists should be character strings stored in one-dimensional arrays. Design a driver function to test your library.

**33.** If you have solved Programming Projects 31 and 32, you have a sort and a search library that you can use on character string arrays. Design an application that is similar to Example Program 2 in this chapter to process lists of character strings.

**34.** Programming Exercise 21 described a square matrix. Three relatively simple standard operations on matrices and square matrices are addition, subtraction, and multiplication. First, in case you don't know about these operations, find a book on matrix algebra and familiarize yourself with them. Then construct a square matrix library that includes functions to add, subtract, and multiply two matrices. Test your library using a driver function.

**35.** We have a text file in which each record consists of an integer student identification number, a student last name, an integer student year, and a three-character student major code. In each record, data values are separated by a blank character. An instance of this file follows.

```
5000 STEWARD 2 CSC
1000 BROWN 2 CSC
3000 JOHNSON 3 MTH
2000 BLACKWELL 1 PHY
```

Design and implement a modular program that reads this file into 4 one-dimensional arrays called `student_idno`, `student_name`, `student_age`, and `student_major`; sorts the data in increasing order by student identification number; and writes them to another text file that will contain the same data ordered by student identification number. You may use a sort algorithm of your choice. Note that if the sort algorithm swaps two array elements of the `student_idno` array, all corresponding elements of the remaining three arrays must also be swapped. For example, for the preceding sample file, the output of your program should be a file that contains the records as follows:

```
1000 BROWN 2 CSC
2000 BLACKWELL 1 PHY
3000 JOHNSON 3 MTH
5000 STEWARD 2 CSC
```

Arrays that are logically related to one another in this manner such that, for a given index value, the respective elements in all the arrays behave in parallel are called **parallel arrays**.

**36.** After you complete Programming Project 35, expand your application by incorporating into it a module that searches the parallel arrays for a user-supplied student identification number value, and if the search is successful, prints on the screen the last name, year, and major of the student whose identification number is the search key. Use the binary search algorithm in your implementation.

# chapter

# 12

# Structures and Enumerations

---

## CHAPTER OBJECTIVES

In this chapter you will learn about:

- **Structures as a derived, programmer-defined, structured data type**
  Declaring structures and structure variables
  Nested structures
  Initializing structure variables
  Operations on structure variables
  Structures as function parameters
  Arrays of structures and structures of arrays

- **Enumerated data types**
  Declaring enumerated data types and variables
  Operations on enumerated variables
  Using enumerated data types

By the time you have completed this chapter, you will have acquired the ability to:

- **Use structures and enumerated data types for better program design**

---

## 12.1   INTRODUCTION

The previous chapter described arrays as a derived, structured data type that is built into the C language. To use arrays in a program, all we have to do is to declare array variables, which is the fundamental characteristic of built-in data types. Programmers do not have to explain anything about the array to the compiler; they do not have to specify what, for example, the data type  int,  double, or a one-dimensional array is. All we have to do is declare variables of these types and use them in programs.

The remaining structured and derived data types in C — structures and unions — behave somewhat differently from arrays. We must declare data types as structures or unions before we can use them. In other words, we must first tell the compiler about such data types. Although the compiler is designed to recognize them, it does not know about their specifics. It knows what a structure is, but it needs to know about the *structure* for that particular structure. So, we can't just go ahead and declare a variable to be of type structure. We must first declare the structure and then declare variables of that structure type; only then we can use such variables. The situation is the same with unions, which are outside the scope of this book.

Another special programmer-defined data type is the enumerated data type. An enumerated data type is not structured. It is an integral data type, such as integers. The values that a variable of an enumerated data type may assume depend on the way the enumerated data type is declared. Therefore, like structures, we must first declare enumerated data types and then declare variables of such types and use them.

This chapter focuses exclusively on programmer-defined data types. You will study structures and use them in problem solving. Next, you will learn about enumerated data types and how they can be used to improve programs.

## 12.2   STRUCTURES

Let us consider an application in which an instructor wants to compute student project score averages, midterm examination score averages, semester averages, and letter grades by using scores for three projects, two midterm examinations, and a final examination. To identify each student, the instructor wants to use a student identification number and a student name. The letter grade field is especially important, and the instructor wants to associate it with other data that belong to each student. Suppose we are asked to develop a program for this application. We know that we must begin by declaring the variables. The following are appropriate declarations:

```
int student_idno;
char student_name[31];
int project1_score;
int project2_score;
```

```
int project3_score;
int test1_score;
int test2_score;
int final_exam_score;
char letter_grade;
```

At this point we realize that all of these variables represent certain characteristics that belong to a student. If rather than merely declaring them, we can also relate them to one another, we would accurately reflect the real-world relationship that they all belong to a student. This approach might even facilitate our programming effort. In C we can bring related data together by using a structure declaration that encompasses all of these variables:

```
struct student_struct {
        int student_idno;
        char student_name[31];
        int project1_score;
        int project2_score;
        int project3_score;
        int test1_score;
        int test2_score;
        int final_exam_score;
        char letter_grade;
}; /* end student_struct */
```

Such a declaration is for a derived and structured data type, called a structure, that is partially defined by the programmer. In this example the name of the data type is `struct student_struct`. By including this declaration in our program, we are informing the compiler about a new data type. So far it does not take any action. This declaration is similar to declaring the data type `int`, except we don't do this, since the data type `int` is built-in and the compiler is already aware of it. Having defined this derived data type, we can now declare variables that are based on it, as in

```
struct student_struct student_record;
```

This variable declaration causes the compiler to reserve memory space for the variable `student_record` and the components of its structure. The conceptual memory structure for the structure variable `student_record` is shown in Figure 12.1. In this figure we are assuming that the components of the variable `student_record` have already been assigned values.

| Structure Variable | Components | Values |
|---|---|---|
| student_record | student_idno | 1100 |
| | student_name | Robert Wells |
| | project1_score | 80 |
| | project2_score | 92 |
| | project3_score | 93 |
| | test1_score | 89 |
| | test2_score | 95 |
| | final_exam_score | 90 |
| | letter_grade | A |

**Figure 12.1**   Conceptual memory structure for the structure variable `student_record` of type `student_struct`

## Declaring Structures

Now it is time to give a definition for a structure.

> A **structure** is a derived data type that represents a collection of related data items called **components** (or **members**) that are not necessarily of the same data type.

A structure is a programmer-defined data type and therefore must be declared in a program. In C there are several ways a structure can be declared. The simplest way of declaring a structure type uses the following syntax:

```
struct StructureTypeName {
        StructureMemberDeclarationsList
}; /* end struct */
```

In this syntax the structure type name is also called the **structure tag**. The structure member declarations list is a list of declarations of its members. *StructureTypeName* is a programmer-defined identifier. To distinguish a structure type from other programmer-defined data types, we will adopt the convention of following the structure type name by the suffix _struct, as in student_struct. The concluding comment /* end struct */ is, of course, an optional style convention.

Some examples of structure type declarations follow.

***Example 12.1*** Suppose we want to declare a structure type called faculty_struct, which has as its members the data items faculty_idno, faculty_name, age, gender, and salary. The following declaration will serve the purpose:

```
struct faculty_struct {
      int faculty_idno;
      char faculty_name[31];
      int age;
      char gender;
      float salary;
}; /* end faculty_struct */
```

***Example 12.2*** The following declaration is for a structure type called class_enrollment_struct, in terms of course_code, academic_year, semester, and enrollment.

```
struct class_enrollment_struct {
      int course_code;
      int academic_year;
      char semester;
      int enrollment;
}; /* end class_enrollment_struct */
```

The rules concerning the placement of structure declarations in the source program are quite similar to those for all declarations in C. They may be declared globally before the function definitions. They may also be placed within function definitions; in this case their declarations must precede their use in the program. If more than one function in your program uses variables of a structure type, you should declare the structure type globally.

### Declaring Structure Variables

After declaring a structure type, we may declare variables that are of that type. A structure variable declaration requires these elements:

1. The keyword struct
2. The structure type name

3.   A list of variable names separated by commas

4.   A concluding semicolon

***Example 12.3***   To declare a variable called `faculty_record` as a variable of type `faculty_struct` of Example 12.1, we write

```
struct faculty_struct faculty_record;
```

When the compiler comes across this declaration in the program, it reserves memory space for the structure variable `faculty_record`.

***Example 12.4***   It is possible to combine the declarations of a structure type and a structure variable by including the name of the variable at the end of the structure type declaration. For example, the declaration

```
struct faculty_struct {
      int faculty_idno;
      char faculty_name[31];
      int age;
      char gender;
      float salary;
} faculty_record;
/* end faculty_struct */
```

is equivalent to both the structure declaration in Example 12.1 and the structure variable declaration in Example 12.3. Of course, in case you have declared the structure type globally, to avoid global variables, you should not combine the declaration of a structure type and variables of that type.

## Declaring Nested Structures

Members of a structure declaration can be of any type, including another structure variable. Such a structure type is called **nested**.

***Example 12.5***   Suppose we have the following structure declaration:

```
struct name_struct {
      char last_name[16];
      char first_name[16];
}; /* end name_struct */
```

We can use this structure type and rewrite the structure declaration of Example 12.1 as

```
struct faculty_struct {
      int faculty_idno;
      struct name_struct faculty_name;
      int age;
      char gender;
      float salary;
}; /* end faculty_struct */
```

In this revised declaration, the member `faculty_name` is a structure variable of type `struct name_struct`. Therefore, the structure type `faculty_struct` has become a nested structure type.

In declaring a nested structure type, we should be careful to place the declaration of the inner structure type before the nested structure type. If the inner structure type will be used only in a nested structure type, the two declarations can be combined. Here is an example.

***Example 12.6***   The structure type `faculty_struct` can be written as

```
struct faculty_struct {
      int faculty_idno;

      struct {
            char last_name[15];
            char first_name[15];
      } faculty_name;
      /* end struct */

      int age;
      char gender;
      float salary;
}; /* end faculty_struct */
```

## Referencing Structure Members

Because a structure variable may have many members, in referencing them we should be able to tell the compiler about the structure type and exactly which member we are trying to access. In C we can use the **component selection operator** (or structure member operator) to do so. The component selection operator is represented by a period, '.'. To reference a structure member, we begin with the name of the structure variable, followed by the component selection operator and the name of the member variable.

***Example 12.7***    The following initialization statements contain examples of structure member references based on the structure type `faculty_struct` of Example 12.5 and the structure variable declaration

```
struct faculty_struct faculty_record;
```

```
faculty_record.faculty_idno = 1200;
strcpy(faculty_record.faculty_name.last_name,"Dixon");
strcpy(faculty_record.faculty_name.first_name,"Robert");
faculty_record.age = 35;
faculty_record.gender = 'M';
faculty_record.salary = 32000.00;
```

Note that because the member variable `faculty_name` is of type `struct name_struct`, the proper reference to the members of `faculty_name` requires the use of the component selection operator twice, as in `faculty_record.faculty_name.last_name`.

### Initializing Structure Variables

In C it is possible to initialize structure variables at compile time. Compile-time initialization of a structure variable requires the following elements:

1. The keyword `struct`
2. The structure type name
3. The name of the structure variable
4. The assignment operator, `=`
5. A set of values for the members of the structure variable, enclosed in braces, and separated by commas
6. A terminating semicolon

The following is an example.

***Example 12.8***    The initialization statements of Example 12.7 are equivalent to the compile-time initialization for the structure variable `faculty_record`:

```
struct faculty_struct faculty_record = {1200, {"Dixon", "Robert"},
                                        35, 'M', 32000.00};
```

This declaration declares the variable `faculty_record` as a structure variable of type `struct faculty_struct`. It also initializes its respective members to the values shown. Note that the values `"Dixon"` and `"Robert"` are for the members `last_name` and `first_name` of the inner structure variable `faculty_name`. They are enclosed in braces. These braces are optional; however, we recommend that you use them to indicate the nesting that is inherent in structure variables.

There are a few rules to keep in mind for initializing structure variables at compile time.

1. The order of values for structure variable members enclosed in braces must match the order of members in the structure type declaration.

2. It is possible to initialize only a subset of the members of a structure variable at compile time. However, that subset must always begin with the first member and continue until your target member without skipping any. In other words, the following partial initialization for the structure variable `faculty_record` of type `struct faculty_struct` is valid:

```
struct faculty_struct faculty_record = {1200, {"Dixon", "Robert"}, 35};
```

This statement will initialize only the first four members of the variable `faculty_struct`. However, if you want to initialize, for example, the members `age` and `gender` without initializing the others, you cannot use compile-time initialization, since these members are not declared in this order from the beginning. You must instead use assignment expression statements, as we did in Example 12.7.

### Operations on Structure Variables

The following operations are permitted on structure variables:

1. Copying the content of a structure variable to another structure variable, provided both are of the same structure type.

2. Passing structure variables or their members to functions.

***Example 12.9***   If we have the following declarations in our program:

```
struct faculty_struct faculty_record_1, faculty_record_2;
```

then the statement

```
faculty_record_2 = faculty_record_1;
```

is legal, since both `faculty_record_1` and `faculty_record_2` are structure variables of the same type. This statement copies the content of `faculty_record_1` to the memory location for `faculty_record_2`.

You will learn how structure variables can be communicated between functions in the next section. Apart from copying and passing to functions, none of the operators that you have studied until this point can be applied to structure variables. These include input-output functions, all arithmetic operators, and comparison operators. Therefore, given the declarations

```
struct faculty_struct f1, f2, f3;
```

all of the following statements are illegal:

```
scanf("%d", &f1);
printf("%d", f2);
f1 = f2 + f3;
if (f1 == f2)
        ..... ;
```

## 12.3    STRUCTURES AS FUNCTION PARAMETERS

Like variables of any other data type, structure variables can be used as formal and actual function parameters. Most of the rules are similar to those described in Chapters 6 and 10. Let us go over them briefly.

In passing structure variables by value to a function, the operating system makes a copy of the entire structure in the data area of the called function. For example, suppose we have a function declaration for which the header is

```
int computed_project_average(struct student_struct s)
```

where `student_struct` is a structure type declared as follows:

```
struct student_struct {
        int student_idno;
        char student_name[31];
        int project1_score;
        int project2_score;
        int project3_score;
        int test1_score;
        int test2_score;
        int final_exam_score;
        char letter_grade;
}; /* end student_struct */
```

The function call in the statement

```
proj_avg = computed_project_average(stu_record);
```

is an example of call by value. It has one actual parameter, `stu_record`. If `stu_record` is a structure variable of type `struct student_struct`, then this function call is legal. As a result of this function call, the operating system will make a copy of the content of the actual variable `stu_record` in the structure variable s in the data area of the function `computed_project_average`.

A nonvoid function of a structure type can return a structure of that structure type under the function's name if we use a `return` statement in the function. For example, the function definition for the function `student_data` given in Figure 12.2 is of type `struct student_struct`.

```
struct student_struct student_data(void) {
      /* Local variables: */

      struct student_struct s;
      char new_line;

      /* Function body: */

      printf("***> Enter student idno          : ");
      scanf("%d", &s.student_idno);
      scanf("%c", &new_line);
      printf("***> Enter student name          : ");
      gets(s.student_name);
      printf("***> Enter first project score : ");
      scanf("%d", &s.project1_score);
      printf("***> Enter second project score: ");
      scanf("%d", &s.project2_score);
      printf("***> Enter third project score : ");
      scanf("%d", &s.project3_score);
      printf("***> Enter first test score      : ");
      scanf("%d", &s.test1_score);
      printf("***> Enter second test score     : ");
      scanf("%d", &s.test2_score);
      printf("***> Enter final exam score      : ");
      scanf("%d", &s.final_exam_score);

      return s;
} /* end function student_data */
```

**Figure 12.2**    A C function that returns a structure variable under function name    ■

For this function, provided `stu_record` is a structure variable of type `struct student_struct` in the calling function, a legal function call is in the statement

```
stu_record = student_data();
```

Note the `return` statement and its return expression, which consists of a local structure variable, `s`, again of type `struct student_struct`.

If all members of a structure variable are not needed for a function to perform its task, we can pass only the required members. However, in this case we must specify the structure members using the component selection operator. For example, the function `computed_semester_average` in Example Program 1 in this chapter has the header

```
int computed_semester_average(int pavg, int mavg, int final_exam)
```

A call to this function is in the following statement:

```
sem_avg = computed_semester_average(proj_avg, midterm_avg,
     student_record.final_exam_score);
```

Here the third actual parameter is `student_record.final_exam_score`, one of the members of the structure variable `student_record`. The corresponding formal parameter in the function definition is `final_exam`, which is of type `int`, because the member `final_exam_score` of `student_record` is also of type `int`.

Finally, it is possible to pass structure variables by using pointers. A function with one pointer parameter of type `struct student_struct` is given in Figure 12.3.

```
void input_student_data(struct student_struct *s) {
        /* Local variables: */

        char new_line;

        /* Function body: */

        printf("***> Enter student idno       : ");
        scanf("%d", &s->student_idno);
        scanf("%c", &new_line);
        printf("***> Enter student name       : ");
        gets(s->student_name);
        printf("***> Enter first project score : ");
        scanf("%d", &s->project1_score);
        printf("***> Enter second project score: ");
        scanf("%d", &s->project2_score);
        printf("***> Enter third project score : ");
        scanf("%d", &s->project3_score);
        printf("***> Enter first test score    : ");
        scanf("%d", &s->test1_score);
        printf("***> Enter second test score   : ");
        scanf("%d", &s->test2_score);
        printf("***> Enter final exam score    : ");
        scanf("%d", &s->final_exam_score);
} /* end function input_student_data */
```

**Figure 12.3**    A C function with a pointer parameter of structure type

In the function of Figure 12.3, the formal parameter `s` is a pointer parameter of type `struct student_struct`. A call to this function can be

```
input_student_data(&stu_record);
```

where the actual parameter `stu_record` is prefixed by the address operator, `&`, and is also of type `struct student_struct`. In the function `input_student_data`, we have references to the members of the structure variable `s`. A typical reference is in the first call to the function `scanf` as `s-> student_idno`.

Here the symbol `->` is a C operator, called the **indirect component selection operator**. The indirect component selection operator is represented using a hyphen and a greater-than sign without an intervening blank. This operator combines the functions of the indirection operator and the component selection operator. Actually, the expression `s->student_idno` is equivalent to `(*s).student_idno`, and both are references to the member `student_idno` of the structure variable `s` using a pointer.

The expression `s->student_idno` is straightforward; however, its equivalent form `(*s).student_idno` needs some explanation. As explained in Chapter 10, any reference to a formal parameter of pointer type in a function must be prefixed by the indirection operator, `*`. Therefore, why did we write `(*s).student_idno`, instead of `*s.student_idno`? The answer can be found in the semantics of the indirection and component selection operators. The indirection operator enables the computer to use a pointer to the memory location of its operand and thus access its content. The component selection operator, on the other hand, instructs the computer to select a particular member of a structure variable. In C the component selection operator has higher precedence than the indirection operator. Therefore, the interpretation of the expression `*s.student_idno` would be "Use a pointer to the `student_idno` member of the structure variable `s`." This action would be wrong, since the formal parameter of the function is the structure variable, `s`, and not its member `s.student_idno`. We actually want the computer to use a pointer to the memory location of the structure variable `s` and then get its member `student_idno`. Therefore, we must alter the precedence of operators and hence use parentheses around `*s`. This way, the computer will follow a pointer to the memory location of the structure variable `s` and then apply the component selection operator to access its `student_idno` member.

You should understand the notation `(*s).student_idno` and that it is equivalent to the simpler expression `s->student_idno`. We suggest that, in most cases, you prefer the indirect component selection operator to the convoluted form that involves the indirection operator and the component selection operator.

The last example that we discussed, the program of Figure 12.3, illustrated passing structure variables using pointers. Clearly, you can declare pointers to structure variables in C. A pointer to a structure is useful, especially when passing structure parameters from a called function to a calling function. Also, it is more efficient to pass a pointer to a structure variable than to pass the structure variable itself by value because, if you pass a structure variable by value, a new copy of the structure variable will be made in the other function's data area. A structure variable generally requires more memory space than a pointer variable.

In returning a structure variable from a function through a parameter, we know that we cannot use value parameters. Therefore, we used pointer parameters in the program of Figure 12.3. What if we are passing a structure variable from a function to a called function? Should we use pointers because pass by pointers is more efficient? The answer is no; pass by pointers, as you know, does not protect your data from inadvertent alterations by the called function, and the small gain in the memory requirements does not justify the risk of leaving your data unprotected. You should use pass by value when you are passing structure variables to a called function.

## REVIEW QUESTIONS

**1.**   A structure in C is a built-in, derived, structured data type. (T or F)

**2.**   The components of a structure type are necessarily of the same data type. (T or F).

**3.**   A structure variable declaration consists of the keyword `struct`, a structure type name, a list of variables separated by commas, and a concluding semicolon. (T or F)

**4.**   In declaring a nested structure type, the declaration of the inner structure type must precede that of the nested structure type. (T or F)

**5.**   Suppose we have the following combined structure type and structure variable declarations:

```
struct faculty_struct {
        int faculty_idno;

        struct {
                char last_name_initial;
                char first_name_initial;
        } name_initials;
        /* end struct */

        int age;
        char gender;
        float salary;
} faculty_information;
/* end faculty_struct */
```

Which of the following is a correct structure variable member reference?
**a.** `faculty_information.first_name_initial.name_initials`
**b.** `faculty_information.name_initials.first_name_initial`
**c.** `first_name_initial.name_initials.faculty_information`
**d.** All of the above.
**e.** None of the above.

**6.**   Assume we have the structure type declaration `faculty_struct` as given in question 5. Which of the following structure variable declarations is legal?
**a.** `struct  faculty_struct  math_faculty  =  {1300,  'B',  ,  37,`
         `'F',  26500.00};`
**b.** `struct faculty_struct math_faculty = {1300, 'B', 'J', 37};`

**c.** struct faculty_struct math_faculty = {, {'B', 'J'} , 37, 'F', 26500.00};

**d.** All of them are legal.

**e.** None of them is legal.

7. Copying the content of a structure variable to another structure variable of the same type and passing a structure variable to functions are legal operations. (T or F)

8. In evaluating expressions, the component selection operator has higher precedence than the indirection operator. (T or F)

## 12.4 EXAMPLE PROGRAM 1: A C Program that Computes Student Test and Project Averages and Letter Grades

In this section we will develop an application program that uses structures. As you will see, this problem can be solved without structure types. However, in most cases using structures facilitates the programming effort and/or produces programs that are more representative of real-world entities and phenomena; in addition, programs with structure types are easier to understand than those without.

***Problem*** An instructor wants us to design a program that reads data values for three student project scores, two midterm examination scores, and a final examination score for a student and then computes and outputs the project score average, the midterm examination average, the semester average, and the letter grade for the student. The program should work for as many students as the instructor has in class.

***Requirements Specification*** Develop a program that does the following:

1. Interactively reads data values for three student project scores, two midterm examination scores, and a final examination score for students who are identified by student identification numbers and names. All scores are on a scale of 100 points.

2. Computes and outputs on the terminal screen the project score average using the formula

    *0.40 × (best of the first two project scores) + 0.60 × third project score*

3. Computes and outputs the midterm examination average by the formula

    *0.35 × first examination score + 0.65 × second examination score*

4. Computes and outputs the semester average for each student using the formula

    *0.30 × project average + 0.40 × midterm examination average + 0.30 × final examination score*

5. Determines and prints the letter grade for each student using the following scheme:

| Semester Average | Letter Grade |
|:---:|:---:|
| 90 – 100 | A |
| 80 – 89 | B |
| 70 – 79 | C |
| 60 – 69 | D |
| 0 – 59 | F |

6.  We also want the program to save the letter grade as a member of the structure variable for the student, presumably to be used in some other related application.

This program should execute and process any number of student data until the user decides to stop. At the end of each processing cycle, the program should ask the user whether to stop or continue and then either repeat the computations for another student or terminate processing.

*Analysis*

**Inputs.** For each student, *student_idno*, *student_name*, *project1_score*, *project2_score*, *project3_score*, *test1_score*, *test2_score*, and *final_exam_score*.

**Outputs.** For each student, *project_average*, *midterm_exam_average*, *semester_average*, and *letter_grade*.

**Formulas.** The formulas for computing project average, midterm examination average, and semester average, and the scheme for determining letter grades are given in the requirements specification.

*Design*   We begin with the initial pseudocode algorithm of Figure 12.4.

---

*while the user wants to continue*
   *begin*
      *call input_student_data*

      *call computed_project_average to compute project_average*
      *call computed_midterm_exam_average to compute midterm_exam_average*
      *call computed_semester_average to compute semester_average*
      *call computed_letter_grade to compute letter_grade*

      *print student_idno*
      *print student_name*
      *print project_average*
      *print midterm_exam_average*
      *print semester_average*
      *print letter_grade*

---

**Figure 12.4**    Algorithm for computing student test and project averages and letter grades (initial pseudocode) *(continued)*   ▶

> ask the user if he/she wants to continue
> end
> end_while

**Figure 12.4**                                                               ■

Obviously, we have identified five simple modules: *input_student_data*, *computed_project_average*, *computed_midterm_exam_average*, *computed_semester_average*, and *computed_letter_grade*. First, we consider the algorithm for the module *input_student_data*, shown in Figure 12.5. This module has no input. It is expected to read and return *student_idno*, *student_name*, *project1_score*, *project2_score*, *project3_score*, *test1_score*, *test2_score*, and *final_exam_score* as its output.

---

*input_student_data(student_idno, student_name, project1_score, project2_score, project3_score,*
*        test1_score, test2_score, final_exam_score):*

*print "Enter student idno:"*
*read student_idno*

*print "Enter student name:"*
*read student_name*

*print "Enter first project score:"*
*read project1_score*

*print "Enter second project score:"*
*read project2_score*

*print "Enter third project score:"*
*read project3_score*

*print "Enter first test score:"*
*read test1_score*

*print "Enter second test score:"*
*read test2_score*

*print "Enter final exam score:"*
*read final_exam_score*

---

**Figure 12.5**    Pseudocode for module *input_student_data*

Next, we design an algorithm for the module *computed_project_average*, shown in Figure 12.6. This module has *project1_score*, *project2_score*, and *project3_score* as its input. It should compute and return *project_average* as its output.

---

*computed_project_average(project1_score, project2_score, project3_score):*
    *set best_of_first_two to project1_score*

    *if project1_score is less than project2_score*
        *set best_of_first_two to project2_score*
    *end_if*

    *compute project_average = 0.40 × best_of_first_two + 0.60 × project3_score*
    *return project_average*

---

**Figure 12.6**     Pseudocode for module *computed_project_average*

In Figure 12.6, after the *if* statement, the variable *best_of_first_two* will contain the value of the highest of *project1_score* and *project2_score*. The next statement is the formula that computes *project_average*.

The module *computed_midterm_exam_average* has *test1_score* and *test2_score* as its input and *midterm_exam_average* as its output. It consists of a single statement:

*compute midterm_exam_average = 0.35 × test1_score + 0.65 × test2_score*

The module *computed_semester_average* is equally simple. It has *project_average*, *midterm_exam_average*, and *final_exam_score* as its input and *semester_average* as its only output. It does its function through the following compute statement:

*compute semester_average = 0.30 × project_average +*
                                         *0.40 × midterm_exam_average +*
                                         *0.30 × final_exam_score*

Figure 12.7 shows the pseudocode for the module *computed_letter_grade*. It receives *semester_average* and returns *letter_grade*. This module consists of a nested *if* statement that is equivalent to the scheme for determining the letter grade.

---

*computed_letter_grade(semester_average):*
    *if semester_average is greater than or equal to 90*
        *set letter_grade to 'A'*
    *else if semester_average is greater than or equal to 80*
        *set letter_grade to 'B'*
    *else if semester_average is greater than or equal to 70*
        *set letter_grade to 'C'*

---

**Figure 12.7**     Pseudocode for module *computed_letter_grade* (continued)    ▶

> else if semester_average is greater than or equal to 60
>     set letter_grade to 'D'
> else
>     set letter_grade to 'F'
> end_if
>
> return letter_grade

**Figure 12.7** ∎

Now that we have devised algorithms for all the modules, we go back to the main program of Figure 12.4 to complete the design and refine it as shown in Figure 12.8.

> set want_to_continue to 'y'
>
> while want_to_continue is equal to 'y'
>     begin
>         call input_student_data
>         call computed_project_average to compute project_average
>         call computed_midterm_exam_average to compute midterm_exam_average
>         call computed_semester_average to compute semester_average
>         call computed_letter_grade to compute letter_grade
>
>         print student_idno
>         print student_name
>         print project_average
>         print midterm_exam_average
>         print semester_average
>         print letter_grade
>
>         print "Do you want to continue? (y/n):"
>         read want_to_continue
>     end
> end_while

**Figure 12.8** Pseudocode for the main program of the software system for computing student test and project averages and letter grades

***Implementation*** Because the student identification number, student name, three project scores, two midterm examination scores, and a final examination score are all data that belong to a given student, it makes sense to structure them in a structure type. We will also include in such a structure a member for the letter grade, as it is one of the problem requirements. The structure type called `student_struct` is declared globally in the program of Figure 12.9, which is the C implementation of the design of Figure 12.8.

```c
/***************************************************************
 Program Filename: prog12_1.c
 Author          : Uckan
 Purpose         : Interactively reads identification numbers,
                   names, project scores, midterm exam scores,
                   and final exam scores for students and then
                   computes and prints project averages, midterm
                   averages, semester averages, and letter grades.
 Input from      : terminal keyboard
 Output to       : screen
 **************************************************************/
#include <stdio.h>

/* Global structure declaration: */

struct student_struct {
        int student_idno;
        char student_name[31];
        int project1_score;
        int project2_score;
        int project3_score;
        int test1_score;
        int test2_score;
        int final_exam_score;
        char letter_grade;
}; /* end student_struct */

/* Function prototypes: */

void input_student_data(struct student_struct *st_rec);
int computed_project_average(struct student_struct st_rec);
int computed_midterm_exam_average(struct student_struct st_rec);
int computed_semester_average(int pr_avg, int mterm_avg,
                               int fin_exam);
char computed_letter_grade(int average);


int main(void) {
        /* Local variables: */
```

**Figure 12.9**    A C implementation of the pseudocode of Figure 12.8 (*continued*)    ▶

```
        struct student_struct student_record;
        char want_to_continue = 'y', new_line;
        int proj_avg, midterm_avg, sem_avg;

        /* Function body: */

        while (want_to_continue == 'y') {
                input_student_data(&student_record);

            proj_avg = computed_project_average(student_record);
            midterm_avg =
                        computed_midterm_exam_average(student_record);
            sem_avg = computed_semester_average(proj_avg, midterm_avg,
                    student_record.final_exam_score);

            printf("Student idno        : %d\n",
                    student_record.student_idno);
            printf("Student name        : %s\n",
                    student_record.student_name);
            printf("Project average     : %d\n",
                        proj_avg);
            printf("Midterm exam average: %d\n",
                        midterm_avg);
            printf("Semester average    : %d\n",
                        sem_avg);
            printf("Final letter grade  : %c\n",
                        (student_record.letter_grade =
                        computed_letter_grade(sem_avg)));

            scanf("%c", &new_line);
            printf("\nDo you want to continue? (y/n): ");
            scanf("%c", &want_to_continue);
        } /* end while */

        return 0;
} /* end function main */

/****************************************************************
 Function Name    : input_student_data
 Purpose          : Inputs identification numbers, student names,
                    project scores, midterm exam scores, and final
                    exam score for students.
 Called by        : main
```

Figure 12.9                                                    ▶

```
  Receives         : None
  Returns          : a structure variable of type student_struct
  ************************************************************/
void input_student_data(struct student_struct *s) {
      /* Local variables: */

      char new_line;

      /* Function body: */

      printf("***> Enter student idno       : ");
      scanf("%d", &s->student_idno);
      scanf("%c", &new_line);
      printf("***> Enter student name       : ");
      gets(s->student_name);
      printf("***> Enter first project score : ");
      scanf("%d", &s->project1_score);
      printf("***> Enter second project score: ");
      scanf("%d", &s->project2_score);
      printf("***> Enter third project score : ");
      scanf("%d", &s->project3_score);
      printf("***> Enter first test score    : ");
      scanf("%d", &s->test1_score);
      printf("***> Enter second test score   : ");
      scanf("%d", &s->test2_score);
      printf("***> Enter final exam score    : ");
      scanf("%d", &s->final_exam_score);
} /* end function input_student_data */

/***********************************************************
  Function Name    : computed_project_average
  Purpose          : Computes a student's project average.
  Called by        : main
  Receives         : a structure variable of type student_struct
  Returns          : project average
  ************************************************************/
int computed_project_average(struct student_struct s) {
      /* Local variables: */

      int best_of_first_two;

      /* Function body: */
```

Figure 12.9

```
            best_of_first_two = s.project1_score;

        if (s.project1_score < s.project2_score)
                best_of_first_two = s.project2_score;
        /* end if */

        return (int) (0.40 * best_of_first_two +
                0.60 * s.project3_score);
 } /* end function computed_project_average */

/**************************************************************
 Function Name    : computed_midterm_exam_average
 Purpose          : Computes a student's midterm exam average.
 Called by        : main
 Receives         : a structure variable of type student_struct
 Returns          : midterm examination average
 **************************************************************/
int computed_midterm_exam_average(struct student_struct s) {
        return (int) (0.35 * s.test1_score + 0.65 * s.test2_score);
 } /* end function computed_midterm_exam_average */


/**************************************************************
 Function Name    : computed_semester_average
 Purpose          : Computes a student's semester average.
 Called by        : main
 Receives         : project average, midterm exam average, final
                    exam score
 Returns          : semester average
 **************************************************************/
int computed_semester_average(int pavg, int mavg, int final_exam) {
        return (int) (0.30 * pavg + 0.40 * mavg + 0.30 * final_exam);
 } /* end function computed_semester_average */


/**************************************************************
 Function Name    : computed_letter_grade
 Purpose          : Computes a student's letter grade.
 Called by        : main
 Receives         : semester average
 Returns          : letter grade
 **************************************************************/
```

Figure 12.9                                                    ▶

```
char computed_letter_grade(int avg) {
      /* Local variables: */

      char grade;

      /* Function body: */

      if (avg >= 90)
            grade = 'A';
      else if (avg >= 80)
            grade = 'B';
      else if (avg >= 70)
            grade = 'C';
      else if (avg >= 60)
            grade = 'D';
      else
            grade = 'F';
      /* end if */

      return grade;
} /* end function computed_letter_grade */
```

**Figure 12.9**                                                                                          ■

The following characteristics are significant in the program of Figure 12.9:

1.   The structure type  student_struct  consists of nine data members. In this program the structure type declaration is placed before any function; hence it is global.

2.   Note that the functions  input_student_data, computed_project_average, and  computed_midterm_average  have parameters of type  student_struct.

3.   In the function  input_student_data, the formal parameter is a pointer to a structure variable of type  student_struct. In the body of this function, all references to structure variable members require the use of the indirect component selection operator,  ->.

4.   The functions computed_project_average and computed_midterm_average  are simple, each with one formal parameter of type  student_struct. Actually, these functions do not need every member of the structure to perform their tasks. For example, for  computed_project_average  we could have decided to pass only the three project scores. Instead, we are passing the entire structure to exemplify structure parameter passing in this application.

Figure 12.10 shows a sample interactive session obtained by running the program of Figure 12.9.

```
***> Enter student idno        : 1100
***> Enter student name        : Thomas Blackwell
***> Enter first project score : 70
***> Enter second project score: 90
***> Enter third project score : 89
***> Enter first test score    : 62
***> Enter second test score   : 88
***> Enter final exam score    : 78
Student idno         : 1100
Student name         : Thomas Blackwell
Project average      : 89
Midterm exam average: 78
Semester average     : 81
Final letter grade   : B

Do you want to continue? (y/n): n
```

**Figure 12.10**    A sample interactive session for the program of Figure 12.9

## 12.5   ENUMERATED DATA TYPES

We know that any data type consists of a set of values and a set of operations. Integer data types are based on a finite set of integer values, which are those that can be represented in a word of two or four bytes. We have a lot of such values, for example, from −32,768 to 32,767, if our data type is  int  and if the computer uses two bytes for their representation.

In many applications we need only a subset of values that a variable of a given data type can represent. For example, to indicate that a value read for the variable  month  is correct, we may declare an integer flag variable as

```
int correct_month;
```

and set it to 1. We indicate that the value is incorrect by setting  correct_month  to 0. Therefore, we use only two integer values, 0 and 1, for this variable. This approach is fine, and we have used it before in our problem-solving efforts. However, 0 and 1 are not very meaningful values, and we may easily forget what represents which state and which values are to be used for the variable  correct_month.

Can we not define a data type for which legal values are  NO  and  YES, rather than 0 and 1, and use a variable of that type as a flag variable? In C, we can, but we need a data type declaration that reads as follows:

```
enum yes_no_enum {
      NO, YES
}; /* end enum yes_no_enum */
```

Now we can go ahead and declare the flag variable `correct_month` as

```
enum yes_no_enum correct_month;
```

with the understanding that the variable `correct_month` may assume only the values `NO` and `YES`. To indicate that the value of month is correct, we set `correct_month` to `YES`:

```
correct_month = YES;
```

Otherwise, we set it to `NO`. This technique renders the flag variable `correct_month` more meaningful and makes the program more readable.

The data type `yes_no_enum` is not known to the compiler until we declare it. If a data type has to be declared in a program, it is a programmer-defined data type. This particular programmer-defined data type is called an enumerated data type or an enumeration in C. Here is how it is defined:

> An **enumerated data type** is a set of integer constant values that are represented by identifiers.

## Declaring Enumerated Data Types and Variables

Like all data types and variables of any data type, an enumerated data type and all variables of that type must be properly declared in a program. The syntax of an enumerated data type declaration is similar to that of a structure type. A simplified syntax is

```
enum EnumerationTypeName {
      EnumeratorList
}; /* end enum */
```

*EnumerationTypeName* (also called **enumeration tag**) is an identifier, and *EnumeratorList* is a list of identifiers and/or a list of assignments separated by commas. These identifiers are considered to be constant values for the declared data type. They are also referred to as **enumeration constants**. Note that the declaration is terminated with a semicolon. The comment `/* end enum */` is, of course, an optional style convention.

Once we declare an enumerated type in our program, we may declare variables of this type. Enumerated type variables can be declared according to the following syntax:

enum *EnumeratedTypeName EnumeratedVariableList*;

In this syntax *EnumeratedVariableList* is a list of identifiers separated by commas.

***Example 12.10***    The declaration

```
enum month_names_enum {
      JANUARY, FEBRUARY, MARCH, APRIL, MAY, JUNE,
      JULY, AUGUST, SEPTEMBER, OCTOBER, NOVEMBER, DECEMBER
}; /* end enum month_names_enum */
```

declares an enumerated data type called `month_names_enum`. A variable `month` subsequently declared to be of type `month_names_enum`

```
    enum month_names_enum month;
```

may assume only the values shown in the enumerator list, which are `JANUARY`, `FEBRUARY`, and so on. The identifiers `JANUARY` through `DECEMBER` are enumeration constants for the data type `month_names_enum`.

When an enumerated data type is declared, the enumerators are set automatically to integer values such that the first enumerator becomes 0, the second 1, and so on. The value of an enumerator, except the first in the list, is the value of the previous enumerator plus 1. In the preceding example, the enumerator `JANUARY` is set to 0, `FEBRUARY` to 1, and finally, `DECEMBER` to 11. The programmer may set enumerators to explicit integer values by using assignments. In explicit value assignments for enumerators in `enum` declarations, all of the following actions are legal:

1.   We can assign constant values to enumerators.
2.   We can assign a value to an enumerator by using previous enumerators in arithmetic expressions.
3.   We can use the same value for more than one enumerator in the list.

***Example 12.11***    Consider the declaration

```
enum department_names_enum {
      SALES = 1, MIS = SALES + 3, ACCOUNTING = 3, MARKETING
}; /* end enum department_names_enum */
```

This declaration sets the enumerator SALES to 1, MIS to 4, ACCOUNTING to 3, and MARKETING to 4. On the other hand, the declaration

```
enum month_names_enum {
      JANUARY = 1, FEBRUARY, MARCH, APRIL, MAY, JUNE,
      JULY, AUGUST, SEPTEMBER, OCTOBER, NOVEMBER, DECEMBER
}; /* end enum month_names_enum */
```

sets JANUARY to 1, FEBRUARY to 2, and finally, DECEMBER to 12.

After an enumerated constant is declared as one of the values for an enumerated data type, it is not possible to change the integer value that has been associated with it. For example, the assignment

```
JANUARY = 2;
```

would be illegal, and we would get a syntax error.

The declaration of an enumerated data type may be global and may precede all function definitions in a source program file. You can declare variables of that type in any function. If, however, an enumerated data type declaration is placed in a function, variables of that data type can be declared and used only in that function. In general, you should declare enumerated data types globally before function definitions in your program.

## Operations on Enumerated Variables

A variable declared to be of an enumerated data type can be used in several operations.

1. You can assign enumeration constants to enumerated variables. For example, given the type declaration

```
enum department_names_enum {
      SALES = 1, MIS = SALES + 3, ACCOUNTING = 3, MARKETING
}; /* end enum department_names_enum */
```

and the variable declarations

```
enum department_names_enum cincinnati_dept, columbus_dept;
```

the following assignment is legal:

```
cincinnati_dept = SALES;
```

2. You can also assign integer values or values of integer expressions in which enumeration constants are used to enumerate variables. However, you should be careful that the value assigned corresponds to an enumeration constant for the enumerated data type. In fact, for such assignments some compilers generate warning messages. Nevertheless, for most compilers assignments such as

```
cincinnati_dept = 1;
cincinnati_dept = SALES + 3;
```

are legal. It would be illegal, however, to write an assignment such as

```
cincinnati_dept = SALES + JANUARY;
```

where JANUARY is an enumeration constant for an enumerated data type other than the one on which the enumerated variable is based.

3. You can input a value for an enumerated variable. However, the value you input cannot be an enumeration constant; it must be an integer. For the input statement

```
scanf("%d", &cincinnati_dept);
```

you can enter the value 1. You may not enter the value SALES; if you do, you will have an error. Again, you must be careful to enter a value that corresponds to one of the enumeration constants.

4. You may output an enumerated variable as in

```
printf("%d", cincinnati_dept);
```

Such an output statement will print the integer counterpart of the value of the variable cincinnati_dept. If the value of the variable is currently SALES, the printf function call will print 1, not SALES.

5. You may compare the value of an enumerated variable to an integer, an enumeration constant of its type, or to another enumerated variable of the same type. The following comparisons are legal:

```
cincinnati_dept > 1
cincinnati_dept == ACCOUNTING
cincinnati_dept >= columbus_dept
```

However, it is illegal to compare an enumerated variable or an enumeration constant to another enumerated variable or constant of a different type. The following comparison is illegal:

```
cincinnati_dept == SUNDAY
```

6. You can pass enumerated variables between functions, as you can any other data type.

A matter of programming style: Use uppercase letters in the names of enumeration constants as you did for named constants. This convention reminds the readers of the program that these elements are constants and not variables.

## Using Enumerated Data Types

The main advantage of the enumerated data types is their ability to make a program more readable. This advantage will become obvious in the following example, which uses an enumerated data type and an enumerated variable.

***Example 12.12***    The code in Figure 12.11 contains a function called `get_month_value`, which reads an integer to represent a month of the year and verifies that it is in the correct range of 1 through 12 before returning it to the calling function. We also used this logic in designing the function `get_a_date` in Example 10.2. In that version we declared the variable `correct_data` as a character variable, initialized it to `'n'`, and used it in a `do-while` loop to validate the entered month value. Here we use an enumerated data type instead.

```c
#include <stdio.h>

enum Boolean_enum {
      FALSE, TRUE
}; /* end enum Boolean_enum */

/* Function prototypes: */

void get_month_value(int *month);


int main(void) {
      int month;

      get_month_value(&month);
      printf("The month is %d", month);
      return 0;
} // end function main


void get_month_value(int *month) {
      enum Boolean_enum correct_data = FALSE;

      do {
            printf("Enter a month as an integer: ");
            scanf("%d", &*month);
```

**Figure 12.11**    Use of an enumerated data type in validating data *(continued)*    ▶

```
                    if (*month < 1 || *month > 12)
                            printf("Incorrect month. Please try again.\n");
                    else
                            correct_data = TRUE;
                    /* end if */
            } while (correct_data == FALSE);
            /* end do-while */
    } /* end function get_month_value */
```

**Figure 12.11**                                                                                    ∎

In the program of Figure 12.11, we declare an enumerated data type called Boolean_enum with two enumeration constants, FALSE and TRUE. Then we declare and initialize the variable correct_data as

enum Boolean_enum correct_data = FALSE;

Now correct_data has become a variable of type Boolean_enum and may assume the values FALSE and TRUE. This declaration initializes correct_data to the value FALSE. The assignment in the else-part of the if statement in the function get_month_value changes correct_data to TRUE only if the value typed for month is in the correct range. You are familiar with the logic of this function. You should note that using values like TRUE and FALSE for correct_data, rather than 'y' and 'n', adds to the readability of the code.

The data type **Boolean** with values *true* and *false* is a fundamental data type in some programming languages, such as Pascal, C++, and Java. In C, Boolean is not a fundamental data type. However, by using an enumerated data type in the preceding application, we have succeeded in simulating it to some extent.

## 12.6 ARRAYS OF STRUCTURES AND STRUCTURES OF ARRAYS

In C we can combine different data types to come up with composite data types and use them conveniently in some applications. Two such composite data types are arrays of structures and structures of arrays.

### Arrays of Structures

In many applications where the use of one-dimensional arrays appears to be appropriate, we have more than one related array. For example, to store student information consisting of student identification number, year, and status, we may declare three arrays, as

```
    int idno[ARRAY_SIZE];
    int year[ARRAY_SIZE];
    char status[ARRAY_SIZE];
```

where `ARRAY_SIZE` is a global named constant declared as

```
#define ARRAY_SIZE 60
```

Thus the array elements `idno[i]`, `year[i]`, and `status[i]` contain information that belong to the $i$th student. Because data stored in the $i$th elements of these arrays belong to the same student, such arrays are called **parallel arrays**.

The use of parallel arrays appears to be a good scheme in problems where data values of different types must be stored for an entity. However, some difficulties occur in processing parallel arrays. For example, in sorting student information stored in three parallel arrays by student identification number, whenever we exchange two elements of the array `idno`, we must also exchange the corresponding elements of the remaining two arrays to maintain them as parallel arrays.

Another approach to solving problems for which parallel arrays seem to be indicated is to use an array of structures. In C the type of an array can be a structure. For example, instead of using three parallel arrays for `idno`, `year`, and `status`, we may declare the following structure type

```
struct student_struct {
      int idno;
      int year;
      char status;
};/* end student_struct */
```

and a one-dimensional array of type `struct student_struct` as

```
struct student_struct student[ARRAY_SIZE];
```

Here the array `student` is of type `struct student_struct`, and it is an array of structures. Having done this, we can reference any member of the structure in a given element of the array using the conventions for arrays and structures. For example, `idno` of the $j$th student has the name `student[j].idno`. Also, we can reference all data for the $j$th student by `student[j]`. Now operations such as those requiring exchange of two elements of the array `student` can be handled easily using only three statements:

```
temp = student[j];
student[j] = student[i];
student[i] = temp;
```

Here `temp` is also a variable of type `struct student_struct`. Had we used three parallel arrays, the same exchange operations would have required nine statements.

In the next section we will develop an application that uses an array of structures.

## Structures of Arrays

If one or more data components of a structure type are arrays, then we have a **structure of arrays**. An example follows.

```
struct grades_struct {
      int list_size;
      char letter_grades[60];
}; /* end grades_struct */
```

In this example we have an array, `letter_grades`, as the component of the structure `grades_struct`. An obvious use of such a structure is in passing arrays to functions by value. As you have learned in Chapter 11, in C the only way to pass arrays to functions is by pointers. The reason is that pass by pointers does not duplicate the array to be passed in the data area of the receiving function, and the available memory is not wasted. However, the array that is passed is not write-protected. In Chapter 11, you have also learned how to use the `const` qualifier to write protect arrays. Another approach is to hide an array in a structure and pass a structure variable to functions by value.

If the array to be passed is hidden in a structure as a data member of that structure, then we can pass it back and forth in any way that we can pass a structure variable — by value, by pointers, and under the function's name. For example, the function `output_grades`, whose prototype follows, is designed to pass a structure variable of type `grades_struct` and, therefore, the array `letter_grades` as a component of that variable:

```
void output_grades(struct grades_struct s);
```

You should note that if you pass an array hidden inside a structure variable this way, you will be write protecting it; but at the same time, you will be duplicating the array in the memory. If you must use this technique, make sure that your array is small and that your computer has enough memory for processing the program.

## REVIEW QUESTIONS

**1.** An enumerated data type is a fundamental data type in C. (T or F)

**2.** In declaring an enumerated data type:
   **a.** We use the keyword `enum`.
   **b.** The keyword `enum` is followed by the name of a variable of that enumerated type.
   **c.** The list of enumerators is enclosed by parentheses.
   **d.** Each enumerator must be an integer constant.
   **e.** All of the above.
   **f.** None of the above.

**3.** An enumerated variable can be assigned the value of an enumeration constant that belongs to another enumerated data type. (T or F)

**4.** Choose the correct statement.
   **a.** A `typedef` in an enumerated data type declaration assigns a synonym to the enumeration tag.
   **b.** The declaration of an enumerated variable must come after the declaration of the corresponding enumerated data type.
   **c.** It is possible to input integer values for enumerated variables.
   **d.** The output of an enumerated variable is an integer value that corresponds to the enumeration constant, which is the variable's current value.
   **e.** All of the above.
   **f.** None of the above.

**5.** We can compare two enumerated variables in a predicate provided they are of the same enumerated data type. (T or F)

**6.** Two one-dimensional arrays are said to be parallel if their respective elements belong to the same entity, and whenever the relative location of an element in one array changes, the relative location of the corresponding element in the other is also changed in parallel. (T or F)

**7.** We have the structure declaration

```
struct books_struct {
      int book_no;
      double price;
}; /* end books_struct */
```

Which of the following is a correct declaration for a one-dimensional array of structures of type `struct books_struct`?
   **a.** `int books_struct books[20];`
   **b.** `struct books_struct books[20];`
   **c.** `struct books[20] books_struct;`
   **d.** `struct books books_struct[20];`
   **e.** None of the above.

**Answers:**   1. F; 2. a; 3. F; 4. e; 5. T; 6. T; 7. b.

---

## 12.7   EXAMPLE PROGRAM 2: A C Program that Processes an Array of Structures

We will design a program to process a list of student records, implemented as a one-dimensional array of structures.

***Problem***   We want to develop an application program that allows the user to perform the actions:

1.  Create an array of structures that stores a list of student records. Each student record consists of student identification number, major code, year, and status.
2.  Print the list of student records stored in the array.
3.  Sort the list in increasing order by student identification number.
4.  Search the list for a given student identification number.

***Requirements Specification***   Develop an interactive C program that does the following:

1.  Displays a menu of choices as

```
+-------------------------------------+
| To create an unordered list -- Type 1 |
| To print the list ----------- Type 2 |
| To sort the list by idno ----- Type 3 |
| To search the list ---------- Type 4 |
| To terminate program -------- Type 5 |
+-------------------------------------+
```

2.  If the user choice is 1, prompts the user to enter values for the number of students — and for each student, an integer student identification number, a 3-byte character string major code, an integer year (1, 2, 3, or 4 for freshman, sophomore, junior or senior, respectively), and a character status code (*'p'*, *'s'*, or *'h'* for probation, satisfactory, or honors) — and reads these values.

3.  If the user choice is 2, prints the list of student records.

4.  If the user choice is 3, sorts the list in increasing order by student identification number, using the selection sort algorithm.

5.  If the user choice is 4, prompts the user to enter a student identification number, reads it, and using it as the search key value, searches the list. Uses the binary search algorithm for searching the list.

6.  If the user choice is 5, terminates the program.

7.  If the user choice is an illegal value (that is, outside the range of 1 through 5), warns the user to enter another value.

8.  If the user choice is 2, 3, or 4 and the list has not yet been created, warns the user to create the list first.

***Analysis***

**Inputs.** User choice; number of students; *idno, major_code, year*, and *status* values for each student; and if user choice is 4, a search key value.

**Outputs.** The menu of choices, appropriate warning messages, list of student records if user choice is 2, and the result of the list search process if user choice is 4.

**Constraints.** The legal values of user choice are 1 through 5.

***Design***    We begin with the pseudocode of Figure 12.12 for the main program.

```
set list_created to FALSE
set continue_processing to TRUE

while continue_processing is equal to TRUE
    begin
        call print_menu_and_get_choice(choice)

        if choice is equal to 1
            call create_student_list(list_size, student_list, list_created)
        else if choice is equal to 2
            call print_student_list(list_size, student_list, list_created)
        else if choice is equal to 3
            call order_student_list(list_size, student_list, list_created)
        else if choice is equal to 4
            call search_student_list(list_size, student_list, list_created)
        else if choice is equal to 5
            begin
                set continue_processing to FALSE
                print "Terminating . . ."
            end
        else
            print "Wrong choice; try again."
        end_if
    end
end_while
```

**Figure 12.12**    A pseudocode for the main program that processes a list of student records

The pseudocode algorithm of Figure 12.12 has references to five modules:

1.  *print_menu_and_get_choice*, which prints the menu of choices on the screen, prompts the user to enter a choice, and reads and returns the choice to the calling program.

2.  *create_student_list*, which creates a *student_list* of size *list_size*, and returns the list together with *list_created*, a flag that informs the main program that the list has been created, to the main program.

3.  *print_student_list*, which prints the list of student records if the list exists.

4.  *order_student_list*, which orders the *student_list* provided the list has been created.

5.  *search_student_list*, which searches the list of student records, again if the list has been created.

The simple logic of *create_student_list* is given in Figure 12.13.

---

*create_student_list(list_size, student_list, list_created):*
    *call input_array(list_size, student_list)*
    *set list_created to TRUE*
    *print "A list of size ", list_size, " has been created."*

---

**Figure 12.13**    Pseudocode algorithm for the module *create_student_list*

Figure 12.14 shows the psedocode for the modules *print_student_list* and *order_student_list*, which are essentially similar.

---

*print_student_list(list_size, student_list, list_created):*
    *if list_created is equal to TRUE*
        *call print_list(list_size, student_list)*
    *else*
        *print "The list has not yet been created."*
    *end_if*

*order_student_list(list_size, student_list, list_created):*
    *if list_created is equal to TRUE*
        *call order_list(list_size, student_list)*
    *else*
        *print "The list has not yet been created."*
    *end_if*

---

**Figure 12.14**    Pseudocode algorithm for the modules *print_student_list* and *order_student_list*

The logic of the module *search_student_list* is a bit more involved and is presented in Figure 12.15.

---

*search_student_list(list_size, student_list, list_created):*
    *if list_created is equal to TRUE*
        *begin*
            *print "Enter a student idno as the search key value: "*
            *read key*
            *call search_list(key, list_size, student_list, success, index)*

---

**Figure 12.15**    Pseudocode algorithm for the module *search_student_list* (continued)    ▶

*if success is equal to TRUE*
  *begin*
    *print "Student ", key, " is in the array."*
    *print idno, major, year, status*
  *end*
*else*
  *print "Student ", key, " is NOT in the array."*
*end_if*
      *end*
    *else*
      *print "The list has not yet been created."*
    *end_if*

Figure 12.15                                                    ■

These modules invoke four lower-level modules: *input_list*, *print_list*, *order_list*, and *search_list*. Of these, *order_list* and *search_list* are essentially the algorithms given in Figures 11.11 and 11.20, respectively. We will simply adapt them for an array of structures. The remaining three modules, *print_menu_and_get_choice*, *input_list*, and *print_list* are so simple that we will directly implement them as functions in our C program. At this point it would be a good exercise for the reader to draw a structure chart corresponding to our design.

***Implementation***    Our implementation will be based on an enumerated type called `Boolean_enum` and a structure type called `student_struct`. The declarations of these global types and the named constant `ARRAY_SIZE` are presented in Figure 12.16.

```
/* Named constant declaration: */

#define ARRAY_SIZE 60

/* Programmer-defined data type declarations: */

enum Boolean_enum {
     FALSE, TRUE
}; /* end enum Boolean_enum */
```

Figure 12.16      Global constant and type declarations for Example Program 2 (*continued*)    ▶

```
struct student_struct {
        int idno;
        char major_code[4];
        int year;
        char status;
}; /* end student_struct */
```

Figure 12.16

We will implement the design using the bottom-up approach. The implementation of the module *print_menu_and_get_choice* is given in Figure 12.17.

```
/*******************************************************************
  Function Name    : print_menu_and_get_choice
  Purpose          : Prints the menu and reads a value for choice.
  Called by        : main
  Receives         : None
  Returns          : choice
 ********************************************************************/
void print_menu_and_get_choice(int *choice) {
     printf("\n");
     printf("+------------------------------------+\n");
     printf("| To create an unordered list -- Type 1 |\n");
     printf("| To print the list ---------- Type 2 |\n");
     printf("| To sort the list by idno ----- Type 3 |\n");
     printf("| To search the list ---------- Type 4 |\n");
     printf("| To terminate program ------- Type 5 |\n");
     printf("+------------------------------------+\n\n");
     printf("Enter your choice: ");
     scanf("%d", &*choice);
} /* end function print_menu_and_get_choice */
```

Figure 12.17    A C implementation of the module *print_menu_and_get_choice*

Next, we present the C functions corresponding to the modules *create_student_list* and *input_list* together in Figure 12.18.

```
/******************************************************************
 Function Name    : create_student_list
 Purpose          : Creates a list of student records.
 Called by        : main
 Receives         : None
 Returns          : list_size, student_list, list_created
 ******************************************************************/
void create_student_list(int *list_size,
                         struct student_struct student_list[],
                         enum Boolean_enum *list_created) {
     /* Function body: */

     input_list(&*list_size, student_list);

     *list_created = TRUE;
     printf("A list of size %d has been created.\n", *list_size);
} /* end function create_student_list */


/******************************************************************
 Function Name    : input_list
 Purpose          : Reads the size of the list of students and the
                    student records, and returns them to the calling
                    function.
 Called by        : create_student_list
 Receives         : None
 Returns          : list_size, arry
 ******************************************************************/
void input_list(int *list_size, struct student_struct arry[]) {
     /* Local variables: */

     int j;
     char new_line;

     /* Function body: */

     printf("Enter number of students: ");
     scanf("%d", &*list_size);

     for (j = 0; j < *list_size; j++) {
          printf("Enter IDNO for the %dth student        : ",
                 j + 1);
          scanf("%d", &arry[j].idno);
```

**Figure 12.18**     C implementations of the modules *create_student_list* and *input_list* (continued)     ▶

```
            scanf("%c", &new_line);
            printf("Enter MAJOR CODE for the %dth student: ",
                   j + 1);
            gets(arry[j].major_code);
            printf("Enter YEAR for the %dth student        : ",
                   j + 1);
            scanf("%d", &arry[j].year);
            scanf("%c", &new_line);
            printf("Enter STATUS for the %dth student       : ",
                   j + 1);
            scanf("%c", &arry[j].status);
      } /* end for */
} /* end function input_list */
```

**Figure 12.18**

In the function `input_list` of Figure 12.18, for example, you should note the declaration for the array of structure of type `student_struct` in the formal parameter list as `student_struct arry[]` and the references to the elements of the array of structure, as in `arry[j].idno`.

Figure 12.19 shows the C functions for the modules *print_student_list* and *print_list*.

```
/* ***********************************************************
  Function Name    : print_student_list
  Purpose          : Prints a list of student records.
  Called by        : main
  Receives         : list_size, student_list, list_created
  *********************************************************** /
void print_student_list(int list_size,
                      const struct student_struct student_list[],
                      enum Boolean_enum list_created) {
      if (list_created == TRUE) {
            printf("Printing the list:\n");
            print_list(list_size, student_list);
            printf("\n");
      }
      else
            printf("The list has not yet been created.\n");
      /* end if */
} /* end function print_student_list */
```

**Figure 12.19**    C implementations of the modules *print_student_list* and *print_list* (continued)    ▶

```
/***************************************************************
 Function Name    : print_list
 Purpose          : Prints the list of student records on the screen.
 Called by        : print_student_list
 Receives         : list_size, arry
 Returns          : None
 ***************************************************************/
void print_list(int list_size, const struct student_struct arry[]) {
     /* Local variables: */

     int t;

     /* Function body: */

     printf("Index    Idno     Major      Year      Status\n");

     for (t = 0; t < list_size; t++)
          printf("%3d%9d       %s%8d         %c\n", t + 1,
                 arry[t].idno, arry[t].major_code, arry[t].year,
                 arry[t].status);
     /* end for */
} /* end function print_list */
```

**Figure 12.19**                                                                    ■

Figure 12.20 displays the C implementations of the modules *order_student_list* and *order_list*. The function  order_list  is a selection sort for an array of structures.

```
/***************************************************************
 Function Name    : order_student_list
 Purpose          : Sorts a list of student records by student idno.
 Called by        : main
 Receives         : list_size, student_list, list_created
 Returns          : student_list
 ***************************************************************/
void order_student_list(int list_size,
                        struct student_struct student_list[],
                        enum Boolean_enum list_created) {
     if (list_created == TRUE) {
          order_list(list_size, student_list);
          printf("The list has been sorted by idno.\n");
```

**Figure 12.20**     C implementations of the modules *order_student_list* and *order_list* (continued)     ▶

```
        }
        else
              printf("The list has not yet been created.\n");
        /* end if */
} /* end function order_student_list */


/* * * * * * * * * * * * * * * * * * * * * * * * * * * * * * * * * * * * * * * * * * * * * * * * *
 Function Name    : order_list
 Purpose          : Sorts an array of structures in increasing order
                    by student idno using the selection sort algorithm.
 Called by        : order_student_list
 Receives         : list_size, array_to_sort
 Returns          : array_to_sort
* * * * * * * * * * * * * * * * * * * * * * * * * * * * * * * * * * * * * * * * * * * * * * * * */
void order_list(int list_size, struct student_struct array_to_sort[]) {
        /* Local variables: */

        int i, index_of_largest, last;
        struct student_struct temp;

        /* Function body: */

        for (last = list_size - 1; last >= 1; last--) {
              index_of_largest = 0;

              for (i = 1; i <= last; i++)
                    if (array_to_sort[i].idno >
                          array_to_sort[index_of_largest].idno)
                          index_of_largest = i;
                    /* end if */
              /* end for */

              temp = array_to_sort[last];
              array_to_sort[last] = array_to_sort[index_of_largest];
              array_to_sort[index_of_largest] = temp;
        } /* end for */
} /* end function order_list */
```

Figure 12.20                                                                                    ■

    In Figure 12.21 we have the C functions for *search_student_list* and *search_list*, which
is the binary search algorithm adopted for the requirements of the present problem. Finally,
in Figure 12.22 we have the function  main  together with the globally declared function prototypes.

```
/******************************************************************
 Function Name    : search_student_list
 Purpose          : Searches a list of student records by idno.
 Called by        : main
 Receives         : list_size, student_list, list_created
 Returns          : None
 ******************************************************************/
void search_student_list(int list_size,
                         const struct student_struct student_list[],
                         enum Boolean_enum list_created) {

    /* Local variables: */

    int index, key;
    enum Boolean_enum success;

    /* Function body: */

    if (list_created == TRUE) {
         printf("Enter a student idno as the search key value: ");
         scanf("%d", &key);

         search_list(key, list_size, student_list,
             &success, &index);

         if (success == TRUE) {
             printf("\nStudent %d is in the array.\n", key);
             printf("   Idno  : %d\n",student_list[index].idno);
             printf("   Major : %s\n",
                     student_list[index].major_code);
             printf("   Year  : %d\n", student_list[index].year);
             printf("   Status: %c\n",
                     student_list[index].status);
         }
         else
             printf("\nStudent %d is NOT in the array.\n", key);
         /* end if */
    }
    else
         printf("\nThe list has not yet been created.\n");
    /* end if */
} /* end function search_student_list */
```

**Figure 12.21**     C implementations of the modules *search_student_list* and *search_list* (continued)     ▶

```
/*******************************************************************
 Function Name    : search_list
 Purpose          : Searches a list of student records using the
                    binary search technique.
 Called by        : search_student_list
 Receives         : search_key, list_size, array_to_search
 Returns          : success, index
 ******************************************************************/
void search_list(int search_key, int list_size,
                 const struct student_struct array_to_search[],
                 enum Boolean_enum *success, int *index) {
     /* Local variables: */

     int first, last, mid;

     /* Function body: */

     *success = FALSE;
     *index = ARRAY_SIZE + 1;
     first = 0;
     last = list_size - 1;

     while (first <= last && *success == FALSE) {
          mid = (first + last) / 2;

          if (array_to_search[mid].idno == search_key) {
               *index = mid;
               *success = TRUE;
          }
          else if (array_to_search[mid].idno > search_key)
               last = mid - 1;
          else
               first = mid + 1;
          /* end if */
     } /* end while */
} /* end function search_list */
```

Figure 12.21

```
/****************************************************************
 Program Filename: prog12_2.c
 Author          : Uckan
 Purpose         : Enables the user to create a list of student
                   records and then print, sort, and search it.
 Input from      : terminal keyboard
 Output to       : screen
 ****************************************************************/
#include <stdio.h>

/* Function prototypes: */

void print_menu_and_get_choice(int *choice);
void create_student_list(int *list_size,
      struct student_struct student_list[],
      enum Boolean_enum *list_created);
void print_student_list(int list_size,
      const struct student_struct student_list[],
      enum Boolean_enum list_created);
void order_student_list(int list_size,
      struct student_struct student_list[],
      enum Boolean_enum list_created);
void search_student_list(int list_size,
      const struct student_struct student_list[],
      enum Boolean_enum list_created);
void input_list(int *list_size, struct student_struct student[]);
void print_list(int list_size,
                const struct student_struct student[]);
void order_list(int list_size, struct student_struct student[]);
void search_list(int key, int list_size,
                const struct student_struct student[],
                enum Boolean_enum *success, int *index);


int main(void) {
      /* Local variables: */

      struct student_struct student_list[ARRAY_SIZE];
      int list_size, choice;
      enum Boolean_enum continue_processing = TRUE,
                        list_created = FALSE;

   /* Function body: */
```

**Figure 12.22**     A C implementation of the main module for Example Program 2 (*continued*)     ▶

```
        while (continue_processing == TRUE) {
            print_menu_and_get_choice(&choice);

            switch (choice) {
                case 1 :
                        create_student_list(&list_size, student_list,
                            &list_created);
                        break;
                case 2 :
                        print_student_list(list_size, student_list,
                            list_created);
                        break;
                case 3 :
                        order_student_list(list_size, student_list,
                            list_created);
                        break;
                case 4 :
                        search_student_list(list_size, student_list,
                            list_created);
                        break;
                case 5 :
                        continue_processing = FALSE;
                        printf("Terminating . . .");
                        break;
                default :
                        printf("Wrong choice; try again.\n");
            } /* end switch */
        } /* end while */

        return 0;
} /* end function main */
```

Figure 12.22                                                                ■

Figure 12.23 is a sample run of the program of Figure 12.22 and all other associated
modules. It comprehensively tests all program features.

```
+-------------------------------------+
| To create an unordered list -- Type 1 |
| To print the list ------------ Type 2 |
| To sort the list by idno ----- Type 3 |
| To search the list ----------- Type 4 |
| To terminate program --------- Type 5 |
+-------------------------------------+

Enter your choice: 7
Wrong choice; try again.

+-------------------------------------+
| To create an unordered list -- Type 1 |
| To print the list ------------ Type 2 |
| To sort the list by idno ----- Type 3 |
| To search the list ----------- Type 4 |
| To terminate program --------- Type 5 |
+-------------------------------------+

Enter your choice: 2
The list has not yet been created.

+-------------------------------------+
| To create an unordered list -- Type 1 |
| To print the list ------------ Type 2 |
| To sort the list by idno ----- Type 3 |
| To search the list ----------- Type 4 |
| To terminate program --------- Type 5 |
+-------------------------------------+

Enter your choice: 1
Enter number of students: 3
Enter IDNO for the 1th student       : 700
Enter MAJOR CODE for the 1th student: csc
Enter YEAR for the 1th student       : 2
Enter STATUS for the 1th student     : h
Enter IDNO for the 2th student       : 600
Enter MAJOR CODE for the 2th student: mth
Enter YEAR for the 2th student       : 1
Enter STATUS for the 2th student     : s
Enter IDNO for the 3th student       : 500
Enter MAJOR CODE for the 3th student: csc
Enter YEAR for the 3th student       : 4
```

**Figure 12.23**    A sample run of the program of Figure 12.22 (*continued*)    ▶

```
Enter STATUS for the 3th student     : p
A list of size 3 has been created.

+-------------------------------------+
| To create an unordered list -- Type 1 |
| To print the list ------------ Type 2 |
| To sort the list by idno ----- Type 3 |
| To search the list ----------- Type 4 |
| To terminate program --------- Type 5 |
+-------------------------------------+

Enter your choice: 2
Printing the list:
Index   Idno    Major    Year      Status
  1      700     csc       2          h
  2      600     mth       1          s
  3      500     csc       4          p


+-------------------------------------+
| To create an unordered list -- Type 1 |
| To print the list ------------ Type 2 |
| To sort the list by idno ----- Type 3 |
| To search the list ----------- Type 4 |
| To terminate program --------- Type 5 |
+-------------------------------------+

Enter your choice: 3
The list has been sorted by idno.

+-------------------------------------+
| To create an unordered list -- Type 1 |
| To print the list ------------ Type 2 |
| To sort the list by idno ----- Type 3 |
| To search the list ----------- Type 4 |
| To terminate program --------- Type 5 |
+-------------------------------------+

Enter your choice: 2
Printing the list:
Index   Idno    Major    Year      Status
  1      500     csc       4          p
  2      600     mth       1          s
  3      700     csc       2          h
```

Figure 12.23

```
+----------------------------------------+
| To create an unordered list –– Type 1 |
| To print the list ––––––––––– Type 2 |
| To sort the list by idno ––––– Type 3 |
| To search the list –––––––––– Type 4 |
| To terminate program –––––––– Type 5 |
+----------------------------------------+

Enter your choice: 4
Enter a student idno as the search key value: 700

Student 700 is in the array.
   Idno  : 700
   Major : csc
   Year  : 2
   Status: h

+----------------------------------------+
| To create an unordered list –– Type 1 |
| To print the list ––––––––––– Type 2 |
| To sort the list by idno ––––– Type 3 |
| To search the list –––––––––– Type 4 |
| To terminate program –––––––– Type 5 |
+----------------------------------------+

Enter your choice: 4
Enter a student idno as the search key value: 650

Student 650 is NOT in the array.

+----------------------------------------+
| To create an unordered list –– Type 1 |
| To print the list ––––––––––– Type 2 |
| To sort the list by idno ––––– Type 3 |
| To search the list –––––––––– Type 4 |
| To terminate program –––––––– Type 5 |
+----------------------------------------+

Enter your choice: 5
Terminating . . .
```

Figure 12.23

## 12.8   SUMMARY

### This Chapter at a Glance

- In this chapter you learned about structures. A structure is a programmer-defined, derived, structured data type that can be used to represent a collection of related data items of different types.

- You studied structure type and variable declarations, how structure members can be accessed, how they can be initialized, and what operations can be used on structures. You learned that structures can be passed between functions and about arrays of structures and structures of arrays.

- This chapter introduced another programmer-defined data type, the enumerated data type, which may significantly improve a program's readability.

### Coming Attractions

- Since Chapter 3 you have been learning about strings. You know about string constants, string variables, and how to input and output strings. You also studied two important functions of the `string` library in C: `strcpy` for copying strings and `strcmp` for comparing strings. However, several additional operations are fundamental in string processing. Also, there are some other important standard library functions in the C `string` library. The next chapter covers them in detail.

## STUDY GUIDE

### Test Your Comprehension

1. Which of the following is *not* a structured data type in C?
   **a.** Structures
   **b.** Unions
   **c.** Arrays
   **d.** Characters

2. Which of the following does *not* correctly describe the syntax for structure type declaration?
   **a.** A structure type declaration must begin with the keyword `struct`.
   **b.** The identifier that follows the keyword `struct` is the structure type name, and it is also called the structure tag.
   **c.** The structure tag is optional; if it is missing, then the keyword `struct` must be preceded by the keyword `typedef`.
   **d.** If `typedef` is not used, the identifiers that follow the list of structure member declarations must be synonyms for the structure tag.

3. Choose the correct statement. A structure variable declaration:

**a.** May precede its structure type declaration.
**b.** Must begin with the keyword combination `typedef struct`.
**c.** May contain only one variable name after the structure type name.
**d.** All of the above are correct.
**e.** None of the above is correct.

**4.** We have the following combined structure type and structure variable declarations:

```
struct faculty_struct {
        int faculty_idno;
        struct {
                char last_name_initial;
                char first_name_initial;
        } name_initials;
        /* end struct */

        int age;
        char gender;
        float salary;
} faculty_record;
/* end faculty_struct */
```

Which of the following is a correct structure variable member reference?
**a.** `faculty_record.salary`
**b.** `faculty_struct.name_initials.last_name_initial`
**c.** `faculty_struct.age`
**d.** `struct faculty_record.age`
**e.** `struct int faculty_record.age`

**5.** The structure type declaration `faculty_struct` is given in question 4. Which of the following compile-time initialization of structure variables is legal?
**a.** `struct cs_fac faculty_struct = {1300,  'B',   ,  37,  'F',`
                                                `26500.00};`
**b.** `struct cs_fac faculty_struct = {1300,  'B',  'J',  37};`
**c.** `struct cs_fac faculty_struct = {,  {'B',  'J'}  ,  37,  'F',`
                                            `26500.00};`
**d.** All of the above.
**e.** None of the above.

**6.** Which of the following operations on structure variables are legal?
**a.** Passing to functions
**b.** Arithmetic
**c.** Input
**d.** Output
**e.** All of the above.
**f.** None of the above.

**7.** Which of the following statements concerning enumerated data types is correct?
  **a.** An enumerated data type is a structured data type.
  **b.** Unless they are explicitly initialized in the list of enumerators, the first enumerator is set to 0, the second to 1, and so on.
  **c.** An enumeration constant can be assigned an integer value, using an assignment statement.
  **d.** It is possible to input enumeration constant values for enumerated variables.
  **e.** All of the above.
  **f.** None of the above.

**Answers:** 1. d; 2. d; 3. e; 4. a; 5. a; 6. a; 7. b.

## Improve Your Problem-Solving Ability

### Debugging Exercises

**8.** Study the following C program, which uses a structure type. Identify all the errors in it, explain why they are errors, and suggest ways to correct them.

```c
#include <stdio.h>

struct employee_struct {
      int employee_number,
      char department_code,
      float salary;
} full_time_employees;
/* end employee_struct */

void input_values(struct employee_struct *e);
void output_results(int emp_no, float salary);


int main(void) {
      input_values(&employee_struct.full_time_employees);

      if (employee_struct.department_code == 'A')
            employee_struct.salary = 1.05 * employee_struct.salary;
      /* end if */

      output_results(full_time_employees.employee_number,
            full_time_employees.salary);
      return 0;
} /* end function main */
```

▶

```
void input_values(struct full_time_employees *s) {
      printf("Enter employee number: ");
      scanf("%d", &*s.employee_number);
      printf("Enter department code: ");
      scanf("%c", &*s.department_code);
      printf("Enter salary: ");
      scanf("%lf", &*s.salary);
} /* end function input_values */

void output_results(int number, float salary) {
      printf("Employee number: %d\n", employee.number;
      printf("Employee salary: %f", employee.salary);
} /* end function output_results */
```

9. In each of the following structure type and structure variable declarations, structure member references, and compile-time initializations, identify and correct any errors. Explain your answer.

   **a.** Declaration of a structure type called  course_struct:

   ```
   struct course_struct {
         int course_number;
         int credit_hours;
         struct {
               char meeting_day_1;
               char meeting_day_2;
               char meeting_day_3;
         } meeting_days;
         struct {
               int hour;
               int minute;
         } meeting_time;
   }
   ```

   **b.** Declaration of a structure variable called   summer_classes, of type course_struct:

   ```
   struct summer_classes course_struct;
   ```

   **c.** Declaration of a structure variable called  weekly_schedule:

   ```
   struct weekly_schedule meeting_days;
   ```

**d.** The reference to the member of the structure variable `summer_classes` of type `course_struct`:

```
summer_classes.credit_hours.meeting_time.hour
```

**e.** The reference to the member of the structure variable `summer_classes` of type `course_struct`:

```
summer_classes.meeting_day_1.meeting_days
```

**f.** The reference to the member of the structure variable `summer_classes` of type `course_struct`:

```
summer_classes.hour.minute
```

**g.** The compile-time initialization of the structure variable `summer_classes` of type `course_struct`:

```
struct course_struct summer_classes = {   };
```

**h.** The compile-time initialization of the structure variable `summer_classes` of type `course_struct`:

```
struct course_struct summer_classes = {230, 3, {'M', 'W', 'F'},
                                       {10, 30}};
```

**i.** The compile-time initialization of the structure variable `summer_classes` of type `course_struct`:

```
struct course_struct summer_classes = {230, 3, {'M', , 'F'},
                                       {10, 30}};
```

**j.** The compile-time initialization of the structure variable `summer_classes` of type `course_struct`:

```
struct course_struct summer_classes = {230, 3, {'M', 'W'}};
```

**10.** Examine the following program, which uses enumerated data types, and indicate any errors you find.

```
#include <stdio.h>

enum fruits_enum {
      APPLE, PEAR, PLUM
}; /* end enum fruits */

enum tropical_fruits_enum {
      MANGO, PAPAYA, ORANGE
}; /* end enum tropical_fruits */
```

▶

```
int main(void) {
      enum fruits_enum northern_fruits;
      enum tropical_fruits_enum southern_fruits;

      APPLE = 1;

      printf("Enter an integer for fruits: ");
      scanf("%d", &northern_fruits);

      if (northern_fruits == APPLE)
            printf("It is an apple.");
      else if (northern_fruits == PEAR)
            printf("It is a pear.");
      else if (northern_fruits == PLUM)
            printf("It is a plum.");
      else if (northern_fruits == MANGO)
            printf("It is a tropical fruit.");
      /* end if */

      return 0;
} /* end function main */
```

◼

### Programming Exercises

Write a C structure type declaration for each of the following structured data types:

**11.** A structure type called `time_struct`, containing integer `hour`, integer `minute`, and integer `second`.

**12.** A structure type called `date_struct`, consisting of integer `year`, integer `month`, and integer `day`.

**13.** A nested structure type called `employee_struct`, containing integer `employee_number` and `date_of_birth`, of structure type `date_struct`, which is similar to the structure type `date_struct` of Programming Exercise 12.

We have the following structure type and variable declarations for exercises 14, 15, and 16:

```
struct date_struct {
      int year, month, day;
}; /* end date_struct */
```

▶

```
struct employee {
      int employee_number;
      char department_code;
      struct date_struct start_date;
      struct date_struct birth_date;

      struct {
            int home_phone_number;
            int work_phone_number;
      } telephones;
      /* end struct */

      float salary;
} full_time_employees;
/* end employee_struct */
```

14. Write expressions to access each of the following structure variable members:
   a. Member employee_number of full_time_employees.
   b. Member year of start_date of full_time_employees.
   c. Member home_phone_number of telephones of full_time_employees.

15. Write a compile-time initialization statement to initialize all numeric members of the structure variable full_time_employees to 0 and the member department_code to 'X'.

16. Draw a figure similar to Figure 12.1 to show the conceptual memory structure for the structure variable full_time_employees.

17. Write a declaration for the enumerated data type major_holidays based on the enumeration constants NEW_YEARS_DAY, PRESIDENTS_DAY, EASTER, MEMORIAL_DAY, INDEPENDENCE_DAY, LABOR_DAY, HALLOWEEN, VETERANS_DAY, THANKSGIVING, and CHRISTMAS, in this order, such that the first enumerator is set to 1.

### Programming Projects

18. Solve Programming Project 39 of Chapter 4, using a structure type called test_scores_struct. It contains three integer test scores, test1, test2, and final_test.

19. Solve Programming Project 23 of Chapter 6, using a structure type called faculty_struct, which consists of two members: faculty_salary and faculty_performance_level.

**20.** Solve Programming Project 21 of Chapter 8, using a structure type called `course_eval_struct`, which consists of an integer `instructor_number`; an integer `course_number`; and five character variables called `question_1`, `question_2`, `question_3`, `question_4`, and `question_5`.

**21.** Design an interactive modular program that does the following:

   **a.** Reads a date into a structure variable of a structure type called `date_struct`, which contains three integer members, `year`, `month`, and `day`. Values entered for `year`, `month`, and `day` should be integers, such as 1998, 5, and 18, for May 18, 1998.

   **b.** Determines whether the date is valid. For example, May 32, 1998, is not valid; neither is February 29, 1998, since 1998 is not a leap year.

   **c.** Prints the date in a nice format.

   A sample program output follows:

```
Enter year  : 1998
Enter month: 5
Enter day   : 32

The date you have entered is not valid.

Enter year  : 1998
Enter month: 5
Enter day   : 18


You have entered: May 18, 1998
```

**22.** Design an interactive modular program that does the following:

   **a.** Reads a five-digit integer consisting of only 0s and 1s, into a structure variable of type `binary_integer_struct`. The structure type `binary_integer_struct` contains five integer members, `digit_1`, `digit_2`, `digit_3`, `digit_4`, and `digit_5`.

   **b.** Reads another five-digit integer of 0s and 1s into another structure variable, also of type `binary_integer_struct`.

   **c.** If both binary integers are valid, computes and outputs their sum.

   A typical program output should be as shown:

```
Enter first binary integer : 00011
Enter second binary integer: 00211
     Warning: 00211 is not a valid binary integer. Try again.
Enter second binary integer: 00111
The sum of 00011 and 00111 is 01010.
```

**23.** Extend Programming Project 22 so that your program, in addition to binary addition of integers, becomes capable of binary subtraction and multiplication.

**24.** Use the enumerated data type `major_holidays` of Programming Exercise 17 to design an interactive, menu-driven, modular program that can

**a.** List all major holidays in a year and their dates.

**b.** Determine and print the next major holiday and its date, given a date expressed as month and day.

**c.** Determine and print the preceding major holiday and its date, given a date.

# 13

# Character Data and Strings

---

**CHAPTER OBJECTIVES**

In this chapter you will learn about:

- **Character data**
  Their internal representation
  Collating sequences
  Automatic conversion rules for character data
  The standard library function `getchar` for character input
  The standard function `putchar` for character output
  The standard C character-handling functions

- **Strings**
  Array and pointer representations for strings
  Compile-time initialization of strings
  Output of strings: the `printf,` `puts,` and `sprintf` functions
  Input of strings: the `scanf,` `gets,` and `sscanf` functions
  String processing and standard string manipulation functions
  Copying strings
  Comparing strings
  Computing length of strings
  Concatenation of strings
  Searching strings for substrings
  Tokenizing strings

By the time you have completed this chapter, you will have acquired the ability to:

- **Solve problems involving character data**

- **Use strings as a data type in problem solving**

---

## 13.1   INTRODUCTION

This chapter is intended to complete the discussion of character data and strings, two related data types that we have been gradually exploring since Chapter 3. Let us recall what we have already covered about character data: We introduced character constants and escape sequences in Chapter 3. Also in Chapter 3 we discussed how to declare character data, how to output character variables using the standard function `printf`, and how to input values for character variables using the standard function `scanf`. Since then, we have been using character data and character variables in many applications.

Strings are another important structured data type frequently used in problem solving. Strings are structured sequences of characters, each considered a single data item. In Chapter 3 we learned about string constants: the fact that, in C, strings are one-dimensional arrays of characters; that we can output string variables using the standard function `printf`; and that we can input values for them using the standard functions `scanf` and `gets`. In Chapter 4 we saw that many operations on strings require the use of the standard library functions in the C library `string`: among them are `strcpy`, which copies a string to a string variable, and `strcmp`, which compares two strings. In Chapter 6 we examined passing strings to functions through parameters. In Chapter 7 we discussed formatted output of strings. With what you have learned about strings, you now have the ability to use them in several applications.

There is more to character data and strings. In this chapter we first focus on character data, their internal representation, the orderings inherent in them, and the automatic conversion rules that the C compilers use for character data. We examine additional C functions for input and output of character data and functions that can be used for handling character data.

Having acquired a good understanding of character data, next we return to strings. We discuss compile-time initialization of strings, as well as string input and output using several standard functions. Then we consider operations on strings, that is, string processing. In addition to copying and comparing stings, other important operations also take strings as their operands. These operations include length computation, concatenation, searching, and tokenization. We also consider how to implement these operations in C programs. Naturally, we can implement any string operation by considering its operand strings as character arrays. It is more efficient, however, to use the standard C string manipulation library functions for string processing. You will become familiar with these functions and learn how they can be used in solving problems that involve strings.

## 13.2   MORE ON CHARACTER DATA

You already know that a character constant is any character in the C character set that is enclosed by single quotation marks, for example, `'a'`, or an escape sequence, such as `'\n'`. You also know that a character variable is one whose type specifier is `char`, as in the declaration

```
char symbol;
```

Such a variable is allocated a memory location that can store any printable or nonprintable character in the character set, including decimal digits, uppercase and lowercase letters, special characters, and escape sequences. An important issue is the internal representation of character data.

## Internal Representation of Character Data

In C each character is represented internally as an integer and, on most machines, in one byte of memory. The integer value stored for a character and how it is stored depend on the character set used by the computer on which your program runs. The two commonly used character sets are **ASCII** (for American Standard Code for Information Interchange) and **EBCDIC** (for Extended Binary Coded Decimal Interchange Code). The ASCII character set is used on most micro- and minicomputers and some mainframes, whereas the EBCDIC system is used primarily on IBM mainframes.

The ASCII character set consists of 128 distinct characters. Each character is represented by a positive integer in the range 0 through 127. Seven bits of the eight bits available in a byte are sufficient to represent all 128 ASCII characters. The remaining bit, that is, the left-most bit, is used for the sign, and does not participate in determining the value of the integer that corresponds to the character represented in the byte. On the other hand, the EBCDIC character set includes 256 characters. If we use all eight bits in a byte, we can represent 256 integers between 0 and 255. Therefore, the EBCDIC system requires the use of eight bits in a byte.

Since data of type `char` in C are represented by integers, like integers they are an integral type. Also like integers, character data can be signed or unsigned. Hence character data can be declared as `signed char` or `unsigned char`, as in the following examples:

```
signed char symbol1;
unsigned char symbol2;
```

Because of these declarations, the variable `symbol1` can store values between −128 and +127, and the variable `symbol2` can store values between 0 and 255. Naturally, we can also declare a character variable simply as of type `char`:

```
char symbol3;
```

Whether a variable of type `char` is, in fact, `signed` or `unsigned` depends on the implementation of the C system and the intrinsic character set of the computer. If the character set is EBCDIC, `char` implies `unsigned char` and you cannot use `signed char`, because you need 256 nonnegative integers to represent the EBCDIC characters. However, if your computer is based on the ASCII character set, either `signed char` or `unsigned char` is sufficient for the 128 nonnegative integers needed by ASCII.

***Example 13.1***    To discover the number of bytes needed for character data; the number of bits in a byte that stores character data; and the maximum and minimum values of `char`, `signed char`, and `unsigned char` types for your system, run the C program of Figure 13.1.

```
#include <stdio.h>
#include <limits.h>

int main(void) {
      printf("Number of bytes for type char              : %d\n",
            sizeof(char));
      printf("Number of bytes for type signed char       : %d\n",
            sizeof(signed char));
      printf("Number of bytes for type unsigned char     : %d\n",
            sizeof(unsigned char));

      printf("Number of bits in a byte of type char, CHAR_BIT: %d\n",
            CHAR_BIT);
      printf("Maximum value of a character, CHAR_MAX      : %d\n",
            CHAR_MAX);
      printf("Minimum value of a character, CHAR_MIN      : %d\n",
            CHAR_MIN);
      printf("Maximum value of a signed char, SCHAR_MAX   : %d\n",
            SCHAR_MAX);
      printf("Minimum value of a signed char, SCHAR_MIN   : %d\n",
            SCHAR_MIN);
      printf("Maximum value of an unsigned char, UCHAR_MAX   : %d",
            UCHAR_MAX);
      return 0;
} /* end function main */
```

**Figure 13.1**   A C program that prints sizes and limits for character data

In the program of Figure 13.1, the first three `printf` function calls use the C operator `sizeof` to determine the number of bytes for data of type `char`, `signed char`, and `unsigned char`. The `sizeof` operator is a unary operator. Its operand is either a type specifier or a variable. If its operand is a type specifier, it returns the number of bytes of storage that the computer uses to store a variable of that type. For example, `sizeof(int)` yields 2 if your machine uses two bytes to store integer data. On the other hand, if the operand is a variable, the `sizeof` operator returns the number of bytes of storage allocated to its operand. For example, assuming we have the array declaration

```
int arr[20];
```

`sizeof(arr)` will return 40, which is the total number of bytes necessary for an array of size 20 if the word length for the type `int` is two bytes on your computer. You can use any data type, or variables of any data type, as the operand of the `sizeof` operator, including arrays, structures, and structure variables.

The remaining `printf` function calls in the program of Figure 13.1 print the values of some named constants declared in the header file `limits.h`. They are `CHAR_BIT`, which is the number of bits in a byte for character data; `CHAR_MAX` and

CHAR_MIN, which the are maximum and minimum values for data of type   char; SCHAR_MAX and SCHAR_MIN, which are the maximum and minimum values for character data of type signed char; and UCHAR_MAX, which is the maximum value for character data of type unsigned char. Figure 13.2 shows the output produced by the program of Figure 13.1 for IBM-compatible systems and the Microsoft Visual C/C++ IDE. On your system the output of this program may show different values.

```
Number of bytes for type char                         : 1
Number of bytes for type signed char                  : 1
Number of bytes for type unsigned char                : 1
Number of bits in a byte of type char, CHAR_BIT: 8
Maximum value of a character, CHAR_MAX                 : 127
Minimum value of a character, CHAR_MIN                 : -128
Maximum value of a signed char, SCHAR_MAX             : 127
Minimum value of a signed char, SCHAR_MIN             : -128
Maximum value of an unsigned char, UCHAR_MAX         : 255
```

**Figure 13.2**    Output of the program of Figure 13.1 for IBM-compatible systems and Microsoft Visual C/C++

If we examine Figure 13.2, we conclude the following about the Microsoft Visual C/C++ environment on IBM-compatible machines:

1.  Character data is stored in 1 byte, which consists of 8 bits.
2.  The types char and signed char are identical. In other words, char defaults to signed char.
3.  The data type char can handle integers from –128 to 127.
4.  The data type unsigned char can store integers from 0 to 255.
5.  Therefore, both char and unsigned char can represent the ASCII characters.

Because both the data types char and unsigned char are adequate for the complete set of ASCII characters, in most applications dealing with character data, we will not need the type unsigned char; we will use char instead.

## Collating Sequences

The first 32 characters in the ASCII character set corresponding to integers 0 through 31 and the last character corresponding to integer 127 are nonprintable characters, such as Esc and Del. The printable ASCII characters are those whose integer values are in the range 32 through 126. Using this fact and the fact that in C characters are stored as integers, we can easily write a program that produces a table of printable ASCII characters.

**Example 13.2**   Provided it is run on an ASCII computer, the C program of Figure 13.3 generates and outputs a table of printable ASCII characters and their integer counterparts.

```
#include <stdio.h>

int main(void) {
      char ascii[13][10];
      int row, column;

      for (row = 0; row < 13; row++)
           for (column = 0; column < 10; column++)
                 ascii[row][column] = ' ';
           // end for
      // end for

      printf("ASCII Character Set\n");
      printf("      |");

      for (column = 0; column < 10; column++)
           printf("%5d", column);
      /* end for */

      printf("\n-----|");

      for (column = 0; column < 10; column++)
           printf("-----");
      /* end for */

      for (row = 3; row < 13; row++)
           for (column = 0; column < 10; column++)
                 if (row == 3 && column < 2)
                       continue;
                 else
                       ascii[row][column] = 10 * row + column;
                 /* end if */
           /* end for */
      /* end for */

      for (row = 3; row < 13; row++) {
           printf("\n%3d  |", row);

           for (column = 0; column < 10; column++)
                 if (row == 12 && column > 6)
                       break;
                 else
                       printf("    %c", ascii[row][column]);
```

**Figure 13.3**    A C program that prints the printable characters of the ASCII character set (*continued*)    ▶

```
                        /* end if */
              /* end for */
      } /* end for */
      return 0;
} /* end function main */
```

Figure 13.3                                                                    ∎

In this program, the declaration

```
char ascii[13][10];
```

declares `ascii` as a two-dimensional character array of 13 rows and 10 columns. The first nested `for` loop initializes each element of the array `ascii` to a space. The five `printf` function calls early in the program print the headers for the ASCII table. The following nested `for` loop generates the table in the two-dimensional array `ascii`.

The assignment expression statement in the second nested `for` loop is interesting:

```
ascii[row][column] = 10 * row + column;
```

This statement computes the value of the integer expression `10 * row + column` and stores the result as an integer in the corresponding element of the character array `ascii`. For example, if the values of `row` and `column` are 9 and 7, respectively, the value that is stored in `ascii[9][7]` will be 97.

The final nested `for` loop prints the rows of the ASCII table using the `printf` function call

```
printf("   %c", ascii[row][column]);
```

Because the array `ascii` is a character array, this `printf` function call uses the conversion specifier `%c` to print the values of its elements as characters, not as integers. For example, if the value of an element is 97, it will print this value as the lowercase letter `a`.

Figure 13.4 shows the partial ASCII character set obtained by running the program of Figure 13.3 on an ASCII-based computer. You can determine the integer counterpart of a character by combining the row and column numbers of a character shown in the table. For example, the character ! is 33 in ASCII.

If you examine the table of Figure 13.4, you will realize that there is an order inherent among the ASCII characters. This order is called a collating sequence.

> A **collating sequence** is the ordering of characters in a character set.

If we disregard the special characters, the ASCII collating sequence is as follows:

$$0 < 1 < ... < 9 < A < B < ... < Z < a < b < ... < z$$

```
ASCII Character Set
     |   0    1    2    3    4    5    6    7    8    9
-----|--------------------------------------------------
  3  |                  !    "    #    $    %    &    `
  4  |   (    )    *    +    ,    -    .    /    0    1
  5  |   2    3    4    5    6    7    8    9    :    ;
  6  |   <    =    >    ?    @    A    B    C    D    E
  7  |   F    G    H    I    J    K    L    M    N    O
  8  |   P    Q    R    S    T    U    V    W    X    Y
  9  |   Z    [    \    ]    ^    _    `    a    b    c
 10  |   d    e    f    g    h    i    j    k    l    m
 11  |   n    o    p    q    r    s    t    u    v    w
 12  |   x    y    z    {    |    }    ~
```

**Figure 13.4**    Table of printable ASCII characters produced by the program of Figure 13.3

In other words, the character representations of decimal digits precede those of uppercase letters of the alphabet, which, in turn, precede the lowercase letters. The collating sequence of the EBCDIC character set is different:

$$a < b < ... < z < A < B < ... < 0 < 1 < ... < 9$$

In EBCDIC lowercase letters come before uppercase letters, which precede the set of decimal digits. The sequences of lowercase and uppercase letters in EBCDIC contain gaps for nonprintable characters.

Why are collating sequences important to us as application programmers? Because the outcome of a conditional expression involving character quantities depends on the character set used by the machine and its collating sequence and may be different in ASCII and EBCDIC.

***Example 13.3***    Suppose we have the declarations

```
char ch1, ch2;
```

If the value of `ch1` is `'0'` and `ch2` is `'5'`, the simple predicate

```
ch1 > ch2
```

yields 0 (false) in both ASCII and EBCDIC. However, if the value of `ch1` is `'a'` and `ch2` is `'5'`, this predicate will compute to 1 (true) in ASCII and 0 (false) in EBCDIC.

Knowledge of the collating sequence of the computer's character set is especially important in sorting alphanumeric data stored as strings, as you will see in the next section.

## Automatic Conversion of Character Data

Because C stores integer values in one byte for character data, it is possible to mix character data with numeric data in expressions. In computing mixed-type expressions, the computer uses the automatic conversion rules discussed in section 5.11.

For example, given the declarations

```
char ch1 = 'a';
char ch2;
int ix = 15;
float fx = 2.5;
```

the expression ch1 + ix + fx is valid. The computer uses the arithmetic conversion rules: because the "longest" type in this expression is float, the result will be 114.5, obtained by adding the integer counterpart of 'a', which is 97 in ASCII, and the values of ix and fx, which are 15 and 2.5, respectively. Therefore, the statement

```
printf("%f", ch1 + ix + fx);
```

will print 114.5.

On the other hand, in executing the statement

```
ch2 = ch1 + ix + fx;
```

the computer will, in addition, perform an assignment conversion. It will convert the value of 114.5 to an integer and store it as 114 in ch2. If we run the statement

```
printf("%c", ch2);
```

we will have r printed on the screen because ch2 is a character variable and its value 114 corresponds to 'r'.

You should realize that such automatic conversions are safe only if the result is a legal value in the machine's character set. If the result computed for a character value is an integer that does not correspond to a character in the machine's character set, you will get unpredictable response.

Under rare circumstances we need to mix character data with numeric data in an expression. An application in which we do this is described in the following example.

**Example 13.4**   Let us write a C function called our_toupper, which converts a lowercase letter to its uppercase counterpart and returns it. The function should return the character unchanged if it is not a lowercase letter, as shown in Figure 13.5.

```
int our_toupper(int letter) {
      if (letter >= 'a' && letter <= 'z')
            return (letter - 'a' + 'A');
      else
            return letter;
      /* end if */
} /* end function our_toupper */
```

**Figure 13.5**     A C function that converts lowercase letters to uppercase

In the function our_toupper of Figure 13.5, the predicate of the if statement, letter >= 'a' && letter <= 'z', is a mixed-type expression containing in-

teger and character data. It computes to 1 (true) if the value of the formal parameter letter is in the range of integers for the letters 'a' through 'z', that is, if letter
corresponds to a lowercase letter. In this case the return statement in the then-part
of the if statement is executed. This return statement has the return expression
letter - 'a' + 'A', and it is also a mixed-type expression. In evaluating it, the
computer converts the characters 'a' and 'A' to their integer counterparts, which
are 97 and 65, respectively. Assuming the value of the variable letter is 100 (that is,
the counterpart of 'd' in ASCII), this expression yields (100 − 97 + 65) = 68, which
is the integer equivalent of 'D'. Therefore, the then-part of the if statement returns
the integer equivalent of the uppercase letter corresponding to a given lowercase letter.
The else-part has a return statement, which returns the value of letter unchanged.
In other words, the function our_toupper converts a lowercase letter to an uppercase and leaves any other character unchanged. You should note that this function will do
its intended task provided your computer uses the ASCII character set.

Figure 13.6 shows a simple program that uses the function our_toupper.

```
#include <stdio.h>

int our_toupper(int x);


int main(void) {
      char letter;

      printf("Enter a lowercase letter: ");
      scanf("%c", &letter);

      printf("Uppercase is: %c", our_toupper(letter));
      return 0;
} /* end function main */
```

**Figure 13.6**   A C program that uses the function our_toupper

## Input and Output of Character Data

In Chapter 3 you learned about the standard functions scanf and printf for input and output of character data. In addition to these, standard C has two other functions,
getchar and putchar, which you can use instead for character input-output. Both
getchar and putchar are declared in the header file stdio.h.

To input a character for a variable of type char declared, for example, as

```
char ch;
```

we can use the scanf function

```
scanf("%c", &ch);
```

Equivalently, we can use the following `getchar` function call:

```
ch = getchar();
```

As you can see, the `getchar` function has no parameters. It returns an integer that is the counterpart of the character read in the computer's character system and stores it in the variable `ch`. When this statement is executed, you should type a character and press the Enter key. In this case the new-line character `\n` generated by the Enter key remains in the input stream. If you type more than one character and press the Enter key, only the first character will be returned by the `getchar` function; the remaining characters and the new-line character will be left in the input stream. To flush the input stream, we can use the function `flush_input_stream`:

```
void flush_input_stream(void) {
        char remnant = getchar();

        while (remnant != '\n')
                remnant = getchar();
        /* end while */
} /* end function flush_input_stream */
```

In the function `flush_input_stream`, which should be executed after a call to `getchar`, the character variable `remnant` is assigned the value that is left in the input stream. The `while` statement keeps reading all excess characters typed one at a time into the variable `remnant`, up to and including the new-line character; this technique flushes the input stream.

A character variable can be output using the function `putchar`, as follows:

```
putchar(ch);
```

The function `putchar` requires one integer parameter. It converts the integer to a character and prints it on the standard output device. This statement is equivalent to the following call to `printf`:

```
printf("%c", ch);
```

Apart from syntactical differences, the function `getchar` differs from `scanf` in that `getchar` returns an integer that is obtained by converting the character typed to its integer counterpart, whereas `scanf` returns an integer representing the number of values it has read from the input stream. For example, assuming `ch` is declared as a character variable, the statement

```
printf("%d", ch = getchar());
```

waits for us to enter a character. If we enter `a`, the function `getchar` stores it in `ch`. Then the function `printf` prints the value returned by `getchar` as an integer because we have used the integer format specifier `%d`. If your machine is an ASCII computer, this value is 97, which corresponds to  a  in the ASCII character set. On the other hand, the statement

```
printf("%d", scanf("%c", &ch));
```

because of the function call to  scanf, waits for us to enter a value for  ch. If we enter  a, the  printf  function call prints 1, which is the number of values read by the function  scanf.

Also, there is a difference between what the  putchar  and  printf  functions return. The  putchar  function returns an integer that corresponds to the character that it prints, whereas the  printf  function returns the number of characters that it has printed. Consider the statement

```
printf("%d", putchar(ch));
```

Assuming that the value that is stored in  ch  is the character  a  and that we are using an ASCII machine, the  putchar  function will print  a  on the screen, and the  printf  function, because of the format specifier  %d, will print 97 instead of  a. However, the following statement behaves differently:

```
printf("%d", printf("You have entered %c", ch));
```

It first prints  You have entered a  to satisfy the inner  printf. Next it prints 18, which is the number of characters printed by the inner  printf.

Example 13.5 uses the  getchar  and  putchar  functions and the standard constant  EOF  for character input and output.

***Example 13.5***   Figure 13.7 shows a C program that interactively reads a character and a text of characters and then determines and outputs the number of occurrences of the character in the text. During the input of the text, the end of the text is marked by an end-of-file character.

```
#include <stdio.h>

int main(void) {
        char character, remnant_char, text_character;
        int character_count = 0;

        printf("Enter the character whose occurrence you ");
        printf("want counted in the text: ");
        character = getchar();
        remnant_char = character;
```

**Figure 13.7**     A C program that determines the number of occurrences of a character in an interactively typed text
(*continued*)   ▶

```
        while (remnant_char != '\n')
                remnant_char = getchar();
        /* end while */

        printf("Type the text, terminate it by the EOF character, ");
        printf("and press Enter: \n");
        text_character = getchar();

        while (text_character != EOF) {
                if (text_character == character)
                        character_count++;
                /* end if */

                text_character = getchar();
        } /* end while */

        putchar('\n');

        printf("\n***> Number of occurrences of the character '%c'",
                character);
        printf(" in the text: %d", character_count);
        return 0;
} /* end function main */
```

**Figure 13.7**                                                                    ■

We note the following about this program:

1. The statement

```
        character = getchar();
```

is used to enter a character, which may be any character including whitespace. We will determine the occurrence of this character in a given text.

2. What follows next is the block of statements

```
  remnant_char = character;

  while (remnant_char != '\n')
        remnant_char = getchar();
  /* end while */
```

which is equivalent to the function `flush_input_stream` developed in this section. Its purpose is to clear the input stream of any extraneous characters the user may type and the new-line character.

3.   The statement

```
text_character = getchar();
```

inputs the first character of the text. If the character typed by the user and saved in `text_character` is anything but the end-of-file character, the predicate of the following `while` statement, `text_character != EOF`, will be nonzero (true). In this case the loop body of the `while` statement is executed. The `if` statement in the loop body determines whether the value of `text_character` matches the value of `character` and accordingly increments `character_count` by 1. The next statement in the loop body is

```
text_character = getchar();
```

This statement reads another text character. The `while` loop is executed until the character entered by the user is the end-of-file character. In this case the loop terminates.

4.   The statement after the `while` loop

```
putchar('\n');
```

causes a new line. Subsequently, the `printf` function calls print the result.

A sample output of this program is shown in Figure 13.8.

```
Enter the character whose occurrence you want counted in the text: a
Type the text, terminate it by the EOF character, and press Enter:
An introduction to problem solving and programming
using C: Structured programming techniques
***> Number of occurrences of the character 'a' in the text: 3
```

**Figure 13.8**     A sample output of the program of Figure 13.7

### Character-Handling Library Functions

The C standard library contains a collection of useful character-handling functions. These functions are declared in the standard header file `ctype.h`. To use them, your source program file must include the preprocessor directive `#include <ctype.h>`. The table of Figure 13.9 describes eight commonly used character-handling library functions.

| Function Prototype | Function Description |
|---|---|
| `int isdigit(int c)` | Returns nonzero if `c` is a digit; returns 0 otherwise. |
| `int isalpha(int c)` | Returns nonzero if `c` is a letter; returns 0 otherwise. |
| `int islower(int c)` | Returns nonzero if `c` is a lowercase letter; returns 0 otherwise. |
| `int isupper(int c)` | Returns nonzero if `c` is an uppercase letter; returns 0 otherwise. |
| `int isspace(int c)` | Returns nonzero if `c` is a whitespace character; returns 0 otherwise. |
| `int ispunct(int c)` | Returns nonzero if `c` is a punctuation character; returns 0 otherwise. |
| `int tolower(int c)` | Returns c as a lowercase letter if `c` is an uppercase letter; returns `c` unchanged otherwise. |
| `int toupper(int c)` | Returns c as an uppercase letter if `c` is a lowercase letter; returns `c` unchanged otherwise. |

**Figure 13.9**    Some useful character-handling library functions declared in the `ctype.h` header file

The first six functions in Figure 13.9 are used for testing characters. For example, the function `isdigit` returns nonzero if its argument is a digit; otherwise it returns zero. In other words, `isdigit` tests for digits. Similarly, the functions `isalpha`, `islower`, `isupper`, `isspace,` and `ispunct` test for alphabetic characters, lowercase alphabetic characters, uppercase alphabetic characters, whitespace characters, and punctuation characters, respectively. Any printable character on the terminal keyboard except digits, alphabetic characters, and whitespace characters are considered to be punctuation characters.

The remaining two functions of Figure 13.9 are `tolower` and `toupper`. The function `toupper` does the same task as the function `our_toupper`, which we developed in Example 13.4; it converts and returns its argument in uppercase if its argument is a lowercase letter. Otherwise, it returns its argument unchanged. The function `tolower` does the opposite. It returns the lowercase counterpart of its argument provided the argument is an uppercase letter; otherwise, it returns the argument without changing it.

You should realize that the standard character handling functions `toupper` and `tolower` return integers. To print the results as characters, we should use, for example, the statement

```
printf("%c", tolower('A'));
```

or the statement

```
putchar(tolower('A'));
```

The following example illustrates the use of the standard character-handling functions listed in Figure 13.9.

***Example 13.6***    The C program in Figure 13.10 prompts the user to enter a character value; reads the typed character; and determines its type as a digit, a lowercase letter, an uppercase letter, a whitespace character, or a punctuation character. In addition, the program prints the uppercase equivalent of the character if it is a lowercase letter and the lowercase counterpart of the character if it is an uppercase letter. The program does its task in a loop as long as the user wants to continue with its execution.

```
#include <stdio.h>
#include <ctype.h>

int main(void) {
        char character, want_to_continue = 'y';

        while (want_to_continue == 'y') {
                printf("Enter a character: ");
                character = getchar();

                printf("***> ");

                if (isdigit(character))
                        printf("'%c' is a DIGIT.\n", character);
                else if (isalpha(character))
                        if (isupper(character))
                                printf("'%c' is an UPPERCASE LETTER.\n",
                                        character);
                        else
                                printf("'%c' is a LOWERCASE LETTER.\n",
                                        character);
                        /* end if */
                else if (isspace(character))
                        printf("'%c' is a WHITE SPACE CHARACTER.\n",
                                character);
                else if (ispunct(character))
                        printf("'%c' is a PUNCTUATION CHARACTER.\n",
                                character);
                /* end if */

                if (isalpha(character)) {
                    printf("***> Character printed in uppercase: %c\n",
                            toupper(character));
                    printf("***> Character printed in lowercase: %c\n",
                            tolower(character));
                } /* end if */

                character = getchar();
                printf("Do you want to continue? (y/n): ");
                want_to_continue = getchar();
                character = getchar();
        } /* end while */
        return 0;
} /* end function main */
```

**Figure 13.10**    A C program that uses standard character-handling functions

The logic of the program of Figure 13.10 is simple. You should note the use of the functions `isdigit`, `isalpha`, `isupper`, `isspace`, `ispunct`, `toupper`, and `tolower`. A sample run of this program is shown in Figure 13.11.

```
Enter a character: a
***> 'a' is a LOWERCASE LETTER.
***> Character printed in uppercase: A
***> Character printed in lowercase: a
Do you want to continue? (y/n): y
Enter a character: T
***> 'T' is an UPPERCASE LETTER.
***> Character printed in uppercase: T
***> Character printed in lowercase: t
Do you want to continue? (y/n): y
Enter a character: 8
***> '8' is a DIGIT.
Do you want to continue? (y/n): y
Enter a character: .
***> '.' is a PUNCTUATION CHARACTER.
Do you want to continue? (y/n): y
Enter a character:
***> ' ' is a WHITE SPACE CHARACTER.
Do you want to continue? (y/n): n
```

**Figure 13.11**    A sample run of the program of Figure 13.10

In addition to the eight standard character-handling functions, C supports five more character-handling functions in its standard library. They are listed in the table of Figure 13.12. These functions are also test functions. They test for alphanumeric characters, hexadecimal digits, control characters, printing characters, and graphic characters, respectively.

| Function Prototype | Function Description |
|---|---|
| `int isalnum(int c)` | Returns nonzero if c is a digit or a letter; returns 0 otherwise. |
| `int isxdigit(int c)` | Returns nonzero if c is a hexadecimal digit; returns 0 otherwise. |
| `int iscntrl(int c)` | Returns nonzero if c is a control character; returns 0 otherwise. |
| `int isprint(int c)` | Returns nonzero if c is a printing character including space;  returns 0 otherwise. |
| `int isgraph(int c)` | Returns nonzero if c is a printing graphic character other than space; returns 0 otherwise. |

**Figure 13.12**    Additional character-handling library functions declared in the  `ctype.h`  header file

## REVIEW QUESTIONS

1.  The ASCII character set
    **a.** Is used primarily on IBM mainframes.

**b.** Consists of 128 distinct characters.

**c.** Represents each character by a positive integer in the range 1 through 128.

**d.** Considers a variable of type `char` necessarily equivalent to the type `unsigned char`.

**e.** All of the above are correct.

**f.** None of the above is correct.

2. The C `sizeof` operator is a unary operator, and it can be used to determine the number of bytes of storage that the computer uses to store a variable or a type specifier, which is the operand of `sizeof`. (T or F)

3. In the ASCII collating sequence,

**a.** Decimal digits precede uppercase letters.

**b.** Uppercase letters precede lowercase letters.

**c.** The first 32 characters and the last character are nonprintable characters.

**d.** Special printable characters are ordered in groups placed between sequences of nonprintable characters, decimal digits, uppercase letters, and lowercase letters.

**e.** All of the above are correct.

**f.** None of the above is correct.

4. The outcome of a conditional expression involving character data depends on the character set used by the computer and its collating sequence. (T or F)

5. In C it is illegal to mix character data with numeric data in arithmetic expressions. (T or F)

6. Suppose we have the following declarations:

```
char x, y;
int a, b;
double c;
```

Assume that the current values of the variables are '1' for $x$, 10 for $a$, 5 for $b$, and –2.5 for $c$. Which of the following arithmetic assignment expression statements involves a safe automatic assignment conversion (that is, the result corresponds to a valid character) on an ASCII machine?

**a.** `y = 3 * x + a * c - b;`

**b.** `y = - 3 * x - a * c + b;`

**c.** `y = x * a + b * c;`

**d.** All of the above.

**e.** None of the above.

7. The function `getchar`

**a.** Is declared in the header file `ctype.h`.

**b.** Can be used to input values for character variables.

**c.** Has the syntax `getchar(ch)`, where `ch` is a character variable.

**d.** Skips whitespace during input.

**e.** All of the above are correct.

**f.** None of the above is correct.

8. Choose the correct statement:

**a.** The call `isdigit(c)` returns nonzero if `c` is a hexadecimal digit.

**b.** The call `isupper(c)` returns `c` as an uppercase letter if it is lowercase.

**c.** The call `ispunct(c)` returns nonzero if `c` is a whitespace character.

**d.** The call `tolower(c)` returns nonzero if `c` is a lowercase letter.

**e.** All of the above.

**f.** None of the above.

**Answers:**   1. b; 2. T; 3. e; 4. T; 5. F; 6. a; 7. b; 8. f.

## 13.3   STRINGS REVISITED

Let us briefly review what we know about strings:

1.   A string is a sequence of characters that is considered a single data item. A string constant is a sequence of characters in a source program, which is enclosed by double quotation marks.

2.   C does not support strings as a data type. However, it allows us to represent strings in one-dimensional arrays of type `char` such that each element of the array stores one character of the string, and the string is terminated by the null character, represented as `'\0'`, which is the symbolic constant `NULL`. Therefore, we can declare a string variable as a one-dimensional character array, as follows:

```
char string1[10];
```

In this example the character array `string1` can store a string of up to nine characters, since a string is always terminated by the null character.

3.   We can initialize string variables at compile time, as in the example:

```
char string1[10] = "Bye";
```

This initialization creates the following structure in storage:

| B | y | e | \0 | \0 | \0 | \0 | \0 | \0 | \0 |
|---|---|---|----|----|----|----|----|----|----|
| [0] | [1] | [2] | [3] | [4] | [5] | [6] | [7] | [8] | [9] |

You should note that the first four elements of the character array are used to store the string `"Bye"`. The fourth element of the array contains the null character `'\0'`. The remaining elements of the array are also initialized to the null character.

4.   We can use the function `scanf`, together with the format specifier `%s`, for interactive input of a string variable provided the string value entered for the string variable does not have embedded whitespace characters. Example:

```
scanf("%s", string1);
```

Similarly, we can use the function `fscanf` and the format specifier `%s` for file-oriented input of string variables.

5.   If the string to be input has embedded whitespace characters, we can resort to the standard `gets` function. Example:

```
gets(string1);
```

6.  We can use the function `printf` and the format specifier `%s` to interactively output string variables. For file-oriented output of string variables, we can use the function `fprintf` and the format specifier `%s`.

7.  We can pass strings to functions through function parameters.

With this background, we continue with our exploration of strings and string processing.

## Strings and Pointers

The usual declaration for a string is the declaration of a one-dimensional character array. It is also possible to declare a string by using a pointer of type `char` to it, as in the following example:

```
char *string1;
```

In this case the number of characters the string pointed to by `string1` can store is not determined until a string value is assigned to it. We can assign a string value to `string1` at compile time:

```
char *string1 = "Hello!";
```

Alternatively, having declared `string1` as a pointer of type `char`, we can use the run-time assignment:

```
string1 = "Hello!";
```

In both cases the computer creates a character array of size seven, which contains the string `"Hello!"`, terminates it with the null character, allocates a memory location for the pointer variable `string1`, and places the address of the character array into the pointer `string1`. We will have the following structure created in the computer's memory:

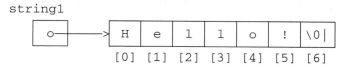

You should note the following:

1.  The assignment `string1 = "Hello!";` is not a string copy, because the variable `string1` is a pointer, not a string.

2.  The pointer `string1` is explicit; the compiler reserves a memory location for it.

On the other hand, if we declare a string as a character array using the array notation, as in

```
char string1[10] = "Hello!";
```

the computer creates a character array of size 10, places the string value `"Hello!"` in it, terminates it with the null character, and initializes all other elements of the character array to `NULL`. The storage structure follows.

```
string1
```

| H | e | l | l | o | ! | \0 | \0 | \0 | \0 |
|---|---|---|---|---|---|----|----|----|----|

```
[0] [1] [2] [3] [4] [5] [6] [7] [8] [9]
```

In this case, the name of the string is `string1`. Because `string1` is an array, its name is a pointer to its first element. This pointer is implicit; the compiler does not create a memory location for it.

In the preceding examples, both in the array and the pointer notations, the name of the string is `string1`. The statement

```
printf("%s", string1);
```

prints the content of the string, which is `"Hello!"`. You can access any element of the character array using either array/subscript or pointer/offset notation. For example, the second element of `string1` has the name `string1[1]` in array/subscript notation and the name `*(string1 + 1)` in pointer/offset notation.

The expression `(string1 + i)` is a legal pointer expression. If the value of `i` is 0, this expression reduces to `string1`, which is the name of the string. We know that it is also a pointer to the string. Therefore, the expression `(string1 + i)` is a pointer expression in which `i` is an offset. It points to the substring of `string1` that begins with `string1[i]` and extends until its end. For example, assuming `string1` contains `"Hello!"`, the `printf` function call

```
printf("%s", (string1 + 1));
```

prints the substring `"ello!"`.

## Compile-Time Initialization of Strings

C has several ways for compile-time initialization of string variables:

1. As explained in Chapter 3, we can declare a string as a character array of constant size and initialize it to a string constant, as in

```
char string1[10] = "Bye";
```

2. We can achieve the same thing by using the notation for array initialization, as in the following example:

```
char string1[10] = {'B', 'y', 'e'};
```

Note that because the uninitialized array elements are automatically set to the null character, we end up with the same storage structure as before, and we have a proper string created in `string1`. The storage structure follows.

| B | y | e | \0 | \0 | \0 | \0 | \0 | \0 | \0 |
|---|---|---|----|----|----|----|----|----|----|

```
[0] [1] [2] [3] [4] [5] [6] [7] [8] [9]
```

3.   We can initialize a string without declaring the array size:

```
char string1[] = "Bye";
```

This declaration creates an array of four elements to store the three characters of the string constant `"Bye"` and terminate them by the null character. The storage structure follows.

```
| B | y | e | \0 |
[0] [1] [2] [3]
```

4.   The compile-time initialization

```
char string1[] = {'B', 'y', 'e'};
```

has exactly the same effect as the initialization

```
char string1[] = "Bye";
```

and creates the same storage structure.

5.   As we saw in the preceding section, we can use the pointer notation for arrays and initialize `string1` as

```
char *string1 = "Bye";
```

In this case, again we end up with the same storage structure, that is, an array of four elements.

Note that the following declaration is incorrect and will result in a compiler error:

```
char string2[5] = "Good bye!";
```

The reason is that the size of the character array `string2` is too small to store 10 characters needed for the constant `"Good bye!"`.

You should realize the difference between a character variable and a string variable that stores a single character. For example, the declaration

```
char ch = 'x';
```

requires a single byte of the memory in which the character `'x'` is stored. If you want to store the character `'x'` as a string constant `"x"`, you must declare at least an array of size 2 as follows:

```
char string3[2] = "x";
```

or you may use the declaration

```
char string3[] = "x";
```

In either case the string constant `"a"` is stored in memory as follows:

```
| a | \0 |
[0] [1]
```

## Output of String Variables

Standard C supports three functions for output of string variables: `printf`, `puts`, and `sprintf`. You already know how to use `printf` to output the value of a string variable. In this section we discuss the functions `puts` and `sprintf`.

**Using `puts` for String Output**   The function `puts` is declared in the header file `stdio.h`. It has one parameter, which is the string variable to be printed. It prints both the string stored in its parameter and a new-line character. Therefore, assuming the string variable `string1` contains the string value `"Good bye!"`, the function call

```
puts(string1);
```

prints `Good bye!` and drops the cursor to the beginning of the next line on the screen.

The `puts` function returns an integer, which is the number of characters in the string that it prints, including the terminating new-line character. For example, the statement

```
printf("%d", puts(string1));
```

first prints the string `Good bye!` because of the `puts` function; then on a new line the `printf` function prints 10, which is the number of characters in the string `"Good bye!"` plus 1, due to the new-line character.

**Using `sprintf` for String Output**   The `sprintf` function is also declared in the standard header file `stdio.h`. This function is similar to `printf` with one exception: instead of printing the string on the standard output device, it stores the output in a string, which is its first parameter. In fact, `sprintf` is not limited to the output of strings and can be used to store any output value in a string.

The format of `sprintf` is as follows:

```
sprintf(String, FormatControlString, PrintList);
```

Here *FormatControlString* and *PrintList* are the same as the parameters of a `printf` function call: *FormatControlString* contains string constants and format specifiers; and *PrintList* consists of constants, variables, or expressions that are to be output. The first parameter *String* is a string that should be properly declared in our program. The output of `sprintf` is copied into that string. Also, like `printf`, the function `sprintf` returns an integer that is the number of characters that have been copied into *String*. Let us consider an example.

***Example 13.7***   Suppose we have the declarations

```
char string3[15] = "Good bye!", string4[15], string5[80];
float fl = 0.25;
int in = 67;
```

The statement

```
sprintf(string4, "%s", string3);
```

copies the content of  string3  into  string4. The statement

```
printf("%d", sprintf(string4, "%s", string3));
```

prints the value 9, which is the length of the string  "Good bye!"  that has been copied into  string4.

On the other hand, the statement

```
sprintf(string5, "Value of fl = %f, and value of in = %d.", fl, in);
```

generates the string  "Value of fl = 0.250000, and value of in = 67."  and copies it into  string5.

## Input of String Variables

C supports three standard input functions that we can use to read values for string variables. They are the  scanf, gets, and  sscanf  functions, all declared in the header file  stdio.h. In Chapter 3 we briefly examined  scanf  and  gets  for string input. In this section we discuss these functions and the function  sscanf  in greater detail.

**Using scanf for String Input**    The standard input function  scanf, together with the format specifier  %s, can be used for input of string variables. However, as we know,  scanf  skips all whitespace characters preceding the string constant typed using the keyboard and terminates the string when it encounters another whitespace character in the input stream. Therefore, it is not possible to input a string value containing whitespace for a string variable using  scanf. For example, given the declaration

```
char string1[15];
```

and the input statement

```
scanf("%s", string1);
```

if we interactively type  Good bye!  and press Enter, any whitespace characters preceding the first word,  Good, will be skipped, and the word  Good  will be assigned to the variable  string1  followed by the null character  '\0',  as follows:

| G | o | o | d | \0 | ? | ? | ? | ? | ? | ? | ? | ? | ? | ? |
|---|---|---|---|----|---|---|---|---|---|---|---|---|---|---|
| [0] | [1] | [2] | [3] | [4] | [5] | [6] | [7] | [8] | [9] | [10] | [11] | [12] | [13] | [14] |

At this time the rest of the string that we have typed,  bye!, and the new-line character  '\n'  remain in the input stream to be used by the next input statement, if any, in the program.

In using  scanf  and the format specifier  %s  to read strings that do not contain whitespace characters, we may indicate the field width using the form *%ws*, where *w* stands for the width of the input field. In this case what happens depends on the actual width of the field in the string that we type on the keyboard:

1.  If the number of characters typed is less than or equal to the field width in the format specifier, provided we have no whitespace in the string, what we have typed will be stored in the string variable, and the new-line character will be consumed.

2.  If we type more characters than the field width, the excess characters and the new-line character will be left in the input stream.

***Example 13.8***   Given the declaration

```
char string1[15];
```

and the statement

```
scanf("%10s", string1);
```

let us assume that we type `Programming` and press Enter. The first 10 characters of `Programming` will be stored in `string1`, and the string will be terminated by the null character, as follows:

| P | r | o | g | r | a | m | m | i | n | \0 | ? | ? | ? | ? |
|---|---|---|---|---|---|---|---|---|---|----|---|---|---|---|
| [0] | [1] | [2] | [3] | [4] | [5] | [6] | [7] | [8] | [9] | [10] | [11] | [12] | [13] | [14] |

The remaining character, `g`, and the new-line character will be left in the input stream. If, however, we type `Program` and press the Enter key, we will have the following picture in the memory and the input stream will be empty:

| P | r | o | g | r | a | m | \0 | ? | ? | ? | ? | ? | ? | ? |
|---|---|---|---|---|---|---|----|---|---|---|---|---|---|---|
| [0] | [1] | [2] | [3] | [4] | [5] | [6] | [7] | [8] | [9] | [10] | [11] | [12] | [13] | [14] |

**Using `gets` for String Input**   For proper input of string values containing whitespace, we can use the `gets` function. The format of the `gets` function call is simple: it has one string parameter. A call to `gets` behaves similarly to a call to `scanf` in that the program execution halts and the user will be expected to type a string terminated by either a new-line or an end-of-file character. Unlike `scanf`, however, `gets` does not skip whitespace characters. It reads characters into its parameter from the standard input device until a new-line or an end-of-file character is encountered and then appends a null character to the string. Also, `gets` returns the string that it has just read.

***Example 13.9***   Given is the partial code:

```
char string1[15];
. . . . . . . . . .
gets(string1);
```

In response to this function call, if we type ␣␣Good bye! <Enter>, where each ␣ represents a space, we will have the following in string1:

| | | G | o | o | d | | b | y | e | ! | \0 | ? | ? | ? |
|---|---|---|---|---|---|---|---|---|---|---|---|---|---|---|
| [0] | [1] | [2] | [3] | [4] | [5] | [6] | [7] | [8] | [9] | [10] | [11] | [12] | [13] | [14] |

The string contains all typed whitespace characters and is terminated by the null character. The new-line character generated by the Enter key does not remain in the input stream.

If we type more characters than can be stored in the string, for example, more than 14 characters for string1 declared as

```
char string1[15];
```

we will be attempting to access string array elements that are outside the legally declared array bounds. We should be careful not to type too many characters, since C does not have array-bounds checking and our system may crash. When using gets, it is possible to terminate the string being typed by an end-of-file character. For example, in a DOS environment for which the end-of-file character is Ctrl-Z, if we type

```
Good mornin^Zg! <Enter>
```

where ^Z is what is printed for Ctrl-Z on the screen, only the first 11 characters will be transferred into the variable string1 and we will have the following:

| G | o | o | d | | m | o | r | n | i | n | \0 | ? | ? | ? |
|---|---|---|---|---|---|---|---|---|---|---|---|---|---|---|
| [0] | [1] | [2] | [3] | [4] | [5] | [6] | [7] | [8] | [9] | [10] | [11] | [12] | [13] | [14] |

The rest of the characters typed into the input stream, ^Zg!, and the new-line character '\n' will remain in the input stream.

Remember that a call to gets returns a pointer to the string, which is its parameter. Consider the following example.

**Example 13.10**   The partial code

```
char string1[15];
. . . . . . . . . . . . . . . . . .
. . . . . . . . . . . . . . . . .
printf("Enter a string: ");
gets(string1);
printf("string1 contains: %s", string1);
```

is equivalent to the following:

```
char string1[15];
.................
.................
printf("Enter a string:\n");
printf("string1 contains: %s", gets(string1));
```

In the latter version we have the `printf` function call

```
printf("string1 contains: %s", gets(string1));
```

in which a call to `gets` is the second parameter. In executing this statement, the computer will do `gets` first and will input the string value typed into `string1`. Next, the `printf` call will be taken up, and it will print `string1 contains: Good bye!`, assuming we have typed `Good bye!` to satisfy the call to `gets`.

**Using `gets` and `sscanf` for Interactive Input**     Another function declared in the header file `stdio.h` is the `sscanf` function. It has the following format:

> sscanf (*String*, *FormatControlString, InputList*) ;

where *String* is a string variable declared in the program. As you can see, this function is essentially similar to `scanf`. The main difference is that the input is read from the string *String* instead of the standard input device. Therefore, a call to `sscanf` must be preceded by a call to the function `gets` so that input typed by the user is stored in a string. Example 13.11 illustrates the use of `sscanf` for interactive input.

***Example 13.11***     Assume that we have the following declarations:

```
char string1[15];
int age;
```

The following partial code can be used to interactively input a value for the variable `age`:

```
printf("Enter your age: ");
gets(string1);
sscanf(string1, "%d", &age);
```

The `gets` function call reads the string typed by the user, containing an integer for the variable `age`, into the string variable `string1`. The subsequent `sscanf` function call extracts the integer value from `string1` and assigns it to `age`. This code is equivalent to the following, which uses `scanf` instead:

```
printf("Enter your age: ");
scanf("%d", &age);
```

The formatted or unformatted interactive input that we have been doing with the scanf function can also be done through the use of gets and sscanf. However, scanf is simpler, and you should prefer it to sscanf in most cases. One of the few instances in which sscanf turns out to be better is when we want to input values for character variables.

***Example 13.12***   Consider the following C program:

```
#include <stdio.h>

int main(void) {
        char first_name_initial, last_name_initial;

        printf("Enter your first name initial: ");
        scanf("%c", &first_name_initial);

        printf("Enter your last name initial: ");
        scanf("%c", &last_name_initial);

        printf("Your initials are: %c. %c.", first_name_initial,
                last_name_initial);
        return 0;
} /* end function main */
```

The problem with this code is that the second scanf function call picks up the new-line character that we must use to terminate the input for first_name_initial in the first scanf function call; thus we are never able to input a value for last_name_initial. This chapter explained a technique to solve this problem, as shown in the following version:

```
#include <stdio.h>

int main(void) {
        char first_name_initial, last_name_initial;
        char garbage;
```

▶

```
        printf("Enter your first name initial: ");
        scanf("%c", &first_name_initial);
        garbage = first_name_initial;

        while (garbage != '\n')
                scanf("%c", &garbage);
        /* end while */

        printf("Enter your last name initial: ");
        scanf("%c", &last_name_initial);

        printf("Your initials are: %c. %c.", first_name_initial,
                last_name_initial);
        return 0;
} /* end function main */
```

■

Here we use a character variable called `garbage` and a `while` loop to get rid of the unwanted new-line character and any other character that the user may have typed into the input stream before we execute the second `scanf` function call.

The same problem can be solved by using `gets` and `sscanf` instead of `scanf`. Let us focus on the following version:

```
#include <stdio.h>

int main(void) {
        char string1[10];
        char first_name_initial, last_name_initial;

        printf("Enter your first name initial: ");
        gets(string1);
        sscanf(string1, "%c", &first_name_initial);

        printf("Enter your last name initial: ");
        gets(string1);
        sscanf(string1, "%c", &last_name_initial);

        printf("Your initials are: %c. %c.", first_name_initial,
                last_name_initial);
        return 0;
} /* end function main */
```

In this program we have `gets`, which enables us to enter a character into `string1`. As we know, because we type a character into `string1` that is only large enough to store a string of size 10, the new-line character will be consumed by `gets` and the second step of interactive input will proceed without any problems.

## Passing Strings to Functions

Because the string data type is a character array in C, the rules for passing strings to functions are quite similar to those for passing arrays to functions. We discussed passing arrays to functions in Chapter 11. Even before that, in Chapter 6 we briefly presented a simple mechanism for passing strings to functions through function parameters. Here we will state the rules for passing strings to functions — mostly as a review of what we already know.

1. C does not permit passing strings by value. The only way to pass strings to functions is by pointers.

2. The string to be passed must be declared as a formal parameter of the function. Here is an example of a function header that contains a string as a formal parameter:

```
void get_string(char string1[])
```

Because the name of a string array without a subscript is a pointer to the string, we can replace the declaration `char string1[];` by `char *string1;` and equivalently write the preceding function header as

```
void get_string(char *string1)
```

3. The function prototype must show that the parameter is a string. For the preceding declaration, the prototype can be written as

```
void get_string(char string1[]);
```

or alternatively as

```
void get_string(char *string1);
```

4. A call to a function with a string parameter must have a string array name without subscripts as its actual parameter, for example,

```
get_string(text_line);
```

where `text_line` is a properly declared string array in the calling function.

5. To write protect a string parameter in the called function, we should use the `const` qualifier, as in the function header

```
void print_string(const char *string1)
```

and the corresponding prototype

```
void print_string(const char *s);
```

## REVIEW QUESTIONS

1. In C which of the following statements is correct?
   **a.** Strings are represented as one-dimensional arrays of type `char`.
   **b.** Strings are terminated by the null character.
   **c.** Strings can be initialized at compile time using character constants.
   **d.** Strings can be initialized at compile time using string constants.
   **e.** All of the above.
   **f.** None of the above.

2. Suppose the string `street_address` contains the string value `"9 Carrie Circle"`. Consider the statement:
   ```
   printf("%s", (street_address + 2));
   ```
   What will be printed by this statement?
   **a.** `Carrie Circle`
   **b.** `Carrie`
   **c.** `Circle`
   **d.** None of the above.

3. Which of the following is an *incorrect* declaration and compile-time initialization for a string?
   **a.** `char name[] = "Bob";`
   **b.** `char *name = "Bob";`
   **c.** `char *name = {'B', 'o', 'b'};`
   **d.** `char name[3] = {'B', 'o', 'b'};`
   **e.** `char name[] = {'B', 'o', 'b'};`

4. The standard function `puts`
   **a.** Is declared in the header file `stdlib.h`.
   **b.** Can be used for string input and output.
   **c.** Has one parameter of string type.
   **d.** First drops the cursor to the beginning of a new line and then prints the value of its parameter.
   **e.** All of the above are correct.
   **f.** None of the above is correct.

5. The standard output function `sprintf`
   **a.** Has three parameters.
   **b.** Behaves like `printf` except it stores the output in its first parameter, which is a string variable.
   **c.** Can be used for copying a string to another.
   **d.** Returns an integer that is the number of characters that have been copied into its first parameter.
   **e.** All of the above are correct.
   **f.** None of the above is correct.

6. The standard input function `scanf` is not suitable for input of strings containing embedded whitespace characters. (T or F)

**7.** The standard C function `gets`
   **a.** Cannot be used to input string variables containing whitespace characters.
   **b.** Is declared in the header file `ctype.h`.
   **c.** Has one string parameter.
   **d.** Does not add the null character to the end of the string that is input using the standard input device.
   **e.** All of the above are correct.
   **f.** None of the above is correct.

**8.** The main difference between `scanf` and `sscanf` is that `sscanf` gets its input from the string variable, which is its first parameter, whereas `scanf` gets its input from the standard input device. (T or F)

**9.** We have the following string declaration:

```
char string1[20];
```

Which of the following input statements will read the string value `Introduction to C` without leaving anything in the input stream?
   **a.** `scanf("%s", string1);`
   **b.** `sscanf(string1, "%s", string1);`
   **c.** `gets(string1);`
   **d.** None of the above.

**Answers:**  1. e; 2. a; 3. d; 4. c; 5. e; 6. T; 7. T; 8. c; 9. c.

## 13.4   STRING PROCESSING

In Chapter 4 we stated that all basic operations on strings require the use of the string manipulation functions of the standard string-handling library; that these functions are declared in the header file `string.h`; and that to use these functions, our program must contain the preprocessor directive `#include <string.h>`.

The fundamental string operations include, but are not limited to

1. Copying strings

2. Comparing strings

3. Computing lengths of strings

4. Concatenating strings

5. Searching strings for substrings

6. Tokenizing strings

For each of these operations, the C string library contains one or more standard functions. In Chapter 4 we introduced two of these functions: `strcpy` for copying strings and `strcmp` for comparing strings. This section discusses additional functions for string processing.

## Copying Strings

In addition to the function `strcpy` that copies one string into another, we have the standard function `strncpy` that copies only the left-most *n* characters of the source string into a target character array. This function has three parameters: a target character array, a source string, and an integer that represents the number of left-most characters of the source string to be copied into the target array. It returns the value of the target array.

The behavior of `strncpy` is somewhat different from that of `strcpy`. The function `strcpy` copies the characters in its second parameter, the source string, to its first parameter, the target array, until the null character is encountered; `strcpy` also copies the null character. Therefore, provided the size of the target array is at least as large as that of the source string, we end up with a proper string in the target array — a character array terminated by the null character. On the other hand, the function `strncpy` transfers the left-most *n* characters of its source string to the target character array, but does not necessarily copy the terminating null character to the end of the target array. If you want to have a string in the target array, in your program you must place the null character in its *(n + 1)*th element.

**Example 13.13**   Let us assume that we have the declarations for two strings

```
char string1[21], string2[21];
```

and that `string1` has the value `"C programming"`. The function call

```
strncpy(string2, string1, 10);
```

copies the first 10 characters of `string1` into the character array `string2`. The statement

```
string2[10] = '\0';
```

places the null character in its 11th element. Now the array `string2` contains a proper string, and the `printf` function call

```
printf("%s", string2);
```

prints the string `"C programm"`.

## Comparing Strings

We know that the standard string library function `strcmp` can be used to compare two strings. A variation of the function `strcmp` is the standard string library function `strncmp`. This function has three parameters: two strings, `string1` and `string2`, and an integer n. The function `strncmp` compares the left-most n characters of the string `string1` to the string `string2` and returns 0, less than 0, or greater than 0 if the string formed by the left-most n characters of `string1` is equal to, less than, or greater than `string2`, respectively.

***Example 13.14***    Suppose we have these declarations:

```
char string1[21], string2[21];
int length;
```

The following partial code illustrates the use of the function `strncmp`:

```
printf("The string formed by ");

if(strncmp(string1, string2, length))
        if(strncmp(string1, string2, length) > 0)  {
                printf("the first %d characters of \"%s\"",
                        length, string1);
                printf(" is greater than \"%s\".", string2);
        }
        else {
                printf("the first %d characters of \"%s\"",
                        length, string1);
                printf(" is less than \"%s\".", string2);
        } /* end if */
else {
        printf("the first %d characters of \"%s\"",
                length, string1);
        printf(" is less than \"%s\".", string2);
} /* end if */
```

If the values of the variables `string1`, `string2`, and `length` are `"database"`, `"data"`, and `4`, respectively, the else-part of the outer `if` statement in the above code will be executed to print `"The string formed by the first 4 characters of "database" is equal to "data"`.

## Computing Length of Strings

The length of a string is the number of characters actually stored in it until the null character `'\0'`, which terminates the string. You should not confuse the length of a string variable with the array size information in its declaration. For example, the declaration

```
char string1[21];
```

declares a string in which we can store a string value of up to 20 characters. If the value that is stored in `string1` is, say, `"database"`, the length of `string1` is 8, which is the number of characters in its content.

To compute the length of a string variable, we use the standard function `strlen`. It has one parameter, which is either a string variable or a string constant. It returns an integer that is the length of its parameter excluding the null character `'\0'`. An example of its use is the call `strlen(string1)`.

*Example 13.15*    Consider the following partial code:

```
char string1[21];

printf("Enter a string of no more than 20 characters: ");
gets(string1);
printf("The length of the string \"%s\" is %d", string1,
       strlen(string1));
```

If in response to the `gets` function call, we enter

    Knowledge base

the final output statement, which contains a call to the function `strlen` will print

    The length of the string "Knowledge base" is 14

## Concatenation of Strings

Concatenation is a special binary operation on strings defined as follows:

> The **concatenation** of a string *string1* of length $m$ and a string *string2* of length $n$ is a string of length $m + n$ obtained by adding *string2* to the end of *string1*.

For example, the concatenation of the string `"data"` and the string `"base"` produces the string `"database"`.

To concatenate two strings, we can use the standard string function `strcat`. This function has two string type parameters and returns another string obtained by concatenating the second parameter to the end of the first. For example, assuming the strings `string1` and `string2` contain the values `"data"` and `"base"`, respectively, the function call

    strcat(string1, string2)

will return the string `"database"`.

*Example 13.16*    Suppose we have the following declarations:

    char string1[21];
    char string2[21];
    char string3[41];

Consider the function call to `strcpy`:

    strcpy(string3, strcat(string1, string2));

Its second parameter is the function call `strcat(string1, string2)`, which will concatenate the content of `string2` to the end of `string1` and return the concatenated string. This string will be copied to `string3`, which is the first parameter of the function call `strcpy`. Thus if the values of `string1` and `string2` are `"knowledge"` and `"base"`, the `printf` function call

```
printf("The concatenated string is: %s", string3);
```

will print

```
The concatenated string is: knowledge base
```

and the statement

```
printf("Its length is: %d", strlen(string3));
```

will print

```
Its length is: 14
```

Note that in this example `string3` is large enough to contain the concatenated string coming from `string1` and `string2`. The string `string3` can store a string of up to 40 characters, and the maximum length of the string obtained by concatenating `string1` and `string2`, each large enough for strings of length 20, is 40. If the target string during copy by `strcpy` has a smaller declared size than the size of the source string, you will exceed the bounds of the array, that is, the target string, and your program and/or the operating system will crash.

Another function that we can use to concatenate strings is the function `strncat`. It has three parameters, which are two strings and an integer. The function call

```
strncat(string1, string2, n)
```

where `string1` and `string2` are assumed to be properly declared strings and `n` is an integer will concatenate the left-most `n` characters of `string2` to the end of `string1` and return the resulting string.

**Example 13.17**   Consider this partial code:

```
char string1[21];
char string2[21];
char string3[41];
int length;
```

▶

```
printf("Enter a string of no more than 20 characters: ");
gets(string1);
printf("Enter another string of no more than 20 characters: ");
gets(string2);
printf("Enter an integer: ");
scanf("%d", &length);

strcpy(string3, strncat(string1, string2, length));

printf("The concatenated string is: %s\n", string3);
printf("Its length is: %d", strlen(string3));
```

∎

Let us assume that we run this code with the following interactive input and output:

```
Enter a string of no more than 20 characters: meta
Enter another string of no more than 20 characters: database
Enter an integer: 4
```

The last two `printf` function calls will then print on the screen

```
The concatenated string is: metadata
Its length is: 8
```

## Searching Strings for Substrings

A typical string operation is searching strings for specified substrings. We may want to determine whether a substring occurs in a given string, and if it does, we may want to compute the relative address of the first character of the substring in the string. For example, the string `"database"` contains the substring `"base"`, and the relative address of the first character of the substring `"base"` in the string `"database"` is 5.

**Determining the Existence of a Substring in a String**   We can use the standard string library function `strstr` for this purpose. It has two parameters and both are strings. A call to `strstr` searches its first parameter for the existence of the second; if the second parameter is a substring of the first, the function returns a pointer to the first occurrence of the substring. Otherwise, the function returns a null pointer. Let us consider two examples.

***Example 13.18***   Assume that we have the declarations

```
char string1[21], string2[21];
```

for two strings. The following  `if`  statement uses a call to the function  `strstr`  to determine the existence of the string  `string2`  in  `string1`.

```
if(strstr(string1, string2) == NULL)
      printf("The string \"%s\" is not a substring of \"%s\".",
            string2, string1);
else
      printf("The string \"%s\" is a substring of \"%s\".",
            string2, string1);
/* end if */
```

***Example 13.19***   To determine the relative position of the start of the first occurrence of a substring in another string and the remainder of the string after the first occurrence of the substring, we may use the following partial code:

```
char string1[21];
char string2[21];
..................
..................
if(strstr(string1, string2) == NULL)
   printf("The string \"%s\" is not a substring of \"%s\".",
          string2, string1);
else {
   printf("The start of the substring \"%s\" in the string \"%s\"",
          string2, string1);
   printf(" is \nposition %d.\n\n",
          (strstr(string1, string2) - string1) + 1);

   printf("The remainder of the string \"%s\" after the first",
          string1);
   printf(" occurrence of \nthe substring \"%s\" is \"%s\".",
          string2, strstr(string1, string2) + strlen(string2));
} /* end if */
```

The reason for the call to the function  `strstr`  in the predicate of the  `if`  statement is obvious. There are two elements in this partial program that need to be explained:

1.   The expression  `(strstr(string1, string2) - string1) + 1`  in the second  `printf`  function call in the else-part of the  `if`  statement is a pointer ex-

pression. Let us assume that `string1` contains the string value `"addisababa"`, and `string2` is `"aba"`, as shown in Figure 13.13. We know that `string1` is a pointer to the first character in the string array and that `strstr(string1, string2)` is a pointer to the first occurrence of `"aba"` in `string1`. In Figure 13.13 this pointer points to the string array element whose subscript is 5. Therefore, the value of the pointer expression `strstr(string1, string2) - string1` is 5, which is the number of string array elements from the beginning of `string1` to the beginning of the first occurrence of `string2` in `string1`. To get the relative address of the first character of `string2` in `string1`, we must simply add 1 to this expression. Hence, we end up with the expression `(strstr(string1, string2) - string1) + 1`, which gives 6 in this example.

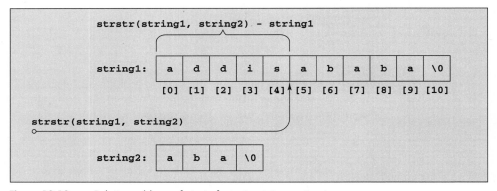

**Figure 13.13**    Relative address of start of `string2` in `string1`

2. The expression `strstr(string1, string2) + strlen(string2)` in the fourth `printf` function call in the else-part of the `if` statement is another pointer expression. As shown in Figure 13.14, the function call `strstr(string1, string2)` is a pointer to the first character of `string2` in its first occurrence in `string1`. In this case it points to the string array element with the subscript 5. If we add to this `strlen(string2)`, which is the length of `string2`, we get a pointer to the remainder of `string1` after the first occurrence of `string2` in it. In Figure 13.14 the function call `strlen(string2)` gives 3. Thus the expression `strstr(string1, string2) + strlen(string2)` becomes a pointer to the string array element whose subscript is 8.

If you run a program containing the above partial code with values of `"addisababa"` and `"aba"` stored in `string1` and `string2`, you get the following result:

```
The start of the substring "aba" in the string "addisababa" is
position 6.

The remainder of the string "addisababa" after the first occurrence of
the substring "aba" is "ba".
```

**Computing the Number of Occurrences of a Substring in a String**   A variation of the string search problem is the problem of determining the number of occurrences of a substring in a string. For example, the substring `"aba"` occurs twice in the string `"addis-ababa"`. The function `strstr` can be used to solve this problem, as shown in the following example.

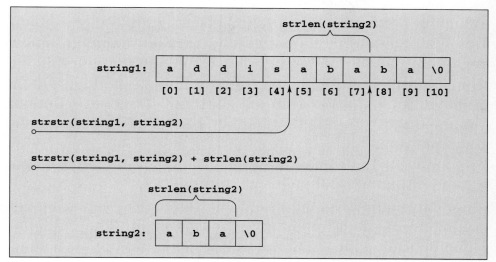

**Figure 13.14**      Pointer to the remainder of `string1` after the first occurrence of `string2`

***Example 13.20***   The function `compute_number_of_occurrences`, given in Figure 13.15, determines the number of times the string `string2` occurs in the string `string1`. The result is returned by the pointer parameter `number`.

```
void compute_number_of_occurrences(const char string1[],
                                   const char string2[], int *number)
{
      char * ptr = strstr(string1, string2);
      *number = 0;

      while(ptr != NULL) {
            *number = *number + 1;
            ptr = strstr(ptr + 1, string2);
      } /* end while */
} /* end function compute_number_of_occurrences */
```

**Figure 13.15**      A C function that determines the number of times a substring occurs in a string

In Figure 13.15 we declare a pointer variable `ptr` of type `char` and initialize it to the pointer returned by the expression `strstr(string1, string2)`. We know that this expression returns a pointer to the first occurrence of the string `string2` in `string1`; it returns `NULL` if `string2` does not exist in `string1`. For example, if `string1` and `string2` are `"addisababa"` and `"aba"`, respectively, `ptr` will be pointing to the substring `"ababa"` of the content of `string1` and it will not be `NULL`.

The predicate of the `while` statement is `ptr != NULL`. Because in our example `ptr` is not `NULL`, this predicate will compute to a nonzero (true) value and the loop body is executed. In the loop body the variable `number` is incremented by 1, and the pointer `ptr` is updated using the expression `strstr(ptr + 1, string2)`.

The first argument of `strstr` in this expression is `ptr + 1`, which is a pointer expression. This expression adds 1 to `ptr`, such that it now points to the next character in the string `"ababa"`. In other words, the expression `ptr + 1` is a pointer to the substring `"baba"`, and the function call `strstr` returns a pointer to the next occurrence of the `string2` value, `"aba"` in the substring `"baba"`. You should note that these operations do not change the contents of the strings `string1` and `string2`.

**Determining the Existence of a Character in a String**    The C string-handling library contains three additional functions that can be used to determine the existence of a character in a string. These functions are `strchr`, `strrchr`, and `strpbrk`.

The function `strchr` has two parameters: a string and a character of type `int`. This function locates the first occurrence of the character in its first parameter, a string, and returns a pointer to the character if found; otherwise, it returns a null pointer. The function `strchr` is quite similar to the function `strstr`. Because any character can be represented as a string of length 1, we may use `strstr` instead of `strchr`.

The second function is `strrchr`. Like `strchr`, it has two parameters: a string and a character. Unlike `strchr`, however, it returns a pointer to the last occurrence of the character in the string.

Finally, there is the standard library function `strpbrk`. It has two string type parameters, `str1` and `str2`, and it locates the first occurrence of any character in `str2` in the string `str1` and returns a pointer to it; otherwise, it returns a null pointer. The following example illustrates the use of `strpbrk`.

***Example 13.21***    The predicate of the following `if` statement involves a call to the function `strpbrk`. This call returns a pointer to the first occurrence in `string1` of any character in `string2`. Assuming `string1` and `string2` are `"addisababa"` and `"bus"`, respectively, the call to `strpbrk` returns a pointer to the fifth character in `"addisababa"`, the character `'s'`, which happens to be the first occurrence of the third character in the string `"bus"`. In this case the then-part of the `if` statement is executed.

```
if(strpbrk(string1, string2) == NULL) {
   printf("The string \"%s\"", string1);
   printf(" does not contain any character of the string \"%s\".",
          string2);
}
else {
   printf("The first occurrence of a character of the string \"%s\"",
          string2);
   printf(" in the string \"%s\" is position %d.",
          string1, (strpbrk(string1, string2) - string1) + 1);
} /* end if */
```

The else-part of the `if` statement consists of two `printf` function calls, and the second contains the pointer expression `(strpbrk(string1, string2) - string1) + 1`, which computes the relative address of the first occurrence in `string1` of any character in `string2`. It also involves a call to `strpbrk`. The reason that this pointer expression does the job of finding a relative address was explained in Example 13.19.

### Tokenizing Strings

Another important string processing application is tokenizing or breaking up a given string into its tokens.

> A **token** is a substring in a string separated (or delimited) by a delimiting character (also called a delimiter).

For example, for the string `"Give every man thine ear, but few thy voice."` and the delimiters space, comma, and period, the tokens are `"Give"`, `"every"`, `"man"`, `"thine"`, `"ear"`, `"but"`, `"few"`, `"thy"`, and `"voice"`. For the same string, if we specify comma and period as delimiters, the tokens become `"Give every man thine ear"` and `"but few thy voice"`.

In order to tokenize a string, we can use the standard string library function `strtok`. Unlike the string functions discussed previously, the function `strtok` requires multiple calls to do its task, that is, to break up a string into its tokens. In fact, it requires one call for each token.

Here is how `strtok` works: Let `str1` be a string to be tokenized and `str2` be a string consisting of the delimiting characters. The first call to `strtok` must have `str1` as its first parameter and `str2` as its second parameter. The function `strtok` searches for the first character in `str1` that is not a delimiting character; this character is the beginning of the first token. Next, the function strtok searches for the first delimiting character in str1. When it finds the character, the function strtok returns a pointer to the first token, replaces the delimiting character with a null character, and saves a pointer to the next character following the token in str1.

The subsequent calls to strtok must have NULL as the first parameter and str2 as the second. The second call will return a pointer to the second token, replace the delimiting character by NULL, and maintain a pointer to the first character following the second token in str1. If there are no more tokens, the null value is returned by strtok.

**Example 13.22**   Let us write a C function that tokenizes a given string string1 according to the delimiter characters stored in another string string2. This function appears in Figure 13.16.

```
void print_tokens(char string1[], const char string2[]) {
      char *ptr;

      ptr = strtok(string1, string2);

      while (ptr != NULL) {
             printf("%s\n", ptr);
             ptr = strtok(NULL, string2);
      } /* end while */
} /* end function print_tokens */
```

**Figure 13.16**     A C function that tokenizes a given string

The function print_tokens of Figure 13.16 has two formal parameters: string1 and string2. It has one local variable, ptr, which is a pointer of type char. We will use this pointer as the pointer to the tokens in string1. We will trace the function body by considering the effect of each statement separately in Figure 13.17.

Let us assume that the strings string1 and string2 contain "we like C" and a space, respectively. In other words, we will use space as the delimiter in tokenizing string1. The initial state in the memory is shown early in Figure 13.17. Remember that both strings are terminated by the null character '\0'.

**Step 1.** The statement

```
      ptr = strtok(string1, string2);
```

is executed. The call to strtok results in the assignment of an address value to ptr, which now points to the beginning of the first token, "we"; placement of the null character in the first space encountered in string1, which is in string1[2]; and creation of a pointer that we will call strtok_ptr in Figure 13.17, which points to the first nonblank character in string1. Now strtok_ptr points to the second token, "like", in string1. You should note that the pointer strtok_ptr is created and maintained by the function strtok; we have no control over it in our program. Furthermore, its actual name is not `strtok_ptr`; we are using this name just to identify it in our trace.

**Step 2.** Because the current value of `ptr` is not `NULL`, the body of the `while` statement in Figure 13.16 is entered. Thus the next statement that is executed is

```
printf("%s\n", ptr);
```

which prints the string `ptr` on the screen. It is the first token, `"we"`.

**Step 3.** The statement

```
ptr = strtok(NULL, string2);
```

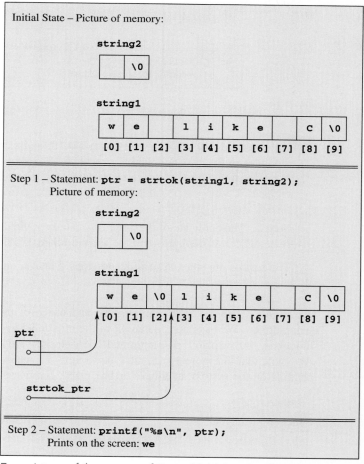

**Figure 13.17**    A trace of the program of Figure 13.16 (*continued*)

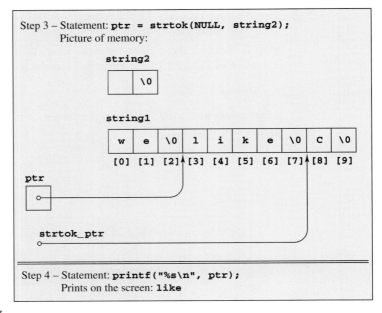

Step 3 – Statement: **ptr = strtok(NULL, string2);**
Picture of memory:

**string2**

| | \0 |
|---|---|

**string1**

| w | e | \0 | l | i | k | e | \0 | C | \0 |
|---|---|---|---|---|---|---|---|---|---|
| [0] | [1] | [2] | [3] | [4] | [5] | [6] | [7] | [8] | [9] |

**ptr**

**strtok_ptr**

Step 4 – Statement: **printf("%s\n", ptr);**
Prints on the screen: **like**

**Figure 13.17**

is the second call to strtok with NULL as its first parameter. This call returns a pointer to the next nonblank character in string1 by copying strtok_ptr to ptr, finds the next space character in string1, which is at string1[7], replaces it with '\0', and updates strtok_ptr such that it points to the next token, "C".

**Step 4.** The predicate of the while statement yields true. Thus the printf function call is executed, printing the second token "like" on the screen.

The rest of the steps are similar to steps 2 and 3, and the execution continues until all tokens are extracted and printed.

Figure 13.18 describes the purpose and usage of the more useful functions in the string library. We have considered all of them in detail in this section. (Three other string functions, strcspn, strspn, and strerror, are not as useful for our purposes.) Also note that in Figure 13.18, the type size_t stands for an integer type, which, depending on the system, is either unsigned long or unsigned int.

| Function Prototypes | Function Description |
|---|---|
| char *strcpy(char *str1, const char *str2) | |
| | Copies the character array str2 into the character array str1 and returns the character array str1. |

**Figure 13.18** Some useful string functions of the string library declared in the string.h header file (continued) ▶

| Function Prototypes | Function Description |
|---|---|
| `char *strncpy(char *str1, const char *str2, size_t n)` | Copies left-most n characters of the character array str2 into the character array str1 and returns the character array str1. |
| `int strcmp(const char *str1, const char *str2)` | Compares the string str1 to the string str2 and returns 0, less than 0, or greater than 0 if str1 is equal to, less than, or greater than str2, respectively. |
| `int strncmp(const char *str1, const char *str2, size_t n)` | Compares left-most n characters of the string str1 to the string str2 and returns 0, less than 0, or greater than 0 if the string formed by left-most n characters of str1 is equal to, less than, or greater than str2, respectively. |
| `size_t strlen(const char *str)` | Determines and returns the length of the strings str, excluding '\0'. |
| `char *strcat(char *str1, const char *str2)` | Concatenates the string str2 to the end of the string str1 and returns the string str1. |
| `char *strncat(char *str1, const char *str2, size_t n)` | Concatenates left-most n characters of the string str2 to the end of the string str1 and returns the string str1. |
| `char *strstr(const char *str1, const char *str2)` | Locates the first occurrence in the string str1 of the string str2 and returns a pointer to the string str2 if the string is found; otherwise returns a null pointer. |
| `char *strchr(const char *str, int c)` | Locates the first occurrence of the character c in the string str and returns a pointer to c in str if c is found; otherwise, returns a null pointer. |
| `char *strrchr(const char *str, int c)` | Locates the last occurrence of the character c in the string str and returns a pointer to c in str if c is found; otherwise, returns a null pointer. |
| `char *strpbrk(const char *str1, const char *str2)` | Locates the first occurrence in the string str1 of any character in the string str2 and returns a pointer to the character if a character from the string str2 is found; otherwise, retuns a null pointer. |

**Figure 13.18**

| Function Prototypes | Function Description |
|---|---|
| `char *strtok(char *str1, const char *str2)` | |
| | Breaks up the string `str1` into its tokens delimited by any character in the string `str2`. The first call to `strtok` must contain `str1` as the first argument; the subsequent calls to tokenize the same string must contain `NULL` as the first argument. Each call returns a pointer to the current token. If there are no more tokens, `NULL` is returned. |

**Figure 13.18**    ■

## REVIEW QUESTIONS

**1.** The function call to `strcpy`

```
strcpy(string2, string1);
```

copies `string2` into `string1`. (T or F)

**2.** Assume that your computer is an ASCII system. Which of the following statements concerning string comparison is correct?
   **a.** `strcmp("data", " data");` returns 0.
   **b.** `strncmp("database", "data", 4);` returns a negative integer.
   **c.** The string `"A15"` is less than `"15A"`.
   **d.** The expression `string1 == "data"`, where `string1` is a string variable, is valid.
   **e.** All of the above.
   **f.** None of the above.

**3.** The value returned by the function `strlen` is the length of the string that is its argument, including the terminating null character. (T or F)

**4.** The result of concatenation of `string1` and `string2` is equal to the result of concatenation of `string2` and `string1`. (T or F)

**5.** Which of the following expressions will correctly store the concatenation of `string1` and `string2` in `string3`?
   **a.** `string3 = strcat(string1, string2);`
   **b.** `strcmp(string3, strcat(string1, string2));`
   **c.** `strcpy(string3, strcat(string1, string2));`
   **d.** `strcpy(strcat(string1, string2), string3);`
   **e.** None of the above.

**6.** Which of the following functions can be used for searching strings?
   **a.** `strstr`
   **b.** `strchr`
   **c.** `strrchr`
   **d.** `strpbrk`

**e.** All of the above.

**f.** None of the above.

**7.** The function call `strstr(string1, string2)` returns a pointer to the first occurrence of `string1` in `string2` if `string1` is a substring of `string2`; otherwise, it returns `NULL`. (T or F)

**8.** A single call to the standard string function `strtok` is enough to completely tokenize a string. (T or F)

## 13.5    EXAMPLE PROGRAM 1: A C Program that Analyzes a Text of Strings

In this application our objective is to design and implement a C program that can be used to analyze a text of strings and determine the number of occurrences of different words in it.

***Problem***    Develop an application program that permits the user to do the following:

1. Enter a text of strings and a string of delimiter characters.

2. Extract tokens from the text, using appropriate string-processing functions, and determine the number of occurrences of each token in the text.

3. Print a list of tokens and the number of their occurrences on the terminal screen in increasing order by the tokens.

***Requirements Specification***    Design and implement an interactive C program that does the following:

1. Prompts the user to enter a text of strings terminated by the back slash character and reads the text into a string.

2. Prompts the user to type a string of delimiter characters terminated by the back slash character and reads the string.

3. Tokenizes the text and determines the number of occurrences of tokens in it. Stores each distinct token and its frequency in an array of structures consisting of a string that stores the token and an integer field that stores its frequency.

4. Sorts the array of structures in increasing order of tokens, using the selection sort algorithm.

5. Prints the sorted list of tokens and their frequencies on the terminal screen.

***Analysis***

**Inputs.**  A text of strings and a string of delimiter characters.

**Outputs.**  A list of tokens and their frequencies.

*Design*    We begin with the initial pseudocode given in Figure 13.19.

---

| | |
|---|---|
| *1* | *prompt user to enter a text of strings and a string of delimiter characters and read them* |
| *2* | *tokenize text, determine token frequencies, and store tokens and their frequencies in a token list* |
| *3* | *sort token list in increasing order of token values, using selection sort* |
| *4* | *display sorted token list on the screen* |

**Figure 13.19**     Initial pseudocode algorithm for a program that analyzes a text of strings

All four steps of the pseudocode of Figure 13.19 must be further refined. Steps 1, 3, and 4 are quite easy to refine and implement. We will give their C implementations directly. Step 2, however, is not trivial, and we will work on it in detail. Figure 13.20 shows a refinement of step 2 as a function called *extract_tokens*. This function has two input parameters: *string1*, which contains the text to be tokenized, and *string2*, which is the string of delimiters. It computes and returns two output parameters: *no_of_tokens*, which represents the number of distinct tokens in *string1*, and a *token_list*, which contains tokens and their respective frequencies.

---

*extract_tokens(string1, string2, no_of_tokens, token_list):*
    *set no_of_tokens to zero*

    *while there are tokens to extract*
        *begin*
            *extract a token and store it in string3*

            *if no_of_tokens is equal to zero*
                *begin*
                    *store string3 as the first element of token_list*
                    *store 1 as the frequency of the first element of token_list*
                    *add 1 to no_of_tokens*
                *end*
            *else*
                *begin*
                    *search for string3 in token_list*

**Figure 13.20**     A pseudocode algorithm for *extract_tokens* (continued)     ▶

```
                              if string3 is found in token_list
                                 add 1 to its frequency
                              else
                                  begin
                                     store string3 as the next element of token_list
                                     store 1 as the frequency of the next element of token_list
                                     add 1 to no_of_tokens
                                  end
                              end if
                         end
                      end if
                 end
              end while
```

**Figure 13.20**                                                                      ■

***Implementation***   Now we are ready to implement the pseudocode algorithms of Figure
13.19 and 13.20 in C. In this implementation, shown in Figure 13.21, we will use the standard functions `strtok`, `strcpy`, and `strcmp`  of the string manipulation library.

```
/ * * * * * * * * * * * * * * * * * * * * * * * * * * * * * * * * * * * * * * * * * * * * * * * * * * * * * * * * * *
   Program Filename: prog13_1.c
   Author         : Uckan
   Purpose        : Tokenizes a string entered by the user and lists
                    the tokens and the numbers of their occurrences
                    in the string in increasing order by the tokens.
   Input from     : terminal keyboard
   Output to      : screen
 * * * * * * * * * * * * * * * * * * * * * * * * * * * * * * * * * * * * * * * * * * * * * * * * * * * * * * * * * * */
#include <stdio.h>
#include <string.h>

/* Named constant declarations: */

#define STRING_SIZE 400
#define ARRAY_SIZE 30

/* Data type declarations: */
```

**Figure 13.21**     A C program that analyzes a text of strings (*continued*)          ▶

```
struct token_list_struct {
      char token[20];
      int no_of_occurrences;
}; /* end struct token_list_struct */

enum Boolean {
      FALSE, TRUE
}; /* end enum Boolean */

/* Function prototypes: */

void get_strings(char str1[], char str2[]);
void sort_array(int list_size, struct token_list_struct
                array_to_sort[]);
void extract_tokens(char str1[], const char str2[], int *no_of_tokens,
                    struct token_list_struct token_list[]);
void output_results(int no_of_tokens,
                    struct token_list_struct token_list[]);


int main(void) {
      /* Local variables: */

      char string1[STRING_SIZE], string2[20];
      struct token_list_struct token_list[ARRAY_SIZE];
      int no_of_tokens;

      /* Function body: */

      get_strings(string1, string2);
      extract_tokens(string1, string2, &no_of_tokens, token_list);
      sort_array(no_of_tokens, token_list);
      output_results(no_of_tokens, token_list);
      return 0;
} /* end function main */


/***************************************************************
 Function Name    : get_strings
 Purpose          : Returns two strings typed by the user.
 Called by        : main
 Receives         : None
 Returns          : string1, string2
 ***************************************************************/
```

**Figure 13.21**                                                                      ▶

```
void get_strings(char string1[], char string2[]) {
      printf("==> Enter a text: \n");
      gets(string1);
      printf("\n==> Enter a delimiter string: ");
      gets(string2);
} /* end function get_strings */



/*****************************************************************
  Function Name    : extract_tokens
  Purpose          : Tokenizes a given string and stores the tokens
                     and the numbers of their occurrences in an array
                     of structures.
  Called by        : main
  Receives         : string1, string2
  Returns          : string1, no_of_tokens, token_list
*****************************************************************/
void extract_tokens(char string1[], const char string2[],
                    int *no_of_tokens,
                    struct token_list_struct token_list[]) {
      /* Local variables: */

      char *ptr;
      char string3[20];
      enum Boolean found;
      int count;

      /* Function body: */

      *no_of_tokens = 0;

      ptr = strtok(string1, string2);

      while (ptr != NULL) {
             found = FALSE;
             strcpy(string3, ptr);
```

Figure 13.21                                                        ▶

```
                if (*no_of_tokens == 0) {
                    strcpy(token_list[0].token, string3);
                    token_list[0].no_of_occurrences = 1;
                    *no_of_tokens = *no_of_tokens + 1;
                }
                else {
                    for (count = 0; count < *no_of_tokens; count++)
                        if (strcmp(token_list[count].token, string3) == 0) {
                            token_list[count].no_of_occurrences++;
                            found = TRUE;
                            break;
                        } /* end if */
                    /* end for */

                    if (found == FALSE) {
                        strcpy(token_list[*no_of_tokens].token, string3);
                        token_list[*no_of_tokens].no_of_occurrences = 1;
                        *no_of_tokens = *no_of_tokens + 1;
                    } /* end if */
                } /* end if */

            ptr = strtok(NULL, string2);
        } /* end while */
} /* end function extract_tokens */


/*****************************************************************
 Function Name    : sort_array
 Purpose          : Sorts an array of structures in increasing order
                    by the values of tokens.
 Called by        : main
 Receives         : list_size, array_to_sort
 Returns          : array_to_sort
 *****************************************************************/
void sort_array(int list_size,
                struct token_list_struct array_to_sort[]) {
    /* Local variables: */

    int count, index_of_largest, last;
    struct token_list_struct temp;

    /* Function body: */
```

Figure 13.21    ▶

```
        for (last = list_size - 1; last >= 1; last--) {
            index_of_largest = 0;

            for (count = 1; count <= last; count++)
                if (strcmp(array_to_sort[count].token,
                    array_to_sort[index_of_largest].token) > 0)
                        index_of_largest = count;
                /* end if */
            /* end for */

            temp = array_to_sort[last];
            array_to_sort[last] = array_to_sort[index_of_largest];
            array_to_sort[index_of_largest] = temp;
    } /* end for */
} /* end function sort_array */


/****************************************************************
 Function Name    : output_results
 Purpose          : Prints on the screen an ordered list of tokens
                    and their numbers of occurrences.
 Called by        : main
 Receives         : no_of_tokens, token_list
 Returns          : None
****************************************************************/
void output_results(int no_of_tokens,
                    struct token_list_struct token_list[]) {
    /* Local variables: */

    int count;

    /* Function body: */

    printf("\n%20s%21s\n", "TOKENS", "NO. OF OCCURRENCES");
    printf("%20s%21s", "------", "------------------");

    for (count = 0; count < no_of_tokens; count++)
            printf("\n%20s%13d", token_list[count].token,
                    token_list[count].no_of_occurrences);
    /* end for */
} /* end function output_results */
```

**Figure 13.21**

■

Let us take a closer look at the program of Figure 13.21.

1.  We have the declarations of a structure type called `token_list_struct` and an enumerated data type called `Boolean`. The structure type `token_list_struct` has two members: a string `token` and an integer `no_of_occurrences`.

2.  The function `main` is simple: it consists of four function calls. It is a direct implementation of the pseudocode of Figure 13.19. Note the declaration of the local variable `token_list`:

```
struct token_list_struct token_list[ARRAY_SIZE];
```

as a one-dimensional array of structures of type `token_list_struct`. This array will contain the tokens to be extracted and their frequencies.

3.  The function `get_strings` prompts the user to enter a text into `string1` and a string of delimiters into `string2` and then returns `string1` and `string2` through its parameters. It uses the input function `gets` for string input.

4.  The function `extract_tokens` is a direct C implementation of the algorithm of Figure 13.20. The statement

```
ptr = strtok(string1, string);
```

extracts the first token from `string1`. The remaining tokens are extracted using the statement

```
ptr = strtok(NULL, string2);
```

in a `while` loop. This issue was discussed in the preceding section.

5.  The function `sort_array` is nothing but a variation of the selection sort algorithm discussed in Chapter 11. The selection sort algorithm is modified to sort an array of structures in which the sort key is a string. Therefore, the function `strcmp` is used in string comparison.

Figure 13.22 is a test run of the program of Figure 13.21.

```
==> Enter a text:
Happiness is not the end of life: character is.

==> Enter a delimiter string: . :
```

**Figure 13.22**    A terminal session of the program of Figure 13.21 *(continued)*    ▶

```
              TOKENS    NO. OF OCCURRENCES
              ------    ------------------
          Happiness            1
          character            1
                end            1
                 is            2
               life            1
                not            1
                 of            1
                the            1
```

Figure 13.22                                              ■

## 13.6   SUMMARY

### This Chapter at a Glance

• In this chapter we continued our earlier discussion of character data. We considered their internal representation, the ASCII and EBCDIC character sets and collating sequences, automatic conversion rules for character data, and C language features for input and output of character data.

• C has a standard character-handling library that includes some useful functions for testing types of characters and for converting letters to uppercase and lowercase. We examined these functions and emphasized those commonly used in applications.

• Next, we focused on strings, which are another structured data type. C does not support strings as a data type. However, we can use character arrays to represent strings. We discussed string declaration, compile-time initialization, and input and output. We explored the standard functions `printf`, `puts`, and `sprintf`, which we can use for string output, and the functions `scanf`, `gets`, and `sscanf`, which we can use for string input. We also discussed the rules for passing strings to functions.

• C relies on the standard string manipulation functions of its string-handling library to process strings. We considered many string manipulation functions and used them to copy strings, to compare them, to compute their length, to concatenate them, to search them for substrings, and to tokenize a string.

### Coming Attractions

• Another important structured data type in C is files. In Chapter 8 we discussed C data files and file processing; however, our discussion was restricted to text files. In the next chapter we return to file processing and discuss two other types of files: binary files that store data in binary form and permit record structuring and random access files that facilitate data retrieval by directly accessing data records.

## STUDY GUIDE

### Test Your Comprehension

1. Choose the *incorrect* statement. The `sizeof` operator
   **a.** Is a unary operator.
   **b.** Has as its operand either a type specifier or a variable.
   **c.** Returns the number of bytes needed to store its operand at compile time.
   **d.** Cannot be used to determine the size of storage for structured data types.

2. In a computer that uses the ASCII character set:
   **a.** The internal representation for '1' is integer 1.
   **b.** The internal representation for '1' is greater than that for 'a'.
   **c.** The internal representation for 'a' is less than that for 'A'.
   **d.** All nonprintable characters are represented by integers that are larger than 128.
   **e.** All of the above are correct.
   **f.** None of the above is correct.

3. Given are the declarations

   ```
   char x = '1', y;
   int a = 10, b = 5;
   double c = -2.5;
   ```

   and the statements

   ```
   y = 2 * x - b * c + a;
   printf("%c", y);
   ```

   Which value will be printed by the `printf` function call?
   **a.** 120
   **b.** 120.5
   **c.** x
   **d.** A space
   **e.** None of the above

4. Choose the correct statement:
   **a.** The function `getchar` can be used to input a character value, whether or not it is a whitespace character, into a character variable.
   **b.** The function `putchar` is for output of character expressions, and `putchar(ch)`, where `ch` is a character expression, is essentially the same as the expression `printf("%c", ch)`.
   **c.** The `putchar` function returns an integer that corresponds to the character that it prints, whereas the `printf` function returns the number of characters that it has printed.
   **d.** All of the above.
   **e.** None of the above.

5. Choose the correct answer:
   **a.** The statement `printf("%d", tolower('x'));` prints x.

**b.** The statement `printf("%d", isdigit('x'));` prints a nonzero integer.
**c.** The statement `printf("%d", isupper('s'));` prints a nonzero integer.
**d.** The statement `printf("%d", isspace('.'));` prints a nonzero integer.
**e.** All of the above.
**f.** None of the above.

**6.** Which of the following string declarations is *not* valid?
**a.** `char string1[10] = {'H', 'i'};`
**b.** `char string1[] = {'H', 'i', '\0'};`
**c.** `char string1[] = "Hi";`
**d.** `char string1[10] = "Hi";`
**e.** `char string1[2] = "Hi";`

**7.** Assume that the variable `str` is a string whose value is `"computer"`. The statement

```
printf(%d", puts(str));
```

prints
**a.** First the string `computer` and then the integer 8.
**b.** First the string `computer` and then the integer 9.
**c.** First the integer 8 and then the string `computer`.
**d.** None of the above.

**8.** Which of the following C input-output functions can be used to copy one string into another string?
**a.** `scanf`
**b.** `puts`
**c.** `sprintf`
**d.** `printf`
**e.** `gets`

**9.** Which of the following statements will read a string of length 10 into the string variable `string1`?
**a.** `getchar(string1);`
**b.** `gets(string1, 10);`
**c.** `scanf("%10c", string1);`
**d.** `scanf("%10s", string1[10]);`
**e.** None of the above.

**10.** Suppose we have the declaration

```
char string1[15];
```

and the statement

```
gets(string1);
```

and we type the string `Structured^Z-programming<Enter>` beginning at the cursor to satisfy the function call to `gets`, where `^Z` represents the end-of-file character and <Enter> represents depressing the Enter key on the keyboard. Which value will be stored in `string1`?
**a.** `Structured-programming`

    **b.** `Structured-pro`
    **c.** `Structured-`
    **d.** `Structured`
    **e.** None of the above.

**11.** The standard string library function
    **a.** `strncpy` copies a source string into a target string.
    **b.** `strcpy` copies the left-most *n* characters of a source string into a target string.
    **c.** `strcmp` compares two strings and returns the first string.
    **d.** `strncmp` compares the first *n* characters of two strings.
    **e.** All of the above are correct.
    **f.** None of the above is correct.

**12.** Choose the correct statement. Assuming `string1` and `string2` contain the values `"column"` and `"sum"`, respectively,
    **a.** `strncat(string1, string2)` returns `"column sum"`.
    **b.** `strcat(string1, string2)` returns `"sumcolumn"`.
    **c.** `strncat(string1, string2, 3)` returns `"colsum"`.
    **d.** `strncat(string1, string2, 3)` returns `"columnsum"`.
    **e.** None of the above.

**13.** The function call `strstr(string1, string2)` returns a pointer to the first occurrence
    **a.** Of `string2` in `string1` if `string2` is a substring of `string1`.
    **b.** Of `string1` in `string2` if `string1` is a substring of `string2`.
    **c.** In `string1` of any character in `string2`.
    **d.** In `string2` of any character in `string1`.
    **e.** None of the above.

**14.** Suppose we want to tokenize the string `"california"` stored in `string1` using the delimiter string `string2`, which contains `"aif"`. The generated token list will be
    **a.** `"cal"`, `"ornia"`
    **b.** `"cal"`, `"orn"`
    **c.** `"california"`
    **d.** `"c"`, `"l"`, `"orn"`
    **e.** None of the above.

**Answers:** 1. d; 2. f; 3. c; 4. d; 5. f; 6. e; 7. b; 8. c; 9. e; 10. d; 11. f; 12. d; 13. a; 14. d.

## Improve Your Problem-Solving Ability

### *Debugging Exercises*

In each of the following C programs or partial code, identify and correct errors of any type.

**15.** The function `our_tolower`, which converts uppercase letters to lowercase:

```
int our_tolower(int letter) {
        if (letter >= 65 && letter <= 90)
                return (letter - 'B' + 'b');
        else
                return letter;
        /* end if */
} /* end function our_tolower */
```

**16.** The main function that uses the function `our_tolower` of Debugging Exercise 15:

```
int main(void) {
      char letter;

      int our_tolower(int x);

      do {
              printf("Enter an uppercase letter (type * to stop): ");
              scanf("%c", &letter);
              printf("Lowercase is: %d", our_tolower(letter));
      } while (letter != '*');
      /* end do-while */
      return 0;
} /* end function main */
```

**17.** The partial code containing a `while` loop:

```
char ch, newline;
ch = ' ';

while (! isdigit(isalpha(ch))) {
        printf("Enter a letter; type any digit to stop: ");
        ch = getchar();
        newline = getchar();
        printf("You have entered: %c", ch);
} /* end while */
```

**18.** The function `replace_string`, which replaces the first occurrence of the substring `string2` in `string1` by `string3`:

```
void replace_string(char *string1, const char *string2,
                    const char *string3) {
      int index, length, i, j;

      if(strstr(string1, string2) == NULL)
            index = 0;
      else
            index = strstr(string1, string2) - string1;
      /* end if */

      length = strlen(string2);
      j = 0;

      for (i = index; i < index + length; i++) {
            string1[i] = string3[j];
            j++;
      } /* end for */
} /* end function replace_string */
```

### *Programming Exercises*

**19.** Write a function called `number_of_uppercase`, which computes and returns under its name the number of uppercase letters in a string that is its only parameter.

**20.** Write a function called `character_count` with two parameters, a string and a character, which determines and returns under its name the number of occurrences of the character in the given string.

**21.** Write a function called `analyze_string` with a string parameter to determine and print the type of each character in the string in the following manner:

```
The 1st character is an uppercase letter.
The 2nd character is a lowercase letter.
. . . . . . . . . . . . . . . . . .
```

**22.** Write a function called `capitalize_text` with one string parameter, which changes every lowercase letter in the string to its uppercase counterpart and returns the string.

**23.** Write a function called `print_special_tokens` with three string parameters: `string1`, `string2`, and `string3`. The function should tokenize `string1` completely using the delimiter string `string2` and print only the tokens that begin with any of the characters in `string3`.

**24.** Write a function called `delete_word` with two string parameters: `text` and `word`. This function should find all occurrences of `word` in `text`, replace each character of the occurrences with the character `*`, and return `text`.

**25.** Rewrite the function `delete_word` of Programming Exercise 24 so that, upon return, the parameter `text` does not contain any occurrences of `word`.

### Programming Projects

**26.** Develop a program that reads a string of words, separated from each other by any number of blanks, and processes the string so that only one blank separates the words. Your program should store the final string in the original string variable and should print its content on the screen.

**27.** Develop an interactive program that reads a text into a string, analyzes the text, and determines and outputs the number of occurrences in the text of each letter in the alphabet without differentiating between upper- and lowercase versions.

**28.** Develop an interactive program that reads a text into a string, reads an integer indicating word length into `word_length`, and determines and outputs all words in the text whose length is equal to `word_length`.

**29.** Develop an interactive program that reads a text into a string called `manuscript` and a series of common words in the English language (such as *a*, *an*, *the*, and *there*), into another string called `common_words`. Your program should tokenize the string `manuscript` and then determine and output the frequency of the words in the string `common_words`.

**30.** Develop a limited-scope text-processing program that reads a text into a string and inserts another string into it immediately after a specified substring. For example, given the string `"This is a structured program."`, your program should generate a string by inserting into it the substring `"and modular"` immediately after the substring `"structured"`. The output of the program will then be `"This is a structured and modular program."`

**31.** Enhance the application program of the preceding problem by incorporating into it the capability to delete any substring from the text. You may use the function `delete_word` of Programming Exercise 25 for this purpose.

**32.** Develop a program that reads a text file of characters and creates another text file containing the data in the input file in encrypted form. Use the simple encryption scheme that replaces each character by a three-digit integer (represented as a string) obtained by subtracting from the constant value of 128 the ASCII integer counterpart of that character. For example, the character 'A' should be converted to the string `"063"`, because in ASCII `'A'` is 65, and when we subtract 65 from 128, we get 63.

**33.** Develop a program that reads a paragraph of text, tokenizes it such that each token is a word, determines whether a token is a palindrome (that is, a word that reads the same forward and backward, such as madam and 1991), and prints all palindromes and the total number of palindromes in the text.

**34.** Develop a program that reads a floating-point value of the form DDDDD.CC, where DDDDD is a dollar amount and CC is cents, and converts the value to a string that expresses the numeric value in its word equivalent, as used in writing checks. For example, if your input is 320.45, your output should be the string `"THREE HUNDRED TWENTY AND 45/100"`.

# Binary and Random Access Data Files

---

**CHAPTER OBJECTIVES**

In this chapter you will learn about:

- **C binary data files**
  Advantages of binary data files
  Specifying binary data files
  Creating binary data files
  Accessing binary data files
  Binary files with structured records

- **Random access files**
  Sequential versus random access to data files
  The `fseek` and `ftell` functions for file streams
  Random creation of text files
  Random access to text files

By the time you have completed this chapter, you will have acquired the ability to:

- **Create and access binary files with structured records**

- **Create and access text files randomly**

---

## 14.1   INTRODUCTION

This chapter is a continuation of the subject of data files that we started in Chapter 8. In Chapter 8 we covered C text data files extensively, and since then we have used them in batch applications. Text files have the advantage of being readable and printable. However, compared to binary files — another file type that C supports — text files require more storage and are not suitable for processing files with structured records.

In this chapter, we first consider binary files. Binary files store data in machine-readable format; therefore, they cannot be created using a text editor. To create them, we must design and run programs. We examine the C features that enable us to create and access binary files in general and binary files with structured records in particular.

Next, we address the issue of access types for data in files. Data in files can be accessed sequentially or randomly. So far, we have used sequential access to data files in our applications. In practice, fast data retrieval calls for random access to data files. C supports random access files, both text and binary, through some standard library functions. We will explore these functions and use them to randomly create and access text data files.

## 14.2   PROCESSING BINARY FILES

In contrast to text files, binary files store data or instructions in binary code that is directly readable by the machine. However, in general, we cannot print binary files directly or browse their content. Despite this, binary data files have some advantages over text data files. Compared to text data files, binary data files store data in a more compact manner and permit reading and writing of data of structured types (arrays and structure variables) and, therefore, structured records.

### A Premise for Binary Files: Files with Mixed Type Data

In some batch applications we may have existing data files whose records contain data of mixed type. Worse yet, data fields may not be separated by blanks. For example, we may have a text file with records typed as

```
1000Kimberly Brown            3.50
```

representing student data, where `1000` is a student identification number, followed by a name, `Kimberly Brown`, and a grade point average, `3.50`, of type `double`. Because records of a text file have no structure, we cannot read them directly into structure variables and subsequently access individual data values.

A rather clumsy solution to this problem is to read a record into a string variable and then tokenize the string into its data fields. To do so, records in the file must be typed according to a specific format. For example, in a student file, assuming that the first four bytes are for student identification number, the value stored in relative positions 5 through 29 is for student name, and the value in relative positions 30 through 33 is for student grade point average, we have a fixed structure. Each record is 33 bytes long and can be read into a string variable declared as

```
char student_record[34];
```

We cannot use the standard string function `strtok` discussed in Chapter 13 to tokenize the string variable `student_record` because we do not have fixed delimiters in this application. We can, however, treat `student_record` as an array of characters and separate the data items contained in it into three string variables declared as

```
char student_idno[5];
char student_name[25];
char student_GPA[5];
```

We still have a problem: `student_GPA` is a string, not data of type `double` on which we can perform arithmetic operations. Fortunately, there is an easy way to solve this problem in the form of some standard string conversion functions. We can use one function, `atof`, which requires a string argument and returns a value of type `double` that is obtained by converting the string argument, if possible, to a value of type `double`. Thus, assuming `GPA` is of type `double`, the statement

```
GPA = atof(student_GPA);
```

will work.

Several string conversion functions are declared in the standard header file `stdlib.h`. Three of them are more useful than the rest. They are `atof`, `atoi`, and `atol`. To use them, your program must contain the preprocessor directive `#include <stdlib.h>`.

The functions `atof`, `atoi`, and `atol` all have a single string argument. The function `atof` converts its argument to `double`, `atoi` converts its argument to `int`, and `atol` converts its argument to `long int`. If conversion is not possible, the behavior of these functions is undefined. A conversion such as `atoi(str)` will work, provided the string variable `str` contains something like "350", which is convertible to integer 350. If `str` contains "JOHN", the function call `atoi(str)` is wrong. You will probably not get a compilation error. In such a situation, what happens depends on the specific compiler. You should certainly try to avoid such conversion attempts.

A more elegant solution to the problem of accessing individual data values in a file with structured records is provided by binary files. Unlike text files, binary files may store structured records, and we can use structure variables to input records from them.

## Fundamentals of Binary Data Files

C supports binary files through its `fread` and `fwrite` functions. With the exception of input and output statements, all file-processing considerations and the standard library functions for file processing that we discussed for text files in Chapter 8 also apply to binary files. The following conventions apply to both binary files and text files:

1. They must be declared as file pointers.
2. They must be opened, using an `fopen` function call, before processing.
3. The function `feof` can be used.
4. The files must be closed with an `fclose` function call.

In fact, as far as the operations listed above are concerned, nothing tells the reader of the program that the file is binary. It is the input and output functions used on a file that identify the file as a binary file. To write data to a binary file, we must use the `fwrite` function. Reading data from a binary file requires the `fread` function.

## Creating Binary Files and the `fwrite` Function

A call to the `fwrite` function has the following format:

> `fwrite(`*AddressOfBuffer*, *LengthOfBuffer*, *NumberOfElements*, *InternalFileName*`);`

where *InternalFileName* is the name of the file, *AddressOfBuffer* is the address of a buffer area in the internal memory considered to be an array, *LengthOfBuffer* is an integer that represents the length in bytes of the buffer area, and *NumberOfElements* is the number of array elements in the buffer area. If the buffer area is not an array, then the parameter *NumberOfElements* must be 1. The `fwrite` function returns the number of array elements that are successfully written.

The `fwrite` function transfers the content of the specified buffer area in the internal memory in binary form to the file and writes *NumberOfElements* elements to the file. Where data are written in the file depends on the write pointer, which points to the position at which the next output will be placed in the file.

The **write pointer** is a pointer maintained by the C system, and the programmer is not directly concerned with its declaration or operations. For a file that has just been opened in output mode, the write pointer points to the first byte in it. If a file has already been written to, the write pointer points to the position that is immediately after the last byte of data that has been written.

The first argument of the `fwrite` function, *AddressOfBuffer*, must be the address of a buffer area in the internal memory. If the buffer area is a string variable, the first argument can be the name of the string variable, since it is a pointer to the string. Thus, for example, given the declarations

```
FILE *outfile;
char str[20];
```

the `fwrite` function call

```
fwrite(str, 20, 1, outfile);
```

is equivalent to the statement

```
fwrite(&str, 20, 1, outfile);
```

and they both transfer 20 bytes from the string `str` to the file `outfile`. However, to write the content of a buffer area declared, say, as of type `int`

```
int test_score;
```

we must use the address operator before `test_score`, as in the following `fwrite` statement:

```
fwrite(&test_score, 2, 1, outfile);
```

This statement will transfer the integer value stored in two bytes in `test_score` to `outfile`.

If we want to write the content of the integer variable `test_score` to `outfile` on a machine in which integers are represented in two bytes, the statement

```
fwrite(&test_score, 2, 1, outfile);
```

will work fine. However, on a machine for which integers require four bytes, this statement will write the binary code in the first two bytes of the memory location for `test_score`. This result is probably not what we intended. Also to ensure greater program portability, it is better to use the `sizeof` operator in the second argument of the `fwrite` statement. Instead of the preceding statement, we can have

```
fwrite(&test_score, sizeof(test_score), 1, outfile);
```

We should note that an `fwrite` statement does not insert a new-line character as a terminator of the output stream. This implies that in binary files a record is the data that are written or read by an output or input statement.

***Example 14.1***   In Example 8.13 we developed a C function named `create_integer_file`, which can be used to create a text file of integers. Here, in Figure 14.1, we have designed a similar function to create a binary file of integers.

```
void create_integer_binary_file(const char file_name[]) {
      /* Local variable declarations: */

      FILE *outdata;
      int test_score;

      /* Function body: */

      if ((outdata = fopen(file_name, "w")) == NULL) {
             fprintf(stderr, "***> Open error on output file %s",
                    file_name);
             exit(-1);
      } /* end if */

      printf("Enter a test score (0 terminates input): ");
      scanf("%d", &test_score);

      while (test_score != 0) {
             fwrite(&test_score, sizeof(test_score), 1, outdata);
```

**Figure 14.1**   A C function that creates a binary file of integers (*continued*)   ▶

```
                    printf("Enter a test score (0 terminates input): ");
                    scanf("%d", &test_score);
            } /* end while */

        fclose(outdata);
    } /* end function create_integer_binary_file */
```

Figure 14.1                                                                        ■

If you compare the function `create_integer_binary_file` to the function `create_integer_file` of Figure 8.6, you will see that they are identical, as expected, except for the file output statement in the body of the `while` loop.

## Accessing Binary Files and the **fread** Function

To read data from an existing file, we must open it in input or input-output mode and use the `fread` function. A call to `fread` has a similar format to `fwrite`:

> `fread(`*AddressOfBuffer*`, `*LengthOfBuffer*`, `*NumberOfElements*`,`
>     *InternalFileName*`);`

Such a call will transfer *LengthOfBuffer* bytes from the file *InternalFileName* in binary form to the main memory buffer whose address is *AddressOfBuffer*. The buffer area is considered to be an array, and the data transferred during input are written to *NumberOfElements* of the array. If the buffer area is not an array, then *NumberOfElements* must be 1.

Reading begins at the position of the read pointer in an input file, which is the relative address of the byte that will be read next. Just like the write pointer, the **read pointer** is also created and maintained by the C system. The read pointer for a file that has just been opened in input mode points to the first byte in the file. After one read operation, the read pointer points to the byte whose relative address is *LengthOfBuffer + 1* in the file.

Assuming we have the declarations

```
FILE *indata;
int test_score;
```

and that the file `indata` has been opened in input mode

```
indata = fopen(file_name, "r");
```

the `fread` function call

```
fread(&test_score, sizeof(test_score), 1, indata);
```

will read, depending on the C environment, two or four bytes from the file indata beginning at the current read position and transfer their content in binary form to the memory location named test_score.

**Example 14.2**    The C function print_integer_binary_file of Figure 14.2 reads records from a binary file of integers and prints them on the monitor screen.

```
void print_integer_binary_file(const char file_name[]) {
      /* Local variable declarations: */

      FILE *indata;
      int test_score;

      if ((indata = fopen(file_name, "r")) == NULL) {
            fprintf(stderr, "***> Open error reading input file %s",
                  file_name);
            exit(-1);
      } /* end if */

      fread(&test_score, sizeof(test_score), 1, indata);

      while(! feof(indata)) {
            printf("\n%d", test_score);

            fread(&test_score, sizeof(test_score), 1, indata);
      } /* end while */

      fclose(indata);
} /* end function print_integer_binary_file */
```

**Figure 14.2**    A C function that prints a binary file of integers on the screen

This function has all the necessary elements for reading files: the file declaration FILE *indata, an fopen function call, file open verification in an if statement, a check for end-of-file using the function feof, and a fclose function call. In addition, in the body of a while loop we have a call to the function fread

```
      fread(&test_score, sizeof(test_score), 1, indata);
```

which reads data from a binary file. This statement tells us that we are processing a binary file.

## Binary Files with Structured Records

The buffer area from which an fwrite function call transfers data during output to a binary file is an area in the internal memory that can contain data of any type. The same is true for the buffer area to which data are transferred during the execution of an `fread` statement on a binary file. Therefore, a binary file can store all data types, including structured data types such as arrays and structures. The structure of the data type stored in a binary file defines the record structure for such a file.

Hence we can use binary files of structured data types to assign structure to data records. For example, to create a file with the following record structure

| student_idno | student_name | student_GPA |
| --- | --- | --- |

as a binary file, we must follow these steps:

1.  We must declare a structure type

```
struct student_struct {
      int student_idno;
      char student_name[26];
      double student_GPA;
}; /* end student_struct */
```

and a structure variable of type `struct student_struct`

```
struct student_struct student_record;
```

2.  We must declare a file as

```
FILE *outdata;
```

and open it in output mode.

3.  We must execute the output statement

```
fwrite(&student_record, sizeof(student_record), 1, outdata);
```

as many times as we have records to write.

Conversely, to access a file that contains structured records of type `struct student_struct`, we must follow these steps:

1.  We must declare the structure type `student_struct` and a structure variable `student_record` of type `struct student_struct`, as shown previously.

2.  We must declare a file as

```
FILE *indata;
```

and open the file `indata` in input or input-output mode.

3.  We must execute the `fread` statement

```
fread(&student_record, sizeof(student_record), 1, indata);
```

as many times as there are records or until we come to the end of the file.

The following program deals with a binary file of structures.

## 14.3    EXAMPLE PROGRAM 1: A C Program that Processes a Binary File of Structures

Suppose we have a file with the following record structure:

| student_idno | student_name | student_age | student_GPA |
|---|---|---|---|

We would like to develop a C program that interactively creates a file of student records with this structure and prints its content in a format that we choose on the screen.

The application is easy, and we don't need an extensive problem analysis for it. What is important here is that our file has structured records and, therefore, must be a binary data file. As for the implementation of the record structure, we will use a structure type. It is called `student_struct` and is declared as follows:

```
struct student_struct {
      int student_idno;
      char student_name[31];
      int student_age;
      double student_GPA;
}; /* end struct student */
```

The C program in Figure 14.3 creates a file of structures of type `student_struct` and prints its content on the screen. It consists of a function `main` and the functions `create_file` and `print_file`.

```
/************************************************************
 Program Filename: prog14_1.c
 Author          : Uckan
 Purpose         : Processes a binary file of structures.
 Input from      : terminal and a binary file of structures
 Output to       : monitor screen and a binary file of structures
 ************************************************************/
#include <stdio.h>
#include <stdlib.h>
```

**Figure 14.3**    A C program that processes a binary file of structures (*continued*)    ▶

```
/* File name definitions: */

#define out_file_name "A:STRUCTUR.DAT"
#define in_file_name "A:STRUCTUR.DAT"

/* Structure declaration for student_struct: */

struct student_struct {
        int student_idno;
        char student_name[31];
        int student_age;
        double student_GPA;
}; /* end student_struct */

/* Function prototypes: */

void create_file(const char fn[]);
void print_file(const char fn[]);


int main(void) {
        printf("Creating output file %s. . .\n", out_file_name);
        create_file(out_file_name);
        printf("%s has been created. . .\n", out_file_name);
        printf("Content of %s:\n", in_file_name);
        print_file(in_file_name);
        return 0;
} /* end function main */


/*****************************************************************
 Function Name    : create_file
 Purpose          : Creates a binary file of structures of type
                    student_struct.
 Called by        : main
 Receives         : file_name
 Returns          : None
 *****************************************************************/
void create_file(const char file_name[]) {
        /* Local variable declarations: */

        FILE *out;
        struct student_struct student_record;
        char waste;
```

Figure 14.3    ▶

```
            /* Function body: */

            if ((out = fopen(file_name, "w")) == NULL) {
                    fprintf(stderr, "***> Open error on output file %s",
                            file_name);
                    exit(-1);
            } /* end if */

            printf("Enter student idno (0 terminates input): ");
            scanf("%d", &student_record.student_idno);
            scanf("%c", &waste);

            while (student_record.student_idno != 0) {
                    printf("Enter student name                 : ");
                    gets(student_record.student_name);
                    printf("Enter student age                  : ");
                    scanf("%d", &student_record.student_age);
                    printf("Enter student GPA                  : ");
                    scanf("%lf", &student_record.student_GPA);

                    fwrite(&student_record, sizeof(student_record), 1, out);

                    printf("Enter student idno (0 terminates input): ");
                    scanf("%d", &student_record.student_idno);
                    scanf("%c", &waste);
            } /* end while */

            fclose(out);
    } /* end function create_file */


    /*****************************************************************
     Function Name    : print_file
     Purpose          : Prints a binary file of structures of type
                        student_struct on the monitor screen.
     Called by        : main
     Receives         : file_name
     Returns          : None
    *****************************************************************/
    void print_file(const char file_name[]) {
            /* Local variable declarations: */

            FILE *in;
            struct student_struct student_record;
```

Figure 14.3                                                              ▶

```
       /* Function body: */

       if ((in = fopen(file_name, "r")) == NULL) {
          fprintf(stderr, "***> Open error while reading input file %s",
                  file_name);
          exit(-1);
       } /* end if */

       fread(&student_record, sizeof(student_record), 1, in);

       while(! feof(in)) {
             printf("    Student idno: %d\n",
                    student_record.student_idno);
             printf("    Student name: %s\n",
                    student_record.student_name);
             printf("    Student age : %d\n",
                    student_record.student_age);
             printf("    Student GPA : %4.2f\n\n",
                    student_record.student_GPA);

             fread(&student_record, sizeof(student_record), 1, in);
       } /* end while */

       fclose(in);
} /* end function print_file */
```

**Figure 14.3**                                                                          ■

We will briefly explain the program of Figure 14.3.

1.   We have two named constant declarations to declare `out_file_name` and `in_file_name` as two string variables, and we initialize both to the string `"A:STRUC-TUR.DAT"`, which is the external name of the file we will create and access.

2.   In the function `create_file`, we declare `out` as a file pointer and `student_record` as a structure variable of type `student_struct`. Next, we open the file `out` as a binary file in output mode using a call to the function `fopen`. We do file open verification in an `if` statement. Subsequently, we prompt the user to enter a student identification number and read interactively the value typed for `student_idno`.

3.   In the body of the `while` loop, we have prompts and interactive input statements to read values for the remaining members of the structure variable `student_record`. Then we have the `fwrite` function call

```
        fwrite(&student_record, sizeof(student_record), 1, out);
```

which writes the data content of the structure variable `student_record` as a record to the file `out`.

4. The `fclose` function call after the `while` statement places an end-of-file marker at the end of the binary file and closes it.

5. In the function `print_file`, our objective is to read the binary file that has been created and print its content on the screen. Therefore we declare `in` as a file pointer and `student_record` as a structure variable of type `student_struct`. Then we open the file `in` in input mode. A record is read by a call to `fread`:

```
fread(&student_record, sizeof(student_record), 1, in);
```

After a record is read, in the body of the while loop its content is printed on the screen, and another record is read. The printing and file record reading operations are repeated until the end of the file is reached.

We suggest that you compile, link, and execute this program and see for yourself that the program creates and accesses a binary file of structured records. It would also be instructive to browse the content of the file STRUCTUR.DAT created in your A drive and verify that the content is not readable.

---

## REVIEW QUESTIONS

1. Binary data files
   **a.** Store data in a compact manner.
   **b.** Permit writing and reading of structured data types.
   **c.** Are supported by C through `fread` and `fwrite` functions.
   **d.** Must be declared as files in a program.
   **e.** All of the above are correct.
   **f.** None of the above is correct.

2. In a binary file a record is the amount of data read or written in one input or output operation. (T or F)

3. Which of the following file-processing functions *cannot* be used for binary files in C?
   **a.** `fread`
   **b.** `fgets`
   **c.** `feof`
   **d.** `fopen`
   **e.** `fclose`

4. The `fwrite` and `fread` functions have four arguments each. The first argument is the address of an internal memory buffer area, the second is the length of buffer area in bytes, the third is the number of array elements in the buffer area, and the last is the internal name of the file. (T or F)

5. Suppose `cost` is a declared variable of type `double`. Which of the following statements will write the content of `cost` to the binary file `output_file`?
   **a.** `fwrite(&cost, output_file);`
   **b.** `fwrite(&cost, sizeof(cost), output_file);`

    **c.** `fwrite(&cost, sizeof(cost), 1, output_file);`
    **d.** `fwrite(cost, sizeof(cost), 1, output_file);`
    **e.** None of the above.

**6.** The write pointer in a binary file points to
    **a.** The position at which the next output will be written.
    **b.** The last byte for a file that has just been opened in output mode.
    **c.** The first byte for an output file after the file is closed.
    **d.** All of the above are correct.
    **e.** None of the above is correct.

**Answers:**     1. e; 2. T; 3. b; 4. T; 5. c; 6. a.

## 14.4     RANDOM ACCESS FILES

Depending on the manner in which data stored in them are accessed, files are classified as sequential access files and random access files.

> In a **sequential access file**, successive read operations access data in the order they exist in the file.

    All data files that we have dealt with in Chapter 8 and in this chapter so far are sequential access files. When we open an existing file for input, the read pointer is at the first byte in it. The first read operation transfers the first data value that we have, beginning at this position, and updates the read pointer to the beginning of the next data in the file. The second read operation transfers the second data value, and so on. To read the $n$th data value in a sequential access file, we must read the first $(n - 1)$ data values preceding it.

    In writing data to a file sequentially, the principle is similar. When we open a file in output mode, the write pointer is at the first byte in it. Therefore, the first write operation writes the data beginning at the first byte and updates the write pointer to point to the byte that follows the data just written. The second write operation writes data after the data written by the first write operation, and so on. In order to write the $n$th data value, we must execute $(n - 1)$ write operations.

***Example 14.3***     Suppose we want to create a text file named `datafile`, consisting of characters. We will use the `put` function for this purpose. The `fopen` function call

```
datafile = fopen("DATA.TXT", "w");
```

opens an empty file that we can represent pictorially as follows:

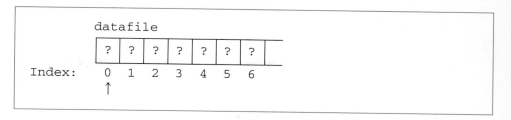

Here the symbol ↑ indicates the write pointer. The first execution of the statement

        fputc(ch, datafile);

where ch is a character variable whose value is J, writes J in the first byte, and advances the write pointer to the next byte:

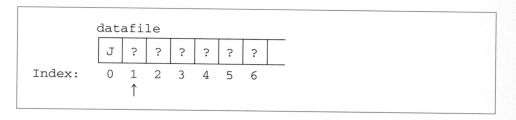

Suppose we execute the statement

        fputc(ch, datafile);

four more times, with ch having the values of A, M, E, and S. We will have in the file the following data:

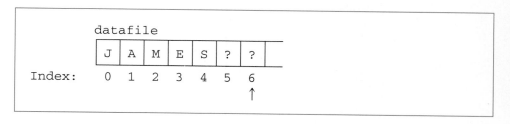

Now, if we close the file using the statement

        fclose(datafile);

the operating system will place an end-of-file marker, represented by ◆ in the following picture:

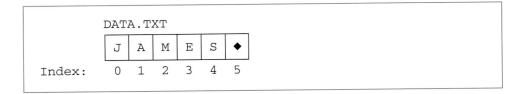

The file is now stored under its external name  DATA.TXT.

Next, let us consider what happens during input. We open the file  datafile  in input mode:

```
datafile = fopen("DATA.TXT", "r");
```

We will have the following picture with the read pointer at the first byte:

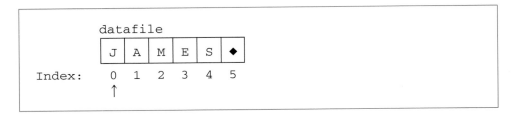

We next execute the input statement

```
ch = fgetc(datafile);
```

The character value  J  stored in the first byte will be transferred to the variable  ch, and the read pointer will advance to the next byte:

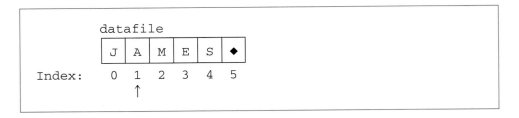

The next  fgetc  statement will read the character value  A. To complete reading the file, we must execute the  fgetc  statement a total of six times.

Sequential access files are fine if our applications call for consecutive access to and processing of every data item in the file. Essentially, the logic of accessing a file sequentially is similar to that of searching an array sequentially. If, however, we want to search a file for a particular data item, the efficiency of the search process becomes roughly the same as that of sequential search of an array, which we know to be rather poor. We also know that we have a better search technique, the binary search algorithm.

We can easily apply the binary search algorithm to an array because we can access an array element directly (or randomly) using array subscripts. To apply binary search to a file, we must have the ability to access data in the file randomly. Random access files give us this ability.

> In a **random access file** we can access a data item in the file directly, without having to access preceding data, by using an offset value from the beginning, end, or the current read/write position of the file.

C supports both sequential and random access files. What makes a file random access is the ability to move write and read pointers randomly in the file. For this purpose, the standard header file `stdio.h` contains the declarations of two functions:

1.  `fseek` function, which can be used to change the read or write pointers in a file stream

2.  `ftell` function, which returns the index of the read or write pointers in a file stream.

The concept of **index** of bytes in files is analogous to the concept of subscripts in C arrays. The first byte in a file has an index value of 0, the second byte has a value of 1, and so on.

### The `fseek` and `ftell` Functions for File Streams

The format of the `ftell` function call is simple:

> `ftell`(*InternalFileName*)

This function returns the index of the read pointer. The `fseek` function call format is more complicated:

> `fseek`(*InternalFileName*, *Offset*, *WhereFrom*);

*Offset* is an integer expression, and *WhereFrom* is one of the following:

1.  The standard constant `SEEK_SET`, which moves the read or write pointer *Offset* bytes from the beginning of the file stream

2.  The standard constant `SEEK_END`, which causes the read or write pointer to move *Offset* bytes from the end of the file stream

3.  The standard constant  SEEK_CUR, which causes the read or write pointer to move *Offset* bytes from its current position.

In summary,  fseek  changes the read or write pointer by *Offset* amount from the beginning, end, or current position in a file. Let us look at an example.

**Example 14.4**    We consider the file  datafile  created in Example 14.3 and open it in input mode:

```
datafile = fopen("DATA.TXT", "r");
```

The read pointer is now at the first byte:

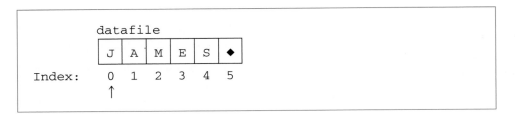

The function call to  ftell

```
ftell(datafile)
```

will return 0, since the read pointer has the index value of 0. Suppose we want to access the third byte from the beginning of the file. First, we must use the  fseek  function to move the read pointer two bytes from the beginning:

```
fseek(datafile, 2, SEEK_SET);
```

This action results in the following picture:

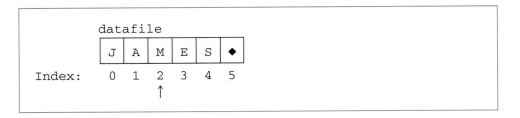

At this point the function call

```
ftell(datafile)
```

will return 2. Now the input statement

```
ch = fgetc(datafile);
```

will read the character  M  to the variable  ch. After this input operation the read pointer will be pointing to the fourth byte in the stream. Next, if we execute the statements

```
fseek(datafile, 1, SEEK_CUR);
ch = fgetc(datafile);
```

the read pointer will move to the fifth byte and the value that is transferred to `ch` will be the character `S`.

The statement

```
fseek(datafile, 0, SEEK_SET);
```

returns the read pointer to the beginning of the file. We can use this statement to go back to the beginning of the file without closing and reopening it.

The statement

```
fseek(datafile, 0, SEEK_END);
```

moves the read pointer to the end of the file, where we have the end-of-file marker. Next, if we execute the call

```
ftell(datafile)
```

in our example, we get 5, which is the number of characters stored in the file excluding the end-of-file marker. You can use this technique to determine the number of characters in a text file.

We can also use the `fseek` and `ftell` functions on files that have been opened in output mode to determine the index of the write pointer and to move the write pointer in the file.

**Example 14.5**    Let us consider how we can create a text file randomly. First, we must open the file:

```
datafile = fopen("DATA.TXT", "w");
```

The operating system will create the external file `DATA.TXT`, and the write pointer will be at the first byte in it:

```
        datafile
        ┌───┬───┬───┬───┬───┬───┬───┬───┐
        │ ? │ ? │ ? │ ? │ ? │ ? │ ? │   │
        └───┴───┴───┴───┴───┴───┴───┴───┘
Index:    0   1   2   3   4   5   6
          ↑
```

Suppose we want to write directly in the third byte of the file the character that is stored in the variable `ch`. We can use these statements:

```
fseek(datafile, 2, SEEK_SET);
fputc(ch, datafile);
```

The call to the function `fseek` will move the write pointer to the byte whose index is 2 (that is, two bytes after its previous position) and, assuming we have M stored in the variable `ch`, will create the following:

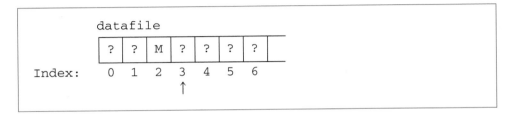

After the output operation the write pointer advances to the next byte. If we now execute the function call

```
ftell(datafile)
```

we will get 3, which is the index of the write pointer after the output operation.

Next, we write the character   J   to the first byte in the file:

```
ch = 'J';
fseek(datafile, 0, SEEK_SET);
fputc(ch, datafile);
```

Here is how our file looks now:

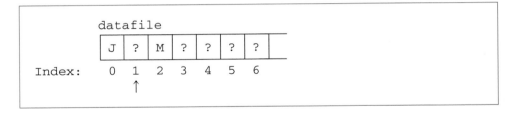

At this point the function call  ftell(datafile)  returns 1.

Finally, we write the character   S   four bytes from the beginning of the file:

```
ch = 'S';
fseek(datafile, 4, SEEK_SET);
fputc(ch, datafile);
```

Now the content of the file is as follows:

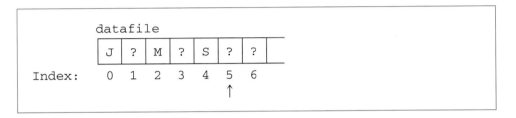

At this point the call `ftell(datafile)` returns 5, the index of the next byte. Now we close the file:

    fclose(datafile);

The file that we have created looks like this:

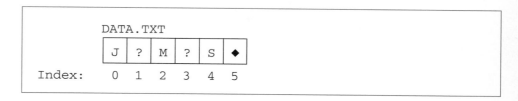

Note that if we print this file or examine it using a text editor, although it is a text file, we may have nonprintable characters where we have not written any data (that is, the positions that contain the symbol ?, implying "garbage"). If we don't want nonprintable characters in our file, and provided we know the number of data items we want to store in it, we may prepare the file by writing blanks to it. Following this step, we may write data randomly. In this case any position to which we have not written data will contain a blank, and we will have a readable and printable file.

Let us summarize what we have discussed so far:

1.   We can create a text file sequentially, without using the `fseek` function, and later process it as a random access file. Also, if we want, in the sequential creation of a text file we may use the `fseek` function. However, we must use the `fseek` function if we want to create a text file sequentially beginning at a position other than the first position in the file. In this case we must vary the offset parameter of `fseek` sequentially.

2.   We can also create a text file randomly using the `fseek` function, as illustrated in Example 14.5.

3.   Having created a text file, we can access it either sequentially or randomly. In accessing a text file sequentially, we may use the `fseek` function and change its first parameter, the offset, in a sequential manner. If we want to access all data items from the beginning of the file, however, we can process a text file without using the `fseek` function.

4.   Random processing of a text file requires the use of the `fseek` function, as shown in Example 14.4.

In C binary files can also be random access files. As in text files, random access during writing and reading binary files necessitates the use of `fseek` and `ftell` functions. We will keep random access binary files outside the scope of our discussion. In the rest of this chapter, we will continue focusing on text files and treat them as random access files.

In practice, random access files are most useful provided they contain structured, fixed-length, records or, at least, fixed-length records. In most cases it is the records in a file that we want to access randomly, and not characters. Systematic random access to records is possible if record length for a file is fixed. In the next two sections, we will consider text files with fixed-length records.

### Random Creation of a Fixed-Length Record Text File

We saw that while creating a text file using random access, we may end up having non-printable and nonreadable characters in the file. To avoid this situation, it is necessary to prepare a blank text file first. Of course, doing so is possible if we know the maximum number of records that we want to store in the file. We also want the text file to have fixed-length records. Thus we need to design a function that prepares a text file consisting of a given number of blank fixed-length records.

This first step of preparation is quite simple. All we have to do is open the file in output mode and write to it a fixed number of blank records, each of a given fixed length and each terminated by the new-line character. Finally, we must close the file. Figure 14.4 is a function named  prepare_random_file  with four formal parameters: a file pointer  out, which is the file's internal name; a character string  file_name, which is the external name of the file;  record_length; and  no_of_records, which represents the number of records in the file.

```
/*********************************************************************
 Function name: prepare_random_file
 Purpose       : Creates a blank random access text file of a
                 specified size, with a specified record length.
 Called by     : main
 Receives      : file_name, record_length, no_of_records
 Returns       : out
 *******************************************************************/
void prepare_random_file(FILE *out, const char file_name[],
                         int record_length, int no_of_records) {
      /* Local variable declarations: */

      int i, j;

      /* Function body: */

      if ((out = fopen(file_name, "w")) == NULL) {
            fprintf(stderr, "***> Open error on output file %s",
                  file_name);
            exit(-1);
      } /* end if */

      for (i = 0; i < no_of_records; i++) {
            for (j = 0; j < record_length; j++)
                  fputc(' ', out);
            /* end for */
      } /* end for */
```

**Figure 14.4**    A C function that creates a blank text file of fixed-length records *(continued)*    ▶

```
        fclose(out);
} /* end function prepare_random_file */
```

**Figure 14.4**                                                                            ∎

In the program of Figure 14.4, we open the file  out  in output mode. The nested
for   loop does the main job. The inner   for   loop writes a record consisting of
record_length blank characters to the file  out. The outer  for  loop repeats these
operations  no_of_record  times. Thus we end up with a blank text file created sequentially.

In our random access text file, we want to access records, rather than characters, randomly, and we want to access them by their relative record numbers. The relative record
number of the first record is 1, the second record is 2, and so on. How do we access a
record by its relative record number? We know that we need the index of the first character of a record to access the appropriate byte to write it randomly. Therefore, we must
be able to convert a given relative record number to an offset that marks the beginning of
that record. We can do this conversion using the following formula:

```
beginning_of_record = (record_number - 1) * record_length;
```

Now we will design a function that will do the following until the user decides to terminate processing:

1.  Prompt the user to enter a relative record number and interactively read the relative
    record number of the record to be written to the file.

2.  Prompt the user to enter a record of length  record_length  and read interac-
    tively what the user types character by character until the user presses the Enter key.

3.  Create and write to the file a fixed-length record, using one of these techniques:

    a.  Pad the record on the right by a sufficient number of blanks if the number of char-
        acters entered by the user is less than  record_length

    b.  Truncate on the right the characters that are in excess of  record_length.

The function that we will name  built_random_file  has four formal parameters: a file pointer  out, an external file name  file_name,  record_length, and
the number of records that can be stored in the file,  no_of_records. The function is
given in Figure 14.5.

```
/******************************************************************
 Function name: build_random_file
 Purpose       : Creates a random access text file from
                 interactively typed data.
 Called by     : main
 Receives      : out, file_name, record_length, no_of_records
 Returns       : out
 ******************************************************************/
void build_random_file(FILE *out, const char file_name[],
                        int record_length, int no_of_records) {
     /* Local variable declarations: */

     char ch, waste, newline = '\n', more_records = 'y';
     int no_of_characters = 0, record_number, beginning_of_record,
         i, j;

     /* Function body: */

     out = fopen(file_name, "r+");

     while (more_records == 'y') {
          if (no_of_characters == 0) {
               printf("Enter record number, between 1 and %d: ",
                      no_of_records);
               scanf("%d", &record_number);
               scanf("%c", &waste);

               while (record_number < 1 ||
               record_number > no_of_records) {
                 printf("Enter record number, between 1 and %d: ",
                        no_of_records);
                 scanf("%d", &record_number);
                 scanf("%c", &waste);
               } /* end while */

               beginning_of_record = (record_number - 1) *
                                     record_length;
               fseek(out, beginning_of_record, SEEK_SET);
               printf("                    ");

               for (i = 0; i < record_length; i++)
                    printf("-");
               /* end for */
```

**Figure 14.5**   A C function that randomly creates a text file of fixed-length records (*continued*)   ▶

```
                    printf("\nEnter a record: ");
                    ch = getchar();
            } /* end if */

            if (no_of_characters < record_length)
                    if (ch != newline) {
                            fputc(ch, out);
                            no_of_characters++;

                            ch = getchar();
                    }
                    else {
                            for (j = 0;
                            j < record_length - no_of_characters;
                            j++)
                                    fputc(' ', out);
                            /* end for */

                            no_of_characters = 0;
                    } /* end if */
            else {
                    while (ch != newline)
                            ch = getchar();
                    /* end while */

                    no_of_characters = 0;
            } /* end if */

            if (no_of_characters == 0) {
                    printf("More records to add or update? (y/n): ");
                    scanf("%c", &more_records);
                    scanf("%c", &waste);
            } /* end if */
    } /* end while */

    fclose(out);
} /* end function build_random_file */
```

Figure 14.5                                                              ■

Because we want to write records to an existing file (prepared in the previous step) without destroying it, we must open it in input-output mode. We use the following `fopen` function call:

```
out = fopen(file_name, "r+");
```

Essentially, the body of the function `build_random_file` of Figure 14.5 consists of a `while` loop that prepares and writes records to the file as long as the user has records to write. In the `while` loop, the function prompts the user to enter a value for `record_number` and reads that value, computes the beginning address of the record, advances the write pointer to the proper byte in the file, prints a scale on the screen to aid the user in typing the record, and prompts the user to enter a record. The characters typed by the user are read and written to the file. The rest of the function is quite straightforward. It allows the user to write records randomly to the file for any relative record number.

The user may rewrite a record corresponding to a given relative record number. In this case the existing record will be overwritten; therefore, the function `build_random_file` of Figure 14.5 can be used not only for building a file initially, but also for updating it any time after it is built. File update is an important operation on data files. Its logic entails finding and reading a record, making changes in its content, and rewriting it to the file. For updating to be possible, the file must be opened in input-output mode, which is the case for our file in this application.

Now that we have two functions, one to prepare a random file and another to write records to it randomly, let us complete the application by designing a main function for it. We will add to the program a function called `print_random_file`, which prints the content of the random file on the screen by processing it sequentially. The functions `main` and `print_random_file` are given in Figure 14.6.

```
#include <stdio.h>
#include <stdlib.h>

// Function prototypes:

void prepare_random_file(FILE *out, const char file_name[],
                         int record_length, int no_of_records);
void build_random_file(FILE *out, const char file_name[],
                       int record_length, int no_of_records);
void print_random_file(FILE *out, const char file_name[],
                       int record_length);


int main(void) {
        /* Local variable declarations: */

        FILE *datafile;
        char file_name[20];
        char waste, any_changes;
        int record_length, how_many;
```

**Figure 14.6**   A C program that randomly creates and updates a text file of fixed-length records *(continued)*   ▶

```
        /* Function body: */

        printf("Enter external name of file to be created: ");
        gets(file_name);
        printf("How many records do you want to write? ");
        scanf("%d", &how_many);
        scanf("%c", &waste);
        printf("Enter record length: ");
        scanf("%d", &record_length);
        scanf("%c", &waste);

        printf("Creating file %s. . .\n", file_name);
        prepare_random_file(datafile, file_name, record_length,
                            how_many);
        build_random_file(datafile, file_name, record_length,
                          how_many);

        printf("%s has been created.\n", file_name);
        printf("Content of %s:\n", file_name);

        print_random_file(datafile, file_name, record_length);

        printf("\nDo you want to make any changes? (y/n): ");
        scanf("%c", &any_changes);
        scanf("%c", &waste);

        if (any_changes == 'y')
             build_random_file(datafile, file_name, record_length,
                               how_many);
        /* end if */

        printf("Final content of file %s:\n", file_name);

        print_random_file(datafile, file_name, record_length);
        return 0;
} /* end function main */
```

Figure 14.6                                                                ▶

```
/********************************************************************
 Function name: print_random_file
 Purpose       : Prints the content of a random access text file
                 on the monitor screen.
 Called by     : main
 Receives      : in, file_name, record_length
 Returns       : in
 ********************************************************************/
void print_random_file(FILE *in, const char file_name[],
                        int record_length) {
     /* Local variable declarations: */

     char ch;
     int relative_record_number = 1, no_of_chars_read = 0;

     /* Function body: */

     if ((in = fopen(file_name, "r")) == NULL) {
          fprintf(stderr, "***> Open error reading input file: %s",
               file_name);
          exit(-1);
     } /* end if */

     printf("Rel. Rec. No.   Record\n");
     printf("------------   -----------------------------\n");
     printf("%7d          ", relative_record_number);

     relative_record_number++;
     ch = fgetc(in);

     while (! feof(in)) {
          no_of_chars_read++;

          if (no_of_chars_read > record_length) {
               printf("\n");
               printf("%7d          ", relative_record_number);
               relative_record_number++;
               no_of_chars_read = 1;
          } /* end if */
```

Figure 14.6     ▶

```
            putchar(ch);
            ch = fgetc(in);
      } /* end while */

      fclose(in);
  } /* end function print_random_file */
```

**Figure 14.6**                                                                ■

Figure 14.7 shows a test run of the program of Figure 14.6, compiled and executed with the functions `prepare_random_file` and `built_random_file` of Figures 14.4 and 14.5. This run creates a text file of three records randomly and updates a record.

```
Enter external name of file to be created: a:student.txt
How many records do you want to write? 3
Enter record length: 30
Creating file a:student.txt. . .
Enter record number, between 1 and 3: 4
Enter record number, between 1 and 3: 0
Enter record number, between 1 and 3: 3
            ------------------------------
Enter a record: 1000 Kimberly Brown        3.50
More records to add or update? (y/n): y
Enter record number, between 1 and 3: 1
            ------------------------------
Enter a record: 2000 John Doe              1.50
More records to add or update? (y/n): y
Enter record number, between 1 and 3: 2
            ------------------------------
Enter a record: 3000 Sharon Willow         3.45
More records to add or update? (y/n): n
a:student.txt has been created.
Content of a:student.txt:
Rel. Rec. No.    Record
------------     ------------------------------
      1          2000 John Doe              1.50
      2          3000 Sharon Willow         3.45
      3          1000 Kimberly Brown        3.50
Do you want to make any changes? (y/n): y
Enter record number, between 1 and 3: 1
            ------------------------------
Enter a record: 2000 John Doe              2.00
More records to add or update? (y/n): n
```

**Figure 14.7**     A sample run of the program of Figure 14.6 (*continued*)     ▶

```
Final content of file a:student.txt:
Rel. Rec. No. Record
------------    ------------------------------
        1       2000 John Doe              2.00
        2       3000 Sharon Willow         3.45
        3       1000 Kimberly Brown        3.50
```

**Figure 14.7**                                                                          ∎

## Random Access to a Fixed-Length Record Text File

Suppose we have a text file consisting of fixed-length records. We want to be able to access records in this file by their relative record numbers. Obviously, the file must be opened in either input or input-output mode. To access a record by its relative record number, we must incorporate into our program a transformation that converts a relative record number to an appropriate byte index. For this requirement, we use the same conversion formula as the one given in the previous section:

```
beginning_of_record = (record_number - 1) * record_length;
```

The variable `beginning_of_record` can be the offset in a `fseek` function call to locate the beginning of the record to be read. Because we know the length of the record, all we have to do is to read `record_length` bytes, beginning at the position of the read pointer, to retrieve the record thus accessed randomly.

The C application program in Figure 14.8 randomly accesses fixed-length records in a text file by their relative record numbers.

```c
#include <stdio.h>
#include <stdlib.h>

// Function prototypes:

void access_random_file(FILE *indata, const char file_name[],
                        int record_length);
void determine_number_of_records(FILE *indata, int record_length,
                                 int *no_of_records);
void access_record(FILE *indata, int record_length,
                   int record_number, int no_of_records);


int main(void) {
        /* Local variable declarations: */
```

**Figure 14.8**    A C program that randomly accesses a text file of fixed-length records (*continued*)    ▶

```
        FILE *indata;
        char file_name[20];
        int record_length;
        char waste;

        /* Function body: */

        printf("Enter external file name: ");
        gets(file_name);
        printf("Enter record length: ");
        scanf("%d", &record_length);
        scanf("%c", &waste);

        access_random_file(indata, file_name, record_length);
        return 0;
} /* end function main */


/*****************************************************************
 Function name: access_random_file
 Purpose       : Randomly accesses a text file of fixed-length
                 records, and prints records on the monitor screen.
 Called by     : main
 Receives      : indata, file_name, record_length
 Returns       : indata
 *****************************************************************/
void access_random_file(FILE *indata, const char file_name[],
                        int record_length) {
        /* Local variable declarations: */

        int no_of_records, record_number;
        char waste, more_access = 'y';

        /* Function body: */

        if ((indata = fopen(file_name, "r")) == NULL) {
                fprintf(stderr, "***> Open error reading input file %s",
                        file_name);
                exit(-1);
        } /* end if */

        determine_number_of_records(indata, record_length,
                &no_of_records);
```

Figure 14.8                                                    ▶

```
        while (more_access == 'y') {
            printf("Record number to be accessed: (between 1 and %d): ",
                    no_of_records);
            scanf("%d", &record_number);
            scanf("%c", &waste);

            access_record(indata, record_length, record_number,
                    no_of_records);

            printf("\nDo you want to access more records? (y/n): ");
            scanf("%c", &more_access);
            scanf("%c", &waste);
        } /* end while */

        fclose(indata);
} /* end function access_random_file */


/****************************************************************
 Function name: determine_number_of_records
 Purpose       : Determines the number of records in a text file
                 of fixed-length records.
 Called by     : access_random_file
 Receives      : indata, record_length
 Returns       : indata, no_of_records
 ****************************************************************/
void determine_number_of_records(FILE *indata, int record_length,
                                 int *no_of_records) {
        /* Local variable declarations: */

        int file_size;

        /* Function body: */

        fseek(indata, 0, SEEK_END);
        file_size = ftell(indata);
        *no_of_records = file_size / record_length;
} /* end function determine_number_of_records */
```

Figure 14.8                                                                    ▶

```
/*****************************************************************
  Function name: access_record
  Purpose       : Randomly accesses a record in a text file of
                  fixed-length records.
  Called by     : access_random_file
  Receives      : indata, record_length, record_number, no_of_records
  Returns       : indata
*****************************************************************/
void access_record(FILE *indata, int record_length,
                    int record_number, int no_of_records) {
      /* Local variables: */

      int beginning_of_record, count;
      char ch;

      /* Function body: */

      if (record_number < 1 || record_number > no_of_records)
            printf("No such record in the file.");
      else {
            beginning_of_record = (record_number - 1) *
                                  record_length;
            fseek(indata, beginning_of_record, SEEK_SET);
            printf("Record accessed: \n");

            for (count = 0; count < record_length; count++) {
                  ch = fgetc(indata);
                  printf("%c",ch);
            } /* end for */
      } /* end if */
} /* end function access_record */
```

Figure 14.8                                                      ∎

In the program of Figure 14.8, we note the following:

1.   In the function access_random_file, we first open the file indata in input mode using a call to fopen. Then we have a call to the function determine_number_of_records, followed by a while loop in which the user is prompted to enter the relative record number of the record to be accessed. The function call to access_record accesses and retrieves the indicated record and prints it on the screen. The body of the while statement is executed as long as the user has more records to access.

2.   The function determine_number_of_records advances the read pointer to the end of the file by an fseek function call, determines file_size in bytes by calling the function ftell, and computes and returns the number of records using the formula:

```
*no_of_records = file_size / record_length;
```

3. The function `access_record` consists of an `if` statement, which verifies that the supplied `record_number` is in the range of 1 through `no_of_records`. If so, it computes `beginning_of_record`, advances the read pointer to the beginning of the record, uses the `fgetc` function to read `record_length` characters and prints them on the screen.

4. The function `main` is a simple function that interactively reads the external file name and the record length and triggers the execution of the function `access_random_file`.

Figure 14.9 is a sample run of the program of Figure 14.8.

```
Enter external file name: a:student.txt
Enter record length: 30
Record number to be accessed: (between 1 and 3): 0
No such record in the file.
Do you want to access more records? (y/n): y
Record number to be accessed: (between 1 and 3): 4
No such record in the file.
Do you want to access more records? (y/n): y
Record number to be accessed: (between 1 and 3): 3
Record accessed:
1000 Kimberly Brown       3.50
Do you want to access more records? (y/n): n
```

**Figure 14.9**    A sample run of the program of Figure 14.8

Before we conclude this section, we should mention that random access files are significantly faster compared to sequential access files and are indicated in most applications using files. However, random access to records in our applications has been by the relative record number of a record to be retrieved. In other words, we have used a relative address to access a record. Such an access is called **access by address**. In practical applications it is more useful to randomly access records by the content of an identifying field of a record. In other words, rather than specifying a retrieval request as "Retrieve the third record in the student file," we prefer "Retrieve the record for John Doe in the student file." This latter access type is called **access by content**. To access a record by content, we must first transform the identifying field value into a relative address. We can achieve such a transformation using indexing or hashing, two techniques that are outside the scope of this book.

## REVIEW QUESTIONS

1. In a sequential access input file:
   **a.** The read pointer is at the first byte immediately after the file is opened.
   **b.** After the third execution of an input statement that reads a character at a time, the read pointer points to the fourth byte in the file.

**c.** To read the last byte in the file, we must read all the data that precede it.

**d.** All of the above are correct.

**e.** None of the above is correct.

2. Random processing of a file is possible through the use of the C file function  `fseek`. (T or F)

3. The function call

```
fseek(indata, -2, SEEK_CUR);
```

moves the read or write pointer to

**a.** The end of the file  `indata`.

**b.** The beginning of the file  `indata`.

**c.** Two bytes after the current position of the read pointer in the file  `indata`.

**d.** Two bytes before the current position of the read pointer in the file  `indata`.

**e.** None of the above.

4. A text data file that has been created randomly may contain unprintable characters. (T or F)

5. Accessing a data file by the relative address of a record is called access by content. (T or F)

**Answers:** 1. d; 2. T; 3. d; 4. T; 5. F.

---

## 14.5    SUMMARY

### This Chapter at a Glance

- In this chapter we continued our discussion of data files. We noted that text files are useful in many batch applications; however, binary data files turn out to be suitable in case data in files are structured.

- We considered binary files and discussed how to create and access them. Then we discussed binary data files with structured records.

- All data files that we have created and used up to this point have been sequential access files in which records are accessed in consecutive order. In many applications accessing data records randomly by their relative locations in the file speeds up processing.

- The characteristic that makes a file random access is the ability to move the read or write pointers in the file to point to the record that we want to access. C provides some standard functions for this purpose and thus supports random access files of text or binary type. We concentrated on random access text files and focused on creating and using them.

### Coming Attractions

- In the final chapter of the book, we will revisit functions. We will see that in C a function can call itself. However, such self-calls must be done in a controlled fashion so that we don't get trapped in an infinite loop.

- If a function is formulated to call itself to solve a smaller version of the problem it is designed to solve and ultimately calls itself so that a self-call is no longer necessary, the function is said to be recursive.

- Recursive functions are useful in solving many iterative problems. A recursive formulation expresses the solution of an iterative problem in terms of a smaller version of itself. Recursion yields elegant and simple solutions to complicated problems and is a very powerful problem-solving technique.

## STUDY GUIDE

### Test Your Comprehension

1. Which of the following statements concerning the function `atof` is *incorrect*?
   **a.** It is a standard C string conversion function.
   **b.** It is declared in the header file `stdlib.h`.
   **c.** It has one argument, which is a string.
   **d.** It returns a value, which is of type `float`.

2. Which of the following file elements indicates that a program is dealing with a binary data file?
   **a.** `fopen` function call
   **b.** File declaration
   **c.** `fgets` function call
   **d.** `fread` function call
   **e.** `fseek` function call

3. In C a binary data file can be a file of
   **a.** Arrays.
   **b.** Structures.
   **c.** Characters.
   **d.** Integers.
   **e.** All of the above.

4. Choose the correct statement.
   **a.** The function `ftell` moves the read or write pointer in a file stream.
   **b.** The function `fseek` returns the index of the read or write pointer in a file stream.
   **c.** The function `ftell` has two arguments: an offset and an origin for the offset.
   **d.** All of the above are correct.
   **e.** None of the above is correct.

5. After the function call

        fseek(indata, 0, SEEK_END);

   the function call `ftell(indata)` returns
   **a.** The number of characters stored in the file, excluding the end-of-file marker.
   **b.** The number of records stored in the file.
   **c.** The length of each record in the file.

**d.** The current index of the read pointer in the file.

**e.** None of the above.

## Improve Your Problem-Solving Ability

### Debugging Exercises

**6.** For each of the following groups of statements or partial programs, find the errors, if any, and suggest ways to correct them.

**a.**
```
if ((my_file = fopen(file_name, "r")) == NULL) {
    fprintf(stderr, "***> Open error on output file %s",
            file_name);
    exit(-1);
} /* end if */
.................
.................
while (student_record.student_idno != 0) {
    .................
    .................
    fwrite(&student_record, sizeof(&student_record), 1,
            my_file);
    .................
    .................
} /* end while */
```

**b.**
```
if ((my_file = fopen(file_name, "w")) == NULL) {
    fprintf(stdin, "***> Open error while reading file %s",
            file_name);
    exit(-1);
} /* end if */

fread(*student_record, sizeof(student_record), 1,
        my_file);
```

**c.**
```
fseek(indata, 0, SEEK_SET);
file_size = ftell(indata);
*no_of_records = file_size / record_length;
```

### Programming Exercises

Consider the `faculty_file` described in the programming exercises in Chapter 8. We want to implement it as a binary file. Again, each record in `faculty_file` consists of the following data items:

• A five-digit faculty identification number

• A faculty name whose maximum length is 25 bytes

• A single-digit faculty rank code (1 for full professor, 2 for associate professor, 3 for assistant professor, and 4 for instructor)

- An annual salary value typed in conventional notation as DDDDD.CC where DDDDD represents the dollar amount and CC stands for cents.

7. Write a function that gets values for the data items of the records of faculty_file interactively and creates a binary file of structure variables based on the structure type faculty_struct. The components of faculty_struct are the data items in the records of faculty_file.

8. Write a function that accesses the records of faculty_file of Programming Exercise 7 sequentially and prints the name of the faculty member whose salary is the largest.

9. Write a function that accesses the records of faculty_file of Programming Exercise 7 sequentially and then computes and returns the average faculty salary.

10. Assume that the records in faculty_file of Programming Exercise 7 are in increasing order by faculty identification number. Write a function that searches faculty_file sequentially to print the record corresponding to a faculty member whose identification number is supplied.

11. Suppose that we have a text file of fixed-length records and that each record consists of a faculty last name and a faculty telephone number. Faculty last name is a 15-byte string, and faculty telephone number is a seven-digit number. The records in the file, called faculty_phones, are arranged in increasing order of faculty last name. A partial content of this file follows.

```
Index:
0123456789012345678901234567890123456789012345678901234567890123456789012345
Data :
BROWN          5290922CANFIELD       5296263DEREK          5298111
```

As you can see, the records are continuous and are not delimited by any character.

Write a function that searches this file sequentially for a supplied faculty last name and returns that faculty member's telephone number.

12. Write a function that receives a faculty last name value, accesses the record of that faculty member in the faculty_phones file of the previous exercise, and updates the telephone number field by replacing the old telephone number with a new one, which is made available to the function as one of its parameters.

### Programming Projects

13. Solve Programming Project 18 of Chapter 8, assuming that the student file is a binary file and that, in each record, the student identification number is immediately followed by a student name with no blanks in between.

14. Solve Programming Project 21 of Chapter 8, assuming that the instructor/course evaluation file is a binary file. Also, assume that each record in the file consists of an instructor number, a course number, and responses to five questions; the data values are not sep-

arated by blanks; and the records in the file are not terminated by the new-line character. A typical record look like this:  500200EEGEE.

**15.** Develop a program that does the following:
  **a.** Creates a text file, called  faculty_file. To create the file, your program should interactively read values for faculty identification number (a four-digit integer) and faculty name (a 30-byte string) and store them in an array of structures. Data input should be terminated when the user types 0 for faculty identification number. Then the program should sort the array of structures in increasing order of faculty identification number. You may use the sorting technique of your choice for this step. Finally, the program should write the content of the ordered array to the  faculty_file  in which records are of fixed length (34 bytes) and are not separated by the new-line character.
  **b.** Gives the user a choice to print the content of the  faculty_file  on the monitor screen or to retrieve and print a faculty record for the faculty member whose identification number is the search key. To print the content of the file, your program should access the file sequentially. To retrieve faculty records, your program should do random access. In retrieving faculty records, you should use binary search on the random access text file.

**16.** Enhance Programming Project 15 by including among its capabilities the three basic file maintenance operations: record insertion, record deletion, and record update. Use the following strategies for these operations:
  **a.** For record insertion, dump the content of the  faculty_file  into an array of structures, add the record to be inserted to the array as its last element, sort the array of structures in increasing order of faculty identification number, and re-create the  faculty_file  by writing the content of the array of structures to it.
  **b.** For record deletion, again dump the  faculty_file  into an array of structures and re-create the file by writing to it all records in the array of structures except the record to be deleted. The record to be deleted is identified by a faculty identification number value. Before starting the delete operation, your program should search the file to ensure that the record to be deleted is in it. Use binary search to locate the record to be deleted.
  **c.** For record update, ask the user to enter a faculty identification number; then search the file using binary search to locate the record to be updated. If the record is found, ask the user to enter a new faculty name; then update the file by rewriting the record. Do not make copies of the content of the file for the update operation.

# 15

# Recursion

---

**CHAPTER OBJECTIVES**

In this chapter you will learn about:

- **Recursion as a problem-solving technique**
- **Recursive functions**
  Recursive valued functions
  Recursive void functions
- **Tracing recursive functions**
- **Recursion versus iteration**

By the time you have completed this chapter, you will have acquired the ability to:

- **Formulate iterative problems recursively**
- **Design recursive C functions**

---

## 15.1   INTRODUCTION

In this final chapter of the book, we discuss recursion and recursive functions. Recursion is a problem-solving technique that expresses the solution of a problem in terms of the solutions of similar but smaller problems. In a sense recursion is similar to top-down design; both techniques split a problem into smaller problems that are similar to the original and solve the problem by first solving its smaller versions. Recursion is a powerful problem-solving technique in computer science and mathematics.

Solving problems by recursion requires the use of recursive functions. A recursive function is one that calls itself repetitively until a final call is made that no longer requires a self-call. The C programming language supports recursive functions and, therefore, recursion. In this chapter we begin by examining the nature of recursion and recursive functions. Then we consider a variety of simple recursive problems and explore the techniques to solve problems recursively.

## 15.2   RECURSIVE PROBLEMS AND RECURSIVE FUNCTIONS

We know that in a modular program a function may call on any function. Moreover, although we have not mentioned it before, C further permits a function to call itself. From a syntactical point of view, the program of Figure 15.1 is correct.

```c
#include <stdio.h>

void prt_integers(int n);


int main(void) {
        int number;

        printf("Enter an integer: ");
        scanf("%d", &number);

        prt_integers(number);
        return 0;
} /* end function main */


void prt_integers(int n) {
        printf("%d\n", n);
        prt_integers(n);
} /* end function prt_integers */
```

**Figure 15.1**   A C function that calls itself

In this program the function `main` calls the function `prt_integers`. Note that the body of the function `prt_integers` has a function call

```
prt_integers (n);
```

thus invoking itself. If you attempt to compile and execute this program, you will see that it will compile without any problems. However, at run time you will be trapped in an infinite loop; the program will keep on printing on the screen the value of `number` that the user enters before the function `prt_integers` is invoked for the first time.

What do we conclude? Do we conclude that, although we can have a function call inside a function to itself, such a call always causes an infinite loop and is, therefore, a useless feature of the language? Not at all! Consider the variation of the preceding program, as given in Figure 15.2.

```
#include <stdio.h>

void print_integers(int n);


int main(void) {
        int number;

        printf("Enter an integer: ");
        scanf("%d", &number);

        print_integers(number);
        return 0;
} /* end function main */


void print_integers(int n) {
        if (n >= 1) {
                printf("%d\n", n);
                print_integers(n-1);
        } /* end if */
} /* end function print_integers */
```

**Figure 15.2**    A function that calls itself recursively

The function `print_integers` in the program of Figure 15.2 also has a function call in its body to itself. However, this call is different from the function call in Figure 15.1 for two reasons:

1.   This time the statement in `print_integers` that calls itself is

```
print_integers(n-1);
```

in which the parameter is 1 less than  n, the value in the previous call. In other words, the problem that the function is expected to solve is a smaller or simpler version of the previous problem. For example, if the user enters 3 when prompted in the function  `main`, the value of  n  will be 3 when we are in the function  `print_integers`  for the first time and the output statement will print 3. The next statement that calls on the function itself will have an actual parameter value of 2, which is less than the first value of  n. Thus we can say that the problem size is gradually diminishing.

2.   In Figure 15.2 the call to  `print_integers`  in  `print_integers`  is enclosed in the then-part of an  `if`  statement. The process of self-call will go on as long as the value of  n  is greater than or equal to 1. Eventually,  n  will become 0, and the calls to the function will stop. Therefore, we will not have an infinite loop this time.

With the program of Figure 15.2, we have solved the simple problem of printing integers beginning with a given integer down to 1. We could have solved this problem using a  `for`  statement, that is, iteration. The solution presented in the program of Figure 15.2 appears to be an alternative to an iterative solution of the same problem. The iterative solution to the problem of printing integers from number down to 1 can be expressed as follows:

> Print integers from  `number`  to 1 by printing the value of  `number`, then one less  `number`, and so on until you print 1.

On the other hand, the solution in Figure 15.2 can be phrased as follows:

> Print integers from  `number`  down to 1 by printing  `number`  and solving the problem of printing integers from  `number` – 1  down to 1 until the problem becomes that of printing 0, in which case do nothing.

This solution is the recursive solution to the problem.

---

A solution to a problem is **recursive** if it is expressible as a smaller version of itself and if ultimately a simple nonrecursive solution can be found.

---

To solve problems recursively, we design functions that call on themselves. Such functions are recursive functions.

---

A function that calls itself to solve a smaller version of its task until a final call that does not require a self-call is a **recursive function**.

---

Note that the function  `prt_integers`  of Figure 15.1 is not a recursive function, whereas the function  `print_integers`  of Figure 15.2 is.

In a recursive solution the part of the solution that expresses the solution in terms of a smaller version of itself is called the **general case**; that part of the solution that is non-recursive is called the **base case**. In the recursive solution of printing integers from num-ber down to 1, the expression "Print number and then solve the problem of print-ing integers from number – 1 down to 1" is the general case. The expression "Do nothing when the problem becomes that of printing 0" is the base case.

## 15.3    A RECURSIVE VALUED FUNCTION THAT COMPUTES FACTORIALS

To understand recursion better, let us consider another example. We return to the problem of computing the factorial of a nonnegative integer. In Example 4.18 we gave the definition of the factorial function in algebra as

$$fact(n) = 1 \times 2 \times ... \times n$$

where $n$ is a nonnegative integer for which we want to compute the factorial. By definition, the factorial of 0 is 1, that is,

$$fact(0) = 1$$

Using these definitions, we presented an iterative solution to the problem. It is repeated here in Figure 15.3 as an integer function called nonrecursive_factorial.

```
int nonrecursive_factorial(int num) {
        int fact = 1, count = 2;

        while (count <= num) {
                fact = fact * count;
                count++;
        } /* end while */

        return fact;
} /* end function nonrecursive_factorial */
```

**Figure 15.3**    A nonrecursive C function that computes the factorial of a nonnegative integer

We can solve the same problem recursively by observing that

$$fact(n) = n \times fact(n - 1)$$

That is, the factorial of an integer can be computed by multiplying it by the factorial of that value minus 1. Here the factorial function, $fact(n)$, is expressed in terms of a smaller version of itself, $fact(n - 1)$. Therefore, this formulation is recursive. To complete it we must also have a base case. The base case is the fact that the factorial of 0 is 1:

$$fact(0) = 1$$

Using the preceding general case and the base case, we can write a C function that computes factorials recursively. Such a function is shown in Figure 15.4.

```
int fact(int num) {
      if (num == 0)
            return 1;
      else
            return (num * fact(num - 1));
      /* end if */
} /* end function fact */
```

**Figure 15.4**     A recursive C function that computes factorial

In Figure 15.4, in the body of the function `fact`, we have a single `if` statement. The then-part of the `if` statement is the C expression of the base case, and the else-part corresponds to the general case. In the else-part the statement

```
return (num * fact(num - 1));
```

recursively calls on the function `fact`. We observe that this recursive formulation is not only more concise and simpler than the corresponding iterative formulation of Figure 15.3 but also more elegant because the code reflects the recursive nature of the problem. In general, this characteristic is true of all recursive formulations.

## 15.4   TRACING RECURSIVE VALUED FUNCTIONS

There is one drawback, however, to recursion as compared to iteration. Recursive solutions tend to be less execution-efficient than iterative solutions. To understand why, and also to see how recursion works, let us trace the recursive function call `fact(4)` in Figure 15.5.

**Step 1.** The function call `fact(4)` brings the program control to the `if` statement in the function `fact`, with 4 as the value of its formal parameter `num`. Because `num` is not equal to 0, the else-part of the `if` statement is executed. It contains the function call `fact(num-1)`. With `num` currently 4, this function call becomes `fact(3)`, another function call to `fact`. Because no value has yet been returned to the calling function, the function call `fact(4)` is incomplete.

**Step 2.** The function call `fact(3)` brings the program control into the function `fact`. Again, because the value of the formal parameter `num` is 3 and, therefore, the predicate of the `if` statement, `num == 0`, is false, the else-part of the `if` statement is executed. Here we have another function call, `fact(2)`. Keep in mind that in addition to `fact(4)`, the function call `fact(3)` is also incomplete.

**Step 3.** Similarly, the function call `fact(2)` triggers another call to `fact` as `fact(1)`. At this point, the calls `fact(4)`, `fact(3)`, and `fact(2)` are incomplete.

**Step 4.** The function call `fact(1)` results in the call `fact(0)`. The list of incomplete function calls becomes `fact(4)`, `fact(3)`, `fact(2)`, and `fact(1)`.

**Step 5.** The function call `fact(0)` renders true for the predicate of the `if` statement, `num == 0`, and the then-part of the `if` statement is executed.

**Step 6.** Therefore, the function call `fact(0)` is complete, and the value 1 is returned to the function `fact` corresponding to the call `fact(0)`. The expression `num * fact(num - 1)` can now be evaluated as 1 * 1, yielding 1.

**Step 7.** This value is returned to the function call `fact(1)`, and this time the expression `num * fact(num - 1)` produces 2 * 1 = 2. Now the list of incomplete function calls includes `fact(4)`, `fact(3)`, and `fact(2)`.

**Step 8.** The value 2 is returned to the function call `fact(2)`, and the expression `num * fact(num - 1)` is evaluated as 3 * 2 = 6. The list of incomplete function calls reduces to `fact(4)` and `fact(3)`.

**Step 9.** The value 6 is returned to the function call `fact(3)`, and the value computed for `num * fact(num - 1)` will be 4 * 6 = 24. The only remaining incomplete function call at this point is `fact(4)`.

**Step 10.** The value 24 is returned to satisfy the function call `fact(4)`.

As you can see, the difficulty in recursion is keeping track of the incomplete recursive function calls. If a programming language supports recursion, then the operating system uses a special data structure called a stack to do this.

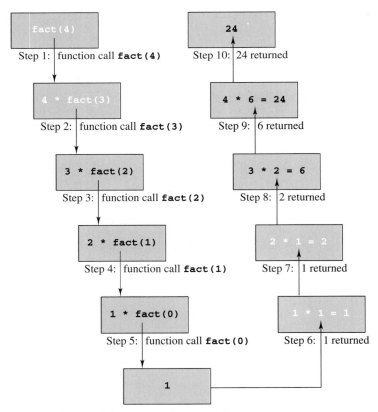

**Figure 15.5**    Manual trace of the recursive function call  `fact(4)`

It should be understood that every time a call to a function is made, the operating system creates a record, called an **activation record**, to keep track of the function calls. To create an activation record, the operating system borrows a main memory segment from the free store. The activation record contains values associated with each data element in the called function together with some additional information. Therefore, for a function that contains a large number of variables, the activation record may use a significant chunk of the free store. When the function's execution is completed, the space used by the activation record is released to the free store.

In executing recursive functions, in general the operating system has to deal with a large number of recursive function calls. For example, in computing the factorial of 4 using the function `fact` in Figure 15.4, the operating system has to keep track of five calls to `fact`. Each call results in the creation of an activation record. The operating system uses a stack to determine which activation record to consider in the proper sequence and release its memory segment to the free store. A **stack** is a last-in-first-out list; the last element that is inserted into it is accessed, processed, and deleted from the list. For example, in processing the function call `fact(4)`, five activation records are created, corresponding to the calls `fact(4)`, `fact(3)`, `fact(2)`, `fact(1)`, and `fact(0)`, in this order, and they are inserted into a stack. Then the operating system accesses the last activation record inserted into the stack, which is the record that corresponds to `fact(0)`, processes it, and frees the memory space reserved for it, and so on.

Fortunately, you don't have to worry about this process while designing your program. In other words, it is the system's task, not yours, to keep track of recursive function calls to complete the processing properly. All you have to do is to express the recursive function definition correctly in your program. However, you should realize that the free store is limited, and because of memory limitations, the operating system may fail to handle recursive function calls that involve a very large number of self-calls. In such cases you must use iterative solutions.

A manual trace of a recursive function is very helpful in understanding how recursion works and in debugging recursive functions. However, it is a tedious debugging technique and cannot be recommended for debugging recursive functions. We can instead insert interactive output statements into a recursive function at its entry and exit points and print the function call and the value returned for each call. This way we can easily see whether the function is behaving properly. Let us reconsider the recursive factorial function of Figure 15.4 in the program in Figure 15.6.

```
#include <stdio.h>

int fact(int);


int main(void) {
        int number;
```

**Figure 15.6**   The recursive function `fact` that traces its execution (*continued*)   ▶

```
         printf("Enter a nonnegative integer: ");
         scanf("%d", &number);

         printf("Factorial of %d is %d.\n", number, fact(number));
         return 0;
} /* end function main */


int fact(int num) {
         int res;

         printf("--> Function call: fact(%d)\n", num);

         if (num == 0)
                 res = 1;
         else
                 res = num * fact(num - 1);
         /* end if */

         printf("<-- %d returned for fact(%d).\n", res, num);

         return res;
} /* end function fact */
```

**Figure 15.6**    ■

In the program of Figure 15.6, we have the recursive function `fact` of Figure 15.4, written with few changes. These changes are the local variable `res`, which is the value the function returns, the output statement

```
printf("---> Function call: fact(%d)\n", num);
```

placed in the function body as the first statement, and the output statement

```
printf("<--- %d returned for fact(%d).\n", res, num);
```

placed just before the `return` statement. We also have a function `main`, in which we call on the function `fact`. If we run this program, we get the output shown in Figure 15.7, corresponding to the function call `fact(4)`. This output traces the recursive function, with results similar to those in Figure 15.5.

```
Enter a nonnegative integer: 4
---> Function call: fact(4)
---> Function call: fact(3)
---> Function call: fact(2)
```

**Figure 15.7**    Output of program of Figure 15.6 (*continued*)    ▶

```
---> Function call: fact(1)
---> Function call: fact(0)
<--- 1 returned for fact(0).
<--- 1 returned for fact(1).
<--- 2 returned for fact(2).
<--- 6 returned for fact(3).
<--- 24 returned for fact(4).
Factorial of 4 is 24.
```

Figure 15.7                                                                    ■

## 15.5   A RECURSIVE void FUNCTION THAT PRINTS A STRING BACKWARD

The example in section 15.4, had a recursive valued function. In view of the function print_integers of Figure 15.2, it is clear that not all recursive functions need to return a value under their name. This section considers another simple problem that can be solved recursively. This time, we will design a function that prints a string backward.

We will assume that strings are represented as one-dimensional character arrays in this application. Given a string variable, *str*, and its length, *length*, the solution of the problem of printing the string backward can be expressed as follows:

Print the last character in *str* whose index is *length* – *1*, then solve the smaller problem of printing backward the string *str* with *length* one less the length of the original string. Do nothing when *length* becomes 0.

In this formulation "Do nothing when *length* becomes 0" is the base case, and "Print backward the string *str* with *length* one less the length of the original string" is the recursive general case. The solution as a C function is given in Figure 15.8.

```
void print_backward(char str[], int length) {
      if(length > 0) {
            printf("%c", str[length - 1]);
            print_backward(str, length - 1);
      } /* end if */
} /* end function print_backward */
```

Figure 15.8    A recursive void function that prints a string backward

In the function print_backward of Figure 15.8, we again have an if statement. The then-part of the if statement is the recursive case; in it, we first print the last character of the string str and then call on the function print_backward, with str as its first argument and length - 1 as its second argument, so that we

can solve the smaller problem of printing backward a shorter string. The else-part of the
`if` statement, which will be executed when length is equal to 0, is the base case, corresponding to doing nothing.

Figure 15.9 shows a main function that reads a string into a string variable and uses
the recursive function `print_backward` of Figure 15.8 to print the string backward.

```c
#include <stdio.h>
#include <string.h>

void print_backward(char str[], int length);


int main(void) {
      char str[41];
      int length;

      printf("Enter a string: ");
      gets(str);

      length = strlen(str);

      print_backward(str, length);
      return 0;
} /* end function main */
```

**Figure 15.9**    A C function that uses the recursive function `print_backward` of Figure 15.8

In the program of Figure 15.9, the length of the string is computed using the standard library function `strlen` of the `string` library.

## 15.6    TRACING `void` RECURSIVE FUNCTIONS

Recursive functions that do not return a value under their name can be traced manually
or by inserting appropriate interactive output statements into the code and running it
through a driver function. In Figure 15.10 we rewrite the function `print_backward`
of Figure 15.8.

```c
1  void print_backward(char str[], int length) {
2     printf("--> Enter function with string \"%s\"", str);
3     printf(" and last index of %d.\n", length);
```

**Figure 15.10**    The recursive `void` function `print_backward` that traces its execution (*continued*)    ▶

```
 4         if(length > 0) {
 5               printf("Character printed: %c\n", str[length - 1]);
 6               print_backward(str, length - 1);
 7         } /* end if */

 8         printf("<-- Exit function with string \"%s\"", str);
 9         printf(" and last index of %d.\n", length);
10  } /* end function print_backward */
```

**Figure 15.10**                                                                              ▪

The version of print_backward given in Figure 15.10 is essentially the same as that in Figure 15.8, with the exception of the output statements on lines 2 and 3, just after the function is entered, and the output statements on lines 8 and 9, just before the function is exited. In addition, the output statement on line 5 that prints the characters of the string is modified to get a better program trace output, as shown in Figure 15.11. You should study this trace carefully to acquire a better understanding of recursion.

```
Enter a string: Bat
---> Enter function with string "Bat" and last index of 3.
Character printed: t
---> Enter function with string "Bat" and last index of 2.
Character printed: a
---> Enter function with string "Bat" and last index of 1.
Character printed: B
---> Enter function with string "Bat" and last index of 0.
<--- Exit function with string "Bat" and last index of 0.
<--- Exit function with string "Bat" and last index of 1.
<--- Exit function with string "Bat" and last index of 2.
<--- Exit function with string "Bat" and last index of 3.
```

**Figure 15.11**    A test run of the programs of Figures 15.9 and 15.10

## 15.7   ADDITIONAL EXAMPLES OF RECURSIVE FUNCTIONS

The best way to learn about recursion is to study a variety of examples. In this section we develop recursive solutions to the problems of generating Fibonacci numbers and consider some one-dimensional array operations, including sorting and searching. We conclude this series of examples by solving an interesting puzzle, that of the Towers of Hanoi, recursively.

## Computing Fibonacci Numbers Recursively

We return to the problem of computing Fibonacci numbers. We solved this problem earlier in section 6.9 and also in Example 10.1 in different ways. These solution were iterative, but it is possible to solve this problem recursively if we recall how Fibonacci numbers are defined. The first and the second Fibonacci numbers are 0 and 1, respectively. Any other member of the Fibonacci sequence can be computed by adding the previous two members. Therefore,

*fibonacci(n) = fibonacci(n – 1) + fibonacci(n – 2)*

This is a recursive definition since *fibonacci(n)* is expressed in terms of two smaller versions of itself, that is, *fibonacci(n - 1)* and *fibonacci(n - 2)*. The equalities

*fibonacci(1) = 0*
*fibonacci(2) = 1*

constitute two base cases for recursion. Now we can write a recursive function to compute Fibonacci numbers as shown in the program of Figure 15.12.

```
#include <stdio.h>

int recursive_fib(int);


int main(void) {
      int seq_number;

      printf("Enter a positive integer: ");
      scanf("%d", &seq_number);

      printf("The %dth Fibonacci number is: %d", seq_number,
            recursive_fib(seq_number));
      return 0;
} /* end function main */


int recursive_fib(int sequence_number) {
      if (sequence_number == 1)
            return 0;
      else if (sequence_number == 2)
            return 1;
      else return (recursive_fib(sequence_number - 1) +
            recursive_fib(sequence_number - 2));
      /* end if */
} /* end function recursive_fib */
```

**Figure 15.12**    A C program that computes Fibonacci numbers recursively

In Figure 15.12 the only statement we have in the body of the function `recur-sive_fib` is a nested `if` statement with three alternatives. The first two alternatives specify the base cases, and the third is the general case for recursion.

## Recursive Processing of One-Dimensional Arrays

Most algorithms on one-dimensional arrays are iterative and can alternatively be formulated as recursive algorithms. Typical of such algorithms are those on sorting and searching, which we covered in Chapter 11. In this section we reconsider some of these algorithms and formulate them recursively.

**Recursive Selection Sort of an Array**    We examined the selection sort algorithm in section 11.5 and presented a C implementation in Figure 11.11. This implementation is iterative. To get a recursive formulation, recall that we first determined the largest element of a list of size *list_size*, and then exchanged it with the last list element. Following this step, we carried out the same process on the unordered list of size *list_size* – *1*; that is, we applied selection sort on the unordered list of size *list_size* – *1*. Thus we have the general case for recursive specification, which can be expressed in pseudocode as follows:

> *find the largest element of the list of size list_size*
> *swap the largest element with the last list element*
> *apply selection sort on the unordered list of size list_size – 1*

Note that in the last line of the pseudocode, the selection sort is applied on a smaller list, which means that the problem size is diminishing. We stop the process when *list_size* becomes 1. This condition is the base case for recursion, and we do nothing when this happens. Now we have a complete recursive formulation expressed in pseudocode in Figure 15.13. We leave its implementation as an exercise to the reader.

> *selection_sort (a list of size list_size):*
>     *if list_size is greater than 1*
>         *begin*
>             *find the largest element of the list*
>             *swap the largest element with the last list element*
>             *call selection_sort (a list of size list_size – 1)*
>         *end*
>     *end_if*

**Figure 15.13**    A recursive formulation for selection sort

**Recursive Sequential Search of an Ordered Array**     The C implementation of the fundamental algorithm that searches an ordered array sequentially was presented in Figure 11.18 as the function `sequential_search_ordered`. This function is iterative. For a recursive formulation, assuming that the list is sorted in increasing order, we observe the following:

1.    If the search key is less than the first element of the array, the search is unsuccessful and we terminate it.

2.    If the search key is equal to the first element of the array, the search is successful and we terminate it.

3.    If the search key is greater than the first element of the array, we apply the sequential search algorithm on the list, beginning with the second element of the array.

Clearly, the first two cases are nonrecursive and can be considered to be the base cases for recursion. The third case involves doing the same thing, that is, sequentially searching a list whose size is one less than the size of the original list; therefore, it is recursive. To keep track of the list that diminishes in size, we use a variable, `first`, which points to the first element of the array to be searched. In the first call to the recursive function, the value of the variable `first`  must be 0, the index of the first element of the array. Figure 15.14 shows a C implementation of the recursive sequential search algorithm.

```
int rec_seq_search(list_item_type search_key,
           const list_item_type array_to_search[], int first) {
      if (search_key < array_to_search[first])
             return -1;
      else if (search_key == array_to_search[first])
             return first;
      else
             return rec_seq_search(search_key, array_to_search,
                    first + 1);
      /* end if */
} /* end function rec_seq_search */
```

**Figure 15.14**     A recursive C implementation of the sequential search algorithm for an ordered list

The function  `rec_seq_search`  is a valued function; it returns the value of `first`  if the search is successful; otherwise, it returns −1, a value that is outside the legal index values for an array. Here  `list_item_type`  is a type alias for a data type, declared using a  `typedef`, as, for example:

```
typedef int list_item_type;
```

We remember that the prototype of the function `sequential_search_ordered` of Figure 11.18 is

```
void sequential_search_ordered(list_item_type search_key,
                               int list_size,
                               const list_item_type array_to_search[],
                               char success[], int *index);
```

which is different from the prototype of the recursive function `rec_seq_search` of Figure 15.14. The interface of the function `rec_seq_search` includes `first`, which must be zero in the first call to the function if the entire list is to be searched. Also, it does not contain the parameters `success` and `index`, needed by the functions that use the sequential search algorithm. To have a similar function interface for the recursive version, we design a function named `rec_sequential_search_ordered`, shown in Figure 15.15.

```
void rec_sequential_search_ordered(list_item_type search_key,
                                   int list_size,
                                   const list_item_type array_to_search[],
                                   char success[], int *index) {
     int first = 0;

     *index = rec_seq_search(search_key, array_to_search, first);

     if (*index == -1)
           strcpy(success, "FALSE");
     else
           strcpy(success, "TRUE");
     /* end if */
} /* end function rec_sequential_search_ordered */
```

**Figure 15.15**    A recursive shell for the function `rec_seq_search` of Figure 15.14

This function sets `first` to 0, calls on the recursive function `rec_seq_search` to receive a value for the variable `index`, and accordingly determines a value for `success`. It serves as an interface between a function that uses `rec_seq_search`, and in a sense, envelops it. A function such as `rec_sequential_search_ordered` is known as a **recursive shell**.

**Recursive Binary Search of an Ordered Array**    The binary search algorithm presented in section 11.6 can be formulated recursively. We consider two integer variables, *first* and *last*, initialized to zero and *list_size − 1*, respectively, pointing to the first and last elements of the list stored in an array. We observe the following:

1.  If, anytime during the search, *first* becomes greater than *last*, the search is unsuccessful and we terminate the algorithm.

2.  Otherwise, if *search_key* is equal to the middle element of the list, the search is successful; in this case, we return *mid*, which is *(first + last) / 2* and terminate the search.

3.  If *first* is not greater than *last* and *search_key* is less than the middle element of the list, we focus on the first half of the list and call on the binary search algorithm with *last* set to *mid – 1*.

4.  If *first* is not greater than *last* and *search_key* is greater than or equal to the middle element of the list, we focus on the second half of the list and call on the binary search algorithm with *first* set to *mid + 1*.

Clearly, the first two cases are nonrecursive base cases and the last two involve recursion, and hence are the general cases. In the two general cases, the problem size is reduced by half. Therefore, this formulation is a proper recursive formulation. The pseudocode for this algorithm is given in Figure 15.16. The implementation of this algorithm in C and the design of a recursive shell for it are left to the reader as exercises.

```
recursive_binary_search (search_key, array_to_search, first, last):
   if first is greater than last
      return –1
   else
      begin
         compute mid as (first + last) / 2
         if search_key is equal to array_to_search[mid]
            return mid
         else if search key is less than array_to_search[mid]
            call recursive_binary_search(search_key, array_to_search, first,
               mid –1)
         else
            call recursive_binary_search(search_key, array_to_search, mid + 1, last)
         end_if
      end
   end_if
```

**Figure 15.16**    A pseudocode algorithm for recursive binary search

## Recursive Solution to the Towers of Hanoi Puzzle

We conclude this set of recursion examples with a classical puzzle known as the Towers of Hanoi, a city in Vietnam. You can buy several versions of this puzzle from toy shops and spend amusing hours trying to solve it. Here is the puzzle:

We have three poles, *first*, *second*, and *third*, and *n* disks of different sizes with holes in the middle so that they can fit on the poles (see Figure 15.17a). Initially, all disks are placed on the first pole such that each disk is placed on top of a disk larger than itself. The challenge is to move the disks, one at a time, from the first pole to the second, using the third pole when necessary. While moving the disks, we are allowed to put a disk on top of another on a pole, provided the disk is always placed on top of a larger disk.

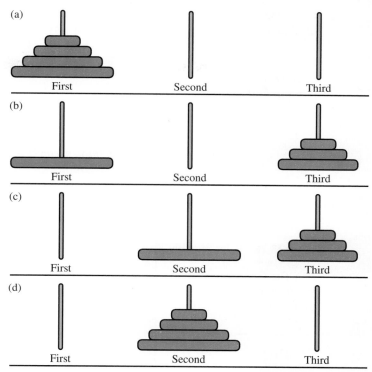

**Figure 15.17**      Recursive solution of the Towers of Hanoi puzzle with four disks

If we have only one disk on pole *first*, the solution of this puzzle is trivial; we simply move the disk from pole *first* to pole *second* without even using the pole *third*. However, if *n* is greater than 1, the puzzle is quite difficult unless we think in terms of a recursive solution:

1.  Suppose we found a way to move the top *n – 1* disks on pole *first* to pole *third*, leaving the largest disk at the bottom on pole *first* (Figure 15.17b).

2.  Now, we can move the largest disk on pole *first* to pole *second* (Figure 15.17c).

3.  We use the method of moving *n – 1* disks from one pole to another, this time from pole *third* to pole *second*, and place *n – 1* disks on top of the largest disk on pole *second*, thus solving the puzzle (Figure 15.17d).

Will this approach work? If you think about it, you will see that it will. The second action above is straightforward and does not involve recursion. It is our base case. The first and the third actions are the solution of the original problem except we are now solving a smaller version of the problem with *n – 1* disks. Let us suppose we have a function called *solve_tower*, with four parameters, *n, first, second,* and *third*, and a call to this function, such as

   *solve_tower (n, first, second, third)*

corresponds to the action of moving *n* disks from the first pole to the second, using the third pole, if necessary. The pseudocode that solves the puzzle is given in Figure 15.18.

```
solve_tower (n, first, second, third):
    if n is equal to 1
        move the disk from pole first to pole second
    else
        begin
            solve_tower (n − 1, first, third, second)
            solve_tower (1, first, second, third)
            solve_tower (n − 1, third, second, first)
        end
    end_if
```

**Figure 15.18**     The recursive formulation of the Towers of Hanoi puzzle in pseudocode

The C implementation is straightforward. The function `solve_tower` and a driver function to test it are given Figure 15.19. Figure 15.20 shows a test run of this program for four disks.

```c
#include <stdio.h>

void solve_towers(int no_of_disks, char first, char second,
                char third);


int main(void) {
        int no_of_disks;

        printf("Enter number of disks: ");
        scanf("%d", &no_of_disks);

        solve_towers(no_of_disks, 'A', 'B', 'C');
        return 0;
} /* end function main */


void solve_towers(int n, char first, char second, char third) {
        if (n == 1)
                printf("Move disk from pole %c to pole %c\n", first,
                        second);
```

**Figure 15.19**     The C implementation of the pseudocode algorithm of Figure 15.18 (continued)   ▶

```
    else {
        solve_towers(n - 1, first, third, second);
        solve_towers(1, first, second, third);
        solve_towers(n - 1, third, second, first);
    } /* end if */
} /* end function solve_towers */
```

**Figure 15.19**                                                                            ■

```
Enter number of disks: 4
Move disk from pole A to pole C
Move disk from pole A to pole B
Move disk from pole C to pole B
Move disk from pole A to pole C
Move disk from pole B to pole A
Move disk from pole B to pole C
Move disk from pole A to pole C
Move disk from pole A to pole B
Move disk from pole C to pole B
Move disk from pole C to pole A
Move disk from pole B to pole A
Move disk from pole C to pole B
Move disk from pole A to pole C
Move disk from pole A to pole B
Move disk from pole C to pole B
```

**Figure 15.20**     The solution of the Towers of Hanoi puzzle for four disks

## 15.8  RECURSION VERSUS ITERATION

If the nature of a problem is recursive, that is, if it is possible to express its solution in terms of the solutions of some simpler versions of itself, then we can design a recursive C function to solve it. Any problem that can be solved recursively can also be solved iteratively, as we have demonstrated with the problems of computing the factorial and Fibonacci numbers.

Why should we prefer recursion to iteration? Recursive formulations are simpler and more elegant because they reflect the nature of the problem directly. For example, the code in the body of the function  recursive_fib  in Figure 15.8 is a single nested  if statement, and it is certainly simpler than the code of the function  compute_fibonacci in Figure 10.3.

There is one drawback to recursion. Recursive solutions may involve a large number of function calls, as illustrated in Figure 15.5 for the recursive function call  fact(4).

Since function calls take more time to execute compared to iterations, recursive formulations may be quite inefficient. For example, the program of Figure 15.12 will compute Fibonacci numbers for relatively small values of `sequence_number` almost as efficiently as the iterative solution of Example 10.1. However, if you try running this program for large values of `sequence_number`, say, 30 to 40, you will see for yourself that it takes quite some time to compute the result, even on a fast computer, and that the iterative solution is significantly faster. Even a call to `recursive_fib` of Figure 15.12 with an argument of 7 results in a total of 25 function calls. Such calls require the generation of a large number of activation records, which explains why recursion is inefficient and places a heavy demand on the available free store.

Therefore, you should prefer recursion to iteration if execution efficiency is not a primary consideration, because recursive programs are easier to design and debug. For example, you should avoid recursion if your problem involves a large number of computations for Fibonacci numbers. However, if you need to compute only a few Fibonacci numbers in an application, recursion will do very well indeed.

## 15.9   SUMMARY

### This Chapter at a Glance

- In this chapter we examined recursion as a problem-solving technique that applies to problems involving iteration. Many problems that are iterative in nature can be solved recursively.

- A recursive solution requires a function that calls on itself to solve a smaller version of the problem. Such functions are recursive functions. C supports recursive functions.

- A recursive formulation must have one or more base cases, which are nonrecursive, and one or more general cases, in which recursive calls are made to solve smaller versions of the original problem.

- Recursive solutions of iterative problems are simpler and more elegant compared to the iterative solutions and are easier to design and debug. However, recursive solutions tend to be less execution-efficient because of the large number of function calls.

### Coming Attractions (or, Shall We Say, the Epilogue)

- Well, for us there are no further coming attractions! All good things must come to an end, and so must this class and this book. This was your introductory exposure to problem solving and C programming. You have developed a good foundation in both, and you are ready to use your acquired knowledge and abilities in solving problems in your chosen fields and professions.

- C is a rich language, and it has other, more advanced features that you may want to study. If you are studying computer science, you are now ready for a course on data abstraction and data structures using C and for other more advanced courses. If you have enjoyed this course, you will also enjoy those based on it. So, go for it!

## STUDY GUIDE

### Test Your Comprehension

1. A recursive function
   a. Must contain a general case that is recursive.
   b. Must include one or more base cases that are nonrecursive.
   c. Can always be expressed iteratively.
   d. All of the above are correct.
   e. None of the above is correct.

2. Choose the *incorrect* statement: Compared to a iterative solution, a recursive solution is
   a. More execution-efficient.
   b. Simpler and more elegant.
   c. Easier to design.
   d. Easier to debug.

3. The solution of the problem of determining the number of different ways to choose $k$ out of $n$ things can be expressed recursively as

$$C(n,\ k) = C(n-1,\ k-1) + C(n-1,\ k)\ \ if\ 0 < k < n$$

   where $n$ and $k$ are integers. (For an iterative formulation of $C(n,\ k)$, see Programming Exercise 15 of Chapter 6.) Which of the following is an appropriate base case for this recursive formulation?
   a. $C(n,\ k) = 1$ if $k = 0$
   b. $C(n,\ k) = 1$ if $k = n$
   c. $C(n,\ k) = 0$ if $k > n$
   d. All of the above.
   e. None of the above.

4. A recursive shell for a recursive function
   a. Is itself a recursive function.
   b. Is needed to initiate a recursive function.
   c. Must have the same prototype as the recursive function that it calls.
   d. Must return a value under its name.
   e. All of the above are correct.
   f. None of the above is correct.

**Answers:** 1. d; 2. a; 3. d; 4. b.

## Improve Your Problem Solving Ability

### Debugging Exercises

In each of the following seemingly recursive function definitions, identify and correct any errors. Explain your answers.

**5.**
```
int p_series(int x) {
    if (x < 4)
            return x;
    else
            return (p_series(x) + p_series(x - 1) +
                        p_series(x - 2));
    /* end if */
} /* end function p_series */
```

**6.**
```
int func(int n) {
    if (n == 0)
            return 0;
    else
            return (n * func(n / 2 * 2));
    /* end if */
} /* end function func */
```

**7.**
```
int xyz(int n) {
    if (n == 0)
            return xyz(n - 1);
    else
            return (n * xyz(n - 2));
    /* end if */
} /* end function xyz */
```

### Programming Exercises

**8.** Given the recursive function

```
int f(int n) {
    if (n == 0)
            return 0;
    else
            return (n + f(n/2));
    /* end if */
} /* end function f */
```

What does the function  f  do? What is the value returned by the function call  f(8)?
Write an iterative version of the function  f.

9. Write a recursive function and a recursive shell for the binary search algorithm of Figure 15.16.

10. Modify the recursive binary search function of the previous programming exercise by inserting into it appropriate interactive output statements to trace its execution.

### Programming Exercises

In programming Projects 11 through 17, first develop a recursive function that does the specified task, next develop an equivalent iterative function, and finally test both the recursive and iterative versions using a simple driver function.

11. A function that computes the number of different ways to choose $k$ out of $n$ things recursively. (**Hint:** See multiple-choice question 3 at the end of this chapter and Programming Exercise 15 in Chapter 6.)

12. A function that computes the $n$th power of a given integer. The problem of raising an integer $x$ to an integer power $n$ where $n >= 0$, can be expressed as follows:

$$x^n = x.x^{n-1} \text{ if } n > 0$$
$$x^0 = 1$$

13. A function that computes and returns the sum of first $n$ elements of an integer array, where $n >= 1$.

14. A function that computes the largest element in a one-dimensional array of integers.

15. A function that copies a one-dimensional array to another one-dimensional array of the same type as the first.

16. A function that prints the contents of a one-dimensional array from the first element to the last.

17. A function that computes the average of values in a one-dimensional array of type `double`.

18. Write a program that uses a Boolean recursive function that returns `true` if a string supplied through its parameter list is a palindrome (that is, a string that reads the same forward and backward, such as "madam" or "poor dan is in a droop"); otherwise, the function should return `false`. Assume that the string is stored in a one-dimensional character array, does not contain any spaces, and consists of lowercase letters. (**Hint:** Use two index variables, *first* and *last*, pointing to the first and last elements of the array, respectively. Compare the elements of the array with index *first* and *last*. If they are not equal, return `false`. If they are equal, repeat the process on the substring in the string beginning with the element with index *first* + *1* and ending with the element with index *last* − *1*.)

# A

# C Reserved Words

The following identifiers are reserved words in the C language and may not be used as programmer-defined identifiers.

| | | | |
|---|---|---|---|
| asm | double | long | typedef |
| auto | else | register | union |
| break | enum | return | unsigned |
| case | extern | short | void |
| char | float | signed | volatile |
| const | for | sizeof | while |
| continue | goto | static | |
| default | if | struct | |
| do | int | switch | |

# B

# C Operators and Character Escape Sequences

## B.1 C OPERATORS AND OPERATOR PRECEDENCE

The following table shows all C operators. Operators at a given precedence level have the same precedence; they have higher precedence than operators described below them and lower precedence than operators described above them.

| PRECEDENCE LEVEL | OPERATOR NAME | SYMBOL | ASSOCIATIVITY |
|---|---|---|---|
| 1 | Function call | `()` | → |
|   | Array subscripting | `[]` | → |
|   | Component selection | `.` | → |
|   | Indirect component selection | `->` | → |
| 2 | Unary plus | `+` | ← |
|   | Unary minus | `-` | ← |
|   | Increment | `++` | ← |
|   | Decrement | `--` | ← |
|   | Logical *not* | `!` | ← |
|   | Complement | `~` | ← |
|   | Indirection | `*` | ← |
|   | Address of | `&` | ← |
|   | Cast | `(type)` | ← |
|   | Size of type or object | `sizeof` | ← |
| 3 | Multiplication | `*` | → |
|   | Division | `/` | → |
|   | Modulus (remainder) | `%` | → |
| 4 | Addition | `+` | → |
|   | Subtraction | `-` | → |
| 5 | Left shift | `<<` | → |
|   | Right shift | `>>` | → |

*(continued)*

▶

| PRECEDENCE LEVEL | OPERATOR NAME | SYMBOL | ASSOCIATIVITY |
|---|---|---|---|
| 6 | Less than | < | → |
| | Less than or equal to | <= | → |
| | Greater than | > | → |
| | Greater than or equal to | >= | → |
| 7 | Equal to | == | → |
| | Not equal to | != | → |
| 8 | Bitwise *and* | & | → |
| 9 | Bitwise exclusive *or* | ^ | → |
| 10 | Bitwise inclusive *or* | \| | → |
| 11 | Logical *and* | && | → |
| 12 | Logical inclusive *or* | \|\| | → |
| 13 | Conditional operator | ? : | ← |
| 14 | Simple assignment | = | ← |
| | Assign sum | += | ← |
| | Assign difference | −= | ← |
| | Assign product | *= | ← |
| | Assign division | /= | ← |
| | Assign remainder | %= | ← |
| | Assign left shift | <= | ← |
| | Assign right shift | >= | ← |
| | Assign *and* | &= | ← |
| | Assign inclusive *or* | \|= | ← |
| | Assign exclusive *or* | ^= | ← |
| 15 | Comma | , | → |

## B.2    C ESCAPE SEQUENCES

| ESCAPE SEQUENCE | NAME | MEANING OF ESCAPE SEQUENCE |
|---|---|---|
| \a | Alert | Sounds a beep |
| \b | Backspace | Backs up one character |
| \f | Formfeed | Starts a new screen or page |
| \n | New line | Moves to beginning of next line |
| \r | Carriage return | Moves to beginning of current line |
| \t | Horizontal tab | Moves to next tab position |
| \v | Vertical tab | Moves down a fixed amount |
| \\ | Back slash | Prints a back slash |
| \' | Single quotation | Prints a single quotation mark |
| \" | Double quotation | Prints a double quotation mark |
| \? | Question mark | Prints a question mark |
| \OOO |  | Prints a character whose ASCII code is a one- to three-digit octal value |
| \XHHH |  | Prints a character whose ASCII code is a one- to three-digit hexadecimal value |

# Appendix

# C

# Standard Header Files and Library Functions

This appendix describes some of the commonly used library functions in the standard header files that come with any ANSI C compiler. Each header file contains prototypes for a set of related library functions. The functions listed in this appendix are categorized by their header files and are described in terms of their prototypes and purpose. In addition to the functions covered in the book, you will also find some that are useful in related applications. For more detailed descriptions of these and many other functions available in the standard C libraries, you should consult the documentation supplied by the vendor of your copy of the C compiler. You may also browse the header files that are stored in a standard subdirectory of the C system and learn more about the functions contained in them.

## C.1 CHARACTER-HANDLING FUNCTIONS IN THE HEADER FILE ctype.h

`isalnum`: `int isalnum (int Character);`
Returns nonzero if `Character` is a digit or a letter; returns 0 otherwise.
`isalpha`: `int isalpha (int Character);`
Returns nonzero if `Character` is a letter; returns 0 otherwise.
`iscntrl`: `int iscntrl (int Character);`
Returns nonzero if `Character` is a control character; returns 0 otherwise.
`isdigit`: `int isdigit (int Character);`
Returns nonzero if `Character` is a digit; returns 0 otherwise.
`isgraph`: `int isgraph (int Character);`
Returns nonzero if `Character` is a printing graphic character other than space; returns 0 otherwise.
`islower`: `int islower (int Character);`
Returns nonzero if `Character` is a lowercase letter; returns 0 otherwise.
`isprint`: `int isprint (int Character);`
Returns nonzero if `Character` is a printing character including space; returns 0 otherwise.
`ispunct`: `int ispunct (int Character);`
Returns nonzero if `Character` is a punctuation character; returns 0 otherwise.

isspace: `int isspace (int Character);`
    Returns nonzero if `Character` is a whitespace character; returns 0 otherwise.
isupper: `int isupper (int Character);`
    Returns nonzero if `Character` is an uppercase letter; returns 0 otherwise.
isxdigit: `int isxdigit (int Character);`
    Returns nonzero if `Character` is a hexadecimal digit; returns 0 otherwise.
tolower: `int tolower (int Character);`
    Returns `Character` as a lowercase letter if `Character` is an uppercase letter; returns `Character` unchanged otherwise.
toupper: `int toupper (int Character);`
    Returns `Character` as an uppercase letter if `Character` is a lowercase letter; returns `Character` unchanged otherwise.

## C.2   MATHEMATICAL FUNCTIONS IN THE HEADER FILE `math.h`

acos: `double acos (double x);`
    Returns in radians the arc cosine of `x`, where `-1 <= x <= 1`.
asin: `double asin (double x);`
    Returns in radians the arc sine of `x`, where `-1 <= x <= 1`.
atan: `double atan (double x);`
    Returns the arc tangent of `x` in radians.
ceil: `double ceil (double x);`
    Returns the smallest integer larger than or equal to `x`.
cos: `double cos (double x);`
    Returns the cosine of `x`, where `x` is in radians.
cosh: `double cosh (double x);`
    Returns the hyperbolic cosine of `x`.
exp: `double exp (double x);`
    Return the exponential of `x` with the base e, where e is 2.718282.
fabs: `double fabs (double x);`
    Returns the absolute value of `x`.
floor: `double floor (double x);`
    Returns the largest integer smaller than or equal to `x`.
log: `double log (double x);`
    Returns the natural logarithm of `x`.
log10: `double log10 (double x);`
    Returns the base-10 logarithm of `x`.
pow: `double pow (double x, double y);`
    Returns `x` raised to the `y` power; if `x` is zero, `y` must be positive, and if `x` is negative, `y` must be an integer.
sin: `double sin (double x);`
    Returns the sine of `x`, where `x` is in radians.

sinh: double sinh (double x);
  Returns the hyperbolic sine of x.
sqrt: double sqrt (double x);
  Returns the square root of x, where x >= 0.
tan: double tan (double x);
  Returns the tangent of x, where x is radians.
tanh: double tanh (double x);
  Returns the hyperbolic tangent of x.

## C.3 GENERAL UTILITIES IN THE HEADER FILE stdlib.h

### String Conversion Functions

atof: double atof (const char *String);
  Converts String to double.
atoi: int atoi (const char *String);
  Converts String to int.
atol: long int atol (const char *String);
  Converts String to long int.

### Functions for Random Number Generation

rand: int rand (void);
  Returns a random number in the range 0 to RAND_MAX, where RAND_MAX is a symbolic constant that must be at least 32767.
srand: void srand (unsigned int Seed);
  Uses Seed as a seed for a new sequence of pseudorandom numbers to be returned by subsequent calls to the function rand. Every time the same Seed value is used in srand, the function rand generates the same sequence of random numbers.

### Functions for Dynamic Variable Allocation and Deallocation

calloc: void *calloc(size_t Array_size, size_t Size);
  Allocates memory space for an array of size Array_size; the size of each element of the array is specified by Size. The function calloc initializes the allocated memory space to all bits zero and returns a pointer to the allocated space or a null pointer. size_t is an unsigned integer type returned by the sizeof operator.
free: void free (void *Pointer);
  Deallocates the memory space pointed to by Pointer and makes it available for further allocation.
malloc: void *malloc (size_t Size);
  Allocates memory space for an object whose size is specified by Size without assigning a value to the object and returns a pointer to the allocated space or a null pointer. size_t is an unsigned integer type returned by the sizeof operator.

## Environment Communication Functions

abort: void abort (void);
> Results in abnormal program termination and returns control to the environment.

exit: void exit (int Status);
> Results in normal program termination and returns Status to the calling environment. An exit Status of 0 or EXIT_SUCCESS implies successful termination; EXIT_FAILURE implies unsuccessful termination. EXIT_SUCCESS and EXIT_FAILURE are symbolic constants defined in the header file stdlib.h.

## Mathematical Functions

abs: int abs (int x);
> Returns the absolute value of x.

## C.4    STRING HANDLING FUNCTIONS IN THE HEADER FILE string.h

strcat: char *strcat (char *String1, const char *String2);
> Concatenates String2 to the end of String1 and returns String1.

strchr: char *strchr (const char *String, int Character);
> Locates the first occurrence of Character in String and returns a pointer to Character in String if Character is found; otherwise, returns a null pointer.

strcmp: int strcmp (const char *String1,
                    const char *String2);
> Compares String1 to String2 and returns 0, less than 0, or greater than 0 if String1 is equal to, less than, or greater than String2, respectively.

strcpy: char *strcpy (char *String1, const char *String2);
> Copies String2 into String1 and returns String1.

strcspn: size_t strcspn (const char *String1,
                         const char *String2);
> Returns the length of the maximum initial segment of String1 that consists entirely of characters not from String2. size_t is an unsigned integer type returned by the sizeof operator.

strerror: char *strerror (int ErrorNumber);
> Returns a pointer to a string that contains ErrorNumber; which is implementation-dependent.

strlen: size_t strlen (const char *String);
> Determines and returns the length of String, excluding '\0'. size_t is an unsigned integer type returned by the sizeof operator.

strncat: char *strncat (char *String1, const char *String2,
                        size_t n);
> Concatenates left-most n characters of String2 to the end of String1 and returns String1. size_t is an unsigned integer type returned by the sizeof operator.

`strncmp:` `int strncmp (const char *String1,`
`const char *String2, size_t n);`

Compares left-most `n` characters of `String1` to `String2` and returns 0, less than 0, or greater than 0 if `String1` is equal to, less than, or greater than `String2`, respectively. `size_t` is an unsigned integer type returned by the `sizeof` operator.

`strncpy:` `char *strncpy (char *String1, const char *String2,`
`size_t n);`

Copies left-most `n` characters of `String2` into `String1` and returns `String1`. `size_t` is an unsigned integer type returned by the `sizeof` operator.

`strpbrk:` `char *strpbrk (const char *String1,`
`const char *String2);`

Locates the first occurrence in `String1` of any character in `String2` and returns a pointer to the character if a character from `String2` is found; otherwise returns a null pointer.

`strrchr:` `char *strrchr (const char *String, int Character);`

Locates the last occurrence of `Character` in `String` and returns a pointer to `Character` in `String` if `Character` is found; otherwise, returns a null pointer.

`strspn:` `size_t strspn (const char *String1,`
`const char *String2);`

Returns the length of the maximum initial segment of `String1` that consists entirely of characters from `String2`. `size_t` is an unsigned integer type returned by the `sizeof` operator.

`strstr:` `char *strstr (const char *String1,`
`const char *String2);`

Locates the first occurrence in `String1` of `String2` and returns a pointer to `String2` if the string is found; otherwise returns a null pointer.

`strtok:` `char *strtok (char *String1, const char *String2);`

Breaks up `String1` into its tokens delimited by any character in `String2`. The first call to `strtok` must contain `String1` as the first argument; the subsequent calls to tokenize the same string must contain `NULL` as the first argument. Each call returns a pointer to the current token. If there are no more tokens, returns `NULL`.

## C.5   INPUT-OUTPUT FUNCTIONS IN THE HEADER FILE `stdio.h`

`fclose:` `int fclose (FILE *Stream);`

Flushes `Stream` and closes the associated file. Returns 0 if `Stream` is successfully closed or `EOF` if any error is detected. `EOF` is a symbolic constant defined in the header file `stdio.h`.

`feof:` `int feof (FILE *Stream);`

Tests the end-of-file indicator for `Stream`. Returns nonzero if the end-of-file indicator is set for `Stream`, otherwise returns zero.

`fgetc:` `int fgetc (FILE *Stream);`

Reads and returns as an integer the next character from the input `Stream` and advances the associated read position for the stream.

fgets: char *fgets (char *String, int n, FILE *Stream);
Reads a maximum of n - 1 characters from Stream into String and returns String if successful. If the first n - 1 characters of Stream contain a new line character or an end-of-file character, only characters preceding the new-line or end-of-file character are read.

fopen: FILE *fopen (const char *FileName,
                    const char *OpenMode);
Opens the file FileName in the mode indicated by OpenMode, and associates a stream with it. The argument OpenMode may be

| | |
|---|---|
| "r" | To open existing text file for reading. |
| "w" | To open new text file for writing. |
| "a" | To open new or existing text file for appending. |
| "r+" | To open existing text file for updating. |
| "w+" | To open new text file for updating. |
| "a+" | To open new or existing file for appending. |
| "rb" | To open existing binary file for reading. |
| "wb" | To open new binary file for writing. |
| "ab" | To open new or existing binary file for appending. |
| "r+b" or "rb+" | To open existing binary file for updating. |
| "w+b" or "wb+" | To open new binary file for updating. |
| "a+b" or "ab+" | To open new or existing binary file for appending. |

fprintf: int fprintf (FILE *Stream,
                      const char *FormatControlString, ...);
Writes output (the values of the variable number of parameters after the second parameter) to Stream using FormatControlString and returns the number of characters transmitted, or a negative value if an output error occurs.

fputc: int fputc (int Character, FILE *Stream);
Writes Character to the output Stream at the position indicated by the associated write position, advances the write position, and returns the character written as an integer. If a write error occurs, returns EOF.

fputs: int fputs (const char *String, FILE *Stream);
Writes the String to the output Stream without the terminating null character and returns a nonnegative integer. If a write error occurs, returns EOF.

fread: size_t fread (void *Pointer, size_t Size,
                     size_t NumberOfElements, FILE *Stream);
Reads from the input Stream up to NumberOfElements elements whose size is Size, transfers them into the array pointed to by Pointer, advances the read position by the number of characters successfully read, and returns the number of elements read. size_t is an unsigned integer type returned by the sizeof operator.

fscanf: int fscanf (FILE *Stream,
                    const char *FormatControlString, ...);
Reads input (the values for the variable number of parameters after the second parameter) from Stream using FormatControlString, converts the values, and

assigns them to input variables; returns the number of input items, or a negative value if an output error occurs. If an input error occurs before any conversion, `fscanf` returns `EOF`.

`fseek: int fseek (FILE *Stream, long int Offset,`
`                    int WhereFrom);`

Sets the read or write position for `Stream` by adding `Offset` to the position specified by `WhereFrom`. The new position is measured in characters from the beginning of the file. The position specified by `WhereFrom` is the beginning of the file if it is `SEEK_SET`, the current value of the file read or write position if `SEEK_CUR`, or the end of the file if `SEEK_END`. If a request cannot be satisfied, `fseek` returns a nonzero value. `SEEK_SET`, `SEEK_CUR`, and `SEEK_END` are symbolic constants defined in the header file `stdio.h`.

`ftell: long int ftell (FILE *Stream);`

Returns the current value of the read or write position for `Stream` in number of characters from the beginning of the file.

`fwrite: size_t fwrite (const void *Pointer, size_t Size,`
`                    size_t NumberOfElements,`
`                    FILE *Stream);`

Writes to the output `Stream` up to `NumberOfElements` elements whose size is `Size`, from the array pointed to by `Pointer`; advances the write position by the number of characters successfully written; and returns the number of elements written. `size_t` is an unsigned integer type returned by the `sizeof` operator.

`getc: int getc (FILE *Stream);`

In general, the function `getc` is equivalent to `fgetc`; it reads and returns as an integer the next character from the input `Stream` and advances the associated read position for the stream.

`getchar: int getchar (void);`

Returns the next character from the standard input stream `stdin`. If the stream is at end-of-file or a read error occurs, returns `EOF`.

`gets: char *gets (char *String);`

Reads characters from the standard input stream `stdin` into `String` until the end-of-file character is encountered or a new-line character is read; returns `String` if successful, and a null pointer if unsuccessful.

`printf: int printf (const char *FormatControlString, ...);`

Writes output (the values of the variable number of parameters after the first parameter) to the standard output stream `stdout` using `FormatControlString`; returns the number of characters transmitted, or a negative value if an output error occurs.

`putc: int putc (int Character, FILE *Stream);`

In general, the function `putc` is equivalent to `fputc`: it writes `Character` to the output `Stream` at the position indicated by the associated write position, advances the write position, and returns the character written as an integer. If a write error occurs, returns `EOF`.

`putchar: int putchar (int Character);`

Writes `Character` to the standard output stream `stdout` at the position indicated by the associated write position, advances the write position, and returns the character written as an integer. If a write error occurs, returns EOF.

puts: `int puts (const char *String);`

Writes String to the standard output stream stdout and appends a new-line character to the output; returns a nonnegative value if successful, and EOF if a write error occurs.

remove: `int remove (const char *FileName);`

Deletes the file whose name is Filename; returns zero if successful, nonzero if not.

rename: `int rename (const char *OldFileName,`
`const char *NewFileName);`

Changes the name of the file OldFileName to NewFileName; returns zero if successful, nonzero if not.

rewind: `void rewind (FILE *Stream);`

Sets the read or write position for Stream to the beginning of the file.

scanf: `int scanf (const char *FormatControlString, ...);`

Reads input (the values for the variable number of parameters after the first parameter) from the standard input stream stdin using FormatControlString and converts the values and assigns them to input variables; returns the number of input items, or a negative value if an output error occurs. If an input error occurs before any conversion, scanf returns EOF.

sprintf: `int sprintf (char *String,`
`const char *FormatControlString, ...);`

Writes output (the values of the variable number of parameters after the second parameter) to String using FormatControlString and returns the number of characters transmitted, or a negative value if an output error occurs.

sscanf: `int sscanf (const char *String,`
`const char *FormatControlString, ...);`

Reads input (the values for the variable number of parameters after the second parameter) from String using FormatControlString, converts the values, and assigns them to input variables; returns the number of input items, or a negative value if an output error occurs. If an input error occurs before any conversion, sscanf returns EOF.

## C.6   DATE AND TIME FUNCTIONS IN THE HEADER FILE **time.h**

clock: `clock_t clock (void);`

Returns the processor time used by the program. To determine the processor time in seconds for a program, divide the difference of the values returned by the clock function at the end and at the beginning of the program by the value of CLOCKS_PER_SEC. clock_t is an implementation-dependent arithmetic type capable of representing time. CLOCKS_PER_SEC is a symbolic constant defined in the header file time.h.

ctime: `char *ctime (const time_t *When);`
  Converts the calendar time pointed to by `When` (see the function time below) to local time in the form of a string of 26 characters, for example:

$$\text{Wed Oct 13 09:03:46 1994\textbackslash n\textbackslash 0}$$

  `time_t` is an implementation-dependent arithmetic type capable of representing time.

time: `time_t time (time_t *When);`
  Returns the absolute time and stores it in `When`. `time_t` is an implementation-dependent arithmetic type capable of representing time.

# INDEX

# G